D1612876

The Intellectual Properties of Learning

The Intellectual Properties
of Learning

A Prehistory from Saint Jerome to John Locke

JOHN WILLINSKY

The University of Chicago Press

CHICAGO AND LONDON

The University of Chicago Press, Chicago 60637
The University of Chicago Press, Ltd., London
© 2017 by The University of Chicago
Published 2017
Printed in the United States of America

26 25 24 23 22 21 20 19 18 17   1 2 3 4 5

ISBN-13: 978-0-226-48792-2 (cloth)
ISBN-13: 978-0-226-48808-0 (e-book)
DOI: 10.7208/chicago/9780226488080.001.0001

Library of Congress Cataloging-in-Publication Data

Names: Willinsky, John, 1950– author.
Title: The intellectual properties of learning : a prehistory from Saint Jerome
to John Locke / John Willinsky.
Description: Chicago ; London : The University of Chicago Press, 2018. |
Includes bibliographical references and index.
Identifiers: LCCN 2017038019 | ISBN 9780226487922 (cloth : alk. paper) |
ISBN 9780226488080 (e-book)
Subjects: LCSH: Learning and scholarship—History. | Learned institutions and
societies—History. | Intellectual property. | Universities and colleges—
Europe—History.
Classification: LCC AZ231 .W55 2018 | DDC 001.2—dc23
LC record available at https://lccn.loc.gov/2017038019

♾ This paper meets the requirements of ANSI/NISO Z39.48-1992
(Permanence of Paper).

Contents

	300	CHRISTIAN MONASTICISM
Jerome (ca. 347–420)		Augustine of Hippo (354–430)
		FALL OF ROME
Benedict of Nursia (480–547)		Boethius (480–524)
Cassiodorus (ca. 485–585)		Radegund of Poitiers (520–587)
Isidore of Seville (ca. 560–636)	600	
Bede (ca. 672/3–735)		
Al-Mansur (714–775)		´ABBASID CALIPHATE
Alcuin (ca.735–804)		CAROLINGIAN RENAISSANCE
Al-Kindī (801–873)		CATHEDRAL SCHOOLS
Al-Farabi (872–951)	900	
Gerbert d'Aurillac (946–1003)		Avicenna (980–1037)
Anselm of Canterbury (ca. 1033–1109)		Peter Abelard (1079–1142)
Bernard of Clairvaux (1090–1153)		Hildegard of Bingen (1098–1179)
Gerard of Cremona (1114–1187)		ARABIC-LATIN TRANSLATION MOVEMENT
Averroës (1126–1198)	1200	UNIVERSITIES
Robert Grosseteste (1175–1253)		Thomas Aquinas (1225–1274)
Francesco Petrarca (1304–1374)		
Desiderius Erasmus (1466–1536)		PRINTING PRESS
Thomas Bodley (1545–1613)	1500	Galileo Galilei (1564–1642)
William Laud (1573–1645)		Federico Cesi (1585–1630)
Henry Oldenburg (ca. 1619–1677)		John Fell (1625–1686)
John Locke (1632–1704)		ROYAL SOCIETY
STATUTE OF ANNE 1710		
	1800	

FIGURE 1. Timeline of book's principal figures and events, 300 to 1710.

for Jan

Preface

This book could be said to have started with a line from John Donlan's poem entitled "An Economics of Happiness."[1] The poem's title is promising enough for an inquiry into scholarly publishing, but that wasn't my initial point of inspiration on first reading it. The poem begins, "I'll see your mistake and double it." This, too, might have proven a poignant spark for considering my own scholarship. But what actually gave me pause was the second line: "Orange King Billy, Our Guide to the Open Bible." I was intrigued by this somewhat obscure reference to William of Orange's Glorious Revolution of 1688, as I later learned, in which he restored Britain to Protestantism after defeating the Catholic convert James II. It signaled the country's return to a Bible made accessible—or open—which is to say, in the English language of the people, rather than the Latin edition of the defeated King James II's Catholicism.

This championing of the *open* Bible spoke to the work that I had been doing over the last decade and a half on finding ways to open scholarly journals to readers beyond the university libraries that could afford to subscribe to them—ways to open them to researchers around the globe, to physicians looking for the latest studies of a new treatment, and to poets seeking to learn more about, say, the role of small magazines in promoting poetic modernism. My work in this area has involved developing the technical means and economic models that can provide scholars and public alike with free

---

1. John Donlan, "An Economics of Happiness," in *Spirit Engine* (London: Brick Books, 2008); the poem is available online.

online access to this body of knowledge. This whole venture of creating open access to research and scholarship was very much an enterprise of the digital era, but King Billy was a reminder of a larger historical story around a struggle for openness and access.

When I asked John Donlan about King Billy and the Open Bible—as he is conveniently married to my cousin Mariam Clavir—he explained that, as a child, he earned a dollar each year on July 12th by carrying a sign that read "Our Guide to the Open Bible" as he walked carefully behind another youngster on horseback playing King Billy in an Orange Parade that was held in a little town north of Toronto. Such an Orange Day commemoration of William's victory is celebrated in a number of Canadian and US communities in what may be these countries' longest-standing annual parade.

This reference to the open Bible and William III, Prince of Orange, soon led me to John Locke, who cast himself at one point as the philosopher of that Glorious Revolution. After six years of political exile in the Netherlands, Locke had returned to London shortly after William and Mary's crowning. While in hiding across the channel, he had completed the manuscripts of two landmark works—*Two Treatises of Government* and *An Essay concerning Human Understanding*—that had much to say about property rights, the nature of knowledge, and the realm of learning generally. I was hardly the first to have that moment of realization: the questions I was working on, around access to research, were not born yesterday. The access issue was not simply a child of the internet, but had a fascinating, illuminating history that might well inform the way forward.

In the *Two Treatises of Government*, published upon his return to England in 1689, Locke sets individual claims to property and liberty against the divine right of kings. In Locke's highly influential account of property rights, he reminds readers that the world was originally given in common to all humankind and that the ownership of things is only justified by what it contributes to the common stock of all. Is that sort of exclusion warranted, a number of us were now asking, in the case of research and scholarship?

In *An Essay concerning Human Understanding*, Locke declares his intention to serve "the Commonwealth of Learning" by clearing away obstructions on the path to knowledge. It left me wondering if the *Essay* might stand as Locke's third treatise of government, dealing with the *common* wealth of learning and how it might best be governed. Following the example of Billy, could Locke be our Guide to Open Learning? Could today's move toward open access be deeply rooted in the history of learning, rather than arising, as it had for me, out of the immediate and profound changes taking place in the shift from print to digital publishing? It was enough to set me off and running with a history inspired by the challenge that Locke set himself in the *Two Treatises*: "It seems to some a very great difficulty, how any one should ever come to have a *property* in any thing."[2] In searching for concrete historical examples of how we had come to have a property in a work of learning, I was drawn further and further into the past. I decided that a reasonable stopping point—and thus the starting point for this book—was the fourth century and Saint Jerome, whose prolific writings and translations established what monasticism could do for learning in the Latin West. In the history that followed from Jerome, it became clear both how anyone within this historical tradition had come to have or find a property in a text, and how the learned properties at the heart of the commonwealth of learning were distinguished and set apart from other goods. It all spoke to a tradition that I was now fully engaged in facilitating for scholarly publishing in the digital era, but without this sense of how it might be deeply rooted in the past.

In the late 1990s I was among those excited by the educational prospects of the internet as a new medium for sharing more of what was known. While a professor of education at the University of British Columbia, I was able to create the Public Knowledge Project in 1998 to explore such prospects with a modest endowment from Pacific Press, which owned Vancouver's two principal newspapers, and gave the money to support work at the intersection of literacy and technology. With the assistance of graduate students Henry Kang and Lisa Korteweg, I then engaged in an experiment with one of the newspapers, the *Vancouver Sun*, to bring research and journalism together in a weeklong series of articles on education and technology. We met with editor-in-chief John Cruikshank and reporter Janet Steffenhagen to plan a series of print articles on local developments backed by online public access to the relevant research. While Janet visited Vancouver schools and libraries to interview teachers, students, and patrons on educational uses of computers, we scrambled to assemble the research needed to put each of the local stories into a larger perspective.

At the time, research was just starting to appear online, but we were shocked and dismayed to discover that publisher agreements with the library precluded our sharing many of the research articles that we thought the public should see. The exceptions that we could use online were a few pioneering

2. John Locke, *Two Treatises of Government*, ed. Peter Laslett (Cambridge: Cambridge University Press, 1988), 2.25.

"open access" journals (before that term was in use). We did create a website to accompany the newspaper articles, which provided research abstracts and a few studies, and we added a forum for comments and discussion. Traffic to the site by readers of the newspaper was little more than a trickle for the week, and the *Vancouver Sun* went no further with our idea of appending research links to its reporting of the news. The experiment did, however, prove to be a turning point in my own work.

This inability to share education research with the public struck me, as a former public school teacher and now a professor preparing teachers, as both wrongheaded and a missed opportunity. How could there be virtually no public access to what so many researchers were doing to better understand and improve public education (not to mention all of the other areas in which research might make a contribution)? Changing what was wrong with the current picture became the goal of the Public Knowledge Project.

Inspired by the open source software movement and early open access journals, we decided that we needed to provide journal editors and publishers with the tools they needed to provide online and open access. To that end, we worked to design and develop an open source version of a journal management and publishing platform. It was first released in 2001 and called Open Journal Systems (OJS). We have been updating and improving it with each new release ever since. Our goal has been to offer free publishing tools that can help others to publish peer-reviewed journals, and more recently monographs, on an open access basis that will contribute to this common wealth of learning.

Having realized that research libraries are natural partners in this work, I joined forces in 2005 with Lynn Copeland and Brian Owen at Simon Fraser University Library. Since then the Public Knowledge Project's technical team, led by Alec Smecher, has developed OJS into a publishing platform that, as I write, is being actively used by over ten thousand journals, almost all of them (given a user's autonomy with open source software) offering open access to their content and more than half of them located in the Global South. Over the course of writing this history of learning, I have been repeatedly struck by my good fortune in also being able to work with the remarkable individuals affiliated with the Public Knowledge Project to help others make the intellectual properties of learning that much more open to that many more people.

Palo Alto and Vancouver

Acknowledgments

This book has benefited by readings and discussions involving Keith Baker, Allan Bell, George Hardin Brown, Gustavo Fischman, Roy Graham, Patrick Inglis, Adithi Iyer, David Jordan, Harper Keenan, Alexander Matthew Key, Emma Lierley, Pat Moore, the sagacious Ray McDermott, Kamran Naim, Josh Ober, Benjamin Paloff, Indira Phukan, Johanne Provençal, James Tully, and Mark Vessey. The anonymous reviewers of the manuscript only reinforced, in their helpful criticisms and welcomed encouragement, my sense of the value and contribution of peer review to our work. I have been greatly assisted in this project by the persistent diligence of Jessica Method, Ellen Mueller, Michael Trottier, and Oded Ziproy. Given the prominent role played by learning's sponsorship throughout this book, I must commend the upholding of this tradition by the Violet Andrews Whittier Fellowship at the Stanford Humanities Center and the Khosla family, who endowed the professorship in public knowledge that I currently hold. I am also indebted to the Stanford University Library, especially to John Mustain and Kathy Kerns, and to the university's Bing Overseas Program at Oxford, where I gained much from the Bodleian Library, as well as from Codrington Library at All Souls College, with the gracious help of Norma Aubertin-Potter and Finoa Godber. I am grateful, as well, for the Simon Fraser University Library's visiting scholar program, with a special nod to Brian Owen, Kevin Stranack, Lynn Copeland, Chuck Eckman, and Gwen Bird. And finally, I am appreciative of Susan H. Karani's exacting editing and suggestions and Gerald van Ravenswaay's superb indexing of the book as well as of how well this project has been served at every point by Elizabeth Branch Dyson, whom I'm proud to call my editor at the University of Chicago Press.

I would also like to acknowledge that, in the spirit of the openness that this book explores, the University of Chicago Press, which has done much in working with me to develop this book, has enabled me to make the final draft of the text available online on an open access basis (discoverable through its title) as a further experiment in the future of scholarly publishing. Earlier versions of portions of this work appeared in *New Media and Society* and *International Journal of Cultural Studies*, coauthored with Johanne Provençal, and in *Policy Futures in Education*.

CHAPTER ONE

The Commonwealth of Learning

In 2015, the scholarly publishing industry had its Napster moment. The quiet world of academic journals had run into something similar to the transgressive peer-to-peer sharing of music files, which so thoroughly rocked the music industry in 1999. This time, it took the form of Sci-Hub, a website and repository bearing the tag line "to remove all barriers in the way of science" and sporting the image of a raven, perhaps one of the Norse god Odin's information-gathering birds, holding a key in its beak. Sci-Hub first caught headlines on June 3, 2015, when Elsevier, the largest of the scholarly journal publishers, filed a lawsuit against the repository, which is now estimated to hold some eighty-two million pirated research articles, in the Southern District of New York Court. Alexandra Elbakyan has been forthright in declaring that she started Sci-Hub in 2011 as a frustrated graduate student in Kazakhstan, unable to obtain the research papers that she needed for her studies. She turned to those willing to send her papers taken from their library collections, in a process that she mysteriously developed into something much larger for others to use. In 2016, readers from every corner of the globe downloaded four million pirated papers a month from Sci-Hub, operating in the deep web outside the reach of court injunctions. That same year, Elbakyan made *Nature*'s "Ten People Who Mattered This Year."[1] If anything says that now is the time to find a sustainable way of opening access to this literature, it is having virtually all of it made freely and *illegally* available online.

---

1. John Bohannon, "Who's Downloading Pirated Papers? Everyone," *Science* 352, no. 6285 (April 28 2016): 508–12; "Ten People Who Mattered this Year," *Nature*, December 19, 2016.

"Of course, if scholarly publishers had a different business model," El-bakyan has stated, "then perhaps this project would not be necessary."[2] That is certainly true, but still I was more than a little surprised to read in the letter that she sent in her defense to Judge Robert W. Sweet, presiding over the case, and for which Elsevier filed an injunction for fifteen-million dollars in damages on May 18, 2017: "What I [have] written here is not just my opinion—this topic is widely discussed in [the] research community. For example, a researcher John Willinsky wrote a book named *The Access Principle: The Case for Open Access to Research and Scholarship* where he discusses this problem."[3] This was not exactly the sort of case I had in mind when I wrote that book, nor do I see Sci-Hub as a viable means of providing public access to this body of work. Still, I stand with those who believe that a new business model is called for when it comes to the circulation of science and scholarship. With this book, I want to add to the pressing sense that now is the time to find a way to open access to science and scholarship. But I want to do so by moving this access question out of the here and now, beyond the Napster-disruptions of the digital era, by asking: *Where in the world did the idea that people have this sort of right to research come from?*

It is not that the growing number of university faculty members and librarians who have been working over the past two decades on this issue have been short of answers to the question of why open access. The populists among them appeal to the taxpayers' investment in government-funded research, which surely earns the public a right to access the resulting work. Philosophers point to how scholars' unrestricted access to research and scholarship is a prerequisite for the work's very claim to knowledge. Jurists hold up learning's special legal status, with the legislative and common law recognition of education and research as copyright and patent exceptions.[4]

The reasons given for pursuing an open access model of scholarly publishing are compelling. Yet they are also largely ahistorical. As such, they only lead to further questions about the origins of scholarship's economic sponsorship, cultural practices, and legal exceptions. In response, this book repre-

2. Alexandra Elbakyan, "Transcript and Translation of Sci-Hub Presentation," Open Access @ UNT, University of North Texas, May 19–20, 2016.

3. In "Letter Addressed to Judge Robert W. Sweet from Alexandra Elbakyan re: Clarification of Details," Elsevier v. Sci-Hub, 1:15-cv-04282, NY Southern District. September 15, 2015. In the letter Elbakyan also cites Timothy Gower, who led a boycott of Elsevier in 2012.

4. For a summary of the case, see Peter Suber, *Open Access* (Cambridge, MA: MIT Press, 2013); John Willinsky, *The Access Principle: The Case for Open Access to Research and Scholarship* (Cambridge, MA: MIT Press, 2006).

sents an immodest attempt to provide a greater historical awareness of how, and under what terms and principles, scholarly knowledge has circulated in the West. It covers the period from late antiquity, when learning in the Christian West was first getting under way, to the early modern era, when our contemporary notion of intellectual property rights first became part of the law, with a recognition of learning's special standing.

Questions about the basis and bearing of such distinctions have only become more pressing today as open access has established itself as a viable publishing model. Since the turn of the twentieth century, open access has moved from being vilified by scholarly publishers as irresponsibly threatening the future of science to official policy for the White House, UNESCO, European Commission, Gates Foundation, and many other organizations involved in supporting research.[5] Faculty bodies at many universities have adopted open access policies to ensure that copies of their published work are publicly available; and they are engaged in editing, reviewing for, and publishing in the thousands of open access journals that are now operating across the disciplines.[6] The large corporate publishing houses, such as Elsevier, Springer Nature, and Wiley-Blackwell, offer a growing suite of open access journals among the thousands of titles they continue to sell by subscription. Open access is now widely recognized as one of the principal pillars in an internet-inspired open science movement that includes open data, open instrumentation, open source software, and open educational resources.

All of this has been very encouraging for open access supporters. But the tension between the commons and commerce in the circulation of learned work is by no means resolved. The vast majority of scholarly journals remains closed to all but subscribing institutions. These subscriptions represent a ten-billion-dollar market for journals in science, technology, and medicine alone, suggesting how much is at stake in moving to open access.[7] And

5. Michael Stebbins, "Expanding Public Access to the Results of Federally Funded Research," White House Office of Science and Technology, Washington, February 22, 2013, online; UNESCO, "Open Access Policy concerning UNESCO Publications," Paris, July 31, 2013, online; European Commission, "Open Access to Scientific Information," Brussels, June 30, 2015, online; "Bill and Melinda Gates Foundation Open Access Policy," Seattle, November 20, 2014, online.

6. See Registry of Open Access Repository Policies and Mandates, University of Southampton, UK, online; Directory of Open Access Journals online.

7. "The annual revenues generated from English-language STM journal publishing are estimated at about $10 billion in 2013 (up from $8 billion in 2008, representing a CAGR of about 4.5%), within a broader STM information publishing market worth some $25.2 billion" (Mark Ware and Michael Mabe, *The STM Report: An Overview of Scientific and Scholarly Journal Publishing*, 4th ed. [London: International Association of Scientific, Technical and Medical Publishers, 2015], 6). On the poor value this market provides subscribers, see Theodore C. Bergstrom, P. N.

in the fields in which open access is growing fastest, authors are being asked to pay open access journals an "article processing charge" (APC) often in the thousands of dollars. Such a price effectively excludes (as well as offends) those working in the grant-starved humanities and social sciences, while forcing many others in the Global South to apply for fee waivers.[8]

Scholarly publishing, much like publishing in general, is undergoing radical changes, much as print thoroughly overtook and overturned the medieval manuscript culture five centuries ago (even as textual illumination in the century after the arrival of print arguably peaked in sheer artfulness). Thus a little historical reflection is in order—that is, reflection on the principles that should guide scholarly publishing going forward, as well as on the pitfalls that should be avoided.[9] After all, scholarly work has always been a good of a different order. It thrives through the widest possible circulation, so that others can make something more of its project.

This book reviews these ideas over what is known as the Long Middle Ages in the West, roughly from the fifth to the eighteenth centuries.[10] The story is told through the lives and learning of individual monks and nuns, clerics and scholars, chancellors and philanthropists. At the same time, it is as much a history of learning through institutional succession. It begins with the enclosed monastic world of late antiquity and the early Middle Ages. The book follows learning through the cathedral schools of the High Middle Ages, into the medieval universities, and on to the academies and societies of the early

Courant, R. Preston McAfee, and Michael A. Williams, "Evaluating Big Deal Journal Bundles," *Proceedings of the National Academy of Sciences* 111, no. 26 (2014): 9425-30.

8. David J. Solomon and Bo-Christer Björk, "A Study of Open Access Journals Using Article Processing Charges," *Journal of the American Society for Information Science and Technology* 63, no. 8 (2012). Add to this mix opportunists spamming academics with sham APC journals: see US Federal Trade Commission, "FTC Charges Academic Journal Publisher OMICS Group Deceived Researchers: Complaint Alleges Company Made False Claims, Failed to Disclose Steep Publishing Fees," press release, August 26, 2016, online. John Bohannon submitted a deliberately flawed paper to 304 open access journals—with 121 chosen from Jeffrey Beall's list of "predatory publishers"—of which 157 accepted the paper, including journals with Elsevier and SAGE: "Who's Afraid of Peer Review," *Science* 342, no. 6154 (2013): 60-65.

9. A rare and admirable application of history lessons to today's situation is found in Jean-Claude Guédon, *In Oldenburg's Long Shadow: Librarians, Research Scientists, Publishers, and the Control of Scientific Publishing* (Washington, DC: Association of Research Libraries, 2001).

10. In writing on the Long Middle Ages, Jacques Le Goff observes that "ruptures in the strict sense, clean breaks with what went before, are seldom observed. The usual case is the more or less long, the more or less profound transformation: the turning point, the internal renaissance" (*Must We Divide History into Periods?*, trans. Malcolm Debevoise [New York: Columbia University Press, 2015], 78.)

modern period.[11] These often chartered and incorporated settings provided the learned with a place to study that was more or less apart from the world. Learning moved into the life of the city over time, and into more secular forms and concerns, while retaining traces of ecclesiastical privilege and support.

During this time the learned were developing what can be thought of, from our perspective, as concepts of *intellectual property* before there was any legal recognition of such property rights.[12] The Christian West inherited many of its ideas about authorship and texts from antiquity.[13] Ancient Greek writers had a sense of authorial ownership; they accused others of plagiarism. The Romans objected to the loss of credit resulting from the theft (*furtum*) of one's literary work.[14] Pliny the Elder's first-century *Natural History* advises its readers that he consulted two thousand volumes in creating this work: "You will count as proof of my professionalism the fact that I have prefaced these books with the names of my authorities"; such a practice, he adds, "abounds with honorable modesty."[15] None of this found its way into the body of Roman law—much as plagiarism, per se, doesn't have a place in copyright law today—but concepts of property and propriety in relation to texts did operate among the literary and learned. These concepts found their way into the law, we might say, only after

11. This is not to deny the contribution of non-Western institutions of learning, such as the fifth-century Buddhist center of higher learning Nalanda Mahavihara in what is now northeast India, which continued to educate students until its destruction at the end of the twelfth century; a revival of it as an international university is currently under way (Amartya Sen, "India: The Stormy Revival of an International University," *New York Review of Books* 62, no. 13 [2015]: 69). Sen affirms the debt of today's global university system to the twelfth-century European emergence of the *studium* (with considerable non-Western input discussed in this book) in defending Nalanda's current autonomy with a reference to how "for many hundreds of years universities in Europe have been helped to become academically excellent by governments that respect their autonomy" (70).

12. Pamela O. Long also investigates "what we now call intellectual property" in the "technical, craft and practical traditions" from antiquity to the seventeenth century, which operated up to the fifteenth century "apart from the world of books and learning": *Openness, Secrecy, Authorship: Technical Arts and the Culture of Knowledge from Antiquity to the Renaissance* (Baltimore: Johns Hopkins University Press, 2001), 1–2.

13. Harold Love points to how following the fall of Rome and the Roman literary order, many classical analytical methods had to be reconstructed in a process that fully emerged only with fifteenth-century humanism: *Attributing Authorship: An Introduction* (Cambridge: Cambridge University Press, 2002), 14–18.

14. Scott McGill points out that plagiarism was not a legal matter then (or today) but a matter of stolen credit: "Plagiarism [in Rome] was understood to accomplish something for its practitioners, namely, to win them credit they did not deserve" (*Plagiarism in Latin Literature* [Cambridge: Cambridge University Press, 2012], 5). The Romans, he demonstrates, had an extralegal sense of intellectual property, using the example of "Seneca the Younger, who notes [in the first century] that Cicero owned the content of his work as its author, while Dorus, the bookseller, only owned the material text of Cicero, over which he had the right of *usus* or usufruct" (16).

15. Pliny the Elder, *Natural History: A Selection*, trans. John F. Healy (London: Penguin, 1991), 6.

printers and booksellers had gained sufficient economic and political force in the early eighteenth century.

I refer to this book as a prehistory because the term *intellectual property* did not enter the English language until the latter half of the eighteenth century (while this book concludes at the beginning of that century).[16] Over the course of this history, which ends with the legal instantiation of intellectual property in 1710, I will demonstrate how the learned have treated texts in ways that foreshadow this later legislated governance of intangible goods. In many ways, scholars have long treated texts like property. For example, the learned were continually assembling a virtual registry of intellectual properties. They maintained that registry not in a single office, of course, but in catalogs, commentaries, compilations, and encyclopedias, distributed among libraries of the works themselves. They surveyed such properties, identifying with great precision who wrote what when, while noting the qualities or properties of the works. If the learned did not commonly refer to a text as a *property* (let alone as an intellectual property), they did refer to it as a *work*. In this sense the text resembles what a craftsperson or artist produces, and possesses value as such.

Adding to this historical sense of a proto-intellectual property is how the production and registry of these properties operated within institutional frameworks. In the history presented here, it begins with monasticism and concludes with the intersecting worlds of university and commerce. The scholars' use of such properties within these institutions is governed by learned norms, rights, and responsibilities, with evidence of this often found in accusations of misuse, misconstrual, misattribution, and forgery.[17] Further distinguishing the standing of these works was their dependence on a system of patronage.

As I worked on this history of learning and its properties, it became clear to me that my original question about expectations of access to learning was

16. The anonymous first instance cited by *Oxford English Dictionary* is from a 1769 *Monthly Review* article—"What a niggard this Doctor is of his own, and how profuse he is of other people's intellectual property"—which supports the definition of the term as "chiefly *Law* property (such as patents, trademarks, and copyright material) which is the product of invention or creativity, and does not exist in a tangible, physical form." The *OED* indicates that *copyright* was first used in the House of Lords in 1735 in relation to author rights, while Chaucer is credited with the fourteenth-century introduction of *patent* referring to a royally conferred right or privilege.

17. See Anthony Grafton for examples of how judgments of forgery dating back to the Renaissance—involving the "sharp sense of literary property and individuality . . . [and] high level of attention to textual detail"—honed the critical skills of philological and rhetorical scholarship: *Forgers and Critics: Creativity and Duplicity in Western Scholarship* (Princeton, NJ: Princeton University Press, 1990), 78.

only one part of the picture. Over the course of this book, I set out an expanded vision of how working with learned texts involves not only rights of access but includes five other distinctive properties as well: accreditation, autonomy, communality, sponsorship, and use.[18] In each chapter I demonstrate how these properties are inherently an intellectual part of learning, from the medieval to early modern periods. It should be clear that I am drawing on the multiple meanings of *property* in association with learning and its texts. For example, I write about how texts use and credit one another for their intellectual qualities or properties; I refer to how people have a property (proprietary) claim on a text they have worked on, which is to say a property right of accreditation, whether they are its author, editor, translator, or commentator. They also have a property right of access and use as a reader. When describing the communality, sponsorship, and autonomy of learned texts, I refer to how a text is financed and valued within a property system, however loosely structured. In the process, I find that these six properties (access, accreditation, autonomy, communality, sponsorship, and use) reflect elements of regulation and economy that suggest a prototypical intellectual property system that has long operated within the culture of learning.

My work with this history has convinced me of three things concerning learning's intellectual properties. First of all, the particular regard for the properties of texts fostered by learning has come to play a major role in the modern legal construct of intellectual property, especially in its application to published work, beginning in the early eighteenth century. This is especially apparent in what is commonly regarded as the legislation that initiated the modern era of copyright, which is the Statute of Anne, passed by the British Parliament in 1710.[19] The statute gives pride of place to learning. It is entitled "An Act for the Encouragement of Learning, by Vesting the Copies

18. An earlier parallel to my work in this book is found in Robert K. Merton's expounding the "ethos of science" in terms of four "institutional imperatives"—universalism, communism, disinterestedness, and organized skepticism (abbreviated CUDOS)—and while the properties that I identify are also very much a matter of institutions, my focus is on the nature of learned work with texts. Merton, "Normative Structures of Science," in *The Sociology of Science: Theoretical and Empirical Investigations*, ed. Norman W. Storer (Chicago: University of Chicago Press, 1973), 267–78.

19. With inventions and patents, the earliest form of legal protection for a work was granted to the architect Flippo Brunellschi in 1421 by the Council of Florence for a cargo ship design; Venice instituted a patent law, granting a ten-year monopoly in 1474 for the building of a "new and ingenious device," as the statute reads, "of great utility and benefit to our commonwealth": cited by Guilio Mandich, "Venetian Patents (1450-1550)," *Journal of the Patent Office Society* 30, no. 3 (1948): 176–77. Long places the origins of the patent concept within intellectual property in "late medieval craft production" (*Openness, Secrecy, Authorship*, 10).

of Printed Books in the Authors or Purchasers of Such Copies, during the Times Therein Mentioned."[20] Printers and booksellers had much to do with the passing of this act, as we shall see, but more than a few of the act's clauses are devoted to enshrining and protecting the intellectual property rights of learning. This act influenced, in turn, the intellectual property clause introduced into the United States Constitution at the original constitutional convention in 1789. This clause empowered Congress "to promote the Progress of Science and useful Arts, by securing for limited Times to Authors and Inventors the exclusive Right to their respective Writings and Discoveries."[21] Learning was front and center at the birth of the current legal sense of intellectual property. That is, however, where this book concludes.

The second thing that has become clear is that from the book's beginning, with Saint Jerome, works of learning can be seen to differ from other types of property, intellectual or otherwise. This difference is marked by the various sorts of institutional, economic, and legal arrangements afforded to learning over the course of this history, as well as by the way that scholars attend, above all, to what is intellectual about the properties at issue. This book presents the historical grounds for thinking of scholarly work as constituting a distinct order of intellectual property. These six properties help to set the learned book apart from a literary work or a craft secret, such as glassblowing. The development of this historical distinction is a crucial one in thinking about the rationale for open access to research and scholarship today. For, while I found that the emphasis on access to learning to be but one of the properties distinguishing this form of work, historical efforts to increase and improve access—through copying and translation, paper and printing, libraries and academies—were among the more constant and inventive activities of learned institutions.

A third factor running throughout this history is the extent to which the intellectual property most at issue for the advancement of learning is not my starting point of access to texts. It is the use of texts. The scholarly norm is that not just the text's authors, but everyone who works with that text, is engaged in supporting and facilitating the use of the work, from the author's original care in its composition, through processes of reviewing and editing, publishing and indexing, commenting and referencing. Breakthroughs, innovations, and other academic achievements often result from the brilliant

20. The Statute of Anne, April 10, 1710, Avalon Project, Lillian Goldman Law Library, Yale University, 2008, online.
21. US Const. art. 1, §8, cl. 8.

use of others' texts, whether by extending, combining, or fault finding. As the modern legal structure of intellectual property is intended to provide an incentive to create works that instruct and delight the public, so with learning the prize comes from the use that others are able to make of a work. The "fair use" exception to copyright infringement, which is permitted under certain conditions, has its origins in the scholar's assumed right to such use of others' work, as well as the additional scholar's obligations of proper crediting.

In addition to the way in which I employ properties in this book, it should also be clear by this point that I use *learning* in the somewhat archaic spirit of Francis Bacon's *The Advancement of Learning* (or, as the 1605 edition had it, *Of the Advancement and Proficience of Learning, or the Partitions of Science*). Learning in this sense encompasses the liberal arts, scholasticism, theology, humanism, and natural philosophy. It involves the study of texts, especially as it gives rise to further texts; it involves recording and publishing observations of the night sky, as well as the day's weather and tides, whether for purposes of comparison with, or the compilation of, others' data.[22] This use of *learning* offers me the further advantage of reconnecting the work of scholar and student, as learning today is more often ascribed to students than to scholars (while historically the "scholars" of the medieval university were students taught by masters).[23] This connection is one of the educationally encouraging results of open access, as more of this scholarly learning is becoming available to current, future, and past students everywhere.

As noted, the term "learning" played a prominent part in the initial copyright legislation. What then of learning's place within today's definition of intellectual property? The lawyers' favorite, *Black's Law Dictionary*, defines intellectual property thus: "A category of intangible rights protecting commercially valuable products of the human intellect" and "a commercially valuable product of the human intellect, in a concrete or abstract form."[24] The

22. Gianna Pomata and Nancy G. Sirais identify how the sciences and humanities in the early modern era were united in "the coupling of empiricism and erudition," or "'learned' empiricism" (introduction to *Historia: Empiricism and Erudition in Early Modern Europe*, ed. Pomata and Sirais [Cambridge, MA: MIT Press, 2005], 7-8). Lorraine Daston notes an early modern "collective empiricism," in which "the library has never ceased to be a site of scientific knowledge, alongside the laboratory and the observatory" ("The Science of the Archive," *Osiris* 27, no. 1 [2012]: 162).

23. A further interest of mine in connecting scholars and students arises out of my years as a schoolteacher and then an education researcher investigating, among other things, student publishing (*The New Literacy: Redefining Reading and Writing in the Schools* [New York: Routledge, 1990]) including, one year, to take hundreds of students through the history of publishing ("To Publish and Publish and Publish," *Language Arts* 62, no. 6 [1985]: 619-23).

24. Bryan A. Garner, ed., *Black's Law Dictionary*, 8th ed. (St. Paul, MN: West, 2004), 824.

emphasis on protecting "commercially valuable products" may well seem to put the work of learning at a disadvantage under this definition. Yet if learning has lost ground in legal thinking about intellectual property, it has by no means disappeared from American law or elsewhere.[25]

In the United States, scholars and students constantly make what is legally recognized as "fair use" of copyrighted material under the exemption reserved for "teaching, scholarship and research," which also allows for criticism and news, within limits in all cases.[26] Then there is the recognition of the "academic exception" within common law, which allows faculty members to retain the copyright associated with their work, including research and teaching materials, rather than having it revert to their employers, which is common in other enterprises.[27] By the same token, there is a patent research exception in common law, which allows researchers to conduct experiments utilizing patented processes without having to license them.[28] A further legal recognition of learning's standing is the Bayh-Dole Act of 1980, which enables researchers and their universities to secure patents for the results of federally funded research to help these inventions reach the public. Still, compared to where learning once stood in those initial eighteenth-century expressions of intellectual property law, it is left with a handful of legal limits and exceptions to protect its best interests. The law intended for "the encouragement of learning" and "to promote the progress of science" has been displaced by interests in, to return to *Black's*, "protecting commercially valuable products of the human intellect."

Just as learning's place within the law has been diminished, so intellectual property does not have much of a place in the education of the young. Little, if anything, is taught about intellectual property in classes devoted to literature, history, social studies, or economics, though it is the means by

25. For an international comparison of educational allowances in copyright law, see Raquel Xalabarder, *Study on Copyright Limitations and Exceptions for Educational Activities in North America, Europe, Caucasus, Central Asia and Israel* (Geneva: World Intellectual Property Organization, 2009).

26. On fair use in the United States, see US Code 17.107: "the various purposes for which the reproduction of a particular work may be considered fair, such as criticism, comment, news reporting, teaching, scholarship, and research."

27. Corynne McSherry, *Who Owns Academic Work? Battling for Control of Intellectual Property* (Cambridge, MA: Harvard University Press, 2001), 101–8.

28. On the common-law patent research exemption and its decline in recent years, see Rebecca S. Eisenberg, "Patent Swords and Shields," *Science* 299, no. 5609 (2003): 1018–19. For the "academic exception," see Chris Triggs, "Academic Freedom, Copyright and the Academic Exception," *Workplace: A Journal for Academic Labor* 13 (2005): 60–79; for a more recent summary of these exemptions, including how "academics form a cognizable class," see Gideon Parchomovsky and Alex Stein, "Intellectual Property Defenses," *Columbia Law Review* 113, no. 6 (2013): 1501.

which the expression of ideas often makes its way to the bank, ends up in court (and then finds its way into the press). If intellectual property issues do arise in the schools—in matters of, say, teachers making questionable copies—it is likely to be dismissed by educators as the business concerns of other people, such as publishers, which is to say not part of education.

But dealing in intellectual property has long been the craft and trade of educators and scholars. What the concept of intellectual property shares with education's project is this involvement in information rights and responsibilities. The topic provides a means of teaching the young about the nature of the law and legal reasoning as it bears on their own creative practices, as well as on the big names in the music business. A greater understanding of intellectual property can serve their own use of media; enable them to take advantage of new licensing models; and, more generally, prepare them for the knowledge-based economy into which they are graduating.[29] So equipped, students might be more likely to lend their support, later in life, to the protections and distinctions that are vital to learning continuing its contribution to the world.

While it is always challenging to draw applicable lessons from historical instances, I do believe in the value of reflecting on the longstanding principles and patterns of scholarly publishing as we go bravely into this digital era. That we have lost sight of how learning stands apart from other enterprises became strikingly apparent not long ago with the arrest of open access advocate Aaron Swartz. On January 10, 2010, this young internet activist and Harvard fellow was charged with wire and computer fraud violations for allegedly entering an unlocked MIT wiring closet and illegally downloading to his laptop roughly 4.8 million scholarly journal articles from the JSTOR database of older journal issues.[30] Carmen Ortiz, US Attorney for the District of Massachusetts, explained Swartz's indictment, for which he was facing up to thirty-five years in prison and a million dollars in fines, by stating that "stealing is stealing, whether you use a computer command or a crowbar, and whether you take documents, data or dollars. It is equally

29. See the Creative Commons approach to copyright, originated by Lawrence Lessig, "The Creative Commons," *Florida Law Review* 55 (2003): 763–78. Or Yochai Benkler's forms of "nonmarket and nonproprietary production" taking place within "the networked information economy," which amount, for him, to a post–Adam Smith "wealth of networks." *The Wealth of Networks: How Social Production Transforms Markets and Freedom* (New Haven, CT: Yale University Press, 2006), 2.

30. "JSTOR Evidence in *United States vs. Aaron Swartz: Overview*" (New York: JSTOR, July 30, 2013), online.

harmful to the victim, whether you sell what you have stolen or give it away."[31]

This one-size-fits-all approach to property is the very point that Swartz was challenging, I think it fair to say, with this act of civil disobedience. The "victim" in this crime, which was JSTOR, allowed that there were property distinctions to be made with learning. For, after initially alerting MIT to the massive downloads, which were explicitly forbidden in its contract with university libraries, JSTOR declined to press charges. In its statement on the affair, JSTOR pointed to its efforts to "offer deeply discounted or free access in furtherance of our mission."[32] The US attorney general's office persisted in the case. On January 11, 2013, two years after his arrest and before the case went to trial, Aaron Swartz, at the age of twenty-six, committed suicide.

The legal grounds for thinking that learned works constitute a different order of intellectual property were only strengthened a year after Swartz's death, when the United States Congress passed the Consolidated Appropriations Act 2014. Deep within its six hundred pages is a requirement that federal agencies with research and development expenditures over $100 million annually develop a public access policy for any research resulting from their funding. This policy will ensure that the public will have "free online public access to such final peer-reviewed manuscripts or published versions within 12 months after the official publication date."[33] As I write, this measure, which has yet to be revoked by President Trump's administration, recognizes that the public sponsorship of research brings into play a different set of rights and responsibilities. Well, not quite. The research is also allowed to remain a private good. The new law requires public access only to the "final peer-reviewed manuscripts" (rather than the published version), with publishers allowed to impose up to a one-year embargo on such access following publication. It might well seem as if the big corporate publishers of this research had successfully lobbied to ensure that their commercial property rights outweighed learning's interests in communality, access, and rights of use, leaving the public with what might well seem a degraded version of this intellectual property.[34]

31. John Schwartz, "Internet Activist, a Creator of RSS, Is Dead at 26, Apparently a Suicide," *New York Times*, January 12, 2014. See Brian Knappenberger's film *The Internet's Own Boy: The Story of Aaron Swartz* (2014), available on YouTube.

32. "JSTOR Evidence."

33. Consolidated Appropriations Act, 2014, H.R. 3547 Sec. 527, 412-12.

34. John Willinsky, "The Publisher's Pushback against NIH's Public Access Policy and Scholarly Publishing Sustainability," *PLoS Biology* 7, no. 1 (2009): e30.

It is another indication of how commercial interests can fray the social contract between university and world.[35] The sciences, in particular, have been pushed in recent years to become centers of "campus capitalism" involving the "commodification of academic research" in "the knowledge factory," to borrow from the titles of three books on the current crisis in higher education.[36] President Barack Obama was among those who cast the campus hookup with capitalism as reflecting the spirit of the country: "And that's what America is all about," Obama declared on January 15, 2014, at North Carolina State University about his National Network for Manufacturing Innovation. "We have always been about research, innovation, and then commercializing that research and innovation so that everybody can benefit."[37]

Is the university to be no more than a network node in manufacturing innovation? Does commercialization alone ensure that everyone benefits from the research conducted by universities? The support for industry-driven, patentable research reflects a "market logic," according to Elizabeth Popp Berman, a sociologist at the State University of New York at Albany, in which the university is an "economic engine" with "science as an economic input."[38] Although I am presenting a history of learned texts rather than patentable inventions, today's intellectual property chase on campuses, spurred by the Bayh-Dole Act in the United States, is increasingly defining the value of

35. On this contractual theme, see David H. Guston and Kenneth Keniston, "Introduction: The Social Contract for Science," in *Fragile Contract: University Science and the Federal Government*, ed. Guston and Keniston (Cambridge, MA: MIT Press, 1994), 13. David B. Downing considers a knowledge contract to be "the set of implicit and explicit obligations that justify both the epistemological and commercial uses of higher education": *The Knowledge Contract: Politics and Paradigms in the Academic Workplace* (Lincoln: University of Nebraska Press, 2005), 5.

36. Daniel S. Greenberg, *Science for Sale: The Perils, Rewards, and Delusions of Campus Capitalism* (Chicago: University of Chicago Press, 2007); Hans Radder, *The Commodification of Academic Research: Science and the Modern University* (Pittsburgh: University of Pittsburgh Press, 2010); and Stanley Aronowitz, *The Knowledge Factory* (Boston: Beacon, 2000). See also Roger L. Geiger, *Knowledge and Money: Research Universities and the Paradox of the Marketplace* (Stanford, CA: Stanford University Press, 2004).

37. Barack Obama, speech on the National Network for Manufacturing Innovation, North Carolina State University, Raleigh, January 15, 2014.

38. Elizabeth Popp Berman, *Creating the Market University* (Princeton, NJ: Princeton University Press, 2012), 173, 175. Berman: "The change in academic science can be seen as resulting from the economic rationalization of political life as much as it resulted from the growing influence of neoliberalism" (175). Sheila Slaughter outlines the "shift away from a public good academic knowledge/ learning regime to an academic capitalist knowledge/learning regime" that increasingly links "state agencies, corporations and universities": "Retheorizing Academic Capital," in *Academic Capitalism in the Age of Globalization*, ed. Brendan Cantwell and Ilkka Kauppinen (Baltimore: Johns Hopkins University Press, 2014), 26, 12.

higher education.[39] While marketing a patent has a role to play in ensuring public access, the patent pursuit in universities—Gatorade, Google, and other success stories notwithstanding—has led to more financial drain than gain.[40]

Yet these complaints about the university's loss of distinction from the commercial sector are not limited to the sciences. The humanities, which play a major role in the prehistory I trace in the chapters that follow, are presently experiencing the creep of market logic. "Thirsty for national profit, nations, and their systems of education, are heedlessly discarding skills that are needed to keep democracies alive," sharply observes Martha Nussbaum, Ernst Freund Distinguished Service Professor of Law and Ethics at the University of Chicago.[41] Nussbaum counters that "democracy needs the humanities" far more than it needs a youth trained for the marketplace.[42] She claims that the humanities provide democracy with "responsible citizens" who possess "the ability to assess historical evidence, to use and think critically about economic principles, to assess accounts of social justice, to speak a foreign language, to appreciate the complexities of the major religions."[43] The history that I present here, however, does not attest to learning's inherently democratic values and practice. It makes clear that learned men contributed to the exclusion of women from higher education, just as they made their peace with European imperialism, finding advantage in the bounty of conquest and the profits of slavery.[44]

39. Janice M. Mueller holds the Bayh-Dole Act responsible for the "patent-centric environment of biotechnological and biomedical research and development": "No Dilettante Affair: Rethinking the Experimental Use Exception to Patent Infringement for Biomedical Research Tools," *Washington Law Review* 76, no. 4 (2001): 5. According to Mueller, the "experimental use" exemption for patents is lost to many labs because of their interest in commercialization.

40. On the hidden cost of the patent chase to the academic mission, see Jacob H. Rooksby and Brian Pusser, "Learning to Litigate: University Patents in the Knowledge Economy," in *Academic Capitalism in the Age of Globalization*, ed. Cantwell and Kauppinen, 74–93. Further, most university patents go unlicensed, with some picked up by "patent trolls" whose accumulate-to-sue model only deters innovation: *AUTM Licensing Activity Survey Highlights* (Deerfield, IL: Association of University Technology Managers, 2012); Heidi Ledford, "Universities Struggle to Make Patents Pay," *Nature* 501, no. 7468 (2013).

41. Martha Nussbaum, *Not for Profit: Why Democracy Needs the Humanities* (Princeton, NJ: Princeton University Press, 2010), 3. Note that I identify faculty members' positions, and where readily available, their extended titles, given the vital role played by institutions and benefactors (and their naming) in this history of learning.

42. Ibid., 2.

43. Ibid.

44. On the educational legacy of imperialism, see, for example, my *Learning to Divide the World: Education at Empire's End* (Minneapolis: University of Minnesota Press, 1996), and on the role of

The critical, reflective questioning that Nussbaum refers to, when it did happen historically, was often the work of a solitary voice rather than a field of study. Think of Bartolomé de las Casas, the fifteenth-century Dominican, historian, and outspoken opponent of imperialism, documenting in protest "the devastation and depopulation of the land" brought on by the Spanish conquest of the Indies.[45] More often—with the example of Locke proving instructive (covered in the final chapters)—the learned conducted their studies alongside the forces of imperialism, providing it with a civilizing veneer; only later did others find elements in their work that served abolitionist and anticolonial causes. Through all of it, whether we consider the current invasion of market logic or the long-term failure to speak truth to power, those engaged in this learning are seeking to establish a place for this form of work, based on what distinguishes the research and scholarship of the academy from other forms of work. The distinctions form part of a historical legacy that those who are seeking to change this institution today might well want to explore and exploit.

I consider both the heroic and the dispiriting actions by those who moved this learning into the world; and I highlight misogynist and ethnocentric shortcomings as well as the efforts to redress them. I offer an episodic rather than a comprehensive history. I have selected nuns, monks, schoolmen, university masters, and scholars for what they demonstrate or have to say about the making of books as the means and ends of learning. Thus this book is not so much about their best ideas as about their manner of working with their own and others' ideas.

This history returns to familiar figures, whether Augustine, Abelard, or Aquinas (among the A's), in the familiar settings of monastery, cathedral school, and medieval university. But I am after something that I believe is less known about these figures and settings, which is what they were able to make of the composing, production, and circulation of learned works within these institutions. And I augment their stories with less familiar figures, such as Alcuin, Averroës, and Avicenna (again the A-team), who deserve to play a more prominent part, I believe, in our understanding of what the West has made of scholarly inquiry and pursuits. The work of these scholars bears on what becomes the concept of intellectual property. They operated within a

slavery in the development of American higher education, Craig Steven Wilder, *Ebony and Ivy: Race, Slavery, and the Troubled History of America's Universities* (New York: Bloomsbury, 2014).

45. Bartolomé de las Casas, *A Short Account of the Destruction of the Indies*, trans. Nigel Griffin (London: Penguin, 2004), 14.

system of rights and responsibilities involving texts and institutions in an evolving (easily breached) social contract with the larger world. We are not done with this legacy, as we continue to work out the standing of research and scholarship as a public good and a force for change. It is part of a history that is often lost to sight within the workings of academic culture today, for all the medieval trappings that it has ceremoniously retained. This historical struggle over the values of learning took many different forms, and it can inform our aspirations for the university's social contract today.

This history offers much on the persistence of learning's hard-earned institutional autonomy, as well as on its sponsorship by a world that often, if inconsistently, valued what such institutions had to offer. At issue is the *commonwealth of learning*, a phrase I take from Locke. His influential theory of property in the *Two Treatises* was, as I noted in the preface, a starting point in my thinking about this project, and it occupies the penultimate chapter of this book, while his political activism around intellectual property legislation forms the basis of the concluding chapter. And while the *Two Treatises* does not deal substantively with anything resembling intellectual property, Locke makes an oblique reference to the concept in the opening of *An Essay concerning Human Understanding*. In the book's "Epistle to the Reader" he famously writes (at least among Locke scholars) of how "the Commonwealth of Learning is not without its Master-Builders, whose mighty Designs, in advancing the Sciences, will leave lasting Monuments to the Admiration of Posterity."[46]

---

46. John Locke, *An Essay concerning Human Understanding*, ed. Peter H. Nidditch (Oxford: Oxford University Press, 1975), 9. Locke also uses "commonwealth of learning" in an unpublished critique of John Norris, complaining of those who "set themselves up as Dictators in ye Commonwealth of learning": cited by Charlotte Johnston, "Locke's Examination of Malebranche and John Norris," *Journal of the History of Ideas* 19, no. 4 (1958): 554. Charles D. Tarlton notes of Locke that "on 7 August, a little more than two weeks before the *Two Treatises* was licensed for publication, he wrote to Philippus van Limbroch that 'the commonwealth of learning here is taking a complete holiday; we have all become politicians'": "'The Rulers Now on Earth': Locke's *Two Treatises* and the Revolution of 1688," *Historical Journal* 28, no. 2 (1985): 294. The expression *commonwealth of learning* was used by others in Locke's day: see John Aubrey, *Brief Lives*, ed. Richard Barber (Woodbridge, Suffolk, UK: Boydell and Brewer, 1982), 162, 315; William Temple cited by George Williamson, "The Restoration Revolt against Enthusiasm," *Studies in Philology* 30, no. 4 (1933): 582; Samuel Hartlib, cited by R. H. Syfret, "The Origins of the Royal Society," *Notes and Records of the Royal Society of London* 5, no. 2 (1948): 96. Edmund Halley writes of Newton's *Principia* being "more serviceable to the Commonwealth of Learning" for the care taken by "the Publisher" (himself) in an advertisement in the *Philosophical Transactions* 16 (1687): 297; see Henry P. Macomber, "A Comparison of the Variations and Errors in Copies of the First Edition of Newton's *Principia*, 1687," *Isis* 42, no. 3 (1951): 231.

The commonwealth of learning offers a powerful guiding image for this book. It suggests a self-governing state (much as the more popular "republic of letters" does), one that the learned have founded for themselves, with their work constituting a wealth held in common. Locke had spent his youth in the Commonwealth of England, initiated by Oliver Cromwell in 1649, whom his father had supported during the Civil War. Since the sixteenth century, a "commonwealth of the people" has been invoked more than once in calls for justice and self-determination against arbitrary uses of power. It has been a way of positing an alternative political and economic structure organized around the collective interests of its members, whether in resisting the agrarian enclosure measures in early modern England or, in this case, working against an unwarranted enclosure of learning.[47]

The commonwealth of learning is about the governance and operating norms of what is, at one level, no more than a trade in works of learning, including, on rare occasions, the lasting Monuments of the Master Builders, as Locke puts it. In what follows, I will show how this commonwealth has worked out what is, in effect, an elaborate intellectual property system entailing the rights and responsibilities associated with the production and circulation of learned works. This system involves the distinctive practices and norms around what I am framing as the properties of learning, namely access, accreditation, autonomy, communality, sponsorship, and the use of such works.

No less relevant to this history is how Locke moves in the *Essay*'s "Epistle" to the sort of labor that constitutes learning's commonwealth, which involves not only building monuments but improving access to knowledge: "But every one must not hope to be a *Boyle*, or a *Sydenham*; and in an Age that produces such Masters, as the Great—*Huygenius*, and the incomparable Mr. *Newton*, with some other of that Strain; 'tis Ambition enough to be employed as an Under-Laborer in clearing the Ground a little, and removing some of the

---

47. Christopher Kendrick, *Utopia, Carnival, and Commonwealth in Renaissance England* (Toronto: University of Toronto Press, 2004), 113–21. Anthony Grafton locates the origins of the Republic of Letters in a similar sixteenth-century framework of "moral duty," "civil code," "intellectual market," "patrons," and "free communication of ideas": "A Sketch Map of a Lost Continent: The Republic of Letters," in *Worlds Made by Words: Scholarship and Community in the Modern West* (Cambridge, MA: Harvard University Press, 2009), 22–27. Adding to this sense of quasi-legal structure, Anne Goldgar writes of its "ethos of service," in which "scholars relied on the 'rights of the Republic of Letters' to ask the services they required": *Impolite Learning: Conduct and Community in the Republic of Letters, 1680–1750* (New Haven, CT: Yale University Press, 1995), 51. On the enclosure parallels between land and the intellectual property, see James Boyle, *The Public Domain: Enclosing the Commons of the Mind* (New Haven, CT: Yale University Press, 2008).

Rubbish that lies in the way to Knowledge."[48] The Under-Laborer here, putting his back into freeing up the way to knowledge, is our humble Locke. The considerable efforts that are needed to improve access to learning are among the principal duties and pleasures of life in this commonwealth.

This book of mine, to dare a shameless comparison, reflects a similar desire. My wish is to speed the plow and clear the path to learning by recounting its past. Some rubbish has also come to obscure long-standing historical distinctions that have set the lasting intellectual properties of learning apart from the fine properties of Apple and Disney, as well as from those of Margaret Atwood and Toni Morrison. 'Tis ambition enough, indeed, as Locke has it, to bring these historic distinctions to the fore. In the *Essay*, Locke clears the way by working through the properties of knowledge; here, I underscore the practices and distinctions that have long constituted the intellectual properties of learning's commonwealth. Our story begins, in the next chapter, with the rise of monasticism, which got off to a powerful intellectual start with the towering and prolific figures of Jerome and Augustine, as the Latin Christian West emerged out of late antiquity, only to face and gradually overcome the contrary forces of Benedict's pervasive monastic *Rule*.

48. Locke, *Essay*, 9–10.

PART ONE

Monastery and School

CHAPTER TWO

The Medieval Monastic Paradox

I realize that to begin a history of intellectual property with the Christian monasteries of late antiquity and the Middle Ages may well call to mind hooded monks silently pacing abbey cloisters with manuscript books in hand, or nuns in wimple and tunic bent over desks, copying and illuminating such works, with Gregorian chants filling the air. Such cinematic images are not out of place as a backdrop to our history, although they do tend to obscure the daily hardship and sacrifice practiced by the monks and nuns whose lives I discuss. Amid the gritty, rough-hewn discomforts of monastic life, monk and nun, abbot and abbess, created a manuscript culture that dominated the intellectual life of the Latin West from the fourth to twelfth centuries. In this first section, I set out the indebtedness of Western scholarship to Christian monasticism. It proves to be remarkable not only in light of the barbaric tenor of the times, but also because abbey and church were not always the great protectors of learning.

"The struggle of Christianity against intellectualism in all its forms," according to Max Weber, was the "hallmark" of this new religion in its early years.[1] "Anti-intellectualism currents in early Christianity" are reflected in the church's original focus on "the poor in spirit, rather than scholars," notes this pioneer of historical sociology, writing in the first decade of the twentieth century at Heidelberg University, for Christianity lacked "the ritualistic and legalistic scholarship of Judaism and the soteriology of the Gnostic

---

1. Max Weber, *Economy and Society: An Outline of Interpretative Sociology*, ed. Guenther Roth and Claus Wittich (Berkeley: University of California Press, 1978), 1:512.

intellectual aristocrats" from the same period of late antiquity.[2] All that Weber is willing to grant the early church, intellectually, is "the strong influence
of monastic rationalism," which he sees evolving into the Protestant ethic of
asceticism that was to prove vital to the success of capitalism.[3]

However dated Weber's sweeping characterizations may seem today, his
analysis points to the enigma by which "intellectualism in all its forms" took
root in the Christian West. The history of monasticism starts out promisingly
enough, with the intellectual flair of Saints Jerome and Augustine in the fourth
and fifth centuries. They were superbly educated holdovers of late antiquity,
and the devotion to learning that they brought to monasticism would be rarely
seen for centuries to come after the fall of Rome and the monastic adoption of
the *Rule of Benedict*, whose extreme asceticism and devotion to prayer became
a dominant force in monasticism from the seventh century onward. It meant
that the learned risked charges of vanity and pride over their studies; their
questioning and curiosity could be said to forge a path to heresy; and their treasured libraries were accused of bringing worldly possessions into conflict
with the pious goal of looking into the face of God.[4]

So how was it that the great and varied learning, which I review in later
chapters, of the Venerable Bede, Hildegard of Bingen, and Anselm of Canterbury was to find its place within the abbey walls of the medieval monastery?
How did the monasteries play such a key role in the ninth-century Carolingian
Renaissance? How did the few available works in Latin of Plato and Aristotle
become commonly available, despite their pagan standing, in many monastic
libraries? How did a monastery not far from Rome become home to the first
printing press outside of Germany, with the classics among its initial offerings?
The paradox of this peculiar medieval institution is that, despite the *Rule*, it
did indeed prove to be well suited to fostering a degree of learning to which

2. Ibid., 510, 512. In contrast to Weber's position, Anthony Grafton and Megan Williams emphasize how "Christians inherited much, intellectually, from the great Jewish community that had
existed at Alexandria before it was destroyed in the Jewish rebellion that erupted in Egypt in about
117": *Christianity and the Transformation of the Book: Origen, Eusebius, and the Library of Caesarea*
(Cambridge, MA: Harvard University Press, 2008), 76.

3. Weber, *Economy and Society*, 513. Weber allows that monastic rationality and asceticism were
eventually transferred through the Protestant Reformation "into everyday life," where they "began
to dominate worldly morality" and thus contributed to "the tremendous cosmos of the modern economic order": Max Weber, *The Protestant Ethic and the Rise of Capitalism*, trans. Talcott Parsons
(New York: HarperCollins Academic, 1991), 181.

4. "The union of hearts and minds in a monastery . . . showed the first hesitant stages of the
creation of an ideal community that would reach fulfillment only in Heavenly Jerusalem at the end
of time" (Peter Brown, *Through the Eye of a Needle: Wealth, the Fall of Rome, and the Making of Christianity in the West, 350–550 AD* [Princeton, NJ: Princeton University Press, 2012], 180).

it was opposed in principle. The well-endowed, self-governing, highly disciplined monastery, operating at a remove from the world, proved to be the perfect spot in which to produce, accumulate, and retain manuscripts. The cathedral and court libraries, on the other hand, were far more susceptible to losses from war, riots, and theft.[5]

To resolve the paradox within their lives, learned nuns and monks sought to demonstrate the value of such learning to the community; they proved that it served the piety and charity of the whole rather than detracting from them; they treated their work as part of a common good to be shared not only within their religious house but among the greater network of monasteries. All of this had an effect on their thinking about manuscripts and texts. It influenced their regard for composing, copying, and compiling these works. The intangible text was thought of as an object. It could be ascribed to the mind of God or to a mortal author, known or unknown; it could be seen to have had multiple hands work on it. The text had a regulated, if often disputed, spiritual and intellectual standing within and outside this community; it was seen as something to be preserved, copied, corrected, assessed, and shared. The body of work that circulated among the network of monasteries that spread across the West reflected at many points, as I go on to show, what can be termed the *intellectual properties of learning*.

Before turning to the lives of the saints, in the form of Jerome, Augustine, Benedict, and Radegund, as well as the statesman Cassiodorus, let me offer a word on the origins of Christian monasticism. The monastic life begins with a vow to turn one's back on the world. It is rooted, in a biblical sense, in Jesus's forty days of solitude and fasting in the desert (Matt. 4:1–11). In Christianity, it originated in the third century, when a number of the pious headed into the desert beyond the edge of the Nile's floodplains to escape persecution and the schisms within the church.[6] The most celebrated and

5. Ronald G. Witt, *The Two Latin Cultures and the Foundation of Renaissance Humanism in Medieval Italy* (Cambridge: Cambridge University Press, 2012), 10–11. Witt cautions that this preservation factor may have led to an exaggerated sense of monastic learning relative to that of other institutions.

6. John M. McCulloh, "Confessor Saints and the Origins of Monasticism: The *Lives* of Saints Antony and Martin," in *The Middle Ages in Text and Texture: Reflections on Medieval Sources*, ed. Jason Glenn (Toronto: University of Toronto Press, 2011), 22–23. Douglas Burton-Christie identifies "the considerable dispute among historians regarding the origins of monasticism, the major influences upon its rise and growth and its effects on the world," while providing a catalog of reasons for monasticism's early desert form, including that it was "a quest for knowledge (gnosis); a flight from taxes; a refuge from the law; a new form of martyrdom; revival of an earlier Jewish ascetical movement; a rejection of classical culture; an expression of Manichean dualism; a response to a call from the

influential among the early monastics was Antony of Egypt. The son of wealthy landowners, he walked away from that world at the turn of the third century to embrace solitude and piety in an abandoned desert fortress. He was followed there by others who believed his holiness could cure their ills, which only drove him deeper into the wilderness.

The hermit's solitary worship, known as eremitic monasticism, was soon supplanted by a more congenial cohabiting of monastics led by Pachomius in fourth-century Egypt, who established religious houses for men and women along the Nile.[7] This cenobitic form of monasticism (from the Greek word for "communal life") drew its scriptural inspiration from the communal association of Jesus's disciples after his ascension to heaven and, perhaps more directly, from Jewish monastic communities outside Alexandria in the first century BCE.[8] Women were active in monasticism from the outset, with those of noble birth and marriage often leading the early monasteries. The gendered segregation of religious communities came about only after considerable debate, leading to double monasteries, as well as women's religious houses.

While this book focuses on the Latin West, monasticism also took hold in the Eastern Roman Empire. Cenobitic, or community-based, monasticism spread through the Greek-speaking regions of Asia Minor, led by Eustathius of Antioch and Basil of Caesarea. Saint Basil, in particular, promoted the value of the monks' constant collective labors over the far less productive and often harrowing mortification of the flesh common to hermit-monks.[9] Basil was an advocate for the value of learning, both sacred and profane: "We must be conversant with poets, with historians, with orators," he wrote, "indeed, with all men who may further our soul's salvation."[10]

Gospels": *The Word in the Desert: Scripture and the Quest for Holiness in Early Christian Monasticism* (Oxford: Oxford University Press, 1993), 4–5.

7. "By the middle of the fourth century," George Ovitt Jr. writes of monasticism's spread, "the deserts of Egypt were heavily populated by men and women who practiced Christian asceticism, and who lived the harsh life credited by Philo to the Therapeutae": "Manual Labor and Early Medieval Monasticism," *Viator* 17 (1986): 4.

8. Joan E. Taylor and Philip R. Davies describe the second-century Essenes as offering "more egalitarian and communal" Jewish monastic communities than did the Therapeutae, who were devoted to worshiping God in contemplative communities around Alexandria, according to the Jewish philosopher Philo: "The So-Called Therapeutae of 'De Vita Contemplativa': Identity and Character," *Harvard Theological Review* 91, no. 1 (1998): 3–24.

9. M. L. W. Laistner, *Thought and Letters in Western Europe, A.D. 500 to 900*, 2nd ed. (Ithaca, NY: Cornell University Press, 1957), 31. There was particular influence of the "exegetical traditions of Philo" and, to a more limited extent, the "ascetic practices of groups like the Therapeutae," a Jewish monastic group, on early Christian practice (76).

10. Basil, "Address to Young Men," in *Three Thousand Years of Educational Wisdom: Selections from the Great Documents*, ed. Robert Ulich, 2nd ed. (Cambridge, MA: Harvard University Press, 1982), 154. Laistner describes how in the East they "sanctioned contemporary higher education

In the Latin West, such learning was more commonly condemned: "The philosophers are the patriarchs of the heretics" is how the Christian writer Quintus Tertullian put it in the third century, referring to Plato and Aristotle.[11] It was Tertullian who asked, "What indeed has Athens to do with Jerusalem? What concord is there between the academy and the Church?"[12] If learning got off to a rockier start in the West, it still had the advantage of a warmer collective sense of *vita communis*, which led to cooperative networks among monasteries in the West through which manuscripts were shared and copied. It was these "transregional communities" that helped to set Europe on its "special path," in the estimation of historian Michael Mitterauer at the University of Vienna.[13] Certainly, the unusually learned monasticism of Jerome demonstrated the scholarly potential of these communities.

THE SCHOLAR-MONK JEROME

Jerome was born in CE 347 in the Roman town of Stridon, not far from the eastern shore of the Adriatic Sea. Having been sent to Rome around the age of twelve to be schooled, he sought the path of monasticism only after making the best of that educational opportunity. After giving the life of a hermit a trial run in the Syrian desert, he returned to Rome to serve Pope Damasus, further his learning, and serve as a spiritual guide to those who would later become his monastic patrons. Having had his fill of Rome by the age of forty-one, he took up residence in a monastery near Bethlehem. There he continued his biblical studies and spiritual counsel for the remainder of his days. Though seeking to distance himself from the Roman society of late antiquity and devote himself to a life of piety, he still proved particularly effective in taking the trappings of a Roman education and applying them to Christian ends.

More than any other of those who were later designated fathers of the church, Jerome was a figure of scholarly labor-without-end, preparing translations, compiling and composing commentaries and prefaces, and offering

as a preparation for the Christian teacher and theologian" (*Thought and Letters*, 46). Monasticism breeds "athletes of Christ . . . striving eagerly," claimed ironic Saint Basil, "to be the last of all": cited by Geoffrey Galt Harpham, *The Ascetic Imperative in Both Culture and Criticism* (Chicago: University of Chicago Press, 1987), 28.

11. Quintus Tertullian, *De anima*, ed. J. H. Waszink (Leiden: Brill, 2010), 7.

12. Quintus Tertullian, *The Prescription against Heretics*, trans. Peter Holmes, in vol. 3 of *The Ante-Nicene Fathers*, ed. Alexander Roberts and James Donaldson (Grand Rapids, MI: Eerdmans, 1951), 433.

13. Michael Mitterauer, *Why Europe? The Medieval Origins of Its Special Path*, trans. Gerald Chapple (Chicago: University of Chicago Press, 2010), 185.

guidance and learned reflection to his patrons through extended letters. Numerous Renaissance portraits depict Jerome as a solitary scholar-monk at his desk, surrounded by a smattering of books, in what is often a stately study of the High Middle Ages, far removed from the modest monastic cell that he actually occupied outside Bethlehem.[14] A lion is often sitting peacefully on the floor, as Jerome was said to have removed a thorn from a lion's paw with his pen, representing the power and diligence of learning to undo the violent beastliness of the world.

One key to Jerome's success was the generous support of his patrons, which included a number of wealthy widow-ascetics with whom he had become friends while in Rome, giving rise to the kinds of unsavory rumors that proliferated there. Their continuing patronage enabled Jerome to fashion an exceedingly fine monastic library, rich not only in Christian literature but with Plato, Aristotle, Cicero, and Virgil, as well as Roman and Jewish histories. He was able to hire secretaries and scribes, operating the equivalent of a scholarly publishing house and a center for advanced studies in scripture, unequaled in late antiquity and for many centuries to follow. If he carried a good deal of his learned manner from Rome to Bethlehem, he also ensured that the fruits of that learning made their way back. He arranged for annual manuscript shipments to Rome, where his friends and patrons would help see the work copied, placed in libraries, and spoken about in ways that were conveyed back to him.[15]

What, then, of the monastic vows of poverty and the renouncing of all property? Hadn't the desert father Theodore of Pherme sold his books and given the money to the poor, following the fourth-century *Sayings of the Desert Fathers* that it was "best of all to possess nothing"?[16] Jerome countered with

14. Among Renaissance portraits of Saint Jerome are those by Vincenzo Catena (used for the cover of this book), Antonio da Messina, Niccolò Antonio Colantonio, Albrecht Dürer, Jan Van Ecyk, Antonello da Messina, and Vittore Carpaccio; Jerome also served during this period as an imagined artist's model for demonstrations of new scholarly apparatuses such as book wheels, book holders, two-sided lecterns, and the box study: Dora Thornton, *The Scholar in His Study: Ownership and Experience in Renaissance Italy* (New Haven, CT: Yale University Press, 1997), 54–68.

15. Mark Vessey, "Erasmus' Jerome: The Publishing of a Christian Author," *Erasmus of Rotterdam Society Yearbook* 14, no. 1 (1994): 74. Vessey: "Jerome was an exceptional Christian writer, the first (in either Greek or Latin) to make serious claims for a specifically religious literary occupation and, of all the fathers, the one most visibly interested in the material production and dissemination of his own texts" (98). Megan Hale Williams: "Alongside his biblical manuscripts, Jerome must have had an even larger and more costly collection of Jewish and Christian works, filling hundreds if not thousands of codices" (*The Monk and the Book: Jerome and the Making of Christian Scholarship* [Chicago: University of Chicago Press, 2006], 154).

16. *The Sayings of the Desert Fathers*, trans. Benedicta Ward (Kalamazoo, MI: Cistercian, 1975), 73.

claims to monastic humility and the charity of his learning, given that he sought, with the assistance of his library, only to help others learn of God's wisdom. This was to become a key motif for learned nuns and monks during the Middle Ages: "I am writing not a panegyric or a declamation but a commentary," Jerome proclaimed in the preface to his third book of *Commentary on Galatians*, "consequently I hope that my own words receive no praise but that others' sage words be understood as they are originally written down. The task is to elucidate obscure points, to touch only briefly on what is already clear, and to linger over things that are difficult to figure out."[17]

Jerome also stressed the labor of learning. He made it clear that he was deeply invested in this work, adding to the sense that a text is a property worked by an intellect, much as farmers cultivate fields. He made it clear to his readers that he toiled without respite on translations, commentaries, and letters: "Stealing the hours of the night," as he put it in his preface to the *Commentary on Ezekiel*, "I am endeavoring by the light of the lamp to dictate these comments . . . and am trying to mitigate with exposition the weariness of a mind which is a stranger to rest."[18] This point in favor of the individual effort by which learning advances was to remain a contentious one. For however sympathetic students may generally feel toward such expressions of studied weariness, monasticism was to favor the particular humility of manual (rather than manuscript) labor and, more generally, of selfless anonymity in all things.

In his bridging of late antiquity and the opening of the Christian medieval era, Jerome brought to Christian learning a strong sense of the author's responsibility for the shape of a work. He carefully identified each of the authors in a miniature catalog of important works for Christians that he constructed; he made a point of listing his own publications in his *On Illustrious Men* (*De viris illustribus*). His scriptural commentaries took up the attribution and composition of the text. He paid attention to authors' language and style, demonstrating to readers how these qualities contributed to an understanding of their work. Consider his defense of Paul's authorship of the Letter to the Hebrews, in light of controversy over this point and its "distance of language and style," in Jerome's words, from Paul's other letters, which lack the polish of this one. Jerome explains his support for the attribution through his understanding of Paul's linguistic background: "It is

17. Jerome, *Commentary on Galatians*, trans. Andrew Cain, vol. 121 of *The Fathers of the Church* (Washington, DC: Catholic University of America Press, 2010), 206.

18. Jerome, "Preface to the *Commentary on Ezekiel*," in *St. Jerome: Letters and Select Works*, vol. 6 of *Nicene and Post-Nicene Fathers of the Christian Church*, ed. Philip Schaff and Henry Wace, trans. W. H. Freemantle, 2nd ser. (Grand Rapids, MI: Eerdmans, 1954), 500.

truly not a wonder, if he is seen more eloquent in his own language, that is
in Hebrew, rather than in a foreign one, that is in Greek, in which language
the other letters are written."[19] Jerome is establishing the relation between author and work. It is not about ascertaining ownership, as apostles and monastics renounce such worldly matters, but about helping readers gain a greater
sense of the author's project through the whole of his work. Out of a similar
respect for the work of the author, Jerome paid such attention to the accuracy
and integrity of copies and translations. He was known to threaten copyists
with damnation for transcription errors, establishing in effect a holy order of
the exact copy of the author's original and complete work.[20] Through these
practices and principles, Jerome sought to establish for Christianity the value
of attending to the intellectual properties of a text within the scope of an author's corpus.[21]

Jerome brought a similar level of concern for the authenticity of the sources
on which he based his translations. He sought out the early Hebrew versions
of biblical texts, rather than relying on Greek translations, for his own Latin
version. This entailed taking the time to learn Hebrew and consult Jewish
scholars to establish the *Hebraica veritas*, as he referred to it, on which to base
his work.[22] As a result, he felt warranted in making the scholar's claim to proprietary mastery of a text, as he sets out in the preface to his translation of
Samuel and Kings: "First read, then, my Samuel and Kings; mine, I say, mine.
For whatever by diligent translation and by anxious emendation we have
learnt and made our own, is ours."[23] This, for me, brings to the fore the property of accreditation from among the six properties that I associate with learn-

19. Jerome, "Beginning of the Prologue to the Letters of Paul the Apostle," trans. Kevin P. Edgecomb (Biblicalia, blog, August 17, 2006) from *Biblia sacra iuxta Vulgatam versionem*, ed. B. Fischer
and R. Weber 4th ed. (Stuttgart: Deutsche Bibelgesellschaft, 1994).

20. Jerome posted this appeal at the beginning of Eusebius's history of the church: "I adjure thee
who mayest copy this book, by our Lord Jesus Christ, and by his glorious advent when he comes to
judge the quick and the dead, to compare what thou shalt write, and correct it carefully by the exemplars which thou hast followed, and also to transcribe this adjuration, and place it in the copy
which thou has written out" (trans. Vessey, "Erasmus' Jerome," 95).

21. Michel Foucault: "Even while Saint Jerome's four principles of [authorial] authenticity might
seem largely inadequate to modern critics, they, nevertheless, define the critical modalities now used
to display the author function": "What Is an Author?" in *Language, Counter-Memory, Practice: Selected
Essays and Interviews*, trans. Donald F. Bouchard and Sherry Simon (Ithaca, NY: Cornell University
Press, 1977), 129.

22. Williams, *Monk and the Book*, 81–95. Williams notes how this reliance does not prevent
Jerome from condemning the Jews for failing to follow God's commandments (226).

23. Jerome, "Preface, The Books of Samuel and Kings," in *St. Jerome: Letters and Select Works*,
491.

ing. For Jerome, the learned earn a claim to a work through their labor, a claim that has much to do with the work's distinctive intellectual properties.

For all the care that Jerome took with these texts, he still faced rebukes from others who shared with him this sense of a right in such works. Augustine of Hippo, his junior by seven years, called him out for showing less than "scrupulous fidelity" in noting his sources, to which Jerome responded by noting that Augustine seemed "not to understand" the nature of the works he was translating.[24] Others charged Jerome with plagiarizing Origen, a third-century Alexandrian theologian. Jerome certainly credited Origen for heroic and tireless biblical commentaries (which Jerome translated into Latin), although he did later obscure his debt to Origen after the man fell from grace within the church.[25] Still, Jerome was prepared to admit to the "incompetence" of his methods. In the preface to his *Commentary on Galatians*, he confesses, "I summoned my secretary and dictated either my own or others' ideas, all the while paying no attention to the method, the words, or the opinions belonging to each."[26]

For all that Jerome did to apply the learning of antiquity to Christian ends, he also managed to cast a big chill on this enterprise. In 384 he wrote a long and decidedly strange letter on virginity to Eustochium, a "desert mother" supervising a nearby Bethlehem monastery. He describes in the letter a feverish nightmare he had had a decade earlier during Lent. He sets the nightmare up by reporting how "for the sake of the kingdom of heaven I cut myself off from home" and yet "could not bring myself to forgo the library which with great care and labor I had got together at Rome."[27] The contradictions were apparent: "I would fast, only to read Cicero afterwards."[28] Then, in his fevered dream, he reports, it was Judgment Day and his assertion that he was a Christian was met with nothing less than "Thou liest; thou art a Ciceronian, not a Christian. For 'where thy treasure is, there will thy heart be also'

24. Augustine, "Letter LXXI (A.D. 403)," in *The Confessions and Letters of St. Augustine*, vol. 1 of *A Select Library of Nicene and Post-Nicene Fathers of the Christian Church*, ed. Philip Schaff (New York: Charles Scribner's and Sons, 1907), 327; Jerome, "Letter LXXV (A.D. 404)," in ibid., 341.

25. Mark Vessey writes of the "imitation and rivalry" that mark Jerome's relation to Origen: "Jerome's Origen: The Making of a Christian Literary Persona," *Studia Patristica: Papers Presented to the International Conference on Patristic Studies* 28 (1993): 145.

26. Jerome, *Commentary on Galatians*, 58. See Williams, *Monk and the Book*, 190–92.

27. Jerome, "Letter 22 to Eustochium, The Virgin's Profession, Written 384 A.D," in *Jerome: Selected Letters*, trans. F. A. Wright (Cambridge, MA: Harvard University Press, 1933), 125.

28. Ibid.

(Matt. 6:21)."[29] Jerome had been betrayed by the very (treasured) works sitting on his desk. He vowed at the time, he tells Eustochium, that he would no longer "possess worldly books or read them."[30]

He may have kept his promise for a decade or so, before allowing once again that "almost all the books of all writers are replete with learning."[31] Still, his report of the dream traveled far and was used to great effect by those who sought to discourage such learning. Yet his more lasting contribution was in staking the scholar's claim to the use of others' work. In a later letter from the year 397 to Magnus, a Roman orator, Jerome points to the apostle Paul's use of both the Greek poet-philosopher Epimenides and the classical dramatist Menander, as an example of how Paul "had learned from the true David to wrench the sword of the enemy out of his hand and with his own blade to cut off the head of the arrogant Goliath."[32] He writes as well of how, in Deuteronomy, God allowed that if one sheared the hair off a captive woman, she could be taken as a wife: "Is it surprising that I too, admiring the fairness of her form and the grace of her eloquence, desire to make that secular wisdom which is my captive and my handmaid, a matron of the true Israel?"[33] He reassures his readers that this "has always been the practice of the learned in this matter."[34] The practice amounts to, in my estimation, an intellectual property right of use. It overrides apprehensions over the pagan origins of these works—which were commonly referred to as Egyptian gold (with more on this below)—by redirecting it to Christian ends.[35]

In all of his learned activity Jerome really does seem like the original Christian man of letters, as suggested by Mark Vessey, professor of English at the University of British Columbia.[36] Jerome was able to forge such a life

29. Ibid., 127. On Jerome as more *Ciceronianus* than *Christianus,* Roger Ray points to Jerome's rhetorical debts to Cicero: "Bede's Vera Lex Historiae," *Speculum* 55, no. 1 (1980): 4.

30. Jerome, "Letter 22 to Eustochium," 128.

31. Cited by Authur Stanley Pease, "The Attitude of Jerome towards Pagan Literature," *Transactions of the American Philological Association* 50 (1919): 165-66.

32. Jerome, "Letter LXX: To Magnus an Orator of Rome," in *St. Jerome: Letters and Select Works,* 149.

33. Ibid.

34. Ibid., 151.

35. "Later in his career [Jerome] responds to a criticism that he is himself too free with his quotations from and use of non-Christian literature and philosophy by listing and analyzing all the instances of the uses of non-Christian literature in Scripture": Paul J. Griffiths, "Seeking Egyptian Gold: A Fundamental Metaphor for the Christian Intellectual Life in a Religiously Diverse Age," *Cresset* 63, no. 5 (2000): 9.

36. Vessey: "Jerome thus not only issued his own works, he also issued a deliberately composed textual image of their author" ("Erasmus' Jerome," 76). Bernard Bischoff writes of the twenty-

out of antiquity's tradition of patronage and authorship, to which he added the monastic qualities of humility, charity, communality, and devotion to labor. Nothing quite like his prolific monastic arrangement would exist again. Its mix of personal patronage, extensive staff support, expansive library, and distribution network was a winning combination for scholarship, although Erasmus did find something similar, as we shall see, in the home he made for himself in the early printing shop.

AUGUSTINE OF HIPPO

Like Jerome, Augustine was both inspired and troubled by his inner liberal-arts demons. Augustine's monasticism was also arranged to be something of a personal convenience. This involved, in his case, friends sharing a life in common, a form of "spiritual communism," as Princeton historian Peter Brown puts it.[37] Augustine, who was born in 354 in Roman Africa, was a popular teacher of rhetoric in Carthage and later in Rome prior to his conversion to Christianity. At the age of eighteen, he had been particularly moved by Cicero's *Hortensius*: "It changed my life," is how he put it in his *Confessions*, and, as a result, "I pined for deathless wisdom."[38] Still, he went on to be "a peddler of glibness in the marketplace," selling to boys "the weapons of their distraction."[39] In his adeptness as a scholar, he also cornered a portion of the liberal arts textbook market, issuing works on grammar, rhetoric, dialectic, arithmetic, geometry, and music. It all came to an end in 386, when in a moment of bookish fervor that took place in a garden in Milan, he put his life in Christ's hands: "I leaped up, not doubting that it was by divine prompting that I should open the book [Paul's epistle to the Romans] and read what first I hit on."[40]

Five years later, he arrived in Hippo and turned his house into a monastery, vowing to live a celibate, contemplative, and communal life. It was more of a retreat into friendship and study than the rigorously disciplined order that marked monasticism after Benedict, although there is a monastic rule, intended to bring greater order to this religious life, attributed by some

---

eight public libraries found in fourth-century descriptions of Rome: *Manuscripts and Libraries in the Age of Charlemagne* (Cambridge: Cambridge University Press, 1994), 7.

37. Brown, *Through the Eye of a Needle*, 180.

38. Augustine, *Confessions*, trans. Gary Wills (London: Penguin, 2002), 3.3.7 45.

39. Ibid., 9.2.2, 186.

40. Ibid., 8.5.29, 181.

to Augustine.⁴¹ In 395, at the age of forty, Augustine agreed to serve the church as bishop of Hippo. Still, he set up a similarly communal life for himself, living among the secular clergy in a religious house beside the church.⁴²

In the *Confessions*, among the most widely read works of the Middle Ages, Augustine lays out how God led him to a Christian sense of learning, purged of vain pride. At one point he credits God with showing him how "the proud [in learning] you rebuff, while favoring the lowly," as "you brought to me a man, himself inflated with raging winds of pride, to acquaint me with certain books of the Platonists, translated into Latin from the Greek."⁴³ Yet such vanity can be easily overcome, he came to realize, by humility. Elsewhere in the *Confessions* he launches a more determined attack, much as Jerome had, on "transgressive knowledge (*curiositas*)," as Gary Wills translates the title of the fifth chapter of book 10.⁴⁴ Curiosity was not to be the driving force of learning. Augustine warned friends about the dangers of "reprehensible curiosity" as well as "vain and perishing curiosity."⁴⁵ He compared "a craving to know" to "cravings of the flesh": "This [craving] also leads men to pry into the arcane elements of nature, which are beyond our scope—knowing them would serve no purpose, yet men make of that knowing its own purpose."⁴⁶

41. Augustine's rule led to the Augustinian monastic order (to which Martin Luther belonged) and included: "Let them work from early morning till noon and take leisure for three hours from noon til three," and "no one should claim anything as his own" (Augustine, "Regula Sancti Augustini, c. 397," in George Lawless, *Augustine of Hippo and His Monastic Rule* [Oxford: Oxford University Press, 1987], 75). See also Augustine, *The Rule of St. Augustine*, trans. Robert Russell (1976), in *Medieval Sourcebook* Fordham University New York, online.

42. "The most important feature of Augustine's intellectual activity in his middle-age, as he himself saw it, was that it took place in a community, the Catholic Church" (Peter Brown, *Augustine of Hippo* [Berkeley: University of California Press, 2000], 267).

43. Augustine, *Confessions*, 7.4.13 147. See also Elizabeth A. Clark: "Granted also that many sayings preserved in these collections [e.g., *Sayings of the Fathers*] suggest a hostility to 'book-culture'; in some, highly educated monks decry their own secular learning, deemed worthless when compared to the 'wisdom' of their unlettered colleagues" (*Reading Renunciation: Asceticism and Scripture in Early Christianity* [Princeton, NJ: Princeton University Press, 1999], 53).

44. Augustine, *Confessions*, 10.5 244.

45. Augustine of Hippo, "Letter 138: Augustine to Marcellinus (411/412)," in *Political Writings*, ed. E. M. Atkins and R. J. Dodaro (Cambridge: Cambridge University Press, 2001), 42; Augustine, "Of True Religion," in *Earlier Writings*, ed. John H. S. Burleigh (Louisville, KY: Westminster John Knox Press, 1953), 251. Similarly, Saint Ambrose, bishop of Milan, wrote during this era: "Why do you desire to examine curiously what is not helpful for your salvation and what you are not allowed to know?" (cited by Richard Newhauser, "Augustinian *Vitium curiositatis* and Its Reception," in *Saint Augustine and His Influence in the Middle Ages*, ed. Edward B. King and Jacqueline T. Schaefer [Sewanee: Press of the University of the South, 1988], 103).

46. Augustine, *Confessions*, 10.5.54-55 244-45. Curiosity also figured in his critique of Manichaeism, after he converted from this Gnostic faith to Christianity: "Let the mind, therefore, refrain from desiring this vain sort of knowledge if it wishes to keep itself chaste for God" (*The Catho-*

His singling out the exploration of the world and its matter amounts to a sweeping condemnation of the natural sciences. This question of when and in what ways learning acts in the service of faith was to haunt Christianity, as Weber noted. Augustine's concerns with curiosity as a driving intellectual force remained a point of Christian censure until the early modern era.[47]

On the other hand and in learning's favor, Augustine defended the Christian use of works authored by those who lack a Christian purpose. In *On Christian Teaching* (*De doctrina christiana*), composed around 396 as he was stepping into the role of bishop, he extols the usefulness of Aristotle while warning his Christian readers not to adopt this Greek's philosophy as a guide to life itself: "The rules about syllogism and definitions and classifications [via Aristotle], on the other hand, greatly help people to understand, provided that they avoid the error of thinking that when they have mastered them they have learnt the actual truth about the happy life."[48] He advises readers on the scholar's rights (and duties) in using others' work: "Any statements by those who are called philosophers, especially the Platonists, which happen to be true and consistent with our faith should not cause alarm, but be claimed for our own use, as it were from owners who have no right to them."[49]

lic and Manichean Ways of Life, trans. Donald A, Gallagher and Idellla J, Gallagher [Washington, DC: Catholic University of America Press, 1966], 21.38, 32–33). Augustine is invoking the "sin of the intellect," as Newhauser names this target in the church's fight against heresy: "Augustinian *Vitium curiositatis*," 103. Caution is Augustine's theme with extra-Christian learning: "Do not venture without due care into any branches of learning which are pursued outside the church of Christ . . . discriminate sensibly and carefully between them" (*Christian Teaching*, 2.38.57 63).

47. Joanna Picciotto credits Francis Bacon with the Christian redemption of curiosity: "By transferring the primal scene of discovery from Eve's eating of the fruit to Adam's naming the creatures—and by linking the act of naming to the work of experiment—Bacon redeemed curiosity from its association with original sin: associated with investigative labor rather than appetite, the first sin became the first virtue" (*Labors of Innocence in Early Modern England* [Cambridge, MA: Harvard University Press, 2010], 3). Current defenders of Augustine's condemnation of curiosity include the Dominican Joseph Torchia: "Augustine, I think, can provide a cogent, much needed voice in a world that takes for granted things like the mapping of the genome, genetic engineering, and screening, cloning, stem cell research" (*Restless Mind: Curiositas and the Scope of Inquiry in St. Augustine's Psychology* [Marquette, WI: Marquette University Press, 2013], 248).

48. Augustine, *On Christian Teaching*, trans. R. P. H. Green (Oxford: Oxford University Press, 1997), 2.37.55 62. Augustine composed *De doctrinia christiana* upon assuming the bishopric of Hippo for the preparation of clergy: Brian Stock, *Augustine the Reader: Meditation, Self-Knowledge, and the Ethics of Interpretation* (Cambridge, MA: Harvard University Press, 1990), 190.

49. Augustine, *On Christian Teaching*, 2.39.60 64. Mark Vessey advises that Augustine "also promotes the idea, explicitly formulated in *De Doctrina Christiana*, that the useful and salutary practice of arts otherwise known as liberal is already exemplified in the sacred texts of Christianity": introduction to *Augustine and the Disciplines: From "Classiacum" to "Confessions,"* ed. Karla Pollmann and Mark Vessey (Oxford: Oxford University Press), 17.

And he provides a property-rights analogy from the Bible to establish why the use of Egyptian gold, as it was referred to, is fair and worthwhile:

> Like the treasures of the ancient Egyptians, who possessed not only idols and heavy burdens, which the people of Israel hated and shunned, but also vessels and ornaments of silver and gold, and clothes, which on leaving Egypt the people of Israel, in order to make better use of them, surreptitiously claimed themselves (they did this not on their own authority but at God's command, and the Egyptians in their ignorance actually gave them the things of which they had made poor use) [Exod. 3:21–22, 12:35–36].[50]

As if not entirely comfortable with the analogy of the Israelites' biblical pilfering, even at God's command (and to recover unpaid wages), Augustine offers what amounts to a natural law theory of intellectual property, making it clear that such property arises out of the commons. For "any statements by those who are called philosophers," he sets out how "these treasures [are] like the silver and gold, which they did not create but dug, as it were, from the mines of providence, which is everywhere."[51] In his work on the concept of free will, Augustine again asserts that "the beauty of truth and wisdom" is common to all people, and cannot "be the private property of any of them," just as the expression of such wisdom "does not exclude those who come by any packed crowd of hearers" and are able to overhear and thereby learn.[52]

On the other hand, Augustine was prepared to address the violation of his own authorial property rights (however limited he envisions them to be). In a letter to Bishop Aurelius of Carthage sometime after 420, Augustine writes of how at times his "books were taken or stolen from me before I had completed them and before I had polished them after having checked them."[53] Urged by the bishop and others to see his pirated, ill-finished works through to a proper publication, he describes how he "took care to complete, with

50. Augustine, *Christian Teaching*, 2.40.60 64–65. See Griffiths, "Egyptian Gold."
51. Ibid., 2.40.60 65.
52. Augustine, "On Free Will" (*De libero arbitrio*), in *Augustine: Earlier Writings*, trans. John H. S. Burleigh (London: SCM Press, 1953), 156, 159.
53. Augustine of Hippo, "Letter 174," in *The Works of Saint Augustine*, vol. 3, *Letters 156–210*, trans. Roland J. Teske (Hyde Park, NY: New City Press, 2004), 132. Peter J. Lucas describes how such acts of piracy had become, by the fifteenth century, step five in what he summarized as the ten-step process of manuscript publication—"(5) an unauthorized copy might escape at this stage without the author's approval" following a showing of "the work to a particular friend privately for comment" and coming before a recopying of the work incorporating corrections and amendments: *From Author to Audience: John Capgrave and Medieval Publication* (Dublin: University College Dublin Press, 1997), 2.

the help of the Lord, this very laborious work" and "corrected" them.[54] It was then that he "gave permission that they be heard, copied, and read by anyone."[55] The principal difference with these property rights, then and today, is that Augustine's objections to the unapproved copying was more of an intellectual and pedagogical issue for him than a commercial matter. "If I had been able to carry out my plan in them," he further assures the bishop about his work on *The Trinity*, "the books would have been less complicated and clearer as much as the difficulty in explaining such important topics and our ability would have permitted."[56]

The need for more time to make the work "less complicated and clearer" is itself a much-played theme in the labor of learning.[57] Augustine's sense that he has a right to sign off on a work—as much a safeguard for readers as for his reputation as a writer—might be taken as early assumption that such writing has rights associated with it. Once released, the author steps aside, and "anyone," as Augustine notes, can read, copy, and hear the work that belongs, after all, to humankind in common.

Yet he also recognizes a continuing responsibility for works once made public. In his final years, he composes a work he entitles *Retractions*, in which he proposes corrections for no fewer than ninety-three of his works: "I have decided, moreover, to write this work that I might put it into the hands of men from whom I cannot recall for correction the writings I have already published."[58]

Although Augustine was revered and read throughout the Middle Ages, the liberal arts education that had formed him as a scholar was largely lost

54. Augustine, "Letter 174," in *Works*, 132.

55. Ibid., 132–33. Possidus, a biographer at work shortly after Augustine's death, further extends this permission: "If anyone wants to make a copy of [any item] he should apply to the church in Hippo, where the best texts can generally be found. Or he may make inquiries anywhere else he can and should make a copy of what he finds and preserve it, and not begrudge lending it in his turn to someone asking to copy it" (cited by Harry Y. Gamble, *Books and Readers in the Early Church: A History of Early Christian Texts* [New Haven, CT: Yale University Press, 1995], 138).

56. Augustine, "Letter 174," in *Works*, 133. Augustine requested that the good bishop share his position with the world by ensuring that "this letter be placed at the beginning of the same books, though set apart" (ibid.).

57. Among the more famously attributed lines in this regard (among John Locke, Mark Twain, Ben Franklin, and others) is from Blaise Pascal in a letter to the Reverend Fathers, the Jesuits: "The present letter is a very long one, simply because I had no time to make it shorter" ("Letter 16 [December 4, 1656]," *The Provincial Letters of Blaise Pascal*, trans. Thomas M'Crie [London: Chatto and Windus, 1857], 305).

58. Augustine, *The Retractions*, trans. Mary Inez Bogan, R.S.M. (Washington, DC: Catholic University of America Press, 1968), 5.

to Western monasticism following the fall of Rome. Almost a century after Augustine's death in 430, the Byzantine Christian Emperor Justinian saw fit to shut down the Neoplatonic School in Athens, at the behest of local Christians perturbed by its teaching of "pagan" philosophy and astronomy.[59] Christians would have to rebuild learning's place in the West, with that process facilitated by the economic, cultural, and political properties of a monasticism deeply influenced by the *Rule of Benedict*, which was to be so effectively championed by Pope Gregory the Great. While the *Rule* cut learning little slack, it instantiated a form of life that, hour by hour, made learning's return inevitable to the religious houses that adhered to its strictures.

THE *RULE* OF SAINT BENEDICT

Within half a century or so of Augustine's death, the young Benedict of Nursia, born in 480 of a noble family, had become increasingly disillusioned with his Roman schooling. A devout Christian, he was struck by the distinct failure of the liberal arts to lead his classmates to more righteous lives. In Pope Gregory's hagiography, composed within decades of the saint's death, the young Benedict is portrayed as rejecting the sheer folly of such schooling: "But when he [Benedict] saw that many of the students rushed headlong into vice, he withdrew from the world he had just entered, lest, in acquiring worldly knowledge, he might also fall down the same terrific precipice. Despising, therefore, the study of letters, he desired only to please God by a holy life."[60] The striking opposition that Gregory sets between the pursuit of learning and the pleasing of God was to pervade the Benedictine regard for learning within monasticism, often overshadowing the more balanced approach to it in the works of Jerome and Augustine.

Gregory gives the divide a fine turn by characterizing Benedict as "skillfully ignorant, and wisely unlearned."[61] The pope biographer, who founded

---

59. Edwards Watts, "Justinian, Malalas, and the End of Athenian Philosophical Teaching in A.D. 529," *Journal of Roman Studies* 94 (2004): 169, 182. Watts notes that the philosophers were later deprived of their property and at that point departed for Persia.

60. Cited by Frederick Homes Dudden, *Gregory the Great: His Place in History and Thought*, vol. 1 (New York: Longmans, Green, 1905), 287.

61. Cited by Putnam Fennell Jones, "The Gregorian Mission and English Education," *Speculum* 3, no. 3 (1928): 337. Jones also notes Gregory's line from his commentary on the Book of Job: "Holy Scripture is incomparably superior to every form of knowledge and science" (338). As if to confirm Benedict's refusal of learnedness, David Knowles judges his command of Latin to be nothing less than "the breakdown of classical grammar" (*The Evolution of Medieval Thought* [New York: Vintage, 1962], 71). In his lectures to young monks, the modern Benedictine Jean Leclercq for more sympathetically sums up Benedict's regard for learning: "Studies undertaken, and then, not precisely scorned, but renounced and transcended, for the sake of the kingdom of God" (*The Love of Learning*

seven monasteries on his own, did much to set monasticism on a path away from the liberal arts throughout the Latin West of his day.[62] As Gregory has it, after young Benedict turned away from his liberal studies, he fled Rome with his childhood nurse in tow. He initially found redemption as a solitary hermit in a cave, presumably after sending his nurse home, where he remained for some three years. His reputation for piety spread and a group of nearby monks asked him to forsake his solitude in favor of leading their monastery. Benedict accepted the invitation, which led to the founding of Monte Cassino in 529, the year that the Platonic Academy in Athens was closed by the Justinian.[63] Under Benedict's guidance, the monastery at Monte Cassino grew, with schools erected to instruct children destined to join the order. In his time as abbot, Benedict is thought to have set down the pious principles of monastic living in *The Rule of Benedict* (*Regula Benedicti*).[64]

Now medieval monasticism did not want for such rule books. Saints Pachomius, Basil, Cassian, and Columbanus all contributed guides for Christian monasteries, which often grew out of their own service as abbots. The

---

and the Desire of God: A Study of Monastic Culture, trans. C. Misrahi [New York: Fordham University Press, 1982], 12).

62. Laistner also notes Gregory's upbraiding of bishops for speaking publicly on secular authors: *Thought and Letters*, 109. Laistner on Gregory's contribution to monasticism: "As an intense admirer of St. Benedict, Gregory strove to increase the number of religious houses not only in Italy and Sicily, but wherever his authority was of sufficient weight, to remedy abuses in existing monasteries and convents, and to secure the general adoption of the Benedictine Rule" (104). Compare to Martin Irvine, who cites Gregory on the Augustinian approach to secular learning: "Although learning in secular books is not in itself useful for the spiritual conflict of the saints, if this learning is united to sacred Scripture, we are taught more precisely in the knowledge of Scripture. Indeed, it is to this end only that the liberal arts are to be taught" (cited in *Making of Textual Culture: 'Grammatica' and Literary Theory, 350–1100* [Cambridge: Cambridge University Press, 2006], 195).

63. Josef Pieper seizes upon the initiation of the Benedictine monastery and the end of Plato's Academy as symbolizing a turn from Antiquity to the Middle Ages (*Scholasticism: Personalities and Problems of Medieval Philosophy,* trans. Richard Winston and Clare Winston [New York: McGraw-Hill, 1964], 16). Pieper cites Hegel, who had little time for the Middle Ages, on the closing of the Academy as "the downfall of the physical establishments of pagan philosophy" (ibid.).

64. *The Rule of Benedict*, trans. Carolinne White (London: Penguin, 2008). Giorgio Agamben observes that "the fourth and fifth centuries of the Christian era witnessed the birth of a peculiar literature that, at least at first glance, does not seem to have had precedents in the classical world: monastic rules" (*The Highest Poverty: Monastic Rules and Form-of-Life,* trans. Adam Koysko [Stanford, CA: Stanford University Press, 2013], 3). He also points to the lack of precedents for monasticism's "temporal scansion," which is to say the strict governance of time as a matter of discipline and regularity for this form of institutional and communal life (19). Saint Benedict is enjoying something of a revival, as I write, with Rod Dreher's *The Benedict Option: A Strategy for Christians in a Post-Christian Nation* (New York: Penguin Random House, 2017) reaching the *New York Times* bestseller list for a week in April 2017 and in which Dreher recommends following an updated version of Benedict's spiritual path by undertaking "a strategic withdrawal" from "mainstream society" to "find new ways to live in community" (2).

fifth-century *Rule for Virgins* of Caesarius of Arles had a large and literate influence on nunneries; it recommended admitting girls "at an age [of six or seven] where they could learn to read and obey," while requiring nuns to read while they worked.[65] Yet Benedict's *Rule* prevailed across the Latin West, in its simplicity, detail, and unfailing devotion to piety.[66] In the later Middle Ages, periods of monastic reform often involved a rededication of the monastery to the *Rule of Benedict*. The *Rule* consists of seventy-three brief chapters dedicated to the order and regulation of monastic life. Yet for all of its attention to the regulation of that life, the *Rule* also wisely allows, in its conclusion, that it is but a "little rule for beginners" and not a complete guide to monasticism.[67]

In its prologue, the *Rule* initially frames the monastery's purpose in educational terms: "And so we intend to establish a school for the Lord's service."[68] Its chapters prescribe appropriate clothing, footwear, and sleeping arrangements, with little on the pursuit of learning beyond a commitment to reading.[69] Abbots are to be elected for the erudition of their teaching, just as deans (in charge of ten monks) are chosen for "their learning and wisdom."[70] But the acquisition of that wisdom and learning does not fall within the *Rule*. Monks are assumed to be literate, with the *Rule* referring to daily reading, mealtime reading, and readings at the night office.

65. Cited by Pierre Riché, *Education and Culture in the Barbarian West: From the Sixth through the Eighth Century,* trans. John J. Contreni (Columbia, SC: University of South Carolina Press, 1976), 112, 116.

66. R. Kevin Seasoltz, O.S.B., writes that "with the Carolingian reform and the Synod of Aix-la-Chapelle in 817, St. Benedict's *Rule* was established as the only legitimate rule of monastic life in the West" ("Monastic Autonomy and Exemption: Charism and Institution," *Jurist* 34, no. 2 [1974]: 316).

67. *Rule,* 73 104. Laistner attributes the widespread success of the *Rule* to how it called for obedience to its strictures while allowing "the widest possible discretion" for the abbot: "This happy combination of authority in certain basic principles with great latitude in dealing with matters of detail" (*Thought and Letters,* 95). This was no less crucial for the succor that the *Rule* gave to discipline and freedom in learned pursuits.

68. *Rule,* Prologue, 9. M. T. Clanchy notes on this passage that "St. Benedict had indeed founded 'a school of the Lord's service,' but it was not a school of this world" (*Abelard: A Medieval Life* [Oxford: Blackwell, 1999], 211). "It was an elementary school ... a school of morals which was as exacting , in its own way, as any Roman [elementary] school ... blows from the strap included": Peter Brown, *The Rise of Western Christendom: Triumph and Diversity, A.D. 200–100,* 3rd ed. (New York: Wiley, 2013), 225.

69. In contrast to the *Regula magistri,* which is thought to have formed the basis of Benedict's *Rule,* and which distinguished scribes (*scriptores*) from craftsmen (*artifices*) and, according to Malcolm B. Parkes, "prescribed that any of their products superfluous to the community's immediate needs should be sold for less than the market rates in the outside world": *Their Hand before Our Eyes: A Closer Look at Scribes,* Lyell Lectures (1999) (Farnham, Surrey, UK: Ashgate, 2008), 6.

70. *Rule,* 64 93, 21 42. The *Rule of Saint Augustine* is also notably free of concerns for learning.

What is to come of all that reading? It "begins with grammar," declares the twentieth-century Benedictine monk Jean Leclercq, and "terminates in compunction, in desire of heaven."[71] There is no suggestion in the *Rule*, for example, that the study of patristic fathers, such as Jerome and Augustine, should lead to an emulation of their intellectual engagement with scripture and secular works. It amounted to a "mortification of the intellect," in the words of John Henry Newman, nineteenth-century leader of the Oxford Movement within the Church of England and a later convert to Catholicism, which is how he identifies the "mission of Saint Benedict."[72] Monastic penitents aspired to no more than, Newman writes, "the bare ordinary use of reason, without caring to improve it or make the most of it."[73]

The *Rule*'s approach to sacred reading (*lectio divina*) provides a primary instance of this monastic paradox in practice and regulation. The *Rule* depicts this divine reading to be a matter of piety alone. It sets out a disciplined, daily, silent, and absorbed time for reading. Yet the sheer amount of time set aside for reading was surely the first step in opening the monastic door to learning. The act of reading figures prominently in the *Rule*'s chapter entitled "Daily Manual Labor." The chapter begins with labor's prophylactic qualities, whether it is manual and literate work: "Idleness is the enemy of the soul and so brothers ought to engage in manual labor at set times and at other times biblical study."[74] At best, this divine study was to be directed toward "a meeting with God in and through his Word," as the contemporary Cistercian monk M. Basil Pennington names it.[75] The *Rule* sets out how reading was to be disciplined and monitored by "one or two older monks," lest that set time slip into idle work, "wasting his time doing nothing or chatting."[76]

Setting aside two to four hours for solitary reading daily (depending on seasonal light) was not the whole of it. The *Rule* specifies that "the brothers' meals should always be accompanied by reading."[77] The mealtime reader for the week "should receive a little to eat and drink before he begins," while

71. Leclercq, *Love of Learning and the Desire of God*, 72.

72. John Henry Newman, "The Mission of Saint Benedict" in *Historical Sketches*, vol. 2 (London: Longmans Green, 1906), 376.

73. Ibid.

74. *Rule*, 48 72.

75. M. Basil Pennington, O.C.S.O., "Lectio and Love: An Introduction to the Cistercian Tradition," in *In the School of Love: An Anthology of Early Cistercian Texts*, ed. Edith Scholl (Kalamazoo, MI: Cistercian Publications, 2006), 15.

76. *Rule*, 48 73.

77. *Rule*, 38 61. "Four hours or so were occupied by liturgical prayer, about the same time by spiritual reading, and manual work took up six hours or so": D. H. Turner, "This Little Rule for Beginners," in *The Benedictines in Britain*, ed. D. H. Turner, Rachel Stockdale, Dom Philip Jebb, and David Rogers (New York: Braziller, 1980), 15.

asking "all the brothers to pray for him, so that God may preserve him from a spirit of pride."[78] Here was the need to wear one's learning lightly. The *Rule* also ensures that each monk had a book to read in his cell. It requires that members gather together at Lent for an annual distribution among them of the monastery's books (excluding the Bible, service books, classical literature, history, and the sciences) for a year.[79] What the *Rule* does not address is the composition of texts, nor their copying, compiling, binding, or other activities associated with books. A library for the storage of books is mentioned, with this communal collection presumably based on donations and gifts.

Now consider how the allotment of a single book over the course of a year could lead, at least for some, to extended ruminations on the nature of the text, moving from study (*lectio*) to meditation (*meditatio*) on its style, structure, and significance. This could inspire notes in the margins that grow into a commentary on parts of the work. Similarly, the disciplined tone of this daily reading proved a boon for the studious. Nuns and monks turned their extended reading opportunities into increasingly learned glosses, compilations, and commentaries. The only activity allotted a greater block of time was manual labor in this well-regulated order, which had its role in preparing the materials needed to make books, if not the actual writing and copying of them by some interpretations. Jerome, you may recall, emphasized the labor of exegesis, while Florentius of Valeranica, a tenth-century scribe, makes vivid the bodily cost of copying in a note he left in the margins of Gregory the Great's *Moralia in Job*: "Because one who does not know how to write thinks it no labor, I will describe it for you, if you want to know how great the burden of writing: it mists the eyes, it curves the back, it breaks the belly and the ribs, it fills the kidneys with pain, and the body with all kinds of suffering. . . . As the last port is sweet to the sailor, so the last line to the scribe."[80]

---

78. *Rule*, 38 61. Rabanus Maurus, ninth-century abbot of Fulda in Germany, for example, advised that the selected reader "must be imbued with learning and conversant with books": cited by George Haven Putnam, *Books and Their Makers during the Middle Ages*, vol. 1 (New York: Hillary House, 1896), 116.

79. The *Rule* states: "During these days of Lent let all receive books from the library, and let them read them through in order" (38 61). The practice formed many monastery-university continuities, judging by the statutes of Oriel College from 1329, which refers to the "common books (*libri communes*)" being brought out on feast day with the senior scholar given his first choice for a year-long loan of a work: cited by Putnam, *Books and Their Makers*, 151.

80. Cited by Raymond Clements and Timothy Graham, *Introduction to Manuscript Studies* (Ithaca, NY: Cornell University Press, 2007), 23 (with thanks to George Hardin Brown for this source). See also Mark Vessey, "Jerome's Origen," 135–45.

Among the *Rule*'s most famous of strictures was the order that one should not "presume . . . to possess anything of his own—nothing whatever, not a book or a writing table or pen or anything at all, for monks should not even count their own bodies and wills as their own."[81] Using the example of the book, the *Rule* not only emphasized the communal nature of property within the monastery, but denounced self-possession and self-expression, both of which infuse our notions of independent scholarly work, as well as authorship more generally. This was consistent with the understated manner in which manuscript books of this era were referenced not by their author's name but by an incipit made up of the opening words of the work. The selfless and communal themes of monasticism, along with the emphasis on humility, meant that writing done within the monastery was not about asserting authorship claims to owning a work. Rather, a sense of authorship emerged in this context as readers drew on the identity of the writer to understand and analyze the Christian value of the work.

Take the authorship of the *Rule of Benedict* itself as an instance. There is no firsthand account of Benedict having composed the *Rule*. Benedict left behind no other writings, and the *Rule* relies, at many points, on an earlier monastic guide, the *Regula Magistri* by one known only as the Master.[82] The authorship of the *Regula Benedicti* was an act of ascription initiated by Gregory the Great. The pope made this sainted authorship an intellectual property of the work. In doing so, Gregory added to the *Rule*'s coherence, integrity, and force, setting it apart from other similar monastic guides. Making it known that it was Benedict's gave it greater standing as a property or entity, giving it spiritual authority and calling for its exacting preservation and transmission.

There are two further pieces to this early monastic paradox. One of them is Benedict's contemporary Cassiodorus, who provides a contrasting figure

81. *Rule*, 33 55. R. W. Southern holds that "when St. Benedict included in his Rule the provision that all things were to be held in common, he was expressing not just an ideal for a religious society, but the ideal for all society": *Medieval Humanism and Other Studies* (Oxford: Blackwell, 1971), 53.

82. R. W. Southern, *Western Society and the Church in the Middle Ages* (London: Penguin, 1970), 221. Southern comments on the extent to which the *Rule*, which he judges the "most influential guide to spiritual life in western history," borrowed from *Regula Magistri*, but adds that "the mind of St. Benedict emerges more clearly than ever from a comparison of his work with its main source" (222, 223). Where Benedict, for example, mentions *school* once, *Regula Magistri* uses it "several times . . . in the sense of a school," according to Riché (*Education and Culture in the Barbarian West*, 112). Riché continues, "according to the *Regula Magistri*, small children grouped in a *decada* were to study their letters three hours a day under the supervision of a learned monk" (113). Additionally, the learning of letters and Psalms is referred to as spiritual work (*in spirituali opera*) (115).

to Benedict and Benedictine monasticism. After failing to establish a Christian school in Rome, Cassiodorus founded a learned monastery with a legendary library. If his approach to monastic life was passed over in favor of the Benedictine asceticism that dominated the early Middle Ages in the Latin West, the learning that he promoted was ultimately to secure a place within monasticism.

CASSIODORUS

Flavius Magnus Aurelius Cassiodorus was a Roman statesman who in 525 floated the idea for a Christian proto-university in Rome. As Cassiodorus describes it in the preface to *The Divine and Human Readings (Institutiones Divinarum et Saecularium Litterarum)*, he had been "extremely sorry that the Divine Scriptures had no public teachers," given that the secular schools "were swarming with students."[83] He sought subscriptions to raise the necessary funds "to receive professors in the city of Rome, just as custom is said to have existed for a long time at Alexandria and is said even now to be zealously cultivated by the Hebrews in Nisibis."[84] His goal was to balance long-term and immediate educational goals "that thereby the soul might obtain eternal salvation and tongue of the faithful be adorned with a holy and completely faultless eloquence."[85] However, the times were not suited to new educational initiatives: "My ardent desire could in no way be fulfilled because of the struggles that seethed and raged excessively in the Italian realm."[86]

Instead, on retiring from active political life, he established the abbey Vivarium and the hermitage Castellum on his estate at Scylacium in southern Italy. Serving as a monastic guidebook, *The Divine and Human Readings* set quite a different tone than the *Rule* of *Benedict*. It calls on "studious brothers" to "restrain your eager desires," and follow the better course of "learning in the proper order what should be read."[87] The book's homage to classical and Christian texts made the work an inspiration for those who sought to improve medieval monastic libraries.[88] Cassiodorus was willing to give each area of

---

83. Cassiodorus, *An Introduction to the Divine and Human Readings*, trans. Leslie Webber Jones (New York: Columbia University Press, 1946), 67.

84. Ibid.

85. Ibid.

86. Ibid.

87. Ibid., 70.

88. Leslie W. Jones, "The Influence of Cassiodorus on Mediaeval Culture," *Speculum* 20, no. 4 (1945): 441.

learning its due and cede any requirement that secular works serve to interpret scripture, as Augustine had encouraged if not always followed.[89]

In addressing the place of "Secular Letters" in monasticism, he begins by
explaining how the word *book* (*liber*) comes from the word "free"—"a book,
in other words, is the bark of a tree, removed and freed"—whereas *art* "is so
called because it limits (*artet*) and binds us with its rules."[90] On this theme
of the book freeing itself from the tree (the pillars of society?), Cassiodorus
was setting out an important scholarly principle in which inquiry is not ultimately rule-bound but must be free to pursue its own course. His interests
in reading clearly went well beyond reciting one's way to heaven's gate, Benedictine style.

Cassiodorus assembled the monastic library at Vivarium out of works he
secured from nearby Rome and from across the Mediterranean in Africa.[91] He
also assembled a respected team of scribes and translators to produce new
and improved editions, including Latin translations of Greek texts, as well as
his own commentaries on scripture, the liberal arts, and secular learning. He
was careful to establish standards for his scribes to follow in editing the texts
they copied, with an exception made for scripture, where nothing was to be
altered and only the most respected of ancient copies was to be used as exemplars.[92] At the age of ninety, he composed *On Orthography*, perhaps comparable to the "house style" of modern-day publishers, as a further guide for
scribes on handling spelling conventions.[93] Cassiodorus' freedom of inquiry
sets this work apart, the fidelity to others' work reflects a respect for their property, and the concern for conventions eased the meaning and learning of others from such properties.

While the community at Vivarium did not survive Cassiodorus' death, at
least the grand library that he and the monks built found refuge in the Lateran
Palace in Rome. Some of its works later made their way from there to France
and England, with copies along the way adding to that vital circulation of
scholarship he had sought to promote.[94] The resulting Vivarium collection
proved an influential source of historical and classical texts, representing

89. R. W. Southern, *The Making of the Middle Ages* (New Haven, CT: Yale University Press, 1953),
165-66.

90. Cassiodorus, *Divine and Human Readings*, 144.

91. Bischoff, *Manuscripts and Libraries in the Age of Charlemagne*, 3.

92. James O'Donnell, *Cassiodorus* (Berkeley: University of California Press, 1979), 211.

93. Riché, *Education and Culture in the Barbarian West*, 168.

94. Bischoff, *Manuscripts and Libraries in the Age of Charlemagne*, 7.

something of a canon that the most progressive monasteries sought to emulate through their collections during the Middle Ages.[95]

Amid the declining stability and security of the Roman world, it was the Benedictine monasteries that held their own through the early Middle Ages. And yet, over that period, as we will see below, nearly everything Cassiodorus imagined for the scholarly contribution and achievement of Christian monasticism found its way into monastic life.[96] But, while the spirit of learning that came to fruition in the monasteries during this time may have been inspired by Cassiodorus, it was marked by the "regularity" of Benedictine monasticism—in adherence to the regulations of the *Rule*—which included the humility and communality that infused monastic walls, cloister, and scriptorium. The Benedictine monastery of the Middle Ages was not a house of learning. Still, it managed to provide a secure home for learning in an insecure era.

SAINT RADEGUND AND THE SISTERS OF LEARNING

The final piece of learning's monastic paradox is the extent to which women were very much a part of the learned achievement of medieval abbey and priory. The unmistakable quality of their contribution was to be, unfortunately, effectively stymied before the Middle Ages had come to an end. They were excluded from cathedral schools, medieval universities, and church hierarchy. But before all of that, there was Radegund of Poitiers. Radegund was a Thuringian princess from a Germanic tribe that had been enslaved in 531 by the Frankish king Chlothar I. Though still a child at the time of their betrothal, Radegund was his war prize. After joining in the harem of the king's wives, she eventually sought the intervention of Germain of Paris. He managed in 550 to convince Chlothar to grant Radegund both her freedom and a plot of land in Poitiers. There, she built the Convent of the Holy Cross, as a refuge for herself and other women of nobility.[97] Radegund's mission at Holy Cross was to enact forceful humility. She addressed her monastic purpose in a letter to the bishops: "I asked myself, with all the ardor of which I am capable, how I could best forward the cause of other women, and how, if our Lord so willed, my own personal desires might be of advan-

---

95. Jones, "Influence of Cassiodorus," 435 n. 2.

96. O'Donnell, *Cassiodorus*, 198.

97. Jane E. Jeffrey, "Radegund and the Letter of Foundation," in *Women Writing Latin: From Roman Antiquity to Early Modern Europe*, ed. Laurie J. Churchill, Phyllis R. Brown, and Jane E. Jeffrey, vol. 2 (New York: Routledge, 2002), 11–12.

tage to my sisters."[98] She declined the role of Holy Cross abbess, although she still exercised her authority by placing the monastery under Caesarius' *Rule for Virgin (Regula virginum)*.

This was a monastic rule that encouraged the development of literacy as a common right and requirement of all monastics. Radegund took this literacy imperative in both literary and liturgical directions. Caesarius' *Rule* also emphasized strict enclosure for the sisterhood, as well as episcopal independence for the monastery, placing it outside the reach of the local bishop and the secular church.[99] The sisters who joined Holy Cross copied manuscripts and built a library in the spirit of Caesarius and Cassiodorus. Pierre Riché, University of Paris historian, notes how Radegund's monastery was "open to more literary and humanistic culture," as well as endowed with a somewhat "relaxed" following of Caesarius' strictures: "The nuns played dice, took baths, and admitted men into the cloister."[100] For her part, Radegund composed, in whole or in part, the poems "Letter to Artachis" and "The Thuringian War." She penned against the ravages of war, drawing on an experience she knew only too well: "A wife's naked feet trod in her husband's blood / And the tender sister stepped over the fallen brother."[101] In turn, she faced objections from the abbess of Caesarius of Arles, who condemned the expansiveness of her literary and learned interests.[102] And certainly Radegund sought a greater reach and impact through her learning: "Whenever the different kingdoms made war on one another," writes her friend Bishop Venantius Fortunatus about her, "she sent such letters to one and then to the other pleading that that should not make war among themselves nor take up arms lest the land perish. And, likewise, she sent to their noble followers to give the high king salutary counsel so that their power might work to the welfare of the people and the land."[103]

98. Cited and translated by Marcelle Thiébaux, ed., *The Writings of Medieval Women: An Anthology* (London: Routledge, 1994), 87.

99. Ibid., 12. On enclosure, Bateson notes how "no nun might leave the walls of the house alive": "Origin and Early History of the Double Monastery," *Transactions of the Royal Historical Society* 13 (1899): 143. E. T. Dailey reports on how the nuns could not accompany the funeral procession of Radegund through the city: "Confinement and Exclusion in the Monasteries of Sixth-Century Gaul," *Early Medieval Europe* 22, no. 3 (2014): 313.

100. Riché, *Education and Culture in the Barbarian West*, 292.

101. Radegund, "The Thuringian War," in *Sainted Women of the Dark Ages*, trans. Jo Ann McNamara (Durham, NC: Duke University Press, 1992), 66. See McNamara's accompanying note on attribution.

102. Riché, *Education and Culture in the Barbarian West*, 293.

103. Venantius Fortunatus, "The Life of the Holy Radegund," in *Sainted Women of the Dark Ages*, trans. Jo Ann McNamara (Durham, NC: Duke University Press, 1992), 93. Marilyn Dunn sees

Monasticism had afforded Radegund a way to pull away from a brutal world that was unlikely to afford her such learning, peace, and respite. It offered her a way, as well, to direct some part of that learning back into the world as a guide and inspiration to others. But then monasticism held its own set of contradictions for women. Its principle of enclosure could literally mean sealing a woman in a windowless room, cut off from the world, as we will see with Hildegard of Bingen in chapter 5. Women were often placed— although *incarcerated* may be a better word for it—in monasteries against their will by their families. In this and other ways, the monastery, while removed from the world, remained within the prejudices of the larger society.

Still, within convent and priory, women managed to find a space open to their leadership and counsel, as well as to their learning and teachings. It was frequently more than they could find at home.[104] Through monasticism, they served as prioress and abbess, if often with male oversight and collaboration. Some women took charge of the double monasteries, that were not all that rare during the early Middle Ages, in which men and women had separate quarters but common work spaces in scriptoria and schoolrooms. (An end was put to establishing any further double monasteries by the Second Council of Nicaea in 787.)[105] Further, this pious incorporation of nuns and monks in gated communities attracted the beneficence of the nobility, who helped create these monastic centers of literacy across the Latin West, during what were otherwise less conducive times for learning. Brown attests to the extent of their achievement by the seventh century: "In the largest and, in many ways, the wealthiest political unit in western Europe, monasticism had become a fully public institution, identified with stability and political success."[106]

Part of that stability was reflected in how nunneries, like the world outside, reflected the social stratifications of society: if the monasteries recruited from

in Radegund "a picture of feminine values of intercession and peacemaking as well [as] humility in domestic tasks around the nunnery," in contrast to "the 'manly' women characteristic[s] of the earliest days of monasticism": *The Emergence of Monasticism: From the Desert Fathers to the Early Middle Ages* (Oxford: Blackwell, 2000), 109.

104. See Suzanne Fonay Wemple, for the "degree of dignity and autonomy unavailable to married women" that monasteries offered: *Women in Frankish Society: Marriage and the Cloister, 500 to 900* (Philadelphia: University of Pennsylvania Press, 1985), 157.

105. Ibid., 160, 162. Wemple writes of how Burgundofara founded Faremoutiers Abbey as the first of the double monasteries around 617, beginning with the nunnery and then adding quarters for the monks (160). Mary Bateson cites Justinan's Codex from 529 on the need for property that had been held in common by monks and nuns to be divided between them that the sexes might better keep their distance: "Double Monastery," 144.

106. Brown, *Rise of Western Christendom*, 231.

across the social classes, they still mirrored feudal class relations—despite the common vow of poverty—with ladies-in-waiting and laborers typically serving prioresses and abbots of noble birth.[107] And if the monastery offered women a refuge from unwanted and unfortunate marriages, its enclosure at a remove from the world weighed more heavily on nuns than on monks.[108] For a monk might journey to obtain the copy of a book or to serve the church, while a nun would be enclosed without remit for years within her abbey. Even then, nunneries were particularly vulnerable to attack from the marauding pillagers of the age. The Vikings prior to the Norman Conquest managed to destroy so many of the religious houses that women occupied in England that only nine convents were still standing across the land when William the Conqueror arrived in 1066.[109]

CONCLUSION

Late antiquity and the early Middle Ages offer a number of starting positions for the intellectual properties of learning within Christian monasticism. Jerome, for example, made much of laboring over texts, with his editing and translating earning him, as I hold, an intellectual property claim to these works. This was not about displacing the original author (who is often God); it was about the scholar's right and obligation to serve readers with more accurate editions, for which he was both credited and supported. Augustine furthered this sense of associated rights, by insisting on authors having a say over the integrity and completeness of a work before it entered that commons of open scholarly use. He also defended a learned right of inquiry,

107. James A. Raftis: "Insofar as studies can be accurately made of this matter, monks seem to have been recruited fairly widely and consistently from all classes": "Western Monasticism and Economic Organization," *Comparative Studies in Society and History* 3, no. 4 (1961): 454.

108. "The great honor paid by Christianity to the celibate life and the wide field of action opened to a princess in a religious house were strong inducements to the sisters and daughters of kings to take the veil": Linda Eckstein, *Women under Monasticism* (New York: Russell and Russell, 1963), 80. Women also served as porters guarding the convent gate and speaking-window, to which relatives would come to visit. They were keepers of the monastery's books (*bibliothecarius*); they served as scribes and illuminators, as well as infirmarians and cellarers. Rebecca L. Garber points to the Dominican *Nonnenbücher*, or sister-books, in which women wrote vitae for different roles, using "conceptions of feminine exemplarity that would accord with the context of the cloistered Dominican nun": *Feminine Figurae: Representations of Gender in Religious Texts by Medieval German Women Writers* (New York: Routledge, 2003), 61.

109. Janet Tibbetts Schulenburg, "The Heroics of Virginity: Brides of Christ and Sacrificial Mutilation," in *Women in the Middle Ages and Renaissance: Literary and Historical Perspectives*, ed. Mary Beth Rose (Syracuse: Syracuse University Press, 1986), 45.

bound by purpose rather than despised curiosity. This afforded the scholar a degree of (academic) freedom to tap, for example, pagan sources to serve some greater good.

Yet in looking ahead through the Middle Ages, we can see that Jerome and Augustine were engaged in a somewhat idiosyncratic form of monasticism. Neither developed an institutional framework for learning that would support and sustain the proto-intellectual property regime they established for themselves. That missing element of monastic regularity and sustainability was introduced by the *Rule of Benedict*. While the *Rule* did not endorse learning, per se, the Benedictine monastery more than made up for that by providing the conditions for learning: the endowment of daily reading time, an insistence on communal book sharing, and, by making manuscripts such an integral part of monastic life, the provisions for book production. The full resolution of the monastic paradox, however, only comes with the Venerable Bede, introduced in the next chapter, who creates a warrant within Benedictine monasticism for learning and scholarship by making clear the extent to which it can serve the salvation of others.

For his part, Cassiodorus demonstrated how far such institutions could go in support of learning, even if monastics and their benefactors opted instead for the Benedictine model and *Rule*. His proto-university was thoroughly dedicated to the preservation and restoration of learned works as valuable properties and part of a canon. If his Vivarium was not to be a model for early Middle Ages monasticism, it still created an ideal of a community fully engaged with the intellectual properties of learning. Cassiodorus celebrated the freedom of the book, and in doing so, he might well have been pointing to the life and works of Radegund. For Radegund demonstrated monasticism's capacities for opening up a space in which women could produce literary works that were unlikely to be otherwise sanctioned in the Christian West. Within this monastic network, the book had taken hold. Works were composed, copied and circulated. They formed part of a regulated life within which their role, as a source of intellectual propriety and freedom, would only grow through the early Middle Ages.

CHAPTER THREE

Learning in the Early Middle Ages

The early Middle Ages, spanning the fifth to tenth centuries, can be thought of as the era of compilation.[1] One influential source for this form was the fifth-century *Saturnalia*, an imaginary symposium populated by Latin and Greek historical, mythological, and grammatical sources by the Roman provincial Macrobius Ambrosius Theodosius: "I have organized the diverse subjects, drawn from a range of authors and a mix of periods . . . in a coherent, organic whole."[2] This "fund of knowledge" in seven books stood as a pillar of late antiquity's encyclopedic tradition.[3] It was this sort of artful assembly of texts, cast in the form of a dialogue, that at once suited medieval monasticism. It represented the selfless humility of an editor culling the work of others, with the resulting work making up for a medieval shortage of sources. "The work of extraction and arrangement," in the estimation of the Oxford historian Richard W. Southern, "was the true medium of the monastic scholars."[4] It

1. Neil Hathaway, "Compilatio: From Plagiarism to Compiling," *Viator* 20 (1989): 19.

2. Macrobius, *Saturnalia*, vol. 1, bks. 1–2, trans. Robert A. Kaster (Cambridge, MA: Harvard University Press, 2011), 5. Adding to this sense of the productive monastery, Georges Duby notes that "virtually all the extant texts from a century-long period between 1030 and 1120 originated in the monasteries," which was the "very period of monasticism's triumph": *The Three Orders: Feudal Society Imagined* (Chicago: University of Chicago Press, 1981), 174, 176.

3. Macrobius, *Saturnalia*, 3.

4. R. W. Southern, *The Making of the Middle Ages* (New Haven, CT: Yale University Press, 1953), 182. When authors' works were commonly and economically bound in a single book, the book would be cataloged by the first title alone, further indicating how familiar readers would be with these compilations; James Stuart Beddie, "The Ancient Classics in the Medieval Libraries," *Speculum* 5, no. 1 (1930): 4.

demonstrated, Southern observes, "the quiet, industrious unambitious mind at work reducing years of reading to an orderly form."[5]

The early and outstanding Christian instance of the compiler's art was the seventh-century *Etymologies* (*Etymologiasive originum*) by Isidore of Seville. Isidore was not a monk, but the bishop of Seville, appointed around 600. He did, however, declare himself Protector of Monks and his well-ordered compilation of sacred and secular, Christian and pagan, sources was intended to inform and enable learning in monastic communities. Earlier in his life, monks had been his teachers, and he later composed for them a relatively lenient monastic rule (*Monastica Regula*), "which he tempered most fittingly for use in this country and for the souls of the weak," as his friend and colleague Braulio of Zaragoza put it.[6]

Isidore was still working on the massive *Etymologies* when he died in 636. As Braulio finished preparing the work, he also helpfully added a table of contents and divided the full work into twenty volumes.[7] It was not long before monastic scribes across Latin Christendom were turning out copies of this compilation of word origins and meanings that covered everything from grammatical forms to domestic furnishings. Within a decade or so of Isidore's death and the book's release, a version of it would be found in Ireland. Nearly a thousand manuscript copies of at least some portion of this work survive to this day.[8]

5. Southern, *Making of Middle Ages*, 183. "The process of collection and arrangement gave an impulse to thought and to methods of enquiry which bore fruit in the schools and universities of the twelfth and thirteenth centuries" (ibid.)

6. Cited by Stephen A. Barney, W. J. Lewis, J. A. Beach, and Oliver Berghof, Introduction to Isidore of Seville, *The Etymologies of Isidore of Seville*, trans. Stephen A. Barney, W. J. Lewis, J. A. Beach, and Oliver Berghof (Cambridge: Cambridge University Press, 2006), 8. Martin Irvine reports that Isidore's *Monastica Regula* included three hours a day for reading and "as well . . . a period when the community would meet to discuss problems posed by *divina lectio* and the abbot was to explain difficult passages for everyone": *Making of Textual Culture: 'Grammatica' and Literary Theory 350–1100* (Cambridge: Cambridge University Press, 1994), 218.

7. In this period before the title page, the *Etymologies* opened with a note to readers, in the case of one early edition, explaining the table of contents: "So that you may quickly find what you are looking for in this work, this page reveals for you, reader, what matters the author of this volume discusses in the individual books" (Isidore, *Etymologies*, 34). Ernst Robert Curtius notes that "the compilation is a literary genre which was highly popular and highly respected in late Antiquity," while noting of Isidore that "to impart knowledge was his aim . . . the only possible literary form for such an aim was to collect and arrange excerpted matter": *European Literature and the Latin Middle Ages,* trans. by Willard R. Trask (London: Routledge, 1953), 456.

8. On an early Irish copy of the *Etymologies* based on an existing fragment, see Michael W. Herren, "Storehouses of Learning: Encyclopaedias and Other Reference Works in Ireland and Pre-Bedan Anglo Saxon England," in *Practice in Learning: The Transfer of Encyclopaedic Knowledge in the early Middle Ages,* ed. Rolf H. Bremmer Jr. and Kees Dekker (Paris: Peeters, 2010), 10. J. N. Hillgarth reports that only Augustine has more manuscripts surviving from before 800 in Ireland than Isidore: "Ireland and Spain in the Seventh Century," *Peritia* 3 (1984): 5.

Although monasteries were often set outside the bishop's realm of influence by papal decree, it was not unusual for a bishop to make a gift to a monastery. Isidore's gift of the *Etymologies*, however, was exceptional, even as it proved something of a Trojan Horse for learning. The Roman education that Benedict of Nursia had fled in disgust as a young man, Isidore of Seville brought in through the monastery gate and placed in the library chest, where its twenty volumes could awaken the (pagan) intellectual interests that Benedict had left behind. *Etymologies* was both source and model for the monastic community. As such, it has been called "arguably the most influential book, after the Bible, in the learned world of the Latin West for nearly a thousand years," by its modern team of editors and translators.[9]

The governing principle of *Etymologies* is that language is itself the source of knowledge. The true sense of the world is to be found in the origins and earlier uses of words: "Adam, as blessed Jerome informs us, means 'human' or 'earthling' or 'red earth,'" to take one example from Isidore's work, "for from earth was flesh made . . . Eve (*Eva*) means 'life' or 'calamity' or 'woe' (*vae*)."[10] This etymological approach required that Isidore do more than merely compile authorities. He had to carefully order, integrate, and weave together pagan and Christian traditions around the origins of words, organizing a coherent whole out of the chaotic richness of language. As for his sources, if he called on scripture more often than Virgil, he cited Aristotle ahead of Augustine, at least in terms of attributions.[11]

To consider an instance, allow me to turn to the grammatical concept of the *negative*, in Isidore's section on "Figures of Words and of Expressions." Here he draws, without noting his source, on a letter by Jerome for this rather unexpected example of expressing the negative in a condition of "wondering": "What! I can scarcely survive; would I wish to fornicate?" [12] He then turns to Ovid (also without attribution, although he acknowledges them both with quotations elsewhere) for a "grieving" negative—"Woe is me, that no love is curable with herbs."[13]

Etymologies represents both the medieval gift economy and the proto-intellectual-property regime. The work was given to the monastic community by Isidore as something borrowed, plundered, synthesized, and created,

9. Barney, Lewis, Beach, and Berghof, Introduction to *Etymologies*, 3.

10. Isidore, *Etymologies*, VII.v.i.4, 162. Note the unfortunate anagram that then ties *Eva* to *vae* (calamity).

11. Barney, Lewis, Beach, and Berghof, Introduction to *Etymologies*, 11, 14.

12. Isidore, *Etymologies*, II.xxi.24 77.

13. Ibid.

from what he found in others' compilations. It was the systematic ordering of that knowledge that constituted the value and advance of this intellectual property. Isidore appears to have been aware, if not consistently, of the attribution and property issues involved in creating such a work. This sort of compilation forms an early test case in the historic formation of the scholar's rights and responsibilities in the use of others' work (even as scholars today continue to work on identifying all who were cited in this work).[14] The textual descendants of *Etymologies*, whether encyclopedias, dictionaries, anthologies, or other reference works, have sustained this mixed record in documenting what is owed to whom.[15]

For his part, Isidore addresses the matter of contribution and credit head-on in book 10 of *Etymologies*. The topic is "certain terms for human beings," one of which is a *plagiarist*: "A plagiarist (*compilator*), one who mixes the words of another with his own, as pigment-makers customarily crush together diverse things mixed up in a mortar (*pila*). The poet of Mantua [Virgil] was once accused of this crime because of his taking verses of Homer and mixing them with his own, and was called by his rivals a plagiarist of the ancients. He answered them, 'It takes great strength to wrest Hercules' club from his hand.'"[16] Clearly aware of the plagiarism charges that accompany compilations—the Latin *compilo* means to plunder, pillage, steal, or snatch—Isidore presents the upside by emphasizing the skill, as well as the Herculean strength, involved in the compilator's art. He is careful to locate the root of *compilator* in the mortar (*pila*), as the bowl within which something new is synthesized, as opposed to the pestle (*pilum*) that crushes what is placed in the *pila*. He is defending, in effect, a right of use. The words of others form an intellectual commons from which some greater scholarly art or value can be created, although still to come was a greater care—and no less scholarly value—in the accrediting sources. And, of course, Isidore's definition of plagiarist turns out to be itself cobbled together, without attribution, from the work of Suetonius, Macrobius, and Jerome, who also wrote on this theme.[17]

14. Barney, Lewis, Beach, and Berghof report in their introduction to *Etymologies* that five of the projected twenty volumes of a scholarly edition published by Belles Lettres in Paris had been completed by 2006. Introduction to *Etymologies*, 11.

15. For example, *Wikipedia* is now thoroughly engaged in these intellectual property questions of giving credit and establishing authority. See "Wikipedia: Verifiability" in *Wikipedia*. Also, on the Victorian use of sources in dictionaries, see John Willinsky, *Empire of Words: The Reign of the OED* (Princeton, NJ: Princeton University Press, 1994).

16. Isidore, *Etymologies*, X.c.44, 216.

17. Hathaway finds that Isidore's entry for *compilator* mirrors an unacknowledged earlier comment on the topic by Jerome, although Jerome bases his etymology for the term on the pestle rather than the mortar: "*Compilatio*," 25, 27, 28.

The medieval compilation was originally known as a *florilegium*, a compound of *flos* (flower) and *legere* (to gather), as if to emphasize the beauty, and sense of gift, associated with gathered flowers. It was to take on greater intellectual authority with the attribution and crediting of its contributors, even if it did not always bear the name of its original humble compiler. By the thirteenth century, the compilation was made up of carefully attributed excerpts in the form we would recognize today as an anthology.[18] The anonymous compilator of the twelfth-century *Florilegium morale oxoniense* states, "I have inscribed the name of its authors next to each of the *dicta*, and arranged with that name similar or dissimilar *dicta*, by the same author or by others . . . that I thought would profit this school."[19] What had also changed since Isidore's day, some six centuries earlier, is that the compilator is now apologetic about intervening in the collection: "To this . . . unworthy type of compilation I have added, although somewhat unwillingly, what little part of my lengthy night labor it was considered to require."[20] Standards had shifted, and yet this compilator felt compelled to remind readers of the learned labors invested in creating a valued intellectual property, involving far more than simple copying one borrowed excerpt after another. While the encyclopedic tradition continued through the Middle Ages and beyond, the eighth century saw the introduction of a new era of monastic scholarship, marked by fresh inquiries and original research, beginning in the north of England with the work of the Benedictine monk Bede.

VENERABLE BEDE

In 679, when Bede was but a young lad of six or seven years of age, he was, "by the care of my kinsmen," as he describes it, "put into the charge of the reverend Abbot Benedict and then of Ceolfrith, to be educated."[21] He had entered the

18. When it comes to the etymology of *compile* (verb), the *Oxford English Dictionary* states that "the history is by no means clear," before citing Isidore's equating of compilator with plagiarist, as well as the fourteenth century Old French for "constructed, built." "Medieval compilers did not conceal that fact that they were deriving their material from classical, patristic, and other medieval sources; they often cite their sources, 'ut Augustinus dicit,' etc.": George Hardin Brown, personal communication, July 1, 2013.

19. Cited by Hathaway, *Compilatio*, 40. The citing was complicated by the extent of anonymous authorship, as Richard Gameson observes that "'signed' manuscripts are the exception not the rule in the early medieval Romanesque periods": "Signed Manuscripts from Early Romanesque Flanders: Saint-Bertin and Saint-Vaast," in *Pen in Hand: Medieval Scribal Portraits, Colophons and Tools*, ed. Michael Gullick (Walkern: Red Gull Press, 2006), 49.

20. Hathaway, *Compilatio*, 40.

21. Bede, *The Ecclesiastical History of the English People,* trans. Bertram Colgrave (Oxford: Oxford University Press, 1969), 5.24 357.

twin Benedictine monasteries of Wearmouth-Jarrow in the north of Anglo-Saxon England. He was to proceed through the holy orders of oblate, novice, and monk over the course of his life, while avoiding the role of abbot. What those fifty-five years at Wearmouth-Jarrow added up to was the quiet, humble triumph of monastic learning. Over the course of his life, Bede produced an amazing variety of works in history, grammar, orthography, rhetoric, hagiography, mathematics, chronology, biblical commentary, geography, and devotional poetry. "Amid the observance of the discipline of the *Rule* and the daily task of singing in the church," Bede writes of this productive life, "it has always been my delight to learn or to teach or to write."[22]

Bede's life amounted to a transformative observance of the *Rule of Benedict*. He made teaching into a respectable vocation for the Benedictine monk and nun, where the *Rule* had limited teaching to abbot and prioress: "It is right that the master should speak and teach," reads the *Rule*, "while the disciple should be made silent and listen."[23] Bede overcame, with some pleasure, the earlier paradox of monastic learning. He successfully challenged Jerome's declaration that "a monk's function is not to teach, but to lament; to mourn either for himself or for the world."[24] Rather, Bede's stance was that learning was a rightful trade for monastics: "I have made it my business, for my own benefit and that of my brothers, to make brief extracts from the works of the venerable fathers on the holy scriptures, or to add notes of my own to clarify their sense and interpretation."[25] Through this educational embrace, Bede resolved the monastic paradox, introduced in the previous chapter, by identifying this selfless, or rather other-directed, property of learning that was engaged in taking up the world and opening what was learned for the benefit of others. "What Bede wanted to do and did superbly," George Hardin Brown, Stanford English and classics professor, notes, "was educate, soberly, quietly, discreetly."[26]

22. Ibid.

23. *The Rule of Benedict*, trans. Carolinne White (London: Penguin, 2008), 7 21.

24. Jerome, "Against Vigilantius," in *St. Jerome: Letters and Select Works*, trans W. H. Fremantle, vol. 6 of *A Select Library of Nicene and Post-Nicene Fathers of the Christian Church*, 2nd ser., ed. Philip Schaff and Henry Wace, (Grand Rapids, MI: Eerdmans, 1954), 15, 423. Jerome goes on to reinforce the point: "Why, you will say, go to the desert? . . . that I may not be disturbed" (ibid.).

25. Bede, *The Ecclesiastical History*, 5.24 357. Some years ago, Robert B. Palmer noted how "modern scholarship has said little about one other extremely important aspect of Bede's genius, which the Middle Ages had long recognized in silence—his lucidity and precision as a textbook writer": "Bede as Textbook Writer: A Study of His *De arte metrica*," *Speculum* 34, no. 4 (1959): 573. Bede's grammar texts demonstrated "a critical synthesis," as well as a "sanity of selection," in Palmer's judgment (584 574).

26. George Hardin Brown, "Bede the Educator," Jarrow Lecture 1996 (Jarrow, UK: St. Paul's Church, 1997), 1.

The value of this learning figures prominently in his celebrated *Ecclesiastical History of the English People*. He reports, for example, that the English were drawn to Irish monasteries in the sixth century by the reputation of the Irish for learned grace and generosity: "There were many in England, both nobles and commons, who ... retired to Ireland either for the sake of religious studies or to live a more ascetic life [and] ... devoted themselves faithfully to the monastic life, while others preferred to travel round to the [monastic] cells of various teachers and apply themselves to study."[27] Such was the force of Irish learning that "in the case of people suffering from snakebite, the leaves of manuscripts from Ireland were scraped, and the scrapings put in water and given to the sufferer to drink."[28] Bede also celebrates the openness with which the Irish shared their learning: "The Irish welcomed them all gladly, gave them their daily food, and also provided them with books to read and with instruction, without asking for any payment."[29]

Bede also did much to celebrate monastic learning in his writing, making it clear that it was integral to the institution. He wrote about the examples of Theodore, a Byzantine Greek who later became archbishop of Canterbury, and Hadrian, a North African who was elected abbot of St. Augustine's Abbey in Canterbury. The two founded a school in England dedicated to the teaching of Greek and Latin: "Because both of them were extremely learned," Bede explains, "in sacred and secular literature, they attracted a crowd of students into whose minds they daily poured the streams of wholesome learning."[30] The reference to learning's wholesomeness is directed against the common charge that it led to sinful pride and paganism (through secular literature). Where Benedict of Nursia fled his studies in sixth-century Rome to seek redemption in monastic solitude and prayer, Bede celebrates Theodore

27. Bede, *Ecclesiastical History*, 3.27 192.
28. Ibid., 1.1 13. Bede reports that Ireland had no snakes, adding further mystery to how such powers were discovered (ibid.). Irish monasteries also played a strong part in the revival of Latin literature, drawing on Virgil among others, as well as the study of grammar: Bernhard Bischoff, "Benedictine Monasteries and the Survival of Classical Literature," in *Manuscripts and Libraries in the Age of Charlemagne*, trans. and ed. Michael M. Gorman (Cambridge: Cambridge University Press, 1994), 137.
29. Bede, *Ecclesiastical History*, 3.27 192. Thomas Cahill refers to Kevin of Glendalough in the sixth century developing "a kind of university city to which came thousands of hopeful students first from all over Ireland, then from England, and at last from everywhere in Europe": *How the Irish Saved Civilization: The Untold Story of Ireland's Heroic Role from the Fall of Rome to the Rise of Medieval Europe* (New York: Doubleday, 1995), 157.
30. Bede, *Ecclesiastical History*, 4.2 205. John Henry Newman credits Pope Vitalian for sending Theodore to Canterbury, regarding it as a historic turning point for monastic learning: "The Benedictine Centuries," *Atlantis* 2 (January–July 1859): 14.

and Hadrian's ability to build a community through their "extremely learned" teaching, as well as by building the library at Canterbury for all to share.[31]

Bede also made much of the library at Wearmouth-Jarrow, which was highly regarded, given it had all of roughly two hundred volumes.[32] Bede credits the library's relatively large size to Benedict Biscop, who had founded Wearmouth and Jarrow in 674 and made repeated journeys to Rome for books.[33] Bede notes with some enthusiasm that Benedict "brought back a large number of books on all branches of sacred knowledge, some bought at a favorable price, others the gifts of well-wishers."[34] Toward the end of Benedict's life, Bede notes, "he gave orders that the fine and extensive library of books which he had brought back from Rome and which were so necessary for improving the standard of education in this church should be carefully preserved as a single collection and not allowed to decay through neglect or be split up piecemeal."[35] Abbot Ceolfrith, who was elected to succeed Benedict, then "doubled the number of books of the libraries in both of the monasteries with an ardor equal to that which Benedict had shown in founding them."[36] Bede reflects that particular sense of the preserved and intact library as forming the natural center or commons of learning's commonwealth.

Bede contributed much to that and other libraries with the seventy or so works that he composed, according to the advertisement with which he concludes the *Ecclesiastical History of the English People*.[37] He not only took

31. Putnam Fennell Jones notes that, "there is no evidence of any such passion for book-collecting in England before the coming of Theodore and Hadrian": "The Gregorian Mission and English Education," *Speculum* 3, no. 3 (1928): 346.

32. David Ganz, "Anglo-Saxon England," in *To 1640*, ed. Elisabeth Leedham-Green and Teresa Webber, vol. 1 of *The Cambridge History of Libraries in Britain and Ireland* (Cambridge: Cambridge University Press, 2006), 95. Ganz includes an extensive list of works, from antiquity and medieval times, that Bede cites, while noting that only one book, a Greek-Latin copy of Acts, is known to have survived from his library (100).

33. Rosalind Love, "The World of Latin Learning," in *The Cambridge Companion to Bede*, ed. S. DeGregorio (Cambridge: Cambridge University Press, 2010), 43. See Michael Lapidge on travel to Rome for books: *The Anglo-Saxon Library* (Oxford: Oxford University Press, 2013), 77.

34. Bede, "Lives of Abbots of Wearmouth and Jarrow," in *The Age of Bede*, trans. D. H. Farmer (London: Penguin, 1965), 188. After Benedict told Egfrid, King of Northumbia, of his studies and books, the king "took to Benedict so warmly that he immediately gave him from his personal property an area of land comprising seventy hides," which was enough for seventy families (188–89).

35. Ibid., 196.

36. Ibid., 201. Although Ceolfrith did trade "the magnificently worked copy of the Cosmographers [mapmakers] which Benedict had bought in Rome" with King Aldrid "for eight hides of land by the River Fresca," it was a charitable act in support of the monastery of St. Paul (ibid.).

37. Bede, *Ecclesiastical History*, 5.24, 357–60.

on the role of publicist with these books, but humbly involved himself in all aspects of their production: "I myself am at once my own dictator, stenographer, and copyist."[38] Working from the commonwealth of the library, Bede skillfully fashioned treatises, compilations, and commentaries for novices and the larger monastic community.

At times, Bede made a point of acknowledging the credit system that accompanies the scholar's right of use. He noted the sources on which he drew in the margins of the page, "lest I be said to steal the sayings of my elders," he wrote, "and to compose these as my own."[39] This talk of theft is an intellectual property constant in this story, with references to such thievery going back to ancient antiquity. To speak of a text as stolen offers its own proof that the text is regarded as a property. More often for Bede, however, such marginal notations of authorship fell to later scholars to fill in, as they treated the text like a running literary puzzle. Beyond the marginal annotation, Bede introduced other refinements into the process by, for example, sending his work out for review and comment to those whose opinion and knowledge he respected.[40] And much as Jerome and Augustine had done, he was careful, in his use of Virgil, Pliny, and other classical writers that he used for Christian ends, to include warnings about thorns among roses and bees amid honey.[41]

As a teacher, Bede emphasized the importance of listening to students, for "when one teaches it is very difficult to prevent some aspect of boastful pride stealing in."[42] He also allowed that "not one and the same teaching is suitable for all," but that what was for all was to "excite the hearts of the hearers to offer their good works to the Lord."[43] Working among those excited hearts, he expanded the scope of monastic learning. He demonstrated a new level of intellectual engagement with natural philosophy and scientific inquiry, where Augustine and others saw temptation and urged caution.

Bede also brought his own experience and observations together with the work of others, such as the Roman naturalist, Pliny the Elder.[44] He held

38. Cited by George Hardin Brown, *A Companion to Bede* (Woodbridge, Suffolk, UK: Boydell and Brewer, 2009), 11.

39. Cited and noted by Brown, "Bede the Educator," 8.

40. Ibid., 3.

41. See Roger Ray, "Bede and Cicero," *Anglo-Saxon England* 16 (1987): 1-15.

42. Cited by T. R. Eckenrode, "Venerable Bede as an Educator," *History of Education* 6, no. 3 (1977): 160.

43. Ibid., 164.

44. Richard C. Dales, *The Scientific Achievement of the Middle Ages* (Philadelphia: University of Pennsylvania Press, 1973), 33. Love points out, in terms of Bede's "rich fusion of distinct intellectual traditions," that he also drew on "a Semitic focus on the 'letter,'" that is, on the text's literal

that the world was a globe with latitudinal bands of climate difference, proposing that those who doubted that the world was round should take the
time to climb a hill and glance around.[45] He considered the periodicity of
the tides, noting "the great fellowship that exists between the ocean and the
course of the Moon," while making precise calculations in days and minutes:
"It is as if [the ocean] *were dragged forwards* against its will *by certain exhalta-
tions of the Moon.*[46] Here, he did not draw on Pliny nor Irish sources which had
addressed the tides. Rather, he collected data over the course of two decades
from a network of correspondents who recorded their local tidal patterns.[47]
It was a rare Medieval instance of collaborative empiricism, and he used the
obvious superiority of the strategy to correct others' accounts of the tides.
This is that particular learned economy of texts, in which value is established through the use and correction of what is otherwise held in common,
whether in texts or in what can be observed of the world.

While Bede held that scientific inquiry must retain a pious purpose, he
introduced a new level of accuracy to observation and explanation. He begins *On the Nature of Things* (*De natura rerum*), another of his schoolbooks,
with a prefatory verse of Augustinian caution: "In brief chapters, I, Bede,
the servant of God, / Have lightly touched on the varied natures of things /
and on the broad ages of fleeting time. You who study the stars above, / Fix
your mind's gaze, I pray, on the Light of the everlasting day."[48] Having stated

---

level: "World of Latin Learning," 41. M. L. W. Laistner contrasts Bede's stance on the classical
tradition to that of the seventh-century Abbot Aldhelm of Malmsebury, whose "poetry is steeped
in Virgil, and in his prose writings he parades tortuous and artificial conceits of the late imperial
rhetorical schools"; Bede is "very sparing " in drawing on "pagan authors": "Bede as a Classical
and Patristic Scholar," in *The Intellectual Heritage of the early Middle Ages: Selected Essays of M. L. W.
Laistner*, ed. Chester G. Starr (Ithaca, NY: Cornell University Press, 1957), 96.

45. Wesley M. Stevens, "Bede's Scientific Achievement," in *Bede and His World: Jarrow Lectures 1979–1993*, vol. 2, ed. Michael Lapidge (Farnham UK: Variorum, 1994), 652.

46. Bede, *The Reckoning of Time*, trans. Faith Wallis (Liverpool: Liverpool University Press,
1999), 82–83.

47. Stevens, "Bede's Scientific Achievement," 657, 662–63. Bede names, among his sources of
data, tidal information from Lindisfarne, Whithorn, and the Isle of Wight, noting the irregularities
in lunar and solar tidal effects, as well as spring tides and neap tides: "Those who live north of me
on the same coastline usually receive and give back each tide sooner that I do, and those to the
south later" (*The Reckoning of Time*, 85).

48. Bede, *On the Nature of Things, and On Times*, trans. Calvin B. Kendall and Faith Wallis (Liverpool: Liverpool University Press, 2010), 71. Augustine objected to the *curiosi* who "look into
spiritual matters with a terrestrial eye," where Bede is careful to look into terrestrial matters with a
spiritual eye: cited by Richard Newhauser, "Augustinian *Vitium curiositatis* and Its Reception," in
Saint Augustine and His Influence in the Middle Ages, ed. Edward B. King and Jacqueline T. Schaefer
(Sewanee, TN: Press of the University of the South, 1988), 111. Newhauser also reports on Augustine objecting in a sermon to those who rely upon empirical evidence (based on their five senses)
in arriving at matters of faith, such as the resurrection of Christ (114).

the ultimate goal, he is then content to focus on what can be learned of the world: "Rains are formed from the little drops of the clouds," he writes in the chapter on precipitation, "they coalesce into bigger drops, no longer supported by the nature of air, sometimes driven by the wind, sometimes dissolved by the sun, they fall down in the form of rain to the earth."[49]

Bede also set a further standard for the scholarly integrity of medieval monasticism, beyond his efforts to properly cite sources and solicit reviews for work in progress. Relatively late in life, he started to learn Greek, which had been largely lost to the Latin West by that point, to be able to better prepare and verify the classical sources he wanted to use for his work.[50] When he was accused of heresy—which was learning's principal occupational hazard in the medieval era—he responded with detailed refutations, defending his autonomy as a thinker. Still, he was not above resorting to ad hominem countercharges that such criticisms were on the order of a ditty "sung stupidly by lascivious rustics at a drinking bout."[51] And finally, he prepared a *Retraction on the Acts of the Apostles*, following the example of Augustine's own late reconsiderations, with Bede, in this case, revising his earlier edition of *Acts*, based in part on his newly acquired Greek.[52]

All told, Bede succeeded in demonstrating the value of a life of monastic learning across a range of fields. It was to prove a critical turning point for monasticism. After Bede, study could be more than a form of penitence, and monasticism could stand for more than a reenactment of the Fall and humankind's expulsion from the Garden of Eden.[53] He had provided an alternative, adding the instructional value of learning to the penitential arithmetic, in which each word copied in the scriptorium reduced one's own or another's time in purgatory. Rather than redeeming past or original sins, Bede made it clear that learning was capable of producing its own fruitful garden, a bookish Eden in which the fruit of the tree of knowledge was held in common.

---

49. Bede, *On the Nature of Things*, 93.

50. Roger Ray, "Who Did Bede Think He Was?" in *Innovation and Tradition in the Writings of the Venerable Bede*, ed. Scott Degregorio (Morgantown: West Virginia University Press, 2006), 20–24.

51. Cited by Ray, "Bede and Cicero," 10. Elsewhere Ray judges that Bede, when faced with criticism, "unleashed a blaze of vituperation in the great tradition," presumably referring to the tradition upheld to this day by the overheated letters section of such periodicals as *New York Review of Books*: *Bede, Rhetoric, and the Creation of Christian Latin Culture*, Jarrow Lecture 1997 (Jarrow, Tyne and Wear, UK: St. Paul's Church, 1997), 10.

52. Arthur G. Holder, "Bede and the New Testament," in *Cambridge Companion to Bede*, 145.

53. "The Benedictine Rule imposes labor on monks in two forms, manual and intellectual, and both are penitences, in conformity with the ideology of the time": Jacques Le Goff, *Time, Work, and Culture in the Middle Ages*, trans. Arthur Goldhammer (Chicago: University of Chicago Press, 1980), 110.

In their subsequent veneration of Bede, monks and nuns recognized how intellectual labor created a common good, if only within the reaches of monasticism and not yet in the world at large.[54]

Bede also demonstrated that the medieval Benedictine monastery was capable of fostering an intellectual life far in advance of the professional intellectuals, whom Jacques Le Goff, an Annales School medievalist, sees emerging in the twelfth century: "A man whose profession it was to write or to teach— and usually both at the same time—a man who, professionally, acted as professor and scholar, in short an intellectual—that man appeared only with the towns."[55] At the turn of the seventh century, Bede spent his days professing what he had learned, and in that sense he earned not his keep but a tenured place for a life of learning within the communal and sustaining work of the monastery. Learning could now enhance the abbey's reputation as disciplined and divinely inspired, reflected in its regular production of illuminated manuscripts. As such, learning was contributing to the reputational economy of bequeathal by which the nobility founded and endowed monasteries (with more on the financing of learning in the next chapter). The enclosure of this learning within monasticism, however, was about to be opened, through the vision of the Emperor Charlemagne, and turned into a larger public good.

CAROLINGIAN RENAISSANCE

In or around 781, Charlemagne, king of the Franks and later emperor of the Romans, approached Alcuin of York to help him educate an empire. Alcuin was an Anglo-Saxon scholar of the trivium (grammar, rhetoric, and dialectics) and *computus* (calculations of time and calendars), as well as keeper of the library at the highly reputed cathedral school of York in England. He had met Charlemagne in Parma earlier that year, catching the king's ear with the scope of his Bede-influenced learning. Charlemagne was captivated by "the most learned man anywhere to be found," in the words of his biogra-

---

54. R. W. Southern points to a "monastic monopoly of intellectual life" in England before the eleventh-century Conquest: "The Place of England in the Twelfth-Century Renaissance," in *Medieval Humanism and Other Studies* (Oxford: Blackwell, 1970), 171. Bischoff notes that despite Benedict's learning "limitation . . . the great historical role which the order of Benedict played in preserving classical Latin literature . . . [it was] not . . . by chance, but rather in response to specific historical conditions": "Benedictine Monasteries," 135. I hold that the *Rule of Benedict* might have limited learning in its intent if it had not also ensured the necessary conditions for it to take place within Benedictine monastery.

55. Jacques Le Goff, *Intellectuals in the Middle Ages*, trans. Teresa Lavender Fagan (Cambridge: Blackwell, 1993), 6.

pher and contemporary, Einhard, a monk who was to serve in the palace school that Alcuin organized for Charlemagne.[56] The king invited Alcuin to direct his educational efforts with the Franks, which included running the court scriptorium, as part of an ambitious cultural revolution for court and kingdom. Alcuin joined a community of scholars that included the Lombard scholar Paulinus II of Aquileia, the grammarian Petrus Pisanus, and the Spanish theologian Theodulf of Orléans, a master of Aristotelian dialectics and the first to make a single book of scripture, as well as a number of Irish monks who had a knowledge of Greek, a rare skill at the time, and introduced into the literate culture both admonishing treatises and penance books.[57]

Monasteries across the empire were able to wear their learning proudly. They celebrated their scriptoria, within which the Carolingian miniscule script developed, which greatly aided reading and studying, through the orderliness of its upper- and lower-case letters, its separation of words, and its attention to the layout of text on the page. The monasteries operated as a network for the circulation and production of manuscripts. It was all part of what is now referred to as the Carolingian Renaissance, extending from the eighth into the ninth century. "We are concerned," Charlemagne wrote in a charter setting out his vision, "to restore with diligent zeal the workshops of knowledge which, through the negligence of our ancestors, have been well-nigh deserted."[58]

Alcuin was given the opportunity to instruct Charlemagne, and under his tutelage, "the emperor spent much time and effort studying rhetoric, dialectic, and especially astrology," Einhard reports.[59] Alcuin was able to call on the king to support his studies: "I, your servant, need some of the rarer learned books which I had in my own country [Northrumbia] through the devoted efforts of my own teacher and through some labor on my own part."[60] He proposed

56. Einhard, "The Life of Charlemagne," in *Einhard and Notker the Stammerer: Two Lives of Charlemagne*, trans. Lewis G. M. Thorpe (London: Penguin, 1969), 79.

57. Johannes Fried, *Charlemagne*, trans. Peter Lewis (Cambridge, MA: Harvard University Press, 2016), 237–40, 243.

58. Cited by Heinrich Fichtenau, *The Carolingian Empire: The Age of Charlemagne* (New York: Harper & Row, 1964), 87. Martin Irvine holds that Charlemagne "effectively made grammatical culture the law of the land": *The Making of Textual Culture: 'Grammatica' and Literary Theory, 350–1100* (Cambridge: Cambridge University Press, 2006), 13.

59. Einhard, "The Life of Charlemagne," 79. Charlemagne is also known to have studied grammar with Pietro of Pisa, who also composed poetry that was issued under the king's name: Ronald G. Witt, *The Two Latin Cultures and the Foundation of Renaissance Humanism in Medieval Italy* (Cambridge: Cambridge University Press, 2012), 19.

60. Alcuin, "To the King on Books, Learning, and Old Age (796)," in *Carolingian Civilization: A Reader*, ed. Paul Edward Dutton (Peterborough, ON: Broadview, 1993), 107.

sending "some of our students to get everything we need," adding that "nothing [is] better for developing a life on the best principles than philosophy,
discipline, and education."[61] In a letter from 799, Alcuin notes how the king,
in examining some of the work he commissioned from Alcuin, had its "errors
noted and sent back for correction."[62] "Yet, you could have corrected it better," Alcuin then adds, "as you have not noted unscholarly statements and un-
orthodox expressions."[63] He then further chastises his majesty by teasing him
on the protocol of this learned economy: "The sponsor of the work should
defend the writer."[64]

Charlemagne also had Alcuin teach the members of his family, with the
emperor's sister Gisela and her daughter Rectruda earning the praise of their
teacher "for the highest devotion in that most holy desire for learning," as
he put it in a letter.[65] Charlemagne also established a magnificent court library that emulated the literary glory of Rome's libraries, contained works
of the church fathers, including the correspondence between Augustine and
Jerome, and provided a written record of oral, legal, and folklore traditions.
Charlemagne envisioned a restored and holy empire, with Latin taught as
its unifying language for administrative and literary purposes. His emphasis on a broadly grammatical education, encompassing rhetoric, poetry, and
history, led to massive copying of Latin literature from the Roman Empire,
accounting for as much as three-quarters of the classical Latin works that
have survived.[66] What we have today of Cicero, Seneca, Horace, Ovid, and others, owes much to the monastic's choice of long-lasting vellum for the pages
of these books. These works were revered for their literary and intellectual
qualities, and their authorship celebrated, with the learned rights of access—
in the spirit of what I am referring to as the intellectual properties of learning—all the more valued given how many of the fragile papyrus rolls of ancient texts had, by that point, crumbled away before anyone had realized their
worth and had a chance to copy them on more lasting materials.[67]

61. Ibid.
62. Alcuin, "To the King on the State of Learning in His Day (799)," in *Carolingian Civilization*, 108.
63. Ibid.
64. Ibid.
65. Cited by Joan M. Ferrante, "The Education of Women in the Middle Ages in Theory, Fact,
and Fantasy," in *Beyond Their Sex: Learned Women of the European Past*, ed. Patricia H. Labalme
(New York: New York University Press, 1980), 10.
66. Witt, *Two Latin Cultures*, 29, n. 52.
67. "Nothing survived of the renown libraries of antiquity, some of which were vast and
which were estimated to have held up to a million volumes. Not a single ancient papyrus roll with
a scholarly text survived the passage of time": Fried, *Charlemagne*, 250–51.

In pursuing these educational goals, Charlemagne challenged the insularity of the monasteries that dotted his kingdom. He charged its members that they "should not be content," as he wrote, "with leading a regular and devout life, but should undertake the task of teaching those who have received from God the capacity to learn, each according to his abilities."[68] Boys from all families were to be taught liturgy, psalms, grammar, computation, and singing in the schools that were to be run by monasteries, with educational centers established in the cathedrals of a number of cities for teaching liberal arts to more advanced students.[69] Charlemagne brought about a vast, coordinated mobilization of educational resources that took Bede's sense of learning as a community service and extended it across the Holy Roman Empire. It was undoubtedly a boon to learning, giving many more people opportunities; but learning also assumed certain political properties in the consolidation and administration of empire in the Christian West, for the first, if not the last, time.

The task of bringing about the monastic transformation fell to Alcuin, who was regarded by some as "a true monk without the monk's vows," as one biographer notes.[70] Alcuin saw to it that the monasteries set up external schools, much as had been done by Irish and Anglo-Saxon monasteries and cathedrals. And these schools needed books, with a corresponding push to expand the productivity of monastic scriptoria. These workshops assembled exemplary copies of the needed works, as well as flocks of goats and sheep to provide the vellum. The period was marked by the production of perhaps ten thousand manuscripts, with much of this growth in learning supported by the larger well-endowed monasteries and churches.[71] Although there was some backlash against this expanded monastic mission, Alcuin prevailed in his educational goal of having the monasteries prepare a new generation

68. Cited by David Knowles, *The Evolution of Medieval Thought* (New York: Vintage, 1962), 71. Charlemagne complains in a letter that the writings "from a number of monasteries" were marked by "an uncultivated language caused by the neglect of learning": cited by Theodore M. Andersson, "A Carolingian Pun and Charlemagne's Languages," in *Along the Oral-Written Continuum: Types of Texts, Relations and their Implications*, ed. Slavica Rankovic (Turnhout, Belgium: Brepolis, 2010), 365. Andersson notes that the title Charlemagne the Corrector was apocryphal but the king's reputation for learning was not (367).

69. Witt records a ninth-century bishop of Lyon complaining that all of the emphasis on singing in the cathedral schools took from the students' studies and was to be, in the words of the bishop, "stupidly and harmfully employed": cited in *Two Latin Cultures*, 36. Still, Wit concludes that "encouraged throughout the empire, these schools likely exercised a positive influence on elementary education and contributed, along with increased political stability, to a modest rise in literacy" (70).

70. Cited by Andrew Fleming West, *Alcuin and the Rise of the Christian Schools* (New York: Scribner, 1899), 64.

71. Fried, *Charlemagne*, 241.

of clerks for local parish churches, rather than simply preparing classes of novitiate to join monastic order.[72]

At the same time that Charlemagne was expanding the monastery's public service, however, he was also reinforcing the enclosure and cultural restraint of women within monasticism: "On no account let them [nuns] dare to write *winileodas* (songs for a friend)," a capitulary in 789 reads, "or send them from the convent."[73] But within the Carolingian Renaissance, the nunneries were no less actively engaged in learning and copying. They possessed growing libraries and engaged in the preparation of new religious works (often composed in collaboration with monks), among them the convent of Notre-Dame in Chelles, for which Charlemagne's sister served as abbess.

For its part, the palace school took on the training of administrators, as court, cathedral, and monastery shared a mission of a Christian education informed by letters and the liberal arts.[74] Alcuin, in the spirit of Bede, prepared treatises and textbooks to supply the empire's schools. He introduced geometry into Christian astronomical calculations of Easter's dates.[75] He revitalized Pliny's and Martianus Capella's astronomy, which was taught alongside that of Bede and Isidore of Seville.[76] It was all supported by the *Liber glossarum*, an encyclopedic alphabetical guide running in excess of a thousand pages, compiled by nuns, some say, from the works of Isidore, Augustine, Jerome, and a half dozen others, with entries on medicine and the natural sciences, among other topics.[77]

In 798, Alcuin was succeeded at court by Theodulf, who was made bishop of Orléans and abbot of a number of monasteries. Theodulf carried on Alcuin's educational campaign. He instructed the churches to extend educa-

---

72. A capitulary from 789 specifies that "in every monastery, instruction shall be given in the psalms, musical notation, chant, the computation of years and seasons, and in grammar; and all books used shall be carefully corrected": cited by Knowles, *Evolution of Medieval Thought*, 72.

73. Cited by Shari Horner, *The Discourse of Enclosure: Representing Women in Old English Literature* (Albany: State University of New York Press, 2001), 35.

74. C. Stephen Jaeger, *The Envy of Angels: Cathedral Schools and Social Ideals in Medieval Europe, 950–1200* (Philadelphia: University of Pennsylvania Press, 1994), 26.

75. Stephen C. McCluskey, "Astronomies in the Latin West from the Fifth to the Ninth Centuries," in *Science in Western and Eastern Civilization in Carolingian Times*, ed. Paul Leo Butzer and Dietrich Lohrmann (Basel: Birkäuser, 1993), 144.

76. Bruce Eastwood, "The Astronomies of Pliny, Martianus, and Isidore of Seville in the Carolingian World," in *Science in Western and Eastern Carolingian Times*, 177.

77. David Ganz, "The *Liber Glossarum*: A Carolingian Encyclopedia," in *Science in Western and Eastern Carolingian Times*, ed. Paul Leo Butzer and Dietrich Lohrmann (Basel: Birkäuser, 1993), 127–35.

tional opportunities as a matter of spiritual principle: "In the villages and townships the priests shall open schools. If any of the faithful entrust their children to them to learn letters, let them not refuse to instruct these children in all charity."[78] In the case of the monastery schools, parents traditionally gave gifts large or small to support the education of their children.[79] In that spirit of charity, Charlemagne made provisions to ensure that on his death his magnificent library would be disbursed for the benefit of the poor, with many volumes ending up in the library of his son Louis the Pious who, with his wife, Judith, remained patrons of learned writers, given the inclusion of their names in dedications in the books from that time.[80]

For his part, Alcuin assumed the position of abbot at the Tours monastery, where he devoted himself to improving the scriptorium's work. He wrote to Charlemagne, for example, about his concern that "punctuation adds greatly to the style of sentences, but its use has almost been lost by copyists owing to their lack of education. It seems to need restoring in the work of copyists, just as fine scholarship and sound learning in general are beginning to be revived through your noble efforts."[81] Alcuin took great care in selecting texts to serve as exemplars that would guide the copying of new editions. He paid special attention to advancing standards of orthography and punctuation, as well as letter forms (in what became known as Caroline minuscule), all of which added to the readability and general quality of the texts.[82] The monastery's considerable efforts in producing uniform Latin editions of key works furthered the sense that each work was an intellectual property, even as they collectively formed part of the communal property of the monastery. He had the monastic commitment to learning inscribed above the scriptorium

78. Cited by Knowles, *Evolution of Medieval Thought*, 72. In the ninth century, the Benedictine monk Rhabanus Maurus prepared a second encyclopedic work *De universo*, assembling, in his words, "many things concerning natural history and etymologies of names and words," and seeking to "create something pleasing and useful," as he "continuously placed together, both the literal and spiritual meaning of each single thing": cited by Mary Carruthers, *The Book of Memory: A Study of Memory in Medieval Culture* (Cambridge: University of Cambridge Press, 1990), 175.

79. "The large entry gifts that monasteries, nunneries, and cathedral chapters expected to accompany new ecclesiastics often seems to have required an outlay comparable to what it would have cost the parents to give a son a share of the inheritance or a daughter a dowry and set them up in the world": Constance Brittain Bouchard, *Sword, Miter, and Cloister: Nobility and the Church in Burgundy, 980-1198* (Ithaca, NY: Cornell University Press, 1987), 59.

80. Bernhard Bischoff, "The Court Library under Louis the Pious," in *Manuscripts and Libraries in the Age of Charlemagne*, 76-78.

81. Alcuin, "To the King on the State of Learning in His Day (799)," 109.

82. West, *Alcuin*, 64-70.

entrance: "Writing books is better than planting vines, for he who plants a vine serves his belly, but he who writes a book serves his soul."[83]

Alcuin was taking a stand on the sacredness of scholarly labor within the Benedictine monastery. While the *Rule of Benedict* paid little mind to learned concerns, Alcuin made it clear that the *Rule*'s regard for discipline, rigor, and humility could and should be brought to bear on this scribal work. So began "the great age of the copying of Latin manuscripts, both patristic and classical," according to Cambridge historian and Benedictine monk David Knowles.[84] These efforts would replenish the supply and circulation of books within monasticism and the Holy Roman Empire.

The Carolingian Renaissance glowed like the tail of a comet across the medieval sky of the Latin West. It was soon eclipsed, however, by the civil wars that engulfed Charlemagne's empire through the ninth and tenth centuries. Yet Charlemagne's educational initiative, guided in good part by Alcuin, had succeeded in placing education back into the public realm, where it was not to be easily dislodged. The schools reemerged from the conflicts most notably in the form of the cathedral schools at Chartres, Orléans, Paris, and elsewhere. They grew into their own educational movement, preparing churchmen and other administrators in scholastic disputation and theological reasoning (leading up to the emergence of universities in the twelfth century).

Sustaining the monastery schools proved more of a challenge. Boisterous schoolchildren among the silence of the cloisters were always going to be a little trying for the monks and nuns.[85] Abbots often agreed to tutor the children of the nobility, perhaps with an eye to later beneficence, but they

---

83. Cited by ibid., 72. Jacques Le Goff makes much of these uniform editions and new script: "It was the basis of a civilization, a development which gradually changed the way knowledge was transmitted and taught . . . the basis for the establishment of the universities" (*My Quest for the Middle Ages*, trans. Richard Veasey [Edinburgh: Edinburgh University Press, 2005], 13). Alcuin's influential retirement into monasticism followed the pattern set by Paolo Diacono, who retired to Montecassino (the monastery of Saint Benedict), after serving as "one of the architects of the Carolingian Renaissance," according to Witt, and whose time as a monk led not only to his composition of "important didactic texts" but a "tradition of scholarship and production of manuscripts that continued, with several interruptions, into the twelfth century": *Two Latin Cultures*, 57.

84. Knowles, *Evolution of Medieval Thought*, 76. Knowles: The "gradual accumulation of clearly (and more correctly) written books was of inestimable value when the more comprehensive revival came two centuries later" (ibid.).

85. In 817, Benedict of Aniane led a council of Frankish abbots that sought to prevent monasteries from operating schools: David Knowles, *The Monastic Order in England: A History of its Development from the Times of St. Dunstan to the Fourth Lateran Council 943–1216* (Cambridge: Cambridge University Press, 1950), 487–88.

would often do so by hiring a schoolmaster and a room set apart from the monastery for these and other children to take their lessons.[86] Charlemagne had shaken the otherworldly remoteness of monasticism with his schooling-on-command but it was a momentary tremor in a long history of monasticism, at least until the late Middle Ages when charitable schools became a common undertaking of monks and nuns.[87]

THE MONASTIC GLOSS

Our story so far has featured a number of landmark works of medieval monasticism, among them has been Jerome's *Vulgate*, Isidore's *Etymologies*, and Bede's *Ecclesiastical History of the English People*. These are, in a sense, the easy cases in exemplifying what's involved in developing a concept of learning's intellectual properties. These works speak to how monasticism gave rise to the composition, production, enhancement, and circulation of works that possessed intellectual qualities that went well beyond the institution's original goal of a pious retreat into salvation. The number of great works was few enough across the centuries that make up the Middle Ages, and dwelling on them, as such, misrepresents the regular life of the mind in abbey, convent, and priory. I opened this chapter with Isidore's compilation, itself a common scriptorium genre, and I close it with the humble gloss as a mainstay of monastic intellectual life.

The medieval art of the *gloss* also begins with reading. A nun or a monk who encounters a difficult or unfamiliar term thinks it helpful to inscribe a translation or a synonym just above the word. To offer an example, a ninth-century reader thought to insert, in a tiny hand, the old Irish word *Cennalar* (headache) above St. Paul's phrase *stimulus carnis* (thorn in the flesh; I Cor 12:7) in the *Codex Paulinus Wirziburgensis*.[88] It was just one of three thousand such

---

86. Roger Bowers, "The Almonry Schools of the English Monasteries, c. 1265-1540," in *Monasteries and Society in Medieval Britain: Proceedings of the 1994 Harlaxton Symposium*, ed. Benjamin Thompson (Stamford, CT: Paul Watkins, 1999), 179. In the fifteenth century, the English abbeys in Burton upon Trent, Evesham, and Reading operated free grammar schools apart from the monastery: Nicholas Orme, *Medieval Schools: From Roman Britain to Renaissance England* (New Haven, CT: Yale University Press, 2006), 286-87.

87. Monasteries ran almonry schools in a room set aside for almsgiving often by the monastery gate: Nicholas Orme, "For Richer, For Poorer? Free Education in England, c.1380-1530," *Journal of the History of Childhood and Youth* 1, no. 2 (2008): 181. The abbots at the English monastery in St. Albans were noted for providing twenty-eight loaves of bread each week to poor scholars in the early fourteenth century, while the Launceton Priory in Cornwall later allowed poor students to sit with the monks for a daily meal: Orme, *Medieval Schools*, 208.

88. "The Würzburg Glosses," *Anglandicus* (Blog), March 7, 2011, online.

glosses in the manuscript, helping to open the work, in this case, to other Irish readers. Or, more elaborately, in the margins of Martianus' *De nuptiis Philologiae et Mercurii*, a scribe added a point of clarification and correction: "According to Hildebertus the sentence is like this: 'I, the Greek, shall not abandon . . .'—taking 'graia' as a nominative. In truth, however, it is a plural accusative, that is: 'In the order of discourse I shall not neglect the things that are Greek.'"[89] I've taken this second example from Mariken J. Teeuwen, a medievalist at the Huygens Institute, University of Utrecht, who notes how scholarship "has long discarded [glosses] as unimportant scribblings of anonymous monks, obscuring the main text."[90] The glosses, for Teeuwen, "tell the story of transmission and transformation of learning" through the early Middle Ages.[91] In taking up this "marginal scholarship," Teeuwen holds that "the margin was the perfect place for dissent and debate: contradictions were displayed and discussed."[92] And the margins worked as "discussion boards" because the books were held and read in common.

Readers' glosses brought Cicero and Boethius to bear on Martianus and then, in other texts, brought Martianus to bear on Boethius.[93] These glosses typically drew on multiple sources in multiple languages, Latin, Greek, Hebrew, and the vernaculars. The marginal notes in Arabic found in a tenth-century copy of Isidore's *Etymologies*, for example, further attest to the work's influence in the al-Andalus region of Iberia.[94] Glosses grew in scope and ambition, sometimes drawing on a shorthand reputedly devised by Cicero's scribe Tiro to make the most of available marginal space.[95]

The glosses spread like a learned vine across and down the vellum page, filling the spaces between the lines and trailing along the margins. By the ninth century, it was common to add glosses that identified the sources of uncredited material in the main text.[96] By the twelfth century, the gloss was

89. Cited and translated by Mariken J. Teeuwen, "The Pursuit of Secular Learning: The Oldest Commentary Tradition on Martianus Capella," *Journal of Medieval Latin* 18 (2008): 36.

90. Mariken J. Teeuwen, "Marginal Scholarship: The Practice of Learning in the early Middle Ages (c. 800—c. 1000)," unpublished project description, Huygens Institute, The Hague, NL, online.

91. Ibid.

92. Mariken J. Teeuwen, "Glossing in Close Co-operation: Examples from Ninth-Century Martianus Capella," in *Practice in Learning: The Transfer of Encyclopaedic Knowledge in the early Middle Ages*, ed. Rolf H. Bremmer, Jr. and Kees Dekker (Paris: Peeters, 2010), 85.

93. Teeuwen, "Pursuit of Secular Learning," 46.

94. Dorothee Metlitzki, *The Matter of Araby in Medieval England* (New Haven, CT: Yale University Press, 1977), 16.

95. Teeuwen, "The Pursuit of Secular Learning," 43.

96. Malcom Beckwith Parkes, "The Influence of Concepts of *Ordinatio* and *Compilatio*," in *Medieval Learning and Literature: Essays Presented to Richard William Hunt*, ed. J. J. G. Alexander

"the principal apparatus of the academic reader," notes Oxford paleographer Malcolm Beckwith Parkes, with scribes recasting the layout of the page to ensure that this "inherited material—the *auctoritates* [authorities]" could be brought forward with each new copy of the work.[97] In preparing to copy a well-glossed text, the scholar-scribe might lay out a marginal space for the glosses to be copied. This would lead to works with a dense border of commentary hemming in the original text. In other cases, scribes carefully wove together the glosses of two or many scholars into full-fledged commentary that might become its own text in another volume.[98]

The gloss could alter the intellectual properties of a text. It might make a classical work safe to read by pointing out its contribution to the Christian pursuit of salvation.[99] It helped to open a work for new readers, setting the text within an interpretative framework, which was established by scholarly references and didactic points. It offered a marginal zone of dispute and dissent in interpretation and learning.[100] In this sense, the gloss formed the intellectual connective tissue, pulling together works and communities of readers within this monastic community.[101] The accumulated glosses around a text were also compiled into separate encyclopedic glossaries, such as the already noted *Liber glossarum*, among the first in Latin to pioneer alphabetical order for easier use by readers.[102]

---

and M. T. Gibson (Oxford: Clarendon, 1976), 116-17. On the influence of gloss on page layout and design, also see Clements and Graham, *Manuscript Studies*, 39-43.

97. Parkes, "*Ordinatio* and *Compilatio*," 116.

98. The scribes also overstepped at times, weaving the gloss *into* the text proper: Clemens and Graham, *Manuscript Studies*, 39.

99. Alastair Minnis, *Medieval Theory of Authorship: Scholastic Literary Attitudes in the Later Middle Ages*, 2nd ed. (Philadelphia: University of Pennsylvania Press, 1988), 29.

100. In addressing the force of learned discourse in modern Europe, Michel Foucault speaks of the commentary's power: "Commentary's only role is to say *finally*, what has silently been articular *deep down*. It must—and the paradox is ever-changing, yet inescapable—say, for the first time, what has already been said, and repeat tirelessly what was, nevertheless, never said": "The Discourse on Language," in *The Archeology of Knowledge and the Discourse on Language*, trans. A. M. Sheridan Smith (New York: Pantheon, 1972), 221. Foucault also sets commentary apart from the academic organization of a *discipline*: "In a discipline, unlike in commentary, what is supposed at the point of departure is not some meaning which must be rediscovered, nor an identity to be reiterated; it is that which is required for the construction of new statements" (223).

101. By the thirteenth century, the academic disciplines of theology and law within the universities had developed their own glossing style and format: Malcolm Beckwith Parkes, "The Influence of the Concepts of *Ordinatio* and *Compilatio* on the Development of the Book," in *Medieval Learning and Literature: Essays Presented to Richard William Hunt*, ed. J. J. G. Alexander and M. T. Gibson (Oxford: Oxford University Press, 1976), 120.

102. Herren, "Storehouses of Learning," 3; Teeuwen, "Pursuit of Secular Learning," 49.

Apart from very avid annotators, such as John the Scot from the ninth century, only a few of those who glossed have been identified.[103] The art of this largely anonymous glossing flourished in the ninth century, particularly among the classical texts that were beginning to attract more attention both at monastic centers such as Corbie and Fleury, and at Laon and other cathedral schools. With sharpened pens in hand and ink nearby, readers found it a duty and a pleasure to identify the relationships among words, meanings, and ideas through marginal notes and diagrams, all within the relative isolation and silence of the monastic learned life. Whether they were teaching masters or pupils prepping for class, or scholars working in the library, they engaged in a common form of reading to learn within the manuscript culture of monasteries and schools, and had no reason to think that this increased interest in the intellectual properties of canonical texts reduced the reader's spiritual experience of the text.

For the reader-scholar-scribe, the page served "a *collecting* purpose, *gathering* as much knowledge . . . as possible from as many sources as possible," as Teeuwen notes of the copious glosses accumulated by editions of Martianus' *De nuptiis*.[104] The glossaries drew on (and directly cited) the biblical commentaries of Jerome, Augustine, and Bede, and integrated them directly into the text commented upon; hence more readers were exposed to the glossaries. It invited a discursive, if marginal, exchange among generations of the learned.[105] The resulting text and paratext were clearly directed toward a different type of reading and engagement than the spiritual *meditatio* or *lectio divina* of the early Middle Ages.[106]

Much of this marginal work had to do with readers reinforcing the accreditation of authorship. The term *author* (*auctor*) is rooted in the classical Latin form of "the seller at auction," according to nineteenth-century Harvard philologist James B. Greenough, which he also relates to "a reliable

---

103. Teeuwen, "Glossing in Close Co-operation," 85.

104. Ibid., 94. Teeuwen: "These scribes [who copied the glosses as part of the texts] were, it seems, the very scholars that studied the text, working together to obtain the maximum result. The scholar jotting down the first layer of glosses was supplemented and corrected by a second scholar, who added glosses in the (sometimes tiny) spaces still left blank" (95).

105. The commentaries of Jerome and Bede, for example, were later transcribed as a marginal gloss in Bishop Hugh's twelfth-century manuscript of the Gospel of St. Mark, with the biblical verses surrounded by Jerome's extended commentary in a smaller hand on the left side and Bede's even more extensive commentary (at least for Mark 1:3) on the right, with additional glosses, one-to-two lines thick, between each line of Mark: *Gospel of Mark Belonging to Bishop Puiset*, British Library, London, online.

106. Parkes, "Influence of the Concepts," 115–16.

guarantor, a good authority."[107] The etymology of the term does a good job of combining the rhetoric involved in selling an idea and the trust an author seeks to instill in readers. Think of Pliny anxiously prefacing his work with a list of the authorities on whom he claimed to have drawn, as much to pitch the work to his readers as to credit his sources. Those who glossed and commented weighed in on the authority of the *auctor* by annotating the text's sources. It had the effect of making the work's author and sources count among the intellectual properties of a work. Readers understood that knowing who and what made up the text added to their understanding of and interest in the text, even as these marginal notes and indexing of sources added to their ability to more readily use the text. These daily, modest, and anonymous undertakings proved of such value that out of them evolved the formal scholarly apparatus of footnotes, tables of contents, and indexes.

CONCLUSION

Across the early Middle Ages, the monastery remained an intellectual center for the composing, compiling, and copying of manuscripts, as well as for creating commentary and glossing the text. What Isidore of Seville introduced into monasticism with his *Etymologies* was a provocation for further inquiry into the nature of language and the world it described. To find such works in the monastic library chest was to be invited to dig deeper into the intellectual properties of texts, to look up the history of words and concepts; to follow Isidore and others in a careful culling of texts to fashion new works (if not always fully credited); to author one's own books for the instruction and delight of others, much as Bede managed to make his life's work, creating a new venerable place for learning within monasticism.

Charlemagne did as much for an empire out of what appears to have been a genuine interest in learning, which created many new opportunities for his subjects. Yet Charlemagne's investment in learning also advanced the empire's administrative order by training a generation of officials in Latin to aid in governing its diversity of peoples. He introduced an educational mission into new settings, perhaps most influentially with the cathedral schools that became a hotbed of scholasticism as an early school of thought in the West. Yet it was Alcuin who made it clear—in his roles as court minister of

---

107. James B. Greenough, "Latin Etymologies," *Harvard Studies in Classical Philology* 4 (1893): 145.

education and abbot—that for all he achieved in educating an empire, the monastery alone offered him the institutional dedication needed to lead a team to skillfully prepare editions of canonical works that furthered the intellectual qualities and properties of learning.

Throughout all of this, nuns and monks continued to humbly gloss the texts that they were reading, looking to further open the text for the next reader, locating a source, sparking debate, enriching engagement. The margins of the text were understood to offer readers a commons for exercising this shared stake in the text. Glosses served texts and readers. Marginalia found its way into future editions or a text of its own. By the ninth century, this greater involvement in the production of intellectual properties, through editing and glossing, had become part of monasticism and its patronage economy. It is an economy that further distinguishes learning's intellectual properties. I turn now to how medieval monastics benefited in myriad ways from grants of land and other endowments of estate. This patronage was responsible for the institutional autonomy and stability so vital to the learning that Isidore, Bede, and Alcuin pursued and that would continue to underwrite learned institutions in the West.

CHAPTER FOUR

The Patronage of Medieval Learning

Prior to the twelfth century, a lord or a noble lady who wished to signal his or her intent to found a monastery might arrange to have a square of turf cut from land that was to be set aside for the establishment of a religious house. The turf was carefully placed on the altar. The donor pronounced a solemn oath before witnesses attesting to the dedication of the land to the church. While a trace of this ritual remains with us in public groundbreaking ceremonies often held when starting a new public building, the medieval practice of presenting turf gave way to a witnessed foundation deed, to which a donor might attach a tree twig from the land.[1] The founders of a monastery could alternatively leave a single glove on the altar, following the common phrase of making gifts "by the hand" (*manu sua*).[2] Or they might place a book, ring, or, more dramatically, a bent knife, indicating that a family was cutting ties to the designated land. Still, the deed that allocated

---

1. Formal charters came into common legal use during the early thirteenth century in Denmark and elsewhere: Linda Rasmussen, "Monastic Benefactors in England and Denmark: Their Social Background and Gender Distribution," in *Religious and Laity in Western Europe, 1000–1400*, vol. 2, ed. Emilia Jamroziak and Janet E. Burton (Turnhout: Brepols, 2010), 78. See also Rosamond McKitterick, *The Carolingians and the Written Word* (Cambridge: Cambridge University Press, 1989), 77.

2. Isidore of Seville explains: "*Mancipatio* is so called because the property is 'taken in the hand' (*manu . . . capitur*). Hence is it appropriate for whoever takes formal possession to grasp the property itself that is given into his possession": *Etymologies of Isidore of Seville*, trans. Stephen A. Barney, W. J. Lewis, J. A. Beach, and Oliver Berghof (Cambridge: Cambridge University Press, 2006), 5.25.31, 122. Benedict's Rule advises novices taking the vows: "Let the novice make his mark, and with his own hand place it on the altar": *Rule of Benedict*, trans. Carolinne White (London: Penguin, 2008), 58 86.

the land to the church might also allow for the donor's continued use or rent of the land for a limited period.[3]

The church altar is where God's gift to humanity is communally celebrated through the Eucharist. It is where the faithful make an offering in return. The founding of a monastery was, above all, a gift made to God. It was part of a medieval "economy of salvation," as David Ganz, a paleographer at King's College, London, describes it.[4] And so I now consider the ways in which this economy both served and shaped learning. In the first instance, it afforded learning a certain autonomy from financial demands that might otherwise keep monastics from prayer and study. Yet it still required the discipline, devotion, and piety that signaled the monastery's value within this salvational economy.

"Lands and property of other kinds were given by royal bounty, to establish monasteries," Bede wrote of King Oswald's pious generosity in seventh-century Northumbria, "and English children, as well as their elders, were instructed by Irish teachers in advanced studies and in the observance of the discipline of a Rule."[5] The charter granted to the monasteries by the landholder not only designated the extent and position of the tract that had been granted, whether cultivated field, pastureland, meadowland, vineyard, or marsh, but might also include mills, toll bridges, peasants, and serfs. It could include the fishing rights to a river, as the brothers Gilbert and Roger Fitz Richard bestowed to the monks of Bec in the early twelfth century.[6] Once established, the monastery benefited from dowries, consisting of further property or something as small as a book that a child might bring on entering the monastery as an oblate. When Heliseus gave a copy of Martianus' *De nuptiis Philologiae et Mercurii* to the monks of St. Germain in the early part

---

3. Arnoud-Jan A. Bijsterveld, *Do ut des: Gift Giving, Memoria, and Conflict Management in the Medieval Low Countries* (Hilversum: Verloren, 2007), 63–70. Bijsterveld, who documents the examples of sod, twig, glove, book, and bent knife, states that the donor might receive a counter-gift of a coin or two to secure and document the gift (65, 77).

4. David Ganz, "Giving to God in the Mass: The Experience of the Offertory," in *The Languages of Gift in the Early Middle Ages*, ed. Wendy Davies and Paul Fouracre (Cambridge: Cambridge University Press, 2010), 18.

5. Bede, *The Ecclesiastical History of the English People*, trans. Bertram Colgrave (Oxford: Oxford University Press, 1969), 3.3 133.

6. David Knowles, *The Monastic Order in England: A History of Its Development from the Times of St. Dunstan to the Fourth Lateran Council, 943–1216* (Cambridge: Cambridge University Press, 1950), 577; J. C. Ward, "Fashions in Monastic Endowment: The Foundations of the Clare Family, 1066–1314," *Journal of Ecclesiastical History* 32, no. 4 (1981): 441, 434.

of the ninth century, the manuscript was inscribed with the terms of the transaction: "Archdeacon Heliseus gave this book to St. Germain for eternal life."[7]

A lord and a lady, having decided to convert to monasticism, would prepare an inventory of their worldly possessions to serve as the charter of their gifts to the monastery in which they planned to spend the remainder of their days. This aristocratic largesse, which peaked during the tenth century, was only the high end of the monastic economy.[8] Monasteries also benefited from the clergy, knights, merchants, and tenants who pooled their resources through public subscription to support this pious form of life.[9] Townspeople flocked to an abbey's initial dedication ceremony, bringing wool for monastic clothing, plates for the table, and hides for leather goods. The people also offered pittances, which the monastics used for holiday food, additional books, or support for the poor.

Reflecting a common theme for commonwealth of learning, the monastery operated as both part of and apart from the prevailing economy. The monastery's land grant made it fully part of a medieval economy that was based on the ownership and transfer of land. Properties changed hands through inheritance, acts of war, rewards for military service, and bequeathals to religious houses. Monastic benefaction eventually assumed the character of the feudal bonds that dominated the High Middle Ages. Where the lord offered protection to the vassal in exchange for military service in the typical feudal arrangement, he agreed to defend the abbot against external threats in exchange for what might be termed extended spiritual advocacy through prayer. More explicitly, a monastery's founding charter frequently called for a reciting of the benefactor's name, as well as those of family members, during daily mass in the abbey chapel.[10] The lord was trading in a surplus good, given the nobility's

7. Cited by Mariken Teeuwen, "The Pursuit of Secular Learning: The Oldest Commentary Tradition on Martianus Capella," *Journal of Medieval Latin* 18 (2008): 37.

8. Van Engen points to how "truly sizable gifts from kings and princes had probably peaked already in the early eleventh century": "The 'Crisis of Cenobitism' Reconsidered," *Speculum* 61 (1986): 278.

9. James G. Clark, "Monastic Confraternity in Medieval England: The Evidence from St. Albans Abbey *Liber Benefactorum*," in *Religious and Laity in Western Europe, 1000–1400: Interaction, Negotiation, and Power*, ed. Emilia Jamroziak and Janet E. Burton (Turnhout, Belgium: Brepols, 2007), 316. Georges Duby speaks of a "stream of pious donations": *Rural Economy and Country Life in the Medieval West*, trans. C. Postan (London: Edward Arnold, 1968), 174.

10. In 1249, the Benedictine Order in Canterbury called for the heads of religious houses to ensure that a private mass for donors was celebrated at least every four days, lest, as Roger Bowers puts it, "the souls of benefactors be defrauded of the expected mitigatory benefits": "The Almonry Schools of the English Monasteries c.1265–1540," in *Monasteries and Society in Medieval Britain*, ed. B. Thompson (Stamford, CT: Paul Watkins, 1999), 189.

possession of more land than they could possibly exploit during their time in this world. Thus, they might well consider investing excess land in the life to come.[11] In the twelfth century, to take one example, Alice de Gant, on marrying Roger de Mowbray, granted her dowry to the Cistercian abbey at Fountains. She received a gold ring from the monks, along with reassurances that, as she wrote, "after my death [they] will perform full service for me in masses and psalms, as is done for a monk of their house."[12]

The initial land awarded a monastery was often sufficient to feed, clothe, and otherwise sustain a religious house, largely through the daily and humble labors of its members, following the *Rule of Benedict*. With subsequent gifts to the monastery—which might include serfs, mills, bridges, and churches accompanied by tithes—as well as through the wise management of the monastic estates' rights and tenures, an abbey would be able to generate sufficient wealth for its members to turn their labors from cultivating fields to preparing manuscripts.[13] These acts of beneficence proved an effective, if initially inadvertent, means of underwriting the labor of learning. And this learning, in time, contributed to the disciplined spirit of monasticism that attracted benefactors. The nobility could see in such learning—as well as in fields of golden wheat, the care of lepers, and hospitality shown travelers—the proof of a religious house's intimacy with God's mercy.[14] The monastics were serv-

---

11. "In a Europe only sparsely settled, in which rulers disposed of lordly rights over vast areas of country which they could not effectively exploit, there were opportunities for lavish gifts of land": R. W. Southern, *Western Society and the Church in the Middle Ages* (London: Penguin, 1970), 229. A. M. Honoré notes the bonds and obligations between lord and tenant made it difficult to say that property was *owned* with the rights that we associate with that kind of ownership today, with this right of gift an early exception: "Ownership," in *Oxford Essays in Jurisprudence*, ed. A. D. Guest (Oxford: Oxford University Press, 1961), 109.

12. Cited by Janet E. Burton, "*Fundator Noster*: Roger de Mowbray as Founder and Patron of Monasteries," in *Religious and Laity in Western Europe 1000–1400*, 35. Roger's own dealings as patron were such that at one point the monks paid off his debts: "The monks of Combe out of love (*caritative*)," as Roger put it, "have acquitted me of 80 marks owed to the Jews" (36).

13. Southern reports on the foundation deed of the priory at St. Mont in Gascony: "It was given by its founder the profits of forty-seven churches, one hamlet, seven manors, four small parcels of land, one vineyard, six arable lots, one wood, one stretch of fishing rights, and various small rents and tolls" (*Western Society and the Church* [London: Penguin, 1970], 233). Ilana F. Silber holds up the twelfth-century Cistercian monastery as "the arch example of economic rationalization and productivity": "Monasticism and the 'Protestant Ethic': Asceticism, Rationality and Wealth in the Medieval West," *British Journal of Sociology* 44, no. 1 (1993): 109.

14. Anne E. Lester reports that providing for the care for the poor and sick appears in Cistercian monastic charters by the early thirteenth century as a "particularly effective form of penitential piety": "Cares beyond the Walls: Cistercian Nuns and the Care of Lepers in Twelfth- and Thirteenth-Century Northern France," in *Religious and Laity in Western Europe, 1000–1400*, 207, 223. The Benedictines in England included hospitality to travelers among their charitable acts:

ing as spiritual surrogates for their benefactors. Their sponsored lives of piety, prayer, and learning represented an investment opportunity in the life to come for the nobility. Monastic support was a way to realize the Gospel's promise: "And every one that hath forsaken houses, or brethren, or sisters, or father, or mother, or wife, or children, or lands, for my name's sake, shall receive an hundredfold, and shall inherit everlasting life" (Matt. 19:29).

Benefactors also made "burial gifts" to monasteries to ensure that they would be placed, on their death, in a burial plot, crypt, or mausoleum on the holy ground of the monastery virtually at heaven's gate.[15] Or a brave knight might promise his estate to the monastery before departing on a crusade, placing the monks in something of a conflict of interest when praying for the knights' safekeeping as part of the chartered contract.[16] The charter might also call for the abbot to remit specified sins or reduce the penances that a sinning benefactor owed the church.[17] Further, women also played a substantial role on both sides of the altar. Some converted to monasticism as a viable alternative to marriage and family life.[18] Among the nobility, wives and daughters turned their dowries and inheritances into convent gifts and founding grants; they used the assets they controlled to inspire monastic reform. Agnes of Burgundy, for example, was a major eleventh-century patron of monasticism, having founded two canons' houses, rebuilt a third, cofounded two abbeys, and donated to other religious houses.[19]

Julie Kerr, *Monastic Hospitality: The Benedictines in England, c. 1070–c. 1250* (Woodbridge, Suffolk, UK: Boydell and Brewer, 2007), 181–82.

15. On securing a monastic mausoleum, see Rasmussen, "Monastic Benefactors in England and Denmark," 79.

16. Constance Brittain Bouchard, *Holy Entrepreneurs: Cistercians, Knights, and Economy Exchange in Twelfth-Century Burgundy* (Ithaca, NY: Cornell University Press, 1991), 76.

17. Bernhard Jussen points out how medieval penitential piety was threefold, involving "(1) the imposing of tariffs on sins, that is, fixed penances for each sin; (2) the conversion of extensive into intensive forms of penance, that is, prayers into psalms, psalms into masses; and (3) the possibility of penance by proxy, that is, by clerics, monks, or surviving spouses": "Religious Discourses of the Gift in the Middle Ages: Semantic Evidences (Second to Twelfth Centuries)," in *Negotiating the Gift: Pre-Modern Figurations of Exchange*, ed. Gadi Algazi, Valentin Groebner, and Bernhard Jussen (Göttingen: Vandenhoeck and Ruprecht, 2003), 182.

18. As Chiara Frugoni observes, "the only place a woman was allowed to have 'a room of her own,' in Virginia Woolf's words, was in a convent": "The Imagined Woman," trans. Clarissa Botsford, in *Silences of the Middle Ages*, ed. Christiane Klapisch-Zuber, vol. 2 of *A History of Women in the West* (Cambridge, MA: Harvard University Press, 1992), 407.

19. Penelope D. Johnson, "Agnes of Burgundy: An Eleventh-Century Woman as Monastic Patron," *Journal of Medieval History* 15, no. 2 (1989): 95, 99. "Wealthy widows, doting parents, and bishops devoted to their mothers and sisters" were the founders of small proprietary nunneries during the Middle Ages, which were then administered by these women: Susan Fonay Wemple, *Women in Frankish Society: Marriage and the Cloister 500–900* (Philadelphia: University of

In this "bookkeeping of the hereafter," benefactors imagined that they were "putting God in their debt," which is how Pope Gregory disapprovingly put it on two occasions at the turn of the sixth century.[20] Patronage could also involve the benefactor having a say in the election of prioress or abbot, perhaps involving a family member.[21] For the good of his soul, a lord, baron, or earl might also assume the monastic office of *advocatus*, which meant assisting in collecting a monastery's revenues from its leased land or the tithes from its church, while defending it against claims made on its possessions and properties.[22] Still, with time, these gifts often became subject to disputes over property transfer, neglect, and misuse, which could be grounds for retracting the gift. Records show that, by the twelfth century, monastic learning was being directed toward producing and marshalling the paperwork needed to defend and reclaim what was originally bequeathed.[23] The donor economy that monasticism developed over the course of the Middle Ages succeeded in making the commonwealth of learning a thing, from the outset, of institutional patronage.

THE PATRONAGE OF LEARNING

The scale of the intellectual property system that I have been describing flourished within the monastic manuscript culture of the Latin West in the Middle Ages. It was part and parcel of the institutionalization of learning

Pennsylvania Press, 1981), 163. Erin Jordan notes that "in the counties of Flanders and Hainaut alone, women were responsible for seventeen of the 30 houses of Cistercian nuns": "Female Founders: Exercising Authority in Thirteenth-Century Flanders and Hainaut," *Church History and Religious Culture* 88, no. 4 (2008): 536.

20. Cited by Valentin Groebner and Bernhard Jussen, *Negotiating the Gift: Pre-modern Figurations of Exchange* (Göttingen: Vandenhoeck and Ruprecht, 2003), 176.

21. Constance Brittain Bouchard, *Sword, Miter, and Cloister: Nobility and the Church in Burgundy, 980–1198* (Ithaca, NY: Cornell University Press, 1987), 247. "Bastard sons and younger brothers of the local lords became bishops or abbots of local churches and monasteries": Norman Cantor, *Inventing the Middle Ages* (New York: William Morrow, 1991), 22. "In addition to the need for eternal life," Southern reminds us, "the economy of a great family required a monastic outlet for its members." *Western Society and the Church*, 228. Southern adds, "The nobility were not easily thwarted in their endless search for a noble and dignified life for their landless children" (235).

22. Bouchard, *Sword, Miter, and Cloister*, 125, 131.

23. Steven Vanderputten: "With the creation of a detailed overview of what the abbey's estate should have looked like in 1116–1120, Abbot Amand proposed an agenda ... [in which] the *Poleticum* and its 'satellite documents' comprised the first step in changing disputed and vague territorial and financial claims into manageable parts of a monastic economy": "Monastic Literate Practices in Eleventh- and Twelfth-Century Northern France," in *Reform, Conflict and the Shaping of Corporate Identities: Collected Studies on Benedictine Monasticism, 1050–1150* (Berlin: LIT Verlag, 2013), 247–81.

during that period. That is, the monastery offered an order and economy that proved to be the most conducive of the era for the production and circulation of works of learning. To highlight just how important the institutional nature of this patronage was to learning at the time, I want to contrast it with the longstanding role played by personal patronage in fostering the arts, politics, and learning. In antiquity, the scholar who lacked sufficient family wealth to finance their studies had to find a patron willing to help underwrite their work, often in exchange for counsel and instruction.

Personal patronage was, at once, intimate, asymmetrical, and sometimes just plain fickle. It could also be treacherous. Plato, for example, was clearly attracted by the prospect of offering counsel to kings, despite the wealth that he had inherited. In Syracuse, he advised the kings Dionysius I and II, in turn, only to lose favor with both of them. When the first Dionysius turned against Plato, he sold the philosopher into slavery, hoping perhaps to recoup the cost of his patronage. Fortunately for Plato, yet another patron redeemed him from this indenture and returned him to Athens, a free if not wiser man. For Plato dared to return to Syracuse, this time to tutor Dionysius II. It led to another narrow escape from the perils of patronage and a hasty retreat back to Athens.

Plato also led one of the great schools of the classical era, but one that operated without what we might characterize today as a sustainable business model. What little is known of the financing of Plato's Academy suggests that it kept overhead down by having participants meet in a public garden outside of Athens (which happened to be named after a mythical hero, not known for his studiousness, by the name of Academus or Hecademus). There's no indication of any endowment or fees to sustain the continuing seminar or symposium led by Plato and attended by colleagues and students, although the master is known to have accepted gifts on occasion.[24] On the other hand, Plato held the Sophists, who collected fees for instruction in rhetoric, in great contempt. In the *Protagoras*, Plato has Socrates inquire of Hippocrates: "Is not a Sophist, Hippocrates, one who deals wholesale or retail in the food of the soul?"[25] He warns his friend that "there is far greater peril in buying knowledge than in buying meat and drink."[26] Suffice it to say that the classical age did not, among its many learned accomplishments,

---

24. Harold F. Cherniss, *The Riddle of the Early Academy* (New York: Russell and Russell, 1962), 61.

25. Plato, "Protagoras," in *The Dialogues of Plato*, vol. 1, 2nd ed., trans. B. Jowett (Oxford: Oxford University Press, 1875), 126.

26. Ibid., 127.

develop particularly robust institutions to sustain that learning beyond the
level of personal patronage that individuals could curry and secure.

During the early Middle Ages, Boethius is the great tragic figure of personal patronage. Born the same year as Benedict of Nursia and a contemporary of Cassiodorus, Boethius received a Roman liberal arts education and
entered the service of Theodoric of the Ostrogoths, ruler of Italy in the early
sixth century. Under Theodoric's patronage, Boethius translated Aristotle's
De interpretatione and *Categories* into Latin, as well as provided commentaries for these works. These books were intended to be only the beginning of
his scholarly contribution: "I shall translate into Latin every work of Aristotle's that comes into my hands, and I shall write commentaries on all of
them," Boethius had promised as a young man, adding, "I shall also translate and comment upon all Plato's dialogues."[27] Such an achievement might
have transformed learning in the Latin West. But, alas, what his patron had
afforded him, he also put to an end. In 523, Boethius was charged by Theodoric with conspiring against him in the service of Byzantine Emperor Justin I.
He was stripped of his position as Master of Offices and placed under house
arrest; during this time he composed his most magnificent work *The Consolation of Philosophy*, which went on to serve the Middle Ages as a major meditative work, as well as a standard Latin grammar text. The king had Boethius
executed the following year at about the age of forty-four.

Medieval monasticism introduced a new element into the patronage of
learning. It established a stable and sustainable model of *institutional endowment* that supported a lifetime of learning for generation after generation of
monastics. Rather than a lord sponsoring the studies of this brilliant poet or
that outstanding scholar in the ancient tradition, he would endow a monastery in perpetuity with a substantial gift of property. Through the accumulation of such bequeathals, monasteries could afford those with an interest in
learning a secure position in a relatively well-endowed institution in which
to pursue their studies.[28] Combined with the papal privileges and canonical
exemptions bestowed on monasteries, the cloisters proved a quiet, seldom-
disturbed place in which to pray and pursue one's studies. Benefactors were
known to interfere occasionally in the life of the monastery, to be sure, but
there was more autonomy than could otherwise be hoped for during that volatile

27. Cited by Seth Lerer, Introduction to Boethius, *The Consolation of Philosophy*, trans. David R.
Slavitt (Cambridge, MA: Harvard University Press, 2008), xiii.

28. After accumulating considerable wealth, the Cluny monasteries, for example, were themselves able to play the role of "patron of the arts on a massive scale, not only in fields of architecture
and sculpture, but in mural painting, music, manuscript illumination, and all aspects of the decora-
tive arts": Edwin Mullins, *Cluny: In Search of God's Lost Empire* (New York: Bluebridge, 2006), 167.

and warring period. The learned were able to develop their studies comfortably within the monastic spirit of humility, selflessness, and devotion, without having to compete for the attention of patrons.

As learning became a part of the disciplined and regulated life of the monastery, it made its own contribution to the house's reputation for piety. This only encouraged abbess and abbot to support such work by acquiring, for example, additional books, as Bede chronicles in the history of his monastery. The support for learning might also involve monastics employing secretaries—as did Hildegard of Bingen and Bernard of Clairvaux—or a further staffing of the scriptoria with scribes, correctors, illuminators, binders, and rubricators (who used red ink to accentuate titles and other portions of the texts), while stocking it with pens, ink, vermillion, bottles, and gold foil.[29] By the same token, the flocks of sheep raised on the monastery's pasturelands provided scribes with parchment, while binders turned to the roebuck and boar hunted in its forests for the leather used to bind and cover the books.[30]

Given the part played by the church altar in the donation of land, we might consider the parallels between what these gifts of land mean for learning and the transubstantiation of the Eucharist.[31] The benefactor's donation was turned, through an act of Holy Communion, into the words and works of learned nuns and monks.[32] The transfer—from tangible land tract to intangible intellectual property—also has a circle-of-gifts quality to it. The land was originally a gift from God to humankind and not only was some portion returned by landholders to its Maker through monastic endowment, but in that form it went on to generate works of great piety and learning. This learning,

29. For the economics of manuscript production leading up the introduction of print, see Joanne Filippone Overty, "The Cost of Doing Scribal Business: Prices of Manuscript Books in England, 1300-1483," *Book History* 11 (2008): 1-32.

30. Jean Leclercq, *The Love of Learning and the Desire for God: A Study of Monastic Culture*, trans. C. Misrahi (New York: Fordham University Press, 1961), 122-23. Thomas Kelly, *Early Public Libraries: A History of Public Libraries in Great Britain before 1850* (London: Library Association, 1966), 14. For the Abbey of the Trinity at Vendôme, the Countess Agnes of Burgundy purchased a book of homilies, as part of her monastic patronage and oversight, noting that its "steep price" was equivalent to 200 sheep: Johnson, "Agnes of Burgundy," 97. More generally, the cost of a manuscript book by the fifteenth century was valued at two cows, a tolerable horse, or ten barrels of beer.

31. The Christian doctrine of transubstantiation has its roots in Saint Ambrose, and while a source of controversy from the ninth to the twelfth centuries, the Lateran Council IV of 1215 made it church doctrine. See James F. McCue, "The Doctrine of Transubstantiation from Berengar through Trent: The Point at Issue," *Harvard Theological Review* 61, no. 3 (1968): 385-430.

32. In another example of the transfer between tangible and intangible *properties* as a point of semantic reference, in Middle English, *tenure* referred solely to rights and obligations associated with the legal holding of property, where it is now used to refer to the protection of the academic freedom and autonomy of university faculty.

in turn, spread word of God's gift, creating a greater understanding and benefit for the larger community. The benefactor's charter often specified that God
or one of the Apostles was the intended recipient of the gift of land: "I fear
the pains of hell," writes a Spanish countess at the beginning of a medieval
Cistercian foundation charter, "and I desire to come to the joys of paradise,
and for the love of God and his glorious Mother, and for the salvation of my
soul and those of my parents, I give to God, St. Mary, and all the saints my
whole inheritance in Retoria."[33]

Further to this circle, knowledge was understood to be a gift of God within
the medieval tradition. As such, it was not to be sold, but enjoyed in common,
much as the world was in its original state.[34] This made the monastery the
right sort of place for the cultivation of knowledge, given that everything there
was held in common. And the fruits of learning were among the most widely
distributed, with manuscripts loaned, copied, and circulated among sister
monasteries, as well as across the larger world of the Latin West. It is true that
monasteries would typically lend a book only when another book was provided as a *pledge*. But it was not so much the manuscript but the intellectual
property of the text that was held in common across the monasteries. The
assumed right to copy the works held by other monasteries created a learning
network among them.

Augustine notes in the opening of *On Christian Teaching* how learning
stands as the public good that keeps on giving: "For all the things which
do not give out when given away are not properly possessed when they are
possessed but not given away."[35] Learning's full value is realized when it is

---

33. Cited by Southern, *Western Society and the Church*, 263.

34. Gaines Post, Kimon Giocarnis, and Richard Kay, "The Medieval Heritage of a Humanistic
Ideal: *Scientia donum dei est, unde vendi non potest*," *Traditio* 11, 220. When Pope Alexander III made
provision in the twelfth century for the appointment in the cathedral schools of grammar teachers
for poor students, he reiterated the medieval principle that knowledge is a gift of God and cannot
be sold: John W. Baldwin, *The Scholastic Culture of the Middle Ages*, 1000–1300 (Long Grove, IL:
Waveland, 1971), 55. Natalie Zemon Davis also refers to how the idea that "knowledge is a gift of
God and cannot be sold" was "still believed in the thirteenth century" in the universities: "Beyond
the Market: Books as Gifts in Sixteenth-Century France," *Transactions of the Royal Historical Society*,
Fifth Series, 33 (1983): 71. "Virtually all medieval thinkers adhered to the common Stoic-Patristic
tradition which described 'the common possession of all things' as a tenet of natural law": Brian
Tierney, "Public Expediency and Natural Law: A Fourteenth-Century Discussion on the Origins
of Government and Property," in *Authority and Power*, ed. Brian Tierney and Peter Lineham (Cambridge: Cambridge University Press, 1980), 176.

35. Augustine, *On Christian Teaching*, trans. R. P. H. Green (Oxford: Oxford University Press,
1997), 1.1 8.

shared with others, as such sharing is rewarded by further learning. Or as Augustine says of God's part in the getting of wisdom: "The material which God had already supplied to me for starting this work [on Christian teaching] will be multiplied, through his own provision, when discussion of it begins. So in this act of service I will not only experience no shortage of material, but in fact enjoy an astonishing abundance of it."[36]

As part of that expansion, the gift of learning made possible by monastic patronage carried with it certain responsibilities for sharing this knowledge with others, given that learning was a path to salvation. The poet and likely abbess Marie de France composed a verse in the late twelfth century that touched on the fruitfulness of this approach to learning:

> To Whom God has given science
> And the eloquence of good speech
> Must not be silent or conceal it
> But willingly show it.
> When a great good is heard by many
> Then it begins to seed
> And when it is praised by many
> Then it bursts into flower.[37]

The historian Natalie Zemon Davis at the University of Toronto cites this verse of Marie de France in her analysis of how books served as gifts during the medieval period, reflecting a sense of knowledge following the "Greek ideal, fortified by Christ's injunction 'Freely ye have received, freely give'" (Matt. 10:8).[38]

EXCESS RENOUNCED AND DISCIPLINED

The endowed economy of medieval monasticism offered a further advantage to learning. It enabled Christianity to confront two vexing problems of excess—*excess wealth* and *excess learning*. These were distinctly Christian

---

36. Ibid.

37. Cited by Davis, "Beyond the Market," 71.

38. Ibid. This element of canon law in the late Middle Ages was "applied not only to professors, who were to take no fees for their teaching," Davis notes, "but even to the sale of notarial and scribal productions" (ibid.). In the seventeenth century, for example, Milton uses the phrase "the divine gift of learning" in his 1641 pamphlet "Animadversions upon the Remonstrant's Defense against Smectymnuus," in *The Works of John Milton, Historical, Political, and Miscellaneous*, vol. 1 (London: Millar, 1753), 102.

dilemmas, and monasticism offered a way to reduce these two threats to salvation. Consider wealth. The Bible could not be more forthright on its spiritual risks: "The love of gold will not be free from sin, for he who pursues wealth is led astray by it" (Eccl. 31:5).[39] And then there was the oft-repeated caution that "it is easier for a camel to pass through the eye of a needle than for a rich man to enter into the kingdom of God" (Mark 10:25, Matt. 19:24, and Luke 18:25). In the face of this gospel, the wealthy appear to have welcomed the opportunity to publicly demonstrate their love of God over gold by founding monasteries. Saint Jerome advises the wealthy that, "when they have laid aside their heavy burden of sins, and the crookedness of their whole body [a feature he ascribes to camels], they can enter through the narrow and straight road that leads to life."[40] As some monastic charters made all too clear, such gifts were intended to compensate for the sins of the benefactor. To devote a parcel of land to the founding of a religious house is to renounce some small part of one's worldly excess, and do so by returning that land to its original state and owner.

Then there was learning, which offered its own danger of excess. There was Saint Paul's admonitions—"Knowledge puffeth up, but charity edifieth" (1 Cor. 8:1) and "The letter killeth, but the spirit giveth life" (2 Cor. 3:6)—to which can be added "Let the woman learn in silence with all subjection" (1 Tim. 2:11). This excess of learning was identified by Saint Benedict, Gregory the Great, and others as everywhere present in the liberal arts of late antiquity. As noted earlier, Augustine had denounced the temptations of curiosity (*vitium curiositas*), citing more broadly the motto "nothing to excess," itself an example of pagan appropriation (from Terence's play *Andria*).[41] The monastery was that much more "the house of discipline," as Augustine referred to the church.[42] The Benedictine *Rule* focused on "the efforts of obedience," which originally offered little place for the advancement of learning.[43]

39. Jacques Le Goff cites this passage in pointing out how "Christianity traditionally placed God in opposition to money": *Your Money or Your Life: Economy and Religion in the Middle Ages*, trans. Patricia Ranum (New York: Zone, 1990), 10.

40. Jerome, *Commentary on Matthew*, trans. Thomas P. Scheck (Washington, DC: Catholic University of America Press, 2008), 3.19.24–26, 220. Jerome goes on to respond to the disciples, who "marvel at the severity of these words," questioning who then will be saved, as "things that are impossible with men are possible with God" (221).

41. Augustine, *On Christian Teaching*, 2.39.58 64.

42. Augustine, "Sermon 399, On Christian Discipline," in *The Works of Saint Augustine*, vol. 10, *Sermons 341–400*, trans. Edmund Hill (Hyde Park: New City Press, 1995), 458. Augustine points out in this context that "'discipline' comes from *disco*, I learn . . . what is learned is how to live a good life; how to live a good life is learned to enable you to live forever" (ibid.).

43. *The Rule of Benedict*, trans. Carolinne White (London: Penguin, 2008), 7.

It was only by applying Aristotle's disciplined methods—particularly *grammatica* trimmed of its excessive literary and rhetorical interests—to the study of God's word that redeemed such learning. This study was dedicated solely to God's glory, rather than to the acquisition of (excessive) learning. It calls to mind how two excessively good composers, Johann Sebastian Bach and George Frideric Handel, signed off their musical scores with "S. D. G." for *Soli Deo gloria* (glory to God alone).[44]

BENEFICENT CODA

To recap, monasticism brought about an intellectual property *transaction* that involved three steps. First, the nobility *transferred* deeds of property to the monastery to enable monastics to devote their lives to prayer. Second, monastics *transformed* these lands, through skilled management and husbandry, into a source of sufficient wealth that enabled some to devote their time to learning, as well as to acquire the necessary parchment, inks, and quills. Third, as monasticism gradually accepted and acknowledged learning as a pious practice, the monastery's production of learned texts could be thought of as *transposing* the original gift of property. It was one form of property giving rise to another, and in ways that would be increasingly valued over the course of the Middle Ages. The institutional endowment of the monastery proved vital to the development of learning in the Latin West but it did not put an end to instances of the learned finding personal patrons, although such patrons tended to favor artists, musicians, and literary talents over learned writers.[45] Still, the institutional patronage of monasticism later became the model for the endowment of the colleges of the medieval universities.

On the other hand, the very success of this monastic gift economy eventually served to undermine the widespread support for this institution. The

---

44. Martin Irvine, *The Making of Textual Culture: 'Grammatica' and Literary Theory, 350–1100* (Cambridge: Cambridge University Press, 1994), 15. Irvine summarizes the concerns of *grammatica:* "'Correct' written Latin, the element of language, texts, and literary genres, normative rules of style, the meanings and value of texts" (ibid.). *Grammatica* is "the discipline that produced the culture of the text in Western societies," and that "all of Western society is thus post-medieval in a significant sense: the grammatical archive continues to shape the understanding of texts, writing, the literary canon, and literacy" (21).

45. Peter J. Lucas identifies the role of the patron in fifteenth-century manuscript production as the eighth step in a ten-step process, noted earlier in this book: "When the work was received by the *destinataire* or patron it was effectively published": *From Author to Audience: John Capgrave and Medieval Publication* (Dublin: University College Dublin Press, 1997), 2.

monasteries of the West gradually accumulated a significant proportion of the arable land of Europe, and they enjoyed great prosperity and prominence.[46] Religious houses were accumulating the very worldliness they had vowed to renounce and turn away from. What, then, of their humility and piety? Among those raising such questions was the Venerable Bede. Although he was full of praise in his *Ecclesiastical History* of the eighth-century royal foundations for new monasteries, he held otherwise in his private correspondence. In a letter to his former pupil Bishop Egbert, he decried the abuse of monastic privileges: "There are many such places, as we all know, that only in the most foolish way deserve the name of monastery, having absolutely nothing of real monastic life to them."[47] He called for an authoritative council to turn wayward monasteries "from luxury to chastity, from vanity to verity, from indulgence of the stomach and gullet to continence and heartfelt piety."[48] He was particularly outraged by those "who commit the graver crime by giving money to the kings and obtaining lands under the pretext of building monasteries in which they can give freer rein to their libidinous tastes; these lands they have assigned to them in hereditary right through written royal edicts, and these charters, as if to make them really worthy in the sight of God."[49] By these means, Bede insists, "they have gained unjust rights over fields and villages, free from both divine and human legal obligations; as laymen ruling over monks, they serve only their own wishes."[50]

The dissipation and irregularity, as well as accumulation of wealth, among monasteries was met by various monastic reform movements. The Cistercian order, founded in 1098, was foremost among them in restoring monasticism to its ascetic roots by establishing monasteries in the remoter regions of the West.[51] In the twelfth century, Bernard of Clairvaux was among those Cistercians who sought to return monasticism to its austere glories: "As a monk I ask my fellow monks the question a pagan poet put to pagans: 'Tell me,

46. Silber, "Monasticism and the 'Protestant Ethic,'" 110.
47. Bede, "Bede's Letter to Egbert," in *Ecclesiastical History*, 349–50. Ian N. Wood refers to this as the "seamy underside" of this gift culture: "The Gifts of Wearmouth and Jarrow," in *The Languages of Gift in the Early Middle Ages*, 93.
48. Bede, "Bede's Letter to Egbert," in *Ecclesiastical History*, 350.
49. Ibid., 351.
50. Ibid.
51. Van Engen, "The 'Crisis of Cenobitism' Reconsidered," 302. J. A. Raftis points to the economic withdrawal of support for monasticism by merchants and entrepreneurs engaged in the commercial exploitation of land and other resources: "Western Monasticism and Economic Organization," *Comparative Studies in Society and History* 3, no. 4 (1961): 469.

O priests, why is there gold in the holy place?' . . . The walls of the church are ablaze with light and color, while the poor of the Church go hungry. . . . Ah Lord! If the folly of it all does not shame us, surely the expense might stick in our throats?'"[52] It may seem, from our perspective today, that the nobility had at times founded monasteries on their lands as extended-stay spiritual spas, time-shares, and retirement homes for the benefit of parents, daughters, sons, brothers, wives, and widows, not to mention themselves, while reserving the right to gain admittance, and for all eternity, by crypt and mausoleum. However, by the late Middle Ages, many of the families that had long stood behind the monasteries began to shift their spiritual sponsorship away from religious houses and toward the building of cathedrals, hospitals, grammar schools, and university colleges, as well as toward supporting artists.[53]

Not only wealth but also learning gradually accumulated within monasticism over the course of the Middle Ages. There came a point when this intellectual wealth overran its place within monasticism and gave rise to new institutional formations, including the glorious cathedral schools of the tenth to twelfth centuries and the medieval universities that first arose in the twelfth century. The elaborate provisions of institutional sponsorship described in this chapter enabled the preparation of editions, compilations, glosses, and commentaries, involving correction, restoration, and standardization, supported by the crafts of transcription, translation, illumination, and bookmaking. The work was paid for in advance. The investment was made without expectations of a return apart from piety and discipline. The intellectual autonomy was limited, hemmed in by heresy charges, but it was by no means insignificant, judging by Radegund's anti-war poetry and Bede's natural history.

The pace and scope of this learning were decidedly modest compared to what was going on during the same period not so very far away in the Islamic Golden Age, which shared similar forms of institutional sponsorship (see chapter 6). Still, the pattern of monastic endowment in the Latin West during the Middle Ages worked for learning and the learned; it demonstrated how well learning was served by this spirit of sponsorship, communality, and autonomy. As a result, learning's intellectual properties bear the watermark of

52. Bernard of Clairvaux, "An Apologia for Abbot William," in *The Cistercian World: Monastic Writings of the Twelfth Century,* trans. Pauline Matarasso (London: Penguin, 1993), 56–57.

53. On the introduction of "disinterested" giving, see Ilana F. Silber, "Gift-Giving in the Great Traditions: The Case of Donations to Monasteries in the Medieval West," *European Journal of Sociology* 36, no. 2 (1995): 234–35.

institutional sponsorship. On the whole and over the long term, this sponsorship of learning reflects the external world's faith in learning and a layperson's
respect for this commonwealth of learning. Still, the relationship between
world and learning could be fraught, often leading to compromised autonomy
for learning, with one outstanding instance of that during the High Middle
Ages found in Peter Abelard, considered in the next chapter, along Anselm of
Canterbury, Bernard of Clairvaux, and Hildegard of Bingen, all representing
the last great age of monastic learning.

CHAPTER FIVE

The Learned Turn of the High Middle Ages

By the eleventh century and the turn of the millennium, learning had, in a number of cases, made its way to the forefront of monastic life. How far reason and analysis had come in the cloisters is exemplified by Anselm of Canterbury. This Benedictine monk served as abbot of Bec before being called upon to be the archbishop of Canterbury in 1093. Anselm boldly advocated a form of faith that could be "defended by reason against the impious."[1] He proposed in a letter to Bishop Fulk of Beauvais that "a Christian should progress through faith to understanding, not reach faith through understanding or, if he cannot understand, fall away from faith."[2] This certainly resonates with the admonition of Saint Augustine, whom Anselm greatly admired, in his commentary on St. John: "Do not seek to understand that you may believe, but believe that you may understand."[3] Yet Anselm was prepared to introduce a new degree of intellectual daring into the relationship between faith and logic. Where Saint Benedict's sixth-century *Rule* prescribed divine study as

1. Anselm, "Letter 136," 315. R. W. Southern regards Anselm as an instance of a new "medieval humanism": "The change took the form of a greater concentration on man and on human experience as a means of knowing God": "Medieval Humanism," in *Medieval Humanism and Other Studies* (Oxford: Blackwell, 1970), 33.

2. Anselm, "Letter 136. To Fulk, Bishop of Beauvais," in *The Letters of Saint Anselm of Canterbury*, vol. 1, trans. Walter Frölich (Kalamazoo, MI: Cistercian, 1990), 315. Anselm asks the bishop to send the letter to a council considering Roscelin's controversial stand on the Trinity, suggesting that, if Anselm's views are requested, they "should be read out in the hearing of the whole assembly" (ibid.).

3. Augustine, "Tractate 29," in *Tractates on the Gospel of John, 28–54*, trans. John W. Rettig (Washington, DC: Catholic University of America Press, 1993), 18.

"the direct route to our creator" for those "who are hurrying towards the heavenly country," Anselm opted to pause.[4] He took the time afforded by life in cloister and cathedral to work out a strictly logical proof of God's existence without calling on scripture for support.

Anselm of Canterbury is a pivotal figure between abbey and school. He has been judged "the last great intellect of the monastic centuries of education," by Johns Hopkins medievalist John W. Baldwin.[5] His manner of reasoning made him one of the fathers of scholasticism, which dominated the cathedral schools and early universities: "No longer belonging to the holy monk in rural isolation," Baldwin writes, "learning has become the property of the urban master who produced his intellectual goods within the *atelier* of his school and sold them to his students at a price to compensate labor and skill."[6] If Anselm led the way, he was hardly alone in inspiring the spread of learning beyond Benedictine monasticism. In addition to Anselm, the three other significant figures of the High Middle Ages whom I consider in this chapter are the scholarly if mystical abbot Bernard of Clairvaux, the talented visionary leader Hildegard of Bingen, and Peter Abelard, who set up one of the major intellectual showdowns of the era, when abbot Bernard sought to have the schoolman Abelard condemned for heresy during the Council of Sens held in 1140.

Much of what is so intriguing about Anselm is that even as he made reason a tool of faith, he did so while upholding the *Rule of Benedict*, despite how little the *Rule* offers the learning he pursued and represented.[7] If the two saints, Benedict and Anselm, differed in their understanding of how best to pursue salvation, Anselm still sought to keep the often ambitious scope of his learning within the Benedictine vow of humility. Consider Anselm's preface to the *Proslogion* finished in 1078, the year he was elected to the position of abbot at the Bec monastery. The preface had become the spot in medieval manu-

---

4. *The Rule of Benedict*, trans. Carolinne White (London: Penguin, 2008), 73 104.

5. John. W. Baldwin, *The Scholastic Culture of the Middle Ages, 100–1300* (Long Grove, IL: Waveland, 1971), 38.

6. Ibid., 56. At the same time, Georges Duby notes that "virtually all the extant texts from a century-long period between 1030 and 1120 originated in the monasteries," which was the "very period of monasticism's triumph": *The Three Orders: Feudal Society Imagined* (Chicago: University of Chicago Press, 1981), 174, 176.

7. Anselm offers this prayer to Benedict, which circulated among the nobility, with a number of women, Benedicta Ward points out, showing interest in his work: "You have placed me under your tutorship, / however ignorant a pupil; / I have vowed to live according to your Rule, / however carnal a monk": "Prayer to St. Benedict," in *The Prayers and Meditations of Saint Anselm with the Proslogion*, trans. Benedicta Ward SLG (London: Penguin, 1973), 197, 275.

scripts in which to confess and apologize for one's presumption in writing what followed. This was called for given the need to recognize that the authority (*auctoritas*) of the author (*auctor*) belongs, in the first instance, to God and kings alone. Yet Anselm was prepared to claim some of that authority for the realm of learning, especially if what was posited could be verified by the commonwealth of the learned.[8]

Anselm opens the preface of *Proslogion* in this spirit of humility. He begins with his reluctance as an author: "After I had published, at the pressing entreaties of several of my brethren, a certain short tract [*Monologion*] ... a number of people (above all the reverend archbishop of Lyons, Hugh, apostolic delegate to Gaul, who commanded me by his apostolic authority) have urged me to put my name to them."[9] Here, with authorship pressed upon him, Anselm appeals directly to God, as the other party in this intellectual labor: "Well then, Lord," he addresses his request for assistance, "that I may understand, as much as You see fit, that You exist as we believe you to exist and that You are what we believe You to be."[10]

Then Anselm takes his famous step. In *Proslogion*, he develops an ontological argument for God's existence. Briefly, the argument holds that God's defining quality is "that than which nothing greater can be thought," as Anselm puts it.[11] And he argues that as we can imagine and understand what is truly supreme, it can be said to exist in the human mind. If the truly supreme being exists in the mind, the argument continues, then such a being must logically and reasonably exist in reality as well. For if such a being did not exist, then the concept of God would be flawed and not supreme.[12] Ergo, God must exist.

8. On this theme, see Alastair Minnis, *Medieval Theory of Authorship: Scholastic Literary Attitudes in the Later Middle Ages*, 2nd ed. (Philadelphia: University of Pennsylvania Press, 1988).

9. Anselm, *St. Anselm's Proslogion, with a Reply on Behalf of the Fool by Gaunilo and the Author's Reply to Gaunilo*, trans. M. J. Charlesworth (Oxford: Oxford University Press, 1965), 103, 105. Anselm explains the title in the preface: "*Proslogion*, that is, an allocution" (105). Bede's *Ecclesiastical History of the English Nation* had been undertaken at the "request" of King Ceolwulf: Preface in *Ecclesiastical History*, 3. In the earlier *Monologion*, Anselm also insisted his authorship was at others' request: "Certain brothers have frequently and earnestly entreated me to write out for them, in the form of a meditation, certain things which I had discussed in non-technical terms with them regarding meditating on the Divine Being": "Monologion," in *Complete Philosophical and Theological Treatises of Anselm of Canterbury*, trans. Jasper Hopkins and Herbert Richardson (Minneapolis: Arthur J. Banning, 2000), 1–2.

10. Anselm, *Proslogion*, 117.

11. Ibid.

12. Ibid. To keep it from seeming too risky a question to even raise, Anselm sets this exercise as a response to Psalm 14 and 53: "The fool hath said in his heart, there is no God." Matthew R. Cosgrove

For our purposes, that Anselm was pressed to publish such an argument testifies to the expansion and drive of learning and logical inquiry within monasticism: "Come now, insignificant man," he begins *Proslogion*, "fly for a moment from your affairs . . . enter into the inner chamber of your soul."[13] The proof is to be found within the soul that remains subject to others' assent, dissent, and encouragement to share. This logic only strengthens the faith out of which it grew. It makes the mind as the final arbiter of faith's soundness. As Anselm concludes, "God cannot be thought not to exist."[14]

Anselm's logical demonstrations of God's divine attributes in *Proslogion* established that this branch of learning offered its own *autonomous* and *authoritative* path to salvation. He counters the predictable charges of heresy in this regard by relating how he only wanted others to experience the intellectual bliss of this approach to God rather than alter what they believe: "Judging, then, what had given me such joy to discover," he writes in the preface, "would afford pleasure, if it were written down, to anyone who might read it, I have written the following tract . . . from the point of view of one trying to raise his mind to contemplate God and seeking to understand what he believes."[15]

As fervently as Anselm insisted that he wrote at the request and for the benefit of others, he still demonstrated proprietary interests in the intellectual quality of the work. In the preface to *Why God Became Man* (*Cur Deus homo*), he opens with just such a concern: "Because of some people who, without my knowledge, began copying out the first parts of this work before it was finished and fully researched, I have been compelled to complete the work . . . in greater haste than would have been opportune."[16] Augustine, you may recall, had expressed a similar sense of having a right over the creation, completeness, and release of his work, reflecting the author's personal investment in, and responsibility for, a work's quality and completeness. Although in Anselm's case, it was not about achieving brevity, or as he puts it in his preface: "For, if I had been allowed to edit it in tranquility and for the appropriate length of time, I would have included further additional material."[17]

neatly summarizes the argument thusly: "If God is 'possible,' i.e., if the notion of God is not logically contradictory, he exists necessarily" ("Thomas Aquinas on Anselm's Argument," *Review of Metaphysics* 27, no. 3 [1974]: 514).

13. Anselm, *Proslogion*, 111.
14. Ibid., 103.
15. Ibid.
16. Anselm, "Why God Became Man," trans. Camilla McNab, in *The Major Works*, ed. Brian Davies and G. R. Evans (Oxford: Oxford University Press, 1998), 261.
17. Ibid.

And again, it is worth noting that this is not about ownership claims over the work or its distribution but a craftsman's right to see the work through properly and thoroughly before turning it over to the use of others.

Anselm's intellectual achievements were a powerful draw for those among the devout who were interested in the life of the mind: "From every country, many noble personages, well-informed clerics, and brave knights came to him in droves . . . [and] consecrated to God's service their persons and their wealth," as his disciple Eadmer observes in his hagiography of Anselm.[18] Anselm's student, Guibert of Nogent, speaks of how his teacher "had free access to the monastery of Fly, where I lived, because of his piety and erudition," and he adds that Anselm's "teachings were incomparable and his life perfectly holy."[19] For Anselm, no less than for Guibert, monastic life was well suited for working out systems of thought on a daily basis over an extended period of time.

Still, the church came to have other plans and needs for Anselm. When he was sixty years of age, the church called on him to restore its threatened endowment in England. In 1093, he left the quietude of the monastery and made the journey across the channel to assume the post of archbishop of Canterbury. This was ostensibly at the bequest of King William II, but Anselm had to take on the king to protect the church's interests at every turn. And the Crown was not above forcing Anselm into exile more than once during his tenure as defender of the church, first under William and then under Henry I.

Despite these new challenges and responsibilities, Anselm of Canterbury continued to write on theological themes. His final text, *The Harmony of the Foreknowledge, the Predestination, and the Grace of God with Free Choice* (*De concordia . . .*), was completed in 1108, just a year before his death at age seventy-six. In his concluding work, he fearlessly takes on once again what appears to be most difficult to establish. He armed himself only with the dialectical reasoning of assertion and response, which was to become the sword and shield of scholasticism. The book begins: "Admittedly, free choice

18. Cited by Jean Leclercq, *Love of Learning and the Desire for God: A Study of Monastic Culture* (New York: Fordham University Press, 1982), 195–96.

19. Guibert of Nogent, *A Monk's Confessions: The Memoirs of Guibert of Nogent*, trans. Paul J. Archambault (University Park: Pennsylvania State University Press, 1996), 61. Further to this matter of learned reputation, Anselm is the sole medieval monastic to earn a section in Anthony J. P. Kenny's *Medieval Philosophy: A New History of Western Philosophy*, vol. 2 of *A New History of Western Philosophy* (Oxford: Oxford University Press, 2005), 40–44.

and the foreknowledge of God seem incompatible."[20] He then goes on to un-
fold the logical necessity of the two concepts coexisting. He concludes this
final work by affirming what had proven to be the life-long pleasure and
communality of learning: "Therefore, since what I know about this topic,
by God's revelation, was especially pleasing to me: knowing that it would
likewise please certain others if I recorded it, I wanted freely to bestow, on
those who are seeking, that which I have freely received."[21]

Anselm made reason far more of an intellectual property of theology for
the pleasure and erudition of others. He allowed that the individual has
the right—nay, the obligation ("come now, insignificant man")—to work out
and test the reasoning that he presented. He recognized others' rights to his
learning. He only asked in return that he be allowed to fully work out his
ideas and determine when they were ready to circulate. His scholasticism
deepened the reach of reason within monasteries and cathedral schools;
it later infused the pedagogy of the universities, beginning in the twelfth
century and continuing well into the early modern era, with humanism its
only rival. It was still present at Oxford, when John Locke attended Christ
Church in the latter half of the seventeenth century. Locke cared little
enough for it, as it had by then been drained of Anselm's pleasure, but that
can happen in the course of six centuries of instruction.

BERNARD OF CLAIRVAUX

Another indicator that learning had made significant gains in the monasteries of the High Middle Ages was the strength of the backlash that it provoked
among more conservative monastics. Monastic wealth and learning were
portrayed as two corrupting influences on the cloisters, diverting religious
houses from their true ascetic mission. Such *irregularity*, on both counts,
led to calls for monastic reform. Among the responses was the founding of
the Cistercian order in 1098 in the Cîteaux Abbey of what is now eastern
France. The Cistercians sought a restorative return to the *Rule of Benedict*,
placing its emphasis on such measures as manual fieldwork in sustaining
the monastery, rather than hiring out such work.[22] The twelfth-century Cis-

---

20. Anselm, "The Harmony of the Foreknowledge, the Predestination, and the Grace of God
with Free Choice," in *Complete Philosophical And Theological Treatises of Anselm of Canterbury*, trans.
Jasper Hopkins and Herbert Richardson (Minneapolis: Arthur J. Banning, 2000), 531.
21. Ibid., 574.
22. Within a century, the Cistercians had some seven hundred monasteries distributed across
the Latin West: David Knowles, *The Monastic Order in England: A History of Its Development from*

tercian monk Arnoul of Bohéries cautioned each monastic sitting before a manuscript that, "when he reads, let him seek for savor, not science."[23] In the early years of the order, Bernard of Clairvaux, born in 1090, served as both inspiration and authority in his own learned challenge to learning's excess. If the Cistercians limited the writing of books to those works and authors to whom explicit permission was granted, Bernard's own prolific flow of commentary and sermon, in book after book, mocked such a restricted view of monastic authorship.[24]

Bernard was particularly intent on restoring the piety of Christian reading against the rising intellectual force of scholasticism that Anselm had inspired. In the place of assertion and defense, Bernard offered a poetic, mystical spiritualism. It reaches a high point, not surprisingly, in his sermon on the visionary Song of Songs, as he turns his loving attention to the Bride, for "she is the soul that thirsts for God" who is every Christian: "She does not ask for freedom or payment or an inheritance or learning, but for a kiss, in the manner of a most chaste bride, who sighs for holy love; and she cannot disguise the flame, which is so evident."[25] It is not learning, then, that quenches the longing for God. Only holy love and the flame of the chaste bride can satiate that need. He cautions that "if anyone who imagines that he has a smattering of knowledge indulges in too close an inquiry, he will find his intellectual powers overcome and his whole mind reduced to subjection [2 Cor. 10:5]."[26] He advises the monks attending his sermons that "today the text we are to study is the book of our own experience; you must therefore turn your attention inward."[27] He advises Hildegard in a letter:

the Times of St. Dunstan to the Fourth Lateran Council 943-1216 (Cambridge: Cambridge University Press, 1950), 526-27. See also Richard Roehl, "Plan and Reality in a Medieval Monastic Economy: The Cistercians," Journal of Economic History 29, no. 1 (1969): 181.

23. Cited by Leclercq, Love of Learning, 73. Ivan Illich draws the connection, in this devotion to reading, to Jewish mysticism and "the desire to live with the book," as he puts it, as such "readings taste to him as sweet as a mother's milk to a babe": In the Vineyard of the Text: A Commentary to Hugh's "Didascalicon" (Chicago: University of Chicago Press, 1993), 59.

24. Emilia Jamroziak, The Cistercian Order in Europe, 1090-1500 (London: Routledge, 2013), 271.

25. Bernard of Clairvaux, "Sermon 7," in Selected Works, trans. G. R. Evans (New York: Harper-Collins, 2005), 114.

26. Bernard of Clairvaux, "Sermon 67," in On the Song of Songs vol. 4, trans. Irene Edmonds (Kalamazoo, MI: Cistercian, 1980), 4.

27. Bernard of Clairvaux, "Sermon 3," in Honey and Salt: Selected Spiritual Writings of Saint Bernard of Clairvaux, trans. Kilian Walsh OCSO (New York: Vintage, 2007), 1.1, 69. Bernard's reference to "the book of our own experience" later becomes a theme for both Bacon and Locke, with more to follow on this. Brian Stock points out that for Bernard "only experience increases one's knowledge": "Experience, Praxis, Work, and Planning in Bernard of Clairvaux: Observations on the Sermones in Cantica," in The Cultural Context of Medieval Learning, ed. John E. Murdoch and

"When the learning and the anointing (which reveal all things to you) are within, what advice could we possibly give?"[28]

Bernard did allow learning a place within the Cistercian restoration of piety: "Perhaps you think that I have sullied too much the good name of knowledge," he writes in another sermon, "that I have cast aspersions on the learned and proscribed the study of letters. God forbid!"[29] Bernard understood that it was too late to return to the "skillfully ignorant and wisely unlearned," as Gregory the Great had characterized Saint Benedict.[30] In another sermon, on knowledge and ignorance, Bernard writes that "there are various and countless things of which one may know nothing without detriment to salvation."[31]

By 1139, Bernard's concern for the growing influence of the Paris schools set him off on a mission to this city. He wanted to restore this growing body of aspiring scholars to the proper faith: "Spare your souls, I beg you brothers. . . . Flee from the midst of Babylon, flee and save your souls (Jer. 48:6; 51:6). Fly to the cities of refuge (Jos. 21:36)."[32] Consider the force of Bernard's image of the rural monastery as the spiritual sanctuary, the anti-city. The very public nature of these new schools was the source of their spiritual risk. It led to "disputes," in Bernard's words, about the Holy Trinity and the nature of God "in towns, villages, and castles, by scholars not only within the schools, but also in the roads and public places . . . and not only among learned or passably instructed persons, but among children even and simple and ignorant persons."[33] Indeed, some left Paris to follow him back to

---

Edith D. Sylla (Dordrecht, Netherlands: D. Reidel, 1975), 226. Stock treats the Latin *experiential* and *experimentum* as synonymous in the work of Bernard, where it was to later develop into the distinctions between experience and experiments (265–68).

28. Bernard, "Letter 2, From Bernard of Clairvaux," in Hildegard of Bingen, *The Personal Correspondence of Hildegard of Bingen*, ed. Joseph L. Baird (Oxford: Oxford University Press, 2006), 21.

29. Bernard, "Sermon 36," in *Honey and Salt*, 2.2, 154. The vanity theme comes up repeatedly in Bernard's sermons: "How can you be proud O Man? [Sir. 10:9] How can you puff yourself up for your smattering of knowledge? [1 Cor. 8:1]?": "Sermon 3," in *Sermons on Conversion*, trans. Marie-Bernard Saïd (Kalamazoo, MI: Cistercian, 1981), 129.

30. Cited by Putnam Fennell Jones, "The Gregorian Mission and English Education," *Speculum* 3, no. 3 (1928): 337.

31. Bernard, "Sermon 36," in *Honey and Salt*, 1.1, 153.

32. Bernard of Clairvaux, "Exhortation to Repentance, and to Seek a Humble Place First and Only after Becoming Worthy to Look to Higher Honor," in *Selected Works*, trans. Gillian R. Evans (Mahwah, NJ: Paulist Press, 1987), 95. On this conversion theme, Evans cites Bernard: "It is better to try to *convert* the Jews than to attack them" (*Bernard of Clairvaux* [Oxford: Oxford University Press, 2000], 109).

33. Bernard of Clairvaux, "Letter 337 (A.D. 1140)," in *Life and Works of Saint Bernard, Abbot of Clairvaux*, vol. 2, ed. John Mabillon, trans. Samuel Eales (London: John Hodges, 1889), 868.

his Cistercian monastery, and took up the monastic vows in "the school of Christ."[34]

Bernard did not believe that the knowledge at issue was entirely misguided. He was opposed to others providing open access to it in schools and towns, as this was bound to cause it to lose its spiritual bearings. Bernard catalogs the failings of a learning that is set apart from this holy charity: "For there are some who long to know for the sole purpose of knowing, and that is shameful curiosity; others who long to know in order to become known, and that is shameful vanity. . . . There are others still who long for knowledge in order to sell its fruits for money or honors, and this is shameful profiteering; others again who long to know in order to be of service, and this is charity."[35]

Bernard could be said to stand with Augustine in condemning idle curiosity and with Bede in keeping learning within monasticism's spiritual compass. But the time of such enclosure for learning was surely passing. It was taking on a new public sense, both charitable and professional, at least for men. The rise of the cathedral schools reflected the extent to which the learned were outgrowing the institutional constraints of monasticism, now that their work was circulating more widely, certainly more than Bernard was comfortable with. To foreshadow the coming of the universities, this new public presence did not put an end to the need for an institutional order that distinguished the properties of their work, economically and politically (in affording a degree of autonomy).

Bernard did have friends among the schoolmen, including the notable scholar Hugo of St. Victor, and he wrote letters in support of those friends when they needed them within the church.[36] Yet he also took on the great schoolman of the age in Peter Abelard. And if Bernard was to win the battle against Abelard, the war against the schools was already lost by 1140. This is when Bernard was invited by the church to bring heresy charges against the apostate at the Council of Sens. Before introducing Abelard (who, as he closes out an age, comes at the end of the chapter though he was born in 1079, eleven years before Bernard), I turn to this book's last great monastic, Hildegard of Bingen, who also greatly expanded the scope of learning

34. Bernard, "Sermon 30," in *Song of Songs*, para. 11.

35. Bernard, "Sermon 36," in *Honey and Salt*, 3.3, 156.

36. Matthew A. Doyle provides a defense of Bernard's acceptance of the schools and his "belief in the validity and benefits of wide learning for the secular clergy": *Bernard of Clairvaux and the Schools: The Formation of an Intellectual Milieu in the First Half of the Twelfth Century* (Spoleto, Italy: Centro Italiano di Studi Sull'alto Medioevo, 2005), 16.

within the cloisters, while extending her gifts to parishioners and court as part of learning's growing circle in the High Middle Ages.

HILDEGARD OF BINGEN

Born on the cusp of the twelfth century in 1098, Hildegard's monastic career began early, at the age of eight, with her dramatic enclosure in the convent. Her parents, born of noble stock, offered her as a tithe to the church. She was sealed in a room with the recluse Jutta of Sponheim to live and pray. Fortunately, Hildegard's life as a nun was not to remain so confined. She first went on to serve as convent "infirmarian" tending to sisters who were unwell through remedies cultivated in the monastery, before assuming the role of intellectual and artistic leader within her community and well beyond.

Working in the infirmary, Hildegard soon supplemented the folkways passed on to her with her own observations and experiments on the healthful benefits of plants and other balms to heal the ailing. In the course of this work, she developed a theory of bodily humors and elements that addressed questions of human sexuality and reproduction, among other topics. She prepared a guide to medicinal herbs that came to be copied and distributed under the title *Physica* and a guide to the treatment of ailments, more broadly, in *Causes and Cures*. She established a reputation in the field of natural remedies that spread through Europe and her name remains closely associated with this field to this day.[37]

In 1136, Hildegard was elected to serve as *magistra*, or a teacher of divine learning, by her sisters, and she was eventually appointed prioress, first at St. Rupertsberg and then at the Eibingen priory on the Rhine. She was well read in secular literature, and went on to write poems, invent alphabets and lexicons, and develop astronomical and astrological theories. She remains among the most celebrated of medieval composers of choral music.[38] She is

37. Hildegard's medical counsel circulated in manuscript before being published in the sixteenth century and continues to this day to be a subject of medical interest: O. Micke and J. Hübner, "Traditional European Medicine—After All, Is Hildegard von Bingen Really Right," *European Journal of Integrative Medicine* 1, no. 4 (2009): 226. Micke and Hüber report that "about three percent of all inhabitants of Germany" trust the "Hildegard medicine" (ibid.). Uehleke Bernhard, Werner Hopfenmuellerd, Rainer Stangeb, and Reinhard Sallera report that the success associated with Hildegard's medical claims is "significantly higher than it could have been by pure chance": "Are the Correct Herbal Claims by Hildegard von Bingen Only Lucky Strikes? A New Statistical Approach," *Research in Complementary Medicine* 19, no. 4 (2012): 187.

38. Jennifer Bain, *Hildegard of Bingen and Musical Reception: The Modern Revival of a Medieval Composer* (Cambridge: Cambridge University Press, 2015).

the author of what is regarded as the earliest extant medieval morality play. She reported that some of this work was inspired by visions she had been having since childhood.[39]

In 1146, at the age of forty-eight, Hildegard decided to act on these visions. She approached the fearsome abbot Bernard of Clairvaux, who had figured in one of her visions "as a man able to stare at the sun" and "a terror to the unlawful foolishness of the world," as she put it.[40] She wrote to him, posing the question of "how much I should say of what I have seen and heard."[41] He responded in brief that "we rejoice in the grace of God which is in you . . . and beseech you to recognize this gift as grace."[42] Bernard's encouragement was amplified two years later when Pope Eugene, in his travels to northern Europe, gave his blessings to the prophetic visions that Hildegard had set down up to that point in *Scivias*. She now had license to share her words, visions, music, lyric, preaching, and teaching. She not only employed secretaries to assist her in her writing, but eventually ventured forth to preach along the Rhine Valley.[43]

"These are great and fearsome matters," she wrote about turning the visions that she had into lessons on the forces of good and evil at play in heaven and earth.[44] These visions are the source and provocation behind much of her verse and prose, as well as the illuminations that she directed the manuscript illustrators to construct for her. She presented these visions

39. The visions have been identified as "indisputably migrainous," judging by their visual aura and other qualities, by the noted neurologist Oliver W. Sacks, *Migraine: Understanding a Common Disorder* (Berkeley: University of California Press, 1985), 106. The influence of migraines had been noted earlier by Charles J. Singer, "The Visions of Hildegard of Bingen," in *From Magic to Science: Essays on the Scientific Twilight* (New York: Boni and Liveright, 1928), 99.

40. Hildegard of Bingen, "Letter to Bernard of Clairvaux," in *Selected Writings*, trans. Mark Atherton (London: Penguin, 2001), 2–3.

41. Ibid., 3.

42. Bernard, "Letter 2, From Bernard of Clairvaux," in Hildegard, *Correspondence*, 21.

43. Constant J. Mews notes how Hildegard "drew on a broader range of human experience than scholastics like Abelard or monks like Bernard. She appealed to those who resented the growing influence of Parisian intellectuals in defining religious belief": "Hildegard and the Schools," in *Hildegard of Bingen: The Context of her Thought and Art*, ed. Charles Burnett and Peter Dronke (London: Warburg Institute, 1998), 109.

44. Hildegard, "Letter to Bernard of Clairvaux," in *Correspondence*, 18. Richard K. Emmerson notes that Hildegard uses "scriptural exegesis to supplement her visions," in an "exceptional" combination, although her exegesis is "generally conventional, homiletic, and highly moralized," invoking themes of "sexual purity or deviance" and demonstrating an "impressive command of monastic learning": "The Representation of Antichrist in Hildegard of Bingen's *Scivias*: Image, Word, Commentary, and Visionary Experience," *Gesta* 41, no. 2 (2002): 102, 106.

as a means of interpreting biblical passages.[45] But they also had their own cosmological order to them, as with the female figure, in *Scivias*, whom she portrays as the Knowledge of God (*Scientia Dei*), pitted against the evil in the world.[46] The illustrations of this and other of her visions are marked by their geometrical order, with striking overlays depicting woman, man, beast, and cosmic force. The images represented for her an "Edifice of Salvation," as she put it, that had been revealed to her by God.[47] It amounts to a reordering of the world, beginning with women's place in that order: "God made the form of woman / to be the mirror of all his beauty, / the embrace of his whole creation."[48] The feminine reflects God's cherished work, rather than the evil Eve-like seductress. An illustration from her later years depicts a handsome naked man, free of genitals, who has declared that, she reports, "I am Reason. . . . everything vital is rooted in me, as Reason is the root for which the sounding word blooms in the world."[49] Reason is the guiding light, as it was for Anselm, vital to an understanding of faith and world.

Hildegard engaged at times in monasticism's regional politics, but she also directed her gifts of prophetic wisdom toward a more orderly arraignment of church and state.[50] She corresponded with popes as well as kings, from Henry II of England to the Holy Roman Emperor Frederick Barbarossa, whom she advised on, as she put it, "how to hold the rod of proper governance in your hand."[51] She assured a prelate that "God established that the female sex is to be governed by faithful teachers," and she established that women could be such teachers, against Saint Paul's oft-cited injunction: "Let the woman learn in silence with all subjection. But I suffer not

45. Peter Dronke, *Women Writers of the Middle Ages: A Critical Study of Texts from Perpetua (†203) to Marguerite (†1310)* (Cambridge: University of Cambridge Press, 1984), 163.

46. Madeline H. Caviness, "Hildegard as Designer of the Illustrations to Her Works," in *Hildegard of Bingen*, 32. See also Beverly Mayne Kienzle, "Hildegard of Bingen's Teaching in her *Expositiones evangeliorum* and *Ordo virtutum*," in *Medieval Monastic Education*, ed. George Ferzoco and Carolyn Muessig (London: Leicester University Press, 2000), 80.

47. Cited by Sarah L. Higley, *Hildegard of Bingen's Unknown Language: An Edition, Translation, and Discussion* (New York: Palgrave Macmillan, 2007), 3. The illustrated figures 2, 7, 10, 11, 15, 16, and 20 include, beneath the main image, a nun sitting at a desk in the cloisters, recording the vision on wax tablets, with her feet comfortably crossed, despite being dwarfed by the vision and uncowed by the blinding light and spewing animals. Hildegard's role in preparing these intricate illuminations is not known; Caviness uses the term "designer": "Hildegard as Designer," 29–62.

48. Cited by Barbara Newman, *Sister of Wisdom: St. Hildegard's Theology of the Feminine* (Berkeley: University of California Press, 1989), 187.

49. Cited by C. T. Clanchy, *Abelard: A Medieval Life* (Oxford: Blackwell, 1999), 178.

50. See Dronke, *Women Writers*, 144–201.

51. Hildegard, "Letter 45 to Frederick Barbarossa," in *Correspondence*, 78.

a woman to teach" (Timothy 1:12–14).[52] Priests sent her pressing queries—
"Please also teach me about the body and blood of Christ"—and provosts
wrote to her, acknowledging the integral role that she played in sustaining
the monastic community: "You have always refreshed me with your consolation in all my tribulations, and because all the things that you have fore-
told have come to pass."[53]

In women's learned contributions to monasticism, we find another demonstration of how the institutional properties of these religious houses—
with their sponsored autonomy and self-discipline, their scriptoria and
shared libraries—eased the path to learning not only for Hildegard of Bingen,
but for Herrad of Landsberg, Hilda of Whitby, Mechthild of Hackeborn, and
other religious women who thrived in convent and priory as students, teachers, administrators, and scholars throughout the Middle Ages.[54] Their contributions to the composing, production, and circulation of learned intellectual
properties were considerable.

Their example also illustrates the limits of this commonwealth's autonomy and its ability to operate outside the mores of the larger society. For
this same period, which saw such learned and creative work from Hildegard
and other sisters, also witnessed the categorical exclusion of women from
the cathedral schools, and then from the medieval universities that were
soon to dominate the intellectual life of the High Middle Ages.[55] The Gregorian church reforms of the late eleventh century and early twelfth centuries
contributed to the cutting off of women from the public life of church and
learning. During this period, Pope Gregory VII approved policies "aimed

52. Ibid., 71.
53. Ibid., 76, 79.
54. On Mechthild of Hackeborn, for example, Barbara Newman points to how she thrived in a
nunnery at Helfta near Eisleben under her sister the abbess "who was renowned for maintaining
a first-class scriptorium, enhancing the library with the purchase and copying of books, [and] promoting education": "Annihilation and Authorship: Three Women Mystics of the 1290s," *Speculum*
91, no. 3 (2016): 592.
55. Lina Eckenstein writes of how the education "secured in so great a measure to women
by convents in the past" was an inspiration to "the modern movement for women's education":
Women under Monasticism (New York: Russell and Russell, 1963), 484. In the eighteenth century
and in Bologna, with its tradition of a forceful student body, women were first able to obtain doc-
torates and hold teaching chairs. Women gained admittance to Oxford in 1879, with the opening
of Lady Margaret Hall and Somerville College, while full "membership of the University" was not
to be theirs until 1920: Vera Brittain, *The Women at Oxford: A Fragment of History* (London: Harrap,
1960). For a review of the historical exclusion of women from the church and other positions of
responsibility and cultural achievement leading up to the early modern period, see David Noble,
A World without Women: The Christian Clerical Culture of Western Science (New York: Oxford, 1993).

at a church virtually free of women at every level but the lowest stratum of the married laity," according to Jo Ann McNamara, a historian at Hunter College.[56] There was an increased emphasis on masculine clerical celibacy; the double monasteries were dissolved; and the new orders of mendicant Franciscan and Dominican friars, so active in learning, did not accept women. The church was increasingly given to portraying women as either the redemptive Mary or the seductive Eve. Still, the enclosed convent remained an intellectual home for women, even as learning increasingly moved into the public domain, where it faced new struggles for autonomy and support.

PETER ABELARD

In *Historia Calamitatum*, Peter Abelard offers what is indeed an account of a calamitous life.[57] He composed this autobiographical letter in his final decade, circa 1132, and it is a tale of, among other things, the great age of cathedral schools, which formed educational centers in Paris, Chartres, Reims, Canterbury, and elsewhere. The schools were attracting a great new interest in learning, both for its own sake (as Bernard of Clairvaux warned) and as a preparation for assuming a role in the officialdom of church or court. Abelard was himself a magnet, bringing to the schools the daring glamour of learning with a touch of tragedy.[58]

Born in 1079 in the west of France, Abelard initially set off to follow in his military father's heavily armored footsteps, along with his brothers. This meant, as Abelard puts it, that his father's sons were to "have instruction in letters before they were trained to arms" as suited a minor nobleman in Brittany.[59] Abelard started down that path by acquiring his letters, only to discover that "the more rapid and easy my progress in my studies, the more eagerly I

56. Jo Ann Kay McNamara, "The Herrenfrage: The Restructuring of the Gender System, 1050–1150," in *Medieval Masculinities: Regarding Men in the Middle Ages*, ed. Clare A. Lees (Minneapolis: University of Minnesota Press, 1994), 7. See Gary Macy on how, by the thirteenth century, "at the same time that theologians and canonists were redefining ordination [to exclude women], they also began the process of expunging the memory of ordained women from Christianity": *The Hidden History of Women's Ordination: Female Clergy in the Medieval West* (Oxford: Oxford University Press, 2008), 110.

57. Peter Abelard, "Letter 1, Historia calamitatum: Abelard to a Friend: The Story of my Misfortunes," in *The Letters of Abelard and Heloise*, trans. Betty Radice (London: Penguin, 1974).

58. As noted earlier, and given what Abelard does for moving the schools forward (toward the coming universities), I have moved him to the end of this chapter, and after the monastics Hildegard and Bernard, though he was born before them.

59. Abelard, "Historia calamitatum," in *Letters of Aberlard and Heloise*, 4.

applied myself, until I was so carried away by my love of learning that I renounced the glory of a military life, and made over my inheritance and rights of the eldest son to my brothers, and withdrew from the court of Mars in order to be educated in the lap of Minerva."[60]

Still, he was his father's son. In his approach to learning, he "preferred the weapons of dialectic," as he describes it, and "chose the conflicts of disputation," to be found at the cathedral school Notre Dame in Paris, "where dialectic had long been particularly flourishing, and [he] joined William of Champeaux, who at the time was the supreme master of the subject."[61] Disputes are bound to arise among such talented disputants, and soon enough the brash Abelard left at Notre Dame to found his own school at Melun, southeast of Paris, at a time when pupils pursued and paid reputable masters for the chance to sit and learn at their feet.

It was on his return to Paris in 1113, to take charge of the school at Notre Dame, that he began his fateful tutoring of the young Heloise, niece of the cathedral's Canon Filbert. It was a turning point for Abelard and Heloise. Their love child and secret marriage led to a nunnery for Heloise and a monastery for Abelard, along with castration at her uncle's instigation.[62] But perhaps more germane to the intersection of learning, gender, and intellectual property is the extent to which the already well-educated and gifted Heloise taught Abelard, beyond the lessons he gave to her. Through their initial meetings and in the course of their continuing correspondence, she demonstrated to him the value of the classical writers in reflecting on philosophical matters and human relationships. M. T. Clanchy, medieval historian at the Warburg Institute, believes that she may be the one who convinced Abelard to become a writer.[63]

Heloise cites Seneca and Cicero, as well as Genesis and Matthew, in her first letter to Abelard. She challenges him to write—"that you will prescribe

60. Ibid.

61. Ibid., 4–5.

62. In that world of rough justice, Abelard reports of those who brutally assaulted him, that "the two who could be caught were blinded and castrated as I had been": "Historia calamitutum," in *Letters of Abelard and Heloise*, 17. Uncle Fulbert's actions were denounced and a property fine levied: John Marenbon, *The Philosophy of Peter Abelard* (Cambridge: Cambridge University Press, 1997), 15.

63. Clanchy, *Abelard*, 169. Clanchy holds that Heloise may have also demonstrated to Abelard what it meant to be "a self-conscious writer" and "a writer in the modern sense of creative author and also in the sense of a stylist and rhetorician, who has been instructed in—and delights in performing variations on—the most advanced maneuvers in Latin" (170). On her influence, John Marenbon observes that "antiquity itself played little part in his thought before about 1120," which is to say before he gets to know Heloise: *Philosophy of Peter Abelard*, 95.

some Rule for us"—for the benefit of the Oratory of the Paraclete convent, for which she served as abbess, even as it was sustained by a bequeathal provided by a friend of Abelard's.[64] Through her letters, Heloise sought in vain to continue the dialogue and connection: "I beg you, think what you owe me."[65] The intellectual slight and loss was as much part of the tragedy of the times as the fate of their love. For all of her influence, what appears distinctly Abelard's is the role of critical reasoning if not skepticism in his theology: "By doubting we are led to inquiry, and by inquiry we attain the truth."[66] His starting point of doubt rather than faith can be contrasted with Anselm's stance: "I do not seek to know in order that I may believe, but I believe in order that I may know."[67] Both were committed to the path, if not yet the rule, of reason. Abelard made great advances in logic, pushing ahead with Anselm's application of reason to faith, working from Aristotle's *Categories* and Porphyry's introduction to it (*Isagoge*, translated by Boethius).[68] He applied this logic to identifying scriptural and doctrinal contradictions. In his *For and Against* (*Sic et non*) from 1121, he offers the 158 conflicting points to be found in the pages of the Bible, without providing a resolution but only a dialectical method of determining the conflict. You can imagine that this may well have struck some as undermining church and priest, especially given his public presence as a teacher.

Abelard first faced censure in 1121, at the Council of Soissons where he was summoned before the papal legate Cardinal Cono of Praeneste: "Without any questioning or discussion they compelled me to throw my book into the fire with my own hands" he writes, "and so it was burnt."[69] This must have been discouraging enough, but he had also come close to being stoned at this sorry event by those who came to see him properly denounced and punished.[70] "I wept much more for the injury done to my reputation," Abelard wrote of it all, "than for the damage to my body, for that I had brought

64. Heloise, "Letter 6, Heloise to Abelard," in *Letters of Abelard and Heloise*, 94.

65. Heloise, "Letter 2, Heloise to Abelard," in *Letters of Abelard and Heloise*, 55. "At all events, I think we should envisage between Abelard and Heloise a literary and intellectual partnership . . . [reflected in] those texts that both he and she cited oftenest . . . [and] in terms of shared pursuits of certain problems": Dronke, *Women Writers*, 112.

66. Peter Abelard, "Sic et Non," in *Educational Documents*, vol. 1, *England and Wales 800–1816*, ed. David William Sylvester (London: Routledge, 1970), 55.

67. Cited by David William Slyvester, Introduction to "Sic et Non," 55.

68. John Marenbon writes of Abelard: "There is throughout his writings the same willingness to challenge accepted views, to find and dwell on awkward question, and to press ideas to their logical conclusion": *Philosophy of Peter Abelard*, 94.

69. Abelard, "Historia Calamitutum," in *Letters of Abelard and Heloise*, 24.

70. Clanchy, *Abelard*, 299. Clanchy identifies Soisons, in 1118, as both a "show trial" and "academic heresy trial" (300).

on myself through my own fault, but this open violence has come upon me only because of the purity of my intentions and love of our Faith which had compelled me to write."[71]

Two decades later, perhaps sensing that the times had changed, Abelard decided to confront his critics again. He asked Archbishop Henry of Sens for the chance to publicly address the accusations that had dogged him for years.[72] Bernard of Clairvaux was selected by the church to prosecute Abelard's theological failings at the Council of Sens where the schoolman-monk would meet his accusers. Although Bernard showed some initial reluctance—"I am but a child in this sort of warfare"—he was soon thoroughly engaged in preparing his brief with the assistance of the most assiduous of his secretaries.[73] Bernard decided that the *capitulum* they composed against Abelard was to be limited to only nineteen of the principal heretical errors in his work: "To answer them all," he observes, "would require volumes. I speak only of those on which I cannot keep silence."[74] As part of his strategy, he secured the presiding judges' support for his case in advance.

In 1141, Bernard must have entered the chambers of the Council of Sens with a great deal of confidence. He was about to put a stop to Abelard's kidnapping of young souls in the midst of Babylon. In attendance at the council were not only church prelates, but also King Louis VII, members of the nobility, and Abelard's fellow teaching masters. Yet for all of Bernard's preparedness, Abelard found a way to subvert this carefully staged disputation on the religious standing of his work. "And so, in the presence of all, face to face with my adversary," Bernard later wrote to the pope, "I took certain headings from his books. And when I began to read these, he refused to

71. Peter Abelard, *Story of Abelard's Adversities*, trans. J. T. Muckle (Toronto: Pontifical Institute of Medieval Studies, 1964), 52. Here are the grounds—referring to his "damage to my body" as "my own fault"—of Heloise's writing of this letter to a friend in which "nearly every line of this letter was filled, I remember, with gall and wormwood": Heloise, "Letter 2, Heloise to Abelard," in *Letters of Abelard and Heloise*, 47.

72. Constant J. Mews, "The Council of Sens (1141): Abelard, Bernard, and the Fear of Social Upheaval," *Speculum* 77, no. 2 (2002): 342-82. There is some dispute over the year of the council, with Mews on the side of 1141, while I follow Clanchy and others with 1140.

73. Bernard of Clairvaux, "Letter 239," in *The Letters of St. Bernard of Clairvaux*, trans. Bruno Scott James (Kalamazoo, MI: Cistercian Publications, 1998), 318. David Knowles on Bernard: "When he attacked Abelard he came forward as one who had come to challenge on his own ground the most brilliant and adored master of his age": "St. Bernard of Clairvaux: 1090-1153," *Dublin Review* 117, no. 105 (1953), 118. Clanchy notes that "in manuscript culture every copy of a book was different and even St. Bernard could not be sure he was reading Abelard's authentic works": *Abelard*, 308.

74. Bernard, "Letter 190 (A.D. 1140)," in *Life and Works of Saint Bernard, Abbot of Clairvaux*, vol. 2, trans. Samuel J. Eales, ed. John Mabillon (London: John Hodges, 1889), 576.

listen and walked out, and appealed from the judges he had chosen, which I do not think was permissible."[75] On leaving, Abelard informed the judges that he would write directly to the pope to defend the fidelity of his faith.[76]

Bernard wasted little time in sending his well-documented *capitulum* to the pope and cardinals, accompanied by a letter in which he refers to Abelard as a "dragon" inflaming disorder and dissent. Bernard, the intrepid dragon slayer, warns that "although he is no longer lurking in his lair: would that his poisonous writings were still lurking in their shelves, and not being discussed at the crossroads!" He continues, "his books have wings . . . his writings 'have passed from country to country, and from one kingdom to another.'"[77] The abbot was alarmed once more by the noisy, public spread of learning, reflected in the growing prominence of the schools across the continent. Further, the archbishop of Sens sent to Rome the court's judgment on the case that had not been heard: Abelard's heresy was nothing less than a "contagion."[78]

The Council of Sens brings the twelfth-century conception of intellectual property rights into sharp focus. Bernard charged Abelard with what is, in effect, intellectual trespassing. He held that Abelard's analysis of scriptural contradictions vastly exceeds the limits of fair use when it comes to the Bible. This is, for Bernard, an infringement of the Holy Book's properties on Abelard's part, namely its divine perfection as the word of God.[79] Abelard aggravates his sin, first of all, by circulating the infringing work through publication, and, secondly, by presuming to teach others how to take such an approach with the Bible.[80]

75. Bernard, "Letter 239," in *Letters of St. Bernard*, 319.

76. The reasons Clanchy offers for this uncharacteristic response from Abelard range from "the stress of the occasion" to "early signs of brain cancer," while also citing Christ's silence before Pontius Pilate: *Abelard*, 312. Clanchy also points out that Abelard was known (by Bernard) to have disciples in Rome (314).

77. Bernard, "Letter 239," in *Letters of St. Bernard*, 318. In this letter, Bernard also casts Abelard as a Goliath facing down the armies of Israel, with Bernard the implied David, able to slay the intellectual giant by throwing at him "certain headings from his [Abelard's] books" (319). Henry, archbishop of Sens, also picks up the crossroads theme in his letter to the pope: "Disputes are carried on about the Holy Trinity and what God is, not only within schools but also at crossroads by public places by boys and simple foolish people, as well as by the learned and students": cited by Clanchy, *Abelard*, 299.

78. Cited by Clanchy, *Abelard*, 318.

79. "Bernard's theological concerns, however, had an important political dimension. He was troubled by the potential of Abelard's teachings to tear the church apart": Mews, "Council of Sens," 344.

80. R. I. Moore writes of the attack on heresy being particularly strong during this period: "Between 1139 and 1148 two of the greatest in a stellar generation of scholars and teachers, Peter Abelard and Gilbert de la Porée, were charged with heresy in high-profile public trials; there were

Bernard's *capitulum* also charges that Abelard "presumptuously prepared to give a reason for everything, even of those things which are above reason."[81] What Anselm of Canterbury unleashed with the application of reason to faith, in his proof of God's existence (without reference to scripture), Abelard had taken a step too far in applying such logic to scripture and the doctrine of the church: "He promises understanding to his hearers, even on those most sublime and sacred truths," Bernard writes, "which are hidden in the bosom of our holy faith."[82] Abelard is said to promise what is not his to offer. He is one "always seeking after new things, who invents what he does not find," as if he were indeed living by the writer's credo.[83] Then there is Bernard's ancient charge against the learned eclecticism that Abelard had acquired, in part, via Heloise: "While he exhausts his strength to make Plato a Christian, he proves himself a heathen."[84]

Abelard later responded to this *capitulum* in a work that came to be known as *Apologia contra Bernardum*, of which only fragments remain. In what has come down to us, he is not given to defending the beliefs that he holds but the integrity of the works in question, reinforcing their standing as intellectual property. Bernard's reading of his books, Abelard holds, is "manifestly mistaken, brother, as if in no way comprehending the import of the words."[85] Against the charge of having written the book *Sentences*, which Bernard denounces as "a crop of blasphemies and errors," Abelard responds, "Thanks be to God ... since such writings either cannot be found or were not mine," and that thus Bernard's own words "prove him wrong without my saying even a word."[86] Yet Abelard also sets the record straight

burnings in Provence, the Rhineland, the Low Countries and northern France; the two most influential churchmen of the age, Peter the Venerable, abbot of Cluny, and Bernard, abbot of Clairvaux, proclaimed heresy among the people a menace to the church": *War on Heresy: Faith and Power in Medieval Europe* (Cambridge, MA: Harvard University Press, 2012), 145.

81. Bernard, "Letter 190," in *Life and Works*, 566.
82. Ibid.
83. Ibid., 567. John R. Sommerfeldt points to how Bernard and Abelard actually hold similar views on this point of logic's limits in the face of belief: *Bernard of Clairvaux: On the Life of the Mind* (New York: Newman, 2004), 127.
84. Bernard, "Letter 190," in *Life and Works*, 576.
85. Peter Abelard, "Apologia," in *Letters of Peter Abelard: Beyond the Personal*, trans. Jan M. Ziolkowski (Washington, DC: Catholic University of America Press, 2008), 122. Abelard adds for good measure by way of trash talk, "So know what you did not know, and learn what you have not learned" (ibid.).
86. Ibid., 118. As if to raise further learned intellectual property issues, Clanchy notes that Abelard "was not telling the whole truth here, as this 'Book of Sentences' does contain Abelard's authentic opinions and it was accepted practice for a master's teachings to be circulated among students in this way": *Abelard*, 308.

by offering a few retractions of what he has written; as such he follows the examples of Augustine, Bede, and others who have treated their earlier work as having this continuing existence, as an intellectual property that they are still responsible for correcting, in others' work and especially in their own.

The charges laid against Abelard at the Council of Sens were different from those mounted at the Inquisition trials that would take place with some regularity within a century's time. In these trials, those accused of heresy were asked to confess, renounce, and repent their beliefs, if under the duress of torture and the threat of imminent death. The Inquisition put the heretic and his sins on trial. At Sens, it was Abelard's books that were accused of corrupting young and old; the books were condemned, and as such, were to be burned. Their texts were held to be toxic. Once they were condemned as an (evil) intellectual force in the world, only then does Abelard become liable for their composition.

On reading the charges and judgment of the council, Pope Innocent II issued two letters to all concerned. The first summarily sentenced Abelard to perpetual silence and his followers to excommunication. The second confined him, as well as his compatriot Arnold of Brescia, to separate religious houses, and called for their "erroneous books to be burned wherever they were found."[87] In censoring Abelard during "these last days and perilous times," the pope cited an earlier fifth-century ruling of the Byzantine emperor Marcian that forbade anyone "to discuss the Christian faith in public."[88] Still, the pope did not sentence Abelard to death, which was later to be the fate of Arnold of Brescia, who was hanged and then burned a decade or so later in 1155 for, among other sins, preaching that the church should renounce all of its property claims.[89]

In Abelard's case, he had friends and admirers in Rome and among the monasteries who intervened on his behalf, suggesting that a change in the church's intellectual climate was afoot. Foremost among his supporters was Peter the Venerable, lord abbot of the Cluny Abbey (although an enemy of God, according to the cantankerous Bernard of Clairvaux). In striking contrast to Bernard's desire to keep learning off the streets, Peter was a monastic who saw learning as a public good. The abbot of Cluny exhorted those "distinguished for their knowledge, love of learning, and eloquence" to be

87. Cited by Clanchy, *Abelard*, 218.
88. Cited by ibid., 319.
89. Elphège Vacandard, "Arnold of Brescia," in *Catholic Encyclopedia*, vol. 1 (New York: Robert Appleton, 1907), online. Arnold also took a leadership role in the republican Commune of Rome that was founded in 1145 and, surviving Arnold's death, lasted to 1193, when the city was again placed under papal authority.

not "so sluggish" in the sharing of their work, but to "hand down in writing to those who are to come after them the marvelous works the Almighty repeatedly accomplishes in different parts of the world."[90] Peter was taken with the fearless and worldly intelligence of Abelard, and reached out to him in his friend's time of need.

Following the pope's condemnation of Abelard, Peter wrote to Innocent II on behalf of his friend the now broken *magister*. He described how Abelard "made his peace with the abbot of Clairvaux [Bernard] and that their previous differences were settled," which seems a remarkable instance of Christian forgiveness on both their parts.[91] Peter further described Abelard heeding others' counsel and removing from his writings "anything offensive to orthodox Christian ears."[92] Abelard had, in Peter's words, "decided to abandon the turmoil of schools and teaching and to remain permanently in your house of Cluny."[93] Peter asked that rather than be arrested, Abelard be allowed to so retire, as his "learning, which is not altogether unknown to you, could be of benefit to our large community of brothers."[94]

Abelard was then able to spend his final year within the shelter of monastic life. In Peter's epitaph on Abelard's death in 1142, Peter pronounced him "the Socrates of the Gauls, Plato of the West, our Aristotle, prince of scholars."[95] That this should be an abbot's greatest praise—and in what sense *our* Aristotle, if not in uniting Abelard's schools and Peter's monasteries—speaks to the broader sense of learning that had found a place within monasticism. Abelard had tended to a more qualified endorsement of the philosophers, at least in his declaration of faith to Heloise: "I do not wish to be a philosopher if it means conflicting with Paul, nor to be an Aristotle if it cuts me off from Christ."[96] Abelard turned to Aristotle, as well as Porphyry and Talmudic scholars, to raise the intellectual stakes within the bounds of Christianity, as he saw it.[97] Had he pursued this work within the quieting brotherhood of the monastery, he would not have posed a problem for the

90. Cited by Jean Leclercq, *The Love of Learning and the Desire for God: A Study of Monastic Culture*, trans. C. Misrahi (New York: Fordham University Press, 1982), 156–57.

91. Peter the Venerable, "Letter (98) to Pope Innocent II," in *Letters of Abelard and Heloise*, 215.

92. Ibid.

93. Ibid.

94. Ibid., 216.

95. Cited by Betty Radice, Introduction to *Letters of Abelard and Heloise*, 42.

96. "Abelard's Confession of Faith," in *Letters of Abelard and Heloise*, 270.

97. "Abelard is one of the few medieval churchmen who shows any understanding of what the Jews suffered at the hands of the Christians. 'We are confined and oppressed, as if the whole world had conspired against us alone. It's a wonder we are allowed to live,' he has a Jew say [in *Dialogue of a Philosopher with a Jew and a Christian*]": Clanchy, *Abelard*, 17.

church. Yet for the twelfth-century Latin West, it was too late to think about cloistering such exercises of logic and reason. Within town and marketplace, a growing segment of the public was clearly interested in what was intellectually at stake for Abelard and others in the public pursuit of learning.

The Council of Sens was monasticism's last great defense of learning's enclosure. There is no small irony in Abelard being condemned to perpetual silence; muteness is the monastery's way, even as it was often overcome by the Bedean spirit of learning. Abelard, too, went on to be heard. At least one historian has designated him the University of Paris's founder-in-effect with that institution gradually taking shape in the decades after his death.[98] The monasteries, as well, were undergoing change. At the Council of Paris in 1212, the prelates of the church declared that monastic libraries should be open to those who had no other access to such learning: "We forbid monks to bind themselves by any oath not to lend books to the poor, seeing that such a loan is one of the chief works of mercy."[99] Taking a far more practical tack to this sense of learned charity, Bernard's own order of Cistercians went on to offer the world a series of improved hydraulic engineering techniques for watermill fulling (pounding) and grinding, agricultural irrigation and drainage, and wastewater and latrine systems.[100] By the thirteenth century, the Cistercians were building among the earliest blast furnaces in the West for smelting iron at Rievaulx Abbey in the north of England.[101] This

98. Gabriel Compayré lists Victor Cousin, John Henry Newman, and Père Denifle, along with "all serious authorities," among those who credit Abelard with "a preeminent part in the foundation of the great Parisian University": *Abelard and the Origin and Early History of Universities* (London: William Heinemann, 1893), 4.

99. George Haven Putman, *Books and Their Makers during the Middle Ages* (New York: Hillary House, 1962), 1:138. "Cathedral libraries" were also public (162–63) and provided grammar teachers for the poor, as a result of Pope Alexander III's policy at the Lateran Council of 1179: Baldwin, *Scholastic Culture*, 39. Thomas Kelly, while noting restrictions in access to the universities, points to fourteenth-century English instances of a Bible bequeathed "for the common use" to the church of St. Nicholas, Newcastle, and a Latin dictionary to the church of Blessed Peter at York "to be placed in a common, safe and honorable place, so that should anyone seek information concerning some point of doubt, scholarship, or disputation, it may easily be found according to the letters of the alphabet": *Early Public Libraries: A History of Public Libraries in Great Britain before 1850* (London: Library Association, 1966), 25.

100. Constance Hoffman Berman, "Medieval Agriculture, the Southern French Countryside, and the Early Cistercians: A Study of Forty-three Monasteries," *Transactions of the American Philosophical Society* 76, no. 5 (1986): 49, 88–89; P. F. Cooper, "Historical Aspects of Wastewater Treatment," in *Decentralised Sanitation and Reuse: Concepts, Systems and Implementation*, ed. Piet Lens, Grietje Zeeman, and Gatze Lettinga (London: IWA Publishing, 2001), 14.

101. Gerald McDonnell, "Cistercian Monks as Metallurgists: Iron Technology at Rievaulx Abbey 1130–1600" (lecture, Ian Ramsey Centre for Science and Religion, Oxford University, 2011, available on iTunes U); R. Vernon, Gerald McDonnell, and A. Schmidt, "The Geophysical Evalua-

very early contribution to the industrial revolution, and perhaps to England's leadership role in it, represents its own sort of culmination of both the practical side of monastic learning and Bernard's original, if limited, blessing of learning in the charitable service of others rather than to oneself.

CONCLUSION

Over the centuries, monastics found various ways to resolve the paradox posed by the *Rule of Benedict* for learning. They did so by establishing the pious and charitable value of encouraging learning within their communities. Radegund, Bede, Alcuin, Anselm, and Hildegard, among those examined here, demonstrate how a Benedictine devotion to the selfless labor of learning could open the road to piety for others. At the same time, learning was slowly moving out into the world, whether through the Carolingian Renaissance's monastic schools, Hildegard's Rhineland preaching tours, or Abelard's establishment of schools wherever students had the chance to gather around him. Europe's intellectual momentum was shifting away from the enclosed space of remote monasteries and into urban centers and secular institutions. Beginning in the eleventh century, scholars in the West started to see a growing number of Greek and Islamic works that were being rendered in Latin for the first time. This wealth of access, which I address in the next chapter, was to permanently alter the direction and institutional setting of learning.

The great era of monastic learning in the Latin West, dating back to Jerome and Augustine, was coming to a close with Anselm, Hildegard, and Bernard of Clairvaux. The monastery had become the great sponsoring agency of learning among the religious; it provided a degree of autonomy, while also offering time and space for studies; it afforded access—both communal and networked—to the works they needed; it created a setting for the accrediting of authors and their ideas through gloss and commentary. The intellectual properties of this learning are both institutional and textual. This mix of qualities, from economic to textual, form part of a monastic legacy that was to serve learning in schools and universities. One sharp failure in the transfer of this legacy—from abbey to school to university—was the unreasonable exclusion of women from this new learning. This tragic loss becomes all the more apparent when considered in light of the learned contributions of Hildegard

tion of an Iron-working Complex: Rievaulx and Environs, North Yorkshire," *Archaeological Prospection* 5, no. 4 (1999): 181–201.

and Heloise reviewed in this chapter. Women continued to find opportunities to develop their talents in nunneries, and were able to contribute much to the age's learning through their scribal efforts.[102] They also thrived in the female semimonastic communities of northern Europe, known as *béguinages*, beginning in the twelfth century, which, if lacking the splendor of great monasteries, gave rise to a number of writers, including the thirteenth-century mystic Marguerite Porete, whose call to give up reason, in the *Mirror of Simple Souls*, led the church to have her burned at the stake.[103]

Compared to Bernard's retreat into monasticism and a poetical mysticism, the new learning, arising from Anselm's scholasticism, Hildegard's polymathic interests, and Abelard's critical turn, was becoming a part of the world. There was a new assertion of the writer's role in creating a purely intellectual artifact at the bequest of others, if still in the service of faith. Hildegard similarly established a new set of monastic practices by preparing practical guides to better health for the larger community, while continuing to serve her religious house with choral music compositions and an illuminated cosmology. It was a time of change for learning. Masters were offering lessons in cathedrals and marketplaces; they were collecting fees from pupils, creating a new level of autonomy, economically and intellectually, for this trade in ideas and ways of thinking. Students were also introducing a new dynamic into learning, much as Heloise pushed Abelard's thinking. They gave the learned book a new standing as something to be possessed as well as mastered. But they also saw books being burned for infringing on the proprietary rights of the church in matters of scriptural interpretation. It suggests that such texts were seen as an autonomous (and sometimes dangerous) force on the world.

Learning's entry into the world was challenged at many points and not just by Bernard of Clairvaux. Women were facing a growing spirit of misogyny in church and state. Their exclusion from the schools (and universities) serves to temper this book's admittedly Whiggish tendency to celebrate

---

102. "The movement of male orders to divest themselves of the *cura monialis* [care of nuns] began during the twelfth century and became general in the thirteenth": Penelope D. Johnson, *Equal in Monastic Profession: Religious Women in Medieval France* (Chicago: University of Chicago Press, 1991), 251. "Monasteries connected with Hirasu, in particular, not only used the services of resident female scribes, but also provided a setting in which women could participate fully in the central activities of their reformed communities, and this meant access to libraries and teachers": Alison I. Beach, *Women as Scribes: Book Production and Monastic Reform in Twelfth-Century Bavaria* (Cambridge: Cambridge University Press, 2004), 133. On monastic women's continuing learning and literacy, see Cynthia J. Cyrus, *The Scribes for Women Convents in Late Medieval Germany* (Toronto: University of Toronto Press, 2009).

103. Donke, *Women Writers*, 202.

gains in learning. It represented a self-serving blind spot among the men who pursued learning during that earlier period, if not to this day in too many cases. Who has access to learning affects its nature and contribution, which is to say its intellectual properties. This is in the sense of both a property right and a property quality. And in the history that I am setting out here, access to learning in the West was about to go through a major seismic shift (in something of another blind spot) as the Latin translations of the great tradition of Islamic science and mathematics began to enter Europe.

PART TWO

University and Academy

CHAPTER SIX

The Translation Movements of Islamic Learning

In the year 967, the young monk Gerbert d'Aurillac left his abbey in the south of France to journey across the Pyrenees into Catalonia. Gerbert was on his way to the cathedral school of Vic. His brilliant mathematical gifts had prompted Atto, the bishop of Vic, to send Gerbert an invitation to join the school. During his three years there, Gerbert appears to have been one of the first Europeans to both examine with some care a series of Arabic works in astronomy, astrology, and mathematics, and later make use of what he learned about operating the Arabic astrolabe (or armillary sphere, which had its origins in ancient Greece) and abacus (originally from China). He was likely guided in these efforts by local Muslim scholars. The cathedral town of Vic fell within the shifting contact zone among Christians, Muslims, and Jews on the Iberian Peninsula during the centuries-long Christian Reconquista, which was aimed at taking back the region from the Islamic caliphate that had been established there in the eighth century.

In his later writings, Gerbert makes no direct reference to Arabic works or Muslim scholars. Still, distinct traces of such learning can be found in his later teachings at the cathedral school in Reims. For example, he shared with his students an abacus designed with Hindu numerals and an astrolabe clearly of Arabic origin.[1] Gerbert's instructional use of these instruments, in the years leading up to his election as Pope Sylvester II, contributed to his reputation of being not just a masterful teacher but, as one thirteenth-century writer

---

1. The oldest known Arabic text on the astrolabe is from the mid-ninth century by Aḥmad Ibn Muḥammad al-Farghānī and can be viewed online at the Qatar Digital Library.

had it, "the best necromancer in France, whom the demons of the air readily obeyed."[2] An odd ascription for a pope, to be sure. But how could it be otherwise? Gerbert had stumbled into a mysterious and suspect world of ideas that lay beyond the confines of Christendom. Hindu numerals, for example, were indeed used for rites of divination and astrology in the medieval Islamic empire. Yet this demonic abacus proved an exceptionally useful teaching aid for those learning the basic operations of arithmetic. In demonstrating the value of the Hindu number system to calculate and compute, Gerbert contributed to its spread throughout the West.

The poet and translator Helen Waddell judges Gerbert to be "not the first wandering scholar, but . . . the most famous," in her study of this medieval archetype.[3] The wandering scholar—known as *vagante* in Latin—along with the wandering monk, poet, and Jew, were common types of the time, and not in a good sense, as our word *vagrant* attests. Gerbert, however, strikes me as belonging to a different order. He did not so much wander as deliberately seek out a spot that he knew would advance his learning. If he wandered into entirely unexpected regions of mathematics at Vic, it was still very much part of his plan to pursue his studies there. In this, he was more of a prototype of the visiting scholar, if not as likely a model for a medieval action figure as the *vagrante*.

Following Gerbert, many an intrepid Christian set off in pursuit of what was by then the legendary manuscripts and artifacts of the Islamic empire. These adventurers sought instances from the great storehouse of Arabic learning which was said to include Islamic, Greek, Persian, Indian, Chinese, Christian, or Jewish sources. On coming upon such works in the contact zone among religions and cultures, many were fortunate enough to be able to collaborate with local Muslims, Mozarabs (Arabic-speaking Christians), and Jews to translate the Arabic texts they found into Latin. After the learned in the West had worked for many centuries with a relatively enclosed and self-contained body of texts, this form of medieval manuscript tourism exposed Europe to a new world of learning from other lands, languages, and traditions during the twelfth and thirteenth centuries. The dispersion of Arabic translations and copies throughout Europe evolved into a Latin translation movement—one that would alter the shape and direction of learning on the Continent.

2. Cited by Charles Burnett, "The Translating Activity in Medieval Spain," in *The Legacy of Muslim Spain*, vol. 2, ed. Salma Khadra Jayyusi (Leiden: Brill, 1992), 1038.
3. Helen Waddell, *The Wandering Scholars of the Middle Ages* (London: Constable, 1927), 73.

Such a consequential movement of learning across languages was not without precedent, in its ability to afford a great boost in access to new forms of knowledge. Four centuries earlier, Islamic scholars had similarly engaged in translating a great variety of Greek, Persian, Hindu, and Hebrew texts into Arabic. Opening access to this array of works led to a great blossoming of learning across the Islamic empire. The West would benefit from the new knowledge and perspective of the Arabic translations and from subsequent Islamic scholarly engagement with these works from the eighth to the twelfth centuries.

The two related translation movements hold their own set of lessons on the intellectual properties of learning. What must first be noted is that the West's great indebtedness to this era of Arabic learning has long been underplayed in European histories of the period.[4] This would seem to reflect some of the "natural" limits of scholarship's autonomy, when it comes to rising above the ethnocentric prejudices of its time and place. These two translation movements point to the dramatic difference that access to learning from other languages and cultures can make. To open great swaths of learning from other traditions for the use of scholars, over the course of a century or two, not only proves immensely productive but can also garner much support from court and public. Then, at the level of the works themselves, at least one of the titles translated across both movements, namely Aristotle's *On the Soul* (*De anima*), prompted much reflection on the nature of the intellect in ways that bear on the properties of learning. Much thought was given in commentary and original work on Aristotle's theme of what is common to all and what is individual in intellectual labor, raising germane questions on the ownership of ideas, as well as taking responsibility for them. As such, these Arabic and Latin translation movements warrant a discussion of the growth of Islamic learning during the first movement from the eighth to twelfth centuries, followed by the wave of Latin translations in the twelfth and thirteen centuries.

---

4. Charles Homer Haskins exemplifies the belittlement of the Islamic contribution to the West: "Between 1100 and 1200, however, there came a great influx of new knowledge into western Europe partly through Italy and Sicily, but chiefly through the Arab scholars of Spain—the works of Aristotle, Euclid, Ptolemy, and the Greek physicians, the new arithmetic, and those texts of Roman law which lay hidden through the Dark Ages": *The Rise of Universities* (Ithaca, NY: Cornell University Press, 1923), 4–5. More recently, Toby E. Huff addresses "The Problem of Arabic Science" by noting, despite its progress, "the failure of Arabic science to give birth to modern science," and its "apparent decline and retrogression": *The Rise of Early Modern Science: Islam, China, and the West*, 2nd ed. (Cambridge: Cambridge University Press, 2003), 47.

Now, I realize that my efforts to credit the Islamic developments and contributions that have not always received their due in the West still demonstrate a certain eurocentricity. My focus is, after all, on how this Islamic history served the Western course of learning, and I use the Latinized names by which Islamic scholars became known in the medieval West and a Christian dating of Islamic history. Allowing for one historical correction at a time, my purpose is to ensure that a history of learning in the West credits the full intellectual force of Islam involving issues of intellectual property creation, access, and use. I address the ramifications of this in the next chapter, in which I show how the cumulative intellectual force of these movements contributed to the emergence of the medieval university.

THE ʿABBASID CALIPHATE'S REVIVAL OF LEARNING

The story begins with the ʿAbbasid caliphate of the Islamic empire, established by al-Saffāh in 750. The caliphate followed decades of rebellion against the ruling Umayyad family, and was to rule from the eighth until the sixteenth century. Beginning with the caliph al-Saffāh, the ʿAbbasid empire grew until it stretched from India to the Iberian Peninsula, while its caliphs ushered in an era of relative wealth and stability for the Islamic people, thanks in good part to improved farming techniques imported from India. A number of ʿAbbasid caliphs took advantage of this prosperity to become great patrons of learning. This involved importing more than agricultural innovations. The caliphs favored those among their people who were ready to learn from the practical, technical, and scientific works of Greece, Persia, and India.[5] Among the early leaders to foster this appetite for learning-from-abroad was the second ʿAbbasid caliph, al-Mansur, who in the latter half of the eighth century supported, among his more consequential moves, the introduction of the Hindu numerical system into Arabic (which would later fascinate Gerbert d'Aurillac). More broadly, al-Mansur, and his son al-Mahdi, together ruling from 754 to 785, were the catalysts of the Arabic translation movement that defined Islamic learning during this period.

5. Bernard Lewis observes that "according to the Arab tradition . . . [the translations began] at the turn of the seventh-eighth centuries . . . [with] some Greek writings on alchemy," while noting that "there was no attempt to translate Greek poetry, drama, or history": *The Muslim Discovery of Europe* (New York: Norton, 1982), 73, 75. In many cases, works by Aristotle and other Greek writers were initially translated into Syriac by Eastern Christian scholars and then rendered in Arabic: F. E. Peters, *Aristotle and the Arabs: The Aristotelian Tradition in Islam* (New York: New York University Press, 1968), 38–39.

As later told by the fourteenth-century Islamic historian, Ibn Khaldun, this Arabic translation movement began with a gift of Euclid. Al-Mansur had apparently "sent [a request] to the Byzantine emperor," Ibn Khaldun writes, "and asked him to send him translations of mathematical works. The emperor sent him Euclid's book and some works on mathematics."[6] Inspired by this start, al-Mansur went on, according to earlier historians, to acquire Aristotle's work on logic and Ptolemy's *Almagest* with an eye to having these works translated into Arabic. He also pursued works in Syriac and Persian, including some that had originated in China and India. He not only issued diplomatic requests for books to other kingdoms but also treated books as the plunder of war.[7] Such expressions of the court's fascination with learning prompted scholars and adventurers to travel throughout the Byzantine and Islamic empires in pursuit of manuscripts by Aristotle, Plato, Euclid, Galen, Ptolemy, and many other lesser-known authors.[8] From lists compiled of these early translations, the range of subjects translated from Greek alone extended from agriculture and alchemy to veterinary science and zoology.[9]

Al-Mansur sought to build Baghdad into the political and cultural capital of his empire. He built a grand palace at the center of the city in a complex that is said to be the site of the legendary House of Wisdom (*Bayt al-ḥikma*). Although few details have survived, it appears that the House of Wisdom was home to a truly magnificent royal library in a city of libraries; it was also a hub for translating Persian and other works into Arabic.[10] Sponsored libraries were the hallmark of Islamic learning during the ʿAbbasid caliphate not just in Baghdad but in various centers across the empire. Their wealthy patrons provided these libraries on occasion with an endowment (*wakf*) for what might be called wandering scholar fellowships: "When a stranger came to [the library] seeking culture," as one description from the time had

6. Ibn Khaldūn, *The Muqaddimah: An Introduction to History*, trans. Franz Rosenthal (Princeton, NJ: Princeton University Press, 1969), 374.

7. L. E. Goodman, "The Translation of Greek Materials into Arabic," in *Religion, Learning and Science in the ʿAbbasid Period*," ed. M. J. L. Young, J. D. Latham, and R. B. Serjeant (Cambridge: Cambridge University Press, 2006), 482. "What was sought was what was useful, but the concept of the useful was itself enlarged" and could include efforts to "complete an author's canon or support the growth of a science": Goodman, "Translation," 479, 483.

8. Dimitri Gutas, *Greek Thought, Arabic Culture: The Graeco-Arabic Translation Movement in Baghdad and Early ʿAbbasid Society (2nd–4th/8th–10th Centuries)* (London: Routledge, 1998), 15–16. Fredrick S. Starr, *Lost Enlightenment: Central Asia's Golden Age from the Arab Conquest to Tamerlane* (Princeton, NJ: Princeton University Press, 2013), 156.

9. Gutas, *Greek Thought, Arabic Culture*, 193–96.

10. George Makdisi, *The Rise of Colleges: Institutions of Learning in Islam and the West* (Edinburgh: Edinburgh University Press, 1981), 24–26. Gutas demonstrates that House of Wisdom was neither an academy nor a conference center: *Greek Thought, Arab Culture*, 59.

it, "if he happened to be in financial straits," the head of the library "gave him paper and money."[11]

The circulation of scholars and works among these libraries was also facilitated by a highway and postal system that the caliphs developed and maintained across the far reaches of the empire. Learning and libraries were also aided at the time by recent innovations in the manufacture of relatively inexpensive paper from flax and linen that was far superior to papyrus for producing and preserving books. The technique was gleaned, as legend has it, from the Chinese prisoners that the ʿAbbasid forces captured at the battle of Talas in 751 against the Tang Dynasty.[12]

The ʿAbbasid caliphs seemed to make it their mission to follow the precept "seek knowledge even as far as China," attributed to the Prophet Muhammad.[13] There were undoubtedly political motives at play in the caliphs' interests in what could be learned from astrology, for example, and there are indications that translation was viewed as a tool of intellectual conquest in empire building.[14] But then the caliphs also supported importing works on astronomy to increase the accuracy of prayer times, the direction of Mecca, and the timing of Ramadan.[15] The openness to new ideas went hand in hand with an acceptance of Jews, Christians, and other infidels in their midst who could assist in this intellectual acquisitiveness. While Arabic provided Islamic territories with linguistic unity, the empire still represented a culturally and intellectually diverse region, dominated by Islam, but still marked by an interest in Hellenic philosophy, Hindu mathematics, Jewish astrology, and Nestorian Christian theology.

The Hellenized Christians in Syria and the Nestorian monks in Iraq, for example, had fled Byzantine persecution, with its eschewal of Greek paganism, and were thus in a good position to traffic in and translate Greek texts, as well as works from Persian and Hindi into Syriac and Arabic.[16] Foremost

11. Cited by Makdisi, *Rise of Colleges*, 26.

12. Jonathan M. Bloom, *Paper before Print: The History and Impact of Paper on the Islamic World* (New Haven, CT: Yale University Press, 2001), 42. China developed paper in the second century (32.)

13. Mark Halstead, "An Islamic Concept of Education," *Comparative Education* 40, no. 4 (2004): 521.

14. Gutas, *Greek Thought, Arabic Culture*, 29–60. Gutas points to how the translation movement, as it represented the "recovery" of an ancient glory to bolster empire, was supported by "the highest posts of the administration" (54).

15. F. Jamil Ragep and Alī al-Qūshjī , "Freeing Astronomy from Philosophy: An Aspect of Islamic Influence on Science," *Osiris* 16, 2nd ser. (2001): 50–51.

16. Dimitri Gutas writes of how in late antiquity "philosophy died a lingering death before Islam appeared," while by the seventh and eighth "centuries—during, that is, the Iconoclastic controversy in Byzantium and the so-called 'Dark Ages'—philosophical treatises were not even copied,

among these translators was the ninth-century Nestorian Christian Ḥunayn ibn Ishaq, a master of Arabic, Greek, Persian, and Syriac. Working with his son Ishaq, he established a new standard for translation. He began by collating and consulting as many editions of the work in the original language as he could find in the process of translating it. Ḥunayn did not leave off with the completion of a translation of a work but went on to extend and build upon it. He followed his translation of Galen, for example, by composing further medical treatises based on the Greek physician's work. Ḥunayn and Ishaq's work contributed to the mix of Greek, Syrian, Persian, and Jewish traditions in medicine that flourished in Gundeshāpūr not far from Baghdad during the ninth century.[17]

Al-Ma'mun, the seventh ʿAbbasid caliph, who ruled in the first half of the ninth century, was another of the great cultural leaders who fully supported the Arabic translation movement. The large cadre of translators, tutors, physicians, and advisors whom al-Ma'mun employed worked on topics in mathematics, astronomy, astrology, and philosophy. They held what were, in effect, conferences that brought together still other learned figures for meetings in al-Ma'mun's palace.[18] These scholars were assisted by various caliphate officials who prided themselves on contributing their own translations to the pool or who commissioned translations of learned and literary works.[19] The

let alone composed": "Origins in Baghdad," in *The Cambridge History of Medieval Philosophy*, ed. Robert Pasnau (Cambridge University Press, 2014), 11. He concludes that "Arabic philosophy internationalized Greek philosophy, and through its success it demonstrated to world culture that philosophy is a supranational enterprise. This, it seems, is what makes the transplantation and development of philosophy in other languages and cultures throughout the Middle Ages historically possible and intelligible" (23). Jerrilyn D. Dodds, María Rosa Menocal, and Abigail Krasner Balbae point out how Christians had earlier shunned these same Greek works in Rome and Constantinople: *The Arts of Intimacy: Christians, Jews, and Muslims in the Making of Castilian Culture* (New Haven, CT: Yale University Press, 2008), 206.

17. Peter Adamson, "Al-Kindī and the Reception of Greek Philosophy," in *The Cambridge Companion to Arabic Philosophy*, ed. Peter Adamson and Richard C. Taylor (Cambridge: Cambridge University Press, 2005), 3. Similarly, in Alexandria, the medical community had its scholar working on translating Aristotle and Galen into Arabic: Jacob Lassner, *Jews, Christians, and the Abode of Islam: Modern Scholarship, Medieval Realities* (Chicago: University of Chicago, 2012), 264.

18. Al-Ma'mun is reported to have dreamt of meeting Aristotle and discussing the *good* with him, with different versions in circulation, at least one of which signals the triumph of Aristotle in Arabic philosophy: Gutas, *Greek Thought, Arab Culture*, 97–104. Compare this to Saint Jerome's dream, discussed in chapter 2, warning him against his love of Cicero. Later caliphs, during the ninth century, such as Ja'far al-Mutawakkil, withdrew their support from learning, Jacob Lassner points out, and placed restrictions on Jews and Christians: "Nevertheless, the legacy of ancient learning lived on," Lassner concludes, "particularly the more practical aspects that found favor with rulers and important notables" (*Jews, Christians*, 268).

19. George Saliba, *Islamic Science and the Making of the European Renaissance* (Cambridge, MA: MIT Press, 2007), 58–62. Gutas in reference to the commissioning of translations: "The

caliph himself is said to have composed treatises in medicine and agriculture. Al-Ma'mun also saw to the building of observatories for studying the heavens, with one constructed just outside Baghdad and another near Damascus. A millennium later, these investments in astronomy earned him the honor of having a crater on the moon named after him.[20]

Having done much to introduce Greek philosophy into Islamic thought through his commissioning of fluid and interpretative translations of these works into Arabic, the Baghdad polymath al-Kindī was among the most distinguished scholars of the period. The translated works included Aristotle's *Metaphysics, Meteorology, On the Heavens*, and a compendium of *On the Soul*, as well as a number of Platonic dialogues and other works.[21] "Al-Kindī's [own] output was vast," Peter Adamson, historian of philosophy at Ludwig Maximillian University of Munich, has written: "A list of his work shows that he wrote hundreds of treatises in a startling array of fields, ranging from metaphysics, ethics, and psychology (i.e., the study of the soul), to medicine, mathematics, astronomy, and optics, and further afield to more practical topics like perfumes and swords."[22] Alas, these works are largely known only through others' reference to them.[23]

What has remained of his work speaks to al-Kindī's intellectual brashness and determination: "We wish to complete the mathematics," he wrote in his work on optics, to "increase that which [the ancients] began and in which there are for us opportunities of attaining all the goods of the soul."[24] Much indebted to Euclid's *Elements* and *Optics*, al-Kindī's reference to the (intangible) goods of the soul suggests, in my reading, a conception of mathematics as a body of work resulting from the labor of scholars from different traditions. As he writes in *On First Philosophy*, "we should not be ashamed to recognize truth and assimilate it, from whatever quarter it may reach us."[25] More than that, al-Kindī advises the Islamic scholars on whose behalf

translation movement made intellectuals, in broad terms, out of all members of the ruling elite" (*Greek Thought, Arab Culture*, 124–25).

20. A crater on the moon was named Almanon in the 1930s to honor al-Ma'mun's support for astronomical observations.

21. Gutas, *Greek Thought, Arab Culture*, 145. Gutas identifies seven stylistic cues that make such translation identifications possible (146).

22. Peter Adamson, "Al-Kindī and the Reception," 33.

23. Ibid.

24. Cited by D. M. Dunlop, *Arab Civilization to A.D. 1500* (New York: Praeger, 1971), 228. Bennison also reports that court intrigue led to the caliph al-Mutawakki having al-Kindī beaten and his library confiscated, with others eventually negotiating its return to him: *Great Caliphs*, 191.

25. Cited by Richard Walzer, "The Rise of Islamic Philosophy," *Oriens* 3, no. 1 (1950):9. Charles Burnett notes that the first al-Kindī work translated into Latin was on astrology: "Al-Kindī, Latin

he speaks—in his use of *we*—to labor over what he clearly sees as a body of work held in common. This right of access is marked by the responsibilities of learning—"to complete the mathematics"—whether that completion involved tidying up loose ends, assimilating Greek and Hindu mathematical traditions, or something far greater.

Al-Kindī's ideas about these goods of the soul also reflect his wrestling with the concept of the intellect that Aristotle developed in *On the Soul*. Aristotle's book was the center of much commentary on the nature of intellect and intellectual work, not only for al-Kindī but for the Islamic philosophers al-Farabi, Avicenna, and Averroës who succeeded him. And it is this thread that I want to follow (if not in all of the overwhelming intricacies of multiple intellects working out complex philosophies), as they employed a concept of intellect that spoke to the nature of learning and the contribution of the learned. These Islamic scholars were fearless in taking up many of the philosophical difficulties that Aristotle left half-resolved in contemplating the nature of thought.

"That part of the soul," writes Aristotle in *On the Soul*, which "is called intellect (by which I mean that whereby the soul thinks and supposes) is before it thinks in actuality none of the things that exist."[26] He further illustrates the intellect's state of readiness "before it thinks" with the analogy of a tablet awaiting someone to use it to express ideas: "The intellect is in a way potentially the objects of thought, but nothing in actuality before it thinks, and the potentiality is like that of the tablet on which nothing is actually written."[27] Thought may seem to arise out of nothing, within this potential intellect, but is incited, for Aristotle, by an external, active intellect: "An intellect characterized by that to bring all things about, and to bring them about in just the way that a state, like light, does. (For in a way, light also *makes* things that are potentially colors, colors in actuality.) Now this latter intellect is separate, unaffected and unmixed, being in substance activity."[28] Thus, the external active intellect allows ideas to be perceived, worked on,

Translations of," in *Encyclopedia of Medieval Philosophy: Philosophy between 500–1500*, ed. Henrik Lagerlund (Dordrecht, Netherlands: Springer, 2011), 676.

26. Aristotle, *De Anima (On the Soul)*, trans. Hugh Lawson-Tancred (London: Penguin, 1986), 3.4.429a, 202.

27. Ibid., 3.4.429b, 203. "The most intensely studied sentences in the history of philosophy are probably those in Aristotle's *De anima* that undertake to explain how the human intellect passes from its original state, in which it does not think, to a subsequent state, in which it does": Herbert A. Davidson, *Alfarabi, Avicenna, and Averroes on Intellect: Their Cosmologies, Theories of the Active Intellect, and Theories of Human Intellect* (Oxford: Oxford University Press, 1992), 3.

28. Aristotle, *De Anima (On the Soul)*, 3.5.430a10, 204–5.

and expounded by shining a light on what has yet to be revealed within the passive intellect. In Aristotle's thinking, the active intellect is not the source of ideas, but the means of illuminating potential ideas and gaining insight from them.

For my purposes, al-Kindī's contribution to this tradition arises out of his adopting Aristotle's notion of the intellect as a blank tablet: "[The soul] makes it apparent so that it will exist for others as something that comes from it," al-Kindī writes. "[This is] like writing in the writer: it belongs [to the writer] as a possible disposition that he obtained and that is established in his soul, after which he brings it into action and uses it whenever he wants."[29] This interest in using the intellect for some greater purpose is what defines a thinker. The thinker then needs to act on this disposition by, say, expressing a line of thinking in a text to be shared with others. This is the form of "intellect that appears from the soul whenever it brings it into action," al-Kindī continues, "at which point it is something that exists for others as something coming from it actually."[30] What originally comes to the soul is something universal and available to all, to restate al-Kindī, while what the intellect makes of the original concept belongs to the writer, even as it is intended for others. In other words, the human intellect works with what is given in common to create something of distinctive benefit for others. With many variations, this is the pattern with learning's intellectual properties as reviewed in this book.

Although the eclectic al-Kindī and his circle did much to further access to learning from near and far, he also understood this work to be in the service of those in power, by which he earned appointments from more than one of the caliphs who ruled during his lifetime. As part of that service, perhaps, he worked out a genealogy that made Muslims the descendants of the ancient Greeks, and Islam the rightful heir of both Greek science and earlier Mediterranean empires (while the West would later recast this Greek genealogy as its own).[31] Al-Kindī was, in effect, exercising his own intellectual acts of aggression in the border skirmishes of his time with the Byzantium Empire. Yet it also needs to be made clear that al-Kindī's thought was a matter of

29. Al-Kindī, "On the Intellect," in *Classical Arabic Philosophy: An Anthology of Sources*, ed. Jon McGinnis and David C. Reisman (Indianapolis: Hackett, 2007), 18.

30. Ibid.

31. Gutas, *Greek Thought, Arab Culture*, 88. Gutas on the imperial translation mission: "The moral is thus there for everybody to draw . . . the superiority of of Islam over Christianity in this context, therefore, is solely based on the Muslim acceptance of the fruits of the translation movement" (ibid.).

high culture, rather than something that pervaded Islam and the empire as a whole. He may well have had the support of more than one caliph, but the empire's religious schools were not noticeably influenced by his work on Aristotle or on Islamic theology, even as he left his mark on Islamic learning.[32]

What followed from the interpretative translations and syntheses of al-Kindī's circle was a great wave of commentaries on the works of Aristotle, as if the Greek philosopher was the light that effectively illuminated and sparked others' potential intellect. The commentary is the most academic of genres, as noted above. It typically and painstakingly works with the intellectual qualities of its subject text. Assessing the text's value and accrediting the author's achievement, the commentator is exercising complete access rights to the text in question. As such, a commentary's title might advertise itself in this way: *The Philosophy of Aristotle, the Parts of His Philosophy, the Rank Order of Its Parts, the Position from which He Started and the One He Reached.*[33] This exemplary title helps to advance my chronology to the tenth century and to the figure of al-Farabi, the author of this commentary. Al-Farabi was a Christian-trained Muslim scholar who was counted among the largely Christian collection of philosophers known as the Baghdad Peripatetics, named as such for their adherence to Aristotle. He went on to earn a reputation as the "second teacher" or "second master," which is to say second to Aristotle.

He was well regarded not only for his philosophy but for his effort to teach humankind about the nature of the world. Committed to furthering, as he put it, "the *principles of instruction* . . . through which the student is led to the certain truth about what he seeks to know,"[34] he wrote a work that students must have found promisingly entitled *The Attainment of Happiness*. It sets out how the "theoretical virtues" and "deliberative virtues" are the means "through which nations and citizens of cities attain earthly happiness in this life and supreme happiness in the life beyond."[35] Al-Farabi was to turn these theoretical virtues, found everywhere in Aristotle's work, into a program of study within Islam.[36] "Therefore, Aristotle saw fit to make known at the outset," al-Farabi

32. Peters, *Aristotle and the Arabs*, xxiii; F. W. Zimmermann, "Al-Kindī," in *Religion, Learning and Science in the ʾAbbasid Period*, ed. M. J. L. Young, J. D. Latham, and R. B. Serjeant (Cambridge: Cambridge University Press, 2014), 368–69.

33. Al-Farabi, *Philosophy of Plato and Aristotle*, trans. Muhsin Mahdi (Ithaca, NY: Cornell University Press, 1969), 71.

34. Ibid., 14.

35. Ibid., 13.

36. David C. Reisman, "Al-Fārābī and the Philosophical Curriculum," in *The Cambridge Companion to Arabic Philosophy*, ed. Peter Adamson and Richard C. Taylor (Cambridge: Cambridge University Press, 2005), 53.

writes in the commentary cited above, "what the certain science is, how many classes it has, in which subjects it exists, how it exists, and by what and from what it exists in every question."[37] Al-Farabi continues classifying the sciences in this paragraph, until he finally arrives at "the art . . . from which the power of all the classes of ways of instruction proceeds."[38] It is ultimately the art of teaching Aristotle that al-Farabi's commentaries cultivate. He did much to ensure that the Greek peripatetic philosopher became a mainstay of medieval higher learning, first among Muslim scholars and then, centuries later, within the medieval universities of Christianity.[39]

Although al-Farabi took on the breadth of Aristotle's work available in the Islamic empire at the time, the commentary he offered on the philosopher's *On the Soul* is, again, what bears directly on my theme. Al-Farabi extends al-Kindi's Neoplatonic treatment by casting the first and active intellect as a finite and fixed body of knowledge, representing a singular truth, that existed in an incorporeal state apart from humanity. He writes that the active intellect is the source of "the first intelligible thoughts common to all men, such as [the principle] that the whole is greater than the parts."[40] Using their Aristotelian tablets, the learned work on articulating, accumulating, possessing, and sharing the knowledge, which is at least potentially common to all. "Excellent discernment," al-Farabi writes, "allows us to come into possession of the knowledge of everything people can know."[41]

Although *to possess knowledge* is a familiar phrase, al-Farabi is clear that the ownership of knowledge is earned through the discerning quality of an intellect willing to weigh and judge the quality of ideas. It is associated with the right to know but entails additional responsibilities that involve earning a claim to that knowledge. Al-Farabi is among those concerned with protecting learning from misuse and distortion. In his commentary on Plato's *Laws*, for example, he identifies how this philosopher "followed the practice

37. Al-Farabi, *Philosophy of Plato and Aristotle*, 81.

38. Ibid.

39. "The relation of the Active Intellect to man is like that of the Sun to vision," al-Farabi writes on this theme, adding that we are not only able to see by virtue of the sun but that our "vision sees the Sun itself which is the cause of its actually seeing": "On the Intellect," in *Classical Arabic Philosophy: An Anthology of Sources*, ed. Jon McGinnis and David C. Reisman (Indianapolis: Hackett, 2007), 84.

40. Cited by Davidson, *Alfarabi, Avicenna, and Averroës*, 51.

41. Al-Farabi, "On the Intellect," 115. Davidson adds on this question knowing everything: "To gain all possible thoughts is no small enterprise for a man of flesh and blood, but the medieval physical universe was finite, and Alfarabi here assumes that wholly comprehensible knowledge does lie within man's power" (49).

of using symbols, riddles, obscurity, and difficulty, so that science would not fall into the hands of those who do not deserve it and be deformed, or into the hands of one who does not know its worth or who uses it improperly."[42] Plato reserved learning for those "trained in that art itself" and "skilled in the science that is being discussed."[43] As stewards of the active intellect's gifts to humankind, the learned walk a fine line between, on the one hand, facilitating access through copying, translation, teaching, and commentary, and, on the other, restricting it to those who could be trusted and trained in its proper use (which I return to below).

During the eleventh century, two Muslim thinkers contributed much to the intellectual properties of learning: the first to the development of a scientific method, and the other to philosophical matters of intellect. The first is Ibn al-Haytham, who lived in Cairo during the early decades of the century. Ibn al-Haytham established a reputation in the study of optics for conducting what we would now call physics experiments. After conducting what is, in effect, a literature review of Euclid and Ptolemy on the topic, he developed a camera obscura to track light's physical properties while he worked out an aesthetic theory to account for the human experience of light.[44] He identified for the first time how objects are visible to us through our perception of the rays of light that reflected off those objects, which he represented geometrically from object to eye.[45] His influential *Book of Optics* was to be consulted in Arabic and Latin by mathematicians and philosophers down to the time of Johannes Kepler in the seventeenth century. His method of carefully building on and testing the work of others became a model of scientific practice in the West.[46]

In addition to breaking new ground in optics, Ibn al-Haytham drew on more recent astronomical observations to reanalyze Ptolemy's second-century

---

42. Al-Farabi, "Plato's Laws," trans. Muhsin Mahdi in *Medieval Political Philosophy: A Sourcebook*, ed. Ralph Lerner and Muhsin Mahdi (New York: Free Press, 1963), 85. Mahdi identifies this as "the only commentary by a Muslim author on a Platonic writing of which we possess the original Arabic text": "The Editio Princeps of Fārābī's Compendium Legum Platonis," *Journal of Near Eastern Studies* 20, no. 1 (1961): 1–2.

43. Al-Farabi, "Plato's Laws," 85.

44. Hans Belting traces the influence of Ibn al-Haytham's optical experiments and theory on the Renaissance refinement of perspective in art: *Florence and Baghdad: Renaissance Art and Arab Science* (Cambridge, MA: Harvard University Press, 2011), 102–11.

45. Peter Adamson, *Philosophy in the Islamic World: A History of Philosophy without any Gaps*, vol. 3 (Oxford: Oxford University Press, 2016), 82.

46. Huff, *Early Modern Science*, 90–91; A. I. Sabra, "Ibn al-Haytham's Revolutionary Project in Optics: The Achievement and the Obstacle," in *The Enterprise of Science in Islam: New Perspectives*, ed. Jan P. Hogendijk and Abdelhamid I. Sabra (Cambridge, MA: MIT Press, 2003), 42.

Almagest: "The contradiction in the configuration of the upper planets that is taken against him," Ibn al-Haytham wrote, "was due to the fact that he assumed the motions to take place in imaginary lines and circles and not in existent bodies."[47] The new observational techniques and standards of Islamic astronomers led to new, more accurate mathematical models of heavenly motion. These models are thought to have contributed to the Copernican revolution in the sixteenth century, even if Islamic astronomers did not seek to dislodge the earth from the center of the universe.

The other eleventh-century Islamic thinker I want to consider is the philosopher and physician known among Latin readers as Avicenna (Ibn Sina). A Persian from central Asia, and perhaps the greatest of Islamic philosophers of the period, Avicenna proved himself an adept student of astronomy, geology, metaphysics, medicine, psychology, optics, and other fields; moreover, he was a rare denier of alchemy's claims as a science. Among the details we have of Avicenna's early life is his gaining access to the library of the Samanid ruler Nuh ibn Mansur: "One day I asked permission to enter the library, look through it, and read its contents. He gave me permission and I was admitted to a building with many rooms. . . . I saw books whose very names are unknown to many and which I had never seen before nor have I seen since. I read those books, mastered their teaching, and realized how far each man had advanced in his science."[48] Avicenna's comments reaffirm how vital access to the intellectual commons of a library is to the mastery of this learned trade compared to the apprentice working with a single master.

Although Avicenna found himself caught up more than once in regime changes that played havoc with the patronage he received as a scholar, he still succeeded in making major contributions to the field of health and healing with his *Canon medicinae*. This compendium of medical wisdom and pharma-

47. Cited by Saliba, *Islamic Science*, 101. Saliba argues that "Classical Greek scientific texts could easily be acclimatized within the current Arabic science of the time, thus transforming the translation process into a simultaneous creative process as well" (18).

48. Cited by David C. Reisman, "Stealing Avicenna's Books: A Study of the Historical Sources for the Life and Times of Avicenna," in *Before and after Avicenna: Proceedings of the First Conference of the Avicenna Study Group*, ed. David C. Reisman and Ahmed H. Al-Rahim (Leiden: Brill, 2003), 121. Ibn Funduq, who composed a mid-twelfth-century biography of Avicenna, a century after the philosopher's death, adds what Reisman believes to be an apocryphal statement on Avicenna's hand in the fiery fate of this library: "It is agreed that this library was burned down and all the books were consumed. An adversary said that Abū ʿAlī [Avicenna] set fire to the library in order that those sciences and [their] precious knowledge would accrue to him alone and that credit for their intellectual benefits (*fawāʾid*) would be cut off from their proper authors" (122). Despite the slander, Ibn Funduq's accusation reinforces the extent to which authors were credited for the intellectual properties of their work, in terms of my book's theme.

cological advice was to one of the more influential and longstanding works translated from Arabic into Latin, serving university masters and students until well into the seventeenth century.[49] Beyond the *Canon*'s practical applications in treating the ill, it introduced philosophical distinctions in medicine between theory and practice: "When we say that practice proceeds from theory," Avicenna explains in *Canon*, it is important to realize "that these two aspects are both sciences," and that one science is needed for "the basic problems of knowledge" and one for "the mode of operation in these principles."[50]

In the realms of practice and theory, Avicenna relied on sharp observation and careful distinctions. With practice, he identified seven conditions for ascertaining a medical treatment's efficacy and sixteen sources of data— from imaginative data to suppositional data—crucial for arriving at conclusions "based on testing and proving."[51] In the case of theory, he was among the first to use the thought experiment or hypothetical case in natural philosophy.[52] And in the name of medical practice and bedside manner, he expanded the goal of physicians, from curing the ill to advising people on how to live healthy lives, an approach that is still very much with us to this day.[53]

In his philosophical work, Avicenna also grappled with Aristotle's treatment of the soul and intellect. He regarded the soul as a source of perfection for the body. He saw it taking shape shortly after a child is born, with the intellect free of innate ideas but open to investigating and abstracting concepts or "intelligibles" from external and internal data. "Man is naturally endowed," Avicenna writes, "to come into possession of knowledge and to perceive things

49. Raphaela Veit points out how Avicenna's *Canon* drew principally on Greek medical texts, as well as reflecting Indian, Persian, and some possible Chinese influences, while efforts were made in the fifteenth and sixteenth century that "padded it out with numerous references to its textual background": "Greek Roots, Arab Authoring, Latin Overlay," in *Vehicles of Transmission, Translation, and Transformation in Medieval Textual Culture*, ed. Robert Wisnovsky, Faith Wallis, Jamie C. Fumo, and Carlos Fraenkel (Turnhout, Belgium: Brepols, 2011), 354, 361.

50. Avicenna, *Canon*, trans. O. Cameron Gruner, in *A Source Book in Medieval Science*, ed. Edward Grant (Cambridge, MA: Harvard University Press, 1974), 716.

51. Cited by Dimitri Gutas, "The Empiricism of Avicenna," *Oriens* 40 (2012): 410. In contrast to Gutas's focus on Avicenna's empiricism, Dag Nikolaus Hasse points to how Avicenna allows for "two ways to acquire universal forms: either by abstraction from particular forms [i.e., empiricist], or by directly receiving them from the active intellect [i.e., Aristotelian]": "Avicenna's Epistemological Optimism," in *Interpreting Avicenna: Critical Essays*, ed. Peter Adamson (Cambridge: Cambridge University Press, 2013), 111.

52. Taneli Kukkonen, "Ibn Sīnā and the Early History of Thought Experiments," *Journal of the History of Philosophy* 52, no. 3 (2014): 433.

53. Harold J. Cook, "Medicine," in *Early Modern Science*, ed. Katharine Park and Lorraine Daston, vol. 3 of *The Cambridge History of Science* (Cambridge: Cambridge University Press, 2006), 409.

by way of the senses and then by way of estimation."[54] This emphasis on the individual's active role in taking hold of a knowledge gleaned from the world gave Avicenna's philosophy an empiricist grounding, setting him apart from al-Kindī and al-Farabi. In analyzing Avicenna's stance, Dimitri Gutas, Yale professor of Islamic Studies, compares the Islamic philosopher to the empiricist John Locke, who similarly referred to how "Experience furnisheth the Understanding with Ideas."[55]

For my purposes, however, the resemblance of note here is between Avicenna's ideas on learning and Locke's theory of property and labor: "He hath mixed his *Labor* with, and joyned to it something that is his own," Locke writes in *Two Treatises of Government*, "and thereby makes it his *Property*."[56] While I discuss the application of Locke's theory to intellectual property in chapter 11, what can be said here in Lockean terms is that Avicenna offers an image of the scholar laboring over a world given in common, resulting in works in which the scholar "might come to have a *property*," in Locke's language, or come "into possession of knowledge," as Avicenna writes, with these works ultimately intended for the benefit of others, or as Locke puts it, "to increase the common stock of mankind."[57]

It should be clear that this Aristotelean wrestling with soul and intellect has much to do with establishing learning's place in the world. These philosophers are offering a commentary, above all, on the soul and intellect of the scholar. Not surprisingly, then, they lend a particular weight to the work of the learned. They set it apart from other practices by giving the intellect a place in the very structure of "the human soul," as Avicenna set it out, between "a faculty related to scientific investigation and so is called the theoretical intellect" for determining "what is necessary, possible and impossible," and "a faculty related to action and so is called the practical intellect," which determines "what is right, wrong, and the permissible."[58] Avicenna was a

---

54. Cited by Gutas, "The Empiricism of Avicenna," 406. Sander Wopke de Boer, *The Science of the Soul: The Commentary Tradition on Aristotle's De Anima, c. 1260–c. 1360* (Leuven, Belgium: Leuven University Press, 2013), 23–24.

55. Gutas, "The Empiricism of Avicenna," 424–25. John Locke, *Essay concerning Human Understanding*, ed. Peter H. Nidditch (Oxford: Oxford University Press, 1975), 2.1.4 105. Gutas speculates that Locke, who likely studied Arabic as part of his medical education, may have encountered Avicenna's work amid the increased interest in Arabic literature during that time (424–25).

56. John Locke, *Two Treatises of Government*, ed. Peter Laslett (Cambridge: Cambridge University Press, 1988), 2.27, 306.

57. Ibid., 2.2 304, 2.37 312; Avicenna is cited by Gutas, "The Empiricism of Avicenna," 406.

58. Ibn Sīnā [Avicenna], "The Soul," in *Classical Arabic Philosophy* 187.

great champion of those whom he described as "the [learned] individual whose soul is strengthened by such intense purity . . . that he blazes with intuition," which is to say "intuition about all or most scientific investigation."[59] And in this case, no one burned more brightly than Avicenna. "The scope of Avicenna's authority overcame the boundaries of the disciplines taught in universities, and the borders of academic faculties," writes Amos Bertolacci, professor of Islamic philosophy at the Scuola Normale Superiore di Pisa. "His thought also entered other fields of Latin culture, like literature (as in the case of Dante Alighieri, among others), and society in general (as its traces in ecclesiastic documents witness)."[60]

These properties of intellect take on a further radical twist in the hands of our final Muslim commentator on Aristotle's *On the Soul*, namely, Averroës (Ibn Rushd). Averroës was a twelfth-century polymath born in Córdoba, the great center of learning in al-Andalus.[61] Islam had established itself in the Iberian peninsula early in the eighth century with learning playing a strong role in the cultural life of many communities there. Córdoba's Great Mosque was endowed by the caliph with teaching positions, while the local schools were free to the young.[62] The collection of books in the Royal Library in the Old Palace (*Alcazar*), which had been established in the tenth century, was by then far greater than any library in Europe. It had been stocked by book buyers in Cairo, Baghdad, Damascus, Alexandria, and elsewhere; the library was equipped with a catalog of its treasures that ran to many volumes.[63]

59. Ibid., 205.

60. Amos Bertolacci, "The Reception of Avicenna in Latin Medieval Culture," *Interpreting Avicenna*, 242.

61. María Rosa Menocal explains that the German nun Hroswitha of Gandersheim named Córdoba an "ornament of the world" in 995, after learning of its splendors from a Muslim ambassador to the German court of Otto the Great: *The Ornament of the World: How Muslims, Jews and Christians Created a Culture of Tolerance in Medieval Spain* (Boston: Little, Brown, 2002), 32.

62. Robert Hillenbrand, "'Ornament of the World': Medieval Córdoba as a Cultural Centre," in *Legacy of Muslim Spain*, ed. Salma Khadra Jayyusi and Manuela Marín (Leiden: Brill, 1992), 120–22.

63. Dorothee Metlitzki, *The Matter of Araby in Medieval England* (New Haven, CT: Yale University Press, 1977), 10. Damascus' Ashrafiya Library affords perhaps the most accurate book count with its thirteenth-century catalog listing over two thousand works; Konrad Hirschler, *Medieval Damascus: Plurality and Diversity in an Arabic Library, The Ashrafiya Library Catalogue* (Edinburgh: Edinburgh University Press, 2016). Martin Levey writes of how millions of volumes may have been in circulation during his period across the Islamic empire, noting that in Córdoba alone, scholars boasted of a library of 250,000 books, although much of it was to be lost: "Owing to the depredations of various groups many libraries were burned and otherwise destroyed" ("Mediaeval Arabic Bookmaking and Its Relation to Early Chemistry and Pharmacology," *Transactions of the American Philosophical Society*, New Series 52, no. 4 [1962]: 6). George F. Hourani reports that the

In such a setting, Averroës created a body of philosophical work, with much of it given to explicating the works of Aristotle. He was referred to as simply "the commentator," much as al-Farabi was known as the "second teacher," both in relation to Aristotle. The translation of Averroës' works into Latin began within decades of his death in 1198. His Aristotelian commentaries were part of the university curriculum during these institutions' earliest years, remaining a part of the curriculum up until the sixteenth century.[64] To gain a sense of what he offered a master who was about to teach a course on Aristotle's *Metaphysics*, consider the opening of his commentary on this book: "We shall start by supplying information on the aim of this science, its usefulness, its parts, its place [in the order of the sciences] and its relationship [with the other sciences], in short, we begin with that the consideration of which may help to get access to this science."[65] Students and teachers alike must have appreciated his systematic, threefold approach to the works of Aristotle: Averroës began with a summary of the philosopher's ideas; then he provided a paraphrase of the work in its entirety; and finally he created a much-revered "long commentary" (*tafsīr*) featuring a line-by-line analysis of five of Aristotle's major works, which also took into account others' commentaries (much as Averroës' commentaries were the subject of other commentaries in Hebrew and other languages). Of these long commentaries, the one he prepared later in life on Aristotle's *On the Soul* introduced a radical interpretation of how the intellect operates between individual souls and ideas held in common. Where others had held that an individual's material intellect was able to receive and absorb ideas that emanated from the external active intellect, Averroës posited that the material intellect, which contains our ideas about the world, is not particular to each of us but is a singular, eternal entity. Individuals can, as he sees it, take more or less part in this external material intellect through study and cogitation that enable

Córdoba library catalog ran to forty-four volumes, even as he is cautious about estimating book totals: "The Early Growth of the Secular Sciences in Andalusia," *Studia Islamica*, no. 32 (1970): 149. Hillenbrand compares this great monastic library at St. Gall, which had six hundred volumes: "'Ornament of the World'", 121. In the fourteenth century, the university in Paris had two thousand manuscripts in its collection: Huff, *Early Modern Science*, 76.

64. "During the fifty years around 1500 numerous Averroistic texts relating to Aristotle were newly translated from the extant Hebrew versions into Latin": Charles B. Schmitt, *Aristotle and the Renaissance* (Cambridge, MA: Harvard University Press, 1983), 23.

65. Averroës, *On Aristotle's* Metaphysics: *An Annotated Translation of the So-Called "Epitome,"* ed. Rüdiger Arnzen (Berlin: Walter de Gruyter, 2010), 21. Attesting to his commentary's value in the West, Burnett notes that more copies of Averroës survive in Latin than in Arabic: "Translating Activity," 1050.

them to share in its ideas: "We have held the opinion that the material intellect is one for all human beings and also on the basis of this we have held
the opinion that the human species is eternal. . . . The material intellect must
not be devoid of the natural principles common to the whole human species, namely, the primary propositions and singular conceptions common to
all."[66] Such an account, which became known as monopsychism, draws on
the confidence that people feel in thinking that others will reason their way
to the same conclusion (or theorem) that they have reached. Averroës builds
his analysis on what is common and shared in human thought, and on how
the world is rendered intelligible across centuries and languages, even as
one's thinking can be refined or redirected, reflecting a greater grasp of what
the material intellect holds and makes available to all.

Averroës points to how the realization "that what is known is the same
in the teacher and the student in this way caused Plato to believe that learning was recollection."[67] For Averroës, teacher and student are not recalling
innate Platonic forms out of which ideas are fashioned, but are tapping
into "the primary propositions and singular conceptions" (which is to say,
the particular ideas) that constitute this external material intellect. People
come to these ideas in the singular, external intellect like so many works in
a great library that is potentially open to all but for which any given volume
or set of ideas can be difficult to grasp and fathom. To gain a thorough sense
of this intellect is, for Averroës, to "made like unto God" in terms of understanding humanity, given that "beings are nothing but his [God's] knowledge and the cause of beings is nothing but his knowledge. How marvelous is that order and how mysterious is that mode of being!"[68] It may seem
marvelously mysterious, indeed, but for Averroës it was where the logic
of human reasoning led. In *On the Harmony of Religions and Philosophy*, he
writes, "the Law urges us to observe creation by means of reason and demands the knowledge thereof through reason. This is evident from different verses of the Qur'an."[69]

66. Averroës, *Long Commentary on the* De anima *of Aristotle*, trans. Richard C. Taylor (New
Haven, CT: Yale University Press, 2009), 322.

67. Ibid., 329.

68. Ibid.

69. Averroës, "On the Harmony of Religions and Philosophy," trans. Mohammed Jamil-al-
Rahman (1921), in *Medieval Sourcebook*, Fordham University, New York, online. Etienne Gilson
credits Averroës's influential defense of Aristotle as "the origins of modern rationalism" in the West
and judges his "conscious reaction against the theologism of the Arabian divines" as influential on
"the evolution even of Christian philosophy": *Reason and Revelation in the Middle Ages* (New York:
Charles Scribner, 1938), 37, 38.

Not surprisingly, this sort of radical mix of philosophy and religion was attacked by other Islamic scholars, as was his social critique of Muslim life, given his stance that, in his words, "our society allows no scope for the development of women's talents. . . . From this stems the misery that pervades our cities."[70] The most vehement of his critics succeeded in having him banished from Córdoba and his works publicly burned. While he was able to find political favor again, some years before his death, his writings remained controversial within Islam. He proved more of an influence on Christian and Jewish thinkers. His work gave rise, most notably, to a group of Latin Averroists at the University in Paris during the thirteenth century, who faced their own set of critics including Thomas Aquinas, who was appalled at Averroës' robbing humanity of the individuality that formed the basis of the soul's immortality (see chapter 7). Averroës may have taken the communal quality of learning too far with his singular intellect. Yet the commentator did much to make a notable interpretation of Aristotle's works universally available across Europe, which forms its own demonstration of his most intriguing and notorious idea (which was still under consideration by some Europeans into the seventeenth century).[71]

Despite the attacks on his work, Avicenna was prepared to defend the right of "the brothers [on] seeing this work [of his] to write down their questions, and perhaps by this the truth concerning this will be found, if I have not yet found it."[72] Still, the censure faced by Averroës, Avicenna, and other Islamic philosophers left them leery of "the unlearned classes," as Averroës names them.[73] Avicenna had earlier warned that "it is not proper for any man to reveal that he possesses knowledge he is hiding from the common people. Indeed he should not even permit an intimation of this. Rather he should inform them of God's majesty and greatness through symbols."[74] Averroës held that "demonstrative books should be banned to the unqualified but not the learned."[75] He condemns Al-Ghazali who "wanted to increase the

70. Cited by Hillenbrand, "'Ornament of the World,'" 122.

71. For Averroës' influence on seventeenth-century English and Italian thinking, including on the "single soul" or "common soul," see Sarah Hutton, "The Cambridge Platonists and Averroes," in *Renaissance Averroism and Its Aftermath: Arabic Philosophy in Early Modern Europe*, eds. Anna Akasoy and Guido Giglioni (Dordrecht, Netherlands: Springer, 2013), 197–211.

72. Averroës, *Long Commentary*, 315.

73. Ibn Rushd [Averroës], "The Decisive Treatise," in *Classical Arabic Philosophy*, 322.

74. Cited by Dimitri Gutas, *Avicenna and the Aristotelian Tradition: Introduction to Reading Avicenna's Philosophical Works* (Leiden: Brill, 2014), 339.

75. Ibn Rushd, "The Decisive Treatise," in *Classical Arabic Philosophy*, 322. Demonstrative books would likely include syllogistic reasoning and other forms of Aristotelian logic.

number of learned men, but in fact increased the number of the corrupted not the learned! As a result one group came to slander philosophy, another to slander religion."[76] The double-edged sword of this risk—to philosophy and religion—suggests that open access was not the goal of this philosophizing. Averroës advises that "a skillful doctor . . . cures the diseases of all the people by prescribing for them rules that can be commonly accepted"; he knows that "he is unable to make them all doctors."[77] (My support for open access to philosophy and medical research, I should add in light of Averroës' objections, is not about the trade-off between treating the ill or making them doctors. It is about treating the ill while respecting the right to learn, without qualifications, about such treatments.)

These Islamic philosophers, from al-Kindī to Averroës, created complex intellectual orders in their efforts to reconcile soul and world. They agreed on some of the properties of ideas, including their potential for being common to all, and thus belonging to no one. Through their labor and intuition, however, they were willing to take possession of these ideas to help others (if only the worthy) find their way to greater understanding, or to collectively see the ideas through to some kind of completion, much as al-Kindī aspired to do with mathematics. They saw their work as rendering intelligible what was given in common to the human intellect by the prime mover. The process began for these Islamic scholars by bringing into the Arabic language a vast series of learned works that had been composed in (or translated into) Greek, Aramaic, Persian, Syriac, and Hebrew. During the twelfth century, this productive infusion of ideas from one culture into another was about to happen again, only this time in Latin.

THE LATIN TRANSLATION MOVEMENT

Although Gerbert introduced elements of Arabic learning into a European classroom in the tenth century, the first known translations of an Arabic text into Latin were completed by Constantine the African in the eleventh century.

76. Ibid.
77. Ibid. Leo Strauss describes the protective writing strategies of those facing persecution for their independence of thought, placing Avicenna and Averroës in the company of Socrates, Plato, Aristotle, Maimonides, Grotius, Descartes, Hobbes, Spinoza, Locke, Bayle, Wolff, Montesquieu, Voltaire, Rousseau, Lessing, and Kant: "Persecution and the Art of Writing," *Social Research* 8, no. 4 (1941): 499. Strauss also points out how al-Farabi highlighted Plato's ability to "safely tell a very dangerous truth provided one tells it in the proper surroundings": "How Farabi Read Plato's Laws," in *What Is Political Philosophy? And Other Studies* (Chicago: University of Chicago Press, 1959), 136.

While a number of Constantine's translations have survived, our knowledge of his life is based on a solitary account a century after his death, which may explain why it resembles a heroic Christian conversion tale. As the story begins, a Muslim merchant from Carthage is plying his trade at the court of the Lombard prince of Salerno. The man learned that many who traveled to Salerno to become physicians were not able to find medical works to support their learning. In what might seem inspired opportunism but proved to be something nobler, he returned to Kairouan, a North African Islamic intellectual center, where he is said to have spent the next few years gathering up copies of Arabic medical works from local physicians.

After a perilous sea voyage that damaged and destroyed some of the manuscripts, he arrived back in Salerno around 1065. He quickly converted to Christianity, took the name Constantine, and joined the Monte Cassino monastery north of Salerno (where Benedict is thought to have composed his *Rule*). The highly literate monks of the scriptorium likely helped Constantine translate those Arabic medical texts into Latin that had survived the journey. He translated Hippocrates' *Aphorisms* and *Prognostics*, Galen's commentaries on Hippocrates and his *Grand Art* (*Megatechne*), and medical works by Algizar (Ibn al-Jazzar) and Isaac Israeli.[78] Constantine's approach to translation is best described as rough adaptation. The translations were intended for physicians seeking to heal the ill, rather than the scholar hoping to learn more about Greek and Islamic medicine. Constantine sometimes identifies himself in the text as the translator while suggesting at other times that he is the author.[79] He was happy to credit Galen and Hippocrates when it suited him, rather than, say, the Persian source from whose text he pulled the words of these two Greeks.

One particularly influential translation was that of the *Book of Fevers* by the tenth-century Jewish physician Isaac Israeli. It remained a part of the medical curriculum at Montpellier, Paris, Bologna, and Oxford until the fourteenth century.[80] This "Constantinian program of translation," in the judgment of Michael McVaugh, a University of North Carolina historian, "did not

78. Michael McVaugh, "Constantine the African," in *Complete Dictionary of Scientific Biography*, vol. 3 (Detroit: Scribner's Sons, 2008), 393.

79. Herbert Bloch credits Constantine and two associates, Afflacius and Atto, with twenty-six translated works or compilations: *Monte Cassino in the Middle Ages* (Cambridge, MA: Harvard University, 1986), 130.

80. Lola Ferre and Raphaela Veit, "The Textual Traditions of Isaac Israeli's *Book on Fevers* in Arabic, Latin, Hebrew, and Spanish," *Aleph: Historical Studies in Science and Judaism* 9, no. 2 (2009): 314. Ferre and Raphaela refer to how the *Book of Fevers* stopped being used "when new translations of medical texts done in Toledo—notably Avicenna's *Canon*—entered the universities" (ibid.)

merely enlarge the sphere of practical competence of the Salernitan physicians; it had the added effect of stimulating them to try to organize the new material into a wider, philosophical framework."[81] Constantine's impulse to share Arab knowledge with others who could benefit from it inspired a number of Latin scholars to develop a knowledge of Arabic, as well as work with Muslim and Jewish writers of Arabic, in undertaking more formal, scholarly transfer of knowledge from Arabic into Latin. What Constantine had initiated, linking monastic scriptorium and medical school, would grow into a flow of Muslim and Jewish learning more generally that was to find its way into the Christian West.

The Jewish physician Moses Sephardi offers a second take on the conversion-translation story. Moses had perhaps been a rabbi in al-Andalus, but at any rate converted to Christianity in 1106 at the age of forty-four. He took on the Latin name Petrus Alfonsi and made his way to England, where his newfound religion—further affirmed by his book *Dialogue Against the Jews*—served him well as court physician to Henry I.[82] He was best known for his *Rule of Life* (*Disciplina clericalis*), which introduced Christians to Arabic thought and literature.[83] But he also undertook important Latin translations, including the ninth-century *Astronomical Tables* (*Zīdj*) by al-Khwarazmi, which recorded the position in Baghdad of the sun, moon, and five planets in relation to the calendar and astrology, as well as latitudes and longitudes for 2,402 locations on earth.[84]

Petrus demonstrated how the techniques of Islamic astronomy and astrology could be used to calculate local tides and harvest times, as well as optimal times for bloodletting and cauterizing a wound. This mix of astronomy, astrology, and medicine was another of the Islamic influences that pervaded European healthcare for centuries.[85] In his letters, Petrus speaks of a universal intellectual compulsion behind his work: "Since it is proper that all those who

81. McVaugh, "Constantine the African," 394.

82. Petrus Alfonsi, *Dialogue against the Jews*, trans. Irven M. Resnick (Washington, DC: Catholic University of America Press, 2006), 42. On Petrus' contribution to the myth of Islamic idolatry, see Bernard Septimus, "Petrus Alfonsi on the Cult of Mecca," *Speculum* 56, no. 3 (1981): 517–33.

83. Metlitzki describes the *Rule* as compiled "partly from the sayings of Arabic philosophers, partly from Arabic proverbs, and Arabian tales," and, as such, that it stands "as a milestone in the development of medieval literature": *Matter of Araby*, 18–19.

84. John Victor Tolan, *Petrus Alfonsi and His Medieval Readers* (Gainesville: University of Florida Press, 1993), 55. Tolan points out that while Adelard, who retranslated the *Zīdj* in 1126, is "more careful in his calculations . . . there are places, too, where Alfonsi's figures are correct and Adelard's are not" (61).

85. Tolan, *Petrus Alfonsi*, 174.

have drunk of any philosophical nectar to love each other, and that anyone who might have anything rare, precious, and useful, which is unknown to others, should impart it generously."[86] Although he was not above feeding the prejudices of his readers against Islam and Judaism, as noted, Petrus called on the learned to generously share what is precious and useful.

Petrus' contemporary, Adelard of Bath, was another who brought together translation and application from Islamic science. Adelard began around 1100 to serve as a tutor at the cathedral school of Laon, he set out while still as a young man on a seven-year quest of *Arabum studia*, traveling through Salerno, Sicily, Misis (Turkey), and Antioch. Although his skills in Arabic have been questioned, he is credited with translating scientific, mathematical, and musical works, which contributed to his unquestioned mastery of quadratic equations, geometry, and astrology.[87] He appears to have conducted medical experiments based on Arabic and Hebrew texts that had been translated into Latin by Constantine the African and others.[88] His own translation of Euclid's *Elements* included supplemental lessons in geometry that he prepared as part of his commentary. He has been called the first English scientist, and he was certainly the country's number one astrologer, given the horoscopes that he cast for those at court.[89] Adelard was also one of learning's great public advocates. In his best-known work of the time, his semiautobiographical *Quaestiones Naturales,* he presents a dialogue between himself, as one given to "investigate the studies of the Arabs," and his irreverent nephew. Adelard dares to oppose the richness of his engagement with Arab teachers to his nephew's captivation with the traditional authority of the church: "For I have learned one thing from my Arab masters, with reason as guide, but you another: you follow a halter, being enthralled by the picture of authority."[90] Among the many parts of that one thing he learned, Adelard makes clear, were Islamic methods of experimentation and observation that gave shape to his own studies and scientific reasoning.

86. Petrus Alfonsi, "Epistola ad peripateticos," in Tolan, *Petrus Alfonsi and His Medieval Readers,* 172–73.

87. Adelard of Bath, *Conversations with His Nephew: On the Same and the Different, Questions on Natural Science, and On Birds,* trans. Charles Burnett (Cambridge: Cambridge University Press, 1998), 3:90, 107. "Adelard's conception of *Arabum studia* was ... nourished—if anything—by *lack* of direct acquaintance with Arabic scholarship" (ibid.).

88. A. C. Crombie, *Robert Grosseteste and the Origins of Experimental Science 1100-1700* (Oxford: Oxford University Press, 1953), 23, 29.

89. Louise Cochrane, *Adelard of Bath: The First English Scientist* (London: British Museum Press, 1994). See Burnett, "Translating Activity," 1038.

90. Adelard of Bath, *Conversations,* 103.

The translation of Arabic texts into Latin was the principal but not the only channel through which this learning entered the West during the period. In the twelfth century, James of Venice and Burgundio of Pisa traveled to Constantinople, where they were able to find a good deal of Aristotle in the original Greek which they translated into Latin. Other scholars sought out and translated the Greek works to be found in Antioch, southern Italy, and Sicily. Yet in the case of Aristotle, there is no mistaking the role played by the commentaries of the Islamic philosophers in making the Greek philosopher so interesting—and so much easier—to teach.[91]

One of the thriving centers for the translation of this wealth of Aristotelian commentary into Latin was the Castilian city of Toledo. The Christians had retaken Toledo without a battle in 1085, on the promise of Alfonso VI, King of Leon and Castile, to protect the religious rights of the city's Muslims and to preserve the city as the center for learning that it had been for al-Andalus. King Alfonso had declared himself "Emperor of Spain and the Two Faiths" (although it clearly should have been three, given the significant number of Jews in the region). His plan for Toledo may have went awry, as its principal mosque was forcibly converted into a cathedral, but as Charles Burnett, professor at the Warburg Institute, explains, "the Islamic élite had left the city, but a rump of learned Muslims may have remained in Toledo."[92] It was not long before the translation of Arabic works into Latin was underway, led initially by works of astrology favored by the kings of Europe.[93] Often working from Arabic texts from the many remaining Islamic libraries, learned Christians, Jews, Mozarabs, and Mudéjars (Muslims living in Christian lands) gathered together and shared their studies of mathematics, astronomy, and other sciences. Toledo gained a reputation as a cultural contact zone. It became a destination city for the young and learned, whose curiosity was piqued by the rumors of great works awaiting translation.[94] Some travelers took up residence and joined in the translation

91. Charles Burnett, "Arabic into Latin: The Reception of Arabic Philosophy into Western Europe," in *The Cambridge Companion to Arabic Philosophy*, ed. Peter Adamson and Richard C. Taylor (Cambridge: Cambridge University Press, 2005), 375.

92. Charles Burnett, "Communities of Learning in Twelfth-Century Toledo," in *Communities of Learning: Networks and the Shaping of Intellectual Identity in Europe, 1100–1500*, ed. Constant J. Mews and John N. Crossley (Turnhout: Brepols, 2011), 10.

93. Ibid., 11.

94. Dodds, Menocal, and Balbale note that twelfth-century Toledo was "poised to become the charismatic center of European intellectual life" and "a warehouse of the great books of mathematics and the sciences": *The Arts of Intimacy*, 202. "Alfred [the Englishman] evidently worked to the dictation of a Mozarab or Jew, turning the text into Latin while the whole or part of it was read

movement; others made quick copies of existing translations. No one left, it seems, without carrying copies of Latin translations, which soon spread throughout European centers of trade and learning.

By the mid-twelfth century, those translating Arabic texts into Latin were among Toledo's principal trades. It was not that such work paid well. For while the company of translators undertook commissions from learned visitors and placed copies of their work with booksellers, records show that they also had to work as tutors to the children of the wealthy and served in civic and church positions. The translators did have something of a patron saint in Archbishop Raymond of Toledo. During his time as church leader, from 1126 to 1152, Raymond supported their work, building his own great Latin archiepiscopal library in the process.[95]

Foremost among the translators, in prolificacy, quality, and modesty, was Gerard of Cremona, a canon of Toledo's cathedral and a physician. He prepared Latin translations of Arabic editions of Ptolemy, Theodosius, Menelaus, and Archimedes, which were often preferred by scholars over translations made from the original Greek.[96] Gerard arrived in Toledo around 1144, having been inspired to make the journey from Italy by rumors that Arabic copies of Claudius Ptolemy's *Almagest*, the legendary second-century work of mathematics and astronomy, were to be found there. He soon acquired two copies of the work, only to spend perhaps a decade, as his Arabic gradually improved, on revising and refining his Latin translation of this work. Given his training as a physician and likely contact with Muslim doctors, Gerard also translated a number of important medical works by Galen from Arabic (some of which are no longer available in the original Greek), as well as al-Kindī's medical work and Avicenna's *Canon medicinae*, with the *Canon* destined to have an especially long run in universities as well as in popularized forms.[97]

---

and explained to him in the vernacular Spanish [Castilian] from the Arabic copy that was being used as the original": Metlitzki, *Matter of Araby*, 41.

95. Menocal, *Ornament of the World*, 195. Burnett identifies the remaining question of "who organized the production and who paid for it" with the West's translation movement more generally: "The Coherence of the Arabic-Latin Translation Program in Toledo in the Twelfth Century," in *Arabic into Latin in the Middle Ages: The Translators and Their Intellectual and Social Context* (London: Routledge, 2009), 7:269–70.

96. Charles Burnett, "The Transmission of Arabic Astronomy via Antioch and Pisa in the Second Quarter of the Twelfth Century," in *The Enterprise of Science in Islam: New Perspectives*, ed. Jan P. Hogendijk and Abdelhamid I. Sabra (Cambridge, MA: MIT Press, 2003), 42.

97. "For about the first two hundred years after its introduction into university curricula in the thirteenth century, the *Canon*, although subjected to occasional criticism, was generally and on the whole rightly esteemed as a sophisticated systematization and summary of almost all available medical learning. By about the mid-seventeenth century, despite the Canon's great historical importance, its irrelevance to current developments in European physiology was clearly appar-

Gerard also prepared the first Latin edition of al-Khwarizmi's *The Compendious Book on Calculation by Completion and Balancing*. It not only introduced the practical mathematical powers of algebra to the West (with translations of other Arabic texts introducing trigonometry and advanced geometry), but was the first to offer a systematic treatment of decimal notation.[98] Al-Khwarizmi's goal had been to introduce what was "easiest and most useful in arithmetic," as the Islamic mathematician put it, "such as men constantly require in cases of inheritance, legacies, partitions, lawsuits, and trade, and in all their dealings with one another, or where the measuring of lands, the digging of canals, [or] geometrical computations . . . are concerned."[99] It is hard to imagine promising anything more mathematically useful at the time, and as for "easiest," well, it may have been for al-Khwarizmi. In astronomy, health, and mathematics, the translation project was less about the rarified classics than the practical and the needed. These were works of demonstrable value, which gave the translation movement its impetus and led to the copying and diffusion of these works throughout Europe.

No less significantly, Gerard worked with "shadow" assistants to bring much of Aristotle into Latin from Arabic, including the *Posterior Analytics*, *Physics*, *On the Heavens*, *On Generation and Corruption*, and *Meteorology*. They also translated the *Book of Causes*, the authorship of which was later downgraded to the Pseudo-Aristotle, although the book still proved an influential contribution to philosophy.[100] Gerard also translated a number of commentaries on Aristotle, some of which had originated in Greek during antiquity, while others were composed by Gerard's contemporary Averroës, working in Córdoba, a couple of hundred miles south of Toledo (which did not fall to the Christian Reconquista until 1236).

The translations of Aristotle, as well as the commentaries, helped to establish the Greek philosopher as "the master of those who know," as Dante put it at the turn of the thirteenth century. Intellectual histories of Europe

---

ent": Nancy G. Siraisi, *Avicenna in Renaissance Italy: The Canon and Medical Teaching in Italian Universities after 1500* (Princeton, NJ: Princeton University Press, 1987), 6. Excerpts and paraphrases of Avicenna also found their way into popular medical works, such as *Prognosticacion, Drawen Out of the Bookes of Ipocras [Hippocrates], Avicen [Avicenna], and Other Notable Auctours of Physycke, Shewynge the Daunger of Dyvers Syckenesses* (London: Robert Wyer, c. 1545).

98. Saliba, *Islamic Science*, 17; Metlitzki, *Matter of Araby*, 35. Al-Khwarizmi originated the concept of an *algorithm*, with the Latin word based on his name.

99. Cited by Starr, *Lost Enlightenment*, 169.

100. Edward Grant points out that *The Book of Causes* attracted commentaries from Albertus Magnus and Thomas Aquinas: *The Foundations of Modern Science in the Middle Ages: Their Religious, Institutional and Intellectual Contexts* (Cambridge: Cambridge University Press, 1996), 31.

through the High Middle Ages make such frequent reference to "Aristotle and the Arabian commentators" that the phrase might be mistaken for the name of a medieval music group.[101] The educational force of this commentary tradition is summed up by Charles Barnett, professor of the history of Islamic influences in Europe at the Warburg Institute: "Arabic texts, therefore, contributed massively to the building up of a coherent curriculum of Aristotelian philosophy."[102] This scale and scope of this new educational program in the sciences and philosophy cried out, as I argue in the next chapter, for a new institutional form in which it could be effectively studied and taught.

All told, Gerard was involved in the translation of at least eighty-five works in medicine, astronomy, mathematics, optics, logic geometry, and natural philosophy, with more than half of them reflecting Islamic authorship. Yet, in the forty years devoted to this work, he did not place his name on a single translation.[103] Fortunately, not long after his death, his self-styled students prepared a list to honor his achievement. They were asserting, in effect, one of learning's principal intellectual property rights (and responsibilities) in the crediting of the labor that goes into authorship, translation, editing, and indexing: "Lest, then, master Gerard of Cremona lie hidden under the darkness of silence," his students wrote, "lest he lose the favor of the renown that he has merited, lest through presumptuous theft an alien heading be affixed to the books translated by him—especially since he himself inscribed none of them with his name—all the works translated by him ... have been listed very carefully by his students."[104] The students point to the service that such accreditation of authorship and translation provides to readers: "So that anyone who is an admirer," the students of Gerard added, "looking

101. References to "Aristotle and the Arabian commentators" are found in Maurice de Wulf, "The Teaching of Philosophy and the Classification of the Sciences in the Thirteenth Century," *Philosophical Review* 27, no. 4 (1918): 368; Burnett, "Arabic into Latin," 380; James Bass Mullinger, *From the Earliest Times to the Royal Injunctions of 1535*, vol. 1 of *The University of Cambridge* (Cambridge: Cambridge University Press, 1873), 175; and Livingstone Thompson, *Modern Science* (Bern: Peter Lang, 2009), 30. They are not to be mistaken for "the pseudo-Aristotle and his Arabian commentators": Brother Azarias, *Aristotle and the Christian Church* (London: Kegan Paul, Trench, 1888), 52. Dante places Aristotle in "Circle one: Limbo (Virtuous pagans)" of the Inferno: "Aristotle, the master of those who know / Ringed by the great souls of philosophy / ... Hippocrates, Galen, Avicenna / And Averroës of the Great Commentary": *Inferno of Dante Alighieri*, trans. John Ciardi (New York: New American Library, 1982), 4:31.

102. Charles Burnett, "Arabic-Latin Translation," 375. Scott L. Montgomery describes how "pedagogic" editions were generally favored for translation, having been "corrected, edited, and sometimes reorganized or even partly rewritten for students": *Science in Translation: Movement of Knowledge through Cultures and Time* (Chicago: University of Chicago Press, 2000), 157–58.

103. Starr, *Lost Enlightenment*, 168; Montgomery, *Science in Translation*, 155.

104. Cited by Burnett, "Arabic-Latin Translation," 254–55.

for one of his works, through the lists he might find it more quickly and become more confident about it."[105] This accreditation is not about, they assert, "clutching at clouds and vanities."[106] It is about recognizing Gerard as the anonymous handmaid of this great transfer of learning to the Latin West.

A second outstanding figure among Toledian translators, and sometime collaborator of Gerard, is Dominicus Gundissalinus, archdeacon of Segovia and resident of Toledo from 1162 to 1181. Gundissalinus' circle included a number of Jewish scholars, most notably the philosopher and historian Avendauth who had fled persecution by the Almohads when they became the rulers of al-Andalus. Gundissalinus, Avendauth, and others saw to the Latin translation of many works from Arabic, including the commentaries on Aristotle's *On the Soul* by al-Kindī, Avicenna, and Averroës. Given how these works are on human intellect, it is worth noting how this additional act of translation—much as with commentary, critique, and citation—demonstrates a further regard for the properties of texts involving both qualities and rights. The translation recognizes and respects the work of the original author, while opening it for a whole new set of readers.

In their translation of Avicenna's *On the Soul*, Gundissalinus and Avendauth add a dedication that emphasizes how valuable this Graeco-Arabic wrestling with soul and intellect is for the state of Christianity. They honor Archbishop John of Toledo's support, while explaining that they had "taken care of your demand to translate this book on the soul by the philosopher Avicenna, in order that, through your generosity and my work, the Latins may attain certainty about . . . [the] true reasons that the soul exists."[107] They comment on how the archbishop regards the Islamic philosopher's work as a theological corrective for "those [Christians] who have abandoned themselves to the senses."[108] The translation movement had the effect of raising interest in a work's intellectual properties, as well as the philosopher's project. There may be something universal about a single thought that can serve Islam and Christianity alike, given shared belief in one God, but still, the translator works to preserve, and open access to, the distinctive intellectual properties that it is believed to embody in one language and then another.

105. Cited by ibid.
106. Cited by ibid., 255.
107. Cited by Alexander Fidora, "From Arabic into Latin into Hebrew: Aristotelian Psychology and Its Contribution to the Rationalisation of Theological Traditions," in *Philosophical Psychology in Arabic Thought and the Latin Aristotelianism of the 13th century*, ed. Luis Xavier López-Farjeat and Jörg Alejandro Tellkamp (Paris: Vrin, 2013), 19.
108. Cited by ibid.

Gundissalinus, however, did not let it go at translating these works. In his efforts to bring greater reason to bear on an understanding of the soul, he prepared a compilation of his own and others' ideas on this theme in *Tractatus de anima*. He brought in Avicenna, as well as Jewish and Christian philosophers (including Avencebrol and Costa ben Luca) whose works were "concealed in Greek and Arabic archives," as he put it: "I have found reasoned arguments among philosophers, and have taken care to collect this in a single treatise" so that "Latins . . . get to know about the soul not only by faith but also through reason."[109] Gundissalinus also took steps to further enhance Gerard's translation of al-Farabi's *Classification of the Science*. He localized it by introducing Latin examples of how the sciences were organized in the West, while further polishing its Latin in the process.[110] He then went on to write the handbook *On the Division of the Sciences* blending Greek, Islamic, and Christian sources, such as Isidore of Seville. This double art of synthesis and classification—in assembling, integrating, and ordering the work of earlier thinkers—was another of the markedly educational properties of intellectual works during this period. It was a way of helping European readers answer the question of what to make of it all, as they confronted the Latin opening of this world of Greek, Indian, Persian, Hebrew, and Arabic learning.

A third and, for my purposes, final figure among the translators of Aristotle and company was Michael Scot, who shifts the scene of translation to Sicily and the emperor's court. Michael first studied Arabic in Toledo, seeing through translations of Averroës, before setting up shop in Palermo, Sicily, in 1225, under the most enlightened of monarchs, Frederick II, King of Sicily and Holy Roman Emperor.[111] Sicily was at the crossroads of Greek, Arabic, Jewish, and Latin intellectual activity, following its capture from Muslim forces in 1091.[112] The Sicilian kings, beginning with Roger II in 1105, sponsored Latin translations from Arabic, and that work continued into the thirteenth century. Frederick appointed Michael Scot as well as Muslim teachers to court positions, where they worked closely with Jewish scholars on a series of translations. This Sicilian school of translation prompted the first

109. Cited by ibid., 20.

110. Burnett, "Communities of Learning," 16.

111. Majid Fakhry, *Averroes: (Ibn Rushd): His Life, Work and Influence* (Oxford: One World, 2001), 133. Fakhry also notes a Jewish Averroist tradition at this time, with Hebrew and Latin translations completed in Toledo, Naples, Arles, and Marseilles (132–33).

112. Dodds, Menocal, and Balbae, *Arts of Intimacy*, 212; Burnett, "Arabic-Latin Translation," 253, 262–63.

Latin editions of Plato's *Menon* and *Phaedo*, as well as further editions of Euclid and Ptolemy.[113] Michael's translations of Aristotle's *Analytics*, *Metaphysics*, and *On the Soul*—which he backed up with his translations of Averroës' commentaries—as well as some nineteen works of natural philosophy, that were to find their way into the scholastic curriculum of the cathedral schools and later the universities.[114] As with Gundissalinus and others in the translation movement, Michael felt sufficiently well equipped by the experience to compose works of his own in astrology, medicine, music, and geography.

For his part, Frederick II added Leonardo of Pisa (also known as Fibonacci) to his count of court intellectuals, only to have him set off for Syria and North Africa to study Islamic advances in mathematics, after which he arrived at his influential sequence of Fibonacci numbers, as they are now known, which he had introduced earlier in his *Book of Calculations* (*Liber abaci*) in 1202.[115] Frederick also set in motion something of an early empire of letters through his wide-ranging correspondence on questions of geometry, astronomy, and philosophy that he conducted with scholars in Egypt, Syria, Iraq, Arabia, Yemen, Morocco, and Spain.[116] He also emerges in the next chapter as among the first founders of a medieval university by royal decree.

With Toledo and Sicily acting as translation gateways, supplemented by Antioch and southern Italy, Europe was subject to a new age of learning. Although the considerable import of Islamic learning generated much excitement among the learned, it was not universally welcomed. Michael Scot, for example, was condemned to a spot on the eighth circle of Dante's *Inferno*: "The one beside him [Eurypylus] with the skinny shanks / was Michael Scott, who mastered every trick / of magic fraud, a prince of mountebanks."[117] Translating Arabic texts struck some as clearly consorting with deceitful infidels. On the Islamic side, Ahmad Ibn Abdun, a jurist in Islamic Seville, instigated a form of intellectual-property backlash by seeking to ban Arabic book sales to Jews and Christians in the early twelfth century. He was particularly

---

113. Gordon Leff, *Paris and Oxford Universities in the Thirteenth and Fourteenth Centuries: An Institutional and Intellectual History* (New York: Wiley, 1968), 130.

114. Rega Wood, "The Influence of Arabic Aristotelianism on Scholastic Natural Philosophy: Projectile Motion, the Place of the Universe, and Elemental Composition," in *The Cambridge History of Medieval Philosophy*, ed. Robert Pasnau (Cambridge: Cambridge University Press, 2009), 53, 248.

115. Fibonacci numbers, which begin 0, 1, 1, 2, 3, 5, 8, 13 (with each number the sum of the previous two), have many mathematical applications that include the golden spiral and the arrangement of leaves on a stem.

116. Metlitzki, *Matter of Araby*, 7.

117. Dante, *Inferno*, Canto XX, 115-17, 311.

offended by translators who took credit for writing what they had only translated into Latin, although there are few indications that his actions had any
effect on the flow of translations.[118]

It must also be remembered that the Latin translation movement oc-
curred under the broadsword shadow of the Crusades, which the West
launched against Islam beginning in the eleventh century. Pope Urban II is
said to have initiated the First Crusade with a sermon in 1095 calling on the
church council, according to Flucher of Chartres, "to persuade all people of
whatever rank, foot-soldiers and knights, poor and rich, to carry aid promptly
to those Christians [in Byzantium] and to destroy that vile race from the
lands of our friends," to which he reassuringly added, "all who die by the
way, whether by land or by sea, or in battle against the pagans, shall have
immediate remission of sins."[119] The nine major Crusades that followed in a
two-century Christian military campaign to recapture the Holy Land must
have made ongoing exchanges between merchant and scholar, and among
Christian, Muslim, and Jew, that much more difficult.[120]

Some scholars, however, sought to do their part for the Crusades. Peter
the Venerable, whom you may recall from chapter 5 as defender and friend
of Peter Abelard, traveled to Spain, prior to the launching of the Second Crusade in 1145. Once there, he commissioned the first Latin translation of the
Qur'an, as well as a life of Muhammad and other Islamic texts (while Muslims
had translated portions of the Christian Bible into Arabic centuries earlier).[121]
Peter sought, in this "Toledan collection," as it became known, to expose the
"errors" of Islam. "I attack you," he wrote, "not as some of us often do by
arms, but by words; not by force, but by reason; not in hatred, but in love. I
love you; loving you, I write to you, writing to you, I invite you to salvation."[122]

118. Burnett, "Translating Activity," 1041.
119. Fulcher of Chartres, "Urban's Speech," in *Muslim and Christian Contact in the Middle Ages*,
ed. Jarbel Rodriquez (Toronto: University of Toronto Press, 2015), 56.
120. In considering the contrast between Crusades and learning, it is worth noting Otto of
Freising who was a leader of the German army on the Second Crusade and a Cistercian monk, and
as such, judged "a scholar and thinker of exceptional learning, intellectual power and piety," according to Giles Constable, "whose high hopes in the crusade were sadly dashed by its failure, and
he could never bring himself to write a connected account of its disasters": "The Second Crusade
as Seen by Contemporaries," *Traditio* 9 (1953): 219–20.
121. Dominique Iogna-Prat points out that "literate Muslims in Baghdad and al-Andalus had
had Arabic versions of the Christian Scriptures for over two centuries": *Order and Exclusion: Cluny
and Christendom Face Heresy, Judaism, and Islam (1000–1150)*, trans. Graham Robert Edwards (Ithaca, NY: Cornell, 2002), 338.
122. Cited by R. W. Southern, *Western Views of Islam in the Middle Ages* (Cambridge, MA: Harvard University Press, 1987), 39. Dominique Iogna-Prat, *Order and Exclusion: Cluny and Chris-*

Peter's suspicions of all things Muslim crept into his observations of the Cluniac monks in Spanish scriptoriums; he referred to the paper they used—in a process borrowed from Arabic craftsmen that had not yet caught on in the West—as "scraps of old rags, or, perhaps, from even viler stuff."[123]

Still, the Christian capture of Antioch and Tripoli during the Crusades led to further translation work of the Arabic works found there, and the twelfth-century Second Crusade, which was largely a disaster for the West, did manage to extend the Latin translation zone deeper into southern Andalusia. The Crusades reflected a Christian sensibility that may go some way in explaining why, amid so much traffic in Arabic texts and Islamic learning, few Muslim scholars were invited or took the initiative to follow that same path into the West. The exceptions are often found in the border regions, such as the Sicilian court of Roger II. Muhammad al-Idrisi, for example, was commissioned by Roger to produce a work of geography in 1138, because as al-Idrisi explains, "it pleased him to know the nature of the land and to know it with certainty and with precision."[124]

Those involved in the Arabic-Latin sharing of this learning demonstrated remarkably little of the prejudices of their times, while their stewardship and curation of this learning points toward more modern conceptions of intellectual property. The translators may have Latinized Ibn Rusd's name—with Averroës based on a Hebrew version—yet every effort was made to properly preserve and credit, as well as faithfully render, his works in translation. The integrity of these works was no less important to those who took issue with Averroës, as Aquinas was to do during the thirteenth century on the very question of intellectual responsibility.

CONCLUSION

As the scholarly project remains more or less part of the larger world of prejudice and politics, it is fair to ask whether the Latin translation movement represented its own crusade, with this one devoted to restoring what

---

tendom Face Heresy, Judaism, and Islam (1000-1150), trans. Graham Robert Edwards (Ithaca, NY: Cornell University Press, 2002), 338.

123. Cited by Jonathan M. Bloom, *Paper before Print: The History and Impact of Paper on the Islamic World* (New Haven, CT: Yale University Press, 2001), 206. Although there are indications that by the eleventh century Christians had acquired the Islamic art of making paper, it did not really take hold in northern Europe until fifteenth century when book production created a great demand for such material (212-13).

124. Al-Idrisi, "A Muslim Geographer in King Roger's Court," in *Muslim and Christian Contact,* 385.

the West believed to be its intellectual property and heritage claims to the philosophical and scientific treasures of ancient Greece. The Graeco-Arabic translations of the ʿAbbasid caliphate had shown similar imperialist tendencies three to four centuries earlier. Yet it was well after the Latin translation movement that scholars in the West set out a claim on the Aryan origins of its Greek heritage (to the exclusion of Semitic and African influences).[125] In that earlier period, however, many European thinkers gave a full and fair measure of credit to al-Farabi, Avicenna, Averroës, and others for their work in astronomy, mathematics, medicine, optics, philosophy, and psychology, as well as for the commentaries that opened many of those Greek treasures for them. The Europeans eagerly borrowed and used, revised and reinvented, what they found with each fresh translation. It amounted to their own demonstration of the *De anima* dilemma that Aristotle had set in motion, and that had vexed the Islamic philosophers. How is one to ascertain the mix between the intellect of individuals and the intellect held in common, amid this massive flow of intellectual properties across cultures and centuries?

In the early twelfth century, Bernard of Chartres, chancellor of the cathedral school, was among those who observed that the itinerant scholars bearing these new translations, sometimes by the cartload, were changing the face of learning in the West: "With humble spirit, eager learning, and peaceful life; in silence and poverty, to explore the most distant lands; many now endeavor to unlock through study what has long been unknown."[126] It was Bernard who was credited by John of Salisbury in 1159 for the observation that we are as "dwarfs perched on the shoulders of giants" and "that we see more and farther than our predecessors, not because we have keener vision or greater height, but because we are lifted up and borne aloft on their gigantic stature."[127] What is often lost in thinking about Western learn-

125. While controversy surrounds Martin Bernal's multi-volume *Black Athena: The Afroasiatic Roots of Classical Civilization*, critics have generally accepted Bernal's assessment, in the first volume, *The Fabrication of Ancient Greece, 1785–1985* (New Brunswick, NJ: Rutgers University Press, 1989), of the extent to which ancient Greece was cast as the foundation of European culture during the nineteenth-century. See Mary R. Lefkowtiz and Guy Maclean Rogers, eds., *Black Athena Revisited* (Chapel Hill: University of North Carolina Press, 1996). Richard Walzer' observes: "The study of this Muslim medieval philosophy is of course no longer part of any philosophical syllabus in Western universities, as it was—in Latin translation—from the twelfth century until the eighteenth" ("Early Islamic Philosophy," in *The Cambridge History of Later Greek and Early Mediaeval Philosophy*, ed. A. H. Armstrong [Cambridge: Cambridge University Press, 1970], 644).

126. Cited by Montgomery, *Science in Translation*, 141.

127. John of Salisbury, *The Metalogicon: A Twelfth-Century Defense of the Verbal and Logical Arts of the Trivium*, trans. Daniel D. McGarry (Berkeley: University of California Press, 1962), 167. Ber-

ing is the extent to which those giants came from outside Christendom and that what these dwarfs are standing on is not so much their shoulders but stacks of the books on which the giants had worked so hard. Those stacks, in turn, were not free-standing. They were housed within systems of patronage and other forms of institutional support that kept them dry and otherwise preserved them. However, as the translations continued to make their way north through twelfth-century Europe, along trade routes and into market towns, it became apparent that the well-established educational structures of monastery and cathedral school would not readily contain or shelve the sheer weight and wealth of this new learning. Those eager to pursue this body of work, master and scholar, must have reflected on how fruitful these homes for learning had been in securing autonomous societal support. In looking about for a way to organize this new trade in higher learning, they would have naturally gravitated toward the emerging guild structures, which brings me to the origins of the European university.

nard's adage has had a life of its own, turning up, among other places, in a letter by Newton and as the motto of Google Scholar: see Robert K. Merton, *On the Shoulders of Giants: The Post-Italianate Edition* (Chicago: University of Chicago Press, 1965).

CHAPTER SEVEN

The Medieval Universities
of Oxford and Paris

Without a surviving notice of a charter, sod-breaking, fanfare, or even a charming anecdote of note, a new educational entity emerged during the twelfth century in Bologna, Paris, and Oxford. In each of these centers, through a seemingly unremarkable series of steps, masters and scholars congregated outside of the episcopal schools, monasteries, or private tutoring arrangements that had otherwise defined the principal educational arrangements in Europe with the sole purpose of pursuing new and ancient forms of learning, prompted, in part, by the manuscripts carted north in fresh Latin translations. Such were their numbers and the scope of their advanced studies, that the masters were not long in organizing themselves into faculties of arts, law, medicine, and theology.[1] By the early years of the thirteenth century, these assemblies were being called studium generale, and were attracting students from every corner of Europe. With new instances appearing in Cambridge, Salamanca, Siena, and Naples, this new organization was capturing the Continent's imagination.

The mystery around the exact origins of the universities has not prevented speculation on why the *studium* appeared when and where it did. Some historians point to the eleventh-century reestablishment of the legal right to incorporate (from Roman law), as the master teachers formed a corporation

---

1. Jacques Le Goff refers to the "'spontaneously born' universities," in contrast to the later "universities *created* by the public authorities," which followed not long after, while emphasizing that historians of this era "still confront a complex and ambiguous variety of institutions": *Time, Work, and Culture in the Middle Ages*, trans. Arthur Goldhammer (Chicago: University of Chicago Press, 1980), 137, 135.

(*universatas*) following the guild model.[2] The new *studium* appeared in the
emerging market centers of the High Middle Ages, where the learned could
readily attract students and find books, as well as profit by following the
example of other guilds.[3] The masters were, in the first instance, practicing
something of a new trade, and as the artisans of that trade, they were ready to
form "the corporation of book users," as Jacques Le Groff names them, to gain
protection and privilege for their practices.[4] Other historians observe how
the universities could satisfy the increasing need of both church and state
for highly literate staff, sufficiently conversant in matters of logic and law to
administer their burgeoning interests.[5] Still others reflect on how cathedral
and canon schools succeeded so well in generating a secular enthusiasm
for scholasticism—embodied by the legendary, if tragic, brilliance of Peter
Abelard—that these schools could not keep up with the intellectual demand
of a growing body of students.[6]

What typically goes missing from this list of likely causes is the great
twelfth- and thirteenth-century influx of Islamic learning through the translation movement, discussed in chapter 6.[7] The works translated into Latin

2. Aleksander Gieysztor, "Management and Resources," in *Universities in the Middle Ages*, ed.
H. de Ridder-Symoens, vol. 1 of *A History of the University in Europe*, ed. Walter Rüegg (Cambridge:
Cambridge University Press, 1992), 108.

3. Davide Cantoni and Noam Yuchtman, "Medieval Universities, Legal Institutions, and the
Commercial Revolution," *Quarterly Journal of Economics* 129, no. 2 (2014): 823–87.

4. Le Goff, *Time, Work, and Culture in the Middle Ages*, 133.

5. Alexander Murray describes a "golden age for careerism," beginning in the twelfth century
featuring "the university ladder": *Reason and Society in the Middle Ages* (Oxford: Oxford University Press, 1978), 220, 27. Alan B. Cobban writes of how "European society had reached that point
in its corporate growth which dictated the establishment of permanent centers of high growth capable of concentrating its available talent for socially useful employment": *The Medieval Universities:
Their Development and Organization* (London: Methuen, 1975), 18.

6. "The schools of Notre Dame occupied the foremost place, and it was from them that the
University [of Paris] sprang": Maurice de Wulf, "The Teaching of Philosophy and the Classification
of the Sciences in the Thirteenth Century," *Philosophical Review* 27, no. 4 (1918): 357. Ronald G.
Witt summarizes the arguments in favor the private schools over the cathedral schools as the origin
of the universities in the case of the Italian peninsula; he describes "the entire institutional growth of
the Bolognese schools" into Bologna's university as "shadowy" (*The Two Latin Cultures and the Foundation of Renaissance Humanism in Medieval Italy* [Cambridge: Cambridge University Press, 2012],
8–9, 363).

7. Charles Homer Haskins identifies a role for translation in the formation of universities, but
leaves aside the Islamic aspect: "This new [Hellenist and Roman] knowledge burst the bonds of the
cathedral and monastery schools ... [and] drew ... youths ... to form ... academic gilds" (*The Rise of
Universities* [Ithaca, NY: Cornell University Press, 1923], 5). John Marenbon presents the coincidence
of university and translation: "The first fifty years of the Paris and Oxford universities also coincided
with the rapid assimilation of Aristotle's non-logical writings" (*Pagans and Philosophers: The Problem Of Paganism from Augustine to Leibniz* [Princeton, NJ: Princeton University Press, 2015], 127).

during this period introduced European scholars to such a wide and sophisticated array of works of Islamic, Hellenic, Hindu, Persian, and Jewish thinkers
that it could not help but define the intellectual moment for the period and
region.[8] In Bologna, Paris, Oxford, and elsewhere, the learned were gathering
to share, discuss, and teach the relatively sudden profusion of a diverse body
of works. Before the thirteenth century was half over, "virtually the whole corpus of Greek science was accessible to the western world," Robert W. Southern estimates, even as he joins those historians who tend to overlook the contributions of Islamic learning to this accessibility, "and scholars groaned [with
pleasure, surely] under its weight as they strove to master it all."[9] Further on
point, Robert Burnett notes that "the preeminence of Arabic sources for Western philosophy can be seen in the fact that, when Giles of Rome criticizes the
errors of the philosophers in teaching Aristotelian philosophy at the University of Paris, all the philosophers named are Arabic or wrote their philosophy
in Arabic (Maimonides), with the exception of Aristotle himself. Even in the
case of Aristotle, Giles uses the Arabic–Latin translations."[10]

Gordon Leff gives due credit to Islamic learning but not as a cause for these new institutions: "If
institutionally the universities are the great new fact in the academic life of Christendom from the
thirteenth century onward, intellectually it consists of the Greco-Arabic corpus of knowledge and
ideas" and "the effects of Averroe's advent were among the most far-reaching in the intellectual
history of the thirteenth century [in the West]" (*Paris and Oxford Universities in the Thirteenth and
Fourteenth Centuries: An Institutional and Intellectual History* [New York: Wiley, 1968], 127, 136).
Ann Blair takes a similar stance: "The translation into Latin for the first time of many texts of Aristotelian philosophy, from Arabic and directly from Greek in some cases, triggered the expansion of
teaching beyond the seven liberal arts … the new disciplines which were added to the curriculum
at the newly founded universities were the three philosophies (physics, metaphysics, and ethics),
themselves considered propaedeutic to study in the higher faculties of medicine, law, and theology" ("Organizations of Knowledge," in *Cambridge Companion to Renaissance Philosophy*, ed. James
Hankins [Cambridge: Cambridge University Press, 2007], 289. As does Ronald G. Witt: "By 1200
contact with an ever-enlarging corpus of scientific and theological writings of ancient Greek and
medieval Islamic origin in translation had awakened European intellectuals to the possibility of
asking a wealth of new questions" (*Two Latin Cultures*, 397).

   8. Burnett supports his claim of "the preeminence of Arabic sources for Western philosophy"
in the Middle Ages with a list of 114 Arabic philosophic works translated into Latin roughly prior
to 1600: "Arabic into Latin: The Reception of Arabic Philosophy into Western Europe," in *The
Cambridge Companion to Arabic Philosophy*, ed. Peter Adamson and Richard C. Taylor (Cambridge:
Cambridge University Press, 2005), 383, 391–400.

   9. R. W. Southern, "Medieval Humanism," in *Medieval Humanism and other Studies* (Oxford:
Blackwell, 1971), 48.

   10. Charles Burnett, "Arabic into Latin: The Reception of Arabic Philosophy into Western Europe," in *The Cambridge Companion to Arabic Philosophy*, ed. Peter Adamson and Richard C. Taylor
(Cambridge: Cambridge University Press, 2005), 383.

These works represented not just topics in philosophy but novel branches of mathematics, astronomy, natural history, and medicine. Most of this work had yet to be reconciled with the tenets of Christianity. It seems reasonable to surmise that cathedral and canon schools were overwhelmed by the stream of Latin translations from Toledo, Sicily, Antioch, and southern Italy. The works themselves called for the development of analytical skills, forms of inquiry, and ways of thinking that went well beyond the traditional study of scripture and the works of church fathers. The cathedral schools were clearly inadequate, as Abelard had already demonstrated earlier in the twelfth century, before the Latin translation movement was fully under way. Something new was required, and while my focus in this chapter is on the medieval universities in Paris and Oxford, in which the teaching masters formed chartered guilds, this was not the only model. In Bologna, the *studium* was far more of a student initiative. It arose out of the contracted *societas* between a master and a fee-paying pupil that became a prominent feature of twelfth-century education in the city. Yet the students also came to organize themselves in Bologna around the "nations" from which they had traveled in hope of being trained in the professions, such as law.[11] The pupil-driven trade in learning, and the *universatas scholarium* that they formed, soon garnered the support of the Holy Roman Emperor Frederick I, who issued a *Privilegium scholasticum* in 1158 guaranteeing Bologna scholars safe conduct in their travels. Such privileges were warranted, his declaration held, for those "who for love of learning choose exile and poverty and divest themselves of their patrimony, while exposing themselves to every peril," even as they "illuminated the whole world with their learning."[12]

In Bologna, the curricular focus was on the Justinian corpus of Roman law. Its study required courses in the art and science of government, as well as canon law, rhetoric, grammar, and *ars nortaria*. This was surely part of Frederick's interest in supporting the university, given his own imperial aspirations and the practical need for administrators of the empire. Yet the interest

11. Hastings Rashdall, *Salerno, Bologna, Paris*, vol. 1 of *The Universities of Europe in the Middle Ages*, ed. F. M. Powicke and A. B. Emden (Oxford: Oxford University Press, 1936), 275, 176. The students later banded together to form a *universitas scholarium*, with the goal of obtaining fair prices for rooms, meals, and books in Bologna: M. W. Strasser, "The Educational Philosophy of the First Universities," in *The University World: A Synoptic View of Higher Education in the Middle Ages and Renaissance*, ed. Douglas Radcliff-Umstead (Pittsburgh: Medieval and Renaissance Studies Committee, University of Pittsburgh, 1973), 3. Witt, *Two Latin Cultures*, 277–78.

12. Pearl Kibre, *Scholarly Privileges in the Middle Ages: The Rights, Privileges, and Immunities of Scholars and Universities at Bologna, Padua, Paris and Oxford* (Cambridge, MA: Mediaeval Academy of America, 1962), 10, 325.

in this learning was not entirely secular. In 1219, Pope Honorius III issued a bull enabling the cathedral archdeacon in Bologna to award a *licentia* (a license to teach) to the students who passed their examinations. The *studium* in Bologna was under way, and it grew into the Middle Ages' dominant intellectual force in the field of jurisprudence.[13]

It was an inspiring model, given the rising bureaucratic needs of the feudal state, and it was not long before universities were founded by royal decree. Alfonso VIII of Castile was among the first, creating a university in Palencia in or around 1210. Not long after, Frederick II, recently crowned Holy Roman Emperor and a strong supporter of Arabic-Latin translations (as noted above), established a more successful instance in Naples in 1224 (known today as Università Federico II). Part of the key to founding a university with staying power, Frederick demonstrated in his famously forceful way, was luring away well-respected masters from other institutions, notably Bologna and Paris, with promises of titles and patronage (initiating another sort of intellectual property market that is still with us).[14]

In terms of teaching, from the outset the medieval university was intellectually dominated by, in a word, Aristotle. This was all the more the case for advanced degrees in law, medicine, and theology, as well as the study of government, citizen, and state.[15] The Philosopher, as he was simply known, was made all the more teachable by the commentaries in Latin of al-Farabi, Avicenna, and Averroës, and later by improved translations of his works from the original Greek. The educational use of pagan philosophers in the universities

13. Walter Ullman, *Law and Politics in the Middle Ages: An Introduction to the Sources of Medieval Political Ideas* (Ithaca, NY: Cornell University Press, 1973), 85. Similar to Ronald G. Witt cited in note 6 above, Ullman refers to the university's origins in the twelfth-century "glossatorial school in Bologna," in which teachers would lecture, and with students, create glosses of the Roman law corpus in what were private lay schools (ibid.).

14. Jacques Verger, *Men of Learning in Europe at the End of the Middle Ages*, trans. Lisa Neal and Steven Randall (Notre Dame, IN: University of Notre Dame Press, 2000), 144. George Makdisi points to similarities between the endowed foundation of colleges, such as the one established by Frederick II, and the Islamic madrasa, given that both being an "incorporated charitable trust" devoted to learning, positioning the *studium* as another aspect of the Islamic legacy in the West: *The Rise of Colleges: Institutions of Learning in Islam and the West* (Edinburgh: Edinburgh University Press, 1981), 225–27. This does not account for the guild formation of the *studium* elsewhere, nor the influence of monasticism on the formation of endowed institutions.

15. "The cosmological revolution which the absorption of Aristotle wrought on the 13th century displayed its great effects in the sphere of governmental science ... Aristotle's concepts of the State as a 'body of citizens sufficing for the purposes of life' seems innocuous enough but nevertheless introduced new dimensions of thought concerning society and its government": Ullman, *Law and Politics*, 269.

understandably troubled the church. The universities were preparing young men for the priesthood, after all (and excluded woman partly on that basis).[16] As a result, the teaching of Aristotle became a battleground in these new organizations' struggle for intellectual autonomy and self-governance. The universities were that much more part of the world and the marketplace, compared to the monasteries that had pursued their own form of autonomy during the Early Middle Ages. But the universities were insistent that their active pursuit of learning required them to stand apart from the business of the world, including that of the local authorities in church and state. The early history of the universities of Oxford and Paris illustrate rather different instances of how the intellectual property of autonomy was established as a necessary aspect of this new learning and these new institutions.

THE UNIVERSITY OF OXFORD

The second half of the twelfth century found "a swarm of wandering scholars" from Western Europe gathering in Oxford, a market town "untrammeled" by any monastic or cathedral agenda.[17] Among the earliest indications of something afoot are the accounts of Petrus Alfonsi and Adelard of Bath (introduced in chapter 6) about the Latin translations that ended up in Oxford in the first half of the twelfth century.[18] There is the account of Daniel of Morley, a Norfolk lad, who first studied at Oxford around 1160 before taking his studies to Paris where he encountered "Arab learning" (*doctrina Arabum*) while studying astronomy there. Told that Toledo was the source of such learning, he went off to the Iberian Peninsula, and, once settled in that city of translation, attended the astronomy lectures of the great Arabic translator Gerard of Cremona.[19] In Daniel's only surviving work, *Philosophia*, from 1175, he describes how "eventually my friends begged me to come back from Spain; so, on their invitation, I arrived in England, bringing

16. "Once priesthood became a prerequisite of higher education, nuns were institutionally disqualified from following monks into new areas of learning and administration, regardless of their natural endowments": Jo Ann Kay McNamara, "The Herrenfrage: The Restructuring of the Gender System, 1050–1150," in *Medieval Masculinities: Regarding Men in the Middle Ages*, ed. Clare A. Lees (Minneapolis: University of Minnesota Press, 1994), 34.
17. Nicholas Barker, *The Oxford University Press and the Spread of Learning* (Oxford: Oxford University Press, 1978), 1; Leff, *Paris and Oxford Universities*, 76.
18. See Charles Homer Haskins, "The Introduction of Arabic Science into England," in *Studies in the History of Medieval Science* (New York: Frederick Ungar, 1924), 113–29.
19. Charles Burnett, "The Translating Activity in Medieval Spain," in *The Legacy of Muslim Spain*, ed. Salma Khadra Jayyusi (Leiden: Brill, 1992), 1045.

a precious multitude of books with me."[20] His *Philosophia* celebrates "the logical arguments of the Arabs," as he puts it, and it is tellingly dedicated to John of Oxford, who was clearly among the more open-minded bishops, given to patronizing such adventuresome learners, with their precious cartloads of books adding to Oxford's ability to attract the learned to this community.[21]

As for the early traces of such books being studied at Oxford, the scant records of the time indicate that Alexander Nequam, grammarian, encyclopedist, commentator, and poet, was introducing his theology students to Aristotle during the 1190s, as well as using texts by Euclid, Galen, and Isaac Israeli, and employing a mariner's instrument, all suggesting Islamic influence.[22] Master John Blund was another who taught Aristotle at Oxford from around 1200, and with the help of Avicenna's commentary and with little effort to reconcile the Greek philosopher's views on the soul, free will, and immortality, with Christianity.[23] Blund's own commentary on Aristotle's *On the Soul* is rich in references to Avicenna and al-Ghazali, with some mention of Plato, Cicero, Boethius, and lesser amounts of Augustine and John of Damascus.[24]

In 1209, Blund was among those masters and scholars who ceased lecturing at Oxford and left for Paris in protest over the town's treatment of two students, while others headed to Cambridge to start a new university. What triggered the exodus was Oxford's mayor and burgess summarily hanging two pupils who were seemingly involved in the murder of a local woman. The masters believed that the students had clerical status, which made them subject to the church law and court alone. The whole matter was complicated by a papal interdict at the time censuring King John and the country as a whole.[25] When the king finally agreed to submit to the authority of Pope Innocent III in 1214, the town of Oxford took it as an opportunity to rebuild the university. Expressing regrets over the hanging, officials approached the

20. Cited by Charles Burnett, *Introduction of Arabic Learning into England* (London: British Library, 1997), 62.

21. Ibid., 63.

22. A. C. Crombie, *Robert Grosseteste and the Origins of Experimental Science 1100–1700* (Oxford: Oxford University Press, 1953), 41.

23. Mary Martin McLaughlin, *Intellectual Freedom and Its Limitations in the University of Paris in the Thirteenth and Fourteenth Centuries* (New York: Arno, 1977), 42.

24. Leff, *Paris and Oxford Universities*, 144.

25. C. H. Lawrence, "Blund, John (*c.*1175–1248)," in *Oxford Dictionary of National Biography*, ed. H. C. G. Matthew and Brian Harrison, online ed. (Oxford: Oxford University Press, 2004). On those who went to Cambridge, Oxford man Rashdall adds, "what attracted them to that distant marsh town we know not": Hastings Rashdall, *English Universities, Student Life*, vol. 3 of *The Universities of Europe in the Middle Ages* (Oxford: Oxford University Press, 1895/1936), 34.

papal legate in England, Nicholas de Romanis, for a settlement that might bring the university back to life. Nicholas complied with a bull on June 20, 1214, that firmly established the scholars' legal rights and town's obligations. It was an attractive package which protected the students from facing civil law and had provisions for discounting rents.[26] Hastings Rashdall, a nineteenth-century historian of European universities, names the ordinance a "charter of privilege," while Southern calls it a "charter of submission."[27] It was both, of course, and, as such, established for the first time the legal and autonomous standing of the university in Oxford.

The charter also made reference to a "chancellor whom the bishop of Lincoln shall set over the scholars."[28] The initial appointment is thought to have been Robert Grosseteste, although some controversy remains on the nature and title of his brief tenure.[29] What is clear is that Grosseteste played a major role in making the Greco-Arabic sciences a part of the university. Born into a modest Suffolk family in 1175, Grosseteste was introduced to the new science while serving the Bishop of Hereford William de Vere who organized within his household a remarkably active study of chronology, astronomy, and astrology.[30] Although aspects of Grosseteste's education are also missing from the record, he appears to have acquired a master's degree at a young age from Oxford and may have studied at Paris (where he may well have picked up the ascription of a swelled head); at some point he certainly encountered the works of Avicenna, al-Ghazali, al-Hazen, and others circulating Europe at the time.[31]

Once established as a master at Oxford, Grosseteste taught theology, while translating Greek texts into Latin and preparing influential commentaries on

26. The papal ordinance established that the town of Oxford would exercise rent controls on behalf of students for two decades, starting with a halving of their rates in 1209 for the first ten years, and then going no higher than those 1209 rates; also, the students were collectively granted 52 shillings annually by the town for the poor among them, as well as an annual dinner for a hundred on St. Nicholas Day (December 6th and the likely anniversary of the student executions); and students were to have the benefit of clergy, which meant submitting to a church court on all legal matters, much as their Parisian counterparts had had for decades: L. W. B. Brockliss, *The University of Oxford: A History* (Oxford: Oxford University Press, 2016), 13–14.

27. Rashdall, *Universities*, 3:35; R. W. Southern, "From Schools to University," in *Early Oxford Schools*, ed. J. I. Catto of *The History of the University of Oxford* (Oxford: Oxford University Press, 1984), 26–31.

28. Ibid., 31.

29. M. B. Hackett, "The University as Corporate Body," in *The Early Oxford Schools*, ed. J. I. Catto, vol. 1 of *The History of the University of Oxford* (Oxford: Oxford University Press, 1984), 45–47.

30. Josiah C. Russell reports on how Roger of Hereford, for example, had adapted Arabic tables in 1176 for tracing the movement of the heavens and the casting of horoscopes suitable to the region: "Hereford and Arabic Science in England about 1175–1200," *Isis* 18, no. 1 (1932): 14–25.

31. Burnett, *Arabic Learning*, 74.

Aristotle.[32] He made the empirical sciences and experimentation part of his teaching, as well as the demonstrative logic of Euclid's geometry and other works.[33] He drew on the commentaries of al-Kindī, al-Farabi, Ibn al-Haytham, and Avicenna. Grosseteste is credited with having composed 120 books on a vast range of topics, which in the sciences included *On the Calendar*, *On the Movement of the Planets*, and *On the Origins of Sound*. His leadership in natural philosophy and the sciences during those early years at Oxford amounted to, in the estimation of Alistair C. Crombie, University of London historian of science, "the methodological revolution to which modern science owes its origin."[34] Grosseteste was inspired by the Latin translation movement, with this great wave of expanded access to scholarly works leading him to develop new principles and techniques in the empirical sciences and the application of logic. His influence on the teaching of natural philosophy at Oxford followed from the case he made for a "science acquired by demonstration," seeking "a cause of the thing known," and which he held is "science most strongly and most properly so called."[35]

Now, to be sure, the scientific methods that Grosseteste introduced were still in their formative years. At one point, he presents the example of "experimental" results demonstrating that the herb scammony (native to Syria and Asia Minor) has been successfully used to treat excess bile. Later scholars have determined that Grosseteste likely lifted this treatment from a work by Avicenna, who presented it himself as no more than something he'd observed and had assumed it was "not by mere chance," as the Islamic scholar put it.[36] Similarly, in his study of light, Grosseteste draws on al-Farabi's

32. Leff, *Paris and Oxford Universities*, 145.

33. Richard W. Southern, *Robert Grosseteste: The Growth of an English Mind in Medieval Europe* (Oxford: Oxford University Press, 1986), v–vii; Robert W. Southern, "Grosseteste, Robert (c.1170–1253)," in *Oxford Dictionary of National Biography*. See also Crombie, *Grosseteste*.

34. Crombie, *Grosseteste*, 9. In a remarkable turn, Crombie both credits the translation movement and deprecates its cultural sources: "The new translations, of which the Greek and Arabic originals had so conspicuously failed to produce a thoroughgoing experimental science in the classical and Mohammedan worlds, provided Western Christendom with the beginnings of a method of rational explanation of empirical facts" (11).

35. Cited by Steven P. Marrone, *William of Auvergne and Robert Grosseteste: New Ideas of Truth in the Early Thirteenth Century* (Princeton, NJ: Princeton University Press, 1983), 228. In the twelfth century, Averroës wrote of "the books of demonstration" and the "demonstrative arts," contrasting them to "persuasive" statements: *Tahafut al Tahafut* (*The Incoherence of the Incoherence*), trans. Simon Van Den Bergh (Cambridge: Gibb Memorial Trust, 2008), 257. When Gerard of Cremona translated Aristotle's *Posterior Analytics*, he called it *The Book of Demonstrations*: Burnett, "Arabic into Latin," 374. Crombie points to how Grosseteste added to "the popularity of optics and mathematical science in the Oxford school": *Grosseteste*, 131.

36. Cited by Bruce S. Eastwood, "Mediaeval Empiricism: The Case of Grosseteste's Optics," *Speculum* 43, no. 2 (1968): 310, 308 n. 19. Richard C. Dales observes that "most of the experiments"

application of geometry, arithmetic, astronomy, and music on this topic.[37] In *On Light* (*De luce*), from 1228, Grosseteste adds certain theological and metaphysical qualities to the study of light's geometry, given that light is the "first corporeal form"—as God's first biblical command was "Let there be light"— and from it the rest of the physical universe is revealed and takes its physical shape.[38] Yet to be fair, in *On Lines, Angles, and Figures* (*De lineis, angulis, et figuris*), completed two years later in 1230–31, Grosseteste privileges the power of Euclidean geometry in making sense of light: "The utility of considering lines, angles and figures is of the greatest utility since it is impossible to know the nature of philosophy without them," he writes in this work on reflection and refraction.[39] Geometry was as much the key to his natural philosophy as the calculus was to be for Newton, in their efforts to look into the mind of God (rather than the face, as monastics aspired to do).

There came such a day for Grosseteste in 1231 when he attended a sermon given by a visiting Dominican friar. The friar's fulminations against the sins of academic pride and vanity moved Grosseteste, at the age of fifty-six, to give up his university post and his parish of Abbotsley. In their stead, he dedicated himself to serving as a teacher (*lector*) for the *studia* of a newly established Franciscan community just beyond Oxford's city walls. Although he did not take the vows of a friar (with more on the Franciscans and Dominicans below) but continued to serve the order for four years, until the church found another role for him. In 1235, the indefatigable Grosseteste was elected Bishop of Lincoln. Although the local bishop was often the bane of the university, Grosseteste was very much its continuing servant.

In 1238 he rescued Adam of Buckfield, the noted Franciscan philosopher, from the Oxford jail after he was arrested for his participation in a student riot.[40] More significantly, in 1240, Grosseteste was able to divert one of the

reported are "those he had read about": "Robert Grosseteste's Scientific Works," *Isis* 52, no. 3 (1961): 401.

37. Ibid., 399. Al-Farabi contrasts his interest in using geometry to *explain* how light works with Aristotle's focus on *describing* light's behavior.

38. Cited by A. Mark Smith, *From Sight to Light: The Passage from Ancient to Modern Optics* (Chicago: University of Chicago Press, 2015), 257.

39. Cited and translated by Amelia Carolina Sparavigna, "Robert Grosseteste and His Treatise on Lines, Angles and Figures of the Propagation of Light," *International Journal of Science* 2, no. 9 (2013): 101. Grosseteste also refers to Aristotle's *Meteorology and Metaphysics*, Euclid's *Elements*, Boethius's *Arithmetic*, and Averroës's *Long Commentary on the* On the Soul: Smith, *From Sight to Light*, 259. Smith also sees traces of al-Kindī in *On Lines*, with Grosseteste citing the Islamic scientist elsewhere (ibid.).

40. Adam of Buckfield went on to teach at Oxford for which he prepared Aristotelian commentaries that were used by Thomas Aquinas in Paris: J. A. Weisheipl, "Science in the Thirteenth

university's bursaries—paid by the town's burgesses in retribution for the 1209 executions—into a loan chest for masters and scholars who were financially short. This university welfare system became an ongoing tradition for ensuring that members of this community were able to continue their studies despite any monetary hardships.[41] More importantly, Grosseteste saw to it that the estate of English baron Alan Basset, which was left to the university in 1243, was used to purchase land that then funded two scholarships for students in need.[42] The students or scholar-priests had to perform a daily mass in the name of Alan Basset and his wife, in yet another of the monastic traditions that were taken up by the *studium*.

As the university continued to attract gifts and endowments, in recognition of its contribution to English life, these donations were often directed toward founding, incorporating, and financing residential colleges, again in the monastic tradition. The residential colleges also took steps to build up their libraries by drawing on the private collections of their members, who were asked to pledge their books to the college following their death or departure from the college. The college library's best copies of a particular volume were often chained to the shelves to ensure access for everyone, while the remainder of the copies were lent out to the fellows. The university's statutes advised the world at large, at more than one point, that "among other works of piety, it is reckoned pious to relieve the needs of scholars."[43]

Although Grosseteste had not spent long with the Franciscans, on his death in 1253, he left a substantial collection of papers, and Latin, Greek, and Arabic books to the convent where he had taught. His bequest formed the core of the

Century," in *The Early Oxford Schools*, ed. J. I. Catto, vol. 1 of *The History of the University of Oxford* (Oxford: Oxford University Press, 1984), 462–63.

41. T. H. Aston and Rosamond Faith, "The Endowments of the University and Colleges to circa 1348," in *Early Oxford Schools*, ed. J. I. Catto, vol. 1 of *The History of the University of Oxford* (Oxford: Oxford University Press, 1984), 267. Support also came from Oxford's Jewish moneylenders, for while Jews were barred from joining the university (until 1856), their money-lending, book trade, and ownership of academic halls made them a vital part of the emerging institution, as did the example of their own devotion to study and book collections (274–75).

42. Aston and Faith, "Endowments," 268. Aston and Faith note how the early colleges were "a community living a common life of a clerical though non-monastic nature" (265). His *Rules of Robert Grosseteste*, c. 1240–42, which he prepared in French to guide the widowed Countess of Lincoln, Margaret de Lacy in estate management, does suggest further monastic parallel: Louise J. Wilkinson, "*The Rules of Robert Grosseteste* Reconsidered: The Lady as Estate and Household Manager in Thirteenth-Century England," in *The Medieval Household in Christian Europe, 800–c. 1550*, ed. Cordelia Beattie, Anna Maslakovic, and Sarah Rees Jones (Turnhout, Belgium: Brepols, 2003), 293–307.

43. Cited by Aston and Faith, "Endowments," 265.

Franciscan convent library in Oxford. For if the Franciscans could own nothing, not even a book, they could *use* the books that they were asked to take care
of, whether to study or prepare a sermon, much as they ate to give themselves
the strength to preach. Grosseteste greatly aided in this use by placing a great
variety of symbols (some four hundred in all) in the margins of many of the
works in his collection, indicating the topics dealt with, such as free will or
the Day of Judgment.[44]

It is worth pausing over the further part played by Franciscans and Dominicans in the medieval organization of learning, particularly at Oxford
and Paris. In 1209, Francis of Assisi had been inspired by a sermon on the
piety of asceticism that led Francis to form an order of mendicant friars
known as Friars Minor, Greyfriars, or Franciscans. He committed the order
to extreme simplicity and humility, leaving little space for learning. Not only
was private property forbidden but communal property, such as books, was
as well: "To live in obedience," Francis's Short Rule had it, "in chastity, and
without anything of their own."[45] The friars were to live on handouts and
not provide for themselves. They were to pray rather than read, to live their
faith rather than interpret it, and thus, or at least initially, had little place
within their lives for educational and intellectual interests.[46] But following the pattern that I observed earlier with the *Rule of Benedict*, the urge to
learn can be hard to contain in certain circumstances. So it was that the Franciscans, as well as the Dominican order which began around the same time,
were soon drawn to the studium generale, ostensibly out of a need for an
informed and persuasive rhetoric with which to combat what they felt
were the heresies and materialism of their times.[47] In 1230, Pope Gregory IX,
who had been a friend of Francis, issued a bull affirming the Franciscan
rule against private and communal property, with the convents that the or-

44. M. W. Sheehan, "The Religious Orders 1220-1370," in *The Early Oxford Schools*, ed. J. I.
Catto, vol. 1 of *The History of the University of Oxford*. (Oxford: Oxford University Press, 1984),
210. To examine a manuscript page displaying these clever indexing icons, see the online illustration entitled "Robert Grosseteste's Indexing Symbols, in a Volume of Works by St. Augustine,
St. John Of Damascus, and Others," *Online Gallery* (London: British Library, 2009). Also, S. Harrison Thomson, "Grosseteste's Topical Concordance of the Bible and the Fathers," *Speculum* 9, no. 2
(1934): 139-44.

45. Francis of Assisi, "The Earlier Rule," in *Francis and Clare: The Complete Works*, trans. Regis J.
Armstrong and Ignatius Brady, 107-35 (Mahwah, NJ: Paulist, 1982), 109.

46. Neslihan Senocak, *The Poor and the Perfect: The Rise of Learning in the Franciscan Order*,
1209-1310 (Ithaca, NY: Cornell University Press, 2012), 30, 32, 50.

47. Barbara H. Rosenwein and Lester K. Little, "Social Meaning in the Monastic and Mendicant
Spiritualities," *Past & Present* 63 (1974): 4. "The friars rejected money; the monks abandoned the
battlefield" of heresy and heterodoxy (32).

der had acquired reverting to church ownership. However, the pontiff specified that the mendicants retained the right to use books, as well as parchment and ink, if still at the discretion of the order's ministers.[48] Amid the rise of market culture, Dominicans preached against individual and collective ownership (*dominium*) in favor of traditional rights of use (*ius utendi*), which, I have been at pains to show, is a mainstay of the commonwealth of learning.[49]

Yet if the friars were drawn to the universities, they had little patience for their worldly guild structure, which tended to antagonize the *seculars* (the masters who took holy orders as clergy) among their colleagues, as the friars would not join their struggle to establish the university's place in the world.[50] The mendicants friars relied, for example, on gifts and donations from their students, while seculars followed the medieval university's guild model of charging for instruction. Still, the friars became a strong presence in the universities. At Oxford, Robert Bacon was among the early Dominican masters, having taken his vows in or around 1229 and continuing to teach theology there until his death in 1248. He worked with Robert Grosseteste at the university and King Henry III appears to have called on his services to assist in the policing of the university cleric's moral purity. While he was not prepared to reconcile Aristotle and Augustine in support of Christian beliefs, as his fellow Dominican Thomas Aquinas was to do at Paris, he still

48. Senocak, *Poor and the Perfect*, 60, 201. Senocak adds that friars were advised "by administrators not use words that indicate ownership" when referring to their collections of books (205). In 1307, the general chapter condemned "the communities of books" that precluded some friars from using the library (207). "Not only did the number of communally owned books increase dramatically, but the collections appear to have gained a greater level of institutional stability. The practice of supplying books with an inscription of communal ownership was beginning to become more common by the end of the twelfth century, especially among the Cistercians and Augustinians": Webber, "Monastic and Cathedral Book Collections," in *To 1640*, vol. 1, *The Cambridge History of Libraries in Britain and Ireland*, ed. Elisabeth Leedham-Green and Teresa Webber (Cambridge: Cambridge University Press, 2006), 123.

49. "Franciscans only wanted to claim *simplex ususfacti*, the power to consume a commodity but not to trade it, alienate it, involve it in the monetary world; they were thereby able to preserve themselves from the non-feudal, profit economy and were, in effect, doing what radical but earlier monastic groups had done: run from the current economy rather than cope with it": Janet Coleman, "Dominium in Thirteenth- and Fourteenth-Century Political Thought and Its Seventeenth-Century Heirs: John of Paris and Locke," *Political Studies* 33 (1985): 95.

50. Rosenwein and Little on the un-guild-like nature of the friars: "The friars in both orders thought of themselves as mendicants, determined to lead full lives each day without stocking supplies for the following day" and "the root of the problem seems to have been two-fold: first, there was a disgust with money itself; and second, the new urban professions lacked moral justification" ("Social Meaning," 21, 25).

demonstrated the Dominican command of the new (ancient) learning with occasional Aristotelian examples in his teaching.[51]

The Dominicans at Paris, led by Aquinas, dominated thirteenth-century teaching of theology after establishing a religious house in the city in 1217.[52] Among their number, John of Paris, born around 1255, claimed that all ecclesiastical property, including that of the university presumably, should be regarded as held in common by all, a position which the church was quick to censure.[53] In 1269, the Franciscan theologian Bonaventure, who studied and taught at the University of Paris, laid out a more nuanced set of property categories "in dealing with temporal goods, namely, ownership, possession, usufruct, and simple use."[54] The friars should take their stand with support for the simple use of things (with no presumption of ownership or rights associated with that), Bonaventure asserted, while clarifying that this did not preclude the church's retention of its extensive properties. Bonaventure was responding to the objections of his secular colleagues in Paris. They criticized the mendicant presumption that their higher poverty was "a more excellent state than that of the Roman church," as Gerard of Abbeville, another Paris theologian, put it in a sermon at the time.[55] A decade later, in 1279, Pope Nicholas III attempted to resolve the question of use with a bull that, among other measures, recognized both a mendicant's "right of use" (to consult the books in a library) and the simple use of food to stay alive.[56]

In the thirteenth century the Franciscans became known for the communal libraries they managed in association with the universities, supported by

51. B. Smalley, "Robert Bacon and the Early Dominican School at Oxford." *Transactions of the Royal Historical Society*, ser. 4, vol. 30 (1948): 15. "The early Oxford Dominicans show a queer blend of resistance and receptivity to new lines in thinking and teaching" (ibid.)

52. K. W. Humphreys, *The Book Provisions of the Medieval Friars 1215–1400* (Amsterdam: Erasmus, 1964), 46; Witt, *Two Latin Cultures*, 406.

53. "Lay property is not granted to the community as a whole as is ecclesiastical property": John of Paris, *On Royal and Papal Power*, trans. J. A. Watt (Toronto: Pontifical Institute of Medieval Studies, 1971), 103. "John of Paris, as a Dominican, is traditionally held to be a staunch defender and follower of Aquinas, but he is doing something more radical than Aquinas and more akin to the Locke this author reads, at any rate, in arguing for the positive support of property rights from the natural law": Coleman, "Dominium in Thirteenth and Fourteenth-Century Political Thought," 96.

54. Bonaventure, *The Works of St. Bonaventure*, ed. Robert J. Karris, vol. 15, *Defense of the Mendicants*, trans. José de Vinck and Robert J. Karris (St. Bonaventure: Franciscan Institute Publications, 2010), 307. Usufruct granted a right to the use of property, including commercial use, that left the property unchanged, and as such corresponds to the intellectual property right of use that I associate with learning, except that critical use can, for example, alter the meaning of the original.

55. Cited by Karris, Introduction to *Works of St. Bonaventure*, 10.

56. Giorgio Agamben, *The Highest Poverty: Monastic Rules and Form-of-Life*, trans. Adam Koysko (Stanford, CA: Stanford University Press, 2013), 125–26. Agamben points to the difference between use as a right and use to stay alive as a distinction between law and fact (126).

Grosseteste-like donations.[57] Among these growing libraries, the friars pioneered a number of organizational innovations to improve the usefulness of their collections. They categorized books by subject; assigned them call numbers; created collection catalogs, including union catalogs across different collections; preserved works in book presses (flattening the humidity-sensitive parchment pages); and sold off less useful works, using the proceeds to strengthen certain areas of their collections.[58] Many aspects of the friars' communal-patronage model of a well-managed research library attuned to the needs of scholars were later adopted by university libraries.

Among the Franciscans at Oxford, Roger Bacon (not be mistaken for the Dominican Robert Bacon, introduced earlier) arrived there after lecturing in Paris on Aristotle's *Physics and Metaphysics* in the 1240s, but before he returned to England where he was likely to have joined the order. At Oxford, Bacon followed the example of Grosseteste by promoting mathematics and the experimental sciences at the university "in the service of theology," to borrow from one of his book titles, but then he also had a strong faith in the powers of astrology.[59] He was among the more ecumenical spirits of his time, bringing together the wisdom of Solomon, Aristotle, and Avicenna as examples of those given to the renewal of learning, while calling for a spirit of cooperation among those committed to a Christian revival.[60]

In England, the Franciscans and Dominicans extended their educational efforts by setting up elementary schools, with the highest-achieving boys sent to their respective order's priory house to study at Oxford.[61] The spiritual element that the friars brought to the university in Oxford attracted the royal patronage of Henry III, who made close to a hundred grants to the two orders,

57. K. W. Humphreys, *The Book Provisions of the Medieval Friars 1215–1400* (Amsterdam: Erasmus, 1964), 47–48. "The advent of friars to the universities at Paris, Oxford, Cambridge and Bologna introduced a new phase in the history of the library" (83).

58. Ibid., 62, 81, 99–118. "The Dominicans, like modern academics, required extensive libraries in which they could glance rapidly over a whole series of books, many of very recent authorship, in order to construct a wide-ranging argument": M. T. Clanchy, *From Memory to Written Record: England 1066–1307*, 2nd ed. (Oxford: Blackwell, 1993), 160.

59. Crombie, *Grosseteste*, 139. "In sharing the same Augustinian theological leaning, the same drive for broad learning, and the same enthusiasm for applying mathematics to the analysis of natural philosophy, Bacon was, in a sense, Grosseteste's alter ego": Smith, *Sight to Light*, 260. Marenbom points out how Roger Bacon's *scientia experimentalis* was something nearer to astrology, alchemy and magic than the experimental sciences in a modern sense," although it did involve work in optics and mathematics: *Pagans and Philosophers*, 128.

60. George Molland, "Bacon, Roger (*c.*1214–1292?)," in *Oxford Dictionary of National Biography*.

61. On the conflict between the orders, Archbishop John Pecham, a Franciscan, failed in his attempt toward the end of the thirteenth century to have the Dominican philosophy of Thomas Aquinas banned from Oxford: Sheehan, "Religious Orders," 204–5.

including allotments of timber and stone, during his long thirteenth-century reign.[62] The friars also received royal pittances to support their students.[63] But the point of general agreement that eventually emerged among masters, secular and mendicant, during that century was on the order that Aristotle brought to learning. The peripatetic philosopher was placed at the head of the Oxford curriculum, but only as he had been carried there on the shoulders of his plentiful commentators, Greek, Islamic, and now European. An "Oxford gloss" on Aristotle was created by the secular and mendicant masters at the university, and they did so with much support from and citing of the Commentator, which is to say, Averroës.[64]

Before the close of the thirteenth century, monastics also began to turn to these new institutions of learning. In 1257, the scholarly Benedictine monk and historian Matthew Paris appeared before King Henry III to defend the *studium* masters against the interference of Henry of Lexington, a bishop of Lincoln who was not as sympathetic to the university as Bishop Grosseteste had been.[65] In 1282 the Cistercians founded the first of Oxford's monastic colleges, having already opened one in Paris, and the Benedictines followed suit at Oxford with the establishment of Gloucester College in 1283 and Durham in 1286.[66] It signaled a recognition that the university's devotion to learning could support the monastic mission despite Bernard of Clairvaux's vehement opposition to the schools of Paris a little more than a century prior.

In introducing his biography of Grosseteste, Southern refers to "the grandeur of the medieval scholastic enterprise" as "one of the greatest achievements of cooperative intellectual effort and social organization at any period in the past."[67] The use and crediting of Islamic scholars by Grosseteste and others in the new universities was a vital element of that cooperative achievement within and across cultures vis-à-vis both the Crusades' violent assault on Islam and the proprietary secrets of other trade guilds. The scholastic masters made their sources and methods plain; it is what they taught to fee-paying students and what they published for those who could afford copies of their manuscript books. The masters and scholars were working

62. Ibid., 211.
63. Ibid., 201.
64. Burnett, *Arabic Learning*, 75–76.
65. Lloyd Simon and Rebecca Reader, "Paris, Matthew (c. 1200–1259)," in *Oxford Dictionary of National Biography*.
66. Sheehan, "Religious Orders," 194.
67. Southern, *Grosseteste*, xxiii–xxiv.

within an intellectual property order that was taking shape within the semi-autonomous commonwealth of learning that was comprised of communal libraries, which recognized rights of copying, compilation, and commentary. What Grosseteste demonstrated above all, and what the friars managed to advance, is how this cooperative intellectual effort thrived on well-organized access to new and traditional forms of knowledge, and on no less well-managed sponsorship and charity. Still, as Paris dramatically demonstrated during the thirteen century, the university was still in the process of establishing the forms of intellectual autonomy that could best serve learning.

THE UNIVERSITY OF PARIS

It hardly needs stating that Paris is not Oxford. To begin with, the university that took shape in that city over the course of the twelfth century was a child of the cathedral school at Notre Dame. The school's chancellor, appointed by the bishop, retained control of the *studium*, if often amid considerable controversy, throughout the thirteenth century and beyond. At the same time, the university masters and scholars swore oaths of fidelity to the ordinances and statutes of their *studium* guild. A further source of tension, common to universities everywhere, was how readily the young, rambunctious, and largely foreign students riled up the townsfolk. King Philip Augustus (the first to hold the title "King of France") had to step in more than once in the case of Paris, and after one such conflagration in 1200 granted the *studium* its own royal charter, which, among the rights and privileges provided, gave scholars some immunity from overbearing civil magistrates.[68]

Issues also arose around the access and use rights of masters and scholars. In 1210, a synod led by Archbishop Peter of Corbeil forbade the teaching or study of Aristotle in all of Paris. It also prohibited the use of related commentaries on natural philosophy by Avicenna, Averroës, and others. Still, the ban appears to have had little effect on the university's program of teaching. After five years, Pope Innocent III felt compelled to intervene. His local legate, Cardinal Robert of Courçon, issued a less restrictive prohibition permitting theology faculty to use Aristotle for private study.[69] In softening

---

68. Kibre, *Scholarly Privileges*, 85–87.
69. John F. Wippel, "The Parisian Condemnations of 1270 and 1277," in *A Companion to Philosophy in the Middle Ages*, ed. Jorge J. E. Garcia and Timothy N. Noone (Oxford: Blackwell, 2002), 66; Senocak, *Poor and the Perfect*, 177.

the prohibition against Aristotle, the cardinal recognized the central place of the philosopher's work in the new method of education, as well the degree of intellectual autonomy that was necessary to encourage masters to serve (rather than resist) the authority of the church.[70] The responsible use of Aristotle was, after all, a frequent subject of scholastic disputation. A master would delve into an Aristotelian dialectic or a grammatical theme, while a bachelor of arts would respond with how this is an appropriate or, more daringly, inappropriate use of Aristotle.[71]

The cardinal also weighed in on the university's fee structure. This was required in light of the Christian belief that as knowledge comes from God, it cannot be sold.[72] The masters did not represent just another guild, but carried forward some part of the communal and pious spirit of monasticism. The cardinal condemned the charging of student fees in theology and canon law, while allowing it for secular subjects such as geometry. If a master of theology was without a church benefice to support himself, however, the cardinal reasonably permitted him to accept gifts of appreciation from pupils.[73] And, finally, the cardinal empowered the *studium* to enter into rent-control agreements with Parisian landlords.[74]

Housing was no small issue for students in Paris (then and now). Fortunately, merchant and noble benefactors were prepared, as they had been in England, to help poor students pursue an education. As early as 1180, the English merchant Jocius de Londoniis founded the Collège des Dix-huit, which provided room and board for eighteen poor students in the Hôtel-Dieu near Notre Dame. It was the students' duty at the college, according to its charter, to carry a cross and holy water at the head of the procession that removed the dead from the hospital. In 1258, the king's chaplain Robert Sorbon contributed a residential college that provided accommodation to poor clergy

70. The popes also intervened in protecting the masters' rights in deciding to whom to grant a license to teach and in preventing the chancellor from demanding payment for that right: Kibre, *Scholarly Privileges*, 89.

71. McLaughlin, *Intellectual Freedom*, 57. McLaughlin points out that these disputations could wander into heresy, using the example of John of Brescain, who was cited in 1247 for errors which "seemed close to the Arian heresy" (58–59). The papal legate deprived John of the right to teach and expelled him from Paris forever (59).

72. In 2015, for example, Johannes Teutonicus reaffirmed the principle that knowledge comes from God in his gloss on canon law, which he taught at Bologna: Gaines Post, Kimon Giocarinis, and Richard Kay, "The Medieval Heritage of a Humanistic Ideal: 'Scientia donum dei escst, unde vendi non potest,'" *Traditio* 11 (1955): 197, 209.

73. John W. Baldwin, *Paris, 1200* (Stanford, CA: Stanford University Press, 2010), 183–84.

74. Ibid., 185.

and scholars who were expected to go on to serve the church.[75] Throughout the thirteenth century, approximately a dozen colleges were founded for students across the Left Bank, with the donors encouraged, in part, by royal favors granted to them by the king.[76]

The university's struggle for autonomy continued over the course of the thirteenth century, with the church proving itself fully prepared to excommunicate masters and scholars, as well as revoke teaching licenses, for various infractions. There were also book burnings, teaching strikes, riots, and at least one student execution, along with a number of other violent deaths. In 1229, for example, a majority of the masters protested the provost of Paris's violent suppression of a student riot. When the masters' concerns were ignored by the responsible city authorities, they decided to put a stop right then and there to the Paris *studium*. This was no bluff. In what became known as the Great Dispersion, the masters began to leave the city for welcoming universities in Toulouse, Oxford, and elsewhere. It was enough of a disruption to catch the attention of Pope Gregory IX, if not immediately.

Within two years of the Paris shutdown, the pope reached out to the masters with a conciliatory bull, *Parens scientiarum*. It named the university the *Parent of the Sciences*. It reasserted that masters and scholars were serving the greater good of the church, and thus warranted privileges that protected their scholarly rights to study. These included a limited immunity from civil authorities and local ecclesiastics, and the right of faculties to determine subjects taught, hours of instruction, hostel rent fees, and dress code.[77] The bull even established procedures and guidelines on teaching of Aristotle: "Those books on natural philosophy which for a certain reason were prohibited in a provincial council, are not to be used at Paris until they have been examined and purged of all suspicion of error."[78]

Gregory followed up the bull that same year with an affirmation that scholars could not be excommunicated by local ecclesiastics, which set a new

75. Astrik L. Gabriel, "Motivation of the Founders at Medieval Colleges," *Miscellanea Mediaevalia* 3 (1964): 66.

76. Baldwin, *Paris*, 184–85. Baldwin identifies the first two college founders as the English merchant Jocius and Robert, Count of Dreux (ibid.). See also Franklin J. Pegues, "Philanthropy and the Universities in France and English in the Later Middle Ages," in *The Economic and Material Frame of the Medieval University*, ed. Astrik L. Gabriel (Notre Dame, IN: International Commission for the History of Universities, 1977), 70.

77. Kibre, *Scholarly Privileges*, 94–95.

78. "Statutes of Gregory IX for University of Paris 1231," in *Translations and Reprints from the Original Sources of History*, vol. 2 (Philadelphia: University of Pennsylvania, Dept. of History, 1902), 10.

standard for academic freedom among medieval universities. But it came at a cost. The pope made it clear that he expected the masters and scholars to be intellectual leaders in the church's defense of the faith. In 1240, Gregory called upon some of the Paris masters to serve in the papal court held in the city to hear the charges of blasphemy brought against the Talmud and the Jewish people. The chosen masters did not prove ardent defenders of others' rights of use and the Talmud was condemned to be burnt in the public squares of the city.[79]

The accord that Gregory struck between church and *studium* was challenged by the righteous within the church who held up examples of what they saw as the university's continuing abuses in teaching Aristotle. They pointed to an anonymous work entitled *Ethics*, of dubious authenticity, which advised students that "we ought not to solve problems after the manner of the theologian but according to the intention of the Philosopher."[80] The church responded with further bans on the reading and teaching of Aristotle and company. Finally, in 1254, the faculty members of the university took a united stand against the church's ongoing interference. They issued an encyclical asserting that the *studium* was not an arm of the local church, as were the cathedral schools. Rather, the *studium* was the intellectual foundation of the church writ large, the masters held, and as such required study and teaching without undue interference.[81] Like the monastery, the university was always careful to position itself as both a part of and apart from church and state.

In 1256, Pope Alexander IV decided to pursue a different tack with the Parisian masters. Alexander again declared the work of the university central to the church, which meant that it needed to be supported, while remaining accountable to the church. The *studium* was, as he put it, "like the tree of life and like a burning lamp in the house of the Lord."[82] At the same time, he solicited

79. Robert Chazan, "Trial, Condemnation, and Censorship: The Talmud in Medieval Europe," in *The Trial of the Talmud: Paris, 1240*, trans. John Friedman and Jean Connell Hoff (Toronto: Pontifical Institute of Medieval Studies, 2012), 1. After hearing appeals from Jewish leaders, Pope Innocent IV later reduced the sentence to a redaction of seemingly offensive passages in the Talmud. Earlier, the Council of Paris had decreed in 1213 that Jews were not allowed to teach their young "this art of writing [used to write down the loans made by their parents]": cited by Sophia Menache, "Communication in the Jewish Diaspora: A Survey," in *Communication in the Jewish Diaspora: The Pre-Modern World*, ed. Sophia Menache (Leiden: Brill, 1996), 46.

80. Cited by McLaughlin, *Intellectual Freedom*, 39.

81. Peter R. McKeon, "The Status of the University of Paris as *Parens Scientiarum*: An Episode in the Development of its Autonomy," *Speculum* 39, no. 4 (1964): 656–57.

82. Citied by McLaughlin, *Intellectual Freedom*, 22. McLaughlin adds that the university "was also a field for the intervention of various authorities, and an arena for their conflicts" (ibid.).

the help of the master Albert the Great to help the church identify what was misguided and heretical among the work of the Parisian masters. In Paris and then at the Dominican *stadium generale* in Cologne, Albert had done considerable work on Aristotle, as well as al-Farabi and Avicenna. He favored the Aristotelian sense of the intellect as something acquired and developed through study, while he opposed Averroës' position on a singular extra-human intellect as the source of all ideas.[83] In undertaking this mission for Pope Alexander, Albert's principal targets were those known as the Latin Averroists, led by the colorful and controversial figure, Siger of Brabant, who ended up facing the Inquisitor for his beliefs, only to be murdered by his secretary in 1282.[84]

Albert was assisted in the *averroista* refutation by his student Thomas Aquinas, whose work on Aristotle had drawn from Islamic commentaries, as well as by the work of Moses Maimonides, the great Jewish philosopher and a contemporary of Averroës from Córdoba. Aquinas' willingness to reach out to pagan, Islamic, Jewish, and Christian thinkers was all about strengthening the intellectual basis of Christianity: "We need such knowledge [as Aristotle proffered]," Aquinas wrote in his unfinished commentary on Aristotle's *Politics* between 1268 and 1272 while at Paris, "since we need to teach everything that reason can know for the perfection of human wisdom called philosophy."[85] In this use of others' work, Aquinas was careful to

83. "The writings of Albertus Magnus in particular show a knowledge of several Arabic philosophical texts of which we do not have evidence of full translations into Latin, such as commentaries on Aristotle's logic and physics": Burnett, "Arabic into Latin," 383.

84. Siger's position on Averroës was ambivalent, at best, and his reputation was later elevated by Dante who places him in the fourth circle of heaven in the *Paradiso*. Herbert A. Davidson identifies nineteen Averroists by name in Paris, Bologna, and Oxford during the thirteenth and fourteenth century, while pointing to the influence of Averroës through to the sixteenth century in northern Italy: *Alfarabi, Avicenna, and Averroes on Intellect: Their Cosmologies, Theories of the Active Intellect, and Theories of Human Intellect* (Oxford: Oxford University Press, 1992), 309-11. The church objected to Averroës's ideas on the perfectibility of reason and knowledge, as well as on humankind sharing a common intellect: Marshall W. Baldwin, "The Popes and Learning in the High Middle Ages (Concluded)," *Manuscripta* 2, no. 1 (1958): 17.

85. Thomas Aquinas, *Commentary on Aristotle's* Politics, trans. Richard J. Regan (Indianapolis: Hackett, 2007), 2. Bernard McGinn sums up Aristotle's influence on Aquinas as follows: "Truth told, Thomas absorbed much from both Aristotle and the Neoplatonists, but he would not have been happy to be terms either an 'Aristotelian' or a 'Neoplatonist'—nor, of course, a 'Thomist'" (*Thomas Aquinas'* Summa theologiae: *A Biography* [Princeton, NJ: Princeton University Press, 2014], 42). "He was more inclined to examine the arguments of thinkers than their faith," David C. Burrell, professor of theology at the University of Notre Dame, notes, and as such "he epitomized the medieval respect for learning, with its conviction that 'truth was where one found it'": "Aquinas and Islamic and Jewish Thinkers," in *Cambridge Companion to Aquinas*, ed. Norman Kretzmann and Eleonore Stump (Cambridge: Cambridge University Press, 1993), 61.

locate his position in relation to theirs, as if to affirm this common project of strengthening the philosophical coherence of human wisdom by identifying the particular positions and stances of those who have contributed to the ideas in question: "I say with Avicenna," writes Aquinas in opposing Averroës, "that the possible intellect begins to exist but does not go out of existence with the body."[86] Or he would anchor an assertion with "this is also the teaching of the Commentator," which is to say Averroës on Aristotle.[87] Aquinas was a diligent scholar in this accreditation process, with tens of thousands of citations to be found in his work.[88]

In making Aristotle safe for Christianity, Aquinas had to confront what was most unchristian about Averroës' influential reading of Aristotle. This included the idea—which Averroës alone found in the Aristotle's *On the Soul*—of an external and immortal intellect shared by humankind but belonging to no one. This struck Aquinas as undermining an individual's responsibility for ideas, heretical or otherwise, in this age of Catholic confession; it also didn't do much for the concept of a soul possessing eternal life, if that soul had no intellect of its own to preserve. In 1270, Aquinas sought, in his own words, to "destroy the error ['in what is falsely named a science'] . . . using the arguments and teachings of the philosophers themselves."[89] He cites both Aristotle and Avicenna in demonstrating that "certain operations of the soul are not through a mediating body," as Averroës held.[90]

86. Thomas Aquinas, "Commentary on Book II of the *Sentences*, Distinction 17, Question 2, Article 1," trans. Richard C. Taylor, in *Philosophical Psychology in Arabic Thought and the Latin Aristotelianism of the 13th Century*, ed. Luis Xavier López Farjeat and Jörg Alejandro Tellkamp (Paris: J. Vrin, 2013), 291. As part of that curation, later scholars have identified the exact locations in the works of Averroës and Avicenna to which Aquinas is referring. What I did not encounter in work on this topic was a consideration of how Averroës's concept of a single external intelligence aligned with the medieval Christian concept of knowledge originating with God.

87. Thomas Aquinas, *The Divisions and Methods of the Sciences*, 4th ed., trans. Armand Maurer (Toronto: Pontifical Institute of Medieval Studies, 1986), 92.

88. McGinn, *Thomas Aquinas' Summa theologiae*, 23.

89. Thomas Aquinas, *Aquinas against the Averroists: On There Being Only One Intellect*, trans. Ralph McInerny (West Lafayette, IN: Purdue University Press, 1993), 145.

90. Thomas Aquinas, "Commentary on Book II of the 'Sentences,' Distinction 17, Question 2, Article 1," trans. Richard C. Taylor, in *Philosophical Psychology in Arabic Thought*, 292. Aquinas, writes, following al-Farabi, that "in every man there is a certain principle of knowledge, namely the light of the active intellect, through which certain universal principles of all the sciences are naturally understood as soon as proposed to the intellect," which is an interpretation, Aquinas reminds us, of "what the Philosopher says (Poster. I, I): 'All teaching and all learning proceed from previous knowledge,'" which Aquinas goes on to cite in support "as Averroës argues, the teacher does not cause knowledge in the disciple after the manner of a natural active cause" (*Summa theologica*, trans. Laurence Shapcote [Raleigh, NC: Hayes Barton, 2006], 1.117.1.4 1045-46).

Aquinas' emphasis on intellectual responsibility not only served the church's interest in personal confession, but it provided the groundwork for considering writers' intellectual property rights in their work. His theology of property and authorship possesses a further relevance for my interests. In *Summa theologica*, Aquinas introduces the Christian conceptions of communal property found in the *Acts of the Apostles*, as well as in the work of the church fathers Basil, Ambrose, and Augustine. He then employs Aristotle's arguments to identify the natural limits of this communality: "Every man is more careful," Aquinas paraphrases Aristotle, "to procure what is for himself alone than that which is common to many or to all."[91] He takes Aristotle's observation to form a natural proof: "It is by this argument that the Philosopher proves (*Polit*. i, 3) that the possession of external things is natural to man."[92] He then allows that these two property types, common and private, coexist, the one by natural law and the other by human reason: "Hence the ownership of possessions is not contrary to the natural law, but a super-addition (*adinventio*) thereto devised by human reason."[93] This is the Aristotelian-Christian synthesis, and it figures in Locke's natural law theory of property considered in chapter 11. And it also speaks to the property distinctions that I consider a part of the commonwealth of learning. For, through no less a careful application of human reason, what prevails in the commonwealth is the common right of use, with authorship, rather than ownership, considered a natural point of inquiry and interest.

Aquinas was also an advocate of a more open or public approach to teaching and disputations. He was for giving controversial issues a hearing rather than hiding them away: "Let him not speak in corners nor to boys who cannot judge."[94] It was in this spirit of making scholarly deliberations more of a

91. Aquinas, *Summa theologica*, 2.2.66.1-2 2684.

92. Ibid. "In general," Aristotle writes, "living together and sharing in common in all human matters is difficult, and most of all in these sorts of things": *The Politics*, trans. by T. A. Sinclair and Trevor J. Saunders (London: Penguin, 1981), 1263a15-16. Additionally, "further, with regard to pleasure, too, it makes an immense difference to consider something one's own. For it is not without reason that each person has affection for himself; this is natural" (1263a40-b1).

93. Aquinas, *Summa theologica*, 2.2.66.2 2686. Averroës does figure in Aquinas's ideas on intellectual property, as he notes that "Averroes argues, the teacher does not cause knowledge in the disciple," which is to say that the pupil is responsible for that knowledge (1.2.117.1 1046).

94. Aquinas, *Against the Averroists*, 145. Typical of those taking exception to Aquinas's approach is his contemporary Franciscan Peter Olivi: "I am astonished to see that Aristotle the pagan and the Arab Averroes, as well as other unbelieving philosophers, are held in great esteem and veneration and allowed so great an authority, especially in discussions about scared authority": cited by John M. Rist, *Augustine Deformed: Love Sin and Freedom in the Western Tradition* (Cambridge: Cambridge University Press, 2014), 140.

public enterprise that the University of Paris passed a measure in 1276, two years after Aquinas' death, requiring that lectures be given in the university's public settings, rather than in "private places."[95] Yet this new level of public accountability only exacerbated the local church's attacks on the Parisian masters' intellectual autonomy.

In 1277, Etienne Tempier, bishop of Paris and former Notre Dame chancellor (and thus chancellor of the university), issued the *Condemnation of 219 Propositions* directed against the University of Paris. Although it was not uncommon at the time to hear of heresies perpetuated by the masters at the university, Tempier's charges added up to a particularly pointed and aggressive attack on the new learning.[96] The targets were, once again, Aristotle, Averroës, and Avicenna, particularly as taught by the recently murdered Siger of Brabant, while Aquinas also figured in the *Condemnation*.[97] Tempier was charging the university's masters and scholars with, as he put it, "certain obvious and loathsome errors, or rather *vanities and lying follies* [Ps. 39:5] which are contained in the roll joined to this letter."[98] In one point after another, the roll presented a caricature of the new learning: "2. That the only wise men in this world are the philosophers"; "5. That man should not be content with authority to have certitude about any question"; and "180. That the Christian Law impedes learning."[99] Tempier singled out specific positions held by Averroës without naming the source—"116. That the intellect is numerically one for all"; and by Aquinas in his support for Aristotle—"27. That the first cause cannot make more than one world."[100] Tempier also proclaimed in the preamble that those who dared to teach such propositions,

95. Cited by McLaughlin, *Intellectual Freedom*, 83.

96. "Sixteen lists of censured theses . . . were issued at the University of Paris during the thirteenth and fourteenth centuries": J. M. M. Thijesen, "What Really Happened on 7 March 1277? Bishop Tempier's Condemnation and its Institutional Context," in *Texts and Contexts in Ancient and Medieval Science*, ed. Edith Sylla and Michael McVaugh (Brill: Leiden, 1997), 85. The University of Oxford faced a similar set of condemnations at the time from Robert Kilwardby, archbishop of Canterbury: Leland E. Wilshire, "Were the Oxford Condemnations of 1277 Directed Against Aquinas?" *New Scholasticism* 48, no. 1 (1974): 125-32.

97. Leland E. Wilshire, "The Condemnations of 1277 and the Intellectual Climate of the Medieval University," in *The Intellectual Climate of the Early University: Essays in Honor of Otto Gründler*, ed. Nancy van Deusen (Kalamazoo, MI: Medieval Institute Publications, 1977), 152.

98. "The Condemnation of 219 Propositions," trans. Ernest L. Fortin and Peter D. O'Neill, in *Medieval Political Philosophy: A Sourcebook*, ed. Ralph Lerner and Mushn Mahdi (New York: Free Press: 1963), 337.

99. Ibid., 338, 352. Giles of Rome prepared a far more detailed critique in *De erroribus philosophorum*, likely written between 1270 and 1277, citing passages from Aristotle, al-Kindī, al-Ghazali, Avicenna, Averroës, and Maimonides: Richard Dale, *Medieval Discussions of the Eternity of the World* (Leiden: Brill, 1990), 154.

100. "Condemnations," 347, 340.

or those who "listened to them," were subject to excommunication.[101] The only hope for the guilty was to confess their sins to Tempier or the university chancellor within seven days of their error, and for that they should still expect "penalties as the gravity of the offence demands."[102]

In the face of the bishop's sweeping condemnation, the Parisian masters once again turned to pope and king for support. Although Pope John XXI had written in support of the *Condemnation*, especially as it applied to the Arts faculty, he passed away within months of its issuance. The proctor of the university's arts faculty John of Malignes appeared before the papal court in 1283 (or perhaps 1284) to challenge the right of Notre Dame's Chancellor Tempier to act as head of the *studium*. John sought to convince the church that Tempier was not the right person to lead the university, as the university was a distinctive gift from God acting in the service of the larger church and, as such, deserved the oversight and protection of the pope rather than a local chancellor: "God himself has wisely provided for man the tree [i.e., Paris] in whose center He opened the noble fount which is divided into four streams . . . whose water is [the masters'] teaching. . . . The streams are the four faculties of arts, medicine, canon law, and theology."[103]

Despite John's plea, Pope Honorius IV upheld the Notre Dame's chancellor's right to govern the university. It was only in 1296, with Pope Boniface VIII, that the university was freed from the oversight of Notre Dame. By this point, Rome was providing various forms of funding directly to the university, including benefices (salaries) to support masters in the arts faculty, and prebends (stipends) for up to five years for clerics studying theology.[104] Likewise, during the final decade of the thirteenth century, King Philip IV shored up the Paris scholars' rights, privileges, and immunities, by placing the students under the king's safeguard in their travels, as well as exempting them from travelers' tolls and customs duties (largely for importing books, one imagines), and from tax assessments for the royal household and the needs of war.[105]

It was clear by this point, at the close of the thirteenth century, that the university of Paris had, through its process of incorporation, managed to set itself apart from other craft and trade guilds, as well as from local bishops, chancellors, and civil laws. The masters constituted themselves as a self-governing body in regulating costumes, lectures, disputations, funerals, the

101. Ibid., 338.
102. Ibid.
103. Cited by McLaughlin, *Intellectual Freedom*, 1.
104. Ibid., 27; Baldwin, *Paris, 1200*, 183.
105. Kibre, *Scholarly Privileges*, 128–30.

rent charged to students, and the pawnbrokers allowed to lend them money. The masters took a particular interest in the production of texts. Here, the city's guild structure came into play. The university masters worked with the guilds organized by scribes, illuminators, and bookbinders.[106] They appointed *peciarii* from within their own ranks to oversee the local book trade, which was led by the *stationarii* who operated bookstalls with new and secondhand manuscripts for rent, sale, and trade. The *peciarii* oversaw the correctness of the exemplars that were used to make copies. They assessed fines against the scribes when students or masters found errors in their copies.[107] They recalled copies of a given text from master and student when questions arose about the integrity and accuracy of texts being taught.

The scribal culture of the university operated what was, in effect, a program of copyrights. The university assumed a right to regulate the texts that could be copied in what was referred to as the *pecia* system that controlled the simultaneous copying of certified parts (or pieces) of a manuscript that could be readily fit together, greatly speeding up production without a loss of quality. Master and pupil had nonexclusive rights to have texts copied and to copies that were as complete and correct as possible. The authors of the texts, whether living or dead, had a right to proper attribution and their texts were owed a certain fidelity. Everyone involved had a right and responsibility to report errors; to improve translations; to prepare new, more accurate editions; to compose compilations; to create glosses; and to fashion commentaries. The manuscripts in circulation at the time constituted the currency and property of the commonwealth of learning. The paratext of the books that made up this commonwealth grew more elaborate. The best of them might include an analytical table of contents, running titles, and other study aids, including content summaries, chapters, paragraphs, footnotes, and indexes. Further, many books were assembled out of compilations of related texts to support a course of study.[108]

106. David Diringer, *The Book before Printing: Ancient, Medieval and Oriental* (New York: Dover, 1982), 208. Robert Steele, "The Pecia," *Library* 4, no. 2 (1930): 230-34.

107. Rashdall writes of students having to report errors in their copies "on pain of perjury," *Universities*, vol. 1, 189. He judges the university book trade "one of the most curious parts of the university system," and gives the further example of how "books above a certain value might only be sold in presence of the university notary" (190).

108. The act of compiling texts is portrayed by Malcolm Beckwith Parkes as a way for "a scholar of very humble talents . . . [to] feel that he was contributing to something of importance": "The Influence of the Concepts of *Ordinatio* and *Compilatio* on the Development of the Book," in *Medieval Learning and Literature: Essays Presented to Richard William Hunt*, ed. J. J. G. Alexander and M. T. Gibson (Oxford: Clarendon, 1976), 115-16.

The control of the book trade in and around the universities was not the only medieval intellectual property regime of its day. In 1291, the Republic of Venice granted legal rights to the Murano Guild of glass producers in Venice enabling them, through regulations and fines, to keep their business secret and secure.[109] This secretiveness, as well as the proprietary regard for knowledge, sets the Murano Guild apart from the *studium*. The knowledge and skills of the university masters are precisely what they have to offer to others in the belief that they can be enjoyed by all men—and only men, alas—willing and able to pay, or to find a patron who would pay, for what was essentially an intellectual property contract between master and scholar.

CONCLUSION

Paris was hardly alone in creating a university system to ensure the quality of access to learned texts. Bologna's bookmaking regulations were particularly detailed, requiring *studium* masters or doctors to transcribe the argument of each *diputatio* or *repetition*. These transcriptions were submitted to the university beadle who, on judging it sufficiently detailed, sent it along to the stationers for copying and circulation.[110] To ensure an adequate supply of books at the time, as contracts from the period reveal, the university employed a number of women as scribes and miniaturists, often working in conjunction with their fathers and husbands.[111] Bologna also took steps to ensure that the transportation of books did not face the tolls and customs levied against other goods, while preventing such works from being seized to pay a scholar's debts.[112]

From the early Middle Ages, with the Lenten distribution of books in Benedictine monasteries, to the *pecia* system of the early universities, organizing

---

109. Tine De Moor, "The Silent Revolution: A New Perspective on the Emergence of Commons, Guilds, and Other Forms of Corporate Collective Action in Western Europe," *International Review of Social History*, supp. 53 (2008): 203. Patrick McCray, *Glassmaking in Renaissance Venice: The Fragile Craft* (Farnham, Surrey, UK: Ashgate, 1999), 150. "Craft secrecy and patents, both manifestations of proprietary attitudes toward craft knowledge, developed rapidly in the specific historical context of medieval urbanism": Pamela O. Long, *Openness, Secrecy, Authorship: Technical Arts and the Culture of Knowledge from Antiquity to the Renaissance* (Baltimore: Johns Hopkins University Press, 2001), 89. Long adds that "there seems to have been no interest in discovering whether the claimant for a patent actually invented the device" (95).

110. Rashdall, *Universities*, 1:190.

111. Chiara Frugoni, "The Imagined Woman," trans. Clarissa Botsford, in *Silences of the Middle Ages*, ed. Christiane Klapisch-Zuber, vol. 2 of *A History of Women in the West* (Cambridge, MA: Harvard University Press, 1992), 400.

112. Kibre, *Scholarly Privileges*, 21.

the quality of access to texts was part of a long tradition of institutional structures that fostered learning, if more than intended in the Benedictine instance. The Venetian glassmakers may be credited as among the first to have
a form of intellectual protection in place by the thirteenth century, but I am
suggesting that a much older tradition of privilege and protection concerned
with the production of knowledge developed through the history of medieval monasteries, schools, and universities.[113] The masters and scholars used
the great educational force of the universities in negotiating with church and
state, as well as within their own institution, to gain specific rights and qualities of access, accreditation, autonomy, communality, sponsorship, and use,
that they deemed necessary for their work with learned texts. These factors
figured in the day-to-day regulation of manuscript production; the constant
battles with local church officials over the university's teachings; and the extraordinary measures occasionally employed on both sides, triggering academic strikes and acts of excommunication. They are part of what Grosseteste achieved in bringing the Islamic empirical sciences and Greek logic to
Oxford and what Aquinas gained in the Aristotelian application of reason to
theology at Paris. And one of them, namely the right of use, became central
to the friars' considerable contribution to this form of higher education.

The momentum achieved by the new learning gave rise to a new type of
educational incorporation in market towns, which further awakened an interest in book learning. Where the universities had thrived initially on the
translation of Islamic and Greek philosophy, including natural philosophy,
they were about to be swept by the broader cultural interest of what we now
call the humanities, even if it lay with the narrower geo-political range of classical antiquity. If this history were not already replete with self-congratulatory
renaissances, beginning with the Carolingian Renaissance earlier in this book,
and in the next chapter the Renaissance itself, I might have introduced the
"renaissance of the twelfth century," as Haskins and others have framed the
period. But it was more of a naissance, as something was born anew with
the universities through this access to Islamic learning that would not be seen
again with anything like the impact it had in this instance.

---

113. "Whatever economic dislocations it brings with it, the trend toward more intellectual
property certainly shows the robustness of the concepts first introduced by those Renaissance
Venetians": Robert P. Merges, "The Economic Impact of Intellectual Property Rights: An Overview
and Guide," *Journal of Cultural Economics* 19 (1995): 111.

CHAPTER EIGHT

The Humanist Revival

In the fourteenth century, Francesco Petrarca, or Petrarch, could be readily cast as the first (humanist) raider of the lost ark in his pursuit of undiscovered classical manuscripts. He journeyed to remote abbeys, priories, convents, and cathedrals to scour the uncatalogued disarray of their decayed manuscript collections. He sought out the lost treasures, the plays, histories, and letters that others in antiquity had referred to in their works, often with great admiration, but of which not a trace or copy of the manuscript had been seen in centuries. For Petrarch, what was at stake in this quest was the Greco-Roman legacy of antiquity as a European intellectual birthright. His manuscript discoveries, his eloquence (as a poet and scholar), and his enthusiasm for this birthright drew many, including wealthy patrons, to the humanist cause. In the universities, humanists introduced through their writing and teaching this new disciplinary field of the humanities (*studia humanitatis*) dedicated to the study of a rediscovered noble and legitimate form of learning (*eruditio legitima et ingenua*).[1]

This humanist movement involved intellectual property at every turn. Humanists studied the qualities that set the Roman histories of Livy apart

---

1. "The Italian humanists of the Renaissance created a new form of culture, inspired by Greco-Roman literature, which they referred to with names like the *studia humanitatis* (the humanities), *studia humaniora* (more humane studies), *studia honestarum artium* (the study of honorable arts), *bonae litterae* (good letters), *bonae artes* (the good arts), *eruditio legitima et ingenua* (noble and legitimate learning)": James Hankins, "Humanism, Scholasticism, and Renaissance Philosophy," in *Cambridge Companion to Renaissance Philosophy*, ed. James Hankins (Cambridge: Cambridge University Press, 2007), 32.

from those of Sallust. They prepared editions and translations that made the literary output of classical and late antiquity available again in Europe. Patrons of the humanities took advantage of the breadth of Greek and Roman literature that was appearing to assemble magnificent libraries, while the fifteenth-century arrival of the printing press made these books far more widely available across the Continent.[2] Outside of the universities, the humanist bent gave rise to a new public formation known as the academies, which sprang up in communities large and small during this period (and which form the subject of the next chapter).

The humanists were putting in place what was in effect a Christianized version of classical antiquity that would eventually be credited as forming a worthy origin of Western Civilization and the very definition of culture. They tied the West's destiny to the glory of Aristotle and Alexander the Great, Cicero and the Roman Empire. In this, the humanists brought forward a political mix of imperial ideology, republican Rome, and virtuous citizenship. Humanists furthered the alignment of Christian and classical texts, to which Augustine and Aquinas, among others, had contributed. Where the European ruling nobility once endowed monastic learning for its otherworldly spiritual order leading to heaven's gate, this time their support was for its overarching, worldly historical narrative.

To demonstrate what this humanist shift in learning represents for the intellectual properties of learning, I examine two of the leading humanists who taken together form European Renaissance bookends born centuries apart. The first is Petrarch, the fourteenth-century father of humanism; the second is Erasmus of Rotterdam, its sixteenth-century prince of print. Their leadership was as much about the place of humanism in the world, as they took learning another step or two into the court and marketplace of public life, while keeping a foot in its past. Petrarch's life was torn between monastic inclinations and political pursuits; Erasmus has been identified as "a monk of convenience," who took his vows only to walk away from the cloisters.[3] They were both similarly associated with and pursued by various universi-

---

2. Ann Blair estimates that "personal libraries increased over tenfold in size from 1450 to 1650 as a result of the lower cost, greater availability, and increasing accumulation of printed books": "Organizations of Knowledge," in *Cambridge Companion to Renaissance Philosophy*, ed. James Hankins (Cambridge: Cambridge University Press, 2007), 297.

3. Bruce Mansfield refers to Erasmus as "a monk of convenience, living outside his monastery," who had then "to discover a personal vocation": *Phoenix of His Age: Interpretations of Erasmus, c. 1550–1750* (Toronto: University of Toronto Press, 1979), 3.

ties, only to reject academic posts in favor of the patronage of the powerful. Carving out their place in this history of mine further determines the ways in which learning works in the world, given that their scholarship—and their open reflection on it—was combined for Petrarch with political engagement and for Erasmus with the commerce of print.

FRANCESCO PETRARCA

Born in 1304 in Tuscan Italy, Petrarch credits his classicist interests to the inspiring walks that he took "through the remains of a broken city," as he refers to Rome in one of his many published letters, in which "the remnant of ruins lay before our eyes."[4] He was moved, as well, by the stirrings of a patriotic fervor: "For who can doubt," he wrote in that same letter, "that Rome would rise again instantly if she began to know herself."[5] Petrarch was intent on helping Rome know herself again as the once and future empire; he came at this as poet, scholar, and, finally, diplomat acting on behalf of the church in his version of a civic humanism with imperialist aspirations that inevitably narrowed the scope of learning.

Jacob Burckhardt, the nineteenth-century Swiss historian who helped make the name *Renaissance* synonymous with civilization, is among the critics of Petrarch's devotion to a "revival of antiquity" and his "one-sided worship of classical antiquity."[6] Burckhardt holds up, by way of contrast, the far more open-minded example of Giovanni Pico della Mirandola, who was "the only man who loudly and vigorously defended the truth and science of all ages," for "he knew how to value not only Averroës and the Jewish investigators but also the scholastic writers of the Middle Ages."[7] In contrast, Petrarch was particularly dismissive of Islamic learning: "Keep your Arab authorities in banishment from any advice to me; I hate the entire race," Petrarch wrote to his physician, who had probably studied Latin medical texts translated from Arabic: "I shall scarcely be persuaded that anything good can come

---

4. Francesco Petrarch, "To Giovanni Colonna," in *Letters on Familiar Matters (Rerum familiarium libri) I–VIII,* vol. 1, trans. Aldo S. Bernardo (New York: Italica Press, 2005), 294.

5. Ibid., 1:293. Hans Baron discusses how Petrarch's historical and political sympathies shifted from republican to imperial Rome over the course of his life: *The Crisis of the Early Italian Renaissance: Civic Humanism and Republican Liberty in the Age of Classicism and Tyranny* (Princeton, NJ: Princeton University Press, 1966), 119–20.

6. Jacob Burckhardt, *The Civilization of the Renaissance in Italy,* trans. S. G. C. Middlemore (London: Penguin, 1990), 135.

7. Ibid.

from Arabia."[8] And elsewhere, Petrarch refers to "that mad dog, Averroes," besmirching the friend of so many students of Aristotle.[9]

Petrarch's ethnocentric version of a Greco-Roman humanism ultimately triumphed over Pico's more inclusive version, which tended toward the occult at many points. For its part, the Islamic legacy was sustained across the universities in astronomy, mathematics, and medicine.[10] But then Petrarch was no less critical of the universities, particularly for their scholasticism. Scholasticism was mired in empty dialectic and endless disputation, for Petrarch, be it over the nature of God or the number of angels who can dance on Aristotle's head. In a letter, this time to a friend from his student days at Bologna, Petrarch allowed only that "dialectic can be part of the journey; but it is certainly not the goal," before slipping in the sting that "there is nothing more deformed than an old dialectician."[11] Scholasticism was part of the failure of the Middle Ages, so called as the era between the glory of Rome and the birth of the European Renaissance. He was no kinder with monasticism, which he saw as clearly fumbling its responsibilities for preserving the classical legacy leading to the loss of so many texts: "Although they had nothing of their own to hand down to those who were to come after, they robbed posterity of its ancestral heritage."[12] Petrarch sought to right all of that, and not just through bombastic assertion but by careful scholarly inquiry into the reconstruction and interpretation of that past.

Among Petrarch's literary discoveries was his uncovering in 1333 of a copy of Cicero's defense oration (*Pro Archia*) on behalf of the poet Archias, for which Petrarch prepared an annotated edition. In Paris, he turned up love poems by Propertius from the first century BCE. He found a manuscript of Livy in the library at Chartres that helped him reconstruct this historian's

8. Francesco Petrarch, "To Giovanni Boccaccio da Certdaldo," *Letters of Old Age (Rerum senilium libri)*, vol. 2, trans. Reta A. Bernardo (New York: Italica Press, 2005), 650. Petrarch continues on this theme: "You learned men, through some strange mental weakness, celebrate them with great, and unless I am mistaken, undeserved trumpeting" (ibid.).

9. Petrarch, "To Luigi Marsili in Paris (ca. 1370)," in *Letters of Old Age*, 1:580. On the political front, Petrarch was troubled by the Ottoman Turks who, having ended Latin rule in Constantinople in 1453, entered the Balkans and appeared poised to make advances on Europe.

10. See for example, F. Jamil Ragep, "Copernicus and His Islamic Predecessors: Some Historical Remarks," *History of Science* 45, no. 1 (2007): 65–81.

11. Petrarch, "To Tommaso da Messina," in *Letters on Familiar Matters*, 1:39, 40.

12. Cited by James Harvey Robinson, *Petrarch: The First Modern Scholar and Man of Letters* (New York: Putnam's Sons, 1907), 25–26. In Petrarch's disdain for matters medieval, Robinson notes, he "disliked dialectics, the most esteemed branch of study in medieval schools; he utterly disregarded Scotus and Aquinas" (37).

work on Rome.[13] Drawing on copies of fragments from a variety of European libraries, he was able to assemble, collate, and correct the first ten books of Livy, as well as books 21–40 of the history (with some still missing to this day), adding annotations and supplements to create a magnificent edition of the Roman historian.[14] Petrarch was rebuilding Rome, one recovered intellectual property at a time.

Petrarch's biggest discovery, however, came in 1345 when he found a manuscript in the cathedral library in Verona that he realized contained Cicero's missing letters to Atticus, as well as to Brutus and to Cicero's brother, Quintus. Composed in the first century BCE, the letters are full of reflections on the arts of writing and statecraft in the Roman Republic. Petrarch copied out the letters himself and then, in an imaginative turn that becomes a poet, he prepared his own letter to Cicero (as he was to do to Homer, Virgil, and others) by way of announcing his find. He told Cicero that he was shocked by how "many quarrels and utterly useless feuds," as revealed in the letters, occupied a man who claimed to have distanced himself from the world; Petrarch wrote that he was "filled with shame and distress at your shortcomings" as he learned to "now recognize the kind of guide you were for yourself."[15] Cicero's letters, along with those of Seneca, ended up giving shape to Petrarch's own writing project. The poet began to compose letters as personal essays on public matters with the unmistakable intention of publishing them. Petrarch credited Cicero with inspiring this form of *civic* humanism. Cicero had declared that as an orator "his duty too it is to arouse a listless nation, and to curb its unbridled impetuosity" and this is what Petrarch most fervently sought to do over the course of his life.[16]

13. Andrew Pettegree, *The Book in the Renaissance* (New Haven, CT: Yale University Press, 2010), 10. James Turner, *Philology: The Forgotten Origins of the Modern Humanities* (Princeton, NJ: Princeton University Press, 2014), 34.

14. A dozen pages of this edition can be viewed online, courtesy of the British Library (Harley MS 2493, Digitized Manuscripts), with the scribe identified as "Francesco Petrarca and other 14th century hands." "Petrarch was not the first person to try this [reconstruction], but he was by far the best in over a thousand years": Rens Bod, *New History of the Humanities: The Search for Principles and Patterns from Antiquity to the Present* (Oxford: Oxford University Press, 2014), 144.

15. Petrarch, "To Marcus Tullius Cicero," in *Letters on Familiar Matters*, 3:317. "The Renaissance begins, for our purposes, with Francesco Petrarch's discovery in 1345 of a copy of Cicero's letters to Atticus": David Wootton, *Modern Political Thought: Readings from Machiavelli to Nietzsche* (Cambridge: Hackett, 2008), 1. Anthony Grafton sees in Petrarch's life of Cicero "the beginnings of a critical history of philosophy": "Availability of Ancient Works," in *The Cambridge History of Renaissance Philosophy*, ed. Charles B. Schmitt et al., 763–91 (Cambridge: Cambridge University Press), 771.

16. Cicero, *De oratore, Books I–II*, trans. E. W. Sutton and H. Rackham (Cambridge, MA: Harvard University Press, 1942), 223. On civic versus stylistic interests in humanism, see Baron, *Crisis of*

Petrarch initially supported his life of learning, discovery, and poetry by accepting the clerical preferments and benefices provided by the patronage of the Colonna family in Rome.[17] His devotion to learning was such in those days that he refused to pursue administrative positions with the church: "I would never approve any conditions," Petrarch wrote to his friend, the poet, Boccaccio, "that would distract me even for a short while from my freedom and from my studies. Therefore, when everyone sought the palace, I either sought the forest or rested in my room among my books."[18] Later in life, however, he played the part of court intellectual for the King of Naples, the Duke of Milan, the Doge of Venice, and the pope.[19] He found the grand life to his liking and accepted the political patronage offered by Italian despots, such as Giovanni Visconti, archbishop of Milan, in whose service he remained for eight years as diplomat and orator-on-demand.

Petrarch did, however, express regrets over the demands of such patronage: "Even in fetters, if fortune condemns me to them, I continue thinking of liberty, and amidst the cities I continue thinking of the country."[20] He had in 1350 declined the Florentines' invitation to occupy a chair at their newly founded university.[21] He had attended university at Montpellier and then Bologna, where he reluctantly studied civil law at his father's urging: "I saw Bologna and I did not cleave to it," he later reflected in a letter to a professor there, as "nature begot me a lover of solitude and not of the marketplace."[22] Still, in 1341, the lover of solitude arranged to have himself crowned Poet Laureate in Rome and extended his stay in Milan, the largest city and marketplace in Italy at the time.[23]

the Early Italian Renaissance; and Jerrold E. Siegel, "Civic Humanism' or Ciceronian Rhetoric?" *Past and Present* 34 (1966): 3-48.

17. Petrarch writes in 1370: "I remained many years with his brother John, the Cardinal Colonna, not, as it were, under a patron, but under a father—nay, not even that, say rather a most affectionate brother, with whom I lived as at home and in my own house" ("Epistle to Posterity," in Henry Reeve, *Petrarch* [Edinburgh: Blackwood and Sons, 1878], 21-22).

18. Petrarch, "To Giovanni Boccaccio da Certdaldo," *Letters of Old Age*, 2:650.

19. Reeve, *Petrarch*, 129.

20. Petrarch, "To Giovanni," in *Letters on Familiar Matters*, 3:35. "Petrarch disclosed a troubled sensibility about accepting certain kinds of patronage throughout his career, and his disclosure affected poets in his wake": William J. Kennedy, "Versions of a Career: Petrarch and His Renaissance Commentators," in *European Literary Careers: The Author from Antiquity to the Renaissance*, ed. Patrick Cheney and Frederick Alfred De Armas (Toronto: University of Toronto Press, 2002), 156.

21. Robinson, *Petrarch*, 115.

22. Petrarch, "To a Certain Famous Man," in *Letters on Familiar Matters*, 1:223.

23. Boccaccio wrote in honor of his friend's crowning, in a metaphor paralleling Locke's description of his scholarly task (cited in my first chapter), that Petrarch "removed the thornbushes and undergrowth with which man's negligence had encumbered the road . . . and so opened the way for himself as well as for those who wished to ascend after him": cited by Baron, *Crisis of the*

Petrarch had a similarly mixed response to the monastic life of learning. His brother Gerard had become a Carthusian lay brother in the monastery at Montrieux, and this rigorously ascetic monastic order was a decided influence on Petrarch's life, just as a number of monasteries proved to be centers of humanist study.[24] Yet it was the life of writing, rather than that of monastic piety and the pursuit of salvation, that provided him with the solace he sought: "While I write I become eagerly engaged with our greatest writers in whatever way I can and willingly forget those among whom my unlucky star destined me to live; and to flee from these I concentrate all my strength following the ancients instead."[25] And Petrarch, for all his devoutness— "Thou, my God, 'Lord of Learning' . . . Thou Whom I must and will prefer to Aristotle"—followed the life of the pen rather than that of prayer.[26]

Petrarch also went on to propose what might be thought of as the natural law of literary use without ownership in a vision of an ecological commons that is improved through communal use: "We must write just as the bees make honey," one of his letters to Boccaccio states, "not gathering flowers but turning them into a honeycombs, thereby blending them into oneness that is unlike them all, and better."[27]

Out of this interest in fruitful engagement with books and their properties, Petrarch managed to assemble one of the largest private libraries of the day,

Early Italian Renaissance, 262. The coronation echoed the honoring of literary greats by Roman emperors: Thomas G. Bergin, *Petrarch* (New York: Twayne, 1970), 54.

24. Demetrio S. Yocum, *Petrarch's Humanist Writing and Carthusian Monasticism: The Secret Language of the Self* (Leiden: Brepols, 2013), 6, 19. "The Carthusians welcoming in their fold many disillusioned academics" (18). "It was in medieval monastic writings that Petrarch found a model for placing these beliefs within a consistent literary program": Brian Stock, "Reading, Writing, and the Self: Petrarch and His Forerunners," *New Literary History* 26, no. 4 (1995): 727. Some abbeys formed networks of pious readers among the laity, especially within women's religious communities, which they supported through the loaning of books: Mary C. Erler, *Women, Reading, and Piety in Late Medieval England* (Cambridge: Cambridge University Press, 2006), 27. "In 1336, Pope Benedict XII had issued the bull *Summa magistri*, which demanded, among other things, that each Benedictine Monastery must provide within its walls instruction in 'primitive sciences,' grammar, logic, and philosophy": David N. Bell, "The Libraries of Religious Houses in the Late Middle Ages," in *To 1640*, vol. 1, in *The Cambridge History of Libraries in Britain and Ireland*, ed. Elisabeth Leedham-Green and Teresa Webber (Cambridge: Cambridge University Press, 2006), 129.

25. Petrarch, "To an Unknown Correspondent," in *Letters on Familiar Matters*, 1:314–15. "For the first time since late antiquity, it is the secular library and not the monastic cell that is the image of this solitude": Brian Stock, *After Augustine: The Meditative Reader and the Text* (Philadelphia: University of Pennsylvania Press, 2011), 80.

26. Francesco Petrarca, "On His Own Ignorance and That of Others," trans. Hans Nachod, in *The Renaissance Philosophy of Man*, ed. Ernst Cassirer, Paul Oskar Kristeller, and John Herman Randall, Jr. (Chicago: University of Chicago Press, 1948), 63. With "Lord of Learning," Petrarch is citing 1 Sam. 2:3.

27. Petrarch, "The Young Humanist of Ravenna," *Letters on Familiar Matters*, 3:302.

claiming, only partly in jest, that "the number of my books is incalculable."[28] Understanding his library to be a privately assembled public good, he proposed in 1362 that he would donate his "daughter," as he referred to it, to the Republic of Venice on his death, in exchange for a house in advance, "not large but respectable," to live out his days.[29] The bequeathal of his library was, he stated, "for the encouragement and convenience of scholars and gentlemen."[30] The *encouragement of learning* is a repeated theme in this book, as you may recall from my first-chapter reference to the title of the Statute of Anne 1710, and as you will hear from Milton and Defoe in the final chapter. Although Petrarch moved into the Venetian house he requested, his books did not go to the city upon his death. They were acquired by his final patron, Francesco da Carrara, Lord of Padua, who ended up selling some and forfeiting the rest as the spoils of a war that he lost.[31] He thus managed to set off another humanist treasure hunt on his death, this time for his own heavily annotated volumes dispersed across Western Europe in private and public collections.[32] In this, too, Petrarch has much to teach us about the political economy of learning, as well as the instabilities and overhead that accompany personal patronage. Erasmus moves this question of learning's sponsorship ahead by nearly a century and a half, with the commerce of print now playing a key role in advancing the humanist take on a life of learning.

DESIDERIUS ERASMUS

In 1500 and at the age of thirty-four—to jump right into the earliest days of his time in the book trade—Erasmus of Rotterdam made arrangements

28. Petrarch, "On the Abundance of Books," in *Four Dialogues for Scholars*, trans. Conrad H. Rawski (Cleveland, OH: Case Western University Press, 1967), 32.

29. Cited by Robinson, *Petrarch*, 30. Petrarch continued that "he did not wish this because his books are very numerous or very valuable, but is impelled by the hope that hereafter that glorious city may, from time to time, add other works at the public expense, and that private individuals, nobles, or other citizens who love their country, or even strangers, may follow his example, and leave a part of their books, by their last will, to the said church" (cited by ibid.). Rudolph Pfeiffer cites Petrarch's use of "daughter" in referring to the library: *History of Classical Scholarship 1300–1850* (Oxford: Oxford University Press, 1976), 13.

30. Cited by Robinson, *Petrarch*, 29.

31. Ibid., 32. Robinson refers to Francesco da Carrara, as "Petrarch's last tyrant-patron" (ibid.).

32. Pfeiffer, *Classical Scholarship*, 13. The humanist Niccolò Niccoli offers a more encouraging example, having spent his large inheritance assembling a magnificent library that, on his death, was destined to be distributed among his creditors, only to have the great patron Cosimo de' Medici purchase it for the monastery library of San Marco in Florence, which opened its doors in 1444 and became a model for other public libraries, as well as a further bridge between medieval and humanist learning: Pettegree, *Book in the Renaissance*, 10, 15.

with the printer John Philippi of Kreuznach to publish a book of his rather hastily assembled collection of 818 proverbs. Erasmus had gathered the proverbs from Latin and Greek sources, and accompanied each with a few lines of explanation and interpretation. He underwrote the printing costs of the *Collection of Old Adages* (*Collectanea adagiorum veterum*), rather than following the more common practice of selling a text to the printer with copies of the book taken in payment. Erasmus dedicated the work to William Blount, Lord Mountjoy, who had graduated from being Erasmus's pupil to becoming his patron, with Blount's support allowing him to retain ownership of the book.[33] Four years later, Erasmus can be found writing from Paris to John Colet, a priest at Salisbury Cathedral, whom he had befriended on an earlier trip to England. Erasmus asked Colet about "the hundred copies of the *Adagia* sent to England at my own expense, and three years ago at that"; he is confident that "all the books have been sold and the purchase price paid to someone."[34] Erasmus was already immersed in the accounts-receivable language of an emerging printing industry, even as he was feeling the exasperations of inadequate quality control: "[The book] is so full of printers' errors that it looks as if it has been deliberately spoiled," he wrote to Colet.[35]

In 1508, while in Turin studying for a Doctor of Divinity degree, Erasmus became that much more involved in the business by joining forces with the printer Aldus Manutius on an expanded and revised edition of his proverb collection, to be entitled *Thousands of Adages* (*Adagiorum chiliades*). Aldus had set up his printing shop in Venice in 1490. That city, along with Florence, was blossoming as a publishing center for works in Latin and the vernacular Tuscan.[36] Yet it was above all the printer Aldus who was to develop a new humanist aesthetic of the page and font with the Aldine press. By the turn of the century, both the Venetian Senate and the pope awarded him, on his request but in recognition of his contribution, a number of ten- and twenty-year printing privileges for both his Greek works and italic type, in an effort to protect

33. James D. Tracy, *Erasmus of the Low Countries* (Berkeley: University of California Press, 1997), 28. Elizabeth L. Eisenstein reports on Erasmus using the printers' complimentary copies of his books "to fool hundreds of patrons into thinking of themselves as dedicatees and (hopefully) providing hundreds of pensions in return": *The Printing Press as an Agent of Change* (Cambridge: Cambridge University Press, 1982), 401.

34. Desiderius Erasmus, "181 / To John Colet, Paris, [about December] 1504," in *The Correspondence of Erasmus, Letters 142 to 297, 1501 to 1514*, vol. 2, trans. R. A. B. Mynors and D. F. S. Thomson, annotator Wallace K. Fergusin, *The Collected Works of Erasmus*, ed. Richard J. Schoeck and Beatrice Corrigan (Toronto: University of Toronto Press, 1975), 88.

35. Ibid.

36. Brian Richardson, *Print Culture in Renaissance Italy: The Editor and the Vernacular Text, 1470-1600* (Cambridge: Cambridge University Press, 1984), 28-30.

these books from being counterfeited.[37] Aldus was making the book a more readable, portable, and attractive object. The Aldine press reached its peak in 1502, the year Aldus proudly released sixteen fine editions, only to have the press close its doors in 1506 for want of sales, especially among its Greek titles.[38] It did reopen a little more than a year later, with Erasmus's encouragement, operating out of Aldus's father-in-law's house in Venice.[39] The Aldine press's faltering reflects the struggle of making a business of learned books, despite the privileges and patrons behind such work.

Aldus had made it his business to open his printshop as a workshop for scholars such as Erasmus, as a means of raising the quality of his Latin and Greek editions.[40] This was definitely the case with *Adages*: "Erasmus sat in one corner of the printing-room, writing the *Adagia* from memory," according to an account reconstructed by the University of Warwick historian Martin Lowry, "and handing the text sheet by sheet to the compositors, too busy, by his own account, to scratch his ears," while "in another corner sat Aldus, quietly reading over the proofs."[41] Any attempt to interrupt Aldus was met, according to Erasmus, by the printer shouting back, "I'm learning!" (*studio*).[42] Erasmus spent nine months on the book, working in what was, by Lowry's account, "a now almost incredible mixture of the sweatshop, the boarding-house and the research institute."[43]

The result was a compilation of 3,260 adages, accompanied by Erasmus's well-documented and occasionally extensive commentaries. The book's success transformed Erasmus into an internationally recognized scholar among

37. Henry George Fletcher III, *New Aldine Studies: Documentary Essays on the Life and Works of Aldus Manutius* (San Francisco: Bernard M. Rosenthal, 1988), 137–56.

38. M. J. C. Lowry, "The 'New Academy' of Aldus Manutius: A Renaissance Dream," *Bulletin of the John Rylands University Library* 58, no. 2 (1976): 397, 399.

39. Fletcher, *New Aldine Studies*, 9.

40. "Aldine books were printed without the marginal commentary or textual apparatus that made scholastic texts so visually offensive to humanist readers ... Aldine books ... would attract a new kind of reader, whose literacy was not circumscribed by the monastery or university": Jennifer Summit, *Memory's Library: Medieval Books in Early Modern England* (Chicago: University of Chicago Press, 2006), 73.

41. Martin Lowry, *The World of Aldus Manutius: Business and Scholarship in Renaissance Venice* (Ithaca, NY: Cornell University Press, 1979), 94. "Throughout his life not more than eight printers managed to form a relationship with him that was more than casual": Peter G. Bietenholz, "Ethics and Early Printing: Erasmus' Rules for the Proper Conduct of Authors," *Humanities Association Review* 26 (1975): 182. See also S. Diane Shaw, "Study of the Collaboration between Erasmus of Rotterdam and His Printer Johann Froben at Basel during the Years 1514 to 1527," *Erasmus of Rotterdam Society Yearbook* 6, no. 1 (1986): 35.

42. Cited by Fletcher, *New Aldine Studies*, 12.

43. Lowry, *Aldus Manutius*, 94.

humanists.[44] The fine press work of Aldus, combined with Erasmus's accessible manner of writing, encouraged an expansion of the humanist audience, at least among that narrow affluent company of men and women who read Latin.[45] Erasmus continued to add adages and extend his commentaries on them, seeing through a further twenty-seven editions until, in 1535, the collection exceeded four thousand adages and a thousand pages. And he continued to correct the text: "I publish in a hurry, and in the nature of things am sometimes obliged to refurbish the whole thing from top to toe," Erasmus had written earlier to John Botzheim in 1523.[46] The book was printed and marketed in various formats, most greatly abridged. It fell within the medieval tradition of *florilegia* or compilation, and proved among the most popular and profitable of Erasmus's titles.[47] It was designed to be read and used: "He equipped [the adages] with sophisticated information retrieval tools," notes Anthony Grafton, Princeton historian. "From the first full edition, the adages were preceded by elaborate indexes that not only listed their topics in alphabetical order, but also rearranged them into categories to indicate the contexts in which to cite them."[48] It became a model for the commonplace books that people started keeping in the sixteenth century in which they kept short passages worthy of citing or modeling in their own work. Today, to step out of this history for moment, with the end of the print era upon us, the early printshop collaborations between printer and scholar take on a certain poignancy. What's called for, however, is not nostalgia over the lost fragrance of ink, but reflection on the collaborative elements between scholarly and

44. Margaret Mann Phillips calls *Adages* "a front-line work for the New Learning": Desiderius Erasmus, *Erasmus on His Times: A Shortened Version of the 'Adages' of Erasmus*, ed. Margaret Mann Phillips (Cambridge: Cambridge University Press, 1967), viii.

45. "The accomplishments of the educated woman (the 'learned lady') is an end in itself, like fine needlepoint . . . It is not viewed as training for anything, perhaps not even virtue": Anthony Grafton and Lisa Jardine, *From Humanism to the Humanities: Education and the Liberal Arts in Fifteenth- and Sixteenth-Century Europe* (London: Duckworth, 1986), 56. Jean-François Cottier points out how the paraphrases "were intended to instruct (*docere*) but equally to move and please (*movere* and *placere*)": "Erasmus's *Paraphrases*: A 'New Kind of Commentary'?," in *The Unfolding of Words: Commentary in the Age of Erasmus*, ed. Judith Rice Henderson (Toronto: University of Toronto Press, 2012), 34.

46. Desiderius Erasmus, "1341A / To John Botzheim, Basel 30 January 1523," in *The Correspondence of Erasmus, Letters 1252 to 1355, 1522 to 1523*, vol. 9, trans. R. A. B. Mynors, annotator James M. Estes, *The Collected Works of Erasmus* (Toronto: University of Toronto Press, 1989), 294.

47. Brian Cummings, "Encyclopaedic Erasmus," *Renaissance Studies* 28, no. 2 (2014): 192. "At times, Adagia seems like a parody of academic study, a pedantic chain of references without limit. At others, it appears like the pure literary pleasure of a mind full of quotation" (196).

48. Anthony Grafton, *The Culture of Correction in Renaissance Europe* (London: British Library, 2011), 158.

productive crafts that are worth preserving and revitalizing through such initiatives as the digital humanities.[49]

An indication of what Erasmus and others valued about learning and printing is found in his treatment of two of his many collected adages—*between friends all is common* and *make haste slowly*—to which I want to give some consideration to here. Starting with the 1508 edition printed by Aldus, Erasmus opened the book with the friends' adage: *Amicorum communia omnia.*[50] Much has been made of this proposition by Kathy Eden, Mark Van Doren Professor of Humanities at Columbia University, who finds it a key to Erasmus's "cultural program for cooperation," as she put it.[51] In support of her point, Eden cites Erasmus's friend and biographer, Beatus Rheanus, who notes that when "he was about to publish *Adagia*, certain scholars said to him, 'Erasmus, you are divulging our secrets.' But he was desirous that these be accessible to all so that they may attain complete scholarship."[52] And while this adage may seem to restrict this openness to a closed circle "between friends," Erasmus's commentary makes it clear, as do his letters and other books, that he sees learning itself as common to all, extending beyond any bounds of friendship.

"There is nothing more wholesome or more generally accepted than this proverb," Erasmus writes in his commentary on "between friends all is common." He supports this by citing those who have used it, noting the differences in their use: Socrates "deduced" from it that "all things belong to all good men, just as they do to the gods"; Martial "pokes fun" at others' hypocritical use of it; Diogenes Laertius and Timaeus both "report" on its origins in Pythagoras, as does Aulus Gellius, who, Erasmus notes, "in his *Attic Nights*, book 1 chapter 9, bears witness that not only was Pythagoras the author of this saying, but he also instituted a sharing of life and property in this way,

49. See, for example, the mix of scholarly and media production values on display in "Mapping the Republic of Letters" led by Paula Findlen, Daniel Edelstein, and Nicole Coleman at Stanford University.

50. Desiderius Erasmus, *Adages Ii1 to Iv100*, trans. Margaret Mann Phillips, *Collected Works of Erasmus*, vol. 31 (Toronto: University of Toronto Press, 1982), 29. This adage had been number 96 in the original edition of 1500.

51. Kathy Eden, *Friends Hold All Things in Common: Tradition, Intellectual Property and the Adages of Erasmus* (New Haven, CT: Yale University Press, 2001), 10. I remain indebted to Eden for seeing so clearly the intellectual property implications of the adages, especially the two that I focus on in this section.

52. Beatus Renanus, "The Life of Erasmus," in Desiderius Erasmus, *Christian Humanism and the Reformation: Selected Writings of Erasmus*, ed. John C. Olin, 3rd ed. (New York: Fordham University Press, 1987), 60.

the very thing Christ wants to happen among Christians."[53] In tying together the pre-Socratic Pythagoras with Christ, Erasmus bridges humanism's potential classicism-Christian gap with this common interest in a communal life.

Erasmus also takes care over how these writers differ in their sense of "possession and legal ownership."[54] In particular, he sets Plato apart from Aristotle, but not by very much: "In the *Laws*, book 5," Erasmus writes, "Plato is trying to show how the happiest condition of a society consists in the community of all possessions."[55] He then turns to Aristotle, who "in book 2 of the *Politics* moderates the opinion of Plato by saying that possession and legal ownership should be vested in certain definite persons, but otherwise all should be in common according to the proverb, for the sake of convenience, virtuous living and social harmony."[56] Ownership is what ensures, as Aristotle has it, responsible care and use.

Yet in a section of Aristotle's *Politics* that Erasmus does not cite, the philosopher makes a claim for individual ownership that scholarship appears to contradict: "The greater the number of owners, the less respect for common property."[57] As the number of humanists, and scholars in general, grows, their work on improving the commons, edition by translation, compilation by commentary, increases the respect for, and the utility of, the whole. Those who expose misattributions, plagiarism, even poor editions, improve the commons. The *tragedy of the commons* (which refers to the temptation of herders to irresponsibly overgraze the village green with extra sheep) takes a different turn

53. Erasmus, *Adages*, 29-30. The *Adages'* editor William Watson Barker corrects in the notes the misattribution to Socrates, which should have been to Diogenes (29). Erasmus also states: "It is extraordinary that Christians dislike this common ownership of Plato's, how in fact they cast stones at it, although nothing was ever said by a pagan philosopher which comes closer to the mind of Christ" (30).

54. Ibid., 4, 30.

55. Ibid., 29. Grafton attributes Erasmus's sense of the "proper way to read" (as reflected in *Adages*: "Read and find the deep and rich sense of the simple") to Giovanni Pico della Mirandola who delivered the "Oration on the Dignity of Man" in 1486, called by some the Renaissance Manifesto (*Commerce with the Classics: Ancient Books and Renaissance Readers* [Ann Arbor: University of Michigan Press, 1997], 110).

56. Erasmus, *Adages*, 30.

57. Aristotle, *The Politics*, trans. T. A. Sinclair and Trevor J. Saunders (London: Penguin, 1981), 2.3 108. In 1558, French jurist Jean Bodin takes up Aristotle's theme: "They deceive themselves who think that persons and property possessed in common will be much cared for," for "public property are habitually neglected": *Six Books of the Commonwealth*, trans. M. J. Tooley (Oxford: Blackwell, 1955), 9. Bodin suggests the need for "some private advantage from looking after" the commons, with that advantage presumably being the building of a reputation through such care, in the case of learning (ibid.).

with learning.[58] Still, if Erasmus more fully aligns both himself and Christ with Plato in his commentary on the adage, he finds in Aristotle a certain flexibility around what is private and common, which, I go on to show, proves closer to the pattern of Erasmus's own life as a scholar in the book business.

Erasmus added the second adage I consider here—"make haste slowly" (*festina lente*)—to the 1508 edition, identifying it as a paradoxical proverb. "It carries with it a pretty riddle," he writes, "particularly as it consists of contradictory terms."[59] In his extended commentary on this adage, he discusses Aldus's printer's mark of a dolphin entwining an anchor, which the press had been using since 1501, borrowing image (and adage) from an old Roman coin.[60] Nothing is more nimble than the dolphin, Erasmus notes, and yet such haste needs to be anchored in accurate sources, careful correction, and thoughtful commentary. The symbol of the dolphin-and-anchor has been, he notes, "sent out beyond the bounds of Christendom [in] all kinds of books in both languages, recognized, owned and praised by all to whom liberal studies are holy."[61]

While Erasmus praises this divine printing program for increasing access to learning, the principle is not, he observes, universally accepted among the learned: "How many good MSS are hidden away, either pushed out of sight by carelessness, or kept secret owing to the ambition of some people who have only one thing at heart—to seem to have the monopoly on learning?"[62] This other tendency of actively fostering a secretive regard for the cultivation of knowledge—closely associated with alchemy and the esoteric arts, as well as the craft guilds—was assiduously opposed in the early modern era by Erasmus among others. This celebrated public quality of learning served both the epistemological principles of science and the interests of the printing trade, which found a great market in publishing the "book of secrets" that shared the recipes, methods, and techniques of legitimate sciences and trades, as well as questionable arts.[63]

58. The oft-cited contemporary statement to this effect is found in Garrett Hardin, "The Tragedy of the Commons," *Science* 162, no. 3859 (1968); but compare Elinor Ostrom, "Revisiting the Commons: Local Lessons, Global Challenges" in *Science* 284, no. 5412 (1999).

59. Phillips, *Erasmus on His Times*, 3.

60. Ibid., 9, 15. Aldus first published the motto "Festina lente" in a dedication to *Astronomici veteres* in 1499, and with a variation on the adage and a prototype of the dolphin and anchor later that year in *Hypnerotomachia Poliphili*: Fletcher, *New Aldine Studies*, 43–44. Fletcher holds that Aldus's first prominent use of the mark was in a 1503 warning directed against Lyonese counterfeiters of his publications (51–52).

61. Phillips, *Erasmus on His Times*, 15.

62. Ibid., 9–10.

63. William Eamon, *Science and the Secrets of Nature: Books of Secrets in Medieval and Early Modern Culture*. (Princeton, NJ: Princeton University Press, 1994), 250–52. Pamela O. Long traces

In his commentary on this adage, Erasmus praises Aldus as "the man who sets fallen learning on its feet (and this is almost more difficult than to originate it in the first place) [and] is building up a sacred and immortal thing, and serving not one province alone but all peoples and all generations."[64] The scholarly editor works "slowly" among the ruins, restoring the coherence and integrity of ancient texts that otherwise represent the tragedy of the (learning) commons, not from overgrazing but from neglect. Erasmus celebrates the reach of the Aldine editions by contrasting print with the legendary library of Alexandria, which had its origins in the third century BCE. He refers to "the greatest glory of Ptolemy," without naming the library directly, which "was between the narrow walls of its own house."[65] By striking contrast, "Aldus is building up a library which has no other limits than the world itself."[66] The ideal of universal access is something of a constant within the commonwealth of learning, and no less so today, within the commonwealth and among related ventures as varied as Google and Wikipedia.[67]

Having praised Aldus, he then begins to "air his grievance" against the "rascally printers," who are taking advantage of Aldus's good name—in what should not seem the least bit strange to our ears and emails—by setting up their own shops in Venice that print "shamelessly incorrect" Aristotle, Cicero, and Quintilian, "to say nothing of the Holy Scriptures."[68] In exposing the tragedy of commerce within the field of learning, he condemns those printers "who would rather let a good book get choked up with six thousand mistakes than spend a few coins on paying someone to supervise the proof-reading."[69] Erasmus even speculates about the need for some form of intellectual property protection or other legal recourse to ensure the quality of learning reflected in the books that are printed: "And if a man imposes books like these on so

the legacy of esoteric knowledge within Neoplatonism during the age of print, pointing out that "print was entirely neutral in one sense: it widely disseminated both the values of secrecy and the values of openness": *Openness, Secrecy, Authorship: Technical Arts and the Culture of Knowledge from Antiquity to the Renaissance* (Baltimore: Johns Hopkins University Press, 2001), 246.

64. Phillips, *Erasmus on His Times*, 10.
65. Ibid.
66. Ibid.
67. "Google's mission is to organize the world's information and make it universally accessible and useful": About, Google Company, online. Robert Darnton holds that "the World Wide Web can accommodate a worldwide library" in describing the scope of the Digital Public Library of America: "A World Digital Library Is Coming True!" *New York Review of Books* 61, no. 9 (2014): 11.
68. Phillips, *Erasmus on His Times*, 10–11.
69. Ibid., 11. Erasmus compares these printers to "the thief, the impostor and the pimp" who set out "to rob them [authors] in the daylight of their good fame," while insisting that it is "less vicious to use one's own body or other people's for gain than to attack the life of another, and what is dearer than life, his reputation" (13).

many thousand readers, he is free to enjoy his profits or rather his robbery?"[70] He judges that "here the laws are nodding"; after all, there are statutes to prevent "selling cloth dyed in Britain as cloth dyed in Venice."[71] He also decries "these swarms of new books," for he judges "the very multitude of them is harmful to scholarship" and "instrumental in provoking profiteering wars between us."[72] By way of "remedy," Erasmus asks that princes and magistrates "expel (as far as possible) those [prolific] idlers," while those "who strive to achieve what is in the public interest but have the means, are helped by grants from the princes, from the Bishops and abbots, from public funds."[73] He holds out little hope of support in this regard from "the merchant class, who have mostly dedicated themselves to the worship of Mammon."[74] This sense of an intrusive commercialism being the bane of scholarship is no less with us today (as I reviewed in the first chapter), but it first emerges here out of a new dependency that printing introduces, which differs from the sponsorship of patronage. Much as Erasmus works on the front line (in the print shop) of a humanist model of commerce, so some struggle today for a commercially viable model of greater access for the digital era.

What sets Erasmus apart from the others I discuss in this book is the degree to which he lived and thrived in this new zone, where learning worked side-by-side with commerce "in the public interest." He is thought to have been the first writer to have made a living by the book trade, and there may have been as many as a million copies of his books printed during his lifetime.[75] His success was facilitated by the new distribution channels established

70. Ibid. 11.

71. Phillips, *Erasmus on His Times*, 11. Erasmus betrays much prejudice in this rant against how "such a sacred trust [is] tended to be [by] obscure and inexperienced monks, nay, even women, employed without selection" (ibid.). This was not his only outburst against women, as he complains in a letter about a share of Froben's business being inherited by the daughters of a former partner: "I do not like that petticoat government in your household. How can a dancer of hornpipes pull his weight in the boat?" (Desiderius Erasmus, "885 / To Johann Froben, Louvain 22 October [1518]," in *The Correspondence of Erasmus, Letters, 842 to 992, 1518 to 1519*, vol. 6, trans. R.A.B. Mynors and D.F.S. Thomson, annotator Peter G. Bietenholz, *The Collected Works of Erasmus* [Toronto: University of Toronto Press, 1982], 158).

72. Phillips, *Erasmus on His Times*, 11, 13.

73. Ibid., 13.

74. Ibid. "The thirteenth and fourteenth centuries saw the secularization of the copying of texts, with the decline of the monastic scriptorium and the rise of the professional scribe; and of course the advent of what we may call the scholar": Anthony J. P. Kenny, "The Character of Humanist Philology," in *Classical Influences on European Culture A.D. 500–1500*, ed. R. R. Bolgar (Cambridge: Cambridge University Press, 1971), 122. For the *pecia* system used in medieval universities to speed up copying prior to print, see Robert Steele, "The Pecia," *Library* 4, no. 2 (1930).

75. Pettegree, *Book in the Renaissance*, 82, 85. Contra this claim see footnote 114 below.

for printed books, led by the twice-yearly Frankfurt Fair that began around 1475 and proved a major point of sales and access for scholarly books.[76] Yet his work with printers also involved promoting the scholarship of others, such as Lorenzo Valla's innovative work on the use of evidence in philology and Thomas More's *Utopia*.[77] But of course, in the contentious age of Reformation and Counter-Reformation, Erasmus's satirical pen was hardly going to please everyone. His work was condemned by the masters of the University of Paris in his own lifetime and he had titles placed on the Index of prohibited books by Pope Paul IV a couple of decades after his death.[78]

In his commentary on "make haste slowly," Erasmus also considers how the economy of learning is distinguished by an "openness of mind . . . among the Italians, at any rate in the matter of literature." This is based on the generosity of the scholarly community that he encountered while working on *Adages* at the Aldine press: "When I, a Dutchman, was supervising the publication of my book of proverbs in Italy, every one of the scholars who were there offered me, without being asked, copies of authors which had never been printed."[79] His emphasis is on how it should be, when learning is held in common, even among strangers. Continuing on this theme, Erasmus offers the contrasting story of a "northern friend of mine" who refused to share with him a book he had seen with a collection of proverbs inscribed in the margins.[80] The friend did not honor the request, reluctantly explaining, "as if it were dragged out of him by torture," how "up to now learned men had

76. Pettegree: "The business model of scholarly books depended on the publishers being able to dispose of a large proportion at the first fair following publication" (ibid., 80–81).

77. In 1508, Erasmus saw to the first printing of Lorenzo Valla's *Novum Testamentum annotationes apprim*, completed in 1444, which formed a model for his own translation of the New Testament; he saw to the publication of *Utopia* and *Epigrammata* by his friend Thomas More (through Froben and other printers).

78. In 1526 the Sorbonne's theology faculty censured Ersamus's *Colloquies*, pronouncing its satiric dialogues heretical in ninety-six passages and its author a pagan: Craig R. Thompson, Introduction to Erasmus, *Ten Colloquies* (Indianapolis: Bobbs-Merrill, 1957), xxvi–xxvii. See also Hilmar B. Pabel: "The Index of Pope Paul IV (1559) singled out Erasmus for censure more than any other heterodox author. It banned all his writings, explicitly identifying a series of genres, including annotations and *scholia*, whether or not his publications opposed religion or had anything to do with religion" ("Sixteenth-Century Catholic Criticism of Erasmus' Edition of St Jerome," *Reformation and Renaissance Review* 6, no. 2 [2004]: 245). But then Erasmus had a (self-interested) hand in censorship when he recommended to Basle's town council in 1524 and 1525 that those handling anonymously published books should face legal penalties: Shaw, "Collaboration between Erasmus and Froben," 120.

79. Phillips, *Erasmus on His Times*, 14.

80. Ibid.

enjoyed the admiration of the public for possessing such things as these, and now they were becoming public property."[81]

It was Erasmus's mission to make this learning into public properties among scholars, aided by the circulation that print could achieve. It was Aldus's art and craft to collaborate with such scholars and printers to create a wider public for humanist learning by making the text more readable and accessible. The learning that emerged from scholar and printer was to be shared through the furthest-reaching means of the day. Thus, this early, close association between the trades of learning and printing. After observing that Aldus achieved warranted fame and riches (while omitting mention of Aldine's 1506 bankruptcy), Erasmus brings to an end his homage to printing within his commentary on the adage "make haste slowly." He transitions with "but enough of digressions," and returns "to the discussion of the proverb."[82] At some level, the desire shared by Erasmus and Aldus "to achieve what is in the public interest" through their books is no digression at all but every part the equal of their proverbial concern to set "fallen learning on its feet." It was not to be Erasmus's final word on the value of printing to learning.

In 1527, Erasmus composed a eulogy for his friend and business partner, the recently departed printer Johann Froben of Basle, Switzerland. He had formed a close working and personal relationship with Froben over the previous thirteen years. Froben had first come to Erasmus's attention when the printer produced a handsome but pirated edition of *Adages* in 1513, replete with Froben's own emendations improving the text and a lovely woodcut border that Froben had added to the title page. There could be no better means of catching the eye of a man who lived to correct his own and others' work.

Erasmus was soon making his way along the Rhine to Froben's Swiss printing shop. This trip was not about challenging the pirate-printer. Rather, a prince of humanists sought an alliance with a prince of printing. Erasmus came to Basle to see the printing of Christian and humanist works through Froben's press. This again meant moving into the printing shop, working each day with the printer and his employees, as they both supervised the printing of the works that Erasmus had written, edited, and otherwise prepared.[83] Together they established Froben's print shop—well placed in Basle,

---

81. Ibid., 15.

82. Phillips, *Erasmus on His Times*, 15.

83. Over the course of his life, Erasmus edited, translated, and saw into publication, works by Cicero, Euripides, Galen, Lucian, Pliny, Plutarch, Seneca, and Suetonius, as well as the church

with its university and relatively central European location—as a center of Christian humanist scholarship during the early decades of the sixteenth century. In his tribute to Froben, Erasmus describes how he was well served by a man who put learning first:

> I loved him more for the sake of liberal studies, for the enhancement and progress of which he seemed called by divine destiny, than for his predilection for me or for his blameless life. . . . He seemed born to give honor, distinction, and advancement to [literary studies] and spared no toil, no vigils, thinking it reward enough if a good author could be put into men's hands in a fitting manner. . . . Whenever he showed me and other good friends the first pages of some great author, how filled with joy he was . . . you would say that he . . . expected no other recompense.[84]

As Erasmus expressed in another of his published letters, he was delighted by this opportunity to work in such a superb printing shop: "I seem to myself to be living in some delightful precinct of the Muses, to say nothing of so many good scholars, and scholars of no ordinary kind. They all know Latin, they all know Greek, most of them know Hebrew too; one is an expert historian, another an experienced theologian; one is skilled in mathematics, one a keen antiquary, another a jurist."[85] He also applauds "how well they get on together! You would say that they had only one soul."[86] He worked hard among them in the printing workshop, and in the miraculous year 1516 was able to see two of his most significant works of scholarly editing printed: the New Testament and the works of St. Jerome.

---

fathers, Ambrose, Arnobius, Athanasius, Basil, Chrysostom, Cyprian, Jerome, Hilary, Irenaeus, Origen, and Prudentius: Shaw, "Collaboration between Erasmus and Froben," 93, 103.

84. Desiderius Erasmus, "1900 / To Jan of Heemstede, [Basel, ? November 1527]," in *The Correspondence of Erasmus, Letters 1802 to 1925, March-December 1527*, vol. 13, trans. Charles Fantazzi, annotator James K. Farge, *The Collected Works of Erasmus* (Toronto: University of Toronto Press, 1982), 421-23. In English, the epitaph Erasmus wrote in Greek (in addition to Latin and Hebrew) reads: "So here the printer Johann Froben sleeps. / To no one letters owes a greater debt. / Mourn not his death: his deathless soul lives on. / His fame lies in the legacy of books" (426).

85. Desiderius Erasmus, "391A / To John Witz, Basel, [second half of February 1516]," in *The Correspondence of Erasmus, Letters 298 to 445, 1514 to 1516*, vol. 3, trans. R. A. B. Mynors and D. F. S. Thomson, annotator by James K. McConica, *The Collected Works of Erasmus* (Toronto: University of Toronto Press, 1976), 243-44.

86. Ibid., 244. Such humanist-printer partnerships were not uncommon, with Grafton pointing to how the sixteenth-century Italian humanist Piero Vettori and French scholar-printer Henri Estienne "working together, solved the basic editorial problems in a way that still commands assent": "Renaissance Readers and Ancient Texts: Comments on Some Commentaries," *Renaissance Quarterly* 38, no. 4 (1985): 622.

The New Testament, published as *Novum instrumentum omne*, consisted of a much revised and annotated updating of Jerome's Vulgate, the late fourth-century Latin edition of the New Testament. This new instrument was the first print edition published with Greek and Latin side by side, supported by annotations both philological and theological: "I have revised the whole of the New Testament from a collation of Greek manuscripts and ancient manuscripts," Erasmus writes in a letter to his friend and fellow monk Servatius Roger, prior to the work's publication, "and have annotated over a thousand places with some benefit to theologians."[87] As a master philologist—as Froben identified him as *Erasmus Rotterdamus, philologis omnibus* in the front matter of some of his books—he consulted a variety of Greek manuscripts of the New Testament, on which he based his revisions and corrections.[88] While he may have overlooked older available editions of the Greek text (thereby breaking a cardinal philological rule), there were those who raised the more forceful criticism of his presumption in correcting the Bible. Even before it was printed, the humanist theologian Maarten van Dorp, university rector of Louvain, tried to dissuade him from it. "You think it wrong," Erasmus paraphrased Dorp's critique in writing back to him in 1515, "to weaken in any way the hold of something accepted by the agreement of so many centuries and so many synods."[89]

Erasmus stood by the evidence that he had found of the corruption, errors, and fabrication that had crept into the New Testament since Jerome's own imperfect rendering: "Which man encourages falsehood more, he who corrects and restores these passages, or he who would rather see an error added than removed?"[90] Even when the author was thought to be God, Erasmus was demonstrating the right and obligation to approach the text with an eye to restoring what he was treating as the original intellectual property. He cast himself as a judge facing conflicting and untrustworthy claimants: "Just as it sometimes happens that an experienced and attentive judge pieces together what really took place from the statements of many witnesses, none of whom is telling the truth, so I conjectured the true reading on the basis of their differing mistakes."[91]

87. Erasmus, "296 / To Servatius Rogerus, Hammes castle, 8 July 1514," in *Correspondence*, 2:300.

88. "Erasmus' achievements [in collating the manuscripts] are nowadays reckoned fairly modest": Mark Vessey, "Erasmus' Jerome: The Publishing of a Christian Author," *Erasmus of Rotterdam Society Yearbook* 14 (1994): 79.

89. Erasmus, "337 / To Maarten van Dorp, Antwerp [end of May] 1515," in *Correspondence*, 3:133.

90. Ibid., 3:134.

91. Erasmus, "325 / To Thomas Ruthall, Basel, 7 March 1515," in *Correspondence*, 3:65. See Seth Lerer on Erasmus and his fellow-humanists in this matter of correction: "textual correction is a moral and, to some degree, a legal action": *Error and the Academic Self: The Scholarly Imagination, Medieval to Modern* (New York: Columbia University Press, 2002), 39. He cites Budé writing to

The most controversial of Erasmus's New Testament corrections became known as the *Comma Johanneum*. It involves a short passage (hence *comma*) in 1 John 5:7-8 which had stood for some time as the biblical basis for a belief in the Trinity.[92] Finding this passage missing from the Greek manuscripts, Erasmus concluded that the two verses were a later Latin interpolation, and did not include them in his 1516 edition of the New Testament. Pulling the rug out from under the Trinity (within a year or so of Martin Luther posting his ninety-five theses on the church door at Wittenberg) could not help but be judged heretical by the church. Ever the scholar, Erasmus allowed that he would reinsert the passage should it be found in a Greek manuscript that he had overlooked, and sure enough, such a Greek copy was soon "discovered" and brought to his attention, leading him to include the verses in the third edition published in 1522, along with a note on his reasonable doubts about this newfound source.[93]

The second significant Erasmus-Froben publication of 1516 was both a complement to his upgrade of Jerome's Vulgate translation, and a considerable scholarly achievement in its own right: a nine-volume edition of Saint Jerome's works (*Opera Hieronymi*). "I had worked myself to death that Jerome might live again," Erasmus quipped in a letter to Cardinal Raffaele Riario in 1515.[94] While others in Froben's shop contributed to this task, he took on the editing of Jerome's letters in four volumes, as well as his *spuria* (works misattributed to Jerome), "but none the less worth reading," as he told another correspondent.[95] The first volume opens with a dedicatory letter to Erasmus's patron William Warham, archbishop of Canterbury and chancellor of the University of Oxford.[96] In it, Erasmus sets out what amounts to an early

---

Erasmus that "it is normal to let a man off these if he owns up" to the errors he made in the text, as he seeks "remittance, forgiveness in the court of Erasmian philological law" (39, 40).

92. 1 John 5:7-8: "For there are three that bear record in heaven, the Father, the Word, and the Holy Ghost: and these three are one. And there are three that bear witness in earth, the Spirit, and the water, and the blood: and these three agree in one." See Levine, "Problem of the Johannine Comma," *Journal of the History of Ideas* 58, no. 4 (1997): 581.

93. Erasmus had written to Colet many years earlier, in 1504, that "it is one thing to guess, another to judge; one thing to trust your own eyes, and another again to trust those of others": Erasmus, "To John Colet, 1504," 88-89. Others have noted the limits of this empiricism, as Erasmus, having found only one incomplete Greek manuscript with Revelations, translated the missing verses into Greek from Latin to include in his bilingual edition of the New Testament (Levine, "Johannine Comma," 580).

94. Erasmus, "333 / To Raffaele Riario, Cardinal of San Giorgio," in *Correspondence*, 3:90.

95. Erasmus, "308 / To Gregory Reisch, [Basel, September 1514]," 3:37. "Although much early Christian literature had been lost, too, authors of the stature of Jerome or Augustine were more liable to damage by over-cultivation than by neglect": Vessey, "Erasmus' Jerome," 79.

96. M. Heather Lewis reports that when Erasmus was about to meet Warham in 1506, he quickly dedicated his translation of Euripides' *Hecuba* to the archbishop who gave him, Erasmus notes,

fifteenth-century intellectual property manifesto on behalf of learning. He seeks to explain why this work by Jerome is actually his to dedicate to Warham, as he has "borrowed from Jerome the wherewithal to repay you [Warham]."[97] It is as if Erasmus raised wheat on Jerome's dormant field to repay Warham's investment in the land. But then Erasmus takes such care of the land in the process that it benefits the many others who will turn to it in the future.

In this, Erasmus demonstrates the scholar's right and responsibility to use and improve upon others' work. This was Jerome's own intellectual property principle for scholarly editing: "In this line of business," Erasmus writes, "Jerome himself has laid down a principle for me in his preface to the books of Kings, repeatedly calling that work his, because anything we have made our own by correcting, reading, constant devotion, we can fairly claim is ours."[98] Erasmus claims as much with Jerome's texts: "On this principle why should not I myself claim a proprietary right in the works of Jerome?"[99] Erasmus offers a further justification: "For centuries they [Jerome's letters] had been treated as abandoned goods; I entered upon them as something ownerless, and by incalculable efforts reclaimed them for all devotees of the true theology."[100] Erasmus is offering a natural law of intellectual property rights. He sees that the editorial labor invested in a work, otherwise held in common but abandoned, earns that editor a property in the work and a credit for the service to the commons. It is rightly identified as Erasmus's edition of Jerome and sold as such. Erasmus does not infringe. Rather, he honors Jerome's rights as author.[101]

---

a "handsome present." "William Warham, Patron of Erasmus," PhD diss., McGill University, 1997, 35. Warham also offered Erasmus a goodly sum to reside in England, Lewis explains, likely influencing his decision to return, which was duly rewarded; although Erasmus did not stay, he did finally receive a benefice from Warham, as rector of Aldington in Kent, which he resigned within the year, with a lifetime pension from his benefactor (54–56, 59–60).

97. Erasmus, "396 / To William Warham, Basel, 1 April 1516," in *Correspondence*, 3:265.

98. Ibid. "In putting rhetorical questions to Warham [on whether it is 'something borrowed rather than my own'] in such boldly legal terms, Erasmus predicts the collision between the two kinds of profit: one is the kind heirs of an intellectual tradition like the one stored in the *Adages* have expected for centuries from their investment in the works of the past; the other is the kind that comes increasingly to be expected of purveyors of literary property": Eden, *Friends Hold All Things*, 173.

99. Erasmus, "396 / To William Warham, Basel, 1 April 1516," in *Correspondence*, 3:265.

100. Ibid. Erasmus writes further on his efforts: "I believe that the writing of his books cost Jerome less effort than I spent in the restoring of them": "396 / To William Warham, Basel, 1 April 1516," in *Correspondence*, 3:262. In another letter on Jerome, he writes, "I have slain with daggers the spurious or interpolated passages, while I have elucidated the obscure parts in my notes": "296 / To Servatius Rogerus," in *Correspondence*, 2:300.

101. Earlier, in this editorial process in 1514, Erasmus wrote to the Carthusian monk Gregory Reisch, to explain that he was doing this because "in my judgment Jerome is almost the only author

In light of his own investment in this edition of Jerome, Froben took the additional step of purchasing, at no small expense, privileges (*Privilegia*) from the pope and the Holy Roman Emperor that called on their authority to ward off pirated editions.[102] In Erasmus's 1516 edition of Jerome, the terms of the privileges appear on back of the first volume's title page, much as the copyright notice does today. At the bottom of the page was the Froben printer's mark, comprising two snakes entwining Hermes' staff, with a dove on top, and the catchy corporate identification "Jo. Fro" divided on either side of the staff (and later "Fro. Ben."). The page proclaims that these privileges had been granted by both Pope Leo X and Holy Roman Emperor Maximilian I forbidding others from printing this work for a period of five years.

This was an early form of intellectual property protection of the sort that Erasmus alluded to in reference to Venetian dyed cloth, cited above.[103] In 1469, the Republic of Venice granted perhaps the first printing privilege, at the request of Johannes de Speyer, a printer from Mainz. It was a sweeping five-year monopoly by which he alone had the right to operate a printing press in the city. The state councillors cited in their proclamation that Speyer's books had already been published "to universal acclaim" and "in the largest type and with the most beautiful letter-forms"; the councillors were pleased that he "chose our city over all the others" to establish this new engine of humanist learning.[104] Speyer died the following year, and the Venetian councillors were wise enough to never again grant such a far-reaching trade monopoly. Subsequent privileges were restricted to certain titles, works, typefaces, and printing

who deserves to be universally read by everybody, at least among the Theologians who wrote in Latin": Erasmus, "To Gregory Reisch, [Basel, September 1514]," in *Correspondence*, 3:37. The property question is further complicated by Erasmus's intense identification with Jerome as the Christian author he seeks to be, as if Erasmus were *possessed* by Jerome's authorship, which is a theme explored by Lisa Jardine: "The merging of Erasmus with Jerome is achieved so brilliantly, with such consummate cultural skill, that it is little wonder that that image has endured so convincingly down to the present day": *Erasmus, Man of Letters: The Construction of Charisma in Print* (Princeton, NJ: Princeton University Press, 1994), 5.

102. Elizabeth Armstrong relates that Froben's agent in Rome, Michael Hummelberg, reported to the printer that originally the price was thirty gold pieces but that, by working through intermediaries he brought the price down six ducats or gold pieces, involving how many bribes we do not know: *Before Copyright: The Book-Privilege System 1498-1526* (Cambridge: Cambridge University Press, 1990), 13. Maximilian's privileges cost in the area of twenty gold pieces (15). The Privileges page in Jerome is available online at the University of Rochester Department of Rare Books, Special Collections and Preservation under the title, *St. Jerome Omnivm Opervm*.

103. Angela Nuovo, *The Book Trade in the Italian Renaissance*, trans. Lydia G. Cochrane (Leiden: Brill, 2013), 196–99.

104. "Johannes of Speyer's Printing Monopoly, Venice (1469)," in *Primary Sources on Copyright (1450-1900)*, ed. L. Bently and M. Kretschmer (Cambridge: University of Cambridge, 2008), online.

techniques, such as those used for musical scores.[105] The trade in printed books had begun amid the granting of privileges and protections.

Of course, Froben's purchased privileges did not prevent others from pirating parts of Jerome's works. And yet Bruno Amerbach, another editor on the Jerome edition, wrote to Erasmus about how he had succeeded in taking the printer Eucharius Cerviconus of Cologne to court in Frankfurt "for neglecting and indeed despising privileges from the highest authorities" by printing some Jerome letters.[106] Amerbach went on to warn Erasmus that "Jean Petit the Paris printer is a new menace; he threatens to counterfeit the whole work. His efforts can be suppressed by one note from you."[107] Erasmus wrote to Josse Bade in Paris, urging him to speak to Petit, and warning that if he proceeded to "print Jerome's works, despising the papal privilege and flouting, what is worse, the canons of decent behavior," then "he will bring harm on himself" with "his plans to damage other people," although to what effect, we do not know.[108]

Seven years later in 1523, Erasmus successfully petitioned the Holy Roman Emperor for a two-year privilege covering all of Froben's publications, with his agent reporting back that it had been granted "gratis and without payment, which is very rare with us."[109] Erasmus's program of support for learned publishing also included promoting book sales. He can be found gently browbeating John Botzheim, in a 1523 letter cited earlier, into buying another edition of *Adages*, after the man complained that he was, in Erasmus's words, "forced to buy the same book twice." Erasmus counters that "if the first edition gave something of value, worth a moderate sum, and the second does the same, you have gained twice."[110]

Erasmus was never far from the business of books. He expressed his praise for those printers who "have a natural love of good literature and are happy to consider these studies of ours and not your own coffers," as he put it in a preface to the printer Matthias Schüer's 1514 edition of his rhetoric textbook, *Copia: Foundations of the Abundant Style* (*De duplici copia, verborum, ac*

105. Nuovo, *Book Trade*, 202.

106. Erasmus, "802 / From Bruno Amerbach, Frankfurt, [second half of March 1518]," in *Correspondence of Erasmus: Letters 594–841, 1517–1518*, ed. P. G. Bietehholz, vol. 5, *The Collected Works of Erasmus* (Toronto: University of Toronto Press, 1979), 352.

107. Ibid.

108. Erasmus, "815 / To Josse Bade, Louvain, 17 April [1518]," in *Correspondence*, 5:388.

109. Cited by Armstrong, *Before Copyright*, 15. Shaw reports the price of privileges was more typically twenty gold pieces, and it was granted free out of respect for Erasmus and Froben: "Collaboration between Erasmus and Froben," 115.

110. Phillips, *Erasmus on His Times*, xvii.

rerum commentariiduo).[111] As we saw earlier, he called on the commonwealth of learning to help him locate the needed sources for his publishing ventures: "In the sacred name of literature, dear Latimer, kindest of men, I beg you for help with the New Testament," as he put it in not an entirely mocking manner.[112] And he promised others that borrowed manuscripts "shall be returned to you intact and spotless."[113]

To those who complained that he was enriching himself through publishing, he protested that he accepted no more than "one third" of what Froben offered him, even as he did much to promote the idea among scholars that their learning was, as if among friends, common to all.[114] He wrote in *Adages* of how "the value of learning to the public is more important to me than the matter of my own reputation."[115] He repaid the favors and friendships by doing much to help other scholars to publish with Froben. He supported the implementation of a liberal arts curriculum in the schools and universities by equipping teachers with a panoply of humanist textbooks, including his *Copia*, and translations of the classics, bolstering the humanist agenda against the reigning scholastic hegemony in the universities.[116] *Learning before earning* might have been Erasmus's proverbial motto, except that he did not invent his own adages, but drew them from the common stock.

In his final years, and following the scholarly tradition of Augustine's and Bede's retractions, Erasmus prepared corrigenda, if more closely aligned with his editorial concerns with errors than his theological position. It consisted of twenty-six folio pages of corrections needed in other publications, as he systematically addressed the errors that he continued to find in his

---

111. Erasmus, "311 / To Matthias Schuër, Basel, 15 October 1514," in *Correspondence*, 3:43.

112. Erasmus, "417 / To William Latimer, [Saint Omer], 5 June [1516]," in *Correspondence*, 3:299.

113. Erasmus, "300 / To Johann Reuchlin, [Basel, August 1514]," in *Correspondence*, 3:8.

114. When accused of being in it for the money, Erasmus wrote in a letter in 1530/31 that "I received something from Froben . . . but I scarcely took one third of the things he offered; and it seems to you that Erasmus is insatiable for money": cited by Shaw, "Collaboration between Erasmus and Froben," 72. When he died in 1536, Erasmus left "a large number of gold vessels and ornaments given him by distinguished persons, as well as a good outfit of furniture, clothes and household utensils," according to biographer Preserved Smith, who attests to how patrons, whom he names in his will, were the source of wealth rather than the printings of his books: "He got nothing for most of them," Smith surmises (*Erasmus: A Study of His Life, Ideals, and Place in History* [New York: Dover, 1923], 262, 258).

115. Erasmus, *Adages*, 35.

116. Grafton and Jardine commend "the remarkable success of Erasmus' program of education in the liberal arts in educational institutions, from the *gymnasia* and the grammar school to the Royal Colleges at Oxford and Cambridge": *From Humanism*, 140. They then cite a sixteenth-century list of a student's thirty-odd books, of which ten are by Erasmus and four likely edited by him (140–41).

earlier works: "As an honest Christian, I should repair my earlier carelessness. . . . I am doing the best I can to reach that place if with no valuable
assets, at least with the lightest possible burden of error."[117] The care and
concerns that Erasmus brought to the production and properties of the
scholar's work in print, in which he berated his own fallibility as much as he
attacked the shortcomings and overreaching of commercial interests in the
book trade, were to become fully part of the early modern story for learning.

CONCLUSION

From Petrarch to Erasmus, and spanning the fourteenth to the sixteenth centuries, humanists recovered, restored, and reconstructed a body of classical
Greco-Roman and Christian texts, while introducing a particular set of disciplinary concerns with the rhetorical, intellectual, and literary properties of
the works that constituted classical antiquity.[118] They authenticated texts on
philological evidence and attended to the sources and contexts with a new
degree of thoroughness. The humanists treated the discovery, correction, and
publication of these properly accredited works as a right and a responsibility.
The new editions, translations, and commentaries circulated that much more
widely through the humanist collaboration with printers and the book trade.
The humanist object of study and the measure of learning were found in the
intellectual properties of these works, rather than, say, the natural properties
of the world, which was the object of the Greco-Arabic sciences.[119]

117. Erasmus, "2095 / To the Reader, Basel, February 1529," in *The Correspondence of Erasmus,
Letters 2082 to 2203, 1529*, trans. Alexander Dalzell, annotator James M. Estes, vol. 15, *The Collected
Works of Erasmus* (Toronto: University of Toronto Press, 2012), 78. Some of his overlooked errors
have stuck, including his mistranslation, from the Greek, of *Pandora's Jar* as *Pandora's Box* in *Adages*, while rendering *to call a skiff a skiff* as *to call a spade a spade*: William Barker, "Editor's Introduction," *The Adages of Erasmus*, ed. William Barker (Toronto: University of Toronto, 2001), xxxix.
"His mistake became a proverb in every European language except Italian": Grafton, *Culture of
Correction*, 159. Elsewhere, Grafton notes how the astronomer Kepler absorbed humanist concerns
with correction, as reflected in his identifying toward the end of his life, "the sources and weak-
nesses of his data, [while he] explained his assumptions, and corrected his own slips and error":
"Kepler as Reader," *Journal of the History of Ideas* 53, no. 4 (1992): 572.

118. "By learning I do not mean that confused and vulgar sort such as is possessed by those
who nowadays profess theology," wrote the humanist Leonardo Bruni, in his educational treatise
for women, circa 1424, "but a legitimate and liberal kind which joins literary skill with factual
knowledge": "The Study of Literature" in *Humanist Educational Treatises*, trans. Craig W. Kallendorf (Cambridge, MA: Harvard University Press, 2008), 48.

119. Ann Blair writes of the fifteenth-century Angelo Poliziano and the "new range of humanist
scholarship" that "his overarching argument was also typical of humanist disciplinary priorities,
in that he hailed the *grammaticus*, rather than the philosopher, as the omniscient scholar capable

The humanist study of Latin and Greek "classics" also reinforced the image of a golden age of empire, with its suggestion that, through such learning, "Rome would rise again instantly if she began to know herself," as I cited Petrarch at this chapter's outset.[120] For Petrarch, such study thrived, as did he, under the patronage of tyrants. This was not the case with other humanists, such as Leonardo Bruni, who sought the political freedom of Periclean Athens or Machiavelli who exposed the workings of power.[121] What is clear is that humanism brought learning further into the world, opening new possibilities for civic engagement, however much this compromised, some have felt, its desire and ability to speak truth to power.[122]

By the sixteenth century, Erasmus had introduced another part of the world into this humanist learning. He promoted, through wit and satire, counsel and wisdom, an education in the humanities for sons and daughters, men and women.[123] He was no less engaged in the scholarly exercise of use rights with others' texts, but this time it was in the company of printers, whose shops housed and fed him. He established new standards of propriety and fair use in the printing of books, warranted by what was held in common by the friends of learning. He sought privileges from church, state, and patron to protect a scholarly book trade for the greater distribution of learned properties.

This trade introduced new risks to learning. Shoddy editions, choked with errors, were hustled to market, while Aldus went bankrupt over his beautiful but unsold Greek editions. In the economic mix of this new age, the learned had to make their way between the patron's library and the bookstall. The two worlds of learning and commerce vied for rights and privileges, sometimes working beautifully together as with Erasmus and Froben for the betterment of scholarship, but not always. The age of print was full of truth and

of studying all texts": "Organizations of Knowledge," in *Cambridge Companion to Renaissance Philosophy*, 290.

120. Petrarch, "To Giovanni Colonna," in *Letters on Familiar Matters*, 1:293.

121. James Hankins, "Humanism and Modern Political Thought," in *Cambridge Companion to Renaissance Humanism*, ed. Jill Kraye (Cambridge: Cambridge University Press, 2007), 131.

122. "It stamped the more prominent members of the new élite with an indelible cultural seal of superiority, it equipped lesser members with fluency and the learned habit of attention to textual detail and it offered everyone a model of true culture as something given, absolute, to be mastered, not questioned—and thus fostered in its initiates a properly docile attitude towards authority": Grafton and Jardine, *From Humanism*, xiii–xiv.

123. Erasmus advises families that "they would do even better to have [their daughters] instructed in the humanities": "The Institution of Marriage," in *Erasmus on Women*, ed. Erika Rummel (Toronto: University of Toronto, 1996), 85. Erika Rummel judges him liberal in his consideration of women and education before concluding that "Erasmus was no feminist" (9).

consequence for learning, and the humanist part of it that I have still to tell is that of the scholarly academies and societies, which I turn to next. The public expansiveness of print was a boon for those with humanist interests, enabling them to foster a new institutional form beyond, but never far from, the gates of the university. These academies and societies became a way for those with humanist and later scientific interests to establish public bodies that played their own role in fostering learning and its publication.

CHAPTER NINE

Learned Academies and Societies

Within a decade or so of when Johann Gutenberg—the famed blacksmith, goldsmith, and booksmith who introduced printing to Europe—first applied oil-based ink to cast-metal letters set in a press in the city of Mainz, two of the town's newly trained printers as well as clerics, Konrad Sweynheim and Arnold Pannartz, headed south carrying the tools of their trade and following the old Benedictines' trail through the Alps to Italy. We are setting our story back to the mid-fifteenth century, to pick up how humanists organized these new forums, much aided by the invention of print, that proved remarkably effective in advancing the interests of learning, and not just for humanists. To return to the itinerant Sweynheim and Pannartz, these two printers ended their journey in a monastery, some fifty miles outside of Rome at the foot of Mount Taleo, which was among those founded, by Benedict of Nursia in the fifth century. Why they decided in or around 1464 to set up the first printing press outside of Germany in the Abbey of Santa Scholastica, named after Benedict's sister, remains something of a mystery.[1] Still, it is clear that Sweynheim and Pannartz were not print revolutionaries

---

1. Cardinal Nicholas of Cusa, a humanist and early promoter of print in Rome, may have, shortly before his death, instigated the setting up of the press, or it may have perhaps been the German monks who had emigrated earlier to this monastery: see Edwin Hall, *Sweynheim and Pannartz and the Origins of Printing in Italy: German Technology and Italian Humanism In Renaissance Rome* (McMinnville, OR: Philip J. Pirages, 1991), 31–35. See also Johannes Röll, "A Crayfish in Subiaco: A Hint of Nicholas of Cusa's Involvement in Early Printing?" *The Library* 16, no. 2 (1994): 135–40. To be sure, Sweynheim and Pannartz were only four to five years ahead of the printers who set up shops in Venice, Florence, Bologna, and other centers in Italy.

storming the Bastille of the scribal ancien régime. They were welcomed, at least by some of the monks, as harbingers of a new medium for Christian humanist learning.

Once settled in the abbey, Sweynheim and Pannartz cut and cast one of the earliest roman typefaces, reflecting the humanist lightness and grace achieved by the region's scribes, which the two printers favored over the Germanic gothic or black-letter type of the north. What they first printed in 1465 was, prosaically enough, Donatus' *Ars Minor*, intended for instruction in the classical Latin of late antiquity. This was much as Gutenberg and his colleagues had begun, with grammars, Bibles, indulgences, treatises on canon law, and other workaday basics. But for their part, Sweynheim and Pannartz set a different course, selecting works for their press intended to be thoughtfully read and studied (although the Bible falls into this class). They followed their printing of Donatus (which had already seen over a hundred printed editions by that point) with the first editions to be printed of three works: Cicero's *De oratore*, the eloquent church father Lactantius' *Divine Institutions*, and Augustine's great theological work *City of God*.

After printing their first four books, Sweynheim and Pannartz appear to have decided that the remoteness of the monastery, which had served scribal scholarship well, was not the best spot for printing and distributing patristic and pagan works. In 1467, they carted their press down to the city of Rome. Their initiation of Italian printing in a remote monastery and their move to the Eternal City shortly thereafter, offers a vivid image of the role that print was playing in moving learning into the larger world. This new technology both served and required the urban marketplace. Yet printed books proved to be more than just another form of market ware. They played a part in the historic rise and spread of academies, as these new secular and public organizations devoted themselves to fostering the intellectual properties of learning.

Once in Rome, Sweynheim and Pannartz published another fifty-one books between 1467 and 1473, with typical print runs of 275 to 300 copies (going as high as 825 copies on occasion, amounting to respectable numbers for scholarly editions to this day).[2] What they printed was directed by a scholar they hired within a year of setting up shop in Rome. This was Giovanni Andrea Bussi, Bishop of Aleria, who has, by virtue of this employment, a claim to being the first editor of a press. Many of Bussi's selections were appearing

---

2. M. D. Feld, "Sweynheim and Pannartz, Cardinal Bessarion, Neoplatonism: Renaissance Humanism and the Two Early Printers' Choice of Texts," in *Printing and Humanism in Renaissance Italy: Essays on the Revival of the Pagan Gods* (Rome: Roma nel Rinascimento, 2015), 68.

for the first time in print (*editiones princips*), and he composed prefaces for twenty-five of them. In introducing an edition of Jerome's letters, for example, Bussi attested to the sacred ends that print was meant to serve, much as Jerome had seen his Latin translations extending access to Scripture. In what also was to become a longstanding scholarly tradition, Bussi petitioned Pope Sixtus IV in 1472 for subsidies to make printing a viable enterprise: "Now finally, failing in nerves and blood, we beg your assistance," Bussi wrote, referring to their house as "full of unsold books, but empty of the necessities of life."[3] Sweynheim and Pannartz were rewarded with benefices by the pope and continued printing another eleven editions until they dissolved their partnership in 1473.

Their book list was a blend of Christian and classical titles, with works of Augustine, Lactantius, and Aquinas, on the one hand, and those of Aristotle, Caesar, Virgil, and much Cicero, on the other. As discussed earlier, patristic writers were not shy about putting the ancients' eloquent turns to work in enriching Christianity's humble expressions of faith.[4] The humanist printing program enabled readers and scholars to consult the classical sources that had inspired these Christian writers, helping them grasp the intellectual crossover and divide between the two traditions. Printing the originals added to the intellectual value of Christian and classical works alike. The result for Sweynheim, Pannartz, and Bussi was a remarkably coherent book list bearing "the general tone of some outline of a course of studies to be pursued by a reasonably pious, relatively enlightened participant in the early Renaissance," in the estimation of Maury D. Feld, historian of the book and Harvard librarian.[5]

As for who was participating in this course of studies, which is to say purchasing and sharing in these books, it was not just the scholars, but poets, members of the legal and medical professions, churchmen, statesmen, monks, and aristocrats (including women), who had begun to gather around a broad range of humanist interests, well before the arrival of print.[6] Those

---

3. Cited and translated by M. D. Feld, "A Theory of the Early Italian Printing Firm, Part I: Variants of Humanism," in *Printing and Humanism in Renaissance Italy*, 67–77. Feld refers to Bussi's "career of impresario for literate systems" (146).

4. Feld, "Sweynheim and Pannartz," 67–77. Clifford W. Maas reports that Romans at the time favored books on papal matters, such as bulls, briefs, and orations, while visitors preferred guides to Rome's sights and the indulgences to be gained at certain churches; "German Printers and the German Community in Renaissance Rome," *The Library*, ser. 5, no. 31 (1976): 122.

5. Feld, "Sweynheim and Pannartz," 74.

6. Virginia Cox records a dozen certain and an additional sixteen possible instances of women's membership in Italian academies between 1500 and 1650; "Members, Muses, Mascots: Women and Italian Academies," in *The Italian Academies, 1525-1700: Networks of Culture, Innovation and*

who met in any sort of regular way, whether in Rome, Florence, Venice, or other spots, took to identifying their group as an *academy*. The name was, of course, a classical allusion to Plato and his friends meeting in the sacred grove of Academus outside of Athens. In this updated Italian case, patronage was often involved in the formation of the academy.

Among the early instances is the Platonic Academy of Florence for which Cosimo de' Medici served as the patron, having helped found it in 1442. It was loosely organized around a communal teaching studio, which attracted young men interested in advanced studies, and became best known for Marsilio Ficino's lectures on Neoplatonic philosophy. The church, as well, had a hand in the formation of academies. Cardinal Besilios Bessarion held influential gatherings at his villa in Rome, although he did so without making claims to having established an academy; he arranged to have his Christian (humanist) defense of Plato printed by Sweynheim and Pannartz in 1469, in a rare instance of them printing a contemporary work. He also served the printers as a distributor of their works through his network and unofficial academy, in accord with, as Feld has it, "the conventions of courtly patronage and munificence."[7]

The Italian academies were the site of readings, performances, and festivals. Many favored humanist studies in philosophy, philology, the classics, and natural history, with the members engaged in editing texts and preparing papers, as well as publishing and purchasing books. At various points, the academies attracted the patronage of the House of Medici and other noble families. The library of many a grand country villa served as the meeting place for local academies. Such gatherings broke down the traditional boundary between patron and learned to be found in monastery and university.

Print came to play a critical role, not surprisingly, in the spread of humanism among a broader community.[8] The printshop was as much a center

Dissent, eds. Jane E. Everson, Denis V. Reidy and Lisa Sampson (Abingdon: Routledge, 2016), 134-36. Holt N. Parker studied the lives of eighty women humanists between the fourteenth and seventeenth century, whom she found could be largely characterized as being of noble birth and Protestant belief, with a love of learning and family interests in humanism; "Women and Humanism: Nine Factors for the Woman of Learning," *Viator* 35, no. 1 (2004): 582-93.

7. M. D. Feld, "A Theory of the Early Italian Printing Firm, Part II: The Political Economy of Patronage," in *Printing and Humanism*, 194.

8. James Hankins, "Humanist Academies and the 'Platonic Academy of Florence,'" in *On Renaissance Academies*, ed. Marianne Pade (Rome: Quasar, 2011), 2–3. "As the humanists' audience expanded from the notaries and rhetoricians of the time of Salutati to the merchant-bankers of the time of Alberti, and as it expanded finally to include the cobblers, carpenters, and druggists who attended the lectures of the Accademica Fiorentina, so gradually, even those subjects which had previously been left to specialists were at last made available to the general reading public—a social

of learning as were the libraries that purchased their stock. Aldus Manutius, with whom Erasmus worked so closely on *Adages*, had come to printing through his initial experience with the academies, first finding membership in a Roman instance. At the turn of the sixteenth century, with his Aldine Press in Venice in full swing, Aldus began to refer to his own "New Academy" in letters and prefaces, suggesting a press-based association of scholars.[9] The Aldine academy may not have been formally incorporated, as many academies were, but this hardly deterred the learned proof correctors, editors, and translators of the Aldine Press from gathering to converse in Greek and collaborating on the finest editions of antiquity for all of Europe to enjoy.[10]

Following the example of guilds and universities, the academies that undertook formal charters of incorporation often chose an artful, allegorical seal or *imprese* that was then displayed on their publications. The academies came at it with a light touch, judging by the Accademia degli Intronati (Academy of the Stunned or Astounded) founded in Siena in 1525; Padua's Accademia degli Infiammati (the Enflamed); and Florence's Accademia degli Umidi (the Humid) from the same period.[11] The academicians were not, however, without serious intent. The Intronati members made it their business, according to an early history from before 1584, to do "everything that is possible to acquire learning . . . of humanities, of law, of music, of poetry, of arithmetic"— and that included a policy to admit women to their circle of learning.[12]

---

category, by the way, for which the humanists deserve much credit": Eric Cochrane, "Science and Humanism in the Italian Renaissance," *American Historical Review* 81, no. 5 (1976): 1056.

9. M. J. C. Lowry, "The 'New Academy' of Aldus Manutius: A Renaissance Dream," *Bulletin of the John Rylands University Library* 58, no. 2 (1976): 378–420. "The Aldine Academy was never more than an undefined company of friends, dreaming of a glorious past and peering hopefully into a golden future which never materialized" (385).

10. David Chambers, "The Earlier 'Academies' in Italy," in *Italian Academies of the Sixteenth Century*, ed. David Chambers and F. Quiviger (London: Warburg Institute, 1995), 12. Amid humanist concerns with correction, Grafton cannot resist poking fun at Aldus's mistranslation in Aeschylus's *Agamemnon*: "Like vultures who in terrible pain for their *feet* [it should be *children*] wheel high above their nests" ("Renaissance Readers and Ancient Texts: Comments on Some Commentaries," *Renaissance Quarterly* 38, no. 4 [1985]: 621).

11. Frances A. Yates, "The Italian Academies," in *Renaissance and Reform: The Italian Contribution* (London: Routledge, 1983), 6, 12.

12. The rules of the Intronati from 1584 are cited by ibid., 13. Yates also addresses women's admission to the academy, as well as Queen Christina's founding of an academy in Rome in the seventeenth century (26). It should be noted that *academy* was also used, on occasion, to refer to the *studium* and *universitas*—that is, the university. On the seven ways in which the term *academy* was used during this period, see James Hankins, "The Myth of the Platonic Academy of Florence," *Renaissance Quarterly* 44, no. 3 (1991): 433–35.

The Accademia della Crusca (the Bran) provides an instance of the cultural influence that humanist academies could have in areas such as language. The academy was founded in Florence in 1584, under the leadership of Lionardo Salviati, with a focus on Tuscan philology and linguistics. The idea for a vernacular dictionary had had an earlier start with the Benedictine monk Vincenzio Borghini, who died before he could see it through, with his friend Salviati realizing that it would take an academy to bring it about. The Accademia della Crusca sought to purify the vernacular Tuscan language, which would eventually develop into Italian. The academy's motto was a line from Petrarch: "She gathers the fairest flower" (*il più bel fior ne coglie*). And this is exactly the task the members set themselves. They gathered illustrative quotes from prior to the fourteenth century, particularly from the three crowns (*tre corone*) of Italian literature: Dante, Petrarch, and Boccaccio.[13] Their intent was to restore the Tuscan tongue to what it was prior to the corrupting influence of Latin.[14]

The Accademia della Crusca completed the preparations for its Italian dictionary *Vocabolario della lingua italiana*, with almost twenty-five thousand alphabetized word forms in a work of 960 pages, to which twenty-one members had contributed.[15] As the work had not been supported by the Medici family, which had been the academy's original hope, it turned to its members, asking them to *subscribe* to the publication of the dictionary by covering a share of the book's printing costs. This was a relatively new form of sponsorship for the learned book. It distributed the necessary patronage for such a project across the academy's membership (some of whom may have been of modest means). The academy also solicited outside sponsors. The subscriber is both sponsor and consumer, interested in both obtaining a copy of the book and making it available to others. It signaled a new property relationship, compared to the tradition of benefactors operating at a distance from abbey and college. As this method of patronage spread, it became common to list subscribers in the front matter, both in gratitude and as endorsers of the work when it went on sale in bookstalls.[16] Print expanded the market for

13. Pietro G. Beltrami and Simone Fornara, "Italian Historical Dictionaries: From the Accademia della Crusca to the Web," *International Journal of Lexicography* 17, no. 4 (2004): 357-58. "The aim was to demonstrate the continuity from ancient to modern Tuscan; in this way, the living Florentine language was documented with quotations from ancient authors" (360).

14. John Considine, *Academy Dictionaries, 1600–1800* (Cambridge: Cambridge University Press, 2014), 18.

15. Ibid., 21.

16. J. R. Woodhouse, "Borghini and the Foundations of the Accademia della Crusca," in *Italian Academies of the Sixteenth Century*, ed. David Chambers and F. Quiviger (London: Warburg Institute, 1995), 165.

learning's intellectual properties while altering the nature of its sponsorship and economics.

When the academy's dictionary was published in 1612, it set a new lexicographic standard, particularly in its citing of "authorities" as evidence of how a word is used in print. The dictionary's definitions were supported by citations from those authors who constituted what the editors saw as the language's golden era. To take a simple example, the definition of the *word* (*vocabolo*) is accompanied by two different uses of the word by Dante, one poetic—"They took the words of the stars," from the *Paradiso*—and one prosaic, from *Convivio*: "In the cities of Italy, many words can be seen to die out, to be born and to change."[17] The definition that the dictionary provides, however, falls decidedly short of the full meanings of *word*: "Term which is used to indicate the particular names of all things."[18] The definition ends by noting: "And also from word (*Vocabolo*) comes dictionary (*Vocabilario*) which is what this book is."[19]

With the dictionary, the humanist sought to describe the world of the Italian language, backed by historical evidence, even as the book ended up defining and giving form to that world. Setting a linguistic standard for a vernacular language served the linguistic authority of elites, as well as the educated classes who served them.[20] It affirmed that the vernacular, no less than Latin, belonged to the published and the powerful. The academy's presumption with the dictionary was challenged at the time, but the criticism was largely aimed at its reliance on archaic exemplars from earlier centuries.[21] In 1623, the Accademia della Crusca revised the *Vocabolario*, in a second edition, which added two thousand new entries and introduced quotations from the

17. Cited by Beltrami and Fornara, "Italian Historical Dictionaries," 361.

18. Ibid., 360.

19. Cited by ibid., 361.

20. Ibid. Arturo Tosi helpfully introduces Antonio Gramsci into the discussion of the *questione della lingua* involving whose language counts given that Italian was "rich in multi-regional literature": "The Accademia della Crusca in Italy: Past and Present," *Language Policy* 10, no. 4 (2011): 290. "Every time the question of the language surfaces, in one way or another, it means that a series of other problems are coming to the fore: the formation and enlargement of the governing class, the need to establish more intimate and secure relationships between the governing groups and the national-popular mass, in other words to reorganize cultural hegemony": Antonio Gramsci, *Selections from Cultural Writings*, eds. D. Forgacs and G. Nowell Smith, trans. W. Boelhower (London: Lawrence and Wishart, 1985), 183–84. On language academies and nation formation, see Shirley Brice Heath, "A National Language Academy? Debate in the New Nation," *International Journal of the Sociology of Language* 11 (1976): 9–43. For how the politics of language and cultural hegemony can play out in contemporary educational settings, see John Willinsky, *The Well-Tempered Tongue: The Politics of Standard English in the High School* (New York: Teachers College Press, 1988).

21. Beltrami and Fornara, "Italian Historical Dictionaries," 362.

relatively contemporary writing of Machiavelli, Castiglione, and the rising star, Galileo. But the academy kept the dictionary and the language rooted in the past it most admired. Its members continued their research into the Italian language, issuing a third three-volume edition in 1691, dedicated to Cosimo III de' Medici. The academy continues its lexicographical and philological activities to this day.[22]

The Accademia della Crusca was first in setting a literary standard for a rising European vernacular language. The French and Spanish soon followed suit with government support for this linguistic consolidation of the nation-state. The English, on the other hand, famously resisted the idea. Proposals by no less than John Dryden, Daniel Defoe, and Jonathan Swift were rejected in turn. In the eighteenth century, Samuel Johnson, who set his own standard for English with his *Dictionary*, wrote in its preface that he found "our speech copious without order, and energetick without rules," adding that "if an academy should be established," he would "hope the spirit of *English* liberty will hinder or destroy" it.[23] Yet Johnson's definitions were supported by citations in the humanist philological tradition, a practice picked up in the following century by the *Oxford English Dictionary*, which began as a project of the Philological Society of London before moving to Oxford University Press.[24] This scholarly practice of working from the authority and evidence of earlier works, which were cited and documented, has long marked the intellectual properties of learning. It was put to novel uses by the academies in establishing Europe's vernacular languages.

THE SCIENTIFIC ACADEMIES

By the seventeenth century, those drawn to the experimental sciences had also begun to turn to academies to advance their learned interests. The prime instance is certainly Galileo's involvement in the Accademia dei Lincei, as its members helped him steer an almost successful course through

22. Considine, *Academy Dictionaries*, 23–25. A fourth edition of the dictionary in six volumes was issued from 1729 to 1738; the academy was refounded in 1811, with work commencing on a fifth edition that had only arrived at the letter "O" when it ended in 1923. The academy is currently employing digital technologies in its preparation of a dictionary of medieval Italian, based on a similar set of historical principles as its first dictionary. See the Accademia della Crusca website in Italian and English.

23. Samuel Johnson, *A Dictionary of the English Language*, vol. 1 (London: Rivington et al., 1785), 7, 5.

24. See John Willinsky, *Empire of Words: The Reign of the OED* (Princeton, NJ: Princeton University Press, 1994).

the intersecting worlds of science, print, and politics. Before joining the Linceans in 1611, Galileo had aligned himself with a number of humanist academies, if principally in his pursuit of de Medici patronage.[25] The Accademia dei Lincei had been founded in Rome in 1603 by Federico Cesi, an eighteen-year-old prince and son of the Marquis of Monticelli. Cesi was keen on forming the academy in collaboration with the Dutch naturalist and astrologer Johannes van Heeck, as well as the mathematician Francesco Stelluti and the engineer Anastasio de Filiis. The members lived in a semi-monastic communality stocked with the latest laboratory equipment of the day, as well as a fine library. It was arguably the first academy devoted to the study of natural philosophy in what amounted to a synthesis of Platonism, Aristotelianism, and atomism. "With the eyes of a lynx [lincei], as it were," the fourteenth-century Oxford philosopher William of Ockham wrote of Aristotle, "he explored the dark secrets of nature and revealed to posterity the hidden truths of natural philosophy."[26]

In Cesi's address "On the Natural Desire for Knowledge," given in 1616, he spoke of how, as a result of the academy, "the public will enjoy many more books and compositions, I say learned and useful, and doubly so . . . coming so to be communicated to everyone the long labors of years and years of observation, experimentation, and contemplation of all these subjects."[27] Galileo affirmed, in turn, how the academicians "expect the more expert to write and publish their labors, to the benefit of the republic of letters."[28] The

25. Galileo may well have been inspired by the patronage that science was attracting at the time, as demonstrated in 1576 by King Frederick II of Denmark in granting Tycho Brahe, "the prince of astronomers," the fiefdom of Hven, a small island in the Danish Sound, complete with observatory, magnificent house, printing press, and paper mill, all of which came to end 1597 with Christian IV assuming the throne of Denmark.

26. William of Ockham, "On the Notion of Knowledge or Science," *Philosophical Writings*, trans. Philotheus Boehner (Indianapolis: Bobbs-Merrill, 1964), 3. The naming is attributed to Cesi's mentor Della Porta, who identified the symbolic powers of the eyes of the lynx (*lincei*), "whose sight passes through a mountain according to all writers": cited by Paula Findlen, *Possessing Nature: Museums, Collecting, and Scientific Culture in Early Modern Italy* (Berkeley: University of California Press, 1994), 316.

27. Federico Cesi, *The Natural Desire for Knowledge*, trans. by Gregory Conti (Vatican City: Pontifical Academy of Sciences, 2003), 151. Mario Biagioli notes how the "protocols of legitimation (social and epistemological)" in the seventeenth-century shift from "patronage networks" to "scientific *corporations*, like the early academies": *Galileo, Courtier: The Practice of Science in the Culture of Absolutism* (Chicago: University of Chicago Press, 1993), 353, 354.

28. Cited by Eamon, *Science and the Secrets*, 232. On the other hand, Mario Biagioli identifies Galileo's "secrecy" as among his "literary tactics," as well as "his systematic withholding of instrument-making techniques to establish a monopoly over telescopic astronomy": *Galileo's Instruments of Credit: Telescopes, Images, Secrecy* (Chicago: University of Chicago Press 2006), 2. On a similar

academicians did more, however, than set expectations. In 1613, two years after joining the academy, Galileo published three letters on sunspots under the academy's imprimatur, identifying himself on the title page as a Linceo. The *History and Demonstrations concerning Sunspots and Their Properties (Istoria e dimostrazioni intorno alle macchie solari e loro accidenti . . .)* contains a remarkable set of drawings, which Galileo made with the help of the Benedictine monk Benedetto Castelli, showing the movement of sunspots and thus illustrating the roughly twenty-five-day rotation of the sun.[29] The Aristotelian model of a fixed heaven was giving way to the evidence of close observation.

It was in the sunspot letters that Galileo made his first public statement in support of Copernicus: "I tell you that this planet [Saturn] also, perhaps no less than the horned Venus, harmonizes admirably with the great Copernican system, to the universal revelation, of which doctrine propitious winds are now seen to be directed toward us, leaving little fear of clouds or crosswinds."[30] In a subsequent letter to Cesi, Galileo thanked him and Lodovico Cigoli for editing out the book's original effrontery, helping him to turn it into something tamer and more acceptable to church censors.[31] He also made it clear in a 1612 letter that he shared the academy's commitment to reaching a wider audience, explaining that he "wrote [*Concerning Sunspots*] in the common language [Italian] because I must have everyone able to read it," noting that not everyone can be "sent through the universities."[32] He also arranged for a Latin translation, so that, as he put it, "foreigners will be able to read this book too."[33] The academy was serving Galileo as editor and publisher, public defender and advocate. The Linceans brokered deals with printers, engravers, and book licensers; they served as publicity agents and laboratory managers.[34] When Cesi arranged a banquet in Galileo's honor

---

theme, Galileo was able to secure a patent in 1594 from the Venetian Senate for a horse-powered water pump (5).

29. See "Galileo's Sunspot Drawings," an online flip-book animation available online at Rice University's Galileo Project.

30. Galileo, "Letters on Sunspots" in Stillman Drake, *Galileo at Work: His Scientific Biography* (Chicago: University of Chicago Press, 1978), 198.

31. Galileo, *Discoveries and Opinions of Galileo*, trans. Stillman Drake (New York: Anchor, 1957), 147-48. See Paula Findlen and Hannah Marcus on "the two decades of correspondence between Galileo and Cesi [which] concerned many of Galileo's publications"; "The Breakdown of Galileo's Roman Network: Crisis and Community, ca. 1633," *Social Studies of Science* 37 (2017): 10.

32. Cited by Freedberg, *The Eye of the Lynx: Galileo, His Friends, and the Beginnings of Modern Natural History* (Chicago: University of Chicago Press, 2002), 125-26.

33. Cited by ibid., 126.

34. "The Linceans spurred Galileo on when he was unwell (which was often), arranged for publication of the work, decided on printing policy, provided the prefatory material, counseled

during a visit to Rome in 1611, he also ensured that the master was able to step into the night air while he was there to make further observations with his telescope of the orbital period of the Medicean stars (Jupiter's moons).[35]

Another instance after Galileo composed an open letter in 1615 to the Grand Duchess Christina of Tuscany, in which he cast the work of science as no less than a pursuit of "the glory and greatness of Almighty God [that] are marvelously discerned in all his works and divinely read in the open book of heaven."[36] Pope Paul IV begged to differ. A year later, he forbade Galileo any further public pronouncements on astronomy. Once again, Cesi and the other Linceans interceded, if somewhat surreptitiously, to enable Galileo to continue publishing. They arranged for him to ghostwrite a lecture for his student Mario Guiducci on his current interests in the Great Comet of 1618, in which he was able to attack a number of popular views. The lecture was given in the Florentine Academy and later published as *Discourse on Comets* (*Discorso delle comete*) in 1619.

This work was rebutted, in turn, by the Jesuit mathematician Orazio Grassi in an anonymous tract. Cesi then encouraged Galileo to respond "quickly," but in a way that "doesn't come out in the form of a duel," as he wrote.[37] In 1623, Galileo responded with *The Assayer* (*Il Saggiatore*), this time published under his own name and as a Lincean.[38] The academy not only succeeded in steering this work through the censors, it provided *The Assayer* with the finest of engraved title pages. It was executed by Francesco Villamena and features the draped muses Natural Philosophy and Mathematics set in a classicist edifice atop a foundation stone bearing a wreathed and crowned lynx. Here was Galileo—both humanist (having given early lectures on Dante and the architecture of Hell) and anti-humanist (later scoffing at the tyranny of old books)—set within the neoclassicist temple of print. The academies' longstanding association with printers was now serving the sciences well.[39]

him on what to include and exclude (not that he always listened), and helped him negotiate the unexpected and ever-trickier demands of the censors": Freedberg, *Eye of the Lynx*, 117.

35. Meredith K. Ray, *Daughters of Alchemy: Women and Scientific Culture in Early Modern Italy* (Cambridge, MA: Harvard University Press, 2015), 147.

36. Galileo, "Letter to the Grand Duchess of Tuscany," in *Discoveries and Opinions of Galileo*, 196.

37. Cited by Freedberg, *Eye of the Lynx*, 140.

38. Drake ranks this "scientific manifesto . . . the greatest polemic ever written in physical science": *Discoveries and Opinions of Galileo*, 227.

39. While my focus is on the academies as a humanist contribution to the sciences, see also Cochrane, "Science and Humanism"; Ann Blair, "Humanist Methods in Natural Philosophy: The Commonplace Book," *Journal of the History of Ideas* 53, no. 4 (1992): 541–51; and Rens Bod, *A New History of the Humanities: The Search for Principles and Patterns From Antiquity to the Present* (Oxford: Oxford University Press, 2014), 198–211.

The *Assayer* achieved considerable success. It even found favor with the newly elected Pope Urban VIII with whom Galileo met, and whose nephew, the Cardinal Francesco Barberini, was already a member of the Accademia dei Lincei.[40] All must have seemed right with the world for the moment. Galileo initiated another grand work, this time bringing Aristotle and Copernicus into conversation, which he had long been wanting to publish. The *Dialogue concerning the Two Chief World Systems* (*Dialogo sopra i due massimi sistemi del mondo*) was published in 1632. However, the death of Cesi two years earlier quickly dissipated the force of the Accademia dei Lincei, leaving Galileo politically vulnerable. His enemies within the church, as well as among the Aristotelians, particularly at Padua, were soon able to turn the pope against him.[41]

In 1633, Galileo found himself, at the age of sixty-nine, appearing before the Inquisition. Among his inquisitors, Cardinal Barberini refused to condemn him, but seven of the ten inquisitors found him guilty of heresy. Galileo was required by their judgment to "abjure, curse, and detest said errors and heresies"; he had to publicly proclaim: "I swear that for the future I will never say again, nor assert orally or in writing such things."[42] The *Dialogue* was banned, although his sentence "to formal prison of the Holy Office at our discretion" was commuted to house arrest at his villa of Arcreti. Pope Urban VIII took unusual steps against Galileo by having him and his work publicly condemned by inquisitors throughout the region, especially before learned audiences.[43] Still, the irrepressible Galileo was not without friends. They were able to assist him in having a manuscript delivered to Leiden, which was published as *Discourses and Mathematical Demonstrations Relating to Two New Sciences* (*Discorsi e dimostrazioni matematiche, intorno à due nuove scienze*) in 1638, some four years before his death at the age of seventy-eight.[44]

---

40. Cardinal Francesco Barberini's was known to have dissected deformed animals, including a two-headed calf, in his home for educational purposes: Findlen, *Possessing Nature*, 213.

41. "Galileo's act provoked the unanimous hostility of all the Aristotelians of all persuasions. Nor is it surprising that they expressed their defenselessness by resorting to force—by appealing to political and ecclesiastical authority in order to censure Telesio, to condemn Galileo, and to break up the new order of the Scolopians, who had dared teach Galilean physics to school children": Cochrane, "Science and Humanism," 1046.

42. "Sentence, 22 June 1633," and "Abjuration, 22 June 1633," in *The Trial of Galileo, 1612–1633*, ed. Thomas F. Mayer (Toronto: University of Toronto Press, 2012), 194.

43. Findlen and Marcus, "The Breakdown of Galileo's Roman Network," 2.

44. Galileo's book was published by the House of Elsevier (as was Hobbes's *Leviathan* later in the century), a Dutch firm operating from 1580 until 1712, with a current Dutch company, discussed in chapter 1, assuming the name and tree-of-knowledge trademark in 1880.

In its time, the members of the Accademia dei Lincei had skillfully managed the properties, as well as the capital requirements, of print for Galileo. This was far more than the Italian universities or the noble patrons of scholars were able to offer those engaging in the new science. Although, to be fair, Cesi was nobility and not without influence, having inherited the title of Duke of Acquasparta.[45] Although Cesi's death unsettled the Accademia dei Lincei, this was not the end of its contributions to science. Its members went on to complete a second of Cesi's extraordinary publishing projects. In 1611, when Galileo first joined the academy, Cesi showed his new recruit hundreds of natural history illustrations that had been created by both Spanish and Indigenous artists in New Spain. It was but a small sample from the enormous collection assembled by Francisco Hernández de Toledo during his extraordinary scientific expedition to Mexico from 1571 to 1577.

Commissioned by King Philip II of Spain as the royal physician for the Indies, Hernández had been instructed to, as the king's letter put it, "consult, wheresoever you go [in New Spain], all the doctors, medicine men, herbalists, Indians, and other persons with knowledge in such matters," with special attention paid to "medicinal plants" and "what their uses are in practice [and] their powers."[46] During the expedition, Hernández wrote to the king requesting further funding for his encyclopedic work, as well as to, in his words, "translate it into Spanish [from Latin], and into Nahuatl for the benefit of the native population."[47]

Had Hernández's proposal been fully realized, it might have given European imperialism a distinctive turn in what was otherwise its presumptive exercise of intellectual property rights over all that it touched. While Hernández did not receive the additional funding, the proposal reflects an important acknowledgment of the intellectual rights and responsibilities involved in working with Indigenous peoples, given what he had learned from

45. Bruce T. Moran writes on the shift from court to academy: "There, credibility emerged as a result of corporate effort combined with experimental practices and the communal determination of 'matters of fact'" ("Courts and Academies," in *Early Modern Science*, ed. Katherine Park and Lorraine Daston, vol. 3 of *The Cambridge History of Science* [Cambridge: Cambridge University Press, 2006], 267). "The new philosophical academies allowed the development of new forms of authentication" concerning "how experimental reports were published": R. W. Serjeantson, "Proof and Persuasion," in *Early Modern Science*, ed. Katharine Park and Lorraine Daston (Cambridge: Cambridge University Press, 2006), 169.

46. "The Instructions of Philip II to Dr. Francisco Hernández," in *The Mexican Treasury: The Writings of Dr. Francisco Hernández*, trans. Rafael Chabrán, Cynthia L. Chamberlin, and Simon Varey (Stanford, CA: Stanford University Press, 2000), 46.

47. Hernández, "Letter 9, March 20, 1575," in *Mexican Treasury*, 56.

them.[48] He did return to Spain with a remarkably comprehensive bilingual survey of plants and animals based on Nahua (Aztec) knowledge, language, and medical practices, reflecting imperialism's remarkable capacity to acquire and credit, if not repay, the learning of others.[49]

By the seventeenth century, Hernández's unpublished collection was gathering dust in the royal archives of Spain. Cesi made it the Accademia dei Lincei's mission to see this rare scientific and medical collaboration between the Spanish and Nahuatl into print. The academy's members set to work ordering, editing, annotating, and adding materials over the next three to four decades. There was much checking and correcting of the illustrations, relying on plants from America obtained from Jesuit and Dominican missionaries and Spanish trade officials. The Linceans turned to those who had served in the region to further review and verify illustrations and captions.[50] Cesi managed to see small parts of the work printed in 1628, just two years before his death. A full edition of the *Mexican Treasury* (*Tesoro Messicano*) was finally published in 1651. This 950-page folio volume, the largest compilation of new world natural history to date, was duly credited to Francisco Hernández, Nardo Antonio Recchi, and Johann Schreck (who was identified as an academy member), with the book's authorship and editing spanning a great many decades.[51] Here was the humanist practice, given to improving textual accuracy and precision by consulting the best sources, at work in natural history.

The academy's involvement in science, along with the place that it created for Nahuatlian learning, marked a cosmopolitan transition for humanist

48. The intellectual property legacy of such expeditions is found today in bio-prospecting: John Merson, "Bio-prospecting or Bio-piracy: Intellectual Property Rights and Biodiversity in a Colonial and Postcolonial Context," *Osiris* 15 (2000): 282–96.

49. Hernández commissioned Indigenous artists to illustrate plants, animals, and minerals; collaborated with local healing shamans at the Mexican missionary hospitals to test the medicinal qualities of local plants and treatments involving Indigenous taxonomies and pharmaceutical knowledge; conducted post mortems and ran experiments; and recorded observations and conversations in Nahuatl, Spanish, and Latin. The medicinal plants were drawn from the Aztec gardens of the hospital at Huaxtepec, which had been cultivated by the Aztec king Nezahualcoyotl of Texcoco a century earlier: Jorge Cañizares-Esguerra, *Nature, Empire, and Nation: Explorations of the History of Science in the Iberian World* (Stanford, CA: Stanford University Press, 2006), 8, 28.

50. Luigi Guerrini, "The 'Accademia dei Lincei' and the New World," unpublished paper, Max Planck Institute for the History of Science, Berlin, 2008, 9–11.

51. The full title is *Rerum medicarum Novae Hispaniae thesaurus, seu, Plantarum animalium mineralium Mexicanorum historia,* which was published in various editions from 1628 to 1651. Its 1628/30 edition is available online through the Internet Archive. Schreck had been heavily involved in an earlier stage of preparing the manuscript, although he died in 1630, while in Beijing as part of the Jesuit mission there. Freedberg notes that its "taxonomic, ethnobotanical, and pharmacological" contributions included species recorded for the first time in Europe, preserving the Nahuatl names and terms, while other species are "now lost or endangered": *Eye of the Lynx,* 275.

literary and historical concerns with classical antiquity.[52] As the seventeenth century progressed, societies devoted to the study of natural history became points of civic pride in London, Paris, and Berlin. They were chartered by the court and granted publishing and patent rights, as well as land and other sustaining gifts. Whether humanist or scientific, or a blend of the two, the academies amounted to a new "intellectual regime," writes Luce Giard, a historian at the Centre de la recherche scientifique in Paris, with "a widening of the social base of culture, a transformation in the means of access to texts and the channels of circulation of knowledge."[53] It may not have been, as Giard holds, a "return of intellectual debate to the community," as if the medieval or early modern universities had ever had a lock on the discussion of ideas, but the academies undoubtedly contributed to learning's public presence, "based on ties of friendship or patronage," as Giard puts it, "between a magnate and his clients, a group of intellectuals, professional and amateur."[54] By the end of the eighteenth century, as many as 2,500 academies had left some sort of trace on the European historical record, from Cardinal Bessarion's informal humanist academy of the 1470s to the Lunar Society of Birmingham founded in 1765.[55] There is, however, one more society that begs further consideration for the part it played in seventeenth-century scholarly publishing.

THE ROYAL SOCIETY OF LONDON

In England, John Wilkins, warden of Wadham College, began hosting an "experimental philosophical club" at the University of Oxford sometime around 1650.[56] Following the English Civil War, Bishop Wilkins had been

52. Compare to Steven Shapin's highlighting of the distinctions between scientific societies and humanist academies: "The new societies . . . made the production of new knowledge, rather than the guardianship of and commentary on the old, central to their identity and they aimed, with varying success, to link the progress of science to civic concerns rather than wholly scholarly or religious ones" (*The Scientific Revolution* [Chicago: University of Chicago Press, 1996], 133).

53. Luce Giard, "Remapping Knowledge, Reshaping Institutions," in *Science, Culture and Popular Belief in Renaissance Europe*, ed. Stephen Pumfrey, Paolo L. Rossi, and Maurice Slawinski (Manchester: University of Manchester Press, 1991), 19.

54. Ibid., 38.

55. David Lux, "The Reorganization of Science 1450-1700," in *Patronage and Institutions: Science, Technology, and Medicine at the European Court, 1500-1750*, ed. Bruce T. Moran (Rochester, NY: Boydell, 1991), 189.

56. John Aubrey in his memoirs, collected in 1685, writes, "Till about the year 1649 when the Experimental Philosophy was first cultivated by a Club at Oxford, it was held a strange Presumption for a man to attempt an Innovation in Learning, and not to be good manners to be more knowing than his Neighbors and Forefathers": *Memoir of John Aubrey, F.R.S. Embracing his Autobiographical Sketches*, ed. John Britton (London: J. B. Nichols, 1845), 93.

outspoken in his efforts to reestablish the university's somewhat compromised intellectual independence (complicated by his marriage to the sister of Lord Protector Cromwell who had himself named chancellor of the University of Oxford in 1650). The club was intended to contribute to this assertion of independence through its embrace of the new experimental science. Its meetings were attended by Christopher Wren, Robert Hooke, and the young student John Locke, as well as by the new cut of professors occupying endowed positions in the sciences: John Wallis, Savilian Professor of Geometry; Seth Ward, Savilian Professor of Astronomy; and Thomas Willis, Sedleian Professor of Natural Philosophy.[57] Henry Oldenburg and Robert Boyle were among the visitors to the club, with Boyle, an early innovator in chemistry, moving his personal laboratory to Oxford in 1656 to be closer to the action.[58] Fees were collected from club members to purchase scientific instruments and equipment "for the furnishing of an elaboratory," as club member Seth Ward wrote in a letter from 1652, "and for making chymicall experiments which we doe constantly every one of us in course undertakings by weeks to manage the worke."[59] Further, Ward points out that "we have conceived it requisite to examine all the books of our public library (everyone takeing his part) and to make a catalogue or index of matters . . . in philosophy physic mathematics."[60]

Wilkins left Wadham in 1659 to take up a Cambridge post, although he soon lost it after the Restoration in 1660, which placed Charles II on the throne. This left Wilkins free to attend the informal meetings of the scientifically minded in London at Gresham College. The college had been endowed by Sir Thomas Gresham, who had done well as financial advisor to kings and queen, and in establishing the Royal Exchange. On his death in 1579, he bequeathed

57. Peter Laslett, "The Foundation of the Royal Society and the Medical Profession in England," *British Medical Journal* (1960): 166–67; Maurice Cranston, *John Locke: A Biography* (New York: McMillan, 1957), 116. In 1667, Thomas Sprat described the basis of membership in the club: "The *University* had, at that time, many Members of its own, who had begun a *free way* of reasoning; and was also frequented by some *Gentlemen*, of Philosophical Minds, whom the misfortunes of the Kingdom, and the security and ease of a Retirement amongst Gown-men, had drawn thither" (*The History of the Royal Society of London, for the Improving of Natural Knowledge* [London: Knapton, 1722], 53).

58. Robert G. Frank, "Medicine," in *The History of the University of Oxford, Seventeenth-Century*, vol. 4, ed. Nicholas Tyacke (Oxford: Oxford University Press, 1997), 549.

59. H. W. Robinson, "An Unpublished Letter of Dr Seth Ward Relating to the Early Meetings of the Oxford Philosophical Society," *Notes and Records: The Royal Society Journal of the History of Science* 7 (1949): 69. Charles Webster, *The Great Instauration: Science Medicine and Reform 1626–1660* (London: Duckworth, 1975), 165, 195.

60. Robinson, "Letter of Dr Seth Ward," 69.

his great house, as well as all the land and revenue associated with the Royal Exchange, to the foundation of a college with seven professorships in law, rhetoric, divinity, music, physics, geometry, and astronomy, with professors obliged to give public presentations on these themes.[61] Gresham College also provided a meeting place for others interested in the sciences, with a dozen or so, including Wren and Boyle, meeting regularly with Wilkins. This group decided that the Restoration that placed the crown on the head of King Charles II (following the death of Cromwell and the collapse of the Protectorate) offered a perfect opportunity. They would ask the new king to be the patron of a new scientific society. After all, Charles was known to have had his own laboratory installed in Whitehall.[62] On November 28, 1660, after Wren's weekly astronomy lecture, those who met formally declared the founding of a society dedicated to "improving natural knowledge."

It took until 1662 for the king to grant an initial charter, which laid out the formal terms of incorporation for the "Royal Society." The initial charter opens by aligning the new learning with the emerging force of British imperialism: "We have long and fully resolved with Ourself to extend not only the boundaries of the Empire, but also the very arts and sciences."[63] It continues with the court's interest in the new science: "Therefore we look with favor upon all forms of learning, but with particular grace we encourage philosophical studies, especially those which by actual experiments attempt either to shape out a new philosophy or to perfect the old."[64] Three of the charter's provisions bear on intellectual property rights: The Society is able to appoint "one or more typographers or printers" to whom it may be granted "faculty to print such things, matters and affairs touching or concerning the aforesaid Society"; the Society has a right to the bodies of

61. As Charles Webster notes, the rules intended to preserve the dedication to learning at Gresham restricted appointments to unmarried scholars leading to "a severe danger that an institution designed to give versatile young scholars the opportunity to energize the intellectual life of London, would lapse into an almshouse for eccentric old bachelors": *Great Instauration*, 52–53.

62. "Sir Robert Moray mentioned that the King had made an experiment of cold, with three glasses filled with sweet water, used for washing . . .": Royal Society Minutes, January 11, 1664, as quoted in Thomas Birch, *The History of the Royal Society of London for Improving of Natural Knowledge from Its First Rise*, vol. 2 (London: Millar, 1756), 5.

63. Translation of the First Charter, Granted to the President, Council and Fellows of the Royal Society of London by King Charles the Second, A.D. 1662, the Royal Society, London, online.

64. Ibid. Roger Hahn sees the scientific academies playing a more radical role: "A transformed notion of 'academy' that ultimately provided the Republic of Letters with a viable institutional framework, at once elitist and community-directed," for what he considers as "the task of building a new order in addition to destroying the old one" (*The Anatomy of a Scientific Institution: The Paris Academy of Sciences, 1666–1803* [Berkeley: University of California Press, 1971], 43).

executed criminals "to anatomize" in order "to obtain the better effect in their philosophical studies"; and its members are allowed, by letter, "to enjoy mutual intelligence and knowledge with all manner of strangers and foreigners . . . without any molestation, interruption or disturbance."[65] The Society had gained rights to print, to bodies, and to correspondence, each of which represented a precious element of intellectual autonomy, given that this was otherwise a period in which such matters were closely watched and controlled by church, Crown, and the Company of Stationers, with more on this to follow.

The charter did not, however, make provisions for the Society's ongoing financial support. A third royal charter in 1669 did provide a tract of land for the purpose of establishing a permanent home for the Society. Yet the members felt compelled to sell it back to the king, as the Society still lacked the resources to erect a building. This penurious state must have been all the more difficult to bear for Society members, given the situation of the Académie des Sciences, founded in Paris in 1666 by Jean-Baptiste Colbert, finance minister for Louis XIV. The Académie provided *gratifications* to support members, as well as the privilege of meeting in the king's library. In return for this patronage, Académie members served the Crown as scientific advisors, cartographers, and engineers. Until 1688, any reports or reviews published by the members appeared under the name of the Académie alone, and its scientific endeavors, from desalination of seawater to hydraulic engineering, had a practical bent to them.[66]

In contrast, the Royal Society possessed a greater degree of autonomy, making it more fully a part of "the world of letters," as the charter expresses it.[67] It was entrusted by the Crown to print works of learning for the benefit of all humankind, much as the universities had been granted, during this period of continuing press censorship and Stationers' Company monopolies

65. First Charter, 1662.

66. Robin Briggs, "The Académie Royale des Sciences and the Pursuit of Utility," *Past and Present* 131 (1991): 46–48. The Académie was "the beneficiary of the most generous patronage of science known during the seventeenth century": Alice Stroup, "Royal Funding of the Parisian Académie Royale des Sciences during the 1690s," *Transactions of the American Philosophical Society* 77 (1987): 1.

67. First Charter, 1662. Noah Moxham recounts of the Académie Royale des Sciences: "Evidently, this [financial sponsorship] enabled Louis to exploit the work of the Académie for his own prestige and the knowledge it produced specifically as a royal possession to be incorporated into the mechanisms of favor and patronage, but it made the work frustratingly useless as a contribution to the wider republic of letters" ("Edward Tyson's Phocaena: A Case Study in the Institutional Context of Scientific Publishing," *Notes and Records: The Royal Society Journal of the History of Science* 66 [2012]: 241).

among printers. The Society was also allowed to carry on the international correspondence needed at the time to establish and verify claims of discovery and invention. Still, it was not long before the Society's first secretary, Henry Oldenburg, ran into the limits of that autonomy. He was briefly imprisoned in 1667 on suspicion of espionage, in light of the unceasing flow of letters from abroad that arrived at the door of this foreigner living on English soil, but then he was also asked by the State Paper Office to translate intercepted letters in the interests of the country's security. More generally, the trust bestowed by the Crown on the Society may have been based on the Royalist tendencies of its initial membership.[68]

Whatever the king's motives for granting this low-cost charter to the Society, its members were happy to bring papers and demonstrations "before their *weekly Meetings*, to undergo a just and full Examination" at Gresham College, as Thomas Sprat, Bishop of Rochester and Society member, wrote in his 1667 history of the Society.[69] These were not gatherings of idle speculation, as Sprat had it. The demonstrable truth of experimentation held sway over talk: "It was in Vain that any man amongst them strive to preferr himself before another," Sprat wrote, "or to seek for any greater glory from the Subtilty of his Wits; seeing as it was the inartificial Process of the *Experiment*, and not the *Acuteness* of any Commentary upon it, which they have had in Veneration."[70] This just and full examination of what actually took place was not, however, entirely straightforward. Many of the experiments were done outside the college. They might be performed, for example, in Boyle's laboratory or in Hooke's lodging, with a witness or two. This would be followed by a report presented to the Society by way of making the experiment public.[71] The meetings, on the other hand, which might bring out as many as forty

68. Lotte Mulligan, "Civil War Politics, Religion and the Royal Society," *Past and Present* 59, no. 1 (1973): 96. J. G. A. Pocock on the original Oxford's experimental philosophical club: "It is tempting to define the politics of the Oxford Scientists at this time as conservative and empirical, authoritarian and latitudinarian [religion by reason]" (Introduction to *The Political Works of James Harrington*, ed. J. G. A. Pocock [Cambridge: Cambridge University Press, 1977], 84).

69. Sprat, *History of the Royal Society of London*, 91.

70. Ibid., 91. Steven Shapin describes this period as displacing "solitary knowers from the center of the knowledge-making scenes and replacing them with a moral economy": *A Social History of Truth: Civility and Science in Seventeenth-Century England* (Chicago: University of Chicago Press, 1994), 27. This civility, for Shapin, relies upon "trust" and "trusteeship," which, he points out, was to form for Locke (discussed in chapter 11) a basis of legitimate sovereignty (11).

71. Steven Shapin, "The House of Experiment in Seventeenth-Century England," in *Never Pure: Historical Studies of Science as If It Was Produced by People with Bodies, Situated in Time, Space, Culture, and Society, and Struggling for Credibility and Authority* (Baltimore: Johns Hopkins University Press, 2010), 77.

or so members in the early years (judging by the records of the anniversary gathering), were not given to endorsing scientific findings or discoveries on behalf of the Royal Society.[72] Just the opposite. The Society's motto—*nullius in verba* (take no one's word for it)—meant that everyone (well, every member) had a responsibility to judge the work for himself. No one should take the Society's word for it.[73]

Still, Sprat boasted of the membership's creditability, as it consisted of "very many Men of particular Professions, yet the far greater Number are *Gentlemen*, free, and unconfin'd."[74] It was the financial independence of gentlemen that protected the Society against the *"two Corruptions* of Learning."[75] The first being how *"Knowledge* still degenerates to consult *present Profit* too soon," while the other, referring to the universities, is "that *Philosophers* have been always *Masters* and Scholars; some imposing, and all the other submitting; and not as equal Observers without Dependence."[76] This well defines the space occupied by academy and society in early modern Europe, which fell between the craft guilds (given to chasing profits) and universities (deferring to authority). The Society did offer, in principle, a more open and public space for learning than university, cathedral school, and monastery, given it was located in London, and initially at Gresham College, a site of public presentations. Yet its membership was a matter of nomination and election, initially restricted to fifty-five in number (expanded to 115 by

72. See Michael Hunter for seventeenth-century anniversary meeting attendance and membership numbers: *Establishing the New Science: The Experience of the Early Royal Society* (Woodbridge, Suffolk, UK: Boydell and Brewer, 1989), 112–14.

73. Adrian Johns points to William Petty's *"Discourse Made before the Royal Society . . . concerning the Use of Duplicate Proportion,* in which Petty writes of it being a "sample of the Royal Society's labors" and adding that "the Society have been pleased to order it to be published: (I dare not say, as approving it, but as committing it to Examination)": "Science and the Book," in *The Cambridge History of the Book in Britain,* vol. 4, *1557–1695,* ed. John Barnard and D. F. McKenzie (Cambridge: Cambridge University Press, 2002), 279, 302–3 note 65.

74. Sprat, *History of the Royal Society,* 67. Hunter provides a Royal Society membership breakdown by occupation for those somewhat active after election, which places "gentlemen" at 14 percent of the membership, and when combined with "aristocrats" adds up to 25 percent of the members having independent means: *Establishing the New Science,* 116.

75. Sprat, *History of the Royal Society,* 67.

76. Ibid. Later in the book, Sprat continues his charge that "men of business [are] against many sorts of *Knowledge*" because they unfairly judge it "inclines men to be unsettled, and *contentious*; That it takes up more of their time," and "makes them unfit for Action" (331). Sprat is following Francis Bacon's defense of learning against such charges in *The Advancement of Learning* (Oxford: Oxford University Press, 1906), 11–19. "Most modern descriptions of the early years of the Royal Society still fail to give a sufficient sense of just how nervous of criticism the publicists of the Society were": Noel Malcolm, *Aspects of Hobbes* (Oxford: Clarendon, 2002), 330.

1663), with allowances for additionally accepting those at the rank of baron or above. It was, however, the Society's publishing program that was to en-sure it a larger public.

Sprat is clear about the Society being on the side of openness, access, and public usefulness. One part of his unrealized plan for the Society was to have it purchase inventions from their inventors and turn these intellectual properties into public goods: "The Royal Society will be able by degrees, to purchase such extraordinary inventions, which are now close lock'd up in *Cabinets*; and then bring them into the common stock, which shall be upon all occasions expos'd to all mens use."[77] His goal of duly rewarding inventors while protecting the public's interests in such inventions is one of the principles that guides intellectual property law. It had also been part of Francis Bacon's vision for science, earlier in the century, with that vi-sion regarded as an inspiration for the formation of the Royal Society: "The *Artificers* should reap the common crop of their Arts," Sprat writes, "but the *publick* should still have a *Title* to the miraculous productions."[78]

Sprat clearly paid homage to Bacon's emphasis on experimentation in his description of the Society, which involved a means of verification that suggested the value of print: "We should not approve any discovery," Bacon wrote, "unless it is in writing."[79] Within two years of being granted its print-ing rights by royal charter, the Society issued the first book to bear its grand seal. The right to print was an important privilege of intellectual autonomy for learning, but the privilege meant little enough if the Society could not pay the printers. In this, the Society principally relied on the unsteady support of its members. Its printing program began with a work of practical inter-est to the state (which proved uncharacteristic of its books), namely John Evelyn's *Sylva, or A Discourse of Forest-Trees and the Propagation of Timber in His Majesty's Dominions*, published in 1664.[80] In his dedication to King

77. Sprat, *History of the Royal Society*, 75.

78. Ibid.

79. Francis Bacon, *The New Organon*, ed. Lisa Jardine and Michael Silverthorne (Cambridge: Cambridge University Press, 2000), 82. For all of Bacon's suspicions of "literature and book-learning," he had been quick to praise the invention of printing (along with gunpowder and the compass) for "what a change have these three made in the world in these times; the one [printing] in the state of learning," while in *De Augmentis* he praises "the art of printing, which brings books within reach of men of all fortunes": Francis Bacon, "In Praise of Knowledge," in *The Works of Francis Bacon*, ed. James Spedding, Robert Leslie Ellis, and Douglas Denon Heath, vol. 8 (London: Longman, 1858), 125; Francis Bacon, "de Augmentis," in *The Works of Francis Bacon*, 5:110.

80. John Evelyn, *Sylva, or A Discourse of Forest-Trees and the Propagation of Timber in His Maj-esty's Dominions* (London: John Martyn and James Allestry, 1664). A facsimile is available online at the Internet Archive. Suggesting its reluctance to become otherwise involved in matters of state,

Charles II, Evelyn describes the book as "the Publique Fruit of your *Royal Society*," alluding to how this work was a collective effort on the part of the Society, which had been inspired by the suggestion of the navy's "principal *Officers* and *Commissioners*."[81] The title page refers to the book "as it was Deliver'd in the Royal Society" and as "Published by express Order of the Royal Society"; after the first edition, Evelyn's standing was noted as a "Fellow of the Royal Society." The front matter also features a very prominent Royal Society seal, with its motto: *Nullius in verba*. The 120-page work, with a single illustration of hand tools, sold out its thousand-copy print run in its second year, with expanded editions following.[82]

Despite the relative success of Evelyn's book, the Society's members, as well as its printers, were unwilling to underwrite the costs associated with the Society's second book. This was Robert Hooke's *Micrographia or, Some Physiological Descriptions of Minute Bodies Made by Magnifying Glasses, with Observations and Inquiries Thereupon,* which was published in 1665 with private funding.[83] It still carried the Society's seal, as well as a dedication to the Society from its author. It is a rather sensational scientific work with its fold-out and full-page etchings, which included a drone fly eye, a flea's anatomy, the point of a needle, the structure of plant *cells* (so named for the first time), and craters on the moon.[84] It sold well enough to go into a second printing.

With future books, the Society experimented with paying subsidies to those booksellers who would carry their books, and buying copies in advance for members.[85] The Society's struggling efforts to make ends meet left

the Society turned down a proposal by founding member Robert Moray to examine, at the king's request, "any philosophical and mechanical invention" for which a patent was being considered, with nothing coming of it then, nor in 1709, when it was proposed again: Birch, *History of the Royal Society*, 116. Christine Macleod, "The 1690s Patents Boom: Invention or Stock-Jobbing?" *Economic History Review* 39, no. 4 (1986): 552. Moray had connections with Charles II, as he traveled in his company during the king's exile, while at this time he had rooms near the king's laboratory.

81. Evelyn, *Sylva*, unpaginated.

82. Gillian Darley, *John Evelyn: Living for Ingenuity* (New Haven, CT: Yale University Press, 2006), 185.

83. Robert Hooke, *Micrographica, or Some Physiological Descriptions of Minute Bodies Made by Magnifying Glasses, with Observations and Inquiries Thereupon* (London: John Martyn and James Allestry, 1665). Available online at Project Gutenberg.

84. Robert D. Purrington, *The First Professional Scientist: Robert Hooke and the Royal Society of London* (Basel, Switzerland: Springer, 2009), 115.

85. Johns, "Science and the Book," 302. For example, the Society agreed to purchase fifty copies for its members and one hundred for others of Johannes Goedaert's *Of Insects: Done into English and Methodized, with the Addition of Notes*, which Society member Martin Lister not only edited, but financed in 1682 (ibid.). Lister is also notable for having two daughters who were illustrators, perfecting their art with microscopes: Anna Marie Roos, "The Art of Science: A 'Rediscovery' of

printers and booksellers "averse to the printing of mathematical books," as one correspondent wrote to Isaac Newton in 1672, with a later letter pointing to how sales of John Wallis's mathematical work failed to cover its printing costs.[86] Then in 1686, the Society offered to include the members' names on each fish engraving they sponsored (at one guinea each) in the lavishly illustrated *Historia Piscium*.[87] While the strategy worked, and the book was printed at Oxford University under the supervision of John Fell (with more on the university's press operations in the next chapter), booksellers were only able to sell a small portion of the five hundred copies printed on varying qualities of paper. The Society was forced to pay its employees, such as Robert Hooke, in copies of the fish book.[88]

The Society's financial ineptitude amid a limited market for such books almost led it to pass up on publishing a scientific landmark. For in 1686, when Newton finally agreed to have *The Principia* (*Philosophiæ naturalis principia mathematica*) printed after much procrastination, the Society's members were simply not prepared to finance yet another title in the same year in which they had supported *Historia piscium*.[89] Fortunately, one member and a man of independent means, Edmond Halley, came forward with a proposal that was documented in the Society minutes for June 2, 1686 as simply: "Printing it [*Principia*] at his own charge, which he engaged to do."[90]

the Lister Copperplates," *Notes and Records: The Royal Society Journal of the History of Science* 65 (2011): 2.

86. Cited by A. N. L. Munby, "The Distribution of the First Edition of Newton's 'Principia,'" *Notes and Records: The Royal Society Journal of the History of Science* 10, no. 1 (1952): 29.

87. Sachiko Kusukawa, "The *Historia Piscium* (1686)," *Notes and Records: The Royal Society Journal of the History of Science* 54, no. 2 (2000): 180, 187. Around half of the 141 members subscribed, with twenty-five subscribers from outside the Society, including John Fell, who saw to the printing at the university (189). Elsewhere, Kusukawa notes that "the cost of producing illustrations could form up to three-quarters of the capital investment of producing a book," while keeping the price of books within the financial reach of students became a reason for not including illustrations: "Illustrating Nature," in *Books and the Sciences in History*, ed. Marina Frasca-Spada and Nick Jardine (Cambridge: Cambridge University Press, 2000), 97.

88. Kusukawa, "*Historia Piscium*," 192. "The Royal Society . . . could be seen as an authoritative center for natural knowledge because it mastered the use of the press": Adrian Johns, *The Nature of the Book: Print and Knowledge in the Making* (Chicago: University of Chicago Press, 1998), 465. He points to how "it came to maintain its own printers, its own journal, its own correspondence networks and its own right to license books" (ibid.).

89. Kusukawa, "*Historia Piscium*," 192. Adrian Johns furthers the intrigue by reporting that the Royal Society suspected the printers of producing extra copies of *Historia Piscium* to sell on the side, increasing the unsold stock borne by the Society: "The Ambivalence of Authorship in Early Modern Natural Philosophy," in *Scientific Authorship: Credit and Intellectual Property in Science*, ed. Mario Biagioli and Peter Galison (London: Routledge, 2003), 75.

90. Cited by Munby, "First Edition of Newton's 'Principia,'" 30.

Newton, in his preface to *The Principia*, speaks of Halley's "tremendous assistance; not only did he correct the typographical errors and see to the making of the woodcuts, but it was he who started me off on the road to this publication."[91] Newton also acknowledges Halley's "subsequent encouragement and kind patronage," as well as how "he never stopped asking me to communicate it to the Royal Society."[92] And if that were not enough, Halley promoted the book by taking such steps as placing an advance notice of its publication in the *Philosophical Transactions* and requesting that Newton call on his Cambridge booksellers to take copies.[93]

The Society decided on a different path with the publishing of a periodical. These pamphlet-length publications, published at relatively regular intervals, were to be found in increasing numbers among booksellers around St. Paul's and in the coffeehouses of London.[94] The Society's secretary Henry Oldenburg saw an opportunity to use its printer to report on the members' scientific work. He had firsthand access to the papers presented, demonstrations performed, and three hundred or so letters received annually. Such a publication might even finance his position with the Society (which went unpaid until 1669). He may have been more immediately inspired in this venture by a letter in November of 1664 from the French astronomer Adrien Auzout, asking him to contribute "what I can concerning England," as he described it to his friend, patron, and Society fellow Robert Boyle, to "a Journal of all what passeth in Europe in matters of knowledge both Philosophical and Political," including notices of new books, experiments, and discoveries, as well as "the disputes which arise among learned men and interesting problems."[95] This

91. Isaac Newton, *The Principia: Mathematical Principles of Natural Philosophy*, trans. I. Bernard Cohen and Anne Whitman (Berkeley: University of California Press, 1999), 383. Newton's 1687 copy, printed by Joesph Streater, is available online at the Cambridge Digital Library.

92. Ibid.

93. Munby, "First Edition of Newton's 'Principia,'" 31. In having Newton place the book with Cambridge booksellers, Halley suggested, in a 1687 letter to Newton, his willingness to try to interest the booksellers in going "halves with me [in sharing the receipts], rather than have your excellent work smothered by their combinations" (cited by ibid., 29).

94. "The other striking advance of the early seventeenth century concerned the publication of weekly and other regularly produced newsletters and periodicals": James Raven, *The Business of Books: Booksellers and the English Book Trade 1450–1850* (New Haven, CT: Yale University Press, 2007), 58.

95. Henry Oldenburg, "356. Oldenburg to Boyle, 24 November 1664," in *The Correspondence of Henry Oldenburg*, vol. 2, 1663–65, trans. A. Rupert Hall and Marie Boas Hall (Madison: Wisconsin University Press, 1966), 319–320. Andrade reports that the Society minutes record Hooke's designs for a journal, possibly from 1663, as "but one perplexity in the history of the early days of the publication": "The Birth and Early Days of the Philosophical Transactions," *Notes and Records of the Royal Society of London* 20, no. 1 (1965): 12. On Boyle's patronage of science, see Michael Hunter, *Boyle: Between God and Science* (New Haven, CT: Yale University Press, 2009), 123.

was the *Journal des sçavans*, which was about to be printed for the first time in Paris on January 5, 1665, inaugurating the new literary genre that we now think of as the learned journal.

Rather than serve as a stringer for the Parisian *Journal*, Oldenburg decided to fashion his own newsbook. He applied to the Society for a license to print a periodical to be entitled *Philosophical Transactions*. The Society's Council ordered on March 1, 1665, "that the Philosophical Transactions, to be composed by Mr. Oldenburg ... be licensed by the Council of the Society, being first reviewed by some of the Members of the same."[96] It was surely an expedited review; the first issue was dated March 6, 1644/45, five dates after the motion passed.[97] Although it was erroneously referred to, at times, as the *Transactions of the Royal Society* (as the Society was to note with dismay in the eighteenth century), Oldenburg was clear from the first volume that "these Rude Collections," as he states in the dedication to the Royal Society, "are only the Gleanings of my *private* diversions in broken hours."[98]

To Oldenburg's credit, he set out in the first issue how the *Philosophical Transactions* was taking a bold new tack in making print an instrument of learning. On page one, he offers a manifesto and vision for this new genre, in the guise of an "introduction": "Whereas there is nothing more necessary for promoting the improvement of Philosophical Matters than the communicating to such, as apply their Studies and Endeavors that way," he asserts, "it is therefore thought fit to employ the Press."[99] The printing press, for Oldenburg, was to do more than convey the results of experiments and discoveries. It would actively promote the development of natural philosophy. Treating science as a form of news—that is, a breaking story still in process—has the effect of both increasing and encouraging access to the formation of this knowledge, not least because a sixteen-page pamphlet is far more affordable than

96. *The Record of the Royal Society of London* (London: Harrison and Sons, 1897), 103. The *Journal des sçavans* ceased publication in its first year, after its right to publish was suspended, but was reinstated with a shift in editor from Denys de Sallo to Abbé Jean Gallois: Thomas Broman, "Periodical Literature," in *Books and the Sciences*, 229. Broman, noting the success of Peter Bayle's *Nouvelles de la Republique des Letteres*, started in 1684, concludes that "the role of science as a form of public knowledge was decisively shaped by the market for periodical literature and by the distinctive structure of the publications" (230-31).

97. The year is represented as 1664/65 because the New Year started on March 25 in Britain at that time, and was only changed to January 1 in 1751, as it had been on the Continent in 1665.

98. Henry Oldenburg, "To the Royal Society," *Philosophical Transactions*, January 1665, unpaginated.

99. Henry Oldenburg, "The Introduction," *Philosophical Transactions* 1, no. 1 (1664/65): 1.

a book. Oldenburg imagined that a monthly publication would appeal, as he continues in this introduction, to "those whose engagement in such Studies and delight in the advancement of Learning, and profitable Discoveries, doth entitle them to the knowledge of what this Kingdom, or other parts of the World, do, from time to time, afford."[100] Oldenburg was asserting the *inherent access rights* of both those who labor over, as well as those who enjoy, such studies. He was doing so amid a political climate in which the king was all too ready to hand out press monopolies in exchange for press censorship, which would otherwise restrict such entitlements.

Oldenburg sought to honor the rightful claim of the scientifically engaged to "the progress of the Studies, Labors, and attempts of the curious and learned in things of this kind."[101] The attempts include failed experiments, disproven hypotheses, and open questions. These are the transactions of science, and with them he *opens* the whole of experimental science to a broader public, outside the closed membership of the Society. Here, then, is the common enterprise of scholarly publishing: Encouraging "those addicted to and conversant with" learning to collaborate on, as Oldenburg writes, "the Grand design of improving Natural knowledge and perfecting all *Philosophical Arts*, and *Sciences*."[102] He concludes that the addicts and conversants are to share what they know for "the Glory of God, the Honor and Advantage of these Kingdoms, and the Universal Good of Mankind."[103] While the intellectual aspirations were grand, the *Transactions* did not likely meet his immediate financial expectations, although the initial issues sold out.[104] Still, what Oldenburg and other journal publishers created was a form of intellectual property that outlived kingdoms in its pursuit of what he named the universal good of humankind. The *Transactions* may have suffered losses well into the nineteenth century, but by the latter half of the twentieth century, the revenue that scholarly societies, generally, were able to obtain from their

100. Ibid.
101. Ibid., 2.
102. Ibid.
103. Ibid.
104. Henry Oldenburg wrote to Boyle that "what was hoped, might have brought me in, about 150 lb. per annum, English and Latin together, will now scarce amount to 50, especially since the Stationers, by reason of the war, refuse to print Latin": "501. Oldenburg to Boyle, 24 March 1665/6," in *The Correspondence of Henry Oldenburg*, vol. 3, 1666-1667, trans. A. Rupert Hall and Marie Boas Hall (Madison: Wisconsin University Press, 1966), 69. The reference to war is the Second Anglo-Dutch War (1665-1667), which would have added to the risks of printing the *Transactions* in Latin with an intended market on the Continent. See also Marie Boas Hall, *Henry Oldenburg: Shaping the Royal Society* (Oxford: Oxford University Press, 2002), 85-86.

journals was sufficient to bear a good part of the organization's expenses.[105]
The Oldenburgian question pressing on us today is how we think "it fit
to employ" the internet much as he deployed the press, given that "there is
nothing more necessary for promoting the improvement of Philosophical
Matters than the communicating to such, as apply their Studies and Endeavors that way."

Oldenburg also organized an early intellectual property registry of inventions. He made a show of sealing and dating letters at meetings to register a claim, while the Society's president deposited inventions in a box,
along with the date received, to further establish inventors' priorities.[106] The
Transactions served a similar purpose. Oldenburg wrote to Newton in 1672
that his letter on "Light and Colors" was read to "the publick meeting of
the R. Society," and the members "voted unanimously, that if you contra-
dicted it not, this discourse should without delay be printed, there being
cause to apprehend that the ingenious & surprising notion therein contain'd (for such they were taken to be) may be easily snatched from you, and
the Honor of it be assumed by forainers."[107] This is the commonwealth of
learning seeking to protect the priority of its members through published
accreditation.[108]

Still, proprietary disputes arose within the Society during this period. In
the 1670s, the members Robert Hooke and Christiaan Huygens each claimed
to have invented a balance spring that added to the reliability of pocket
watches.[109] After Huygens revealed his invention by sharing diagrams of his

105. Aileen Fyfe presents the consistent financial losses suffered by the *Transactions*, from the
Society taking it on in 1752 to the end of the nineteenth century, reflecting the Society's sense of
it as a responsibility, in Oldenburg's initial terms, rather than the revenue source that it would
later grow into for the society: "Journals, Learned Societies and Money: *Philosophical Transactions*, ca. 1750-1900," *Notes and Records: The Royal Society Journal of the History of Science* (2015):
doi: 10.1098.

106. Rob Iliffe describes how with mathematical inventions, an elaborate encoding technique
was developed for putting the world on notice that a new technique was under development, without revealing anything substantial about it in advance: "'In the Warehouse': Privacy, Property, and
Priority in the Early Royal Society," *History of Science* 30 (1992): 34-36.

107. Henry Oldenburg, "41. Oldenburg to Newton, 8 February 1671/1," in *The Correspondence
of Isaac Newton*, vol. 1, 1661-1775 (Cambridge: Cambridge University Press, 1959), 107. Newton's
paper appeared in the *Philosophical Transactions* 6, no. 80 (1671/72): 3075-87.

108. See N. Moxham for discussion of the late seventeenth-century shift in which "*Transactions* had to absorb functions of registration and research communication that the Society had at
certain times been resolved to keep separate": "Fit for Print: Developing an Institutional Model
of Scientific Periodical Publishing in England, 1665-ca. 1714," *Notes and Records: The Royal Society
Journal of the History of Science* (2015): doi: 10.1098.

109. Ilffe, "'in the Warehouse,'" 34-36.

design at a Society meeting, Hooke claimed that he had deliberately kept his own design of the balance spring out of the *Transactions* because he did not trust Oldenburg, "since I looked on him as one that made a trade of intelligence."[110] Huygens may have had the stronger case, only to find that his seeming friend, the French watchmaker Isaac Thuret, claimed the balance spring as his own invention in the course of implementing Huygens' designs.[111] This mix of craft, commerce, and science, amid charges of theft and betrayed trust, soured the Royal Society on including craft and trade matters in its program.[112] Society fellows soon discovered, however, that the purest of mathematical interests could give rise to no less acrimony over priority claims of invention. This was certainly the case with the Newton-Leibniz conflict over the discovery of the calculus during the second decade of the eighteenth century, to slip beyond the historical scope of this book.[113]

Charges of usurpation and plagiarism were rampant at the time. Adrian Johns, Allan Grant Maclear Professor of History at the University of Chicago, provides a bemusing *who's who* of plagiarism within natural philosophy, naming both the accused and the accuser: "Isaac Newton (by Robert Hooke), Robert Hooke (by John Flamsteed) . . . and John Wallis (by almost everyone)."[114] The very cries of *usurpation* suggest a shared grasp of intellectual property rights (and wrongs). This was natural philosophy's contribution to the growing public recognition of authorship—as a point of honor, integrity, and contention—in what is called the Age of Dryden. But then within the realm of learning, a text's authorship had long been an object of analysis and interpretation among learned readers, most vividly, perhaps, among the Renaissance humanists.

Yet the properties of authorship were also of growing interest in the open and public pursuit of experimental science. During the 1660s, for example, the English philosopher Thomas Hobbes was having none of the Royal Society's pretense of openness around its experiments. Hobbes took exception to the closed nature of the Society's meetings: "Cannot anyone who wishes come," Hobbes asks, "since, as I suppose, they meet in a public place, and give his opinion on the experiments [*experimenta*] which are seen, as well

110. Robert Hooke, "Postscript," in *Lampas, or Descriptions of Some Mechanical Improvements of Lamps and Waterpoises* (London: John Martyn, 1677), 53.

111. Ibid., 50, 54.

112. Iliffe, "'In the Warehouse,'" 54.

113. "Newton carried out its investigation, arranged its evidence, and wrote its report . . . Not surprisingly, the committee, or court, found in Newton's favor": Richard S. Westfall, *Never at Rest: A Biography of Isaac Newton* (Cambridge: Cambridge University Press, 1983), 725.

114. Johns, *Nature of the Book*, 461.

as they?" And again: "By what law would they prevent it? Is this Society not constituted by public privilege?"[115] This right of access to the sources of a knowledge claim is commonly used today, as I noted in the first chapter, in the case made for open access.

The question Hobbes raised of who can witness the Society's demonstrations was more than rhetorical. There is, to begin with, Hobbes's own exclusion from the Royal Society, given his work in optics and mathematics, as well as his friends and supporters among the membership. What kept him out appears to be his mathematical disputes, dating back to the 1650s, with founding members John Wallis, Seth Ward, John Wilkins, and Robert Boyle. Still, the Society's interest in increasing access to learning managed to triumph. In 1675, Society Fellow and Hobbes's friend John Aubrey wrote to the philosopher to say that Robert Hooke was interested in publishing, on behalf of the Society, any mathematical and scientific papers he might have on hand.[116] Hobbes responded that he "could be content it should be published by the society much rather than any other," but that he could not forgive how the Society had allowed that the "evill words and disgraces put upon me by Dr. Wallis are still countenanced without any publique Act of the Society to do me Right."[117] It was, of course, the Society's stance not to pronounce on such public disputes (unless they involved the Society's president, in the case of Newton).

The force of Hobbes's question about access to these experiments—"By what law would they prevent it?"—applies, as well, to the Society's exclusion

---

115. Thomas Hobbes, "Physical Dialogue (1661)," in *Leviathan and the Air Pump: Hobbes, Boyle, and the Experimental Life* by Stephen Schaffer and Simon Schaffer (Princeton, NJ: Princeton University Press, 1985), 113. Quentin Skinner notes common critiques of the Society's experimentation: "Few of the other early Fellows of the Royal Society did experimental work with anything like Boyle's competence. The Society indeed became very sensitive to the criticism, which Pepys mentions and Petty amongst others tried to meet, that much of their early and isolated experimental work tended to look rather useless, even (as Stubbe was to insist) wholly ridiculous" ("Thomas Hobbes and the Nature of the Early Royal Society," *Historical Journal* 12, no. 2 [1969], 228). Also relevant to my discussion in chapter 12, Hobbes also objected, in his final year, to the "privilege of stationers [that] is (in my opinion) a very great hindrance to the advancement of all humane learning": Adrian Johns, "Science and the Book," in *The Cambridge History of the Book in Britain, 1557–1695*, ed. John Barnard and D. F. McKenzie, vol. 4 (Cambridge: Cambridge University Press, 2002), 292, 293.

116. Noel Malcolm, "Hobbes and the Royal Society," in *Perspectives on Thomas Hobbes*, ed. G. A. J. Rogers and Alan Ryan (Oxford: Oxford University Press, 1988), 44.

117. Cited by ibid., 45. John Wilkins and Seth Ward recount Hobbes's critique of the universities: "He may better assert, that there are Universities in the *Moone*, and that they maintain all those Positions, then impose them upon us. *There* it will be hard to prove the contrary, We *now* challenge him to make proofe of what he hath delivered, and Promise to give him satisfaction": *Vindiciae academiarum Containing, Some briefe Animadversions upon Mr Websters Book, Stiled "The Examination of Academies"* (Oxford: Leonard Lichfield, 1654), 60.

of the philosopher Margaret Cavendish. A contemporary of Boyle, Cavendish published on natural philosophy, as well as related works of fiction, all without the fellowship of a society devoted to such interests.[118] The point is brought home in the frontispiece for her *Philosophical and Physical Opinions*, published in 1655. The engraving by Peter van Schuppen portrays Cavendish sitting at a desk, with the verse inscribed beneath: "Studious She is all Alone ... Her Library on which She looks / It is her Head her Thoughts her Books."[119] She dared to dedicate the book to the "two universities," in the express hope that they might reach out to encourage those confined "like Birds in Cages, to Hop up and down in Houses," for otherwise "in time we should grow irrational as idiots."[120] In 1666, she published *Observations upon Experimental Philosophy*, in which she criticizes how "our age [is] more for deluding experiments than rational arguments, which some call a 'tedious babble.'"[121] In 1667, Cavendish made a request to visit the Royal Society, which was granted after some debate among the members. At Gresham College, Boyle demonstrated for her that air possessed weight and acids dissolved flesh (Samuel Pepys disparagingly noting in his diary that "her dress so antick, and her deportment so ordinary that I do not like her at all").[122] Although she expressed her appreciation for the visit at the time, she declined to support the Royal Society when she was approached the following year in her capacity as the Duchess of Newcastle with such a request.[123]

118. "I had neither Learning nor Art to set for these Conceptions. . . . But I can assure you Noble Readers, I was very Studious . . . for all that time my Brain was like an University, Senate, or Council-Chamber, wherein all my Conceptions, Imaginations, Observations, Wit, and Judgment did meet to Dispute": Marchioness of Newcastle [Margaret Cavendish], "An Epistle to the Reader," in *Philosophical and Physical Opinions* (London: William Wilson, 1663), unpaginated. Ray reports that Cavendish was "associated with the Newcastle Circle society" and "was part of a network of scientists and philosophers that included William and Charles Cavendish, Thomas Hobbes and Descartes": *Daughters of Alchemy*, 159.

119. Cavendish, *Philosophical and Physical Opinions*.

120. Ibid. Cavendish points out, in her dedication to the "Most Famously Learned," of "the two most famous universities of England" in *Philosophical and Physical Opinions*, that women "are shut out of all power, and Authority by reason we are never imployed either in civil nor marshall affaires, our counsels are despised, and laught at, the best of our actions are troden down with scorn, by the over-weaning conceit men have of themselves and through a dispisement of us."

121. Margaret Cavendish, *Observations upon Experimental Philosophy*, ed. Eileen O'Neill (Cambridge: Cambridge University Press, 2001), 196.

122. Samuel Pepys, "29th May, 1667," in *Diary and Correspondence of Samuel Pepys, F.R.S.*, ed. J. Smith, vol. 3 (Philadelphia: J. B. Lippincott, 1855), 139. Gerald Dennis Meyer, *The Scientific Lady in England 1650–1760: An Account of Her Rise, with Emphasis on the Major Roles of the Telescope and Microscope* (Berkeley: University of California Press, 1955), 10–11. Women were not admitted to the Society until 1945.

123. Hunter, *Establishing the New Science*, 167–68.

The Royal Society of London for Improving Natural Knowledge was decidedly clubbish, with its tenuously financed publications managing to do considerably more for public access to learning than its restricted membership. Still, there was no mistaking the popularity of this concept of societies as a portable model for those with an interest in learning in its more communal aspects. In 1722, John Macky, in his breezy travelogue *A Journey Through England*, wrote of his London encounter with "an Infinity of CLUBS or SOCIETIES, for the Improvement of Learning and keeping up good Humour and Mirth."[124]

CONCLUSION

The earlier Italian humanist academies of the European Renaissance were gatherings of professors, monks, clergy, professionals, merchants, and nobility, men and women (although not in all academies) of a certain class who came together to share books, present papers, and take on projects often involving the new invention of print. This combination of academy and print brought learning and its books into the marketplace, subject to subsidies, subscriptions, and privileges that mark the economy and incorporation of learning. For the Accademia della Crusca, this involved setting a humanist standard for the Italian language. The Accademia dei Lincei helped move heaven and earth to advance Galileo's work and recover that of Hernández. The Royal Society of London used book and journal to promote the intellectual properties of learning, if more successfully in an epistemological than an economic sense.

The intellectual autonomy achieved by the academies was often through print. The church could be both academy patron, as exemplified by Cardinal Bessarion's humanist printing program, and avenging prosecutor through the offices of the Inquisition, as we saw with Galileo. The state may have

124. [John Macky], *A Journey through England in Familiar Letters*, 2nd ed. (London: J. Hooke, 1722), 287. Steven Shapin writes of the spread of such societies later in the eighteenth century: "The 'lit and phils' [literary and philosophical societies] of the Midlands and North of England represented serious attempts at middle-class cultural self-expression, bringing together enlightened medical men, dissenting divines, and a locally elite audience of culturally adventurous manufacturers and tradesmen": "Property, Patronage, and the Politics of Science: The Founding of the Royal Society of Edinburgh," *British Journal for the History of Science* 7, no. 1 (1974): 3. The Royal Society of Edinburgh for the Advancement of Learning and Useful Knowledge was founded in 1783. Peter Clark points to how British these organizations are: "Clubs and societies became one of the most distinctive social and cultural institutions of Georgian Britain" (*British Clubs and Societies 1580–1800: The Origins of an Associational World* [Oxford: Oxford University Press, 2000], 2).

chartered the academies, as well as granted them printing privileges in an era of censorship. Yet the state also required a degree of deference to its own mission. All told, the academies proved able defenders of learning. They complemented and challenged the universities, proving a source of much original work in humanism and the experimental sciences, while building out a broader engagement with the public, commerce, and the authorities.

The academies experimented with learning's long-standing intellectual properties within the new marketplace of printers and booksellers. The values of commerce often conflicted with learned properties of autonomy, access, and communality. Yet the learned were both a reliable source and market for books; they were given to promoting their value and encouraging others in assembling private and public libraries. During this period, the universities were also swept up in the political impact and learned potential of print. Hence, I now step back historically to the sixteenth century and the havoc that the Reformation wreaked on learning, for all its liberation of the soul, before turning to the century-long struggle of the English universities and their presses to find their place in the print market.

CHAPTER TEN

Early Modern Oxford and Cambridge

The founding of Christ Church at the University of Oxford in 1525 was a revealing moment in the university's gradual shift from a medieval to an early modern institution. As colleges go, Christ Church is something of a bastard child of the Reformation. The college was born of the dissolution of a religious house that stood for centuries above the meadow where the River Cherwell meets the Thames in Oxford. In the seventh century, Didan, King of Oxford, endowed a convent on the spot for his daughter Frideswide (or Frithuswith) and a dozen other devout daughters of the local nobility. The convent was also given "the estates and villages of St. Mary and a third part of the city of Oxford to provide the nun's food," as a twelfth-century hagiography of Frideswide records, and she did serve as its prioress until her death in 727.[1] In 1002, a group of Danes took refuge in the priory church in which Frideswide was buried during the St. Brice's Day Massacre, only to have the English burn it to the ground. The church was gradually restored, and in the twelfth century the Priory of St. Frideswide was made a religious house

---

1. Cited by John Blair, "St. Frideswide Reconsidered," *Oxoniensia* 52 (1987): 75. Blair suggests that Frideswide may have been abbess of a double house of nuns and monks (92). In 2002 St. Frideswide's shrine, among those destroyed during the Reformation, was restored from discovered fragments and placed in Christ Church Cathedral; an Edward Burne-Jones's stained glass window from 1858 was added, depicting the saint's life, including her escape from King Algar's matrimonial designs. His apparent proposal: "King Algar desires you as partner for his bed and kingdom ... but if you refuse the king his honourable offer you will be dragged to a brothel and suffer great dishonor"; the king was struck blind on entering Oxford, in a forceful message about separation of state and monastery that deterred Henry II in 1180 and Edward I in 1275 from entering the city, which was reason enough for university officials to adopt her as patron saint (76).

for Augustinian canons regular, which is to say male clerics who shared everything in common.[2] During this time both town and university adopted St. Frideswide as patron saint and instituted an annual scholarly procession on October 19th in her honor, while a fair held in her name attracted manuscript merchants from London.[3]

A CARDINAL ALMOST FOUNDS A COLLEGE

Things remained relatively unchanged for the Priory until 1525, when Cardinal Thomas Wolsey, Lord Chancellor of England under Henry VIII, decided that it was an ideal location for the sort of college that might commemorate his contributions to the country.[4] Such was his power that he was able to suppress (or dissolve) St. Frideswide Priory, with the king's support and a bull from Pope Clement VII. The lands and possessions of St. Frideswide were insufficient, however, to fulfill the cardinal's vision. To remedy that and then some, he saw to the suppression of a further twenty monasteries, declaring that "neither God was served, nor religion kept" by these religious houses.[5] Wolsey's architectural plans for his Cardinal College, as he intended to name it, included a sizeable cloistered quadrangle, as if to remind Oxford masters and students of their monastic indebtedness. The cardinal employed, according to a nineteenth-century cathedral handbook, "many hundred workmen, including artists of all kinds" for this project.[6] He made it clear in the new college statutes that scholars would go out into

2. George Henry Cook, *Letters to Cromwell and Others on the Suppression of the Monasteries* (London: John Barker, 1965), 14.

3. John Blair, "Frithuswith [St. Frithuswith, Frideswide] (*d.* 727), Abbess of Oxford," in *Oxford Dictionary of National Biography*, ed. H. C. G. Mathew and Brian Harrison, online ed. (Oxford: Oxford University Press, 2004). James Raven, *The Business of Books: Booksellers and the English Book Trade 1450–1850* (New Haven, CT: Yale University Press, 2007), 60.

4. On the founding of colleges at the time, R. W. Hoyle reports: "In the fifteenth and early sixteenth centuries, no one had the money with which to establish a monastery on the classic high medieval lines. For those who wished a permanent memorial to themselves and their ancestors, there were cheaper options, including colleges and almshouses": "The Origins of the Dissolution of the Monasteries," *Historical Journal* 38, no. 2 (1995): 276–77.

5. Cited by David Knowles, *Bare Ruined Choirs: The Dissolution of the English Monasteries* (Cambridge: Cambridge University Press, 1976), 59. Not everyone agreed with such a sweeping condemnation of the monasteries. The closing of the Tonbridge monastery had the townspeople petitioning, unsuccessfully, for its continuance, while being told that the monastic closures would result in, among other things, scholarships for students from communities such as theirs to the new Oxford college (ibid.).

6. Richard John King, *Handbook to the Cathedrals of England, Eastern Division* (London: John Murray, 1881), 63.

the world well equipped to reach the simpler souls of their parishes with their sermons.[7]

However, Wolsey did not get very far with his building plans before it was his turn to face the heavy hand of royal suppression. In 1529, the immoderate Henry VIII grew impatient with the cardinal's lack of influence in Rome, and placed him under arrest. The charges included his having overrun the papal bulls that he had been granted following his closures of the monasteries.[8] By the medieval right of *escheat*, Henry then assumed ownership of the college lands and unfinished buildings.[9] In 1532, Henry refounded Wolsey's college as "King Henry the VIII's College in Oxford," dedicating it to St. Frideswide.[10]

In 1535, Henry further asserted the Crown's supremacy over ecclesiastical institutions by conducting royal visitations to the universities in Oxford and Cambridge.[11] On the first Reformation visit to Oxford, Richard Layton arrived on the king's behalf and proceeded to scour the university for books reflecting papal allegiance. Layton reported back to his majesty, with some color, that he had banished works of the "Dunce" (the thirteenth-century theologian Duns Scotus) from "Oxforde for ever."[12] "We found all the gret quarant [of New College] court full of the leiffes of Dunce," he wrote, "the wynde blowying them into evere corner."[13] Such visits purged the university libraries of any books that could be accused of containing traces of popery. The royal visitors put an end to the teaching of Peter Lombard's *Sentences* and other scholastic mainstays, which were perhaps due for retirement, and introduced free public lectures on the new theology.[14] What Oxford and

7. Astrik L. Gabriel "Motivation of the Founders at Medieval Colleges," *Miscellanea Mediaevalia* 3 (1964): 71.

8. Knowles, *Bare Ruined Choirs*, 59; Hoyle, "Origins of the Dissolution," 299.

9. Joseph Wells, *Wadham College* (London: Routledge/Thoemmes, 1898), 11. *Escheat* is a common-land doctrine, in which the land that an owner has lost legal right to—as Wolsey had by being arrested for delaying Henry's divorce—reverts to the superior feudal lord, rather than standing ownerless.

10. Richard Rex and C. D. C. Armstrong, "Henry VIII's Ecclesiastical and Collegiate Foundations," *Historical Research* 75, no. 190 (2002): 394.

11. F. Donald Logan judges the visit a clear "intrusion of the power of the state into the affairs of the English universities": "The First Royal Visitation of the English Universities, 1535," *English Historical Review* 106, no. 421 (1991): 861.

12. Cited by Ronald Harold Fritze, "'Truth Hath Lacked Witnesse, Tyme Wanted Light': The Dispersal of the English Monastic Libraries and Protestant Efforts at Preservation, ca. 1535–1625," *Journal of Library History* 18, no. 3 (1983): 278.

13. Cited by ibid.

14. Logan, "First Royal Visitation," 866, 873.

Cambridge lost in autonomy they gained in endowment, privileges, and increased presence in English life, as those who governed expressed a belief in learning's contribution to the state.[15]

In 1536, Parliament passed the Act for the Dissolution of the Lesser Monasteries. The ostensible aim was monastic reformation, beginning with the elimination of those failed religious houses whose worth had slipped below £200: "that the possessions of such religious houses, now being spent, spoiled, and wasted for increase and maintenance of sin, should be used and converted to better uses," as the act put it.[16] The displaced monastics were to join larger, seemingly better managed houses. Henry had proclaimed his support for the monastic *ideal* in this initial act of suppression. Still, a second act came three years later, in 1539, directed against the "Greater Monasteries," which included some 552 religious houses across England. The two acts were accompanied by a series of legal and political maneuvers seeking voluntary, if often coerced, surrender of monastic properties with, at best, a pension provision for homeless monastics. It also closed the doors on the colleges operated by monastic houses in Oxford, including Durham College and Gloucester College, as well as Canterbury College, which possessed a notable manuscript collection.[17]

By 1541, Henry had effectively put an end to monasticism in England, with much credit going to his ruthlessly efficient chief minister, Thomas Cromwell.[18] Many of the manuscripts in abbey collections were lost in the shuffle,

15. "Just as the Church in England became the Church of England, so the universities in England became the universities of England": Mark H. Curtis, *Oxford and Cambridge in Transition 1558–1642* (Oxford: Oxford University Press, 1959), 6–7, 50.

16. "Act for the Dissolution of the Lesser Monasteries" (1536), *Life in Tudor Times*, online. Knowles notes that there were indeed "decayed and disorderly houses" among the English monasteries of the day: *Bare Ruined Choirs*, 83.

17. Kristen Jensen, "Universities and Colleges," in *Cambridge History of Libraries in Britain and Ireland*, ed. Elisabeth Leedham-Green and Teresa Webber (Cambridge: Cambridge University Press, 2006), 346. At the time, monasticism had been developing links with both scholasticism and humanism, and monk-scholars were involved not only in theological studies but engaged in questions concerning mathematics and astronomy: James G. Clark, "University Monks in Late Medieval England," in *Medieval Monastic Education*, ed. George Ferzoco and Carolyn Muessig (London: Leicester University Press, 2000), 62. At the abbeys of St. Albans and Bury, they were also making inroads in historical studies in the best tradition of Bede. To support this learning, printing presses were installed in the Benedictine abbeys of Abingdon in 1525 and Tavistock in 1528, with Franciscan and Dominican friars playing a prominent role in the early printing trade: David N. Bell, "The Libraries of Religious Houses in the Late Middle Ages," in *To 1640*, ed. Elisabeth Leedham-Green and Teresa Webber, vol. 1 of *The Cambridge History of Libraries in Britain and Ireland* (Cambridge: Cambridge University Press, 2006), 127, 135, 136.

18. On Cromwell's part, Knowles writes: "It is possible that the Dissolution would have taken place less violently and less rapidly had another than Cromwell been in power": *Bare Ruined Choirs*, 89.

left to perish, sold off for the king's benefit, or saved for his royal library, with few enough smuggled out for protection. In less than a decade, Henry put an end to the form of life that had created, assembled, and preserved manuscript culture in England, while inadvertently creating a commercial market for surviving manuscripts.

In 1546, Henry turned his attention back to the Oxford college-on-the-priory that he had abruptly seized from Wolsey. He founded the college yet again, this time to do double duty. It was to be the Cathedral Church of the Oxford diocese, within the newly independent Church of England, and a college of the university, which he named Christ Church (*Aedes Christi*).[19] He endowed a number of studentships, and appointed himself *visitor* to what was now one of the university's best-endowed of colleges.[20] In a letter from the time, Henry linked the property transfer, from monastery to college, to his "regard onlie to pull down sin by defacing the monasteries . . . [whereas] I judge no land in England better bestowed than that which is given to our Universities."[21] The universities and learning ensure the future, he further asserts, "for by their maintenance our realme shall be well governed when we be dead and rotten. I love not learning so ill that I will impair the revenewes of anie one House by a penie, whereby it may be upholden."[22] To be fair to the other university, he founded Trinity College at Cambridge that same year, through a similar pattern of dissolution. He also added Regius professorships in Hebrew and medicine at Oxford, having already endowed eight such positions at both Cambridge and Oxford.

Henry died in 1547 and was succeeded by his nine-year-old son Edward VI. Power was in the hands of Edward's advisors, who were caught up in the righteous fervor of the Reformation and the eradication of any trace of English popery. On Christmas Day in 1549, the Privy Council issued an order for the destruction of Catholic service books, "which were but a preferring of Ignorance to knowledge and darkness to light."[23] As small as that may seem, it gave terrible license to the king's representatives. On their next royal visitation to Oxford, they decimated the so-called "Catholic" holdings of the

19. The college's full and proper title recognizes its benefactor to this day: "The Dean, Chapter and Students of the Cathedral Church of Christ in Oxford of the Foundation of King Henry the Eighth."

20. David Horan, *Oxford: A Cultural and Literary Companion* (New York: Interlink, 2000), 19.

21. Cited by G. C. Brodrick, *A History of the University of Oxford* (London: Longmans, Green, 1886), 79.

22. Cited by ibid.

23. R. M. Thompson, *A Descriptive Catalogue of the Medieval Manuscripts of Merton College* (Cambridge: D. S. Brewer, 2009), xl. The order in council is cited in Fritze, "Dispersal of the English Monastic Libraries," 278.

university's libraries. Writing of this visit, Anthony à Wood, historian of the university and Locke's contemporary, described how the "public Library" of the university and "those [books] belonging to the Colleges" were ravaged by "certain ignorant and zealous coxcombs."[24] He notes that "a cartload of MSS [manuscripts] and above were taken away."[25] These coxcombs recalled enough of their own Catholic education to identify, mock, and burn the medieval philosophers they now so despised. The royal visitors cast out from Oxford libraries, Wood writes, "the works of the Schoolmen, namely of P. Lombard, Th. Aquinas, Scotus and his followrs, with Criticks also," parading them about Oxford: "Certain rude young men should carry this great spoil of books about the city on biers; which being so done, to set them down in the common market place and in there burn them, to the sorrow of many, as well of the Protestants as of the other party. This was by them stiled 'the funeral of Scotus and Scotists.'"[26] Although reporting more than a century after the fact, Wood gives a vivid sense of the assault on learning: "Many MSS, guilty of no other superstition than red letters in their fronts or titles, were either condemned to the fire or jakes [a privy]. Others also that treated of controversial or scholastical Divinity were let loose from their chains, and given away or sold to Mechanicks for servile uses . . . such books wherein appeared Angles, or Mathematical Diagrams, were thought sufficient to be destroyed, because accounted Popish, or diabolical, or both."[27]

What good were such book chains, given they were looted, as well, when the books most needed protection against this head-on assault on learning's autonomy? The Reformation may have opened the Bible to a new world of interpretation, but the attack on the universities was one of its low points, betraying institutional vulnerabilities, in the association of patronage, religion, and learning within the English context. Still, more was at stake in the religious and political fervor of these times than the destruction

24. Anthony Wood, *The History and Antiquities of the University of Oxford*, trans. John Gutch, vol. 2 (Oxford: Oxford University Press, 1746), 107.

25. Ibid.

26. Ibid., 107–8. As a result, "in all this King's reign, was seldom seen any thing in the University but books of Poetry, Grammar, idle songs and frivolous stuff," Wood continues his lament, and "learning also which now was low, and by considerable persons despised, became a scorn to the vulgar, and especially for this reason, because books were dog cheap, and whole Libraries could be bought for an inconsiderable nothing" (108).

27. Ibid., 106–7. J. C. T. Oates points out that Cambridge was spared the "official [book] purges" of the Edwardian delegation in 1559, and earlier in 1535, with Henry VIII's injunctions against works of Catholic theology. Yet the library lost some books to acts of individual zealous vandalism: *Cambridge University Library: A History, From the Beginnings to the Copyright Act of Queen Anne* (Cambridge: Cambridge University Press, 1986), 79–81.

of manuscripts. No fewer than five of those who served as chancellors of Cambridge University during the Tudor era were executed for treason (if not directly because of the position they held at the university).[28] Although its libraries suffered, the heads of those leading the University of Oxford were largely spared the violent politics of the Tudor era.

During the remainder of the sixteenth century, Oxford's pillaged university library, which occupied the floor above the divinity school, fell into further disrepair and neglect. Christ Church acquired the library's benches and desks, while the rooms themselves—given the shortage of space then as now in universities—were claimed by the Faculty of Medicine. The university library now stood as "the void at the heart of the University," as James Fenton put it in his 1999 Creweian Oration as Professor of Poetry, speaking in praise of those Oxonian benefactors who did so much to fill that void.[29] Fortunately, the "inconstancy of mankind," noted by Wood, works both ways.[30] What Oxford's library suffered in the name of the Reformation during the fifteenth century was put back together again in the next century by the unsurpassable library revivalist Thomas Bodley, scholar, statesman, and benefactor.

BODLEY BUILDS A UNIVERSITY LIBRARY

On February 23, 1597/98, Thomas Bodley wrote in his broad sprawling hand what must still stand as one of the boldest letters ever sent to a vice chancellor of the University of Oxford. His letter was just the sort of thing that would be identified, and deleted, as spam today. It opens humbly enough: "Sir, although you know mee not, as I suppose, yet for the farthering of an offer, of evident utilitie, to your whole university, I will not be so scrupulous, in craving your assistance."[31] A determined Bodley wrote, "For the benefit of posteritie, I would shew some token of affection that I have evermore boarne, to the studies of good learning."[32] Such talk of posterity's benefit has long been part of learning's terms of patronage, but for Bodley this beneficence

28. Among the Cambridge chancellors, Cardinal Fisher, for example, went to his death on Tower Hill for refusing to recognize the spiritual supremacy of Henry VIII in 1535. Craig R. Thompson, *Universities in Tudor England* (Washington, DC: Folger Shakespeare Library, 1959), 4.

29. James Fenton, "Creweian Oration," *Oxford Gazette*, supp. 4517 (June 25, 1999).

30. Wood, *History*, 107.

31. Thomas Bodley, "Letter 1 to the Vice Chancellor," in *Letters of Sir Thomas Bodley to the University of Oxford, 1598-1611*, ed. G. W. Wheeler (Oxford: Oxford University Press, 1927), 4.

32. Ibid.

took a very specific institutional form. He was moved to action by what "hath bin heretofore a publike library in Oxford."³³ The "hath bin" is noteworthy, for by the close of the sixteenth century, a library that served the entire university (as opposed to the individual college libraries) was no longer in existence. Bodley planned to step in and right the matter. He sought to "take charge and cost upon me, to reduce it again to his former use: and to make it fitte, and handsome with seates, and shelfes, and Deskes, and all that may be needful, to stirre up other mens benevolence, to helpe to furnish it with bookes."³⁴

In 1559, nearly forty years earlier, Thomas Bodley had been admitted to Magdalen College as a commoner. On graduating in 1563, he took up a fellowship at Merton. His great facility in languages, aided by having grown up on the Continent, earned him an appointment as Merton's first lecturer in Greek. He was also able to contribute to the emerging area of Hebrew studies and serve as bursar and garden master. But he was also drawn to the larger world and left Oxford in 1576 to pursue a diplomatic career. What made his fortune was his marriage to Ann Ball in 1586, as she was the widow of a prosperous sardine merchant and the heiress of a wealthy father.³⁵

The forcefulness of Bodley's tone in that initial letter is matched by the breathtaking alacrity of its intent, as he seeks "to beginne, assoone as timber can be gotten."³⁶ He also proposes assigning the rent secured from his Manor of Hindons and houses in London "to be disbursed every yere in buing of bookes, in officers stipends, and other pertinent occasions," while hoping that there is nothing illegal about such a property assignment.³⁷ As part of his take-charge attitude, he asks for the records of previous donations to the library, as well as the relevant statutes. He assures the university that his goal was to create "an excellent benefit for the use and ease of studentes: and a singular ornament in the University."³⁸ And then he signs the letter, "your affectionat frend, Tho: Bodley."³⁹

33. Ibid. It may be tempting to read this as "heretofore a pub[-]like library in Oxford," but it should be read, of course, as "public" which is an important concept here.
34. Ibid.
35. W. H. Clennel dryly sums up how the marriage "laid the foundation of Bodley's subsequent career [as generous library patron]. They had no children": W. H. Clennel, "Bodley, Sir Thomas (1545–1613)," in *Oxford Dictionary of National Biography*, ed. H. C. G. Matthew and Brian Harrison, online ed. (Oxford: Oxford University Press, 2004).
36. Bodley, "Letter 1 to the Vice Chancellor," in *Letters*, 4.
37. Ibid.
38. Ibid., 4.
39. Ibid., 5.

By Bodley's fourth letter to the university, on June 25, 1600, he reports that he "began now to busy my selfe and my frendes, about gathering in Bookes of such as will bee benefactours."[40] And to prove the point, he provides a list of those benefactors whom he had won over to the Oxford library's cause as a postscript. The list began with the Earl of Essex's gift of three hundred volumes, and included fourteen lesser benefactors, including "Mr Tho Cornwallis the groome porter" who committed "fower powndes in money."[41] Bodley was unrelenting in soliciting support for the library. He wrote to acquaintances abroad to obtain works in Chinese, Persian, and Arabic, and hired a book-buying agent to travel the continent and make purchases in his name on behalf of the library. He found that Catholic collectors were eager to see their religious heritage recognized and preserved through their contribution of literary and liturgical manuscripts.[42] He had a vellum-paged Register of Benefactors to replace the older practice of the university chaplain reciting donors' names during mass, following the ancient monastic tradition.[43]

In a sixth letter to the university, in March 27, 1602, Bodley felt compelled to address the somewhat delicate question of why there was not yet "free accesse uunto the Librarie."[44] His goal was a collection that would "minister more contentment to students and strangers," while continuing to attract benefactors with its unparalleled opportunity "to manifest their loue unto the Uniuersitie, as to bring suche a place of publike studie."[45] He goes on to discuss the reform of university statutes governing admittance to the library, in his desire to expand admittance beyond the current "Graduates, and to the sonnes of Lordes of the Parliament house" to include "any gentleman stranger," if properly accompanied by a graduate, with the idea that providing for "their accesse unto the place" was vital for the university "in helping

40. Bodley, "Letter 4: To the Right Worthy Mr Dr Thornton," in *Letters*, 7.

41. Ibid., 8.

42. Jennifer Summit, *Memory's Library: Medieval Books in Early Modern England* (Chicago: University of Chicago Press, 2008), 217. Summit also notes how the Bodleian librarian Thomas James used the *Index* of prohibited books as a buying guide, which as James put it: "That we may know what Books, and what Editions to buy, their prohibition being a good direction to guide us therein" (cited by ibid., 222). Bodley, a contemporary of Shakespeare, deliberately kept plays out of the library's collection: Wright, "Some Early 'Friends' of Libraries," *Huntington, Library Quarterly* 2, no. 3 (1939): 356.

43. Wright, "Some Early 'Friends' of Libraries": 356.

44. Bodley, "Letter 6: [Endorsed] To the Right Worshipfull My Very Special Good Frind Mr. Doctour Riues Vicechancellor of the Uniuersitie of Oxford," in *Letters*, 11.

45. Ibid., 11.

to furnishe their stoarehouse with books."[46] Bodley insists that "when any gentleman of sort, shall at any time request, for his furtherance in some studie, to come in of himself . . . to become a freeman of the Librarie," he should be able to take the oath and enter.[47] It was to be a public library after all, at least for gentlemen, and it opened on November 8, 1602, as Bodley's Library.[48] This public right of access was not consistently conveyed to the public, however, as both Thomas Hardy and Virginia Woolf had occasion to note.[49]

In this sixth letter, Bodley also introduced another of his bold and daring steps in reconstructing the university library. He put forward Thomas James, as a "humble suitor," for election to the post of library keeper. James was a fellow of New College, whom Bodley had, "upon special presumption," as he admits, begun employing in 1600 to assist him in putting together the library.[50] James had given proof of his commitment to the new library by donating sixty books and some manuscripts to it. When the university willingly approved James as keeper of the books, Bodley, in yet another monastic

46. Bodley, "Letter 6 to the Vice Chancellor," in *Letters*, 12.

47. Ibid., 12–13. The modern oath that "readers" to this day are asked to recite aloud to a library official: "I hereby undertake not to remove from the Library, nor to mark, deface, or injure in any way, any volume, document or other object belonging to it or in its custody; not to bring into the Library, or kindle therein, any fire or flame, and not to smoke in the Library; and I promise to obey all rules of the Library." The libraries were originally unheated, as a safety measure, and continue, in my experience, to sustain the legacy of their original chilliness. The current guide to the library states that, if this library is "firstly" open to members of the university, it is open "also, to 'the whole community of the learned'" interested in "serious study": *Reader's Guide to the Bodleian Library* (Oxford: Oxford University Library Services, 2009), 3. The Annual Report, 2007–2008, states that there were 31,000 external registered readers and 37,000 from the university for that period (Oxford: Oxford University Library Services, 2008), 30.

48. The first "Extraneus" reader was John Basire, "a Frenchman," who was admitted to the library in 1603. Thomas Bodley, *Letters of Sir Thomas Bodley to Thomas James, First Keeper of the Bodleian Library*, ed. G. W. Wheeler (Oxford: Oxford University Press, 1926), 76. The *Oxford English Dictionary* credits Bodley with the first published use of "public library" in that initial 1597 letter; yet the *OED* also refers to "in the older British universities, a library open to all members of the university," labeling this use "obscure." In this tradition, it is common today for university libraries to offer services to walk-in users.

49. "Jude's eyes swept all the views in succession," including the "roof of the great library," Thomas Hardy writes in his Oxford novel, while noting of "Christminster" that its "buildings and their associations and privileges were not for him": *Jude the Obscure*, ed. Cedric Watts (Peterborough: Broadview, 1999), 151–52. "That a famous library has been cursed by a woman," Virginia Woolf notes of her exclusion from an unnamed Oxbridge library in *A Room of One's Own*, "is of complete indifference to a famous library. Venerable and calm, with all its treasures safe locked within its breast, it sleeps complacently and will, so far as I am concerned, so sleep for ever": *A Room of One's Own and Three Guineas* (London: Hogarth, [1928] 1948), 7.

50. Bodley, "Letter 6 to the Vice Chancellor," in *Letters*, 13.

touch at Oxford, granted him an exemption on the statutory stipulation that librarians remain celibate (a requirement dropped in 1856).[51]

On December 12, 1610, Bodley reported to James that he had succeeded in his pursuit of James's idea to approach the Stationers' Company to secure privileges for the renewed library.[52] The Stationers' Company was the trade guild or livery company for stationers, printers, booksellers, and others involved in London's book trade, and had been granted a royal charter by Queen Mary in 1557 that provided it with a virtual monopoly over the trade.[53] Bodley was able to secure a commitment from the Company to provide the library with "a perfect copy of every book printed by one of its members."[54] The Stationers' Company of London, "out of zeale to the advancement of good learning . . . granted to the University of Oxford, for ever, one copy of every new book in quires that they might borrow or copy any book deposited, for reprinting."[55]

This precedent of printers depositing copies in the public library of the university signaled a recognition that the library, acting as both a national archive and a commons for all, operated at a remove from the book trade economy. The deposit policy was to be enshrined in English law before the century was out, and with time has spread around the world. Of course, within six months of securing this agreement with the Company, Bodley complained that "those of the companie haue taken hitherto no constant speedy order."[56] Further, the books that did arrive often arrived unbound, with "many idle bookes, and riffe raffes among them," as Bodley put it; the unreliability and disarray of shipments revealed the decided downside of additional cataloging, shelving, and preservation issues that were to come of legal deposit.[57]

51. Wright, "Some Early 'Friends' of Libraries," 359.

52. Bodley, "200. Bodley to Thomas James, 16 Feb. 1611," in *Letters to Thomas James*, 205.

53. The name "stationers" may have arisen during the thirteenth century from the fixed position of the stalls assigned in university towns. The Stationers' Company originally formed in 1403 among manuscript crafts and trades people: Peter W. M. Blayney, *The Stationers' Company and the Printers of London, 1501–1557*, vol. 1. (Cambridge: Cambridge University Press, 2013), 4–8.

54. Wheeler appears to be quoting the Stationers' Company grant in his note to this letter (*Letters of Sir Thomas Bodley*, 205).

55. The deed is cited by Ian Philip, *The Bodleian Library in the Seventeenth and Eighteenth Centuries* (Oxford: Oxford University Press, 1983), 27. Philip calculates that this deposit system brought in about 20 percent of what was being published in 1615–16 (28). James may have been inspired by François I's Montpellier Ordinance of 1537 requiring (if seldom honored) the placing of books in the French king's library before they were sold: R. C. Barrington Partridge, *The History of the Legal Deposit of Books* (London: Library Association, 1938), 18.

56. Bodley, "216. Bodley to Thomas James, 23 July 1611," in *Letters to Thomas James*, 217.

57. Ibid., 219.

Just weeks before his death in 1613, Bodley sent a final, brief letter to James, proving himself, if a bit curmudgeonly, to be learning's great champion to the very end. He chastises his librarian for what he saw as a wasteful two-week Christmas closing of the library: "There should be that accesse, for students to that place, as was formerly allowed by the ancient statutes: which never permitted so large vacations." Bodley was the "louing and very assured frind" of the library as he signed off his letter.[58] And very assured indeed, he had been, from when he "firste tooke in hand to builde vpon the ruines of youre publique Librarie," as he put it in a 1609 letter to the vice chancellor of the university.[59] In a final monastic stroke, Bodley was interred in the Merton College chapel following his death on January 28, 1613.

When Francis Bacon sent a copy of the *Advancement of Learning* to the library in 1605, he credited Bodley with "having built an ark to save learning from deluge."[60] Bacon was also inspired by Bodley's building of the university's public library to imagine adding a great public laboratory to it, which might serve as a repository, as he wrote to Bodley, that such a center of learning did "deserve in propriety, any new instrument or engine, whereby learning should be improved or advanced."[61] As noted, the Royal Society later toyed with the idea of such a repository to little effect. What did work for the library was the manuscript donation program. Anthony Wood remarked that, during the Reformation, "lovers of Antiquity, interposing themselves, recovered divers of them [manuscripts] from ruin," and then, many years later, these works "were at length brought by private persons and by them given to the public Library when restored by Sr. Thom. Bodley."[62] Bodley's efforts resulted in donations of close to eight hundred medieval manuscripts, which demonstrated the ability of a fine library's growing collection to attract yet other contributions, with the Bodleian gradually acquiring the world's largest university collection of medieval manuscripts.

58. Bodley, "231. Bodley to Thomas James, 3 Jan. 1613," in *Letters to Thomas James*, 231.

59. Bodley, "Letter 15: To the right worshipfull my deerest frendes Mr. Doctor Kinge vicechancellor the Doctors Proctors and the rest of the Convocation house in Oxon," in *Letters of Sir Thomas Bodley*, 19.

60. Francis Bacon, "To Sir Thomas Bodley, Upon Sending his Book of Advancement of Learning," in *The Works of Francis Bacon*, vol. 5 (London: J. Johnson et al., 1803), 288.

61. Ibid. Vaisey notes that Bacon's presentation copy of the *Advancement* was sold in the 1650s as a duplicate: "Thomas Hyde and Manuscript Collecting at the Bodleian," in *The Foundations of Scholarship: Libraries and Collecting, 1650-1750; Papers Presented At a Clark Library Seminar, 9 March 1985*, ed. David Vaisey and David McKitterick (Los Angeles: William Andrews Clark Memorial Library, University of California, Los Angeles, 1992), 16.

62. Wood, *University of Oxford*, 107.

The Bodleian was "the first expression of the Elizabethan university's recovered self-confidence," opines James McConica of the Pontifical Institute of Medieval Studies in Toronto; he sees it as "a learned quarry of a cosmopolitan, Protestant and humanist culture—scriptural, patristic, oriental, classical and medieval."[63] Bodley fashioned what was, in effect, a pyramid benefactor scheme in which donors recruited donors. Having established this tradition of giving to the library, Bodley was at the same time granting manuscript collectors a more expansive license to pursue the objects of their desires. They were now able to think of their interests in these works as a matter of assembling a trust on behalf of learning and the nation, in a legacy that would be preserved and used. Much as Grosseteste had done centuries earlier at Oxford, Bodley found a way to improve the institutional organization of learning's public sponsorship. At the same time that he took steps to ensure that the university library attracted benefactors by serving as a trusted archive, he also ensured that the library provided for public access to its collection. While past and present works were being reassembled in the Bodleian Library, the future of learned publishing was also taking shape at Oxford and Cambridge through the exercise of their printing privileges.

THE KING GRANTS PRINTING PRIVILEGES TO THE UNIVERSITIES

On July 20, 1534, King Henry issued a letters patent granting the University of Cambridge the right to name three stationers responsible for operating a university-owned printing press. The king's grant was in response to the university's earlier petition, submitted to Cardinal Wolsey in 1529, requesting such powers "for the suppression of error" and for the allowance of three booksellers in Cambridge.[64] The *suppression of error* played to both the Crown's religious concerns with heresy and the scholar's interests in textual transgressions. The university officials' appeal may have taken on a new urgency in 1534, four years after the initial request, as Henry formally declared the English Church free of Rome and pope. The patent that the king issued held that the university "shall have lawful and incontestable power to print

---

63. James McConica, "Humanism and Aristotle in Tudor Oxford," *English Historical Review* 94, no. 371 (1979): 316. McConica continues on the Bodleian: "With its refined gothicism and spacious, well-lit galleries, its architecture is the visible expression of the rhetorical culture it was meant to nourish; and its *scopus* was the infidelity of Rome" (ibid.).

64. Charles Henry Cooper, Entry for "1529," in *Annals of Cambridge*, vol. 1 (Cambridge: Warwick, 1842), 329.

there all manner of books (*omnimodos libros*)" that were approved by the
"Chancellor or his deputy and three doctors"; as well, the university could
elect three "Stationers or Bookprinters."[65] Its representatives could sell other
approved books as well, including foreign books, reflecting the international
Latin scope of the academic community at a time when the London book
trade sought to restrict competition from abroad.[66] The patent created a distinct set of intellectual property rights for Cambridge by enabling it to govern the printing and importing of educational books.

Still, Cambridge did not establish a press for nearly half a century, as the
community was well served by books arriving from the Continent through
its local stationers. By the time that English universities did become heavily
involved in printing during the seventeenth century, they had to contend
with the Stationers' Company control of the book market by virtue of its
royal charter. In addition, sweeping privileges had been granted to some individual printers, beginning with Richard Tottell's Chancery patent, granted
in 1553 by Edward VI, entitling him to "to printe all manner of the common laws of they realme" for seven years.[67] The Stationers' Company, on the
other hand, granted a limited number of houses in London licenses to print,
and the company managed a register of book titles for which these houses
had an exclusive right in perpetuity to sell or trade.[68]

To understand the Stationers' Company's monopoly, one needs to appreciate that when its members had approached Queen Mary in 1557, it was
with a willingness to police, as the Stationers' Charter put it, "certain seditious and heretical books rhymes and treatises [which] are daily published
and printed" for which they were granted a right "to make search whenever
it shall please them in any place ... for any books ... which are or shall be
printed contrary to the form of any statute."[69] In return for this service to
Crown and church, the charter restricted the right to print to those who
"shall be one of the Stationery of the aforesaid city, or has therefore license

65. Cited by David McKitterick, *Four Hundred Years of University Printing and Publishing in
Cambridge* (Cambridge: Cambridge University Press, 1984), 36.

66. Ibid., 35.

67. Cited by Blayney, *Stationers' Company*, 2:644.

68. Raven, *Business of Books*, 47. Raven states about book patents more generally: "Some patent grants served to pay off problematic courtiers, to dispense patronage to political advantage,
and to create occasional and well-publicized charity, but patent allocation was never systematized"
(75).

69. "Stationers' Charter, London (1557)," *Primary Sources on Copyright (1450-1900): Britain*,
ed. L. Bently and M. Kretschmer (Cambridge: University of Cambridge, 2008), online, xxxi. Raven,
Business of Books, 64.

of us."[70] In a classic tradeoff, the Crown granted commercial privilege to consolidate political power.

Under Elizabeth, legislation was passed requiring that each book contain a notice of its license to be printed as issued by the Queen, Privy Council members, or the university chancellors. Two years later, the Star Chamber limited printing to London, Oxford, and Cambridge.[71] While this measure seemed to set up a neat divide between commerce and learning, between the commercial press in the country's center and the learned presses on the periphery, the difference between the two types of presses was not so clear. All presses need to finance an adequate supply of paper in advance of printing, for example, and in that sense a learned press is no less of a speculative business proposition than a commercial press. To make a go of it, the universities' printers had to find ways to sell books in the broader market dominated by London's Stationers' Company.[72]

The University of Cambridge finally appointed its first university printer in 1583, after ignoring for almost fifty years the printing privileges granted to the universities in 1534. Thomas Thomas was to be its first printer, with the university stipulating that "his paper Incke and Letters shalbe as good" as any printer's, while his books were to be "solde at a reasonable Price . . . by the judgment of the vice-chancellor."[73] Thomas was not to print anything "seditious" or anything not "allowed" by the chancellor or vice chancellor, while "one perfecte copie or booke well and sufficientile bounde" was to be deposited in the university library.[74] Setting up this press did not go unnoticed in London. Shortly after Thomas set up his printing press in Cambridge, the Stationers' Company sent a few of its members to pay him a less-than-friendly visit. They promptly carted off his press and related cabinetry.[75] The company was willing to allow the university to license the printing of any book, but insisted that the printers of such books were still subject to the Company's

---

70. "Stationers' Charter, London (1557)," xxxi.

71. Raven, *Business of Books*, 66–67.

72. Nor did London printers ignore learning, as they undertook such magnificent instances as John Day's 1570 edition of *The Elements of Geometrie of the Most Auncient Philosopher Euclide of Megara*, featuring 1,300 diagrams, 38 fold-out flaps, and six bifolia to be pasted on the illustrations for a three-dimensional effect, which was financed by its translator Henry Billingsley, a successful haberdasher and later Lord Mayor of London: Elizabeth Evenden, *Patents, Pictures and Patronage: John Day and the Tudor Book Trade* (Farnham, Surrey, UK: Ashgate, 2008), 116.

73. Cited by John Morris, "Restrictive Practices in the Elizabethan Book Trade: The Stationers' Company v. Thomas Thomas 1583–8," *Transactions of the Cambridge Bibliographical Society* 4, no. 4 (1967): 285.

74. Cited by ibid., 285–86.

75. Ibid., 277, 281.

control of book trade. The university chancellor wrote to the Lord Treasurer of England in defense of its rights, referring to its "ancient privilege ... for the mysterie of printing."[76] The chancellor and his cosignatories pointed to how printing was "to the greate benefit of the vuniuersitie and advauncement of Learning," and on such grounds they succeeded in obtaining a return of the press and furniture.[77] In 1591, the Stationers' Company agreed to allow Cambridge printers to record titles in the Stationers' Register which prevented others from claiming a right to those works.[78] A few university printers were admitted to the company, and books published in association with the universities were listed in the company's catalog.

At about the same time, a group at the University of Oxford submitted to the chancellor Robert Dudley, Earl of Leicester, a *Supplicatio* requesting that Oxford set up a press. They began by pointing out that there is "no university, however small, in Germany and France that does not have a printing press" and in light of which they sought a grant from the queen "to favor and secure a printing house in the University of Oxford."[79] It was a matter of both pride and contribution, as they wrote of rescuing "many excellent manuscripts . . . from perpetual obscurity" that they might be "distributed in other parts of Europe to the great credit of the whole nation."[80] The *Supplicatio* also refers to scholarly authors who cannot afford "to live in London at their own expense while putting their works into print," noting that such books were needed "to shake off the imputation of idleness which foreigners daily lay against them."[81] They also asserted that "a settlement of learned men" leads to books being "printed more correctly and texts more diligently collated."[82] As a result, the local Oxford stationer Joseph Barnes was allowed to step into the role of university printer with the benefit of a £100 loan from the university and approval of the Crown. On the title pages of the books he printed, he identified himself as "printer to the University," or "printer to

76. Cited by ibid., 288.

77. Cited by ibid.

78. Ian Gadd notes that the Printing Act of 1662 "acknowledged that the universities themselves might maintain their own 'Register Booke' of such rights," for which Cambridge's survived for the period 1656 to 1692, with no indication if Oxford kept one: "The Press and the London Book Trade," in *Beginnings to 1780*, ed. Ian Gadd, vol. 1 of *The History of Oxford University Press* (Oxford: Oxford University Press, 2013), 578.

79. "Supplicatio," trans. Simon Neal and Andrew Hegarty, in *Beginnings to 1780*, ed. Ian Gadd, vol. 1 of *The History of Oxford University Press* (Oxford: Oxford University Press, 2013), 651.

80. Ibid.

81. Ibid., 652.

82. Ibid.

the 'famous' University" for at least a portion of the 260 works he had printed. He was able to find outlets among booksellers at St. Paul's in London for the books, and eventually placed a son in the business there. Yet, after thirty-five years in the business, Barnes died deeply in debt in 1618.[83]

By the seventeenth century, the English book trade was awash in printing patents, privileges, and restrictions. These measures had everything to do with the pursuit of commercial advantage, as well as censorship by church and Crown. They had little to do with authors' rights or what I am framing as the intellectual properties of the work published.[84] The patents and privileges were bestowed by the Crown, as a matter of royal prerogative that survived Parliament's best efforts to end such fiats and favors with its Statute of Monopolies in 1623. The statute declared monopolies as "altogether contrary to the Lawes of this Realme," especially as they seldom involved "the true and first inventor."[85] The decades, if not centuries, that separated the royal grants awarded to different bodies led to endless contention over whose rights prevailed, which the king was then asked to decide.[86]

In the case of upholding the universities' printing privileges, Oxford found a champion in 1630, with its election of William Laud to the position of chancellor of the University of Oxford. An archbishop of Canterbury and former president of St. John's College, Laud worked tirelessly to bring greater order to every level of learning at Oxford.[87] He began by sorting out

83. Jason Peacey, "'Printers to the University' 1584-1658," in *Beginnings to 1780*, ed. Ian Gadd, vol. 1 of *The History of Oxford University Press* (Oxford: Oxford University Press, 2013), 53-54.

84. "By 1580, most European countries had settled into a given regime in respect of both censorship (whether pre-censorship or censorship after the fact) and of privileges or commercial protection": Ian Maclean, *Scholarship, Commerce, Religion: The Learned Book in the Age of Confessions, 1560-1630* (Cambridge, MA: Harvard University Press, 2012), 135.

85. "Statute of Monopolies, 1623 Chapter 2 21 Ja 1," in *Henry III. To James II. A.D. 1235-6—1685*, in vol. 1 of *The Statutes: Revised Edition* (London: Eyre and Spottiswoode, 1870), 693.

86. In 1588, the Stationers' Company exercised its rights to search and seize the Psalms, Geneva Bible, and New Testament printed by John Legate, Printer to the University of Cambridge, only to have to promptly return them and make amends for its printing rights were trumped by those of the university: B. J. McMullin, "The Bible Trade," in *History of the Book*, 461. "The problem of credit that piracy generated was thus substantial. From the mathematical sciences it spread throughout natural philosophy and beyond . . . It may well be that no renowned author escaped unscathed": Johns, "Science and the Book," in *History of the Book*, 291.

87. Laud reformed Oxford's statutes to bring about what Anthony Milton summarized as "the revival and strengthening of the university's traditional requirements on discipline, residence, and teaching": "Laud, William (1573-1645), *Archbishop of Canterbury*," *Oxford Dictionary of National Biography*, ed. H. C. G. Matthew and Brian Harrison, online ed. (Oxford: Oxford University Press, 2004).

the university's statutes, which, he dryly observed, "had lain in a confused heap for some ages, and extremely imperfect in all kinds."[88] No matter was too small for Laud's attention, be it dress code—from footwear (no spurs) to hair length (not long)—or the printing quality of local printers. In 1631, he was called upon to pass judgment on the King's Printers Robert Barker and Martin Lucas for their printing of the "Wicked Bible," in which they inadvertently (perhaps) omitted the word "not" from the seventh command-ment: "Thou shall not commit adultery." In condemning this work before the Court of High Commission, Laud added to the printers' sins by citing the Wicked Bible's excessive price and poor quality of paper. He craftily of-fered, as archbishop, to commute their fines, if they were able to secure a fine and proper Greek typeface to help advance his goal, which was "to set up a Greek press in London and Oxford for the printing of the library man-uscripts."[89] The two printers went for it, but the scheme resulted in only a few learned editions—including one with Greek commentaries on the Book of Job—before the Long Parliament, instituted in 1640, declared the Court of High Commission unconstitutional, hence rendering Laud's judgment against Barker and Lucas invalid.

In the second year of his chancellorship, Laud succeeded in obtaining a letters patent from Charles I, enabling Oxford to appoint three *typographi* with the "power and capacity to print . . . all manner of books . . . approved by the judgment of the Chancellor."[90] Laud had made it clear in a letter earlier that year to the university's vice chancellor that there were two ad-vantages he sought through this patent: "The one that you [the University of Oxford] might enjoy this privilege for Learning equally with Cambridge; and the other, that having many excellent Manuscripts in your Library, you might in time hereby be encouraged to publish some of them in Print, to the great honor of that Place, this Church and kingdom."[91] Laud's advice recalls Erasmus's adage "make haste slowly": "Let your Privilege settle a while, and gather strength quietly," he soundly counseled.[92] That said, Laud was not about to stand idly by; rather, he found ways to strengthen the uni-

88. William Laud, *History of the Chancellorship*, vol. 5 of *The Works of the Most Revered Father in God, William Laud* (Oxford: John Henry Parker, 1853), 13.

89. Hugh Trevor-Roper, *Archbishop Laud, 1573–1645*, 3rd ed. (London: Macmillan, 1988), 274.

90. "Patents to the University of Oxford (12 November 1632)," trans. Simon Neal and Andrew Hegarty, in *Beginnings to 1780*, 654.

91. Laud, *History of the Chancellorship*, 79.

92. Ibid., 80.

versity's printing privileges by securing a revised patent in 1633. It specified "that the same University may be encouraged to publish original scripts of books in divers languages, both vernacular and foreign, that have hitherto lain hidden in libraries in the same University, and to compose afresh and issue books . . . to the increase of the Christian religion, good letters, and arts."[93] The revised patent granted the university exclusive rights, if only for twenty-one years, to print works from its manuscript collection. And for works "composed afresh" by the masters and scholars, the sole right to print and reprint was limited to ten years.[94] Note how bringing to light historic works from the university's libraries was seen to require a larger incentive, likely due to the high price and low sales for these national treasures.

In 1634, Laud introduced statutes "Concerning the Printers of the University," in which he graciously thanked King Charles for having "wonderfully enlarged the University's privileges in regard of printing," before turning with a vengeance to "the mechanical artificers (concerned for the most part with their own profit to the detriment of quality in their work) [who] pay the least possible attention to fine lettering or beauty or elegance, but thrust into publication any old work, however rough and uncorrected."[95] Laud's defense of typesetting elegance is matched by his constant concern over the correctness of the text. He was repositioning the English arts of fine printing. He must have seen opportunities for the university's books, as the Thirty Years War was increasingly disrupting the once vibrant book trade of Holland and northern Europe generally.

He sought to have "a Head Printer (*Architypographus*) placed over the University's public press"; the *architypographus* was to be, the statutes specified, "well instructed in Greek and Latin literature and expert in matters philological," and prepared to supervise "the breadth of margins, as well as to perfect the errata of the correctors," among so many other details of learned publishing.[96] It took until 1658 to find an *architypographus* worthy of Laud's vision in the form of Samuel Clarke, a renown and well-published

93. "Revised Patent to the University of Oxford (13 March 1633)," trans. Simon Neal and Andrew Hegarty, in *Beginnings to 1780*, 657.

94. Ibid., 658.

95. "University Statutes (1634–6), Title 18, Section 5," trans. Simon Neal and Andrew Hegarty, in *Beginnings to 1780*, 660.

96. Ibid. In this regard, David McKitterick notes that in comparison to the rest of Europe in the sixteenth and seventeenth centuries "there was no suggestion of a university press in the sense gradually developed in England": "University Printing at Oxford and Cambridge," in *History of the Book*, 190, 195.

orientalist.[97] The chancellor had made print a statutory and scholarly office of the university. More generally, the Laudian Code of Statutes specified in 1636 that the learned press should be subsidized by any surplus remaining in the buildings and maintenance fund generated by fees levied on matriculation and degrees. Laud had made student fees a permanent fixture of the university's finances in the code, although there was no such surplus to be had until the 1650s.[98] Only then could funds "be expended in fitting up and maintaining the public press of the University (an object alike honorable and beneficial to the University), and in bringing at last to the light a world of manuscript volumes, both in Greek and Latin, at present buried in the public library, and which surely but ill deserve to be for ever wrestling with the moths and worms."[99]

A Great Charter, based on a wide range of Laudian reforms, was granted to the University of Oxford by Charles I in 1636. The charter notes the conflicts that had arisen between university and Stationers' Company rights, and declares its intent "to increase the aforesaid University's privileges both old and new (as far as in our power), and utterly to remove and delete all such ambiguities."[100] To that end, the charter affirms the university's right to print "all books of whatever kind" approved by the chancellor or his delegate, without regard for "the charters of the Stationers of our City of London."[101] Laud had managed to set learned publishing apart from the London market monopolies, much to the chagrin of the printers who belonged to the Stationers' Company. But it did not stop there. He used the university's privileges to shrewdly negotiate with the company and the King's Printers covenants of forbearance, in which the university agreed not to exercise its right to

---

97. John Johnson and Strickland Gibson, *Print and Privilege at Oxford to the Year 1700* (Oxford: Oxford University Press, 1946), 24–33. McKitterick notes that Cambridge appointed a similar overseer of the press, while he judges Laud's reform of the press as "characterized by a lack of flexibility, and by a lack of understanding of how the book trade functioned": "University Printing," 192, 197.

98. Nicolas Barker, *The Oxford University Press and the Spread of Learning: An Illustrated History, 1478–1978* (Oxford: Oxford University Press, 1978), 32–33; John Feather, "A Learned Press in a Commercial World," in *Beginnings to 1780*, 247.

99. *Oxford University Statutes*, trans. G. R. M. Ward, vol. 1 (London: William Pickering, 1845), 214–15. In 1846, the statute directing surpluses in building and maintenance to the press was revoked, in favor of remunerating preachers for the delivery of sermons "before the University": *Oxford University Statutes*, trans. G. R. M. Ward, vol. 2 (London: William Pickering, 1851), 260–61.

100. "The Great Charter of the University of Oxford (3 March 1636), Excerpt," trans. Simon Neal and Andrew Hegarty, in *Beginnings to 1780*, 665.

101. Ibid., 666.

print the Bible, grammars, and almanacs in exchange for £200 annually. As Laud informed the vice chancellor in 1637, "for certainly it will be more beneficial to the university for the advance of a learned press to receive £200 a year than to print grammars, and almanacks, &c. And more honour, too ... that this money which you yearly receive may be kept safe, as a stock apart, and put to no other use, than the settling of a learned press."[102] The forbearance fees were initially used to purchase type, matrices, and punches for Hebrew, Arabic, Greek, and Syriac. The type was then loaned to its printer as an in-kind subvention for books printed in these languages.[103]

In 1637, Laud had reason to think that the university was "now upon a very good way toward the setting up of a Learned *Press*," as he put it, poignantly adding at the age of sixty-four, "I should be very glad to see it begun in my own Life-time, if it might be."[104] He had managed to extract what extra value he could from the Crown's sponsorship of learning in an age of commercial privileges. Three years later, in the period leading up to the English Civil War, he was charged with high treason for both favoring the Roman Church and assuming extraordinary powers at Oxford and elsewhere (the press was not mentioned).[105] In 1645, after a final trial failed to convict Laud, Parliament intervened, passing a bill that resulted in his execution.[106]

After the Restoration of 1660 placed Charles II on the throne, Laud's vision of a learned press acquired a second life. In 1662, John Fell, then dean of Christ Church and later vice chancellor of the university, was appointed one of the six press delegates to oversee the day-to-day operations of the university's contract printers and consider the role of printing within the university more generally. Fell was able to convince Gilbert Sheldon to create a place for the press in the new theater, designed by Christopher Wren, that was to be Sheldon's gift to Oxford. The theater was intended as "a more convenient place for the Publique Acts, and other uses of the University," as Sheldon's letter of endowment put it, and the rents from the purchased

102. Laud, *History of the Chancellorship*, 161–62.

103. Laud wanted the church fathers printed in their original Latin, Greek, Coptic, etc.: Michael Hunter, *Science and the Shape of Orthodoxy: Intellectual Change in Late Seventeenth-Century Britain* (Woodbridge, Suffolk, UK: Boydell and Brewer, 1995), 206.

104. Cited by Peacey, "'Printers to the University,'" 63.

105. Andrew Hegarty, "The University and the Press, 1584–1780," in *Beginnings to 1780*, 170.

106. "Few excellent men have ever had fewer friends to their persons," Edward Hyde, Earl of Clarendon, "yet all reasonable men absolved him from any foul crime that the law could take notice of, and punish": *The History of the Rebellion and Civil Wars in England*, vol. 5 (Oxford: Oxford University Press, 1839), 31.

lands were not only for the upkeep of the building but "may be employed for the best advantage and encouragement of the Learned Presse these designed, and allready at Worke, which I pray God prosper."[107] Fell took control of printing at the Sheldonian in 1670, when he and Wren were made curators of the theater.[108] He had placed the printing of learned books at the heart of the university. His goal was to "set up in this place a press freed from mercenary artifices, which will serve not so much to make profits for the booksellers as to further the interests and conveniences of scholars," as he put it to a friend.[109]

Fell decided to create a new partnership to run the university's printing interests. He brought together Thomas Yates, principal of Brasenose College, along with two other Oxford men from London: Leoline Jenkins, a judge in the Court of the Admiralty and a defender of the university's historical privileges; and Joseph Williamson, secretary of state, *London Gazette* editor (which had begun its life in 1665 as the *Oxford Gazette*), and member of Parliament.[110] Fell put an end to the forbearance arrangement with the Stationers' Company as part of an ambitious program for a learned press. He drew up a page worth of titles in 1672 that, as he put it, "We propose to Print, if we may be encouraged."[111]

The list began with "the greek Bible" drawing on various editions "neuer yet collated," and included liturgical manuscripts "of venerable antiquity, never yet Extant [in print]" and "books in seueral parts of learning; & treatises of learned men now liuing in Latine and English." It also included, likely reflecting the Royal Society's influence, "a history of insects, more perfect than any yet Extant." The prospectus also calls for "publick assistance"

---

107. Gilbert Sheldon, "For the Reverend Dr. Fell, Vice-Chancellor, of the University of Oxford, to be communicated to ye University in Convocation" (May 28, 1669), in *The Oxford University Calendar: 1824* (Oxford: J. Parker), 359. In 1668, five presses were installed in the basement of the Sheldonian Theatre, which was then in the final stages of construction, with the presses continuing to operate there for twenty-three years: Barker, *Oxford University Press*, 15. In 1672, the press moved into its own New Print House adjoining the theater with a Little Print House attached to it (19). Mary Ould, "The Workplace: Places, Procedures, and Personnel 1668–1780," in *Beginnings to 1780*, 195–96, 199.

108. Vivienne Larminie, "The Fell Era, 1658–1686," in *Beginnings to 1780*, 88.

109. Cited by ibid.

110. Johnson and Gibson see Fell's takeover of the press—which they term more than once a *coup d'état*—as evidence of how "Fell was avowedly autocratic, his autocracy in dealing with others being only equaled by his austerity in dealing with himself": *Print and Privilege*, 48. They cite Jenkins on Fell's dedication: "Were it not that you ken Mr. Dean extraordinarily well, Sir, it were impossible to imagine how assiduous and Drudgeing he allows himself to be about his Presse" (49).

111. Cited by Harry Carter, *A History of the Oxford University Press* (Oxford: Oxford University Press, 1975), 63.

for "a designe of this nature" having not just "the Advancement of learning" in mind but "the emprovement of trade, & repute of the Nation." Fell set out the methods of financing from benefactors, promising public acknowledgement as well as the option of having loans repaid double with an equivalent value of books, while offering to print any work that could attract three hundred subscribers.

Although some objected to the deal—the delegates' minutes later referred to Fell and his partners as "ye farmers of the Universitys privilege for printing"— the university agreed to lease to Fell and partners its printing rights, press room, and equipment for £200 annually in 1671.[112] The next year *Oxonii, e Theatro Sheldoniano*, as the press was identified on the title page, issued its first scholarly work, William Beveridge's massive two-volume collection of Eastern church canons in parallel Greek and Latin, known as the *Synodicon*. Fell included the London bookseller Robert Scott in the project, given his strong European connections, and had the university cover the corrector's costs and provide materials.[113] The book proved a financial liability for both Fell and Scott, causing Fell to rethink the subsidization of learned printing.[114] He decided to propose a new forbearance covenant with the Stationers' Company, only this time for an annual fee of £100 with the university's retention of the right to print Bibles. Fell was in the midst of preparing an edition of the Bible, distinguished, as he described it, by "practical annotations fitted for the use of every Christian reader."[115]

Fell's press went on to find a level of commercial success through which to cross-subsidize works of scholarship. Fell published *Ladies Calling*, in bridal-gift binding, and *Art of Contentment*, both by the clergyman Richard Allestree, although released anonymously. More surprising was the success of the two-volume catalog of the Bodleian's print books published in 1674.[116] The university's delegates of the press gave the catalog a great boost

---

112. "July 24, 1672," *The First Minute Book of the Delegates of the Oxford University Press, 1668–1756*, ed. John Johnson and Strickland Gibson (Oxford: Oxford University Press, 1943), 9.

113. "Die Lunae viz 7 Sept: 1668," and "Martij 13: 1668 [1669]," in *First Minute Book*, 3, 5.

114. Barker, *Oxford University Press*, 20.

115. Cited by Vivienne Larminie, "Fell Era, 1658-1686," in *Beginnings to 1780*, 96.

116. Librarian Thomas Hyde prepared the catalog over a nine-year period and complained of working on it in the unheated library (given the risks of fire): Barker, *Oxford University Press*, 21. Hyde was given an initial £140 for his work composing it, later supplemented with an additional £60 once the work had proven itself profitable (ibid.). It is not clear if Hyde shared the bonus with his under-librarian Emmanuel Pritchard, who did much of the work. Hyde indexed the collection by author, against those who thought it should have been by subject: Leedham-Green and McKitterick, "Private and Public Libraries," in *The Cambridge History of the Book in Britain*, vol. 4, *1557–1695*, ed. John Barnard and D. F. McKenzie (Cambridge: Cambridge University Press, 2002), 335. Bodley's librarian Thomas James prepared the first such catalog for a public library in Europe,

by decreeing that "no person haue leaue to propose a Dispensation to study in the Library; but shall bring a Certificat from the Janitor that he has bought and payd for one Copie of ye Catalogue."[117] Other libraries used the seven-hundred-page catalog for tracking their own holdings, inserting interleaves to record additional works. Newton owned a copy, as did Locke, who used it not only for identifying books in his own collection but also for recording reviews, prices, and other information.[118] Fell and Yates were paid £725 by the university to print a thousand copies of the catalog, though the run took two decades to sell out.[119] Fell was still learning the book market but became quick to respond "it will not sell" to proposed books, as noted by Humphrey Prideaux, Fell's editorial assistant.[120]

In a further enterprising step, Fell and Yates decided to publish an almanac, noting Cambridge's success with the format.[121] The Oxford almanac was issued in both a forty-eight-page and a single-sheet edition in 1673. It was distinguished by having its moon phases and eclipses calculated by no less than the Savilian Professor of Astronomy at Oxford (although that did not prevent the ghastly omission of Good Friday in the first almanac's calendar).[122] This was followed by the Fell and Yates's Bible. It appeared in 1675, printed in Oxford "at the Theater." It, too, got off to a rocky start. Yates had to personally invest over £4,000 in the printing.[123] Fell's pursuit of greater spelling consistency—by substituting an *i* wherever possible for *y*—met with derision. The

which was printed in 1605 with Bodley underwriting the printing, as well as helping with the classification scheme and serving as corrector: Ian Gadd, "The Learned Press: Printing for the University," in *Beginnings to 1780*, 280.

117. "December 8, 1674," in *First Minute Book*, 11.

118. John Harrison and Peter Laslett, *The Library of John Locke* (Oxford: Oxford University Press, 1965), 30–31.

119. Barker, *Oxford University Press*, 21.

120. Cited by Richard Sharpe, "Selling Books from the Sheldonian," *Library* 11, no. 3 (2010): 278.

121. "The Cambridge press became identified, far beyond university and other educational or scholarly circles, with almanacs . . . as principal supplier of by far the widest selling printed matter in the late seventeenth century": David McKitterick, *Printing and the Book Trade in Cambridge: 1534–1698*, vol. 1 in *A History of Cambridge University Press* (Cambridge: Cambridge University Press, 1992), 387.

122. Paul Luna and Martyn Ould, "The Printed Page," in *Beginnings to 1780*, 520–521. Carter, *History of the Oxford University Press*, 78–79. The first almanac, for 1674, was over a yard wide while the more modest *Oxford Almanack* proved a great success, with a continuous run from 1676 to this day: Luna and Ould, "The Printed Page," 520–21. The almanac of 1674, engraved by Robert White, a student of David Loggan, engraver to the university, features a wildly allegorical, almost hallucinatory, vision of the university and is worth searching for online (with subsequent almanacs offering naturalistic architectural depictions).

123. Scott Mandelbrote, "The Bible Press," in *Beginnings to 1780*, 486.

King's Printers undercut it by selling a comparable edition of the Bible at a loss.[124] Their printing of schoolbooks did not go well either, and they decided to radically alter how they were using their printing privileges. They decided to bring in experienced London printers to whom they would sublet the most lucrative privileges. In 1678, Fell and Yates approached four members of the Stationers' Company: William Leake, Thomas Guy, Peter Parker, and Moses Pitt. It was an unlikely crew. Three of them were known Bible smugglers, given to selling cheap Dutch copies in England, and one had been sued by Fell.[125] It had all the makings of a Western film. The town's failed business-scholars out of desperation bring in guns-for-hire to take on the ruthless city stationers. Fell and Yates agreed to sublet the rights they leased from the university to the four stationers—namely, to print Bibles, Psalters, almanacs, and schoolbooks—along with the presses in the Sheldonian Theatre.[126]

For a dozen years, the four booksellers printed Bibles in various formats on as many as eleven presses, putting out tens of thousands of copies. They offered readers different options for illustrations, bindings, qualities of paper, indices, and kindred tables; they advertised type and paper sizes; they made modifications to meet the accession of James II as a Catholic king.[127] The King's Printers did not sit idly by, but launched appeals against Oxford's "gang of four" with the King in Council, the Court of Chancery, the Court of the King's Bench, and in quo warranto proceedings, none of which succeeded.[128] John Wallis, Oxford's first keeper of the archives and Savilian Chair of Geometry notes that in 1691 "the Price of Bibles for the Advantage of the Publick, was brought down to less than Half of what they were before sold at."[129] Among Oxford's four London stationers, Pitt ended up in debtors' prison and Leake died in 1681.[130] Guy and Parker persisted, creating what was, in effect, an Oxford Bible Press.[131]

124. John Wallis, "A Copy of the Account, which Dr. Wallis Gave to Dr. Bernard, one of the Delegates for Printing, Jan 23 1691," in *Philosophical Experiments and Observations of the Late Eminent Dr. Robert Hooke* (London: W. and J. Innys, 1726), 219; McMullin, "Bible Trade," 463.

125. Mandelbrote, "Bible Press," 488.

126. Larminie, "Fell Era," 100.

127. Mandelbrote, "Bible Press," 488–89; McKitterick, "University Printing," 200–201, 205.

128. Mandelbrote, "Bible Press," 490–93.

129. Wallis, "Copy of the Account," 221.

130. Pitt ran up debts importing Latin works and fumbled a subscription offer with his multivolume *English Atlas* despite endorsements from the king, the Royal Society, and the two universities: E. G. R. Taylor, "'The English Atlas' of Moses Pitt, 1680–83," *Geographical Journal* 95, no. 4 (1940): 292–99.

131. A century later, Oxford Bible Press had revenues amounting to nearly ten times that of the learned press that it was underwriting. Falconer Madan notes that from 1675 to 1700 the press

In the meantime, Fell and Yates concentrated on operating a learned press, which they installed next door to the Sheldonian Theatre in the New Print House. Fell was to see 150 scholarly books into print in his fifteen years with the press, including editions of the church fathers Clement of Alexandria and Cyprian of Carthage, which Laud had desired to see in print.[132] Fell also set up an annual challenge for student translations of classical texts, published as "new year books" for the students of Christ Church.[133] On his death in 1686, his assembly of press machinery, matrices, and typefaces reverted to the chancellor, masters, and scholars of the university.[134]

Years later, in 1718, Fell's struggles with the university press were evocatively summed up by Arthur Charlett, a press delegate: "The vending of books we never could compasse; the want of vent [sales] broke Bishop Fell's body, public spirit, courage, purse and presse."[135] In the early twentieth century, Oxford University Press paid its own homage to the man: "Fell made the great collection of type-punches and matrices from which the beautiful types known by his name are still cast at Oxford; he promoted the setting up of a paper mill at Wolvercote, where Oxford paper is still made; he conducted the long, and ultimately successful, struggle with the Stationers and the King's Printers, from which the history of Oxford Bibles and Prayer Books begins (1677)."[136] Fell had found a viable approach for funding a learned press by subleasing valuable privileges and printing popular works to subsidize learned editions. Although I have concentrated on Oxford's story here, David McKitterick, librarian and fellow of Trinity College, Cambridge, concludes that "by the late 1690s, both universities could boast

---

produced about four scholarly editions (of an unknown number of copies), while between 1808 and 1815 the Oxford Bible Press produced 460,500 Bibles; 386,600 New Testaments; 400,000 Common Prayer Books; 200,00 Psalters, etc., with a total value of £213,000; during that time the learned side of the press produced books worth £24,000. In 1883, the Bible press was folded into Oxford University Press: *A Brief Account of the University Press at Oxford with Illustrations Together with a Chart of Oxford Printing* (Oxford: Oxford University Press, 1908), 16–17: Mandelbrote, "Bible Press," 498.

132. Jacqueline Rose, *Godly Kingship in Restoration England: The Politics of The Royal Supremacy, 1660–1688* (Cambridge: Cambridge University Press, 2001), 135. "The exchange of books and the rediscovery of medieval and later manuscripts fed literary and antiquarian interests among many contemporary aristocracy, gentry, and clergy. They supplied both raw materials and audience for the developing press": Larminie, "Fell Era," 97.

133. Madan, *Brief Account of the University Press*, 28–29.

134. Barker, *Oxford University Press*, 16–17.

135. Cited by Matthew Kilburn, "The Fell Legacy 1686–1755," in *Beginnings to 1780*, 120.

136. *Some Account of the Oxford University Press, 1468–1926* (Oxford: Oxford University Press, 1926), 15.

learned presses, under their own control, run by professional printers, and with provision for their continued existence in an institutional manner."[137]

The seventeenth century saw a major transformation in print's service to learning. Archbishop Laud initiated a trade in privileges which was to eventually create a place for learned books in print's early modern market economy of capital investment and perpetual monopolies. John Fell, identified at the time as "that great Assertor of University's Rights," extended that model through business partnerships with London stationers by which he was able to float a learned press.[138] Such assertions enabled Laud's dream of "the public press of the University" to be realized. The Commonwealth of Learning had to come to terms with the "Stationers Common-wealth," to use the poet George Wither's satirical coinage from 1624.[139]

The university differed from the monastery by moving learning to the center of an institution that was still in pursuit of God's blessings. This was especially true of such devout faculty as Archbishop Laud and Bishop Fell. The university's Bible press, which Fell established, not only subsidized the learned press, but furthered the spread of the holy word among at least the literate at home and through missionaries abroad.[140] A Bible press was the perfect complement to a learned press; together, the two could take advantage of the emerging market economy of early modern monopoly capitalism in what was still an age of faith. What Laud and Fell initiated, the employees of the Oxford University Press went on to adeptly master within the market intricacies of the modern world. As a source of university sponsorship, it is without peer among learned presses, and it more than holds its own among global corporate publishers.[141]

---

137. McKitterick, "University Printing," 204. McKitterick observes that Cambridge authors preferred London printing "for not only were the printers there demonstrably better accustomed to scholarly printing, the London trade also offered easier access to an international readership": *Printing and the Book Trade in Cambridge,* 386.

138. Johnson and Gibson, *Print and Privilege,* 47.

139. George Withier, *The Schollers Purgatory* (London: G. Wood, 1624), title page.

140. Mandelbrote, "Bible Press," 490.

141. In 2012, Oxford University Press (OUP) was ranked the twenty-first largest publisher in the world, with revenues of $1,125 billion, with Cambridge University Press ranked 43rd and second among university presses, with revenue of $396 million: "The World's 60 Largest Book Publishers, 2012, *Publisher's Weekly* (July 19, 2013). OUP transferred $50 million "to the rest of the university" in 2013: *Annual Report of the Delegates of the University Press, 2013–14* (Oxford: Oxford University Press, 2014), 35. This *Annual Report* gives dictionaries twenty-five mentions and "educational" resources twenty-one mentions, with no reference to Bible publishing, although it continues in multiple formats.

CONCLUSION

I have introduced the influences of the Reformation and the age of print on the institutional properties of learning at Oxford. Henry VIII's dissolution of the monasteries put an end to the scholar-monks' revival of learning; monastic colleges were dissolved, if only to endow new colleges; and monastic manuscripts were dispersed and destroyed, if only to have a surviving portion donated to and preserved in the Bodleian and other libraries. What the manuscripts lost in spiritual force, in moving from religious house to university library, they gained in intellectual property value, as scholars cataloged, preserved, edited, and attended to their every detail, while seeing a number of them scripts into print. Among the continuities running through this disruptive history of Reformation and Civil War are learning's archangels of patronage and privilege. The beneficence bestowed on learning is found in the royal scholarships at Christ Church, the manuscript collections of Thomas Bodley's library, and the university press privileges bestowed by the Crown and exploited by William Laud and John Fell. What Bodley's public library of the university demonstrated, much as William Laud sought with his public press, was a new level of institutional commitment to learned curation and public access. Ideally, university library and press served each other well around the properties of access, communality, sponsorship, and use, even as the press continued to seek financial stability.

Part of the challenge speaks to what sets Bodley apart from Laud and Fell. Bodley was old school, favoring the sponsorship of learning. His bequeathal brought outside wealth to bear on the revitalization of learning, if in the form of the public library at Oxford. His endowment ensured and enabled learning over the long term, not only through his property gifts, but also in founding a library that would continue to attract gifts, publisher deposits, and public support.

Laud and Fell, on the other hand, were part of the new commercial economy of print. The press was certainly the adept "instrument or engine" that Francis Bacon had advised Bodley to look out for, "whereby learning should be improved or advanced."[142] Yet Laud and Fell struggled, much as the Royal Society did at the time, to find sufficient advantage in the privileges granted learning to sustain a press, amid a print market rife with such privileges.

142. Francis Bacon, "To Sir Thomas Bodley," 253.

It took a Bible press (in the hands of London booksellers) to sufficiently subsidize learned printing, much as it had taken monastic piety to stock the scriptorium. From Bodley's benefaction to Fell's privileges, we can see how the university maintained the spectrum of medieval and early modern sponsorship among learning's properties. Add to this the academies' introduction of membership subscription to the subsidizing of book publishing and you have the cumulative history of learning's intellectual property economy in the early modern period.

While the Reformation and Civil War played havoc with the university's autonomy, Bodley, Laud, and Fell further secured learning's place within a political economy of patronage, privilege, and, increasingly, market capitalism. The seventeenth century was marked by the all-too-cozy exchange of printer monopolies for book censorship in Britain. By century's end, this compromised intellectual property regime was running out of political steam. To give an early instance, in 1645, the radical pamphleteer John Lilburne denounced not only how he was "unjustly imprisoned" but "that insufferable, unjust and tyrannical Monopoly of Printing, whereby a great company ... suppress every thing which hath any true Declaration of the just Rights and Liberties of the free-borne people of this Nation."[143]

By the 1690s, Parliament was hard pressed to renew, once more, the Book Licensing Act of 1662 that enforced censorship and granted print monopolies. The act ran counter to the Whig banner *Liberty and Property* that had won the day with the Glorious Revolution of 1688. If book licensing offended liberty, new ideas about property were also being floated, not least of all by Christ Church alumni John Locke whose natural law theory was to later have great consequence for intellectual property law. Given the press's political force in the English Civil War, Restoration, and Revolution, it was a time for rethinking the liberties and properties of the printed word. During the 1690s, Locke was among those who successfully lobbied for the end of book licensing. He proposed reforms on behalf of readers and authors of learned books, and those reforms were to figure, after his death, in the Statute of Anne 1710, entitled "An Act for the Encouragement of Learning," which launched the age of intellectual property.

143. John Lilburne, *England's Birth-Right Justified* (London: Larner's Press, 1645), 10.

PART THREE

Locke and Property

CHAPTER ELEVEN

A Theory of Property

Finally, I turn to John Locke, which is where this project began for me. In his life and philosophy, Locke brings together many of learning's properties. A good example of this is how Locke, over a better part of his life, benefited from the two principal modes of sponsorship that dominate this history of learning—namely, institutional endowment and personal patronage. In the first instance, Locke was a royal scholarship student, from his childhood at Westminster School until well into his maturity at Oxford. He only lost his fellowship at Christ Church at the age of fifty-two when his anti-monarchist politics resulted in the Crown ending this support. The politics in question were inspired by Anthony Ashley Cooper, later Earl of Shaftesbury, the patron whom Locke acquired in 1667, when he went to work for him as a physician and then as a hired pen. Lord Shaftesbury, a large-scale landholder and radical Whig politician, managed to involve Locke in colonialism, slavery, near-insurrection, and political exile, as well as equip him with a supportive annuity. The tension between the fellowship's scholarly repose and patronage's overheated politics has its counterpart in the havoc among conflicting interpretations of Locke's theory of property. He set out his ideas in a chapter of the *Two Treatises of Government*, and contributed to the conflict by successfully shrouding the origins of the book in mystery.

The *Two Treatises* has had a profound, but by no means singular, influence on later thinking about liberal democracy and human rights, including property and intellectual property rights. The book has been championed and excoriated by socialists and capitalists, progressives and conservatives, historians and philosophers (of which the footnotes that follow will give a taste).

I join the melee by holding that Locke's theory turns out to be particularly useful for consolidating my historical claims about the intellectual properties of learning, both as learning infuses our concept of intellectual property and as it constitutes a distinct class of such property. In this chapter, I demonstrate how the qualities that I have been attributing to learning align with what Locke makes of property. I add to the weight of this reading of Locke by linking it, in the next chapter, to his short-lived but arguably effective political campaign on behalf of learning's distinctive properties in the British legislative debates over book regulation at the end of the seventeenth century.

Not only was the *Two Treatises* published anonymously in 1689, but there are no preliminary notes or drafts to be found for the *Two Treatises*; Locke made no references to the writing of the book in his extant letters and papers (where these exist for his other books).[1] Nor does he explain at any point the gap introduced in the book's preface: "Reader, Thou hast here the Beginning and End of Discourse concerning Government; what Fate has otherwise disposed of the Papers that should have filled up the middle and were more than all the rest, 'tis not worth while to tell thee."[2] Locke only acknowledged his authorship of the *Two Treatises* (and others of his anonymously published works) in his last will and testament.[3]

All that is certain about the publication of the *Two Treatises* is that it was licensed for publication in London by J. Fraser on August 23, 1689, without an identified author. The licensing took place under an extension of the 1662 Act for Regulating Printing, which was part of the Crown's ongoing efforts, as noted earlier, to combine privileges with press censorship (with Locke's role in defeating this act addressed in the next chapter). The book was printed for the London bookseller Awnsham Churchill at the Black Swan in Ave-Mary-Lane, by Amen-Corner with a publication date of 1690.

The book appeared on the heels of the Glorious Revolution of 1688. William of Orange defeated the Catholic James II and, with Mary, was crowned on February 13, 1689. In the preface to the *Two Treatises*, Locke claims that the book is "sufficient to establish," as he puts it, "the Throne of Our Great Restorer, Our present King *William*; to make good his Title, in the Consent of the People, which being the only one of all lawful Governments, he has

1. See also Peter Laslett, "The English Revolution and Locke's *Two Treatises of Government*," *Cambridge Historical Journal* 12, no. 1 (1956): 47.

2. The *First Treatise* ends in mid-sentence with asterisks—"From Adam ****" (1.169).

3. John Locke, "Will," *Correspondence of John Locke*, ed. E. S. de Beer, vol. 8 (Oxford: Oxford University Press, 1989), 425–427.

more fully and clearly than any Prince in Christendom."[4] This is to make the book a manifesto for "the true original, extent, and end of civil government" (to cite the subtitle of the second treatise) and a guidebook for the Glorious Revolution. What has since been discovered, or rather surmised—given Locke's successful cover-up—is that the *Two Treatises* contains more than a few clues, including Locke's secretiveness about it, that suggest it was composed while Locke was engaged, with Lord Shaftesbury, in the inflammatory Exclusion Crisis taking place around 1680.[5]

Locke had become involved with Shaftesbury during the latter half of the 1660s, when he may well have been growing weary of Oxford's prevailing scholasticism, given to medieval disputation without end or import, or as Locke puts it in the *Essay*, the "running out of disputes into an endless train of syllogisms."[6] Anthony Ashley Cooper, who would later become the First Earl of Shaftesbury, asked Locke to join his household in London in 1667, first as a physician—involving the daring draining of his lord's hydatid cyst—and then as a political advisor.[7] During his time with Shaftesbury, Locke retained his Royal Fellowship at Christ Church, as well as his rooms at the college, returning in 1675 to complete the requirements of a bachelor's degree in medicine.

Among his early political duties, Locke assisted Shaftesbury and his fellow Lords Proprietors of the province of Carolina in composing the *Fundamental Constitutions of Carolina*, first issued in 1669. It served to introduce our philosopher to American colonialism and the slave trade, with the *Constitutions* recognizing a freeman's "absolute power and authority over his negro slaves," with allowances for freedom of religion.[8] In 1672, Locke

4. John Locke, *Two Treatises of Government*, ed. Peter Laslett (Cambridge: Cambridge University Press, 1988), 155. Henceforth, when I cite from this work, I will include the treatise and paragraph number immediately after the text.

5. After World War II, a large store of Locke's papers was sold to the Bodleian Library by the descendants of Locke's cousin, Peter King, to whom Locke had originally willed his papers. The papers revealed some of his involvement in the political intrigues of the Exclusion Crisis of 1680. Peter Laslett presents a detailed argument on how Locke "actually wrote the book for Shaftesbury's purposes," in his lordship's struggle against Charles II around 1680, which makes the book "an Exclusion Tract, not a Revolutionary Pamphlet": Introduction to *Two Treatises of Government*, 61.

6. John Locke, *An Essay concerning Human Understanding*, ed. Peter H. Nidditch (Oxford: Oxford University Press, 1975), 4.7.11

7. Later in life, Locke arguably found a second patron in Lady Damaris Masham at whose Oates estate outside of London he spent his final years, on returning from exile abroad in 1689, and with whom he shared philosophical interests (if not perhaps something more than that at an earlier point): see Jacqueline Broad, "A Woman's Influence? John Locke and Damaris Masham on Moral Accountability," *Journal of the History of Ideas* 67, no. 3 (2006): 489–510.

8. The Fundamental Constitutions of Carolina: March 1, 1669, Avalon Project, Yale University, online.

followed his patron's lead and counsel by investing in the newly formed Bahamas Company for a three-year period, and then the Royal African Company (which held a monopoly over the English slave trade until 1712), resulting in profits that Shaftesbury turned into a generous annuity for Locke.[9] This Middle Passage profiteering carries its own lesson on learning, as it strikingly contradicts the *Two Treatises'* opening line—"Slavery is so vile and miserable an Estate of Man"—as well as one of the primary property principles in the book holding that "every Man has a *Property* in his own *Person*: This no body has any right to but himself" (2.27). Locke is attacking the monarchist Robert Filmer, whom he accuses of advocating the enslavement of the English people by upholding the divine right of kings. Locke's tactic reveals a gross insensitivity to the actual horrors of the Atlantic slave trade, as well as to the abolitionist implications of his own stand on people possessing an inviolate property in themselves. It serves as another warning of learning's limits and shortsightedness in realizing its own ideals. It falls to the constant scrutiny of later generations to reinterpret and run with the full force and application of our better ideas.

During the 1670s, Shaftesbury was a leading force behind the Exclusion Bill, to prevent the king's Catholic brother from ascending to the throne. By the end of the decade, Locke's patron was on the verge of insurrection, before being forced to flee to Holland, where he died of ill health in 1679. Four years later, Locke also fled to Holland to escape arrest and perhaps the fate of Algernon Sidney, a member of the Long Parliament who was executed in 1683 for his unpublished manuscript that critiqued absolute monarchy. During the first year of Locke's exile, the Earl of Sunderland wrote to John Fell, Dean of Christ Church (whom you may recall from chapter 10), to complain that Locke's studentship "was never intended for the maintenance and support of such as seek to overthrow the government, and to bring the King's sacred person into contempt."[10] Locke was expelled in 1684, at age 52, and his days at Oxford were at an end.

---

9. William A. Pettigrew, "Free to Enslave: Politics and the Escalation of Britain's Transatlantic Slave Trade, 1688–1714," *William and Mary Quarterly*, ser. 3, vol. 64, no. 1 (2007): 3, 5. Pettigrew points out that the Royal African Company was founded by Charles II with his brother James having "vast holdings" in it (10). According to Pettigrew, "Liberal institutions proved instrumental in escalating the worst brutalities of British imperialism. Lockean motifs operating in England, such as the sovereignty of Parliament, can be more directly implicated in the development of Atlantic slavery than slavery can in the increased interest in republican ideology in America less than a century later" (8).

10. Cited by Roger S. Woolhouse, *Locke: A Biography* (Cambridge: Cambridge University Press, 2007), 210.

Locke remained in exile for nearly five years. During that time, James II's assumption of the throne in 1685, following the death of his brother Charles, triggered a revolt among the English that, under William of Orange's leadership, overthrew James II in 1688. Only after William and Mary were installed on the throne in 1689 did Locke feel it safe to return to London. Once back, this little-known fifty-seven-year-old unemployed scholar wasted little time in seeing into print not only the *Two Treatises* but also *An Essay concerning Human Understanding*, which appeared under his name that same year. In addition to that, a friend arranged to have Locke's *A Letter concerning Toleration* printed anonymously in 1689, as well.[11]

Lord Shaftesbury's patronage threw Locke headlong into the radical struggle for democracy in late seventeenth-century Britain, bringing into a sharp light ideas about natural law and human rights that he had been considering in a more contemplative fashion at Oxford. The combination shaped the *Two Treatises*, which went on to have a considerable influence on ideals of liberal democracy, as well as intellectual property. Some judge the book a work of considered political philosophy (reflecting in good part Locke's earlier Oxford life): "Three hundred years after its publication," writes James Tully, Distinguished Professor of Political Science, Law, Indigenous Governance and Philosophy at the University of Victoria, "the *Two Treatises* continues to present one of the major political philosophies of the modern world."[12] Others take it to exemplify his patron's commissioned pamphleteering, as if he had "disinterred his Shaftesburyean tract and published it anonymously late in 1689," in the words of John G. A. Pocock, a Johns Hopkins University historian.[13]

11. Unbeknownst to Locke, in 1689, his friend Philip van Limborch saw into print an English translation (by William Popple) of Locke's *Epsitola de Tolerantia* published in the Netherlands in April of 1689: Woolhouse, *Locke*, 270–74.

12. James Tully, "Rediscovering America: The *Two Treatises* and Aboriginal Rights," in *An Approach to Political Philosophy: Locke in Contexts* (Cambridge: Cambridge University Press, 1993), 137. Among those holding to the accomplishment of Locke's book, Jeremy Waldron believes the *Two Treatises* stands among Locke's "mature" works and, as such, is "as well-worked-out a theory of basic equality as we have in the canon of political philosophy": *God, Locke, and Equality: Christian Foundations of John Locke's Political Thought* (Cambridge: Cambridge University Press, 2002), 1.

13. J. G. A. Pocock, "The Myth of John Locke and the Obsession with Liberalism," in *John Locke*, ed. J. G. A. Pocock and Richard Ashcraft (Los Angeles: William Andrews Clark Memorial Library, 1980), 5. Maurice Cranston identifies Locke's book as "a revolutionary manifesto," and one which he finds "inferior to [Hobbe's] the *Leviathan*; it is not written as philosophy but propaganda—a party book against a party book" (referring to Locke's critique of Robert Filmer's *Patriarcha*): "The Politics of John Locke," *History Today* 2, no. 9 (1952): 621, 622.

Locke may well have decided, on returning from his years of exile (1683–89), that the Glorious Revolution had created a place for the *Two Treatises* which he may not have had an opportunity to complete or publish, or feared to do so amid the earlier, largely vitriolic, pamphleteering and lewd versifying that had swirled around the philandering crypto-Catholic Charles II in the late 1670s.[14] Still, it might also seem that becoming caught up in the firefight surrounding Charles forged and tempered Locke's Oxonian arguments for a democracy founded on human rights and based on the consent of the people—arguments he had begun to develop prior to meeting Shaftesbury.[15] The influences of Locke's Oxford and then London years suggest the gains and risks of learning moving out of the cloisters and spires and into the world.

Nor was it simply a matter of patrons leading the learned astray. This was a period in which the learned were lending European imperialism a hand in the colonial acquisition of medicinal treatments, flora and fauna specimens, historical artifacts, cultural icons, and art objects. In the ancient and new world, there were to be universities, fine libraries and endowed colleges built on wealth gained from sugar plantations and human trafficking.[16] We are still working through what this imperial legacy means for the properties of learning and our knowledge of the world.[17] This history suggests that learning is not inherently self-correcting; it does not simply arrive at the right answer (attitude, belief, theory) with time and support. Rather, learn-

14. Tim Harris, *London Crowds in the Reign of Charles II: Propaganda and Politics from the Restoration until the Exclusion Crisis* (Cambridge: Cambridge University Press, 1987). The scurrilous verses that circulated in manuscript form during the Crisis came to be published in 1696 after the book licensing act lapsed: see Rachel Weil, "Sometimes a Scepter Is Only a Scepter: Pornography and Politics in Restoration England," in *The Invention of Pornography: Obscenity and the Origins of Modernity, 1500–1800*, ed. Lynn Hunt (New York: Zone, 1996), 125.

15. At Christ Church, and before Shaftesbury entered his life, Locke composed a manuscript (which went unpublished until 1967) in which he sets out, if in a milder manner, a series of democratic principles, including how "the magistrate's power" is "derived from, or conveyed to him by, the consent of the people" and that "man naturally [is] the owner of an entire liberty, and so much master of himself": *Two Tracts on Government*, ed. and trans. Philip Abrams (Cambridge: Cambridge University Press, 1967), 122, 125.

16. As one who gained great advantage from spending time in the Codrington Library at All Souls, Oxford, let me cite from the historical note on its website concerning "a substantial legacy of £10,000 received by the College in 1710 from Christopher Codrington, sometime Fellow and governor general of the Leeward Islands. His family wealth principally derived from sugar plantations—worked by slaves—in Antigua and Barbados." See also Craig Steven Wilder. *Ebony and Ivy: Race, Slavery, and the Troubled History of America's Universities* (New York: Bloomsbury, 2014).

17. See, for example, John Willinsky, *Learning to Divide the World: Education at Empire's End* (Minneapolis: University of Minnesota Press, 1998).

ing is about the process of correction without end, punctuated by moments of consensus and agreement.

"OF PROPERTY"

The significance of Locke's ideas about property in the *Two Treatises* lies in the timing and timelessness of his book. The *Two Treatises* was published two decades before the British Parliament passed, in 1710, the first intellectual property legislation based on recognizing the rights of authors and learning (with Locke's role in the statute discussed in the next and final chapter). Yet the importance of Locke's chapter on property to my history has as much to do with how it remains a touchstone to this day for intellectual property jurisprudence. His book continues to be regularly cited across a broad body of literature on copyright and patent law.[18]

Locke sets out the challenge in opening the chapter "Of Property": "It seems to some a very great difficulty, how any one should ever come to have a *Property* in any thing" (2.25). Locke's approach here is, first of all, to establish that the act of owning things is not a given fact of nature; rather, he argued, ownership needs to be explained and justified. His second task was to define ownership as the possession of a stake or *entitlement in* something, rather than outright and entire *possession of* the thing. Though Locke describes the "great difficulty" of explaining ownership, he does situate the origins of property rights within the scope of natural law.[19] It is a law that is susceptible

18. Between 1990 and 2010, *Two Treatises of Government* was cited 147 times in the scholarly literature dealing with intellectual property: "Intellectual Property Collection," HeinOnline, Getzville, online. Let me offer two of the richer examples of how this continues to be used: In considering how a natural-rights theory of intellectual property can protect free speech interests, Wendy J. Gordon argues that a "Lockean concern with protecting the public from harm" offers a natural limit on "current intellectual property systems [that] give rights in excess of what a Lockean model would justify": "A Property Right in Self-Expression: Equality and Individualism in the Natural Law of Intellectual Property," *Yale Law Review* 102 (1993): 1569, 1608. Benjamin G. Damstedt holds that "revisiting Locke for a theory of intellectual property has become vital" in establishing a more just patent system, for which he proposes what he terms "a Lockean fair use right" for drug patents to ensure greater equity of access to needed medications in the Global South: "Limiting Locke: A Natural Law Justification for the Fair Use Doctrine," *Yale Law Journal* 112, no. 5 (2003): 1180, 1183.

19. "It is the clear-sightedness that made Locke's achievement (assuming it was largely his) so remarkable, and enabled him to publish the most satisfying work presented by anyone in this natural rights tradition": Richard Tuck, *Natural Rights Theories: Their Origin and Development* (Cambridge: Cambridge University Press, 1979), 171. See also J. R. Milton, "Laws of Nature," in *The Cambridge History of the Seventeenth Century*, vol. 1, ed. Daniel Garber and Michael Ayers (Cambridge: Cambridge University Press 1998), 684.

to change through the consensual social contracts of communities, civil governments, moneyed economies, and other structures.[20] Locke's turn to natural law was part of an early Enlightenment revival of what Thomas Aquinas had been championing, centuries earlier, as Christian faith expressed through reason, with even earlier roots of this concept traceable back to Plato.[21]

In just that spirit, Locke begins his chapter with the two pillars on which his argument on property rests: "Whether we consider natural *Reason* . . . Or *Revelation*" (2.25).[22] He then points out how in the biblical beginning of the world there was no property, and he moves forward through various property developments to his own day.[23] His focus is on the possession of property in arable land, and on acorns, deer, cloth, silk, ropes. As an avid collector and reader of travel books, he has gathered evidence for property's natural law through what he has read of the Indigenous peoples of the Americas.[24] He also regards the historical introduction of money

20. On the originality of Locke's position, Tully points out that he "gathered together many of the arguments of the early seventeenth century," while noting the force of this effective gathering was such that "his theory set the terms for many of the later theories that were used to justify the establishment of European property in America": "Aboriginal Property and Western Theory: Recovering a Middle Ground," *Social Philosophy and Policy* 11, no. 2 (1994): 158. "Locke's philosophy is a workaday synthesis of the ideas of the more creative, more revolutionary thinkers of the earlier seventeenth century": Christopher Hill, *The Century of Revolution, 1603–1714*, 2nd ed. (New York: Norton, 1980), 252.

21. "Participation of rational creatures in the eternal law is called natural law": Thomas Aquinas, "Summae theologiae," 1a2ae 91, art 2, in *Political Writings*, ed. R. W. Dyson (Cambridge: Cambridge University Press, 2002), 86. On Locke's link to Aquinas, see Frederick C. Copleston: "We can trace a connection between the medieval philosophy of law and that of John Locke, while the latter's empiricism was not so entirely alien to medieval thought as one might be inclined to think": *Medieval Philosophy* (London: Methuen, 1952), 2.

22. Thomas Sprat declared in his early history of the Royal Society (to which Locke was elected in 1678): "The universal Disposition of this *Age* is bent upon a *rational Religion*" (*The History of the Royal Society of London, for the Improving of Natural Knowledge* [London: Knapton et al., 1722], 374).

23. Stephen Buckle provocatively suggests that Locke's "Of Property" presents "a natural history of property": *Natural Law and the Theory of Property: Grotius to Hume* (Oxford: Oxford University Press, 1991), 188. This ties in well with Locke's membership in the Royal Society of London, as well as his earlier involvement with Oxford's Experimental Philosophical Club, with that membership leading him to send out numerous natural history inquiries across the seas (in the corresponding scientific spirit of Bede, Newton, and later, Darwin), with recipients kindly sending him specimens and descriptions of Native American remedies (Sarah Irving, *Natural Science and the Origins of the British Empire* [London: Pickering and Chatto, 2008], 121–22). He also attempted unsuccessfully to assess barometric pressure in mining shafts for the Royal Society, but he saw through to publication the late Robert Boyle's *The General History of the Air* in 1692, in which Locke included his daily Oxford weather reports from 1667 to 1683.

24. John Locke recommends "books of Travel" in "Some Thoughts concerning Reading and Study for a Gentleman," in *Political Essays*, ed. Mark Goldie (Cambridge: Cambridge University Press, 1997), 353.

into property relations as a critical turning point, amounting to a social contract instituted through the consent of the people. This enables him to introduce a political arithmetic by which to calculate the contribution of private property rights to the welfare of the whole community. In Locke's hands, individual property rights are grounded in natural law and people's consent, which provided a thorough check on the divine right of kings and the arbitrary exercise of power by the likes of Charles II.

Having provided a little of the context behind Locke's "Of Property," I now want to demonstrate how this vastly influential statement on property rights, involving the tangibility of acorns and apples, can also serve as a guide to that distinctive class of intellectual property associated with learning. This is only to point out how my claims for learning fit within the scope of at least one substantial theory of property rights, as it was articulated in the years before this prehistory concludes and as this theory continues to have import. To that end, I identify seven property principles from within Locke's chapter. For each, I begin with a phrase from Locke that characterizes the principle, followed by a summary of its meaning and import, before applying it to what I have made, throughout this book, of learning's intellectual properties while footnoting other readings of the principle.

Locke's Theory of Property in Seven Principles

1. THE GREAT COMMON OF THE WORLD: In the beginning, according to Locke, "God gave the World to Men in Common" (2.34). The original state of nature is a world without property distinctions or ownership claims.[25] Locke not only relies on the reasonableness of this proposition but offers his

---

25. Tully traces the world-held-in-common theme through Francisco Suárez, Hugo Grotius, Samuel von Pufendorf, John Selden, and Richard Cumberland, leading up to Locke's use of it: *A Discourse on Property: John Locke and his Adversaries* (Cambridge: Cambridge University Press, 1980), 66–79. Questions abound about Locke's encounter with Diggers and Levellers radicalism, the literature on which he likely encountered through his Dutch friend Benjamin Furley during his time in exile: John Harrison and Peter Laslett, *Library of John Locke* (Oxford: Oxford University Press, 1965), 50–54. To take one example of the Diggers stance, Gerrard Winstanley, failed cloth merchant and Diggers leader, insisted during the English Civil War "that the earth was made to be a common Treasury of livelihood for all, *without respect of persons*, and was not made to be bought and sold: And that mankind . . . was not made to acknowledge any of his own kinde to be his teacher and ruler": *A Letter to the Lord Fairfax and His Council of War . . . That the Common People Ought to Dig, Plow, Plant, and Dwell Upon the Commons, without . . . Paying Rent to Any* (London: Giles Calvert, 1649), 9. Ellen Meiksins Wood judges that Locke "both appropriates *and*, on critical issues, deliberately neutralizes the radical 'discourse' of his time": "Radicalism, Capitalism and Historical Contexts: Not Only a Reply to Richard Ashcraft on John Locke," *History of Political Thought* 15, no. 3 (1994): 323.

readers its place in the Bible: "T'is very clear, that God, as King *David* says, *Psal.* CXV. xvi. *has given the Earth to the Children of Men*; given it to mankind in common" (2.25). By pointing out that God gave the world in common to humankind, Locke is arguing that the introduction of property rights into such a world needs to be warranted, whether by natural law or the consent of all (to whom the world was given). This first principle undermines the prevailing monarchial assumption of Robert Filmer, which is that God entrusted the world to kings, as His representative on earth, with each king a descendent of Adam.[26] In his attack on this conception of absolute monarchy, Locke provides a biblical basis for a democratic starting point and in which the children of men and women have an equal claim to a world within which they will have property rights.

This first principle holds for this Western history of learning, if in a somewhat different manner than suggested by Locke's emphasis on it as an original state, rather than one to be sustained. The abbey book chest and scriptorium, in which learning had its origins in the West, were part of the monastic compact under the *Rule of Benedict* to recreate and to sustain that original world held in common. This communal principle continued to play a part in the medieval axiom that knowledge is a gift of God (not to be owned or sold), which Thomas Aquinas at the University of Paris and others felt should affect the payment of masters in the medieval universities, and which was still a point of reference for the Italian humanists.[27] Works of learning were certainly for sale, especially in the marketplace created by print, but this was always accompanied by private and institutional arrangements to place copies in the communal state of private and public libraries. To hold learning in common like this proved to be a productive basis of scholarship, even as it was based on recognizing and maintaining authors' claims to their work. In this, learning is regarded as if it is always given in common to all, as part of the original gift, even if who is included in that *all* remains an ideal rather than the reality, to this day.

2. A PROPERTY IN HIS OWN PERSON: Locke begins the process of establishing how an individual gains a right in property with a second natural law principle: "Though the Earth, and all inferior Creatures, be common

26. Robert Filmer writes that "this lordship which Adam by creation had over the whole world and by right descending from him the patriarchs did enjoy": "Patriarcha," in *Patriarcha and other Writings*, ed. Johann P. Sommerville, (Cambridge: Cambridge University Press, 1991), 6–7.

27. On the medieval regard for the gift of knowledge (introduced in chapter 7), see Gaines Post, Kimon Giocarinis, and Richard Kay, "The Medieval Heritage of a Humanistic Ideal: '*Scientia donum dei est, unde vendi non potest,*'" *Traditio* 11 (1955): 195–234.

to all Men, yet every Man has a *Property* in his own *Person*: This no body has any right to but himself" (2.27).[28] The principle of self-possession is complicated by Locke's belief that God has a maker's right over humankind: "For Men being all the Workmanship of one Omnipotent, and infinitely wise Maker... they are his Property" (2.6).[29] We are each a joint shareholder with God in our own life.[30] A person's autonomy and self-possession, which is critical to Locke's concept of governance by democratic consent, leads him to use the term *property* in a far more encompassing sense than suggested by the term *ownership*: For as he puts it, "Property, that is, his Life, Liberty and Estate" is what each person holds "equally with any other Man," by "all the Rights and Privileges of the Law of Nature" (2.87).[31]

This second principle speaks to the individual's right to education. Learning is a means through which to develop and exercise this inherent property-in-oneself. Charlemagne was among the first to honor this on a large scale in the West by employing Alcuin to direct an empire's schooling program. This self-possession is also a right of intellectual independence (and against indoctrination) when it comes to learning, as it proved to be for Radegund and Hildegard. It is no less a right of accreditation, for all that one achieves through learning is a property right to which one has a claim. For many of the figures in this book, the identification of self and property led to an all-encompassing sense of learning as their life, liberty, and estate, in Locke's terms. Taken collectively, this right in oneself was the basis of membership in the commonwealth of learning, much as it was for the democratic state that

28. The right of self-possession was to prove a basic concept in the fight for democracy, abolitionism, and feminism. See Boston Women's Health Collective's *Our Bodies, Ourselves* (Boston: New England Fress Press, 1971). Anne Philips credits Locke in her recent work on this theme: *Our Bodies: Whose Property?* (Princeton, NJ: Princeton University Press, 2010), 20, 34. Carole Pateman calls for qualifying this Lockean property in oneself, as it can then be alienated in damaging ways for democratic life: "Self-Ownership and Property in the Person: Democratization and a Tale of Two Concepts," *Journal of Political Philosophy* 10, no. 1 (2002): 20–53.

29. An earlier example is found in Richard Overton who refers to self-ownership in a 1646 Leveller pamphlet he wrote while imprisoned for pamphleteering: "To every Individall in nature, is given an individuall property by nature, not to be invaded or usurped by any: for every one as he is himself, so he hath a selfe propriety." *An Arrow against All Tyrants and Tyranny, Shot from the Prison of New-gate into the Prerogative Bowels of the Arbitrary House of Lords* (London: Martin Claw-Clergy, 1646), 3. Cf. note 21.

30. Waldron sees God's ownership claim bearing on human equality: "Since our relation to God (the relation which grounds our equality) is to be understood in terms of our being owned by Him," it forms part of Locke's "commitment to basic equality [which] is an important working premise of his whole political theory": *God, Locke, and Equality*, 162, 152.

31. A. John Simmons: "Locke characterizes all of a person's rights as 'property'": *The Lockean Theory of Rights* (Princeton, NJ: Princeton University Press, 1992), 232.

Locke envisioned. This sense of having a property in oneself figures in an author's claim to a work being her own, as well as in the coherence of an author's body of work. Still that self-expression is to be appreciated—building on the first principle of communality and following Bede—for what it contributes to the learning of others and how they are able to use it themselves.

3. LABOR WAS TO BE HIS TITLE TO IT: Locke holds that, in the original state of nature, one gains a property in something by working on it. This I take to be his third principle of property: "The *Labor* of his Body, and the *Work* of his Hands, we may say, are properly his. Whatsoever then he removes out of the State that Nature hath provided, and left it in, he hath mixed his *Labor* with, and joyned to it something that is his own, and thereby makes it his *property*" (2.27).[32] Or, as Locke combines the second and third of these principles: "Man (by being Master of himself and *Proprietor of his own Person*, and Actions or *Labor* of it) had still in himself *the great Foundation of Property*" (2.44). A natural right to the fruits of one's labor has long made sense to people.[33] For Locke, the principle is not merely a social convention, as it was for natural law theorists Hugo Grotius and

---

32. In the eighteenth century, Adam Smith also found *labor* a convincing source of property rights: "The property which every man has in his own labor, as it is the original foundation of all other property, so it is the most sacred and inviolable" (*An Inquiry into the Nature and Causes of the Wealth of Nations*, vol. 1, ed. Edwin Cannan [London: Methuen, 1904], 1.10.2 123). In turn, Marx was to make much of the loss of this proprietary relationship between self-possession and labor: "External labor, labor in which man alienates himself, is a labor of self-sacrifice, of mortification. Lastly, the external character of labor for the worker appears in the fact that it is not his own, but someone else's, that it does not belong to him, that in it he belongs, not to himself, but to another ... it is the loss of his self": *Economic and Philosophic Manuscripts of 1844*, trans. Martin Milligan (Moscow: Progress Publishers, 1959), 30. I find Nozick's objection to the labor-mixing property principle—illustrated by pouring a can of tomato soup into the ocean and claiming said ocean—unpersuasive, as it misses Locke's concern for "the Industrious and Rational, (and [whose] *Labour* was to be *his* Title to it;)" (2.34): *Anarchy, State, and Utopia* (New York: Basic, 1974), 175. Cf. John Donne: "A man does not become proprietary of the sea because he hath two or three boats fishing in it": "Sermon ... to the Honorable Company of the Virginia Plantation" (1622).

33. "In modern times, however, the claim of him who creates has been urged by a long line of writers beginning with Locke and culminating in the socialists": Roscoe Pound, *An Introduction to the Philosophy of Law* (New Haven, CT: Yale University Press, 1954), 110. For Jeremy Waldron, Locke's labor theory suffers "a slight lacuna ... [that] Hume and Kant have been quick to exploit," which is that one has to take possession of a thing prior to investing labor in it: *The Right to Private Property* (Oxford: Oxford University Press, 1988), 173. Tully points out how, in the nineteenth century, "the early English and French socialists took it [*Two Treatises*] as the major philosophical foundation of modern socialism: the worker's right to the product of their labor and possession regulated by need," while in the twentieth century the book has been held up as championing private property rights: *Discourse on Property*, x.

Samuel de Pufendorf during that era.[34] Labor also had a religious value for the Calvinist in Locke: "The strain of physical labor," Cambridge historian John Dunn points out in his work on the *Two Treatises*, and "the sweat of their brow" is a "palpable index of salvation."[35] Labor was a form of prayer among the monastics, with the Calvinist difference that labor leads to individual rather than communal ownership.[36] Yet this labored right of ownership is not without its limits, as I discuss in the next two principles, entailing property matters of sufficiency and spoilage.

With learning, a number of Benedictine nuns and monks were able to establish that study was a form of labor that fulfilled their monastic vows by creating a communal good that sustained the pious community, rather than leading to ownership or prideful vanity. Yet both Jerome and Erasmus made bold proprietary claims for their labors with the word of God and, in Erasmus's case, with Jerome's works. Gerard of Cremona, who worked on so many texts during the Latin translation movement, left his work unsigned, only to have his students properly credit his work. This speaks to how having a property in a work does not exclude others from contributing to its value through their own scholarly efforts.[37] The Locke scholars, whose labor occupies this chapter's footnotes, further demonstrate the inexhaustibly productive and selective right to work on others' work.[38] The goal is to bring order to this proliferation of texts and meanings within the commons by honoring, correcting, and discrediting others' labors. Locke refers

34. "Alienation of original rights by consent . . . was the solution favored by Locke's predecessors in the natural law tradition, Hugo Grotius and Samuel Pufendorf": Waldron, *Right to Private Property*, 149–51.

35. John Dunn, *The Political Thought of John Locke: An Historical Account of the Argument of the Two Treatises of Government* (Cambridge: Cambridge University Press, 1969), 220.

36. The Benedictine motto was *ora et labora* (pray and work) and its corresponding *laborare est orare* (to work is to pray). Dunn only adds to this association by pointing to more than once Locke's unpublished essay from 1693 on the sensibility of assigning the hours of the day to work and study in an eerie resemblance to the Rule of St. Benedict (ibid., 231 note 6, 235). In the essay, Locke recommends spending "half the day employed in useful labor" which would "supply the inhabitants of the earth with the necessaries and conveniences of life," and "six hours in the day well directed in study would carry a man as far in the improvement of his mind as his parts are capable of": "Labor," in *Political Essays*, 326, 327.

37. In the *Essay concerning Human Understanding*, Locke defines the labor involved in knowledge work as "the perception of the connexion and agreement, or disagreement and repugnancy of any of our Ideas": *Essay*, 4.1.2 525.

38. Among all of these differences of opinion over Locke, it is good to keep in mind Gordon J. Schochet's point: "Locke himself was not nearly so clear as our beliefs about him would suggest." Introduction in *Life, Liberty and Property: Essays on Locke's Political Ideas*, ed. Gordon J. Schochet (Belmont, CA: Wadsworth, 1971), 1.

to the "labor of thought," as well as "learned and laborious inquiries" in the *Essay*, but makes no reference to property claims in reference to such labor, as he does with the labor invested in harvesting wheat and barley.[39]

4. ENOUGH, AND AS GOOD: Locke identifies a natural limit to the property claims that can be made in the name of self and labor with what is referred to as a sufficiency proviso. The proviso asserts that one person's property claims cannot unduly limit others' ability to make similar claims: "For this *Labor* being the unquestionable Property of the Laborer, no Man but he can have a right to what that is once joyned to, at least where there is enough, and as good, left in common for others" (2.27). Although what may count as *enough, and as good* is open to interpretation, he does state that "he that leaves as much as another can make use of, does as good as take nothing at all" (2.33). It is easy enough to imagine that the original state of nature offered enough, and as good of pretty well everything for everyone.[40] In Locke's day, it was common, and all too convenient, to think that the New World offered enterprising Europeans some part of that original state of sufficiency: "In the beginning all the world was *America*" (2.49) is how Locke puts it, with more on this assumption below. Still, this proviso advanced the equality of individual rights, against the presumption that property rights are available on an all-you-can-take basis.

The sufficiency proviso is of considerable importance to the learned. Ensuring that there is enough and as good, however, is not for them a check on acquisitiveness. Rather, it is the goal of cooperation and coordination within the commonwealth of learning. From the monastic book chest to the university stacks, from the scholar to the student, the library ensures that each has *enough, and as good* as any other for their studies. The Benedictine scriptorium made copying a pious act of provision for just such a principle. Al-Ma'mun sponsored a multilingual translation movement to make Islamic

---

39. Locke, *Essay*, 2.11.2 156, 4.20.2 707. At other points, he makes the proprietary point that language is "no man's private possession, but the common measure of commerce and communication" (3.11.11, 514); he shows sympathy for those who cannot afford books (or the leisure and languages to read them) (4.20.2, 707); he also refers to the *possession* of ideas: "So much as we ourselves consider and comprehend of truth and reason, so much we possess of real and true knowledge" (1.3.24 66).

40. Jeremy Waldron argues that *enough, and as good* is not a proviso or limit at all but "is seen by Locke as a *fact about* acquisition in the early ages of man" and "thus the 'enough and as good' clause cannot be construed as a necessary condition, or as a restriction, on appropriation without concluding that it is downright inconsistent with what Locke claimed to be the fundamental duty of the law of nature": "Enough and as Good Left for Others," *Philosophical Quarterly* 29, no. 117 (1979): 321–22, 326.

learning the equal of any in the world of his day. Books were chained to library shelves to ensure that the best editions were available. And Bodley sought to fulfill the sufficiency proviso, by doing his best to arrange for a copy of each book printed to be added to the library, while Bodleian regulations at Oxford continue to prevent books from being signed out of the library, so that readers never go without.

5. NOTHING WAS MADE TO SPOIL: Locke adds a second natural-law curb on property rights, which is a prohibition against waste: "Nothing was made by God for Man to spoil or destroy" (2.31). Without proper use, there is no right of property in, say, the apples picked from a tree: "But if they perished, in his Possession, without their due use . . . he offended against the Common Law of Nature" (2.37). Restating this principle, Locke advises that if anything is "to be looked on as Waste . . . [it] might be the Possession of any other" (2.38). For "he took more than his share, and robb'd others" (2.46). Taken together, the sufficiency and spoilage provisos place a strong limit on absolute or unqualified property claims under natural law.

The spoilage proviso also takes on a certain priority with learning. Petrarch and his humanist colleagues devoted themselves to recovering, assembling, and preserving the artifacts of classical learning that were otherwise lost and left to molder away. Print only added to their revitalized use. More generally, the efforts of Isidore of Seville, al-Farabi, Grosseteste, and Erasmus to classify, index, compile, and annotate texts were directed toward ensuring that works can be located, comprehended, and used to their full advantage. Again, the libraries of Islam and the West discussed here were devoted to collecting and preserving what had been achieved for purposes of access and use. Within the accumulation of learned works, a great many works are destined to go uncited and unused. These works do not represent so much waste as the vast number of attempts that it requires for breakthroughs in learning, combined with the indeterminacy, at any given point, of what will prove useful at a later stage.

6. FROM THE CONSENT OF MEN: The sixth principle moves Locke's property theory from natural law to social contract. Locke advises that people can put "an end to the State of Nature between Men" by "agreeing together mutually to enter into one Community, and make one Body Politic" (2.14). The point of this agreement, for Locke, is the protection of property rights: "The great and *chief end*, therefore, of Mens uniting into Commonwealths, and putting themselves under Government, *is the Preservation of their Property*" (2.124). This preservation is facilitated by "the *Invention of Money* and the tacit Agreement of Men to put value on it" and this "introduced

(by Consent) larger Possessions, and a Right to them" (2.36). And if "the *Use of Money* . . . had made Land scarce" (2.45), then the resulting "larger possessions" (2.36) can still satisfy the sufficiency proviso, by providing enough, and as good for others through employment opportunities, tax revenues, and the production of a greater variety and quantity of goods at cheaper prices.[41] Money can also help people avoid the spoilage proviso: "A man may fairly possess more land than he himself can use the product of, by receiving in exchange for the overplus, Gold and Silver" (2.50). With the formation of political communities by consent, natural law is not abandoned but supplemented by human laws that serve all: "The positive Laws of the Society, [are] made conformable to the Laws of Nature for the public good," Locke writes of property in the *First Treatise*, "*i.e.* the good of every particular Member of that Society, as far as by common Rules it can be provided for" (1.92).

This history of learning has long been about people entering into compacts that further their studies, whether inadvertently, with the *Rule of Benedict*, or intentionally, with the incorporation of the studium generale. The history of these learned incorporations, which were increasingly focused and explicit in their learned interests, reflect a series of arrangements with the larger world. The world agreed to support—if more in principle than practice, if never sufficiently nor consistently—the founding of monasteries, schools, and colleges that afforded the learned a degree of autonomy in the service of learning. More specifically, Federico Cesi reached a temporary accord with the church on behalf of Galileo's risky work; William Laud and John Fell traded in printing privileges with the Stationers' Company; John Wilkins and friends convinced King Charles II to charter their Royal Society. The purpose of "uniting into Commonwealths [of learning], and putting themselves under Government," as Locke had it, may well have been "the Preservation of their [intellectual] Property," which is to say the life, liberty, and estate of learning.

7. INCREASE THE COMMON STOCK: What I take to be the seventh principle of Locke's theory of property is his proto-utilitarian justification of "the increase of lands, and [property owners'] right imploying of them" (2.42).[42] This principle enables the modern improving landowner (think:

41. See James Tully, "Property, Self-Government and Consent," *Canadian Journal of Political Science* 28, no. 1 (1995): 121.

42. "One way of understanding the significance of Locke's rationalism is to approach him as a social theorist and to see the two sides of Locke—the natural law rationalist and the utilitarian rationalist—not as competing philosophical theories but as complementary aspects of a coherent social theory": David Resnick, "Rationality and the *Two Treatises*," in *John Locke's Two Treatises*

Locke's patron Lord Shaftesbury) to continue to acquire land as long as the accumulation can be shown to offer a bounty to all humankind (his two provisos notwithstanding). Locke is advocating the most efficient exercise of property rights for the greatest good: "God and his Reason commanded him to subdue the Earth," as it will "improve it for the benefit of Life" (2.32). In an early instance of political arithmetic, he does the math on "the Benefit Mankind receives from" such "husbandry" (2.43):

> He who appropriates land to himself by his labor, does not lessen, but increase the common stock of mankind: for the provisions serving to the support of human life, produced by one acre of inclosed and cultivated land, are (to speak much within compasse) ten times more than those which are yielded by an acre of land of an equal richness lyeing wast in common. And therefor he that incloses land, and has a greater plenty of the conveniencys of life from ten acres, than he could have from an hundred left to Nature, may truly be said to give ninety acres to Mankind . . . I have here rated the improved land very low, in making its product but as ten to one, when it is much nearer an hundred to one. (2.37)

Locke only added this section on the yield-gain calculus to the *Two Treatises* during the preparation of his fourth and final edition of the book (published posthumously in 1713). He sought to emphasize the public payoff of appropriation, enclosure, and cultivation against the undermining of human equality resulting from land accumulation. Everyone is the beneficiary of a tenfold, make that a hundredfold, increase in agricultural productivity. This is why, then, "Men have agreed to a disproportionate and unequal Possession of the Earth" (2.50). Now, one may still want to consider the corollary of this principle, namely, that acts of enclosure and privatization that lead to anything less than this hundredfold level of public benefit are on less solid ground and the property should, as such, be returned to the commons.[43]

This seventh principle again has a parallel within the commonwealth of learning. Whereas the act of enclosing land, Locke insists, "does not lessen but increase the common stock" (2.37), so efforts to improve and preserve the learned holdings of a library are intended to increase the common stock

---

of Government: New Interpretations, ed. Edward J. Harpham (Lawrence: Kansas University Press, 1992), 88.

43. The hundredfold test that I suggest here is at least consistent with Richard Ashcraft's judgment that "Locke's chapter on property" is "one of the most radical critiques of the landowning aristocracy produced during the last half of the seventeenth century": *Revolutionary Politics and Locke's* Two Treatises of Government (Princeton, NJ: Princeton University Press, 1986), ix.

of learning.[44] The difference between learning and land is that the library increases productivity by opening access for the many of this commonwealth, which is not the case with Locke's cultivated fields. Those who glossed the manuscripts also sought to increase the common stock with their annotations and commentaries. Or take the example of Henry Oldenburg, who employed the press to greatly multiply the reach of the membership-only transactions of the Royal Society.

Print multiplied access, and the spread of learning followed. Now, it needs to be recognized that to increase what the commonwealth of learning gives to humankind "ten times more," if not "much nearer an hundred," as Locke claims for the cultivation of land (2.37), may take "such Masters, as . . . the incomparable Mr. Newton, with some other of that Strain," to step back to the era of Locke's *Essay*.[45] In the cultivation of learning—as the history I have laid out in this book demonstrates—increases to the common stock result from people exercising intellectual property rights of access, accreditation, autonomy, communality, sponsorship, and use. So it was then and as it needs to be now by those who represent, if not yet sufficiently, a far more diverse, global commonwealth of learning. Throw into the mix a new standard for increasing the common stock of learning through open access to the literature, and you have the promise of a ten times if not a hundred-fold increase in value and use.

Through these seven property principles, Locke delivers on his promise to explain how anyone might come to have a property in anything. In the process, he makes property rights the basis of individual sovereignty arising out of a commons to which each has an equal right. Locke's adept combining of natural law, theology, and social contract in the *Two Treatises* is responsible, I imagine, for a good part of this theory's continuing appeal. He may have largely conceived of the sovereign individual as a male landholder of the sort represented by his patron Shaftesbury (or himself, with his small inherited landholding), yet his principles of liberal democracy and property rights have played their part in the spread of democratic governance, consistent with his statement—if not his beliefs and actions, according to our

---

44. "Roman jurists recognized that certain things were not subject to acquisition. . . . It might be that from their nature they could only be used, not owned, and from their nature they adapted to general use. These were *res communes*": Pound, *Philosophy of Law*, 110. Pound contrasts this with "nineteenth-century dogma that everything must be owned" (111).

45. "Epistle to the Reader," *Essay*, 10. In scholarly work, the extent to which the common stock is increased is calculated today by the number of times a work is cited: Eugene Garfield, "The History and Meaning of the Journal Impact Factor," *Journal of the American Medical Association* 295, no. 1 (2006): 90–93.

standards—that "the People have a Right to act as Supreme" (2.242). This is the note on which Locke concludes the *Two Treatises*.

THE RIGHT OF RESPONSIBLE USE

In addition to the uncertainties surrounding Locke's writing the *Two Treatises of Government*, controversy surrounds the book's historical influence. At the very least there is the question of what it meant to Thomas Jefferson and the founding of the United States.[46] But no less germane to questions of property is the part that Locke's theory played in the colonial dispossession of the Indigenous peoples of America during the eighteenth and nineteenth centuries, following from Locke's claims that the cultivation of land warrants proprietary claims to it. For as much as I have made of the value that learning gains from its autonomy, I want to be just as adamant about learning's responsibilities for grappling with its consequences, as well as contributions, to the world from which it stands apart. The property rights of use carry with them liabilities that can, on occasion, call for corrective action on the part of the learned.

This was brought home to me in the course of working on the Locke section of this book. I gradually came to realize that one of the scholars whom I encountered and have already cited, James Tully, is continuing to work out an exemplary path of responsible use in his work on Locke. His scholarly career holds its own set of lessons on the intellectual properties of learning, and so I conclude this chapter with Tully's inspired move from the study of Locke to the scholarly support of the Indigenous peoples who are reestablishing rights they lost to extremely damaging uses of Locke's theory of property.

To appreciate Tully's approach to Locke, let me first briefly present the prevailing interpretation of the *Two Treatises* in the 1970s that he inherited as a graduate student in political philosophy at Cambridge. At the outset

---

46. As Thomas Jefferson reflects in his final years on the Declaration of Independence: "All its authority rests then on the harmonizing sentiments of the day, whether expressed in conversation, in letters, printed essays, or in the elementary books of public right, as Aristotle, Cicero, Locke, Sidney, etc." ("To Henry Lee, Monticello, May 8, 1825," in *Writings*, ed. Merrill D. Peterson [New York: Library of America, 1984], 1501). Isaac Kramnick argues of the *Declaration of Independence*, "Locke lurks behind its every phrase": *Republicanism and Bourgeois Radicalism: Political Ideology in Late Eighteenth-Century England and America* (Ithaca, NY: Cornell University Press, 1990), 293. Also see Steven M. Dworetz, *The Unvarnished Doctrine: Locke, Liberalism, and the American Revolution* (Durham, NC: Duke University Press, 1990); Thomas L. Pangle, *The Spirit of Modern Republicanism: The Moral Vision of the American Founders and the Philosophy of Locke* (Chicago: University of Chicago Press, 1990); Jerome Huyler, *Locke in America: The Moral Philosophy of the Founding Era* (Lawrence: University of Kansas Press, 1995).

of the 1950s, Leo Strauss, political theorist and classicist at the University of Chicago, condemned Locke's *Two Treatises* as a book that "justifies the emancipation of acquisitiveness" and did so in ways that betray Locke's position as the "most famous and most influential of all modern natural right teachers."[47] A decade later in the 1960s, political theorist C. B. Macpherson, at the University of Toronto, accused Locke—particularly in his treatment of money as a matter of compact and consent—of being the slippery and elusive promoter of "possessive individualism" and absolute property rights.[48]

In 1980, Tully published *A Discourse on Property: John Locke and His Adversaries*, proving himself to be, among students of Locke, far more cognizant of the humane and communitarian side of Locke in the *Two Treatises*, refuting both capitalist and libertarian readings of the book. With this step, Tully manages to do number of things of relevance for my project. He stresses the persistent moral limits that Locke sees as inherent in property rights. These limits are particularly germane to learning's intellectual properties, in which property rights are about collective standards around accreditation and use, rather than absolute or unqualified possession. He uncovers a communitarian strand in Locke's concept of property use: "There is, therefore, no right in land, as such," Tully writes, "but only a use right in improved land conditional upon the use of its products."[49] While Tully's original reading faced a barrage of criticism, to which he responded by altering such views as the dominance of communal rights, while he maintained his emphasis on Locke's position that "the Regulating and Preserving of Property" is "only for the Publick Good" (2.3).[50] This is the Locke who during the 1690s took on the

47. Leo Strauss, *Natural Right and History* (Chicago: University of Chicago Press, 1950), 165, 242. "Locke still thought that he had to prove that the unlimited acquisition of wealth is not unjust or morally wrong" (246). Strauss, who would otherwise deny Locke's claim on natural law, holds that "the need for natural right is as evident today as it has been for centuries and even millennia" (2). Strauss also ranked Locke (as he had been driven into exile) among the persecuted writers, who as a result "concealed their views only far enough to protect themselves as well as possible from persecution; had they been more subtle than that, they would have defeated their purpose, which was to enlighten an ever-increasing number of people who were not philosophers" ("Persecution and the Art of Writing" *Social Research* 8, no. 4 [1941]: 500).

48. "Locke has justified the specifically capitalist appropriation of land and money": C. B. Macpherson, *The Political Theory of Possessive Individualism: Hobbes to Locke* (Oxford: Oxford University Press, 1962), 208. Macpherson was much criticized for his portrayal of Locke, with Isaiah Berlin caricaturing Macpherson's portrayal thusly: "Locke is a capitalist wolf in medieval, natural law, sheep's clothing" ("Hobbes, Locke and Professor Macpherson," *Political Quarterly* 35, no. 4 [1964]: 461 note 1).

49. Tully, *Discourse on Property*, 123.

50. G. A. Cohen, for example, refers to Tully's "welfarist intentions" as "a misuse of Locke's texts" and to his "extravagant conclusion" on community ownership: *Self-Ownership, Freedom, and Equality* (Cambridge: Cambridge University Press, 1995), 188, 194. In response to his critics,

Stationers' Company in successfully advocating an end to the printer monopolies and censorship.

Yet over the course of the decade following the publication of his Locke book, Tully came to realize the extent to which Locke had been influenced by arguments defending settler land claims against Indigenous peoples during that earlier period.[51] As a result, Tully realized, Locke constructed a theory of property that is premised on Indigenous peoples not having a property in the traditional territories on which they have always lived. For want of cultivating that land, they were wasting it. In Tully's words, Locke failed to credit the "planning, coordination, skills and activities involved in native hunting, gathering, fishing, and non-sedentary agriculture," all of which "did not 'waste' the land" but used it in "more ecologically benign ways."[52] At the same time, Tully saw how Indigenous peoples were using the arguments of Locke's theory of civil government to actively resist the abrogation of their rights. They used Locke's theory "once again to criticize and transcend the ideological constraint that he placed upon it," Tully writes, and "to expose injustice and justify resistance to it."[53] Learning's right of use enables just such moves with Locke. Using the *Two Treatises* in this way, both to critique its failures and

---

which included changes in his thinking, James Tully writes: "This constant activity of working on and changing one's understanding—of past thought and one's relation to it, and using this exercise as a way of freeing oneself from the customary and stultifying ways of thought in the present—is what the history of political philosophy is about" ("Differences in the Interpretation of Locke on Property," in *An Approach to Political Philosophy: Locke in Contexts* [Cambridge: Cambridge University Press, 1993], 125).

51. Tully uncovers likely sources for Locke's line of argument in a series of colonial pamphlets responding to New England land disputes from 1630 to 1690; they were composed by John Winthrop, John Cotton, and other Puritans who defended their "natural rights" to the territories of Indigenous peoples without their consent: "The arguments and the very terms used in the pamphlets [advocating 'appropriation by cultivation']," Tully writes, "are strikingly similar to chapter five [Of Property] of the *Two Treatises*. No author puts forward an account that is as theoretically sophisticated as Locke's, but the basic terminology, premises, and conclusions for such a theory are present" ("Rediscovering America: The Two Treatises and Aboriginal Rights," in *Approach to Political Philosophy*, 149).

52. Ibid., 156, 163. Locke could have known better, having in his collection Gabriel Sagard's *Histoire du Canada et voyages que les Frères mineur recollects* (Paris: Claude Sonnius, 1636), a record of missionary life among the hospitable and compassionate Huron people who educated Sagard in the fruitful, productive use of the land: Anne Talbot, *"The Great Ocean of Knowledge": The Influence of Travel Literature on the Work of John Locke* (Leiden: Brill, 2010), 21-44. As for the academic influence of Locke's misreading, see Laslett crediting Locke as a founder of "the field of comparative anthropology," with the larger nod to the *Essay*: "Introduction," 98; and Waldron names him "a pathfinder" of "political anthropology"; "John Locke: Social Contract versus Political Anthropology," *Review of Politics* 51, no. 1 (1989): 9.

53. Tully, "Rediscovering America," 176. Tully emphasizes Locke's checks and balances in his "enduring delegation of constitutional government, limited by the popular rights to dissent from and resist abuses of political power" (ibid.).

build on its principles—that is, to play it against itself—has the further advantage of being able to address the many generations of readers who, after all, share this work in common given how often it is taught to students. At issue is the importance of returning to emblematic works, not to somehow correct them retroactively, but to work with and against their legacy in what we continue to take for granted.

Tully was able to direct his reinterpretation and new understanding of the *Two Treatises* to some greater public use by serving as advisor to the Mohawk people and the Royal Commission on Aboriginal Peoples established by the Canadian government in 1991. The *Report of the Royal Commission* cites Tully on how "Locke draws the immensely influential conclusion that Europeans are free to settle and acquire property rights to vacant land in America by agricultural cultivation without the consent of the Aboriginal people."[54] Tully went on to work out a political philosophy in which "a just and practical relationship of negotiation between the Aboriginal and non-Aboriginal people of Canada" can be established "that brings reconciliation."[55] In 1999, he joined forces with Bear Clan Mohawk scholar Gerald Taiaiake Alfred to found the Indigenous Governance Program at the University of Victoria. The program is preparing a new generation of Indigenous leaders, even as the long overdue treaty negotiations between the First Nations peoples and the Canadian government are now underway in British Columbia. In Tully's work with the Nisga'a Nation and the Haida Nation on the treaty negotiation process, he notes how political *consent* and *dissent*, so critical to Locke's project, are now being redefined in a recognition of rights beyond anything Locke had dreamt of in his philosophy.[56] By the same token, Indigenous scholars are introducing into the universities new ways and means of learning where once their people were, at best, objects of sympathetic ethnological study, much as Locke cast them in the *Two Treatises*.[57]

54. *Report of the Royal Commission on Aboriginal Peoples* (Ottawa: Department of Indian and Northern Affairs, 1996), 48, which at this point is citing James Tully, "Aboriginal Property and Western Theory," 159.

55. This is from the modified version of the paper James Tully prepared for the Royal Commission: "The Negotiation of Reconciliation," in *Public Philosophy in a New Key*, vol. 1 (Cambridge: Cambridge University Press, 2008), 224.

56. James Tully, "Conclusion: Consent, Hegemony, Dissent in Treaty Negotiations," in *Consent among Peoples*, ed. J. Webber and C. MacLeod (Vancouver: University of British Columbia Press, 2010), 248–49.

57. See, for example, Sandy Grande, *Red Critical Theory: Native American Social and Political Thought* (Lanham, MD: Rowman and Littlefield, 2004); Devon Abbott Mihesuah and Angela Cavender Wilson, eds., *Indigenizing the Academy: Transforming Scholarship and Empowering Communities* (Lincoln: University of Nebraska Press, 2004); and Linda Tuhiwai Smith, *Decolonizing Methodolo-*

While working on this book, I had the chance to sit down with Professor Tully in his office at the University of Victoria to discuss what I saw as his shift from the close study of Locke's political philosophy to the application of that scholarship to First Nations property rights in Canada. I explained to him that I saw something heroic in his own turn from Locke to those who suffered his misuse. The shift on his part seemed a particularly responsible exercise of the scholar's right of use. That is, in uncovering the extent to which Locke's *Two Treatises* had been used to legitimate government and private land claims made against Indigenous peoples, this leading Locke scholar felt compelled to set a corrective course with his scholarship by seeking to redress this insidious use of Locke. No one was more knowledgeable about Locke than Tully, but to continue to work directly on Locke's political philosophy was no longer a responsible use of this expertise, given the option of assisting with Indigenous land right claims. Tully was a little taken aback by my somewhat schematic reading of his career path, as he had not, he indicated, looked at it in just that way. Still, he was appreciative, although I am hardly alone in commending his work.[58]

Within a few years of his publishing the *Two Treatises of Government*, John Locke became involved in the reform of printing regulations in Britain. He mounted what was, in effect, a lobbying campaign to put an end to book censorship and the perpetual monopolies of the Stationers' Company, which he also proposed that it be replaced with legislation far more sympathetic to the interests of learning. Although Locke died in 1704, his campaign was a part of all that contributed to the first modern intellectual property law, the Statute of Anne 1710. His lobbying for learning, as well as the passing of this act, is what I discuss next and finally in this prehistory of intellectual property.

---

gies: Research and Indigenous Peoples, 2nd ed. (London: Zed Books, 2012). For intellectual property issues, see Catherine Bell and Val Napoleon, eds., *First Nations Cultural Heritage and Law: Case Studies, Voices, and Perspectives* (Vancouver: University of British Columbia Press, 2009).

58. For example, David Armitage praises Tully for pursuing a "public philosophy with a practical intent": "Probing the Foundations of Tully's Public Philosophy," *Political Theory* 39, no. 1 (2011): 125.

CHAPTER TWELVE

An Act for the Encouragement
of Learning

On January 2, 1693, after publishing a few years earlier two major philo-sophical statements—one on intellect and knowledge (*Essay*), the other on property (*Two Treatises*)—Locke decided to do something about the state of intellectual property in Britain. On that day, Locke wrote to his friend Ed-ward Clarke, then a Whig member of Parliament from Taunton (and mar-ried to a relative of his) with his concerns about the book trade. Parliament was considering the renewal, once again, of the thirty-year-old Licensing of the Press Act of 1662. It had last been approved in 1685, under James II, for another seven years. In his letter, Locke asked Clarke to consider the dam-age done by the Stationers' Company monopolies granted by this act:

> I wish you would have some care of Book buyers as well as all of Book sellers
> and the Company of Stationers who haveing got a Patent for all or most of the
> Ancient Latin Authors (by what right or pretence I know not) claime the text to
> be theirs and soe will not suffer fairer and more correct Editions than any thing
> they print here or with new Comments to be imported . . . whereby these most
> usefull books are excessively dear to schollers.[1]

The awarding of these patents could keep, he protests, a new edition of *Aesop's Fables* from being printed. The edition of *Aesop* he likely had in mind, he fails to mention, is the English-Latin edition of the *Fables* that he had prepared some years before for educational purposes, only to face just such patent

---

1. John Locke, "1586. Locke to Edward Clarke, 2 January 1693," in *Correspondence of John Locke*, ed. E. S. de Beer, vol. 4 (Oxford: Oxford University Press, 1989), 614-15.

hurdles.[2] Locke's letter, however, was too little too late. The Licensing of the Press Act was renewed in March of 1693.[3] It was, however, for only a two-year term, making it clear that members of Parliament had lost their enthusiasm for book licensing. Locke must have understood it as such. He began to campaign in earnest against any further renewal of the act. As part of that effort, Locke worked with Edward Clarke as well as John Freke, a lawyer and further Whig lobbyist, and John Somers, who held the parliamentary post of lord keeper of the great seal and was a member of the Privy Council.[4] In his letters, Locke refers to this group as his "Colledg" (college).

The original passing of the Licensing of the Press Act in 1662 had been the latest measure of English press regulation, which dated back to actions taken by Henry VIII in the 1530s.[5] The chamber required that books be licensed before being printed, while it also restricted the number of master printers, as well as the importing of books from abroad.[6] During the English

2. Locke's printer Awnsham Churchill requested the right from the Stationers' Company to print what became Locke's *Æsop's Fables, in English & Latin, Interlineary, for the Benefit of Those Who Not Having a Master, Would Learn Either of These Tongues* (London: A. and J. Churchill, 1703), which was granted on December 12, 1695, enabling him to print one thousand copies without having to pay the Company for this privilege, although the book was only published eight years later: Donald F. McKenzie and Maureen Bell, *A Chronology and Calendar of Documents Relating to the London Book Trade, 1641–1700* (Oxford: Oxford University Press, 2005), 199, 207. On the other hand, Roger L'Estrange, who had earlier served Charles II as press licensor, published a "registered" edition of the fables in 1692 with Awnsham Churchill and a number of other printers: *Fables, of Aesop and Other Eminent Mythologists: With Morals and Reflection* (London: R. Sare, A. & J. Churchill, et al., 1692).

3. In the House of Lords, eleven dissenting Peers issued a statement of protest against the act, as it "subjects all Learning and true Information to the arbitrary Will and Pleasure of a mercenary, and, perhaps ignorant, Licenser, destroys the Properties of Authors in their Copies; and sets up many Monopolies": *A Complete Collection of the Lords' Protests, from the First upon Record in the Reign of Henry the Third, to the Present Time*, vol. 1 (London, 1768), 163.

4. Locke was, during his period of exile (1683–89), part of a similarly informal group known as "Collegium privatum medicum" in Amsterdam; Locke also reports that Lady Masham "gives her service to the Colledg" ("1845. Locke to John Freke and Edward Clarke, 8 February [1695]," *Correspondence*, 5:265).

5. Ronan Deazley, "Commentary on Henrician Proclamation 1538," in *Primary Sources on Copyright (1450–1900)*, ed. L. Bently and M. Kretschmer (Cambridge: University of Cambridge), online.

6. This licensing of books can be traced back to Henry VIII's November 16, 1538, proclamation requiring, in light of "wronge teachynge and naughtye printed bokes," that books receive "his maiesties special licence": cited by Alfred W. Pollard, "The Regulation of the Book Trade in the Sixteenth Century," *Library* 7, no. 25 (1916): 22–23. See Adrian Johns's helpful table of "measures regulating the press, 1586–1710 (*The Nature of the Book: Print and Knowledge in the Making* [Chicago: University of Chicago Press, 1998], 232). Johns cautions that "evasion, at least, was extensive; just as a large proportion of published books were never entered [in the Stationer's Register] so a large proportion lacked licenses" and that whenever it "lapsed pamphlets and piracies seemed to flourish" (234).

Civil War, which ran from 1642 to 1651 and saw the Star Chamber abolished, Parliament passed a similar Licensing Order of 1643. Enter John Milton, otherwise a supporter of the Parliamentarians' struggle against the Royalists. The poet Milton found his compatriot's Licensing Order objectionable in the extreme. In an unlicensed 1644 pamphlet entitled *Areopagitica,* he offered a defense of the learning threatened by licensing. The pamphlet was boldly identified as "A SPEECH of Mr. JOHN MILTON For the Liberty of Unlicenc'd PRINTING, to the PARLAMENT OF ENGLAND."[7] It followed on the heels of his much contested and anonymous tract in favor of divorce. The Stationers' Company cited this earlier tract as reason enough to continue the tradition of book regulation.

In *Areopagitica,* Milton argues that restrictions on press freedom "will be primely to the discouragement of all learning and the stop of Truth."[8] It will be to the detriment of "the purest efficacy and extraction of the living intellect [i.e., the author] that bred" the books in the first place.[9] He tied his fight to the interests of learning and writing, as such licensing constitutes a "dishonor and derogation to the author, to the book, to the privilege and dignity of learning."[10] Milton asks, "How can a man teach with authority, which is the life of teaching, how can he be a doctor in his own book ... under the correction of his patriarchal licenser?"[11] If Milton's pamphlet did little to incite a revoking of the Licensing Order, his impassioned, eloquent defense of press freedom, learning, and the author's intellectual property rights were likely influences on both Locke (who had a copy of Milton's political works) and Daniel Defoe in the years leading up to the Statute of Anne 1710. In particular, Milton's theme that learning is something to be encouraged in any regulation of the press—given that book licensing is "the

---

7. John Milton, "Areopagitica," in *Milton's Prose Writings*, ed. K. M. Burton (London: Dent, 1958), 149.

8. Ibid.

9. Ibid., 149. Milton refers to "learning" twenty-eight times in the course of his essay, treating it as a source of non-commercial property: "Truth and understanding are not such wares as to be monopolized and traded in by tickets and statutes and standards. We must not think to make a staple commodity of all knowledge in the land, to mark and license like our broadcloths and our woolpacks" (168–69). Mark Rose argues that Milton's essay is "a key document in the emergence of the bourgeois public sphere," in which Milton "portraying himself as a private man addressing the public at large through parliament, participates in the discourse of the public sphere": "The Public Sphere and the Emergence of Copyright: Areopagitica, the Stationers' Company, and the Statute of Anne," *Tulsa Journal of Technology and Intellectual Property* 12 (2009): 132.

10. Milton, "Areopagitica," 167.

11. Ibid., 167.

greatest discouragement and affront, that can be offer'd to learning and to learned men"—was clearly echoed in the 1710 statute.[12]

Press regulation continued during the English Civil War and then into the Commonwealth and Protectorate under Cromwell that lasted until the Restoration in 1660. The growing political influence of newsbooks made them a favorite target among the censors. The press faced further restrictive measures from Parliament in 1647 and 1649 (with Milton at this point serving Cromwell as Latin Secretary, placing him in the very role of book licenser).[13] Then, with the Restoration of the Crown, a chastened Parliament instituted a new round of book licensing measures in 1662. This was in the form of "An Act for Preventing the Frequent Abuses in Printing Seditious Treasonable and Unlicensed Books and Pamphlets and for Regulating of Printing and Printing Presses." The Licensing of the Press Act 1662, as it was known, restricted printing to London, York, and, in recognition of the universities' historic rights, Oxford and Cambridge.[14]

The act continued the close censorious and monopolistic association of Crown, church, and Stationers' Company. It was regarded by the Whig opposition to Charles II as a perfect example of Restoration excess. Parliament allowed the act to lapse in 1679, amid the hostilities that Charles II was facing during the Exclusion Crisis from Lord Shaftesbury and others. It was probably clear that the ensuing Whig-Tory pamphlet war was unlikely to be contained by any licensing regime. The Licensing of the Press Act of 1662 was renewed again in 1685, when the not-to-be-excluded James II took the throne. Just as a similar act had endured the Civil War earlier in the century, the 1662 act initially survived the Glorious Revolution of 1688 that deposed James II. Yet book licensing must have struck some as not entirely consistent with the Bill of Rights of 1689, which limited the power of the monarchy.

---

12. Milton, "Areopagitica," 166. In 1667, the book licensor Rev. Thomas Tomkyns is said to have reluctantly granted a license to *Paradise Lost*, given the light it accorded Satan: David Masson, "Introduction: Biographical and Expository," in *Poetical Works of John Milton*, vol. 2, ed. David Masson (London: Macmillan, 1890), 6.

13. Referring to Milton's licensing of *Mercurius Politicus*, a weekly semiofficial Commonwealth newsbook, and on Milton's continuing influence on debates over press regulation, at least up to 1707, see Ernest Sirluck, "Areopagitica and a Forgotten Licensing Controversy," *Review of English Studies* 11, no. 43 (1960): 260–74.

14. Astbury reports that during the 1690s, the universities entered into an agreement with the Stationers' Company not to compete on the sales of English Stock-books, which included cheap editions of schoolbooks, psalm-books, and almanacs, further reflecting the univesities' struggle to find the right trade off of privileges to make a go of scholarly publishing: "The Renewal of the Licensing Act in 1693 and Its Lapse in 1695," *Library* ser. 5, vol. 33, no. 4 (1978): 297 note 2.

There was pressure, particularly from the Whigs, to put an end to press regulation and monopoly once and for all.

LOCKE'S MEMO

The times were ripe by 1694 for Locke's "college" to weigh in on book licensing. Edward Clarke was appointed that year to the Commons committee to review laws about to expire, the 1662 Licensing Act among them. To assist Clarke in preventing this act from being renewed yet again, Locke prepared a memorandum. He begins by sounding the familiar trumpet, after Milton, in favor of a free press: "I know not why a man should not have liberty to print what ever he would speake."[15] To have to obtain a license to print a work in advance was like "gagging a man for fear he should talk heresy or sedition."[16] Yet he recommended some stipulations. He specifies that the printer or author be clearly identified in the book to ensure that someone will "be answerable for" any transgressions of the law they have committed with the book.[17] The risk of that transgression, however, is little enough for Locke, compared to the misuse that exudes from the Licensing of the Press Act: "By this act England loses in general," as he puts it at one point. "Scholars in particular are ground [down] and nobody gets [anything] but a lazy ignorant Company of Stationers. To say no worse of them. But anything rather than let mother church be disturbed in her opinion or impositions, by any bold voice from the press."[18]

Locke then moves into what matters at least as much to him as press freedom. This is the current "restraint of printing the classic authors."[19] He sarcastically asks after the value of such restraint: "Does [it] any way prevent the printing of seditious and treasonable pamphlets, which is the title and pretense of this act."[20] He is not objecting to the prosecution of sedition, though he might well have, having been a candidate for such charges when he fled

15. John Locke, "Liberty of the Press (1694-5)," in *Political Essays*, ed. Mark Goldie (Cambridge: Cambridge University Press, 1997), 331. Geoff Kemp notes that Spinoza and Milton precede Locke in this fight: "The 'End of Censorship' and the Politics of Toleration, from Locke to Sacheverell," *Parliamentary History* 31 (2012): 52–53. Astbury observes that Locke's critique resembles that of other contemporary pamphlets on many points, with some found in Locke's collection of these works: "Renewal of the Licensing Act," 307.

16. Locke, "Liberty of the Press."

17. Ibid., 331.

18. Ibid., 335.

19. Ibid., 334.

20. Ibid.

to Holland in 1683. Rather, what bothers him is how badly learning is served by the Stationers' Company: "Scholars cannot but at excessive rates have the fair and correct editions of these books and the comments [commentaries] on them printed beyond [the] seas"; they are left with "scandalously illprinted" local editions, given the lack of competition.[21] To bring the point home, Locke refers to an imported edition of "Tully's Works" (Marcus Tullius Cicero) which he found to be "a very fine edition, with new corrections made by Gronovius, who takes the pains to compare that which was thought the best edition"; the work was "seized and kept a good while in [the Company's] custody," before it was sold with the booksellers "demanding 6s. 8d. per book."[22] The problem is the overly broad and exclusive patents issued to the Stationers' Company without end or limit on Cicero's works.

Locke's overarching concern for scholars' access rights leads him, finally, to a backhanded commendation of at least one of the current act's clauses. The act requires that a copy of every book printed be sent to, as he puts it, "the public libraries of both universities." This was initially instituted, you may recall, by Thomas Bodley for the university library at Oxford. Locke complains that this requirement of sending books to the libraries "will be found to be mightily if not wholly neglected" by the Stationers' Company, however keenly it otherwise supported the act.[23] The public libraries' book deposit policy at Oxford and Cambridge represents a recognition of learning's distinct economic and political position, which has long been sustained by such compacts.

In the face of the Stationers' Company's perpetual monopolies, Locke calls for term limits on intellectual property rights, much as he qualified property rights in the *Second Treatise* with his sufficiency and spoilage provisos. "And for those [printers and booksellers] who purchase copies from authors that live now and write," he states in his Licensing Act memo, "it may be reasonable to limit their property to a certain number of years after the death of the author or the first printing of the book as suppose 50 or 70 years."[24] This would allow for new editions of older works, compared to current difficulties, he points

21. Ibid., 332.

22. Ibid., 332–33.

23. Ibid., 336.

24. Ibid., 337. Joseph Lowenstein judges that Locke's "opposition to perpetual copyright is one of the most consequential aspects of Locke's critique of the licensing bill," while pointing out that it was inspired by the "limited-term privilege" of "the old institution of the patent": *The Author's Due: Printing and the Prehistory of Copyright* (Chicago: University of Chicago Press, 2002), 230. In 1998, the US Copyright Act extended the length of copyright from fifty to seventy years after the author's death.

out, when "the Company of Stationers have a monopoly of all the classic authors."[25] Locke also objected to restrictions on importing books. This opposition aligns with his spoilage proviso with regard to property rights. Foreign books could augment English learning, but instead the ban effectively wasted this potential. His friend Edward Clarke took up this theme of waste in his report to the House of Lords by identifying how delays and other restrictions on book importers caused by the act meant that, as he vividly puts it, "part of his Stock lie dead; or the Books, if wet, may rot and perish."[26]

When Locke bemoans in his memo that the act is "so manifest an invasion on the trade, liberty, and property of the subject," I take it that what is under siege are the intellectual property rights of the learned and learning.[27] As Locke sees it, access to this literature must be facilitated, rather than impeded by such unfair trade practices as perpetual monopolies and book blockades: "That any person or company should have patents for the sole printing of ancient authors," he writes in the memo, "is very unreasonable and injurious to learning."[28] This was, of course, Milton's theme, in objecting to a licensing of the press that inevitably discourages learning.

LOCKE'S FURTHER REFLECTIONS ON THE PRESS

Not long after Locke's memo, in 1695, Clarke began to work with his fellow legislator Robert Harley on a "Bill for the better Regulating of Printing and Printing Presses." Their proposed bill had the virtue of exempting from state licensing those books exploring heraldry, science, and the arts. It offered no protection of Stationers' Company monopolies or the universities' printing privileges.[29] Locke had not been involved in the drafting of Clarke and Harley's first go at the new bill, but he jumped in soon enough with proposed amendments to it.[30] Although a number of Locke's suggestions for

25. Locke, "Liberty of the Press," 332.

26. "Commons Reasons for Disagreeing to the Clause for Reviving the Printing Act," *Journal of the House of Lords* 15 (1695): 546.

27. Locke, "Liberty of the Press," 336.

28. Ibid., 337. Locke continues: "Tis very absurd and ridiculous that anyone now living should pretend to have a property in or a power to dispose of the property of any copies or writings of authors who lived before printing was known and used in Europe" (ibid.).

29. Cited by Astbury, "Renewal of the Licensing Act," 321. Among those calling for a renewal of the Licensing Act was John Wallis, book licenser and professor of geometry at Oxford, who warned that the university's loss of privileges in printing profitable books would leave it unable to subsidize costly scholarly works (a refrain still heard from university presses today): Astbury, "Renewal of the Licensing Act," 322.

30. Ibid., 312.

the bill have since been lost, what is clear is that he was now prepared to make far more of the author's intellectual property rights than he had in his earlier memo. He proposed to Clarke that the new bill "secure the author's property in his copy" for a limited time.[31] He tied this safeguarding of the author's property in the work to a registration process that, in the first instance, protected the rights of learning. The printed book was initially to be deposited *"for the use of the publique librarys of the said Universities."* After this deposit, the bill "shall vest a privileg in the Author . . . for __ years from the first edition."[32] The exact number of years he left up to Parliament to set, although he had earlier advocated fifty to seventy years after the death of the author.

Consider how Locke frames his case. Books are intended for the *use* of others through, for example, the public libraries of the universities, while authors are vested with a limited privilege in their books as an incentive to produce further works. There is no sense of outright or absolute ownership. He is treating intellectual property as something one has an interest in or some claim on, much like how in the *Two Treatises* he writes of "how one . . . comes to have a *Property* in any thing."[33] In the case of books, the author has a property in a book that earns the author a limited-term privilege with the book (as well as a longer-term accreditation for having written it, which is not part of the proposed legislation). He also proposes that authors have a further right to control any subsequent editions of their work. In drafting a clause to this effect, he left it to Parliament—democrat that he is—to decide the duration of the author's rights, so that no book "within [blank] years after its first edition [would] be reprinted with or without the name of the author to it without authority given in writing by the author or somebody entitled by him."[34] At the time of writing this, he was likely engaged in revising

31. Locke, "Appendix, Documents relating to the termination of the Licensing Act, 1695," in *Correspondence*, 5:795.

32. Ibid., 5:796.

33. John Locke, *Two Treatises of Government*, ed. Peter Laslett (Cambridge: Cambridge University Press, 1988), 2.27.

34. Locke, "Liberty of the Press," 338. The "[blank]" is Locke's. An earlier anonymous pamphlet complained of how, despite that "the Property of English Authors hath been always owned as Sacred among the Traders," those who wrote commentaries on books "have been compelled to pay [licensors] their extravagant Demands, for using the Bible Text to Comment upon"; as well, "many learned Authors have been defrauded of their Rights thereby, who, after many years Pain and Study, and afterwards by a bare Delivery of their Books to be Licensed or Transcribed, have been barred by surreptitious Entries made in the said Register": *Reasons Humbly Offered to Be Considered before the Act of Printing Be Renewed (unless with Alterations) Viz. for Freedom of Trade in Lawful Books, and Setting Severe Penalties on Scandalous and Seditious Books against the Government* (London, 1692), 3.

the third editions of both the *Essay concerning Human Understanding* and the *Two Treatises*.[35] In giving authors control of subsequent editions, he is advocating for the authors' interests and responsibilities in correcting and improving their work with each new edition.

The Stationers' Company lobbied vigorously against Clarke and Harley's "Better Regulating of Printing" bill, and it stalled and died on the floor of the Commons in 1695. The Company, which sought a straightforward renewal of the Licensing Act of 1662, protested that the reforms proposed by Clarke and Harley were "wanting as to the Security of [our] Property," which was a fair enough estimation of their intent.[36] Drawing on Locke's theme of the loss to learning, Clarke retaliated by circulating objections to the Company's unfair trade practices. Yet even with the failure of this bill, the House of Commons and the House of Lords still took the dramatic step of voting that year not to renew the Licensing of the Press Act of 1662. The act expired on May 3, 1695, putting an end to well over a century of oppressive and easily corrupted press regulation. The great nineteenth-century historian and politician Thomas Babington Macaulay declared the act's expiry meant nothing less than that "English literature was emancipated, and emancipated for ever, from the control of the government."[37] Closer to the ground and the practical outcome of ending regulation, Sir William Trumbull wrote in a letter at the time, of how "since the Act for Printing Expired London swarmes with seditious Pamphletts."[38]

Locke's part in the defeat of the Licensing Act led his biographer, Maurice Cranston, a political science professor at the London School of Economics, to praise his subject's political realism, for "unlike Milton, who called for liberty in the name of liberty, Locke was content to ask for liberty in the name of trade, and unlike Milton, he achieved his end."[39] It does suggest that philosophers might join with the poets who are "the unacknowledged legislators

35. The *Essay*'s "Epistle to the Reader" contains Locke's reflections on revisions made across five editions (1689-1706) up to the last year of his life, with provisions in his will for the final edition; a remarkably detailed publishing history of Locke's works is available in Jean S. Yolton, *John Locke: A Descriptive Bibliography* (Bristol: Thoemmes, 1998).

36. Cited by Raymond Astbury, "The Renewal of the Licensing Act in 1693 and Its Lapse in 1695," *Library* ser. 5, vol. 33, no. 4 (1978): 312.

37. Thomas Babington Macaulay, *The History of England, from the Accession of James II*, vol. 4 (Philadelphia: Butler, 1856), 377.

38. Cited by Astbury, "Renewal of the Licensing Act," 317.

39. Maurice Cranston, *John Locke: A Biography* (Oxford: Oxford University Press, 1957), 387. "Clearly, the Commons' objections owed much to Locke's Memorandum of 1694, even though his expressions of animosity towards Court and Church as the leading champions of preprinting censorship were expunged": Astbury, "Renewal of the Licensing Act," 315.

of the world," as Shelley had it in his defense of poetry.[40] What mattered to Locke "in the name of trade" was the trade in learning, which he had occasion to address briefly that same year of 1695 with the publication of his last substantial publication, *The Reasonableness of Christianity as Delivered in Scriptures*.

In this book, Locke sets out the various ways in which reason serves revelation, while seeking to correct another common misconception about morality and ethics. Our knowledge of such matters has for too long, he notes, been treated as a "private Possession" alone, when it is always already something more than that:

> Thus the whole stock of Human Knowledge is claimed by every one, as his private Possession, as soon as he (profiting by others Discoveries) has got it into his own mind; And so it is: But not properly by his own single Industry, nor of his own Acquisition. He studies, 'tis true, and takes pains to make a progress in what others have delivered; But their pains were of another sort, who first brought those Truths to light, which he afterwards derives from them. He that Travels the Roads now, applauds his own strength and legs that have carried him so far in such a scantling of time. And ascribes all to his own Vigor, little considering how much he owes to their pains, who cleared the Woods, drained the Bogs, built the Bridges, and made the Ways passable; without which he might have toiled much with little progress.[41]

There may be little original in Locke pointing out that we stand on the shoulders of giants or at least owe a debt to those who came before. However, he is also setting out how the "whole stock of Human Knowledge" operates as a commons, within which individuals may make "progress" through their studies and pain but that they owe consideration to those who "made the Ways passable." It is the very business of learning to create a public record of those "who first brought those Truths to light," as he puts it here. The intellectual properties of learning are about the rights and responsibilities required "to make a progress in what others have delivered," just as this history of ideas captured in scholars' bibliographies keeps them from claiming any of it as a "private Possession."

40. Percy Shelley, *A Defense of Poetry*, ed. Mary Shelley (Indianapolis: Bobbs-Merrill, 1904), 90.

41. John Locke, "The Reasonableness of Christianity as Delivered in Scriptures," in *Writings on Religion*, ed. Victor Nuovo (Oxford: Oxford University Press, 2002), 199–200. With thanks to Joanna Picciotto who "made the Ways passable" for me by pointing out this passage in Locke: *Labors of Innocence in Early Modern England* (Cambridge, MA: Harvard University Press, 2010), 265.

Upon his death in 1704, Locke provided in his will for the distribution of a number of his titles to the Bodleian Library of the University of Oxford, as if to recognize the public claim on these works. In the will, he refers to how the Reverend Dr. Hudson, Library Keeper of the Bodleian Library, had written to him "desireing of me for the said Library the books whereof I was the Author."[42] Locke explains that he had earlier sent those works "publishd under my name," only to receive back a note indicating that these books "were not understood fully to answer the request."[43] With this last will and testament, Locke states that "I do hereby further give to the publick Library of the University of Oxford these following books . . . [including] two Treatises of Government (whereof Mr. Churchill has published severall editions, but all very incorrect)."[44] As such, he settled his debt to the public property rights of learning, much as he paid homage to the scholar's eternal lament of corrections needed. The Statute of Anne, though he did not live to see its passing, would reflect his balancing the rights of authors and learning.

PIRACY'S INTERLUDE

Immediately following on the expiry of print licensing in 1695, the streets of London were filled with the sight and sound of those hawking newspapers, cheap pirated editions of books and magazines, scandalous and obscene pamphlets. As Locke had held, the existing libel and blasphemy laws were brought to bear with search warrants and arrests. As well, new laws were added, such as the 1698 Act for the More Effectual Suppressing of Blasphemy and Prophaneness.[45] The Stationers' Company denounced, with increasing rancor and outrage, a market flooded with cheap reprints of its titles. Its members cast such acts as *piracy*. The term started to be used in the 1680s for those who "stole" titles assigned to others in their Register.[46]

42. Locke, "Will," in *Correspondence*, 8:425.
43. Ibid.
44. Ibid., 8:426.
45. Kemp, "The 'End of Censorship,'" 55. The act made it a crime to deny the Holy Trinity in speaking, writing, or teaching, which Locke had done, in effect, a few years earlier simply by not mentioning it in *The Reasonableness of Christianity*. Locke was not prosecuted nor the book suppressed, although he engaged in an exchange of published letters, beginning in 1696, with Bishop Stillingfleet, who attacked his *Essay* as a threat to the faith.
46. Adrian Johns, *Piracy: The Intellectual Property Wars from Gutenberg to Gates,* (Chicago: University of Chicago Press, 2009), 41. On the origins of the term, John Fell refers, in a 1674 letter, to the Stationers' Company as "land-pirats," for treading on the university's "propertie in Printing": cited by Johns, *Nature of the Book*, 344. The *Oxford English Dictionary* credits J. Mennes' *Recreation for Geniuses Head-peeces* in 1654 with first use of *piracy* in this sense.

It was, in fact, a free market for almost the first time in print materials. Gone were the monopolies that the Company's well-established printers and booksellers had enjoyed over the past century and more. The so-called pirates were not above citing lofty principles, to borrow a vivid instance from London bookseller Benjamin Motte a couple of decades later: "The World has an absolute and indisputable power over all that appear in print." Motte was defending his printing of an abridged edition of the *Philosophical Transactions* in 1722 (although he was ready to sue when his copyright on Jonathan Swift was infringed by a Dublin printer).[47]

The Stationers' Company was having none of the world-has-a-right bunk. It turned to Parliament for remedy. But reintroducing regulation was an up-hill battle. In the years following the Licensing Act's expiry, the Company promoted one unsuccessful parliamentary bill after another. In 1704, the year of Locke's death, a Bill to Restrain the Licentiousness of the Press was introduced into Parliament. As the force behind the bill, the Stationer's Company hid its economic interests behind the shield of the community's moral safety. The members of the House of Commons readily saw through it and were not inclined to return to Company monopolies. Across Europe, and especially in the haven for learning that was Holland, unlicensed printing and reprinting appeared to have a certain intellectual excitement going for it, amid the blustering, nose-thumbing piracy of a free press.[48]

Some were also prepared to speak out in support of authors' rights in book publishing, which had not played a part in the seventeenth-century licensed press. Among them was Daniel Defoe. This was well before he'd found his legs as a novelist, when he was still a pamphleteer and journalist. In 1703, Defoe published an anonymous defense of press liberty, *Essay on the Regulation of the Press*, which began: "All Men pretend the Licentiousness of the Press to be a publick Grievance, but it is much easier to say it is so, than to prove, or prescribe a proper Remedy."[49] Defoe had already, a year earlier in 1703, proven Locke's point about the sufficiency of post-publication prosecution. Defoe was

47. Cited by Johns, *Nature of the Book*, 353.

48. Among the reprint examples that Johns introduces is that of Locke's works which found pirating printers in "Dublin, Glasgow, Amsterdam, The Hague, Rotterdam, Geneva, Brussels, Paris, Leipzig, Uppsala, Jena, Mannheim, Milan, Naples, Stockholm (by order of the Swedish Riksdag, no less), and, ultimately, Boston" (50). Johns refers to "chain reactions of reappropriation, generally unauthorized, and often denounced," before concluding that "no piracy, we might say, no Enlightenment" (ibid.).

49. Daniel Defoe, *An Essay on the Regulation of the Press* (Oxford: Luttrell Society and Blackwell, 1948), 3.

charged with libel, after releasing an anonymous satirical pamphlet taking on the Church of England's regard for Dissenters. He was sentenced to be publicly pilloried on three occasions, but Defoe was not one to let an opportunity go to waste, and composed a *Hymn to the Pillory*—"HAIL! *Hi'roglyphick* State *Machin"*—which he had distributed during his time in the stocks, while arranging for his books to be sold nearby. Flowers were thrown at Defoe's feet, rather than rotten eggs.[50] Still, he ended up doing prison time for libel.[51]

In his *Essay on the Regulation of the Press*, Defoe follows Milton and Locke in pressing the point that the *"License of the Press"* was not consistent with "the Encouragement due to Learning" or "the Liberty of this Nation."[52] The encouragement of learning comes up more than once in Defoe's tract as the very thing about the press that needs to be protected. Defoe bemoans how "pirating Books in smaller Print, and meaner Paper" was, among other things and concurring with Milton, "a Discouragement to Learning."[53]

As it goes with the freedom to turn ideas to new purposes, this encouragement-of-learning theme was picked up by printers and booksellers as a promising line of attack on an unregulated press and print piracy. Beginning in 1706, the Stationers' Company was likely behind three anonymous petitions to Parliament, starting with the one-page *Reasons Humbly Offer'd for a Bill for the Encouragement of Learning, and the Improvement of Printing*.[54] This petition opens with a concern for the "Many Learned Men [who] have been at great Pains and Expence in Composing and Writing of Books." It takes a Lockean stance on the author's "undoubted Right to the Copy of his own Book, as being a Product of his own Labor." The petition reflects the Miltonic worry that "Learned Men will be wholly Discouraged from Propagating the most useful Parts of Knowledge." It introduces, in closing, the requisite

---

50. Paula R. Backscheider, *Daniel Defoe: His Life* (Baltimore: Johns Hopkins, 1989), 118. Daniel Defoe, *Hymn to the Pillory: An Online Edition*, ed. Jess McCarthy, online (2013).

51. Defoe was not alone in facing charges, as John Feather lists thirty-six works prosecuted for blasphemy, breach of parliamentary privilege, and like offences, between the end of licensing in 1695 and the Statute of Anne: "The Book Trade in Politics: The Making of the Copyright Act of 1710," *Publishing History* 8 (1980): 26.

52. Defoe, *Regulation of the Press*, 15. Defoe continued to protest, in his *Review*, the "Piracies, and Invasions of Property": cited by Ronan Deazley, "Commentary on Defoe's Essay on the Regulation of the Press (1704)" in *Primary Sources on Copyright (1450-1900): Britain*, ed. L. Bently and M. Kretschmer (Cambridge: University of Cambridge, 2008), online.

53. Defoe, *Regulation of the Press*, 27.

54. "Reasons Humbly Offer'd for a Bill for the Encouragement of Learning and Improvement of Printing" (London, 1706), in *Primary Sources on Copyright (1450-1900)*, ed. L. Bently and M. Kretschmer (Cambridge: University of Cambridge, 2008), online.

image of a bereft author's widow, in this case "of the late Arch-Bishop Til-lotson," who was generously provided for by "Booksellers," only to have this support threatened by print piracy.

In 1709, a further petition to Parliament presented "REASONS Humbly Offer'd," yet again, "for a "BILL for Encouragement of Learning."[55] This time the title additionally called for the "Securing the Property of Copies of Books to the Rightful Owners thereof." Learning became the focus of this battle over print regulation to a degree that far exceeded its slight and tenuous market share in the book trade.[56] The Stationers' Company's piracy complaints had recently been exacerbated by a flood of reprints from Scottish printers taking advantage of the 1707 Act of Union to forge a Great Britain of enterprising booksellers.[57] The 1709 petition was one of the last of what had been perhaps a dozen attempts on the part of the Stationers' Company, the Church of England, and even Oxford University to reinstate the Licensing Act or something very much like it.[58] In 1710, Britain's brief interlude of unregulated printing came to an end.

THE STATUTE OF ANNE 1710

If print piracy was the driving force behind this legislation, the Statute of Anne still amounts to far more than a legal remedy for a greatly disrupted if vibrant marketplace. Nor was it a return to the seventeenth-century compact among Crown, church, and guild. This new legislation combined the author's natural rights in a text with the public good of learning. In an initial draft, the Statute of Anne refers to "Books and Writings" as "the undoubted Property" of authors, with such property regarded as (in a Lockean phrase) "the Product of their Learning and Labor."[59] In the final version, the author's

---

55. "Reasons Humbly Offer'd for the Bill for the Encouragement of Learning, and for Securing the Property of Copies of Books to the Rightful Owners thereof" (London, 1709), in *Primary Sources on Copyright (1450–1900)*, ed. L. Bently and M. Kretschmer (Cambridge: University of Cambridge, 2008), online.

56. John Feather, *A History of British Publishing* (London: Routledge, 1988), 57–60.

57. "The invention of copyright was largely a response to a piracy feud overflowing with national resentments, namely the attempt of Scottish reprinters to compete with London's book trade": Johns, *Piracy*, 13.

58. 8 Anne, c.19. See *The Statute of Anne*, April 10, 1710, Avalon Project, Lillian Goldman Law Library, Yale University, 2008, online. Feather lists eleven unsuccessful bills relating to the book trade brought before Parliament between 1695 and 1710: "Book Trade in Politics," 22. Johns calculates that the Stationers' Company called on Parliament fifteen times seeking some form of legislative protection: *Nature of the Book*, 353.

59. Cited by R. Deazley, "Commentary on the *Statute of Anne* 1710," in *Primary Sources on Copyright (1450–1900): Britain*, ed. L. Bently and M. Kretschmer (Cambridge: University of Cambridge),

earning of this right is left implicit, for it is not being legislated; the author's property claim in a text is left to natural and common law. On the other hand, learning's role in motivating this legislation is made explicit in the statute's subtitle, which begins "An Act for the Encouragement of Learning."

The statute opens with the Stationers' Company's complaint that "printers, booksellers, and other persons have of late frequently taken the liberty of printing . . . books and other writings, without the consent of the authors or proprietors of such books and writings," which leads "too often to the ruin of them and their families."[60] Authors, as the natural owners of their compositions, have a right to profit from this labor. They are characterized as "learned men" who strive to "compose and write useful books."[61] Thus, the author (or assignee) "shall have the sole liberty of printing and reprinting such book and books for the term of fourteen years."[62] The author may forever be credited for having written the book—again, this natural right was not being legislated—but the exclusive right to make copies of the work was restricted to an initial period of fourteen years, with the prospect of renewing it for another fourteen years (while works registered prior to the statute are granted a continuing exclusive right to copy for twenty-one years). The statute requires that books "before such publication, be entered in the register book of the Company of Stationers, in such manner as hath been usual." This use of term limits with monopoly rights had been deployed for some time with patents granted for inventions. Such rights were regarded as a temporary "encouragement," or incentive, intended to ward off "ruin" while author and inventor prepared further contributions.

These limits also reflect the troubled politics of monopolies in this emerging liberal democracy, harking back to the Statute of Monopolies of 1624. That statute was an early parliamentary victory against King Charles I in curbing the widely abused royal prerogative of granting trade monopolies to

---

online. Additionally, the "Discouragement to Learning," a phrase used by Milton and Defoe, was in the original draft of the statute (ibid.).

60. Feather establishes the degree to which the Stationers' Company influenced the final wording of the statute—it did bear the expenses associated with seeing the statute through Parliament—which did not include being able to make changes to the term limit on copyright: "Book Trade in Politics," 36.

61. This language dates back to the Company's 1706 petition, which begins, "Whereas many Learned Men have been at great Pains and Expense . . .": "Reasons Humbly Offer'd for the Bill for the Encouragement of Learning, London (1706)," in *Primary Sources*. While any author was to a degree learned, in early eighteenth-century Britain, the Company had in this earlier petition referred to "a Gentleman [who] has spent the greatest Part of his Time and Fortune in a Liberal Education" (ibid.).

62. 8 Anne, c.19.

favored subjects of the realm. It dared to declare that such privileges bore the "untrue pretences of publique good" and were nothing less than "mischeivous to the State by raising prices of commodities."[63] The 1624 Statute pronounced these monopolies null and void. Only legitimate inventions—"anie manner of New manufacture"—warranted a patent and for a restricted period of fourteen years (or twenty-one if prior to the statute), with an exception made for gunpowder, given its importance for national security, and print, given the role of monopolies in securing censorship. However, the 1624 Statute did not actually put an end to the Crown's habit of granting monopoly privileges. Thus, the Statute of Anne was a further parliamentary assertion of elected authority against royal prerogative; Parliament's endorsement of access to learning in the emerging spirit of the Enlightenment brought this point home.

Four of the statute's roughly ten provisions address the encouragement of learning. These provisions grant learning distinct property rights (with two of the measures continuing rights that had been granted in the Licensing Act of 1662). Among the new rights, the statute first of all offers a remarkably direct remedy to Locke's concerns over the price of learned books: "The Vice-Chancellors of the Two Universities . . . the Rector of the College of *Edinburgh* . . . have hereby full Power and Authority . . . to Limit and Settle the Price of every such Printed Book . . . as to them shall seem Just and Reasonable."[64] But, to be fair, this right is also extended to the archbishop and lord chief justice, and thus was to apply beyond the university.

Other privileges are granted to the universities on behalf of learning. Continuing the earlier recognition of the value of a well-stocked intellectual commons, set apart from the book-selling market, the statute expands the requirement of the earlier act that printers and booksellers provide a copy of each new book to university and state libraries: "Copies of each Book . . . upon the best Paper . . . be Delivered . . . for the Use of the Libraries of the Universities of *Oxford* and *Cambridge,* the Libraries of the Four Universities in *Scotland,* the Library of *Sion College* in *London,* and the Library commonly called the Library belonging to the Faculty of Advocates at *Edinburgh.*"[65] If

---

63. The complaint in the *Statute* was that the patents were granted "uppon misinformacions and untrue pretences of publique good many such grauntes have bene unduly obteyned and unlawfully putt in execucion to the great greivance and inconvenyence of your Majesties subjects": "Statute of Monopolies, Westminster (1624)," in *Primary Sources on Copyright (1450-1900),* ed. L. Bently and M. Kretschmer (Cambridge: University of Cambridge), online.

64. 8 Anne, c.19.

65. Ibid.

the power of vice chancellors to re-set book prices was repeated in 1735, the *legal deposit* of books in libraries has only grown into a common legislative requirement throughout the world.[66]

The Statute of Anne also disallowed restrictions on importing "any books in Greek, Latin, or any other foreign language printed beyond the seas," as if to address Locke's concern that restricting access to foreign scholarship discourages learning.[67] And finally, in a fourth measure, the statute declares that nothing herein should "prejudice or confirm any right that the said universities" had "to the printing or reprinting any book or copy already printed, or hereafter to be printed."[68]

The statute certainly refers more generally and more often to "the author of any book" and "any such book," rather than focusing exclusively on learned men. It ensures the rights of the "proprietors of such books and writings," the booksellers and printers to whom authors commonly sold the rights to their work. Yet along with authors and proprietors, learning was very much in mind of the legislators at the threshold of Britain's age of copyright in 1710, when they passed legislation "vesting the copies of printed books in the authors or purchasers of such copies, during the times therein mentioned."[69] The Statute of Anne grants and affirms privileges for the learned that are perpetual and without limit. The learned could expect books to be priced fairly; they could import cheaper and better editions from abroad; they could prepare such editions themselves and have them printed at the university press; and they could go to the university library and find what they need on the shelves. These legislated privileges are acts of good faith in the value of learning; they anticipate that increases in learning will provide return enough to the society as a whole. These were the grounds on which the larger world

---

66. Richard Bell, "Legal Deposit in Britain (Part 1)," *Law Librarian* 8, no. 1 (1977): 5.

67. 8 Anne, c.19.

68. Ibid. The universities' printing activities were called to account on occasion. John Twigg discusses how in 1640 during the Civil War, John Pym complained of how the presses "published and maintained in the Universities" were spreading Royalist works, while Cambridge's licensing of Royalist books led to the arrest of the college master, Richard Holdsworth: *The University of Cambridge and the English Revolution, 1625–1688* (Cambridge: Boydell and Brewer, 1990), 84–86.

69. 8 Anne, c.19, 2. In 1486 the city of Venice issued a patent to Marcus Sabellicus for his book *Historiae rerum venetarum ab urbe condita*, which recognized his right in this property but without creating a legal category of ownership for authors, as the Statute of Anne does. Pamela O. Long notes that such patents "rarely prevented piracy" and were a "commercial privilege" with little connection to "the originality of the author's expression": *Openness, Secrecy, Authorship: Technical Arts and the Culture of Knowledge from Antiquity to the Renaissance* (Baltimore: John Hopkins University Press, 2001), 11.

had supported learning in the past by sponsoring abbeys, convents, schools, and universities.

A similar appreciation for how learning forms a clear and worthy goal of intellectual property law was introduced into the United States Constitution nearly eight decades later, in 1789. This initial constitutional convention gave Congress the power "to promote the Progress of Science and useful Arts, by securing for limited Times to Authors and Inventors the exclusive Right to their respective Writings and Discoveries."[70] Subsequent United States legislation spelled out the exceptions and privileges for learning, as I discussed in the first chapter.[71]

In 1710, British legislation bound authors, booksellers, and printers, as well as the universities and their libraries, within a legal structure that forms one of the pillars of today's intellectual property regime (involving copyrights, patents, trademarks, and trade secrets). The Statute of Anne recognizes learning as the source of a valued class of properties. Learning has been instrumental, as I hope that I have demonstrated, in the historical formation and appreciation of intellectual property as a concept, even as it suggests a class of properties that stand apart from other types of intellectual property in ways that I have identified in terms of rights associated with access, accreditation, autonomy, communality, sponsorship, and use. These six properties operate as rights and cultural practices, involving texts and institutions, that have changed over time and by place. They provide a framework for this history of learning, and given their continuing value for learning, are worth recapping here.

Access: The ability to access works of learning is the right that launched this book. I have identified many historical figures and institutions that have contributed to this learned access. Jerome cultivated a network of friends from Bethlehem to Rome through which to circulate his work; Benedict allowed for the annual dispersion of books from the monastic library chest; Islamic libraries instituted fellowships for itinerant scholars; and benefactors stocked the Bodleian Library in early modern Oxford with their treasured manuscript collections. The presumed right and responsibility of access motivated the translation of Arabic texts into Latin during the twelfth

---

70. U.S. Const. art. 4, § 8, cl. 8.

71. "When, in the late eighteenth century, Americans created their first copyright regime—first through state enactments and then by the federal 1790 Copyright Act—they used the British Statute of Anne as their doctrinal blueprint. Despite a few changes and omissions, the degree of similarity on the level of basic concepts, structure, and text between the 1790 Copyright Act and the 1710 British statute is remarkable": Oren Bracha, "The Statute of Anne: An American Mythology," *Houston Law Review* 47 (2010-11): 877-78.

and thirteenth centuries, much as it inspired the humanist recovery of Latin and Greek manuscripts beginning in the fourteenth. Wandering scholars were driven by the prospects of discovery, sharing, and copying. Yet the learned excluded and occluded access at historic points. Recall Margaret Cavendish's appeal to the universities against their banishing of women (not to mention other religions and cultures), or Erasmus' encounter with a sheer lack of trust and generosity among colleagues. Still, the ongoing institutional efforts to improve, restore, and expand access came to be reflected in the Statute of Anne clauses on book deposit, importing, and pricing.

Accreditation: Scholars are also driven by the desire to credit (and contest) others' work. The careful handling of credits signifies scholarly work, much like a silversmith's hallmark authenticates the work. Jerome and Augustine made a point of crediting Cicero and Virgil to demonstrate what antiquity can do for Christianity, while Cassiodorus built a model library to a similar end. Bede notes the church father footsteps he followed in breaking new ground for learning. Masters at medieval universities readily acknowledged how Avicenna and Averroës eased their way to Aristotle, natural history, and medicine. Learning is based on a credit economy with reputation its currency. One polishes another's star to shine more brightly oneself, just as who one references in the bibliography forms its own identifiable constellation within that great firmament held in common.

Autonomy: Learning appears to thrive by stepping away from the flow of life. In the Middle Ages, popes enabled abbeys to be self-governing communities. Medieval university masters left town when the town was thought to interfere. Yet standing apart can make one vulnerable, as Bernard of Clairvaux pressed on Abelard. Dissatisfied kings can disband monasteries, if only to endow colleges with limited autonomy (which can be susceptible to over-zealous royal visits). Universities gained printing rights in Britain, only to stumble over London's commercial book-trade monopolies. Negotiating sustainable autonomy became part of these institutions' intellectual property work, as demonstrated by Anselm, Hildegard, Abelard, Locke, and others.

Communality: Learning had a communal start in the West, as the *Rule of Benedict* called for a sharing of book, table, and pen. The doors of the vast Islamic libraries seem to have always been open. The humanist patrons' private libraries and the public libraries of the ancient universities both honored a collective right of access and use among the learned. It inspired much copying, translation, editing, and, above all, commentary, which further opened the communal properties of these shared works. Erasmus tirelessly improved the common stock of adages for wider circulation in both expensive and cheap, often pirated, editions. Oldenburg made the Royal Society's clubbish concerns with improving natural knowledge the stuff of coffeehouses and bookstalls, thinking it "necessary for promoting the improvement of Philosophical Matters."

Sponsorship: Among these properties, sponsorship provided the foundation for learning's incorporation in the West. The abbeys, convents, priories, schools, colleges, and academies were chartered through the kindness of strangers, family, nobility, court and church. The benefactors who founded and funded these institutions enabled them to stand that much closer to heaven, and apart from the world, on their patrons' behalf. Such beneficence, if never consistent nor certain, was sustained across the long Middle Ages, with women of a certain standing often playing key roles. Later, tuition and print complicated the funding model, amid the privileges and monopolies of the age of commerce. Still, institutional sponsorship offered the steadier grip compared to the personal patronage enjoyed and suffered by Boethius, Averroës, Petrarch, Locke, and others.

Use: The sixth and final property in this set was known in Roman law as *usufruct*, and allowed for uses that did not alter the property. Except that with learning, use alters a work's properties. When a scholar judges (uses) another's work that deals with yet a third scholar's book, the properties of each may be slightly, permanently altered (with that third scholar as likely to be Aristotle as anyone, after the Latin Translation Movement). On the other hand, the church pronounced it a decided misuse of scripture when Abelard pointed out biblical contradictions, while Aquinas was condemned for overuse of Aristotelian reasoning in theological matters. Hernández, on the other hand, assumed that to make use of Aztec medical practices was to owe these people a reciprocal translation of his findings into Nahuatl. Access, accreditation, autonomy, and communality all serve this property right of use, as does the sponsorship of institution and library.

CONCLUSION

The history of learning's properties in the West, as I have presented it in this book, spans some 1,400 years. I have been selective and illustrative, often drawing on the more familiar figures among nuns and monks, humanists and printers, masters and scholars, in the hope of raising something afresh about how their work reflects this sense of an intellectual property. This history is not progressive or linear. Many of the ideas about learning were inherited from antiquity and thus present from the outset, with Saint Jerome's labors in his well-stocked cell. What was new with the rise of the Latin West, I have tried to make clear, is the development of institutional frameworks that served learning well, from monasticism to university and academy. It is a history distinguished by its philosophical and scientific debt to Islamic scholarship; to translation's cooperative contact zone; to the contributions of otherwise excluded women; to the support for libraries; to publishing's struggle with privilege, monopoly, and censorship; and to its intricate involvement in European imperialism.

While this book does end on the triumphant note of "An Act for the Encouragement of Learning," it is worth observing that this early eighteenth-century encouragement did not extend in Britain at the time to admitting women to higher education (with Oxford first granting women degrees only in 1920); or Jews (admitted in 1856 to Oxford); or "dissenters" from outside the Church of England (admitted in 1854), or Indians (admitted in 1871), and the list goes on. On these and other points that have come up, the learned did not get it right or fairly or honestly. If I have favored the success stories here, it has been to capture the values and ideals, as well as the cautions, that might guide us going forward. Education has always done better with articulating the promise and potential of a finer world than with realizing the full extent of that improvement—particularly on issues of equality of opportunity—within its own dominion. I can say that as one who has spent his life as a teacher, as well as a student of education, all too aware of our shortcomings in the face of our best hopes.

My aim for this book has been to demonstrate the debt that the current concept of intellectual property, as economically and legally powerful as it is today, owes to the history of learning. The figures who populate this history made the intangible qualities of texts a reality—in fact, the reality of their lives. They valued texts as distinctive entities, works of labor and insight. This led to an evolving set of rights and responsibilities, institutions and economies, geared toward the advancement of learning in the form of books and other artifacts. Their work also managed to convince many of those who were not otherwise involved in this learning to see its intrinsic value for the larger world, and thus to sponsor and provide privileges and protections to the study of Christian theology, the liberal arts, and natural philosophy. This form or work stood apart from the production of other sorts of tangible and intangible goods. It is not that other crafts and guilds lack intellectual property claims. It is only that with learning, much of the energy and care, as well as the technique and method, is devoted to articulating the intellectual nature and value of the properties. How could the field of learning not give substance and form to a concept of intellectual property as an intangible good? How could it not foster a set of rights and responsibilities that are distinct and separate from other human enterprises?

As Locke felt compelled at the end of the seventeenth century to lobby for the legislative reform of intellectual property rights on behalf of his interests as a scholar, so this is no less of a critical time to rethink the legal structure of intellectual property. For that reason, I close with an epilogue in which I suggest how a history such as this might inspire greater access and use of research and scholarship going forward into the digital era.

EPILOGUE

Although this prehistory of learning's intellectual properties concludes with the Statute of Anne 1710, my hope is that it might inform today's discussions of open access to research and scholarship. With the global embrace of digitization, the entire field of publishing faces myriad changes, not least of all within that small branch known as scholarly communication. Yet amid this scramble for sustainable new business models, the digital era does seem to hold great promise for learning, and in ways reminiscent of the earlier translation movements, the initiation of universities, and the advent of printing. These prior breakthroughs for learning each offered greater access to a far broader literature, new methods of inquiry and scholarly standards, and different forms of sponsorship. This time the increases in access are not only about learned books and journals, but about data, sources, archives, and instruments; and this time the access is on a global and public scale, all of which speak to a far more open and diverse commonwealth of learning.

What is missing today, however, is what learning appears to have achieved in 1710. Learning held the place of honor at the birth of intellectual property law with the Statute of Anne. The statute may well have been something of a cover for Stationers' Company interests, yet learning was still more than a front for this legislation. The learned author, book, and reader were recognized and accepted as the reason for such a statute. Their interests were protected in the authoring of such works, as well as in their pricing, importing, depositing, and printing. Today, learning's earlier legal prominence has been overshadowed by the economic engines of corporate patents and commercially exploited copyright. Something of this market logic has also invaded the universities, particularly in the sciences (as I reviewed in the opening chapter). The question is how, within the prevailing climate do, we restore the original constitutional imperative to promote the progress of science and the useful arts for the encouragement of learning?

My first suggestion in that regard is to give serious consideration to creating through legislation a distinct legal class or category for the intellectual property associated with learning, whether that property be scholarly journals, learned books, historical sources, data sets, or other sorts of learning. Today's legal system offers learning a ragbag of copyright and patent exceptions, exemptions, and embargoes (also reviewed in the opening chapter). Much greater coherence and consistency can be brought to advancing the interests and value of learning by constituting a legal category for this class of intangible goods to which certain rights of access and use apply.

I am taking this strategy of "tailoring of intellectual property rights" from legal scholar Michael W. Carroll at Washington's American University. Carroll presents a generic case for establishing a new property class as a way to improve the return on the "copyright bargain" made in granting such privileges.[1] The creation of different legal categories of intellectual property, Carroll points out, is currently employed to separate inventions, covered by patents, from expressions of ideas, covered by copyright. A second example is provided by musical compositions, which are licensed at a set rate to anyone who seeks to use the work, so that permission is not required each time a song is played. A third instance follows from the Bayh-Dole Act of 1980, which allows universities and faculty members to seek patent protection for federally funded inventions to help realize greater public benefits from such work.

I am proposing something broader, less of an exception and more of a recognition that learning is one of the mainstays of what intellectual property law is intended to encourage. Such a legislative change would create a class of intellectual property for the research and scholarship produced by public or nonprofit research and education institutions. In the case of copyright, it could require that a Creative Commons license be applied to ensure communal access and enable a wide range of uses, while protecting the accreditation of the work. Such a law might consolidate and extend

1. Michael W. Carroll, "One Size Does Not Fit All: A Framework for Tailoring Intellectual Property Rights," *Ohio State Law Journal* 70, no. 6 (2009): 1376. Carroll lays out the social costs of having a uniform law compared to (a) tailoring for greater efficiency and public benefit through legislation, which I focus on here, but also (b) through judicial interpretation and administrative rules, which are currently being applied to research and scholarship in ways, I argue in the first chapter, that do not protect learning from undue commercial exploitation.

tax exemptions for this body of work to further encourage sponsorship; it might reinforce the autonomy of this work not only in matters of academic freedom, but around the authors' or inventors' intentions with it, which can still involve pursuing a commercial route for their intellectual property.

This would enable the best-selling authors among academics—consider the Scholarly Stephens, Hawking and Greenblatt—to continue to contribute to the healthy state of commercial book publishing, or allow graduate students, such as Larry Page and Sergey Brin, to scale up a patent's public value through commercialization. At the same time, this new class of intellectual property could also offer a standard means of a non-commercial public interest patenting, which has been exercised in the past on an ad-hoc basis, for example, with the SARS (Severe Acute Respiratory Syndrome) outbreak of 2003.[2]

This may seem to still leave the question of how to finance universal open access to scholarly publishing. To begin with, we might take a feather from Thomas Bodley's hat, in calling for a special arrangement between library and publisher in support of learning. However, in this case, research libraries can offer publishers and scholarly societies a better deal than Bodley did with the London printers in the seventeenth century. Rather than suggest that publishers and societies deposit a free copy in the library, libraries can offer publishers and societies the equivalent of their previous subscription fees to make their journals open access. After all, libraries gain little advantage from the exclusivity of a journal subscription. The library community has been among the strongest supporters of open access, with wider access improving the learning commons as a whole, while offering occasional value to the tax-payers that support many such libraries. As for the threat of free-riding, the evidence to date is on the side of library participation, as these institutions lead a new generation of just such open access collaborations among scholars and presses.[3]

2. The British Columbia Cancer Agency (BCCA), the Center for Disease Control, and the University of Hong Kong filed "defensive patents" on diagnostic tests and treatments utilizing the genetic sequence of the SARS coronavirus to ensure that what was patented remained open and available: Matthew Rimmer, "The Race to Patent the SARS Virus: The TRIPS Agreement and Access to Essential Medicines," *Melbourne Journal of International Law* 5, no. 2 (2004): 338. While the BCCA's policy is to support both "public use and commercial application" of its research, with SARS, the agency was "trying to pre-empt the nonsense that has gone on in the past" by "making sure the market is not cornered," according to Samuel Abraham, BCCA's vice president for research. Abraham is cited by Peg Brickley, "Preemptive SARS Patents," *Genome Biology* 4 (2003).

3. Examples of current cooperative publishing initiatives include the Library Publishing Coalition, with over a hundred libraries in the US hosting over four hundred open access journals, as

The research funding agencies have also begun to explore new collaborative models. A leading instance is the open access biomedical journal *eLife*, which the Wellcome Trust, Howard Hughes Medical Institute, and Max Planck Society collaborated on endowing.[4] Such organizations, most of which have open access mandates, are in a position to pay publishers directly, if the researchers they fund select one of its journals, for open access. The cooperative spirit echoes the earlier scholar-in the-press-room ventures of Erasmus, Aldus, and Froben, as well as Laud's and Fell's arrangements with the Stationers' Company. As this history reveals, it takes time to find learning's advantage amid changing technologies and markets, with the gains reflecting a set of common principles and properties that are largely preserved through the course of these changes.

This concept of universal access to this distinct class of works begs, I realize, a further, if never final, question. What will it mean to make this body of work public for the first time on such a scale? If we open it, will they come? We do have the example of the Latin translation movement, which lead to Aristotle and the Commentators rocking Europe with their books touring the Continent to sold-out bookstalls and packed university classes. What, then, should we expect of the digital era's great opening of this body of learning, if not changes in how schools educate, how professionals are trained, how the media report the news, how democracies deliberate and states develop policies and laws?

In 2000, JSTOR, the online archive principally of humanities and social science journal back issues, undertook a two-year pilot by giving access to sixteen high schools for which they found a "very positive impact on students' scholarship," with teachers testifying how this access refreshed their teaching.[5] Since then, large-scale studies of what happens when research is made open access have shown that it leads to a substantial growth in the readership of

well as the Open Library of the Humanities, Knowledge Unlatched, OAPEN, and the University of California Press Collabora. The SCOAP3 version involves the cooperation of 3,000 libraries in purchasing open access to particle physics journals: Salvatore Mele et al., "SCOAP3 and Open Access," *Serials Review* 35, no. 4 (2009): 264–71. Also see Open Access 2020 (OA2020) online, coordinated by the Max Planck Library. Our modest efforts, through the Public Knowledge Project, in proposing new models are available online at the Open Access Publishing Cooperative Study.

4. Declan Butler, "Three Major Biology Funders Launch New Open Access Journal, but Why Exactly?" Newsblog, *Nature*, June 27, 2011.

5. "JSTOR Participation Information Meeting for Secondary Schools": JSTOR, New York, online. A more recent example of what access can mean for such students is found in the high school sophomore Jack Andraka, who discovered a remarkably effective and inexpensive pancreatic diagnostic: Jack Andraka, "Why Science Journal Paywalls Have to Go," *Student Blog* (PLOS, February 18, 2013).

such work, as well as increased use of scholarly work.[6] In Latin America, where all journals have generally been open access since shortly after the turn of the century, representing another sort of Latin Translation Movement, Juan Pablo Alperin, assistant professor of publishing at Simon Fraser University, found that fully a quarter of the readers of this scholarly work are from *outside* the academic community, with the public showing only somewhat less interest in the arts and humanities than in work from the biomedical field.[7] In the United States, where only half the literature, if that, is publicly available, we have studied what happens when a sample of over four hundred physicians and public health staff are provided with relatively complete open access for a year.[8] A third of the physicians and two thirds of the public health staff in the study accessed research articles on roughly a weekly basis in their roles as clinicians, educators, researchers, learners, administrators, and advocates, suggesting both the value of increased access and a need to make the use of such work a greater part of professional education and practice.

The proportion of published research that is open access is increasing each year. This growth is bound to inform and unsettle people's thinking, as the tentative and conditional quality of this learning becomes part of the fabric of our lives. The access has the potential to excite and engage a broader segment of the population out of interest, curiosity, and learning for its own sake. It will be misunderstood and misused, as we are seeing with climate change studies, as well as derided and perhaps defunded. Such situations will demand strong and compelling defenses of learning's autonomy and value. And cases will arise that will make it easier to call for increased support for research. If the history assembled here—inspired by questions of learning's properties and driven by the seeming potential of online access to enhance those properties—emboldens a broader discussion about what matters for the future of scholarly communication in advancing the value of this civic and public good, then this labor has more than justified itself. For as much

6. Steve Hitchcock, "The Effect of Open Access and Downloads ('Hits') on Citation Impact: A Bibliography of Studies," OpCit Project (2013), online.

7. Juan Pablo Alperin, "The Public Impact of Latin America's Approach to Open Access" (Ph.D. dissertation, Stanford University, 2015), online. Juan is a member of the Public Knowledge Project.

8. Laura Moorhead, Cheryl Holzmeyer, Lauren Maggio, Ryan Steinberg, and John Willinsky, "In an Age of Open Access to Research Policies: Physician and Public Health NGO Staff Research Use and Policy Awareness," *PLOS One* (2015): doi: 10.1371, online.

as this book has taught me to appreciate Erasmus's wit on editing Saint Jerome—"I had worked myself to death that Jerome might live again"—and his wisdom in focusing on publishing when he came to write about the adage "make haste slowly," it has been my great pleasure to realize with Erasmus & Co. the extent to which "between friends all is common."[9]

9. Erasmus's line is from his letter: "To Raffaele Riario, Cardinal of San Giorgio," in *The Correspondence of Erasmus, Letters 298 to 445, 1514 to 1516*, vol. 3, trans. R. A. B. Mynors and D. F. S. Thomson, annotator James K. McConica, *The Collected Works of Erasmus* (Toronto: University of Toronto Press, 1976), 90. The two adages, you might recall, are discussed in chapter 8.

Bibliography

Abelard, Peter. *Letters of Peter Abelard: Beyond the Personal.* Translated by Jan M. Ziolkowski. Washington, DC: Catholic University of America Press, 2008.

———. *Story of Abelard's Adversities.* Translated by J. T. Muckle. Toronto: Pontifical Institute of Medieval Studies, 1964.

Abelard, Peter. *Sic et Non.* In *Educational Documents*, vol. 1, *England and Wales, 800–1816*, edited by David William Sylvester, 55–56. London: Routledge, 1970.

Abelard, Peter, and Heloise. *The Letters of Abelard and Heloise.* Translated by Betty Radice. London: Penguin, 1974.

Adamson, Peter. "Al-Kindī and the Reception of Greek Philosophy." In *The Cambridge Companion to Arabic Philosophy*, edited by Peter Adamson and Richard C. Taylor, 32–51. Cambridge: Cambridge University Press, 2005.

Adamson, Peter. *Philosophy in the Islamic World: A History of Philosophy Without Any Gaps.* Vol. 3. Oxford: Oxford University Press, 2016.

Adelard of Bath. *Conversations with His Nephew: On the Same and the Different, Questions on Natural Science, and On Birds.* Translated by Charles Burnett. Cambridge: Cambridge University Press, 1998.

"Advertisement." *Philosophical Transactions* 47 (1752–53) [unpaginated].

Agamben, Giorgio. *The Highest Poverty: Monastic Rules and Form-of-Life.* Translated by Adam Koysko. Stanford, CA: Stanford University Press, 2013.

Alcuin. "To the King on Books, Learning, and Old Age (796)." In *Carolingian Civilization: A Reader*, edited by Paul Edward Dutton, 104–6. Peterborough, ON: Broadview, 1993.

———. "To the King on the State of Learning in His Day (799)." In *Carolingian Civilization: A Reader*, edited by Paul Edward Dutton, 106–8. Peterborough, ON: Broadview, 1993.

Alfonsi, Petrus. *Dialogue against the Jews.* Translated by Irven M. Resnick. Washington, DC: Catholic University of America Press, 2006.

———. "Epistola ad peripateticos." In John Victor Tolan, *Petrus Alfonsi and His Medieval Readers*, 66–68. Miami: University of Florida Press, 1993.

Alperin, Juan Pablo. "The Public Impact of Latin America's Approach to Open Access." PhD diss., Stanford University, 2015.

Andersson, Theodore M. "A Carolingian Pun and Charlemagne's Languages." In *Along the Oral-Written Continuum: Types of Texts, Relations and Their Implications*, edited by Slavica Rankovic, 357–69. Turnhout, Belgium: Brepolis, 2010.

Andrade, E. N. Da C. "The Birth and Early Days of the Philosophical Transactions." *Notes and Records of the Royal Society of London* 20, no. 1 (1965): 9–27.

Andraka, Jack. "Why Science Journal Paywalls Have to Go." *Student Blog* (PLOS), February 18, 2013.

Anselm. *Complete Philosophical and Theological Treaties of Anselm of Canterbury.* Translated by Jasper Hopkins and Herbert Richardson. Minneapolis: Arthur J. Banning, 2000.

———. *The Letters of Saint Anselm of Canterbury.* Vol. 1. Translated by Walter Frölich. Kalamazoo, MI: Cistercian, 1990.

———. *The Major Works.* Edited by Brian Davies and Gillian R. Evans. Oxford: Oxford University Press, 1998.

———. "Prayer to St. Benedict." In *The Prayers and Meditations of Saint Anselm with the Proslogion*, translated by Benedicta Ward, 196–200. London: Penguin, 1973.

———. *St. Anselm's Proslogion, with a Reply on Behalf of the Fool by Gaunilo and the Author's Reply to Gaunilo.* Translated by M. J. Charlesworth. Oxford: Oxford University Press, 1965.

Aquinas, Thomas. *Aquinas against the Averroists: On There Being Only One Intellect.* Translated by Ralph McInerny. West Lafayette, IN: Purdue University Press, 1993.

———. *Commentary on Aristotle's* Politics. Translated by Richard J. Regan. Indianapolis: Hackett, 2007.

———. "Commentary on Book II of the *Sentences*, Distinction 17, Question 2, Article 1." Translated by Richard C. Taylor. In *Philosophical Psychology in Arabic Thought and the Latin Aristotelianism of the 13th Century*, edited by Luis Xavier López Farjeat and Jörg Alejandro Tellkamp, 279–96. Paris: J. Vrin, 2013.

———. *The Divisions and Methods of the Sciences.* 4th ed. Translated by Armand Maurer. Toronto: Pontifical Institute of Medieval Studies, 1986.

———. *Political Writings.* Edited by R. W. Dyson. Cambridge: Cambridge University Press, 2002.

———. *Summa theologica.* Translated by Laurence Shapcote. Raleigh, NC: Hayes Barton, 2006.

Aristotle. *De Anima (On the Soul).* Translated by Hugh Lawson-Tancred. London: Penguin, 1986.

———. *The Politics.* Translated by T. A. Sinclair and Trevor J. Saunders. London: Penguin, 1981.

Armitage, David. "Probing the Foundations of Tully's Public Philosophy." *Political Theory* 39, no. 1 (2011): 124–30.

Armstrong, Elizabeth. *Before Copyright: The Book-Privilege System 1498–1526.* Cambridge: Cambridge University Press, 1990.

Aronowitz, Stanley. *The Knowledge Factory.* Boston: Beacon, 2000.

Ashcraft, Richard. *Revolutionary Politics and Locke's Two Treatises of Government.* Princeton, NJ: Princeton University Press, 1986.

Association of University Technology Managers. *AUTM Licensing Activity Survey Highlights.* Deerfield, IL: AUTM, 2012.

Astbury, Raymond. "The Renewal of the Licensing Act in 1693 and Its Lapse in 1695." *Library*, ser. 5, vol. 33, no. 4 (1978): 296–322.

Aston, T. H., and Rosamond Faith. "The Endowments to the University and Colleges to circa 1348." In *The Early Oxford Schools*, vol. 1 of *The History of the University of Oxford*, edited by J. I. Catto, 265–309. Oxford: Oxford University Press, 1984.

Aubrey, John. *Brief Lives.* Edited by Richard Barber. Woodbridge, Suffolk, UK: Boydell and Brewer, 1982.

———. *Memoir of John Aubrey, F.R.S., Embracing His Auto-biographical Sketches, a Brief Review of His Personal and Literary Merits, and an Account of His Works: With Extracts from His Correspondence, Anecdotes of Some of His Contemporaries, and of the Times in Which He Lived.* Edited by John Britton. London: J. B. Nichols, 1845.

Augustine. *The Catholic and Manichean Ways of Life.* Translated by Donald A. Gallagher and Idellla J. Gallagher. Washington, DC: Catholic University of America Press, 1966.

———. *The Confessions and Letters of St. Augustine.* Translated by J. G. Cunningham. Vol. 1 of *A Select Library of Nicene and Post-Nicene Fathers of the Christian Church.* Edited by Philip Schaff. New York: Charles Scribner's and Sons, 1907.

———. *Earlier Writings.* Edited by John H. S. Burleigh. Louisville, KY: Westminster John Knox Press, 1953.

———. *On Christian Teaching.* Translated by R. P. H. Green. Oxford: Oxford University Press, 1997.

———. *Political Writings.* Edited by E. M. Atkins and R. J. Dodaro. Cambridge: Cambridge University Press, 2001.

———. "Regula Sancti Augustini, c. 397." In George Lawless, *Augustine of Hippo and His Monastic Rule,* 65–120. Oxford: Oxford University Press, 1987.

———. *The Retractions.* Translated by Mary Inez Bogan. Washington, DC: Catholic University of America Press, 1968.

———. *The Rule of St. Augustine,* trans. Robert Russell (1976), in Medieval Sourcebook, Fordham University, New York, online.

———. *Tractates on the Gospel of John, 28–54.* Translated by John W. Rettig. Washington, DC: Catholic University of America Press, 1993.

———. *The Works of Saint Augustine.* Translated by Roland J. Teske, Edmund Hill, et al. 35 vols. Hyde Park, NY: New City Press, 1995.

Averroës (Ibn Rushd). *Aristotle's "Metaphysics": An Annotated Translation of the So-Called "Epitome."* Edited by Rüdiger Arnzen. Berlin: Walter de Gruyter, 2010.

———. "The Decisive Treatise." In *Classical Arabic Philosophy: An Anthology of Sources,* edited by Jon McGinnis and David C. Reisman, 309–29. Indianapolis: Hackett, 2007.

———. *Long Commentary on the* De anima *of Aristotle.* Translated by Richard C. Taylor and Thérèse-Anne Druat. New Haven, CT: Yale University Press, 2009.

———. "On the Harmony of Religions and Philosophy." Translated by Mohammed Jamil-al-Rahman (1921). In *Medieval Sourcebook,* Fordham University, New York, online.

———. *Tahafut al Tahafut (The Incoherence of the Incoherence).* Translated by Simon Van Den Bergh. Cambridge, UK: Gibb Memorial Trust, 2008.

Avicenna. "Canon." Translated by O. Cameron Gruner. In *A Source Book in Medieval Science,* edited by Edward Grant, 715–19. Cambridge, MA: Harvard University Press, 1974.

———. "Healing: Metaphysics X." Translated by Michael E. Marmura. In *Medieval Political Philosophy: A Sourcebook,* edited by Ralph Lerner and Muhsin Mahdi, 98–111. New York: Free Press, 1963.

———. "On the Division of the Rational Sciences." Translated by Mushin Mahdi. In *Medieval Political Philosophy: A Sourcebook,* edited by Ralph Lerner and Mushin Mahdi, 95–97. New York: Free Press, 1963.

———. [Ibn Sīnā]. "The Soul." In *Classical Arabic Philosophy: An Anthology of Sources,* edited by Jon McGinnis and David C. Reisman, 175–208. Indianapolis: Hackett, 2007.

Azarias [Patrick Francis Mullany]. *Aristotle and the Christian Church.* London: Kegan Paul, Trench, 1888.

Backscheide, Paula R. *Daniel Defoe: His Life.* Baltimore: Johns Hopkins University Press, 1989.

Bacon, Francis. *The Advancement of Learning and New Atlantis.* London: Oxford University Press, 1906.

———. *The New Organon.* Edited by Lisa Jardine and Michael Silverthorne. Cambridge: Cambridge University Press, 2000.

———. *Novum Organum, with the Great Instauration.* Translated by Peter Urbach and John Gibson. Chicago: Open Court, 1994.

———. *The Works of Francis Bacon.* Vol. 5. London: J. Johnson et al., 1803.

———. *The Works of Francis Bacon.* Vols. 5, 8. Collected and edited by James Spedding, Robert Leslie Ellis, and Douglas Denon Heath. London: Longman, 1860.

Bain, Jennifer. *Hildegard of Bingen and Musical Reception: The Modern Revival of a Medieval Composer.* Cambridge: Cambridge University Press, 2015.

Baldwin, John W. *Paris, 1200.* Stanford, CA: Stanford University Press, 2010.

———. *The Scholastic Culture of the Middle Ages, 1000–1300.* Long Grove, IL: Waveland, 1971.

Baldwin, Marshall W. "The Popes and Learning in the High Middle Ages (Concluded)." *Manuscripta* 2, no. 1 (1958): 16–23.

Barker, Nicolas. *The Oxford University Press and the Spread of Learning: An Illustrated History, 1478–1978.* Oxford: Oxford University Press, 1978.

Barker, William. Introduction to *The Adages of Erasmus,* edited by William Barker, ix–xlvii. Toronto: University of Toronto Press, 2001.

Barney, A., W. J. Lewis, J. A. Beach, and Oliver Berghof. Introduction to *The Etymologies of Isidore of Seville,* translated by Stephen A. Barney, W. J. Lewis, J. A. Beach, and Oliver Berghof, 3–28. Cambridge: Cambridge University Press, 2006.

Baron, Hans. *The Crisis of the Early Italian Renaissance: Civic Humanism and the Republican Liberty in the Age of Classicism and Tyranny.* Princeton, NJ: Princeton University Press, 1966.

Basil. "Address to Young Men." In *Three Thousand Years of Educational Wisdom: Selections from the Great Documents,* edited by Robert Ulich, 2nd ed., 330–79. Cambridge, MA: Harvard University Press, 1982.

Bateson, Mary. "Origin and Early History of the Double Monastery." *Transactions of the Royal Historical Society* 13 (1899): 137–98.

Beach, Alison I. *Women as Scribes: Book Production and Monastic Reform in Twelfth-Century Bavaria.* Cambridge: Cambridge University Press, 2004.

Beddie, James Stuart. "The Ancient Classics in the Medieval Libraries." *Speculum* 5, no. 1 (1930): 3–20.

Bede. *The Age of Bede.* Translated by D. H. Farmer. London: Penguin, 1965.

———. *The Ecclesiastical History of the English People.* Translated by Bertram Colgrave. Oxford: Oxford University Press, 1969.

———. *On the Nature of Things, and On Times.* Translated by Calvin B. Kendall and Faith Wallis. Liverpool: Liverpool University Press, 2010.

———. *The Reckoning of Time.* Translated by Faith Wallis. Liverpool: Liverpool University Press, 1999.

Bell, Catherine, and Val Napoleon, eds. *First Nations Cultural Heritage and Law: Case Studies, Voices, and Perspectives.* Vancouver: University of British Columbia Press, 2009.

Bell, David N. "The Libraries of Religious Houses in the Late Middle Ages." In *To 1640,* vol. 1 of *The Cambridge History of Libraries in Britain and Ireland,* edited by Elisabeth Leedham-Green and Teresa Webber, 126–51. Cambridge: Cambridge University Press, 2006.

Bell, Richard. "Legal Deposit in Britain (Part 1)." *Law Librarian* 8, no. 1 (1977): 5–8.

Belting, Hans. *Florence and Baghdad: Renaissance Art and Arab Science.* Cambridge, MA: Harvard University Press, 2011.

Beltrami, Pietro G., and Simone Fornara. "Italian Historical Dictionaries: From the Accademia della Crusca to the Web." *International Journal of Lexicography* 17, no. 4 (2004): 357–84.

Benkler, Yochai. *The Wealth of Networks: How Social Production Transforms Markets and Freedom.* New Haven, CT: Yale University Press, 2006.

Bennison, Amira K. *Great Caliphs: The Golden Age of the 'Abbasid Empire.* New Haven, CT: Yale University Press, 2009.

Bergin, Thomas G. *Petrarch.* New York: Twayne, 1970.

Bergstrom, Theodore C., P. N. Courant, R. Preston McAfee, and Michael A. Williams. "Evaluating Big Deal Journal Bundles." *Proceedings of the National Academy of Sciences* 111, no. 26 (2014): 9425–30.

Berlin, Isaiah. "Hobbes, Locke and Professor Macpherson." *Political Quarterly* 35, no. 4 (1964): 444–68.

Berman, Constance Hoffman. "Medieval Agriculture, the Southern French Countryside, and the Early Cistercians: A Study of Forty-Three Monasteries." *Transactions of the American Philosophical Society* 76, no. 5 (1986): 1–179.

Berman, Elizabeth Popp. *Creating the Market University*. Princeton, NJ: Princeton University Press, 2012.

Bernal, Martin. *The Fabrication of Ancient Greece, 1785–1985*, vol. 1 of *Black Athena: The Afroasiatic Roots of Classical Civilization*. New Brunswick, NJ: Rutgers University Press, 1989.

Bernard of Clairvaux. "An Apologia for Abbot William." In *The Cistercian World: Monastic Writings of the Twelfth Century*, translated by Pauline Matarasso, 42–58. London: Penguin, 1993.

———. "Exhortation to Repentance, and to Seek a Humble Place First and Only after Becoming Worthy to Look to Higher Honor." In *Selected Works*, translated by Gillian R. Evans, 21–37, 95–96. Mahwah, NJ: Paulist, 1987.

———. *Honey and Salt: Selected Spiritual Writings of Saint Bernard of Clairvaux*. Translated by Kilian Walsh. New York: Random House, 2007.

———. *The Letters of St. Bernard of Clairvaux*. Translated by Bruno Scott James. Kalamazoo, MI: Cistercian, 1998.

———. *Life and Works of Saint Bernard, Abbot of Clairvaux*. Vol. 2. 2nd ed. Edited by John Mabillon, translated and edited with additional notes by Samuel J. Eales. London: John Hodges, 1889.

———. *On the Song of Songs*, vol. 4 of *Sermons*. Translated by Irene Edmonds. Kalamazoo, MI: Cistercian, 1980.

———. *Selected Works*. Translated by G. R. Evans. New York: HarperCollins, 2005.

———. *Sermons on Conversion*. Translated by Marie-Bernard Saïd. Vol. 25 of *Cistercian Fathers*. Kalamazoo, MI: Cistercian, 1981.

Bernhard, Uehleke, Werner Hopfenmuellerd, Rainer Stangeb, and Reinhard Sallera. "Are the Correct Herbal Claims by Hildegard von Bingen Only Lucky Strikes? A New Statistical Approach." *Research in Complementary Medicine* 19, no. 4 (2012): 187–90.

Bertolacci, Amos. "The Reception of Avicenna in Latin Medieval Culture." In *Interpreting Avicenna: Critical Essays*, edited by Peter Adamson, 242–69. Cambridge: Cambridge University Press, 2013.

Biagioli, Mario. *Galileo, Courtier: The Practice of Science in the Culture of Absolutism*. Chicago: University of Chicago Press, 1993.

———. *Galileo's Instruments of Credit: Telescopes, Images, Secrecy*. Chicago: University of Chicago Press, 2006.

Biddle, Justin B. "Tragedy of the Anticommons? Intellectual Property and the Sharing of Scientific Information." *Philosophy of Science* 79, no. 5 (2012): 821–32.

Bietenholz, Peter G. "Ethics and Early Printing: Erasmus' Rules for the Proper Conduct of Authors." *Humanities Association Review* 26 (1975): 180–95.

Bijsterveld, Arnoud-Jan A. *Do ut des: Gift Giving, Memoria, and Conflict Management in the Medieval Low Countries*. Hilversum: Verloren, 2007.

Bill and Melinda Gates Foundation. "Bill and Melinda Gates Foundation Open Access Policy." Seattle, November 20, 2014, online.

Birch, Thomas. *The History of the Royal Society of London for Improving of Natural Knowledge from Its First Rise*. Vol. 2. London: Millar, 1756.

Bischoff, Bernard. "Benedictine Monasteries and the Survival of Classical Literature." In *Manuscripts and Libraries in the Age of Charlemagne*, translated and edited by Michael M. Gorman, 134–60. Cambridge: Cambridge University Press, 1994.

Blair, Ann. "Humanist Methods in Natural Philosophy: The Commonplace Book." *Journal of the History of Ideas* 53, no. 4 (1992): 541–51.

———. "Organizations of Knowledge." In *Cambridge Companion to Renaissance Philosophy*, edited by James Hankins, 287–303. Cambridge: Cambridge University Press, 2007.

Blair, John. "Frithuswith [St. Frithuswith, Frideswide] (*d.* 727), Abbess or Oxford." In *Oxford Dictionary of National Biography*, edited by H. C. G. Matthew and Brian Harrison, online ed. Oxford: Oxford University Press, 2004.

———. "St. Frideswide Reconsidered." *Oxoniensia* 52 (1987): 71-127.

Blayney, Peter W. M. *The Stationers' Company and the Printers of London, 1501-1557.* Vol. 1. Cambridge: Cambridge University Press, 2013.

Bloom, Jonathan M. *Paper before Print: The History and Impact of Paper on the Islamic World.* New Haven, CT: Yale University Press, 2001.

Bod, Rens. *A New History of the Humanities: The Search for Principles and Patterns from Antiquity to the Present.* Oxford: Oxford University Press, 2014.

Bodin, Jean. *Six Books of the Commonwealth.* Translated by M. J. Tooley. Oxford: Blackwell, 1955.

Bodley, Thomas. *The Autobiography of Sir Thomas Bodley.* Oxford: Bodleian Library, 2006.

———. *Letters of Sir Thomas Bodley to the University of Oxford, 1598-1611.* Edited by. G. W. Wheeler. Oxford: Oxford University Press, 1927.

———. *Letters of Sir Thomas Bodley to Thomas James, First Keeper of the Bodleian Library.* Edited by G. W. Wheeler. Oxford: Oxford University Press, 1926.

Boethius. *The Consolation of Philosophy.* Translated by David R. Slavitt. Cambridge, MA: Harvard University Press, 2008.

Bohannon, John. "Who's Afraid of Peer Review?" *Science* 342, no. 6154 (2013): 60-65.

———. "Who's Downloading Pirated Papers? Everyone." *Science,* 352, no. 6285 (April 28, 2016): 508-12.

Bok, Derek. *Universities in the Marketplace: The Commercialization of Higher Education.* Princeton, NJ: Princeton University Press, 2004.

Bonaventure. *The Works of St. Bonaventure.* Edited by Robert J. Karris. Vol. 15, *Defense of the Mendicants,* translated by José de Vinck and Robert J. Karris. St. Bonaventure, NY: Franciscan Institute Publications, 2010.

Boston Women's Health Collective. *Our Bodies, Ourselves.* Boston: New England Free Press, 1971.

Bouchard, Constance Brittain. *Holy Entrepreneurs: Cistercians, Knights, and Economy Exchange in Twelfth-Century Burgundy.* Ithaca, NY: Cornell University Press, 1991.

———. *Sword, Miter, and Cloister: Nobility and the Church in Burgundy, 980-1198.* Ithaca, NY: Cornell University Press, 1987.

Bowers, Roger. "The Almonry Schools of the English Monasteries, c. 1265-1540." In *Monasteries and Society in Medieval Britain: Proceedings of the 1994 Harlaxton Symposium,* edited by Benjamin Thompson, 177-222. Stamford, CT: Paul Watkins, 1999.

Boyle, James. *The Public Domain: Enclosing the Commons of the Mind.* New Haven, CT: Yale University Press, 2008.

Bracha, Oren. "The Statute of Anne: An American Mythology." *Houston Law Review* 47 (2010-11): 877-918.

Brickley, Peg. "Preemptive SARS Patents." *Genome Biology* 4 (2003), online.

Briggs, Robin. "The Académie Royale des Sciences and the Pursuit of Utility." *Past and Present* 131 (1991): 38-88.

Brittain, Vera. *The Women at Oxford: A Fragment of History.* London: Harrap, 1960.

Broad, Jacqueline. "A Woman's Influence? John Locke and Damaris Masham on Moral Accountability." *Journal of the History of Ideas* 67, no. 3 (2006): 489-510.

Brockliss, L. W. B. *The University of Oxford: A History.* Oxford: Oxford University Press, 2016.

Brodrick, G. C. *A History of the University of Oxford.* London: Longmans, Green, 1886.

Broman, Thomas. "Periodical Literature." In *Books and the Sciences in History,* edited by Marina Frasca-Spada and Nick Jardine, 225-38. Cambridge: Cambridge University Press, 2000.

Brown, George Hardin. *Bede the Educator.* Lecture 1996. Jarrow, UK: St. Paul's Church, 1997.

———. *A Companion to Bede.* Woodbridge, Suffolk, UK: Boydell and Brewer, 2009.

Brown, James R. "Privatizing the University: The New Tragedy of the Commons." *Science* 290 (2000): 1701-2.

Brown, Peter. *Augustine of Hippo: A Biography*. Berkeley: University of California Press, 2000.

———. *The Rise of Western Christendom: Triumph and Diversity, A.D. 200-100*. 3rd ed. New York: Wiley, 2013.

———. *Through the Eye of a Needle: Wealth, the Fall of Rome, and the Making of Christianity in the West, 350-550 AD*. Princeton, NJ: Princeton University Press, 2012.

Bruni, Leonardo. "The Study of Literature." In *Humanist Educational Treatises*, translated by Craig W. Kallendorf, 47-63. Cambridge, MA: Harvard University Press, 2008.

Buckle, Stephen. *Natural Law and the Theory of Property: Grotius to Hume*. Oxford: Oxford University Press, 1991.

Burckhardt, Jacob. *The Civilization of the Renaissance in Italy*. Translated by S. G. C. Middlemore. London: Penguin, 1990.

Burnett, Charles. "Adelard of Bath and the Arabs." In *Arab into Latin in the Middle Ages: The Translators and the Social Contexts*, 89-107. Farnham, Surrey, UK: Ashgate, 2009.

———. "Al-Kindī, Latin Translations of." In *Encyclopedia of Medieval Philosophy: Philosophy between 500-1500*, edited by Henrik Lagerlund. Dordrecht, Netherlands: Springer, 2011.

———. "Arabic into Latin: The Reception of Arabic Philosophy into Western Europe." In *The Cambridge Companion to Arabic Philosophy*, edited by Peter Adamson and Richard C. Taylor, 370-404. Cambridge: Cambridge University Press, 2005.

———. *Arabic into Latin in the Middle Ages: The Translators and Their Intellectual and Social Context*, 249-88. London: Routledge, 2009.

———. "Communities of Learning in Twelfth-Century Toledo." In *Communities of Learning: Networks and the Shaping of Intellectual Identity in Europe, 1100-1500*, edited by Constant J. Mews and John N. Crossley, 9-18. Turnhout, Belgium: Brepols, 2011.

———. *Introduction of Arabic Learning into England*. London: British Library, 1997.

———. "The 'Sons of Averroes with the Emperor Frederick' and the Transmission of the Philosophical Works by Ibn Rushd." In *Averroes and the Aristotelian Tradition: Sources, Constitution, and Reception of the Philosophy of Ibn Rushd (1126-1198)*, edited by Gerhard Endress, Jan Aertsen, and Klaus Braun, 259-99. Leiden: Bill, 1999.

———. "The Translating Activity in Medieval Spain." In *The Legacy of Muslim Spain*, vol. 2, edited by Salma Khadra Jayyusi, 1036-58. Leiden: Brill, 1992.

———. "The Transmission of Arabic Astronomy via Antioch and Pisa in the Second Quarter of the Twelfth Century." In *The Enterprise of Science in Islam: New Perspectives*, edited by Jan P. Hogendijk and Abdelhamid I. Sabra, 23-51. Cambridge, MA: MIT Press, 2003.

Burrell, David C. "Aquinas and Islamic and Jewish Thinkers." In *Cambridge Companion to Aquinas*, edited by Norman Kretzmann and Eleonore Stump, 60-84. Cambridge: Cambridge University Press, 1993.

Burton, Janet E. "*Fundator Noster*: Roger de Mowbray as Founder and Patron of Monasteries." In *Religious and Laity in Western Europe 1000-1400*, edited by Emilia Jamroziak and Janet E. Burton, 2:23-39. Turnhout, Belgium: Brepols, 2010.

Cahill, Thomas. *How the Irish Saved Civilization: The Untold Story of Ireland's Heroic Role from the Fall of Rome to the Rise of Medieval Europe*. New York: Doubleday, 1995.

Cañizares Esguerra, Jorge. *Nature, Empire, and Nation: Explorations of the History of Science in the Iberian World*. Stanford, CA: Stanford University Press, 2006.

Cantoni, Davide, and Noam Yuchtman. "Medieval Universities, Legal Institutions, and the Commercial Revolution." *Quarterly Journal of Economics* 129, no. 2 (2014): 823-87.

Cantor, Norman. *Inventing the Middle Ages*. New York: William Morrow, 1991.

Carroll, Michael W. "One Size Does Not Fit All: A Framework for Tailoring Intellectual Property Rights." *Ohio State Law Journal* 70, no. 6 (2009): 1361-434.

Carruthers, Mary. *The Book of Memory: A Study of Memory in Medieval Culture*. Cambridge: Cambridge University Press, 1990.

Carter, Harry. *History of the Oxford University Press*. Oxford: Oxford University Press, 1975.

Cassiodorus. *An Introduction to the Divine and Human Readings*. Translated by Leslie Webber Jones. New York: Columbia University Press, 1946.

Cavendish, Margaret. *Observations upon Experimental Philosophy*. Edited by Eileen O'Neil. Cambridge: Cambridge University Press, 2001.

———. *Philosophical and Physical Opinions*. London: William Wilson, 1663.

Caviness, Madeline H. "Hildegard as Designer of the Illustrations to Her Works." In *Hildegard of Bingen: The Context of Her Thought and Art*, edited by Charles Burnett and Peter Dronke, 29–62. London: Warburg Institute, 1998.

Cesi, Federico. *The Natural Desire for Knowledge*. Translated by Gregory Conti. Vatican City: Pontifical Academy of Sciences, 2003.

Chambers, David, and F. Quiviger, eds. *Italian Academies of the Sixteenth Century*. London: Warburg Institute, 1995.

Chazan, Robert. "Trial, Condemnation, and Censorship: The Talmud in Medieval Europe." In *The Trial of the Talmud: Paris, 1240*, translated by John Friedman and Jean Connell Hoff, 1–91. Toronto: Pontifical Institute of Medieval Studies, 2012.

Cherniss, Harold F. *The Riddle of the Early Academy*. New York: Russell and Russell, 1962.

Christie, Andrew F., and Robin Wright. "A Comparative Analysis of the Three-Step Tests in International Treaties." *IIC-International Review of Intellectual Property and Competition Law* 45, no. 4 (2014): 409–33.

Cicero. *De oratore, Books I–II*. Translated by E. W. Sutton and H. Rackham. Cambridge, MA: Harvard University Press, 1942.

Clanchy, C. T. *Abelard: A Medieval Life*. Oxford: Blackwell, 1999.

———. *From Memory to Written Record: England 1066–1307*. 2nd ed. Oxford: Blackwell, 1983.

Clark, Elizabeth. *Reading Renunciation: Asceticism and Scripture in Early Christianity*. Princeton, NJ: Princeton University Press, 1999.

Clark, James G. "Monastic Confraternity in Medieval England: The Evidence from St. Albans Abbey *Liber Benefactorum*." In *Religious and Laity in Western Europe, 1000–1400: Interaction, Negotiation, and Power*, edited by Emilia Jamroziak and Janet E. Burton, 315–31. Turnhout, Belgium: Brepols, 2007.

———. "University Monks in Late Medieval England." In *Medieval Monastic Education*, edited by George Ferzoco and Carolyn Muessig, 56–71. London: Leicester University Press, 2000.

Clark, Peter. *British Clubs and Societies 1580–1800: The Origins of an Associational World*. Oxford: Oxford University Press, 2000.

Clements, Raymond, and Timothy Graham. *Introduction to Manuscript Studies*. Ithaca, NY: Cornell University Press, 2007.

Clennel, W. H. "Bodley, Sir Thomas (1545–1613)." In *Oxford Dictionary of National Biography*, edited by H. C. G. Matthew and Brian Harrison, online ed. Oxford: Oxford University Press, 2004.

Cobban, Alan B. *The Medieval Universities: Their Development and Organization*. London: Methuen, 1975.

Cochrane, Eric. "Science and Humanism in the Italian Renaissance." *American Historical Review* 81, no. 5 (1976): 1039–57.

Cochrane, Louise. *Adelard of Bath: The First English Scientist*. London: British Museum Press, 1994.

Cohen, G. A. *Self-Ownership, Freedom, and Equality*. Cambridge: Cambridge University Press, 1995.

Coleman, Janet. "Dominium in Thirteenth- and Fourteenth-Century Political Thought and Its Seventeenth-Century Heirs: John of Paris and Locke." *Political Studies* 33 (1985): 73–100.

"Commons Reasons for Disagreeing to the Clause for Reviving the Printing Act." *Journal of the House of Lords* 15 (1691–96): 546.

Compayré, Gabriel. *Abelard and the Origin and Early History of Universities.* London: William Heinemann, 1893.

"The Condemnation of 219 Propositions." Translated by Ernest L. Fortin and Peter D. O'Neill. In *Medieval Political Philosophy: A Sourcebook,* edited by Ralph Lerner and Mushn Mahdi, 335–54. New York: Free Press: 1963.

Considine, John. *Academy Dictionaries, 1600–1800.* Cambridge: Cambridge University Press, 2014.

Constable, Giles. "The Second Crusade as Seen by Contemporaries." *Traditio* 9 (1953): 213–79.

Cook, George Henry. *Letters to Cromwell and Others on the Suppression of the Monasteries.* London: John Barker, 1965.

Cook, Harold J. "Medicine." In *Early Modern Science,* edited by Katharine Park and Lorraine Daston, 408–34, vol. 3 of *The Cambridge History of Science.* Cambridge: Cambridge University Press, 2006.

Cooper, Charles Henry. "1529." In *Annals of Cambridge,* vol. 1. Cambridge, UK: Warwick, 1842.

Cooper, P. F. "Historical Aspects of Wastewater Treatment." In *Decentralised Sanitation and Reuse: Concepts, Systems and Implementation,* edited by Piet Lens, Grietje Zeeman, and Gatze Lettinga, 11–38. London: IWA Publishing, 2001.

Copleston, Frederick C. *Medieval Philosophy.* London: Methuen, 1952.

Cosgrove, Matthew R. "Thomas Aquinas on Anselm's Argument." *Review of Metaphysics* 27, no. 3 (1974): 513–30.

Cottier, Jean-François. "Erasmus's *Paraphrases*: 'A New Kind of Commentary'?" In *The Unfolding of Words: Commentary in the Age of Erasmus,* edited by Judith Rice Henderson, 27–45. Toronto: University of Toronto Press, 2012.

Cox, Virginia. "Members, Muses, Mascots: Women and Italian Academies." In *The Italian Academies, 1525–1700: Networks of Culture, Innovation and Dissent,* edited by Jane E. Everson, Denis V. Reidy and Lisa Sampson, 132–69. Abingdon: Routledge, 2016.

Cranston, Maurice. *John Locke: A Biography.* Oxford: Oxford University Press, 1957.

———. "The Politics of John Locke." *History Today* 2, no. 9 (1952): 619–22.

Crombie, A. C. *Robert Grosseteste and the Origins of Experimental Science 1100–1700.* Oxford: Oxford University Press, 1953.

Cummings, Brian. "Encyclopaedic Erasmus." *Renaissance Studies* 28, no. 2 (2014): 183–204.

Curtis, Mark H. *Oxford and Cambridge in Transition, 1558–164.* Oxford: Oxford University Press, 1959.

Curtius, Ernst Robert. *European Literature and the Latin Middle Ages.* Translated by Willard R. Trask. London: Routledge, 1953.

Cyrus, Cynthia J. *The Scribes for Women Convents in Late Medieval Germany.* Toronto: University of Toronto Press, 2009.

Dailey, E. T. "Confinement and Exclusion in the Monasteries of Sixth-Century Gaul." *Early Medieval Europe* 22, no. 3 (2014): 304–35.

Dale, Richard. *Medieval Discussions of the Eternity of the World.* Leiden: Brill, 1990.

Dales, Richard C. "Robert Grosseteste's Scientific Works." *Isis* 52, no. 3 (1961): 381–402.

———. *The Scientific Achievement of the Middle Ages.* Philadelphia: University of Press, 1973.

Damstedt, Benjamin G. "Limiting Locke: A Natural Law Justification for the Fair Use Doctrine." *Yale Law Journal* 112, no. 5 (2003): 1179–221.

Dante Alighieri. *The Inferno.* Translated by John Ciardi. New York: New American Library, 1982.

Darley, Gillian. *John Evelyn: Living for Ingenuity.* New Haven, CT: Yale University Press, 2006.

Darnton, Robert. "A World Digital Library Is Coming True!" *New York Review of Books* 61, no. 9 (2014): 8–11.

Daston, Lorraine. "The Science of the Archive." *Osiris* 27, no. 1 (2012): 156–87.

Davidson, Herbert A. *Alfarabi, Avicenna, and Averroes on Intellect: Their Cosmologies, Theories of the Active Intellect, and Theories of Human Intellect.* Oxford: Oxford University Press, 1992.

Davis, Natalie Zemon. "Beyond the Market: Books as Gifts in Sixteenth-Century France." *Transactions of the Royal Historical Society*, ser. 5, vol. 33 (1983): 69–88.

Deazley, Ronan. "Commentary on Defoe's Essay on the Regulation of the Press (1704)." In *Primary Sources on Copyright (1450–1900): Britain*, edited by L. Bently and M. Kretschmer. Cambridge: University of Cambridge, 2008, online.

———. "Commentary on the *Statute of Anne* 1710." In *Primary Sources on Copyright (1450–1900): Britain*, edited by L. Bently and M. Kretschmer. Cambridge: University of Cambridge, 2008, online.

De Boer, Sander Wopke. *The Science of the Soul: The Commentary Tradition on Aristotle's De Anima, c. 1260–c. 1360.* Leuven, Belgium: Leuven University Press, 2013.

Defoe, Daniel. *An Essay on the Regulation of the Press.* Oxford: Luttrell Society and Blackwell, 1948.

———. *Hymn to the Pillory.* Online ed. Edited by Jess McCarthy, 2013.

De Moor, Tine. "The Silent Revolution: A New Perspective on the Emergence of Commons, Guilds, and Other Forms of Corporate Collective Action in Western Europe." *International Review of Social History*, supp. 53 (2008): 179–212.

De Wulf, Maurice. "The Teaching of Philosophy and the Classification of the Sciences in the Thirteenth Century." *Philosophical Review* 27, no. 4 (1918): 356–73.

Diringer, David. *The Book before Printing: Ancient, Medieval and Oriental.* New York: Dover, 1982.

Dodds, Jerrilyn D., María Rosa Menocal, and Abigail Krasner Balbae. *The Arts of Intimacy: Christians, Jews, and Muslims in the Making of Castilian Culture.* New Haven, CT: Yale University Press, 2008.

Donlan, John. *Spirit Engine.* London, ON: Brick Books, 2008.

Donne, John. *The Works of John Done.* Vol. 6, edited by Henry Alford. London: John Parker, 1889.

Donoghue, Frank. *The Last Professors: The Corporate University and the Fate of the Humanities.* New York: Fordham, 2008.

Downing, David B. *The Knowledge Contract: Politics and Paradigms in the Academic Workplace.* Lincoln: University of Nebraska Press, 2005.

Doyle, Matthew A. *Bernard of Clairvaux and the Schools: The Formation of an Intellectual Milieu in the First Half of the Twelfth Century.* Spoleto, Italy: Centro Italiano di Studi Sull'alto Medioevo, 2005.

Drake, Stillman. *Galileo at Work: His Scientific Biography.* Chicago: University of Chicago Press, 1978.

Dreher, Rod. *The Benedict Option: A Strategy Christians in a Post-Christian Nation.* New York: Penguin Random House, 2017.

Dronke, Peter. *Women Writers of the Middle Ages: A Critical Study of Texts from Perpetua (†203) to Marguerite (†1310).* Cambridge: Cambridge University Press, 1984.

Duby, Georges. *Rural Economy and Country Life in the Medieval West.* Translated by C. Postan. London: Edward Arnold, 1968.

———. *The Three Orders: Feudal Society Imagined.* Translated by Arthur Goldhammer. Chicago: University of Chicago Press, 1981.

Dudden, Frederick Homes. *Gregory the Great: His Place in History and Thought.* Vol. 1. New York: Longmans, Green, 1905.

Dunlop, D. M. *Arab Civilization to A.D. 1500.* New York: Praeger, 1971.

Dunn, John. *The Political Thought of John Locke: An Historical Account of the Argument of the Two Treatises of Government.* Cambridge: Cambridge University Press, 1969.

———. "The Politics of Locke in England and America in the Eighteenth Century." In *John Locke: Problems and Perspectives; A Collection of New Essays,* edited by John W. Yolton, 45–80. Cambridge: Cambridge University Press, 1969.

Dunn, Marilyn. *The Emergence of Monasticism: From the Desert Fathers to the Early Middle Ages.* Oxford: Blackwell, 2000.

Dworetz, Stephen M. *The Unvarnished Doctrine: Locke, Liberalism, and the American Revolution.* Durham, NC: Duke University Press, 1990.

Eamon, William. "From the Secrets of Nature to Public Knowledge: The Origins of the Concept of Openness in Science." *Minerva* 23, no. 3 (1985): 321–47.

———. *Science and the Secrets of Nature: Books of Secrets in Medieval and Early Modern Culture.* Princeton, NJ: Princeton University Press, 1994.

Eastwood, Bruce. "The Astronomies of Pliny, Martianus Capella, and Isidore of Seville in the Carolingian World." In *Science in Western and Eastern Carolingian Times,* edited by Paul Leo Butzer and Dietrich Lohrmann, 169–74. Basel, Switzerland: Birkäuser, 1993.

———. "Mediaeval Empiricism: The Case of Grosseteste's Optics." *Speculum* 43, no. 2 (1968): 306–21.

Eckenrode, T. R. "The Venerable Bede as an Educator." *History of Education* 6, no. 3 (1977): 165–66.

Eckstein, Linda. *Women under Monasticism.* New York: Russell and Russell, 1963.

Eden, Kathy. *Friends Hold All Things in Common: Tradition, Intellectual Property and the Adages of Erasmus.* New Haven, CT: Yale University Press, 2001.

Einhard. "The Life of Charlemagne." In *Einhard and Notker the Stammerer: Two Lives of Charlemagne,* translated by Lewis G. M. Thorpe, 49–90. London: Penguin, 1969.

Eisenberg, Rebecca S. "Patent Swords and Shields." *Science* 299, no. 5609 (2003): 1018–19.

Eisenstein, Elizabeth L. *The Printing Press as an Agent of Change.* Cambridge: Cambridge University Press, 1982.

Elbakyan, Alexandra. "Letter Addressed to Judge Robert W. Sweet from Alexandra Elbakyan re: Clarification of Details." *Elsevier v. Sci-Hub,* 1:15-cv-04282. NY Southern District (September 15, 2015).

———. "Transcript and Translation of Sci-Hub Presentation." Open Access @ UNT, University of North Texas, May 19–20, 2016.

Emmerson, Richard K. "The Representation of Antichrist in Hildegard of Bingen's *Scivias*: Image, Word, Commentary, and Visionary Experience." *Gesta* 41, no. 2 (2002): 95–110.

Erasmus, Desiderius. *Christian Humanism and the Reformation: Selected Writings of Erasmus.* Edited by John C. Olin. New York: Fordham University Press, 1987.

———. *Collected Works of Erasmus.* 65 vols. Edited by Richard J. Schoeck, and Beatrice Corrigan. Toronto: University of Toronto Press, 1974–2016.

———. *Erasmus on His Times: A Shortened Version of the "Adages" of Erasmus.* Edited and translated by Margaret Mann Phillips. Cambridge: Cambridge University Press, 1967.

———. *Erasmus on Women.* Edited by Erika Rummel. Toronto: University of Toronto, 1996.

Erler, Mary C. *Women, Reading, and Piety in Late Medieval England.* Cambridge: Cambridge University Press, 2006.

European Commission. "Open Access to Scientific Information." Brussels, June 30, 2015, online.

Evans, Gillian R. *Bernard of Clairvaux.* Oxford: Oxford University Press, 2000.

Evelyn, John. *Sylva, or A Discourse of Forest-Trees and the Propagation of Timber in His Majesty's Dominion.* London: John Martyn and James Allestry, 1664.

Evenden, Elizabeth. *Patents, Pictures and Patronage: John Day and the Tudor Book Trade.* Farnham, Surrey, UK: Ashgate, 2008.

Fakhry, Majid. *Averroës (Ibn Rushd): His Life, Works and Influence.* Oxford: Oneworld, 2001.

al-Farabi. "The Enumeration of the Sciences." Translated by Fauzi M. Najjar. In *Medieval Political Philosophy: A Sourcebook,* edited by Ralph Lerner and Mushin Mahdi, 22–30. New York: Free Press, 1969.

———. "On the Intellect." In *Classical Arabic Philosophy: An Anthology of Sources,* edited by Jon McGinnis and David C. Reisman, 68–77. Indianapolis: Hackett, 2007.

———. *Philosophy of Plato and Aristotle.* Translated by Muhsin Mahdi. Rev. ed. Ithaca, NY: Cornell University Press, 1969.

———. "Plato's Laws." Translated by Muhsin Mahdi. In *Medieval Political Philosophy: A Sourcebook*, edited by Ralph Lerner and Muhsin Mahdi, 83–94. New York: Free Press, 1963.

Feather, John. "The Book Trade in Politics: The Making of the Copyright Act of 1710." *Publishing History* 8 (1980): 19–44.

———. *A History of British Publishing*. London: Routledge, 1988.

———. "A Learned Press in a Commercial World." In *Beginnings to 1780*, vol. 1 of *The History of Oxford University Press*, edited by Ian Gadd, 242–77. Oxford: Oxford University Press, 2013.

Feld, M. D. *Printing and Humanism in Renaissance Italy: Essays on the Revival of the Pagan Gods*. Rome: Roma nel Rianascimento, 2015.

Fenton, James. "Creweian Oration." *Oxford Gazette*, supp. 4517 (June 25, 1999).

Ferrante, Joan M. "The Education of Women in the Middle Ages in Theory, Fact, and Fantasy." In *Beyond Their Sex: Learned Women of the European Past*, edited by Patricia H. Labalme, 9–42. New York: New York University Press, 1980.

Ferre, Lola, and Raphaela Veit. "The Textual Traditions of Isaac Israeli's *Book on Fevers* in Arabic, Latin, Hebrew, and Spanish." *Aleph: Historical Studies in Science and Judaism* 9, no. 2 (2009): 309–34.

Fichtenau, Heinrich. *The Carolingian Empire: The Age of Charlemagne*. New York: Harper and Row, 1964.

Fidora, Alexander. "From Arabic into Latin into Hebrew: Aristotelian Psychology and Its Contribution to the Rationalisation of Theological Traditions." In *Philosophical Psychology in Arabic Thought and the Latin Aristotelianism of the 13th century*, edited by Luis Xavier López-Farjeat and Jörg Alejandro Tellkamp, 17–40. Paris: Vrin, 2013.

Filmer, Robert. "Patriarcha." In *Patriarcha and Other Writings*, edited by Johann P. Sommerville. Cambridge: Cambridge University Press, 1991.

Findlen, Paula. *Possessing Nature: Museums, Collecting, and Scientific Culture in Early Modern Italy*. Berkeley: University of California Press, 1994.

Findlen, Paula, and Hannah Marcus. "The Breakdown of Galileo's Roman Network: Crisis and Community, ca. 1633." *Social Studies of Science* 47 (2017): 1–27.

Fletcher III, Henry George. *New Aldine Studies: Documentary Essays on the Life and Works of Aldus Manutius*. San Francisco: Bernard M. Rosenthal, 1988.

Fortunatus, Venantius. "The Life of the Holy Radegund." In *Sainted Women of the Dark Ages*, translated by Jo Ann McNamara, 70–105. Durham, NC: Duke University Press, 1992.

Foucault, Michel. *The Archeology of Knowledge and the Discourse on Language*. Translated by A. M. Sheridan Smith. New York: Pantheon, 1972.

———. *Language, Counter-Memory, Practice: Selected Essays and Interviews*. Translated by Donald F. Bouchard and Sherry Simon. Ithaca, NY: Cornell University Press, 1977.

Francis of Assisi. "The Earlier Rule." In *Francis and Clare: The Complete Works*, translated by Regis J. Armstrong and Ignatius Brady, 107–35. Mahwah, NJ: Paulist, 1982.

Frank, Robert G. "Medicine." In *Seventeenth Century*, vol. 4 of *The History of the University of Oxford*, edited by Nicholas Tyacke, 359–448. Oxford: Oxford University Press, 1997.

Freedberg, David. *The Eye of the Lynx: Galileo, His Friends, and the Beginnings of Modern Natural History*. Chicago: University of Chicago Press, 2002.

Fried, Johannes. *Charlemagne*. Translated by Peter Lewis. Cambridge, MA: Harvard University Press, 2016.

Fritze, Ronald Harold. "'Truth Hath Lacked Witnesse, Tyme Wanted Light': The Dispersal of the English Monastic Libraries and Protestant Efforts at Preservation, ca. 1535–1625." *Journal of Library History* 18, no. 3 (1983): 274–291.

Frugoni, Chiara. "The Imagined Woman." Translated by Clarissa Botsford. In *Silences of the Middle Ages*, edited by Christiane Klapisch-Zuber, 336–422, vol. 2 of *A History of Women in the West*. Cambridge, MA: Harvard University Press, 1992.

Fyfe, Aileen. "Journals, Learned Societies and Money: *Philosophical Transactions*, ca. 1750–1900." *Notes and Records: The Royal Society Journal of the History of Science* (2015): doi:10.1098.

Gabriel, Astrik L. "Motivation of the Founders at Medieval Colleges." *Miscellanea Mediaevalia* 3 (1964): 61–72.

Gadd, Ian. "The Learned Press: Printing for the University." In *Beginnings to 1780*, vol. 1 of *The History of Oxford University Press*, edited by Ian Gadd, 278–306. Oxford: Oxford University Press, 2013.

———. "The Press and the London Book Trade." In *Beginnings to 1780*, vol. 1 of *The History of Oxford University Press*, edited by Ian Gadd, 569–99. Oxford: Oxford University Press, 2013.

Galilei, Galileo. *Discoveries and Opinions of Galileo*. Translated by Stillman Drake. New York: Anchor, 1957.

Gamble, Harry Y. *Books and Readers in the Early Church: A History of Early Christian Texts*. New Haven, CT: Yale University Press, 1995.

Gameson, Richard. "Signed Manuscripts from Early Romanseque Flanders: Saint-Bertin and Saint-Vaast." In *Pen in Hand: Medieval Scribal Portraits, Colophons and Tools*, edited by Michael Gullick, 31–73. Walkern, Herts, UK: Red Gull, 2006.

Ganz, David. "Anglo-Saxon England." In *To 1640*, vol. 1 of *The Cambridge History of Libraries in Britain and Ireland*, edited by Elisabeth Leedham-Green and Teresa Webber, 91–108. Cambridge: Cambridge University Press, 2006.

———. "Giving to God in the Mass: The Experience of the Offertory." In *The Languages of Gift in the Early Middle Ages*, edited by Wendy Davies and Paul Fouracre, 18–32. Cambridge: Cambridge University Press, 2010.

———. "The *Liber Glossarum*: A Carolingian Encyclopedia." In *Science in Western and Eastern Carolingian Times*, edited by Paul Leo Butzer and Dietrich Lohrmann, 127–38. Basel, Switzerland: Birkäuser Verlag, 1993.

Garber, Rebecca L. *Feminine Figurae: Representations of Gender in Religious Texts by Medieval German Women Writers*. New York: Routledge, 2003.

Garfield, Eugene. "The History and Meaning of the Journal Impact Factor." *Journal of the American Medical Association* 295, no. 1 (2006): 90–93.

Garner, Bryan A., ed. *Black's Law Dictionary*. 8th ed. St. Paul, MN: West, 2004.

Geiger, Roger L. *Knowledge and Money: Research Universities and the Paradox of the Marketplace*. Stanford, CA: Stanford University Press, 2004.

Gerber, Ben S., and Arnold R. Eiser. "The Patient-Physician Relationship in the Internet Age: Future Prospects and the Research Agenda." *Journal of Medical Internet Research* 3, no. 2 (2001), online.

Giard, Luce. "Remapping Knowledge, Reshaping Institutions." In *Science, Culture and Popular Belief in Renaissance Europe*, edited by Stephen Pumfrey, Paolo L. Rossi, and Maurice Slawinski, 19–47. Manchester: University of Manchester Press, 1991.

Gieysztor, Aleksander. "Management and Resources." In *Universities in the Middle Ages*, edited by H. de Ridder-Symoens, vol. 1 of *A History of the University in Europe*, edited by Walter Rüegg, 108–43. Cambridge: Cambridge University Press, 1992.

Gilson, Étienne. *Reason and Revelation in the Middle Ages*. New York: Charles Scribner, 1938.

Goldgar, Anne, *Impolite Learning: Conduct and Community in the Republic of Letters, 1680–1750*. New Haven, CT: Yale University Press, 1995.

Goodman, L. E. "The Translation of Greek Materials into Arabic." In *Religion, Learning and Science in the ʿAbbasid Period*," edited by M. J. L. Young, J. D. Latham, and R. B. Serjeant, 477–97. Cambridge: Cambridge University Press, 2006.

Gordon, Wendy J. "A Property Right in Self-Expression: Equality and Individualism in the Natural Law of Intellectual Property." *Yale Law Review* 102 (1993): 1533–609.

Grafton, Anthony. "Availability of Ancient Works." In *The Cambridge History of Renaissance Philosophy*, edited by Charles B. Schmitt, Quentin Skinner, Eckhard Kessler, and Jill Kraye, 763–91. Cambridge: Cambridge University Press, 1988.

———. *Commerce with the Classics: Ancient Books and Renaissance Readers.* Ann Arbor: University of Michigan Press, 1997.

———. *The Culture of Correction in Renaissance Europe.* London: British Library, 2011.

———. *Forgers and Critics: Creativity and Duplicity in Western Scholarship.* Princeton, NJ: Princeton University Press, 1990.

———. "Kepler as Reader." *Journal of the History of Ideas* 53, no. 4 (1992): 561–72.

———. "Renaissance Readers and Ancient Texts: Comments on Some Commentaries." *Renaissance Quarterly* 38, no. 4 (1985): 615–49.

———. *Worlds Made by Words: Scholarship and Community in the Modern West.* Cambridge, MA: Harvard University Press, 2009.

Grafton, Anthony, and Lisa Jardine. *From Humanism to the Humanities: Education and the Liberal Arts in the Fifteenth- and Sixteenth-Century Europe.* London: Duckworth, 1986.

Grafton, Anthony, and Megan Williams. *Christianity and the Transformation of the Book: Origen, Eusebius, and the Library of Caesarea.* Cambridge, MA: Harvard University Press, 2008.

Graham, Timothy. *Introduction to Manuscript Studies.* Ithaca, NY: Cornell University Press, 2007.

Gramsci, Antonio. *Selections from Cultural Writings.* Edited by D. Forgacs and G. Nowell Smith. Translated by W. Boelhower. London: Lawrence and Wishart, 1985.

Grande, Sandy. *Red Critical Theory: Native American Social and Political Thought.* Lanham, MD: Rowman and Littlefield, 2004.

Grant, Edward. *The Foundations of Modern Science in the Middle Ages: Their Religious, Institutional and Intellectual Contexts.* Cambridge: Cambridge University Press, 1996.

"The Great Charter of the University of Oxford (3 March 1636), Excerpt." Translated by Simon Neal and Andrew Hegarty. In *Beginnings to 1780*, vol. 1 of *The History of Oxford University Press*, edited by Ian Gadd, 660–67. Oxford: Oxford University Press, 2013.

Green, Peter. "Politics of Royal Patronage: Early Ptolemaic Alexandria." *Grand Street* 5, no. 1 (1985): 151–63.

Greenberg, Daniel S. *Science for Sale: The Perils, Rewards, and Delusions of Campus Capitalism.* Chicago: University of Chicago Press, 2007.

Greenough, James B. "Etymologies." *Harvard Studies in Classical Philology* 4 (1893): 143–49.

Griffiths, Fiona J. "Nun's Memories or Missing History in Alsace (c. 1200): Herrad of Hohenbourg's *Garden of Delights*." In *Medieval Memories: Men, Women and the Past, 700–1300*, edited by Elisabeth M. C. Van Houts, 132–49. Harlow, Essex, UK: Longman, 2001.

Griffiths, Paul J. "Seeking Egyptian Gold: A Fundamental Metaphor for the Christian Intellectual Life in a Religiously Diverse Age." *Cresset* 63, no. 5 (2000): 6–17.

Guédon, Jean-Claude. *In Oldenburg's Long Shadow: Librarians, Research Scientists, Publishers, and the Control of Scientific Publishing.* Washington, DC: Association of Research Libraries, 2001.

Guerrini, Luigi. "The 'Accademia dei Lincei' and the New World." Unpublished paper. Max Planck Institute for the History of Science, Berlin, 2008.

Guibert of Nogent. *A Monk's Confessions: The Memoirs of Guibert of Nogent.* Translated by Paul J. Archambault. University Park: Pennsylvania State University Press, 1996.

Guston, David H., and Kenneth Keniston. "Introduction: The Social Contract for Science." In *Fragile Contract: University Science and the Federal Government*, edited by David H. Guston and Kenneth Keniston, 1–41. Cambridge, MA: MIT Press, 1994.

Gutas, Dimitri. *Avicenna and the Aristotelian Tradition: Introduction to Reading Avicenna's Philosophical Works.* Leiden: Brill, 2014.

———. "The Empiricism of Avicenna." *Oriens* 40 (2012): 391–436.

———. *Greek Thought, Arabic Culture: The Graeco-Arabic Translation Movement in Baghdad and Early 'Abbāsid Society (2nd-4th/8th-10th Centuries)*. London: Routledge, 1998.

———. "Origins in Baghdad." In *The Cambridge History of Medieval Philosophy*, edited by Robert Pasnau, 11-25. Cambridge: Cambridge University Press, 2014.

Hackett, M. B. "The University as Corporate Body." In *The Early Oxford Schools*, vol. 1 of *The History of the University of Oxford*, edited by J. I. Catto, 37-96. Oxford: Oxford University Press, 1984.

Hahn, Roger. *The Anatomy of a Scientific Institution: The Paris Academy of Sciences, 1666-1803*. Berkeley: University of California Press, 1971.

Hall, Edwin. *Sweynheim and Pannartz and the Origins of Printing in Italy: German Technology and Italian Humanism in Renaissance Rome*. McMinnville, OR: Phillip J. Pirages, 1991.

Hall, Marie Boas. *Henry Oldenburg: Shaping the Royal Society*. Oxford: Oxford University Press, 2002.

Halley, Edmund. "Advertisement." *Philosophical Transactions* 16 (1687): 297.

Halstead, Mark. "An Islamic Concept of Education." *Comparative Education* 40, no. 4 (2004): 517-29.

Hankins, James. "Humanism and Modern Political Thought." In *Cambridge Companion to Renaissance Humanism*, edited by Jill Kraye, 118-41. Cambridge: Cambridge University Press, 2007.

———. "Humanism, Scholasticism, and Renaissance Philosophy." In *Cambridge Companion to Renaissance Philosophy*, edited by James Hankins, 30-48. Cambridge: Cambridge University Press, 2007.

———. "Humanist Academies and the 'Platonic Academy of Florence.'" In *On Renaissance Academies*, edited by Marianne Pade, 31-46. Rome: Quasar, 2011.

———. "The Myth of the Platonic Academy of Florence." *Renaissance Quarterly* 44, no. 3 (1991): 429-75.

Hanning, Robert W. *The Vision of History in Early Britain: From Gildas to Geoffrey of Monmouth*. New York: Columbia University Press, 1966.

Hardin, Garrett. "The Tragedy of the Commons." *Science* 162, no. 3859 (1968): 1243-48.

Hardy, Thomas. *Jude the Obscure*. Edited by Cedric Watts. Peterborough, ON: Broadview, 1999.

Harnad, Stevan. Registry of Open Access Repository Policies and Mandates. University of Southampton, UK, July 27, 2015, online.

Harris, Tim. *London Crowds in the Reign of Charles II: Propaganda and Politics from the Restoration until the Exclusion Crisis*. Cambridge: Cambridge University Press, 1987.

Harrison, John, and Peter Laslett. *The Library of John Locke*. Oxford: Oxford University Press, 1965.

Haskins, Charles Homer. "The Introduction of Arabic Science into England." In *Studies in the History of Medieval Science*. New York: Frederick Ungar, 1924.

———. *The Rise of Universities*. Ithaca, NY: Cornell University Press, 1923.

Hasse, Dag Nikolaus. "Avicenna's Epistemological Optimism." In *Interpreting Avicenna: Critical Essays*, edited by Peter Adamson, 109-18. Cambridge: Cambridge University Press, 2013.

Hathaway, Neil. "Compilatio: From Plagiarism to Compiling." *Viator* 20 (1989): 19-44.

Heath, Shirley Brice. "A National Language Academy? Debate in the New Nation." *International Journal of the Sociology of Language* 11 (1976): 9-43.

Hegarty, Andrew. "The University and the Press, 1584-1780." In *Beginnings to 1780*, vol. 1 of *The History of Oxford University Press*, edited by Ian Gadd, 158-90. Oxford: Oxford University Press, 2013.

Hernández, Francisco. *The Mexican Treasury: The Writings of Dr. Francisco Hernández*. Translated by Rafael Chabrán, Cynthia L. Chamberlin, and Simon Varey. Stanford, CA: Stanford University Press, 2000.

Herren, Michael W. "Storehouses of Learning: Encyclopaedias and Other Reference Works in Ireland and Pre-Bedan Anglo Saxon England." In *Practice in Learning: The Transfer of Encyclopaedic*

Knowledge in the Early Middle Ages, edited by Rolf H. Bremmer Jr. and Kees Dekker, 1–18. Paris: Peeters, 2010.

Hiaschmann, Nancy, and Kristie M McLure, eds. *Feminist Interpretations of John Locke*. University Park: Pennsylvania State University Press, 2007.

Higley, Sarah L. *Hildegard of Bingen's Unknown Language: An Edition, Translation, and Discussion*. New York: Palgrave Macmillan, 2007.

Hildegard of Bingen. *The Personal Correspondence of Hildegard of Bingen*. Edited by Joseph L. Baird. Oxford: Oxford University Press, 2006.

———. *Selected Writings*. Translated by Mark Atherton. London: Penguin, 2001.

Hill, Christopher. *The Century of Revolution, 1603–1714*. 2nd ed. New York: Norton, 1980.

Hillenbrand, Robert. "'Ornament of the World': Medieval Córdoba as a Cultural Centre." In *Legacy of Muslim Spain*, edited by Salma Khadra Jayyusi and Manuela Marín, 112–35. Leiden: Brill, 1992.

Hillgarth, J. N. "Ireland and Spain in the Seventh Century." *Peritia* 3 (1984): 1–16.

Hippocrates. *Prognosticacion, Drawen Out of the Bookes of Ipocras, Avicen, and Other Notable Auctours of Physycke, Shewynge the Daunger of Dyvers Syckenesses*. London: Robert Wyer, ca. 1545.

History and Proceedings of the House of Commons from Restoration to Present Times, vol. 6. London: Richard Chandler, 1742.

Hitchcock, Steve. "The Effect of Open Access and Downloads ('Hits') on Citation Impact: A Bibliography of Studies." OpCit Project (2013). Online.

Holder, Arthur G. "Bede and the New Testament." In *Cambridge Companion to Bede*, edited by Scott De Gregorio, 142–55. Cambridge: Cambridge University Press, 2010.

Holland, Suzanne, Karen Lebacqz, and Laurie Zoloth, eds. *The Human Embryonic Stem Cell Debate: Science, Ethics, and Public Policy*. Cambridge, MA: MIT Press, 2001.

Honoré, A. M. "Ownership." In *Oxford Essays in Jurisprudence*, edited by A. G. Guest, 107–28. Oxford: Oxford University Press, 1961.

Hooke, Robert. *Lampas, or Descriptions of Some Mechanical Improvements of Lamps and Waterpoises*. London: John Martyn, 1677.

———. *Micrographica, or Some Physiological Descriptions of Minute Bodies Made by Magnifying Glasses, with Observations and Inquiries Thereupon*. London: John Martyn and James Allestry, 1665.

Horan, David. *Oxford: A Cultural and Literary Companion*. New York: Interlink, 2000.

Horner, Shari. *The Discourse of Enclosure: Representing Women in Old English Literature*. Albany: State University of New York Press, 2001.

Hourani, George F. "The Early Growth of the Secular Sciences in Andalusia." *Studia Islamica*, no. 32 (1970): 143–56.

Hoyle, R. W. "The Origins of the Dissolution of the Monasteries." *Historical Journal* 38, no. 2 (1995): 275–305.

Huff, Toby E. *The Rise of Early Modern Science: Islam, China, and the West*. 2nd ed. Cambridge: Cambridge University Press, 2003.

Humphreys, K. W. *The Book Provisions of the Medieval Friars 1215–1400*. Amsterdam: Erasmus, 1964.

Hunter, Michael. *Boyle: Between God and Science*. New Haven, CT: Yale University Press, 2009.

———. *Establishing the New Science: The Experience of the Early Royal Society*. Woodbridge, Suffolk, UK: Boydell and Brewer, 1989.

———. *Science and the Shape of Orthodoxy: Intellectual Change in Late Seventeenth-Century Britain*. Woodbridge, Suffolk, UK: Boydell and Brewer, 1995.

Hutton, Sarah. "The Cambridge Platonists and Averroes." In *Renaissance Averroism and Its Aftermath: Arabic Philosophy in Early Modern Europe*, edited by Anna Akasoy and Guido Giglioni, 197–211. Dordrecht, Netherlands: Springer, 2013.

Huyler, Jerome. *Locke in America: The Moral Philosophy of the Founding Era*. Lawrence: University of Kansas Press, 1995.

Hyde, Edward. *The History of the Rebellion and Civil Wars in England*, vol. 5. Oxford: Oxford University Press, 1839.

Ibn Khaldun. *The Muqaddimah: An Introduction to History*. Translated by Franz Rosenthal. Princeton, NJ: Princeton University Press, 1969.

al-Idrisi. "A Muslim Geographer in King Roger's Court." In *Muslim and Christian Contact in the Middle Ages: A Reader*, edited by Jarbel Rodriguez, 384–86. Toronto: University of Toronto Press, 2015.

Iliffe, Rob. "'In the Warehouse': Privacy, Property, and Priority in the Early Royal Society." *History of Science* 30 (1992): 29–68.

Illich, Ivan. *In the Vineyard of the Text: A Commentary to Hugh's "Didascalion."* Chicago: University of Chicago Press, 1993.

Iogna-Prat, Dominique. *Order and Exclusion: Cluny and Christendom Face Heresy, Judaism, and Islam, 1000–1150*. Translated by Graham Robert Edwards. Ithaca, NY: Cornell University Press, 2002.

Irvine, Martin. *The Making of Textual Culture: 'Grammatica' and Literary Theory, 350–1100*. Cambridge: Cambridge University Press, 2006.

Irving, Sarah. *Natural Science and the Origins of the British Empire*. London: Pickering and Chatto, 2008.

Isidore of Seville. *The Etymologies of Isidore of Seville*. Translated by Stephen A. Barney, W. J. Lewis, J. A. Beach, and Oliver Berghof. Cambridge: Cambridge University Press, 2006.

Jaeger, C. Stephen. *The Envy of Angels: Cathedral Schools and Social Ideas in Medieval Europe, 950–1200*. Philadelphia: University of Pennsylvania Press, 1994.

Jamroziak, Emilia. *The Cistercian Order in Medieval Europe, 1090–1500*. London: Routledge, 2013.

Jardine, Lisa. *Erasmus, Man of Letters: The Construction of Charisma in Print*. Princeton, NJ: Princeton University Press, 1994.

Jefferson, Thomas. *Writings*. Edited by Merrill D. Peterson. New York: Library of America, 1984.

Jeffrey, Jane E. "Radegund and the Letter of Foundation." In *Women Writing Latin: From Roman Antiquity to Early Modern Europe*, vol. 2, edited by Laurie J. Churchill, Phyllis R. Brown, and Jane E. Jeffrey, 11–24. New York: Routledge, 2002.

Jensen, Kristen. "Universities and Colleges." In *To 1640*, vol. 1 of *The Cambridge History of Libraries in Britain and Ireland*, edited by Elisabeth Leedham-Green and Teresa Webber, 345–62. Cambridge: Cambridge University Press, 2006.

Jerome. "Beginning of the Prologue to the Letters of Paul the Apostle." Translated by Kevin P. Edgecomb (Biblicalia, blog, August 17, 2006) from *Biblia sacra: Iuxta Vulgatam versionem*, edited by B. Fischer and R. Weber, 4th ed. Stuttgart: Deutoche Bibelgescellscaft, 1994.

———. *Commentary on Galatians*. Translated by Andrew Cain, vol. 121 of *The Fathers of the Church*. Washington, DC: Catholic University of America Press, 2010.

———. *Commentary on Matthew*. Translated by Thomas P. Scheck. Washington, DC: Catholic University of America Press, 2008.

———. "Letter 22 to Eustochium, The Virgin's Profession, Written 384 A.D." In *Jerome: Selected Letters*, translated by F. A. Wright, 53–159. Cambridge, MA: Harvard University Press, 1933.

———. *St. Jerome: Letters and Select Works*. Translated by W. H. Freemantle. Vol. 6 of *Nicene and Post-Nicene Fathers of the Christian Church*, 2nd ser., edited by Philip Schaff and Henry Wace. Grand Rapids, MI: Eerdmans, 1954.

"Johannes of Speyer's Printing Monopoly, Venice (1469)." In *Primary Sources on Copyright (1450–1900)*, edited by Lionel Bently and Martion Kretschmer. Cambridge: University of Cambridge, 2008, online.

John of Paris. *On Royal and Papal Power*. Translated by J. A. Watt. Toronto: Pontifical Institute of Medieval Studies, 1971.

John of Salisbury. *The Metalogicon: A Twelfth-Century Defense of the Verbal and Logical Arts of the "Trivium."* Translated by Daniel D. McGarry. Berkeley: University of California Press, 1962.

Johns, Adrian. "The Ambivalence of Authorship in Early Modern Natural Philosophy." In *Scientific Authorship: Credit and Intellectual Property in Science*, edited by Mario Biagioli and Peter Galison, 67–90. London: Routledge, 2003.

———. *The Nature of the Book: Print and Knowledge in the Making*. Chicago: University of Chicago Press, 1998.

———. *Piracy: The Intellectual Property Wars from Gutenberg to Gates*. Chicago: University of Chicago Press, 2009.

———. "Science and the Book." In *The Cambridge History of the Book in Britain*, vol. 4, *1557–1695*, edited by John Barnard and D. F. McKenzie, 274–303. Cambridge: Cambridge University Press, 2002.

Johnson, John, and Strickland Gibson, eds. *The First Minute Book of the Delegates of the Oxford University Press, 1668–1756*. Oxford: Oxford University Press, 1943.

———. *Print and Privilege at Oxford to the Year 1700*. Oxford: Oxford University Press, 1946.

Johnson, Penelope D. "Agnes of Burgundy: An Eleventh-Century Woman as Monastic Patron." *Journal of Medieval History* 15, no. 2 (1989): 93–104.

———. *Equal in Monastic Profession: Religious Women in Medieval France*. Chicago: University of Chicago Press, 1991.

Johnson, Samuel. *A Dictionary of the English Language*. London: Rivington et al., 1785.

Johnston, Charlotte. "Locke's Examination of Malebranche and John Norris." *Journal of the History of Ideas* 19, no. 4 (1958): 551–58.

Jones, Leslie W. "The Influence of Cassiodorus on Mediaeval Culture." *Speculum* 20, no. 4 (1945): 433–42.

Jones, Putnam Fennell. "The Gregorian Mission and English Education." *Speculum* 3, no. 3 (1928): 335–48.

Jordan, Erin. "Female Founders: Exercising Authority in Thirteenth-Century Flanders and Hainaut." *Church History and Religious Culture* 88, no. 4 (2008): 535–61.

"JSTOR Evidence in *United States vs. Aaron Swartz*: Overview." New York: JSTOR, July 30, 2013, online.

Jussen, Bernhard, "Religious Discourses of the Gift in the Middle Ages: Semantic Evidences (Second to Twelfth Centuries)," in *Negotiating the Gift: Pre-Modern Figurations of Exchange*, ed. Gadi Algazi, Valentin Groebner, and Bernhard Jussen, 173–92. Göttingen, Germany: Vandenhoeck and Ruprecht, 2003.

Kelly, Thomas. *Early Public Libraries: A History of Public Libraries in Great Britain before 1850*. London: Library Association, 1966.

Kemp, Geoff. "The 'End of Censorship' and the Politics of Toleration, from Locke to Sacheverell." *Parliamentary History* 31 (2012): 47–68.

Kendrick, Christopher. *Utopia, Carnival, and Commonwealth in Renaissance England*. Toronto: University of Toronto Press, 2004.

Kennedy, William J. "Versions of a Career: Petrarch and His Renaissance Commentators." In *European Literary Careers: The Author from Antiquity to the Renaissance*, edited by Patrick Cheney and Frederick Alfred De Armas, 146–64. Toronto: University of Toronto Press, 2002.

Kenny, Anthony J. P. "The Character of Humanist Philology." In *Classical Influences on European Culture A.D. 500–1500*, edited by R. R. Bolgar, 119–28. Cambridge: Cambridge University Press, 1971.

———. *Medieval Philosophy*. Vol. 2 of *A New History of Western Philosophy*. Oxford: Oxford University Press, 2005.

Kerr, Julie. *Monastic Hospitality: The Benedictines in England, c. 1070—c. 1250*. Woodbridge, Suffolk, UK: Boydell and Brewer, 2007.

Kibre, Pearl. *Scholarly Privileges in the Middle Ages: The Rights, Privileges, and Immunities of Scholars and Universities at Bologna, Padua, Paris and Oxford*. Cambridge: Medieval Academy of America, 1962.

Kienzle, Beverly Mayne. "Hildegard of Bingen's Teaching in Her *Expositiones evangeliorum* and *Ordo virtutum.*" In *Medieval Monastic Education*, edited by George Ferzoco and Carolyn Muessig, 72–86. London: Leicester University Press, 2000.

Kilburn, Matthew. "The Fell Legacy 1686-1755." In *Beginnings to 1780*, vol. 1 of *The History of Oxford University Press*, edited by Ian Gadd, 106–37. Oxford: Oxford University Press, 2013.

al-Kindī. "On the Intellect." In *Classical Arabic Philosophy: An Anthology of Sources*, edited by Jon McGinnis and David C. Reisman, 16–17. Indianapolis: Hackett, 2007.

King, Richard John. *Handbook to the Cathedrals of England, Eastern Division*. London: John Murray, 1881.

Kingsley, Charles. *Alton Locke, Tailor and Poet: An Autobiography*. London: Macmillan, 1881.

Knappenberger, Brian. *The Internet's Own Boy: The Story of Aaron Swartz*. Los Angeles: Luminant Media, 2014, online.

Knowles, David. *Bare Ruined Choirs: The Dissolution of the English Monasteries*. Cambridge: Cambridge University Press, 1976.

———. *The Evolution of Medieval Thought*. New York: Vintage, 1962.

———. *The Monastic Order in England: A History of Its Development from the Times of St. Dunstan to the Fourth Lateran Council, 943-1216*. Cambridge: Cambridge University Press, 1950.

———. *The Religious Orders in England*. Cambridge: Cambridge University Press, 1959.

———. "St. Bernard of Clairvaux: 1090-1153." *Dublin Review* 177, no. 105 (1953): 104–21.

Kraemer, Joel L. "The Islamic Context of Medieval Jewish Philosophy." In *Cambridge Companion to Medieval Jewish Philosophy*, edited by Daniel H. Frank and Oliver Leaman, 38–68. Cambridge: Cambridge University Press, 2003.

Kramnick, Isaac. *Republicanism and Bourgeois Radicalism: Political Ideology in Late Eighteenth-Century England and America*. Ithaca, NY: Cornell University Press, 1990.

Kukkonen, Taneli. "Ibn Sīnā and the Early History of Thought Experiments." *Journal of the History of Philosophy* 52, no. 3 (2014): 432–59.

Kusukawa, Sachiko. "The *Historia Piscium* (1686)." *Notes and Records: The Royal Society Journal of the History of Science* 54, no. 2 (2000): 179–97.

———. "Illustrating Nature." In *Books and the Sciences in History*, edited by Marina Frasca-Spada and Nick Jardine, 90–113. Cambridge: Cambridge University Press, 2000.

Laistner, M. L. W. "Bede as a Classical and Patristic Scholar." In *The Intellectual Heritage of the Early Middle Ages: Selected Essays of M. L. W. Laistner*, edited by Chester G. Starr, 93–116. Ithaca, NY: Cornell University Press, 1957.

———. *Thought and Letters in Western Europe, A.D. 500 to 900*. 2nd ed. Ithaca, NY: Cornell University Press, 1957.

Lapidge, Michael. *The Anglo-Saxon Library*. Oxford: Oxford University Press, 2013.

Larminie, Vivienne. "The Fell Era, 1658-1686." In *Beginnings to 1780*, vol. 1 of *The History of Oxford University Press*, edited by Ian Gadd, 79–104. Oxford: Oxford University Press, 2013.

Las Casas, Bartolomé de. *A Short Account of the Destruction of the Indies*. Translated by Nigel Griffin. London: Penguin, 2004.

Laslett, Peter. "The Foundation of the Royal Society and the Medical Profession in England." *British Medical Journal* (1960): 165–69.

Lassner, Jacob. "The English Revolution and Locke's *Two Treatises of Government.*" *Cambridge Historical Journal* 12, no. 1 (1956): 40–55.

———. *Jews, Christians, and the Abode of Islam: Modern Scholarship, Medieval Realities*. Chicago: University of Chicago Press, 2012.

Laud, William, *History of the Chancellorship*, vol. 5 of *The Works of the Most Revered Father in God, William Laud*. Oxford: John Henry Parker, 1853.

Lawrence, C. H. "Blund, John (c.1175–1248)." In *Oxford Dictionary of National Biography*, edited by H. C. G. Matthew and Brian Harrison, online ed. Oxford: Oxford University Press, 2004.

Leclercq, Jean. *The Love of Learning and the Desire for God: A Study of Monastic Culture*. Translated by C. Misrahi. New York: Fordham University Press, 1982.

Ledford, Heidi. "Universities Struggle to Make Patents Pay." *Nature* 501, no. 7468 (2013): 471–72.

Leedham-Green, Elisabeth, and David McKitterick. "Ownership: Private and Public Libraries." In *1557–1695*, vol. 4 of *The Cambridge History of the Book in Britain*, edited by John Barnard and D. F. McKenzie, 323–38. Cambridge: Cambridge University Press, 2002.

Leff, Gordon. *Paris and Oxford Universities in the Thirteenth and Fourteenth Centuries: An Institutional and Intellectual History*. New York: Wiley, 1968.

Lefkowtiz, Mary R., and Guy Maclean Rogers, eds. *Black Athena Revisited*. Chapel Hill: University of North Carolina Press, 1996.

Le Goff, Jacques. *Intellectuals in the Middle Ages*. Translated by Teresa Lavender Fagan. Oxford: Blackwell, 1993.

———. *Must We Divide History into Periods?* Translated by Malcolm Debevoise. New York: Columbia University Press, 2015.

———. *My Quest for the Middle Ages*. Translated by Richard Veasey. Edinburgh: Edinburgh University Press, 2005.

———. *Time, Work, and Culture in the Middle Ages*. Translated by Arthur Goldhammer. Chicago: University of Chicago Press, 1980.

———. *Your Money or Your Life: Economy and Religion in the Middle Ages*. Translated by Patricia Ranum. New York: Zone, 1990.

Lerer, Seth. *Error and the Academic Self: The Scholarly Imagination, Medieval to Modern*. New York: Columbia University Press, 2002.

———. Introduction to Boethius, *The Consolation of Philosophy*, translated by David R. Slavitt. Cambridge, MA: Harvard University Press, 2008.

Lessig, Lawrence. "The Creative Commons." *Florida Law Review* 55 (2003): 763–78.

Lester, Anne E. "Cares beyond the Walls: Cistercian Nuns and the Care of Lepers in Twelfth- and Thirteenth-Century Northern France." In *Religious and Laity in Western Europe, 1000–1400*, vol. 2, edited by Emilia Jamroziak and Janet E. Burton, 197–224. Turnhout, Belgium: Brepols, 2010.

L'Estrange, Roger. *The Character of a Papist in Masquerade: Supported by Authority and Experience, in Answer to "The Character of a Popish Successor."* London: H. Brome, 1681.

———. *Fables, of Aesop and Other Eminent Mythologists: With Morals and Reflection*. London: R. Sare, A. & J. Churchill, et al., 1692.

Levey, Martin. "Mediaeval Arabic Bookmaking and Its Relation to Early Chemistry and Pharmacology." *Transactions of the American Philosophical Society*, new ser., 52, no. 4 (1962): 1–79.

Levine, Joseph M. "Problem of the Johannine Comma." *Journal of the History of Ideas* 58, no. 4 (1997): 573–96.

Lewis, Bernard. *The Muslim Discovery of Europe*. New York: Norton, 1982.

Lewis, M. Heather. "William Warham, Patron of Erasmus." PhD diss., McGill University, 1997.

Lilburne, John. *England's Birth-Right Justified*. London: Larner's Press, 1645.

Locke, John. *Æsop's Fables, in English & Latin, Interlineary, for the Benefit of Those Who Not Having a Master, Would Learn Either of These Tongues*. London: A. and J. Churchill, 1703.

———. *Correspondence of John Locke*. Edited by E. S. de Beer. 9 vols. Oxford: Oxford University Press, 1989.

———. *An Essay concerning Human Understanding*. Edited by Peter H. Nidditch. Oxford: Oxford University Press, 1975.

———. *Political Essays*. Edited by Mark Goldie. Cambridge: Cambridge University Press, 1997.

———. *Two Tracts on Government*. Edited and translated by Philip Abrams. Cambridge: Cambridge University Press, 1967.

———. *Two Treatises of Government*. Edited by Peter Laslett. Student ed. Cambridge: Cambridge University Press, 1988.

———. *Writings on Religion*. Edited by Victor Nuovo. Oxford: Oxford University Press, 2002.

Logan, F. Donald. "The First Royal Visitation of the English Universities, 1535." *English Historical Review* 106, no. 421 (1991): 861–88.

Long, Pamela O. *Openness, Secrecy, Authorship: Technical Arts and the Culture of Knowledge from Antiquity to the Renaissance*. Baltimore: Johns Hopkins University Press, 2001.

Love, Harold, *Attributing Authorship: An Introduction*. Cambridge: Cambridge University Press, 2002.

Love, Rosalind. "The World of Latin Learning." In *The Cambridge Companion to Bede*, edited by Scott De Gregorio, 40–53. Cambridge: Cambridge University Press, 2010.

Lowenstein, Joseph. *The Author's Due: Printing and the Prehistory of Copyright*. Chicago: University of Chicago Press, 2002.

Lowry, Martin J. C. "The 'New Academy' of Aldus Manutius: A Renaissance Dream." *Bulletin of the John Rylands University Library* 58, no. 2 (1976): 378–420.

———. *The World of Aldus Manutius: Business and Scholarship in Renaissance Venice*. Ithaca, NY: Cornell University Press, 1979.

Lucas, Peter J. *From Author to Audience: John Capgrave and Medieval Publication*. Dublin: University College Dublin Press, 1997.

Luna, Paul, and Martyn Ould. "The Printed Page." In *Beginnings to 1780*, vol. 1 of *The History of Oxford University Press*, edited by Ian Gadd, 510–45. Oxford: Oxford University Press, 2013.

Lux, David. "The Reorganization of Science 1450–1700." In *Patronage and Institutions: Science, Technology, and Medicine at the European Court, 1500–1750*, edited by Bruce T. Moran. Rochester, NY: Boydell, 1991.

Macaulay, Thomas Babington. *The History of England, from the Accession of James II*, vol. 4. Philadelphia: Butler, 1856.

Maclean, Ian. *Scholarship, Commerce, Religion: The Learned Book in the Age of Confessions, 1560–1630*. Cambridge, MA: Harvard University Press, 2012.

Macky, John. *A Journey through England in Familiar Letters*. 2nd ed. London: J. Hooke, 1722.

Macleod, Christine. "The 1690s Patents Boom: Invention or Stock-Jobbing?" *Economic History Review* 39, no. 4 (1986): 549–71.

Macomber, Henry P. "A Comparison of the Variations and Errors in Copies of the First Edition of Newton's *Principia*, 1687." *Isis* 42, no. 3 (1951): 230–32.

Macpherson, C. B. *The Political Theory of Possessive Individualism: Hobbes to Locke*. Oxford: Oxford University Press, 1962.

Macrobius. *Saturnalia*. Vol. 1, bks. 1–2. Translated by Robert A. Kaster. Cambridge, MA: Harvard University Press, 2011.

Macy, Gary. *The Hidden History of Women's Ordination: Female Clergy in the Medieval West*. Oxford: Oxford University Press, 2008.

Madan, Falconer. *A Brief Account of the University Press at Oxford with Illustrations Together with a Chart of Oxford Printing*. Oxford: Oxford University Press, 1908.

Mahdi, Muhsin. "The Editio Princeps of Fārābī's *Compendium Legum Platonis*." *Journal of Near Eastern Studies* 20, no. 1 (1961): 1–24.

Makdisi, George. *The Rise of Colleges: Institutions of Learning in Islam and the West*. Edinburgh: Edinburgh University Press, 1981.

Malcolm, Noel. *Aspects of Hobbes*. Oxford: Clarendon, 2002.

———. "Hobbes and the Royal Society." In *Perspectives on Thomas Hobbes*, edited by G. A. J. Rogers and Alan Ryan, 43–66. Oxford: Oxford University Press, 1988.

Maloney, Erin K., et al. "Sources and Types of Online Information That Breast Cancer Patients Read and Discuss with Their Doctors." *Palliative and Supportive Care* 13, no. 2 (2015): 107-14.

Mandelbrote, Scott. "The Bible Press." In *Beginnings to 1780*, vol. 1 of *The History of Oxford University Press*, edited by Ian Gadd, 480-509. Oxford: Oxford University Press, 2013.

Mandich, Guilio "Venetian Patents (1450-1550)," *Journal of the Patent Office Society* 30, no. 3 (1948): 166-224.

Mansfield, Bruce. *Phoenix of His Age: Interpretations of Erasmus, c. 1550-1750*. Toronto: University of Toronto Press, 1979.

Marenbon, John. *Pagans and Philosophers: The Problem of Paganism from Augustine to Leibniz*. Princeton, NJ: Princeton University Press, 2015.

———. *The Philosophy of Peter Abelard*. Cambridge: Cambridge University Press, 1997.

Marrone, Steven P. *William of Auvergne and Robert Grosseteste: New Ideas of Truth in the Early Thirteenth Century*. Princeton, NJ: Princeton University Press, 1983.

Marx, Karl. *Economic and Philosophic Manuscripts of 1844*. Translated by Martin Milligan. Moscow: Progress, 1959.

Mass, Clifford W. "German Printers and the German Community in Renaissance Rome." *Library* 5, no. 31 (1976): 118-26.

Masson, David. "Introduction: Bibliographical, Biographical, and Expository." In *Poetical Works of John Milton*, edited by David Masson, 2:1-124. London: Macmillan, 1890.

Mayer, Thomas F., ed. *The Trial of Galileo, 1612-1633*. Toronto: University of Toronto Press, 2012.

McCluskey, Stephen C. "Astronomies in the Latin West from the Fifth to the Ninth Centuries." In *Science in Western and Eastern Civilization in Carolingian Times*, edited by Paul Leo Butzer and Dietrich Lohrmann, 139-60. Basel: Birkäuser, 1993.

McConica, James. "Humanism and Aristotle in Tudor Oxford." *English Historical Review* 94, no. 371 (1979): 291-317.

McCray, Patrick. *Glassmaking in Renaissance Venice: The Fragile Craft*. Farnham, Surrey, UK: Ashgate, 1999.

McCue, James F. "The Doctrine of Transubstantiation from Berengar through Trent: The Point at Issue." *Harvard Theological Review* 61, no. 3 (1968): 385-430.

McCulloh, John M. "Confessor Saints and the Origins of Monasticism: The Lives of Saints Antony and Martin." In *The Middle Ages in Text and Texture: Reflections on Medieval Sources*, edited by Jason Glenn, 21-32. Toronto: University of Toronto Press, 2011.

McDonnell, Gerald. "Cistercian Monks as Metallurgists: Iron Technology at Rievaulx Abbey 1130-1600." Lecture. Ian Ramsey Centre for Science and Religion, Oxford University, 2011. iTunes U online.

McGill, Scott. *Plagiarism in Latin Literature*. Cambridge: Cambridge University Press, 2012.

McGinn, Bernard. *Thomas Aquinas's "Summa theologiae": A Biography*. Princeton, NJ: Princeton University Press, 2014.

McKenzie, Donald F., and Maureen Bell. *A Chronology and Calendar of Documents Relating to the London Book Trade, 1641-1700*. Oxford: Oxford University Press, 2005.

McKeon, Peter R. "The Status of the University of Paris as *Parens Scientiarum*: An Episode in the Development of Its Autonomy." *Speculum* 39, no. 4 (1964): 651-75.

McKitterick, David. *Four Hundred Years of University Printing and Publishing in Cambridge*. Cambridge: Cambridge University Press, 1984.

———. *Printing and the Book Trade in Cambridge: 1534-1698*. Vol. 1 of *A History of Cambridge University Press*. Cambridge: Cambridge University Press, 1992.

McKitterick, Rosamond. *The Carolingians and the Written Word*. Cambridge: Cambridge University Press, 1989.

McLaughlin, Mary Martin. *Intellectual Freedom and Its Limitations in the University of Paris in the Thirteenth and Fourteenth Centuries*. New York: Arno, 1977.

McMullin, B. J. "The Bible Trade." In *The Cambridge History of the Book in Britain*, vol. 4, *1557–1695*, edited by John Barnard and D. F. McKenzie, 455–73. Cambridge: Cambridge University Press, 2002.

McNamara, Jo Ann Kay. "The Herrenfrage: The Restructuring of the Gender System, 1050–1150." In *Medieval Masculinities: Regarding Men in the Middle Ages*, edited by Clare A. Lees, 3–29. Minneapolis: University of Minnesota Press, 1994.

McSherry, Corynne. *Who Owns Academic Work? Battling for Control of Intellectual Property*. Cambridge, MA: Harvard University Press, 2000.

McVaugh, Michael. "Constantine the African." In *Complete Dictionary of Scientific Biography*, 3:393–95. Detroit: Scribner's Sons, 2008.

Mele, Salvatore, Heather Morrison, Dan D'Agostino, and Sharon Dyas-Correia. "SCOAP3 and Open Access." *Serials Review* 35, no. 4 (2009): 264–71.

Menache, Sophia, "Communication in the Jewish Diaspora: A Survey." In *Communication in the Jewish Diaspora: The Pre-modern World*, edited by Sophia Menache, 15–58. Leiden: Brill, 1996.

Mendelson, Michael. "Saint Augustine." In *Stanford Encyclopedia of Philosophy*, edited by Edward N. Zalta. Stanford, CA: Metaphysics Research Lab, 2010, online.

Menocal, Maria Rosa. *The Ornament of the World: How Muslims, Jews and Christians Created a Culture of Tolerance in Medieval Spain*. Boston: Little, Brown, 2002.

Merges, Robert P. "The Economic Impact of Intellectual Property Rights: An Overview and Guide." *Journal of Cultural Economics* 19 (1995): 103–17.

Merson, John. "Bio-prospecting or Bio-piracy: Intellectual Property Rights and Biodiversity in a Colonial and Postcolonial Context." *Osiris* 15 (2000): 282–96.

Merton, Robert K. "The Normative Structure of Science." In *The Sociology of Science: Theoretical and Empirical Investigations*, edited by Norman W. Storer, 267–78. Chicago: University of Chicago, 1973.

———. *On the Shoulders of Giants: The Post-Italianate Edition*. Chicago: University of Chicago Press, 1965.

Metlitzki, Dorothee. *The Matter of Araby in Medieval England*. New Haven, CT: Yale University Press, 1977.

Mews, Constant J. "The Council of Sens (1141): Abelard, Bernard, and the Fear of Social Upheaval." *Speculum* 77, no. 2 (2002): 342–82.

———. "Hildegard and the Schools." In *Hildegard of Bingen: The Context of Her Thought and Art*, edited by Charles Burnett and Peter Dronke, 89–110. London: Warburg Institute, 1998.

Meyer, Gerald Dennis. *The Scientific Lady in England 1650–1760: An Account of Her Rise, with Emphasis on the Major Roles of the Telescope and Microscope*. Berkeley: University of California Press, 1955.

Micke, O., and Hübner, J. "Traditional European Medicine—After All, Is Hildegard von Bingen Really Right?" *European Journal of Integrative Medicine* 1, no. 4 (2009): 226.

Mihesuah, Devon Abbott, and Angela Cavender Wilson, eds. *Indigenizing the Academy: Transforming Scholarship and Empowering Communities*. Lincoln: University of Nebraska Press, 2004.

Milton, Anthony. "Laud, William (1573–1645). *Archbishop of Canterbury*." In *Oxford Dictionary of National Biography*, edited by H. C. G. Matthew and Brian Harrison, online ed. Oxford: Oxford University Press, 2004.

Milton, John R. "Animadversions upon the Remonstrants Defense against Smectymnuus." In *The Works of John Milton, Historical, Political, and Miscellaneous*, vol. 1, edited by Richard Baron, 80–108. London: Millar, 1753.

———. "Areopagitica." In *Milton's Prose Writings*, 145–85. London: Dent, 1958.

———. "Laws of Nature." In *The Cambridge History of the Seventeenth-Century Philosophy*, vol. 1, edited by Daniel Garber and Michael Ayers, 680–701. Cambridge: Cambridge University Press, 1998.

Minnis, Alistair J. *Medieval Theory of Authorship: Scholastic Literary Attitudes in the Later Middle Ages*. 2nd ed. Philadelphia: University of Pennsylvania Press, 1988.

———. "Nolens auctor sed compilator reputari: The Late-Medieval Discourse of Compilation." In *La méthode critique au moyen âge*, edited by Mireille Chazan and Gilbert Dahan, 47-63. Turnhout, Belgium: Brepols, 2006.

Mitterauer, Michael. *Why Europe? The Medieval Origins of Its Special Path.* Translated by Gerald Chapple. Chicago: University of Chicago Press, 2010.

Montgomery, Scott L. *Science in Translation: Movement of Knowledge through Cultures and Time.* Chicago: University of Chicago Press, 2000.

Moore, R. I. *War on Heresy: Faith and Power in Medieval Europe.* Cambridge, MA: Harvard University Press, 2012.

Moorhead, Laura, Cheryl Holzmeyer, Lauren Maggio, Ryan Steinberg, and John Willinsky. "In an Age of Open Access to Research Policies: Physician and Public Health NGO Staff Research Use and Policy Awareness." *PLOS One,* 2015, doi:10.1371.

Moran, Bruce T. "Courts and Academies." In *Early Modern Science,* edited by Katherine Park and Lorraine Daston, 251-71. Vol. 3 of *The Cambridge History of Science,* Cambridge: Cambridge University Press, 2006.

Morris, John. "Restrictive Practices in the Elizabethan Book Trade: The Stationers' Company v. Thomas Thomas 1583-8." *Transactions of the Cambridge Bibliographical Society* 4, no. 4 (1967): 276-90.

Moxham, Noah. "Edward Tyson's Phocaena: A Case Study in the Institutional Context of Scientific Publishing." *Notes and Records: The Royal Society Journal of the History of Science* 66, no. 3 (2012): 235-52.

———. "Fit for Print: Developing an Institutional Model of Scientific Periodical Publishing in England, 1665-ca. 1714." *Notes and Records: The Royal Society Journal of the History of Science* 69, no. 3 (2015): doi:10.1098.

Mueller, Janice M. "No Dilettante Affair: Rethinking the Experimental Use Exception to Patent Infringement for Biomedical Research Tools." *Washington Law Review* 76, no. 4 (2001): 1-66.

Mulligan, Lotte. "Civil War Politics, Religion and the Royal Society" *Past and Present* 59, no. 1 (1973): 92-116.

Mullinger, James Bass. *From the Earliest Times to the Royal Injunctions of 1535.* Vol. 1 of *The University of Cambridge.* Cambridge: Cambridge University Press, 1873.

Mullins, Edwin. *Cluny: In Search of God's Lost Empire.* New York: Bluebridge, 2006.

Munby, A. N. L. "The Distribution of the First Edition of Newton's 'Principia.'" *Notes and Records: The Royal Society Journal of the History of Science* 10, no. 1 (1952): 28-39.

Murray, Alexander. *Reason and Society in the Middle Ages.* Oxford: Oxford University Press, 1978.

al-Musawi, Muhsin J. *Medieval Islamic Republic of Letters: Arabic Knowledge Construction.* Notre Dame, IN: University of Notre Dame Press, 2015.

National Science Board. "Science and Engineering Indicators 2014." Arlington, VA: National Science Foundation.

Newhauser, Richard. "Augustinian *Vitium curiositatis* and Its Reception." In *Saint Augustine and His Influence in the Middle Ages,* edited by Edward B. King and Jacqueline T. Schaefer, 99-124. Sewanee, TN: Press of the University of the South, 1988.

Newman, Barbara. "Annihilation and Authorship: Three Women Mystics of the 1290s." *Speculum* 91, no. 3 (2016): 591-630.

———. *Sister of Wisdom: St. Hildegard's Theology of the Feminine.* Berkeley: University of California Press, 1989.

Newman, John Henry. "The Benedictine Centuries." *Atlantis* 2 (January-July 1859): 1-43.

———. *Historical Sketches,* vol. 2. London: Longmans Green, 1906.

Newton, Isaac. *The Correspondence of Isaac Newton.* Vol. 1, *1667-1775.* Cambridge: Cambridge University Press, 1959.

———. *Philosophiæ Naturalis Principia Mathematica.* London: Joseph Streater, 1687.

———. *The Principia: Mathematical Principles of Natural Philosophy*. Translated by I. Bernard Cohen and Anne Whitman. Berkeley: University of California Press, 1999.

Noble, David. *A World without Women: The Christian Clerical Culture of Western Science*. New York: Oxford University Press, 1993.

Nozick, Robert. *Anarchy, State, and Utopia*. New York: Basic, 1974.

Nuovo, Angela. *The Book Trade in the Italian Renaissance*. Translated by Lydia G. Cochrane. Leiden: Brill, 2013.

Nussbaum, Martha. *Not for Profit: Why Democracy Needs the Humanities*. Princeton, NJ: Princeton University Press, 2010.

Oates, J. C. T. *Cambridge University Library: A History, from the Beginnings to the Copyright Act of Queen Anne*. Cambridge: Cambridge University Press, 1986.

Obama, Barack. "Remarks by the President on the National Network for Manufacturing Innovation." Speech, North Carolina State University, Raleigh, January 15, 2014.

O'Brien, William. "March-In Rights under the Bayh-Dole Act: The NIH's Paper Tiger?" *Seton Hall Law Review* 43 (2013): 1403-32.

Ockham, William of. *Philosophical Writings*. Translated by Philotheus Boehner. Indianapolis: Bobbs-Merrill, 1964.

O'Donnell, *Cassiodorus*. Berkeley: University of California Press, 1979.

Oldenburg, Henry. *Correspondence of Henry Oldenburg*. Edited by A. Rupert Hall and Marie Boas Hall. 12 vols. Madison: University of Wisconsin Press, 1966.

———. "The Introduction." *Philosophical Transactions* 1, no. 1 (1664/65): 1-2.

———. "To the Royal Society." *Philosophical Transactions* 1 (1665) [unpaginated].

Orme, Nicholas. "For Richer, for Poorer? Free Education in England, c. 1380-1530." *Journal of the History of Childhood and Youth* 1, no. 2 (2008): 169-87.

———. *Medieval Schools: From Roman Britain to Renaissance England*. New Haven, CT: Yale University Press, 2006.

Ostrom, Elinor. "Revisiting the Commons: Local Lessons, Global Challenges." *Science* 284, no. 5412 (1999): 278-82.

Ould, Mary. "The Workplace: Places, Procedures, and Personnel 1668-1780." In *Beginnings to 1780*, vol. 1 of *The History of Oxford University Press*, edited by Ian Gadd, 193-240. Oxford: Oxford University Press, 2013.

Overton, Richard. *An Arrow against All Tyrants and Tyranny, Shot from the Prison of New-gate into the Prerogative Bowels of the Arbitrary House of Lords*. London: Martin Claw, 1646.

Overty, Joanne Filippone. "The Cost of Doing Scribal Business: Prices of Manuscript Books in England, 1300-1483." *Book History* 11 (2008): 1-32.

Ovitt, George, Jr. "Manual Labor and Early Medieval Monasticism." *Viator* 17 (1986): 1-17.

Oxford University Statutes. Vols. 1-2, Translated by G. R. M. Ward. London: William Pickering, 1845-51.

Pabel, Hilmar B. "Sixteenth-Century Catholic Criticism of Erasmus' Edition of St Jerome." *Reformation and Renaissance Review* 6, no. 2 (2004): 231-62.

Palmer, Robert B. "Bede as Textbook Writer: A Study of His *De arte metrica*." *Speculum* 34, no. 4 (1959): 573-84.

Pangle, Thomas L. *The Spirit of Modern Republicanism: The Moral Vision of the American Founders and the Philosophy of Locke*. Chicago: University of Chicago Press, 1990.

Parchomovsky, Gideon, and Alex Stein. "Intellectual Property Defenses." *Columbia Law Review* 113, no. 6 (2013): 1483-1542.

Parker, Holt N. "Women and Humanism: Nine Factors for the Woman Learning." *Viator* 35, no. 1 (2004): 581-616.

Parkes, Malcolm Beckwith. "The Influence of the Concepts of *Ordinatio* and *Compilatio* on the Development of the Book." In *Medieval Learning and Literature: Essays Presented to Richard*

William Hunt, edited by J. J. G. Alexander and M. T. Gibson, 115–41. Oxford: Oxford University Press, 1976.

———. *Their Hand before Our Eyes: A Closer Look at Scribes*. Lyell Lectures 1999. Farnham, Surrey, UK: Ashgate, 2008.

Partridge, R. C. Barrington. *The History of the Legal Deposit of Books*. London: Library Association, 1938.

Pascal, Blaise. *The Provincial Letters of Blaise Pascal*. Translated by Thomas M'Crie. London: Chatto and Windus, 1857.

Pateman, Carole. "Self-Ownership and Property in the Person: Democratization and a Tale of Two Concepts." *Journal of Political Philosophy* 10, no. 1 (2002): 20–53.

"Patents to the University of Oxford (12 November 1632)." Translated by Simon Neal and Andrew Hegarty. In *Beginnings to 1780*, vol. 1 of *The History of Oxford University Press*, edited by Ian Gadd, 652–55. Oxford: Oxford University Press, 2013.

Peacey, Jason. "'Printers to the University': 1584–1658." In *Beginnings to 1780*, vol. 1 of *The History of Oxford University Press*, edited by Ian Gadd, 50–77. Oxford: Oxford University Press, 2013.

Pease, Arthur Stanley. "The Attitude of Jerome towards Pagan Literature." *Transactions of the American Philological Association* 50 (1919): 150–67.

Pegues, Franklin J. "Philanthropy and the Universities in France and England in the Later Middle Ages." In *The Economic and Material Frame of the Medieval University*, edited by Astrik L. Gabriel, 69–80. Notre Dame, IN: International Commission for the History of Universities, 1977.

Pennington, M. Basil. "Lectio and Love: An Introduction to the Cistercian Tradition." In *In the School of Love: An Anthology of Early Cistercian Texts*, edited by Edith Scholl, 15–19. Kalamazoo, MI: Cistercian, 2006.

Pepys, Samuel. *Diary and Correspondence of Samuel Pepys. F.R.S.* Edited by J. Smith. Philadelphia: J. B. Lippincott, 1855.

Peters, F. E. *Aristotle and the Arabs: The Aristotelian Tradition in Islam*. New York: New York University Press, 1968.

Petrarch, Francesco. *Letters of Old Age (Rerum Senillium Libri)*. 2 vols. Translated by Reta A. Bernardo. New York: Italica, 2005.

———. *Letters on Familiar Matters (Rerum Familiarium Libri)*. 3 vols. Translated by Aldo S. Bernardo. New York: Italica, 2005.

———. "On His Own Ignorance and That of Others." Translated by Hans Nachod. In *The Renaissance Philosophy of Man*, edited by Ernst Cassirer, Paul Oskar Kristeller, and John Herman Randall Jr., 47–133. Chicago: University of Chicago Press, 1948.

———. "On the Abundance of Books." In *Four Dialogues for Scholars*, translated by Conrad H. Rawski, 30–44. Cleveland, OH: Case Western University Press, 1967.

Pettegree, Andrew. *The Book in the Renaissance*. New Haven, CT: Yale University Press, 2010.

Pettigrew, William A. "Free to Enslave: Politics and the Escalation of Britain's Transatlantic Slave Trade, 1688–1714." *William and Mary Quarterly*, ser. 3, vol. 64, no. 1 (2007): 3–38.

Pfeiffer, Rudolph. *History of Classical Scholarship 1300–1850*. Oxford: Oxford University Press, 1976.

Philip, Ian. *The Bodleian Library in the Seventeenth and Eighteenth Centuries*. Oxford: Oxford University Press, 1983.

Philips, Anne. *Our Bodies: Whose Property?* Princeton, NJ: Princeton University Press, 2010.

Picciotto, Joanna. *Labors of Innocence in Early Modern England*. Cambridge, MA: Harvard University Press, 2010.

Pieper, Josef. *Scholasticism: Personalities and Problems of Medieval Philosophy*. Translated by Richard Winston and Clare Winston. New York: McGraw-Hill, 1964.

Plato. "Protagoras." In *The Dialogues of Plato*, vol. 1, 2nd ed., translated by B. Jowett. Oxford: Oxford University Press, 1875.

Pliny the Elder. *Natural History: A Selection*. Translated by John F. Healy. London: Penguin, 1991.

Pocock, J. G. A. Introduction to *The Political Works of James Harrington*, part 1, edited by J. G. A. Pocock, 1-154. Cambridge: Cambridge University Press, 1977.

———. "The Myth of John Locke and the Obsession with Liberalism." In *John Locke*, edited by J. G. A. Pocock and Richard Ashcraft, 3-24. Los Angeles: William Andrews Clark Memorial Library, 1980.

Pollack, Andrew. "Myriad Genetics Ending Patent Dispute on Breast Cancer Risk Testing." *New York Times*, January 27, 2015, online.

Pollard, Alfred W. "The Regulation of the Book Trade in the Sixteenth Century." *Library*, ser. 3, vol. 7, no. 25 (1916): 18-43.

Pomata, Gianna, and Nancy G. Sirais. Introduction to *Historia: Empiricism and Erudition in Early Modern Europe*, edited by Gianna Pomata and Nancy G. Sirais, 1-38. Cambridge, MA: MIT Press, 2005.

Post, Gaines, Kimon Giocarinis, and Richard Kay. "The Medieval Heritage of a Humanistic Ideal: 'Scientia donum dei est, unde vendi non potest.'" *Traditio* 11 (1955): 195-234.

Pound, Roscoe. *An Introduction to the Philosophy of Law*. New Haven, CT: Yale University Press, 1954.

Purrington, Robert D. *The First Professional Scientist: Robert Hooke and the Royal Society of London*. Basel, Switzerland: Springer, 2009.

Putnam, George Haven. *Books and Their Makers during the Middle Ages*. New York: Hillary House, 1962.

Radder, Hans. *The Commodification of Academic Research: Science and the Modern University*. Pittsburgh: University of Pittsburgh Press, 2010.

Radegund. "The Thuringian War." In *Sainted Women of the Dark Ages*, translated by Jo Ann McNamara, 65-70. Durham, NC: Duke University Press, 1992.

Radice, Betty. Introduction to *The Letters of Abelard and Heloise*, translated by Betty Radice, xiii-lxxxvii. London: Penguin, 1974.

Raftis, James A. "Western Monasticism and Economic Organization." *Comparative Studies in Society and History* 3, no. 4 (1961): 452-69.

Ragep, F. Jamil. "Copernicus and His Islamic Predecessors: Some Historical Remarks." *History of Science* 45, no. 1 (2007): 65-81.

Ragep, F. Jamil, and Alī al-Qūshjī. "Freeing Astronomy from Philosophy: An Aspect of Islamic Influence on Science." *Osiris* 16 (2001): 49-71.

Rashdall, Hastings. *The Universities of Europe in the Middle Ages*. Edited by F. M. Powicke and A. B. Emden. 3 vols. Oxford: Oxford University Press, 1936.

Rasmussen, Linda. "Monastic Benefactors in England and Denmark: Their Social Background and Gender Distribution." In *Religious and Laity in Western Europe, 1000-1400*, vol. 2, edited by Emilia Jamroziak and Janet E. Burton, 77-91. Turnhout, Belgium: Brepols, 2010.

Raven, James *The Business of Books: Booksellers and the English Book Trade 1450-1850*. New Haven, CT: Yale University Press, 2007.

Ray, Meredith K. *Daughters of Alchemy: Women and Scientific Culture in Early Modern Italy*. Cambridge, MA: Harvard University Press, 2015.

Ray, Roger. "Bede and Cicero." *Anglo-Saxon England* 16 (1987): 1-15.

———. *Bede, Rhetoric, and the Creation of Christian Latin Culture*, Jarrow Lecture 1997. Jarrow, Tyne and Wear, UK: St. Paul's Church, 1997.

———. "Bede's Vera Lex Historiae." *Speculum* 55, no. 1 (1980): 1-21.

———. "Who Did Bede Think He Was?" In *Innovation and Tradition in the Writings of the Venerable Bede*, edited by Scott Degregorio, 11-36. Morgantown: West Virginia University Press, 2006.

Reader's Guide to the Bodleian Library. Oxford: Oxford University Library Services, 2009.

Reasons Humbly Offered to Be Considered before the Act of Printing Be Renewed (unless with Alterations) Viz. for Freedom of Trade in Lawful Books, and Setting Severe Penalties on Scandalous and Seditious Books against the Government. London, 1692.

"Reasons Humbly Offer'd for the Bill for the Encouragement of Learning" (London, 1706). In *Primary Sources on Copyright (1450-1900),* edited by L. Bently and M. Kretschmer. Cambridge: University of Cambridge, 2008, online.

"Reasons Humbly Offer'd for the Bill for the Encouragement of Learning, and for Securing the Property of Copies of Books to the Rightful Owners thereof" (London, 1709). In *Primary Sources on Copyright (1450-1900),* edited by L. Bently and M. Kretschmer. Cambridge: University of Cambridge, 2008, online.

The Record of the Royal Society of London. London: Harrison and Sons, 1897.

Reeve, Henry. *Petrarch.* Edinburgh: Blackwood and Sons, 1878.

Reisman, David C. "Al-Fārābī and the Philosophical Curriculum." In *The Cambridge Companion to Arabic Philosophy,* edited by Peter Adamson and Richard C. Taylor, 52-71. Cambridge: Cambridge University Press, 2005.

———. "Stealing Avicenna's Books: A Study of the Historical Sources for the Life and Times of Avicenna." In *Before and after Avicenna: Proceedings of the First Conference of the Avicenna Study Group,* edited by David C. Reisman and Ahmed H. al-Rahim, 91-126. Leiden: Brill, 2003.

Resnick, David. "Rationality and the *Two Treatises.*" In *John Locke's "Two Treatises of Government": New Interpretations,* edited by Edward J. Harpham, 82-117. Lawrence: Kansas University Press, 1992.

"Revised Patent to the University of Oxford (13 March 1633)." Translated by Simon Neal and Andrew Hegarty. In *Beginnings to 1780,* vol. 1 of *The History of Oxford University Press,* edited by Ian Gadd, 655-59. Oxford: Oxford University Press, 2013.

Rex, Richard, and C. D. C. Armstrong. "Henry VIII's Ecclesiastical and Collegiate Foundations." *Historical Research* 75, no. 190 (2002): 390-407.

Richardson, Brian. *Print Culture in Renaissance Italy: The Editor and the Vernacular Text, 1470-1600.* Cambridge: Cambridge University Press, 1984.

Riché, Pierre. *Education and Culture in the Barbarian West: From the Sixth through the Eighth Century.* Translated by John J. Contreni. Columbia: University of South Carolina Press, 1976.

Rimmer, Matthew. "The Race to Patent the SARS Virus: The TRIPS Agreement and Access to Essential Medicines." *Melbourne Journal of International Law* 5, no. 2 (2004): 335-74.

Rist, John M. *Augustine Deformed: Love, Sin, and Freedom in the Western Tradition.* Cambridge: Cambridge University Press, 2014.

Robinson, H. W. "An Unpublished Letter of Dr Seth Ward Relating to the Early Meetings of the Oxford Philosophical Society." *Notes and Records: The Royal Society Journal of the History of Science* 7 (1949): 68-70.

Robinson, James Harvey. *Petrarch: The First Modern Scholar and Man of Letters.* New York: Putnam's Sons, 1907.

Roehl, Richard. "Plan and Reality in a Medieval Monastic Economy: The Cistercians." *Journal of Economic History* 29, no. 1 (1969): 180-82.

Rogers, G. A. J. "Locke's *Essay* and Newton's *Principia.*" *Journal of the History of Ideas* 39, no. 2 (1978): 217-32.

Röll, Johannes. "A Crayfish in Subiaco: A Hint of Nicholas of Cusa's Involvement in Early Printing?" *Library* 16, no. 2 (1994): 135-40.

Romm, James S. "Aristotle's Elephant and the Myth of Alexander's Scientific Patronage." *American Journal of Philology* 110, no. 4 (Winter 1989): 566-75.

Rooksby, Jacob H., and Brian Pusser, "Learning to Litigate: University Patents in the Knowledge Economy." In *Academic Capitalism in the Age of Globalization,* edited by Brenda Cantwell and Ilkka Kaupin, 74-93. Baltimore: Johns Hopkins University Press, 2014.

Roos, Anna Marie. "The Art of Science: A 'Rediscovery' of the Lister Copperplates." *Notes and Records: The Royal Society Journal of the History of Science* 65 (2011): 1–22.

Rose, Jacqueline. *Godly Kingship in Restoration England: The Politics of the Royal Supremacy, 1660–1688.* Cambridge: Cambridge University Press, 2001.

Rose, Mark. "The Public Sphere and the Emergence of Copyright: Areopagitica, the Stationers' Company, and the Statute of Anne." *Tulsa Journal of Technology and Intellectual Property* 12 (2009): 123–44.

Rosenwein, Barbara H., and Lester K. Little. "Social Meaning in the Monastic and Mendicant Spiritualities." *Past and Present* 63 (1974): 4–32.

The Rule of Benedict. Translated by Carolinne White. London: Penguin, 2008.

Russell, Josiah C. "Hereford and Arabic Science in England about 1175–1200." *Isis* 18, no. 1 (1932): 14–25.

Sabra, A. I. "Ibn al-Haytham's Revolutionary Project in Optics: The Achievement and the Obstacle." In *The Enterprise of Science in Islam: New Perspectives*, edited by Jan P. Hogendijk and Abdelhamid I. Sabra, 85–117. Cambridge, MA: MIT Press, 2003.

Sacks, Oliver W. *Migraine: Understanding a Common Disorder.* Berkeley: University of California Press, 1985.

Sagard, Gabriel. *Histoire du Canada et voyages que les Frères mineurs recollects.* Paris: Claude Sonnius, 1636.

Saliba, George. *Islamic Science and the Making of the European Renaissance.* Cambridge, MA: MIT Press, 2007.

The Sayings of the Desert Fathers. Translated by Benedicta Ward. Kalamazoo, MI: Cistercian Publications, 1975.

Schaffer, Stephen, and Simon Schaffer. *Leviathan and the Air Pump: Hobbes, Boyle, and the Experimental Life.* Princeton, NJ: Princeton University Press, 1985.

Schmitt, Charles B. *Aristotle and the Renaissance.* Cambridge, MA: Harvard University Press, 1983.

Schochet, Gordon J. Introduction to *Life, Liberty and Property: Essays on Locke's Political Ideas*, edited by Gordon J. Schochet. Belmont, CA: Wadsworth, 1971.

Schulenburg, Janet Tibbetts. "The Heroics of Virginity: Brides of Christ and Sacrificial Mutilation." In *Women in the Middle Ages and Renaissance: Literary and Historical Perspectives*, edited by Mary Beth Rose, 29–72. Syracuse, NY: Syracuse University Press, 1986.

Schwartz, John. "Internet Activist, a Creator of RSS, Is Dead at 26, Apparently a Suicide." *New York Times*, January 12, 2014.

Seagrave, S. Adam. "How Old Are Modern Rights? On the Lockean Roots of Contemporary Human Rights Discourse." *Journal of the History of Ideas* 72, no. 2 (2011): 318, 325.

Seasoltz, R. Kevin. "Monastic Autonomy and Exemption: Charism and Institution." *Jurist* 34, no. 2 (1974): 316–55.

Sen, Amartya. "India: The Stormy Revival of an International University." *New Review of Books* 62, no. 13 (2015): 69–71.

Senocak, Neslihan. *The Poor and the Perfect: The Rise of the Franciscan Order, 1209–1310.* Ithaca, NY: Cornell University Press, 2012.

Septimus, Bernard. "Petrus Alfonsi on the Cult of Mecca." *Speculum* 56, no. 3 (1981): 517–33.

Serjeantson, R. W. "Proof and Persuasion." In *Early Modern Science*, edited by Katharine Park and Lorraine Daston, 132–75. Cambridge: Cambridge University Press, 2006.

Shapin, Steven. *Never Pure: Historical Studies of Science as If It Was Produced by People with Bodies, Situated in Time, Space, Culture, and Society, and Struggling for Credibility and Authority.* Baltimore: Johns Hopkins University Press, 2010.

———. "Property, Patronage, and the Politics of Science: The Founding of the Royal Society of Edinburgh." *British Journal for the History of Science* 7, no. 1 (1974): 1–41.

———. *The Scientific Revolution.* Chicago: University of Chicago Press, 1996.

———. *A Social History of Truth: Civility and Science in Seventeenth-Century England.* Chicago: University of Chicago Press, 1994.

Sharpe, Richard. "Selling Books from the Sheldonian." *Library* 11, no. 3 (2010): 275-320.

Shaw, S. Diane. "Study of the Collaboration between Erasmus of Rotterdam and His Printer Johann Froben at Basel during the Years 1514 to 1527." *Erasmus of Rotterdam Society Yearbook* 6, no. 1 (1986): 31-124.

Shaw, Stanford J. *History of the Ottoman Empire and Modern Turkey,* vol. 1. Cambridge: Cambridge University Press, 1976.

Sheehan, M. W. "The Religious Orders 1220-1370." In *The Early Oxford Schools,* edited by J. I. Catto, 193-224, vol. 1 of *The History of the University of Oxford.* Oxford: Oxford University Press, 1984.

Shelley, Percy. *A Defense of Poetry.* Edited by Mary Shelley. Indianapolis: Bobbs-Merrill, 1904.

Siegel, Jerrold E. "'Civic Humanism' or Ciceronian Rhetoric?" *Past and Present* 34 (1966): 3-48.

Silber, Ilana F. "Gift-Giving in the Great Traditions: The Case of Donations to Monasteries in the Medieval West." *European Journal of Sociology* 36, no. 2 (1995): 209-43.

———. "Monasticism and the 'Protestant Ethic': Asceticism, Rationality and Wealth in the Medieval West." *British Journal of Sociology* 44, no. 1 (1993): 103-23.

Simmons, A. John. *The Lockean Theory of Rights.* Princeton, NJ: Princeton University Press, 1992.

Singer, Charles J. "The Visions of Hildegard of Bingen." In *From Magic to Science: Essays on the Scientific Twilight,* 199-239. New York: Boni and Liveright, 1928.

Siraisi, Nancy G. *Avicenna in Renaissance Italy: The Canon and Medical Teaching in Italian Universities after 1500.* Princeton, NJ: Princeton University Press, 1987.

Sirluck, Ernest. "Areopagitica and a Forgotten Licensing Controversy." *Review of English Studies* 11, no. 43 (1960): 260-74.

Skinner, Quentin. "Thomas Hobbes and the Nature of the Early Royal Society." *Historical Journal* 12, no. 2 (1969): 217-39.

Slaughter, Elizabeth. "Retheorizing Academic Capital." In *Academic Capitalism in the Age of Globalization,* edited by Brendan Cantwell and Ilkka Kauppinen, 10-32. Baltimore: Johns Hopkins University Press, 2014.

Smalley, B. "Robert Bacon and the Early Dominican School at Oxford." *Transactions of the Royal Historical Society,* ser. 4, vol. 30 (1948): 1-19.

Smith, A. Mark. *From Sight to Light: The Passage from Ancient to Modern Optics.* Chicago: University of Chicago Press, 2015.

Smith, Adam. *An Inquiry into the Nature and Causes of the Wealth of Nations.* Vol. 1, edited by Edwin Cannan. London: Methuen, 1904.

Smith, Linda Tuhiwai. *Decolonizing Methodologies: Research and Indigenous Peoples.* 2nd ed. London: Zed Books, 2012.

Smith, Preserved. *Erasmus: A Study of His Life, Ideals, and Place in History.* New York: Dover, 1923.

Snape, R. H. *English Monastic Finances in the Later Middle Ages.* Cambridge: Cambridge University Press, 1926.

Solomon, David J., and Bo-Christer Björk. "A Study of Open Access Journals Using Article Processing Charges." *Journal of the American Society for Information Science and Technology* 63, no. 8 (2012): 1485-95.

Some Account of the Oxford University Press, 1468-1926. Oxford: Oxford University Press, 1926.

Sommerfeldt, John R. *Bernard of Clairvaux: On the Life of the Mind.* New York: Newman, 2004.

Southern, R. W. "From Schools to University." In *The Early Oxford Schools,* edited by J. I. Catto, 1-37, vol. 1 of *The History of the University of Oxford.* Oxford: Oxford University Press, 1984.

———. "Grosseteste, Robert (c. 1170-1253)." In *Oxford Dictionary of National Biography,* edited by H. C. G. Matthew and Brian Harrison. Oxford: Oxford University Press, 2004, online ed.

———. *The Making of the Middle Ages.* New Haven, CT: Yale University Press, 1953.

——. *Medieval Humanism and Other Studies*. Oxford: Blackwell, 1971.

——. *Robert Grosseteste: The Growth of an English Mind in Medieval Europe*. 2nd ed. Oxford: Oxford University Press, 1992.

——. *Saint Anselm and His Biographer: A Study of Monastic Thought and Life 1059–1130*. Cambridge: Cambridge University Press, 1966.

——. *Western Society and the Church in the Middle Ages*. London: Penguin, 1970.

——. *Western Views of Islam in the Middle Ages*. Cambridge, MA: Harvard University Press, 1987.

Sparavigna, Amelia Carolina. "Robert Grosseteste and His Treatise on Lines, Angles and Figures of the Propagation of Light." *International Journal of Science* 2, no. 9 (2013): 101–7.

Sprat, Thomas. *The History of the Royal Society of London, for the Improving of Natural Knowledge*. London: Knapton, 1722.

Stahl, William Harris. *The Quadrivium of Martianus Capella: Latin Traditions in the Mathematical Sciences, 50 B.C.–A.D. 1250*. Vol. 1 of *Martianus Capella and the Seven Liberal Arts*. New York: Columbia University Press, 1971.

Starr, S. Frederick. *Lost Enlightenment: Central Asia's Golden Age from the Arab Conquest to Tamerlane*. Princeton, NJ: Princeton University Press, 2013.

"Stationers' Charter, London (1557)." In *Primary Sources on Copyright (1450–1900)*, edited by L. Bently and M. Kretschmer. Cambridge: University of Cambridge, 2008, online.

"Statute of Monopolies, 1623 Chapter 2 21 Ja 1." In *Henry III to James II A.D. 1235–1685*, vol. 1 of *The Statues*, rev. ed. London: Eyre and Spottiswoode, 1870.

"Statute of Monopolies, Westminster (1624)." In *Primary Sources on Copyright (1450–1900): Britain*, edited by L. Bently and M. Kretschmer. Cambridge: University of Cambridge, 2008, online.

"Statutes of Gregory IX for University of Paris, 1231." In *Translations and Reprints from the Original Sources of History*, 2:7–11. Philadelphia: University of Pennsylvania, Department of History, 1902.

Stebbins, Michael. "Expanding Public Access to the Results of Federally Funded Research." White House Office of Science and Technology, Washington, February 22, 2013, online.

Steele, Robert. "The Pecia." *Library* 4, no. 2 (1930): 230–34.

Stevens, Wesley M. "Bede's Scientific Achievement." In *Bede and His World: Jarrow Lectures 1979–1993*, edited by Michael Lapidge, 2:645–88. Farnham, Surrey, UK: Variorum, 1994.

Stock, Brian. *After Augustine: The Meditative Reader and the Text*. Philadelphia: University of Pennsylvania Press, 2011.

——. "Experience, Praxis, Work, and Planning in Bernard of Clairvaux: Observations on the *Sermones in Cantica*." In *The Cultural Context of Medieval Learning*, edited by John E. Murdoch and Edith D. Sylla, 219–68. Dordrecht, Netherlands: Reidel, 1975.

——. "Reading, Writing, and the Self: Petrarch and His Forerunners." *New Literary History* 26, no. 4 (1995): 717–30.

Strasser, M. W. "The Educational Philosophy of the First Universities." In *The University World: A Synoptic View of Higher Education in the Middle Ages and Renaissance*, edited by Douglas Radcliff-Umstead, 1–23. Pittsburgh: Medieval and Renaissance Studies Committee, University of Pittsburgh, 1973.

Strauss, Leo. "How Farabi Read Plato's Laws." In *What Is Political Philosophy? And Other Studies*, 134–54. Chicago: University of Chicago Press, 1959.

——. *Natural Right and History*. Chicago: University of Chicago, 1950.

——. "Persecution and the Art of Writing." *Social Research* 8, no. 4 (1941): 488–504.

Stroup, Alice. "Royal Funding of the Parisian Académie Royale des Sciences during the 1690s." *Transactions of the American Philosophical Society* 77 (1987): 1–167.

Suber, Peter. *Open Access*. Cambridge, MA: MIT Press, 2013.

Summit, Jennifer. *Memory's Library: Medieval Books in Early Modern England*. Chicago: University of Chicago Press, 2008.

"Supplicatio." Translated by Simon Neal and Andrew Hegarty. In *Beginnings to 1780*, vol. 1 of *The History of Oxford University Press*, edited by Ian Gadd, 650-52. Oxford: Oxford University Press, 2013.

Syfret, R. H. "The Origins of the Royal Society." *Notes and Records of the Royal Society of London* 5, no. 2 (1948): 75-137.

Talbot, Ann. *"The Great Ocean of Knowledge": The Influence of Travel Literature on the Work of John Locke*. Leiden: Brill, 2010.

Tarlton, Charles D. "'The Rulers Now on Earth': Locke's Two Treatises and the Revolution of 1688." *Historical Journal* 28, no. 2 (1985): 279-98.

Taylor, E. G. R. "'The English Atlas' of Moses Pitt, 1680-83." *Geographical Journal* 95, no. 4 (1940): 292-99.

Taylor, Joan E., and Philip R. Davies. "The So-Called Therapeutae of 'De Vita Contemplativa': Identity and Character." *Harvard Theological Review* 91, no. 1 (1998): 3-24.

Taylor, Richard C. "The Agent Intellect as 'Form for Us' and Averroes's Critique of al-Fārābī." *Tópicos* 29 (2005): 34.

———. "Separate Material Intellect in Averroes' Mature Philosophy." In *Words, Texts and Concepts Cruising the Mediterranean Sea*, edited by Gerhard Endress, Rüdiger Arnzen, and J. Thielmann, 289-309. Louvain, Belgium: Peeters, 2004.

Teeuwen, Mariken. "Glossing in Close Co-operation: Examples from Ninth-Century Martianus Capella Manuscripts." In *Practice in Learning: The Transfer of Encyclopaedic Knowledge in the Early Middle Ages*, edited by Rolf H. Bremmer Jr. and Kees Dekker, 85-99. Paris: Peeters, 2010.

———. "Marginal Scholarship: The Practice of Learning in the Early Middle Ages (c. 800–c. 1000)." Project description, Huygens Institute, The Hague, online.

———. "The Pursuit of Secular Learning: The Oldest Commentary Tradition on Martiannus Capella." *Journal of Medieval Latin* 18 (2008): 36-51.

Tertullian, Quintus. *De Anima*. Edited by J. H. Waszink. Leiden: Brill, 2010.

———. "The Prescription against Heretics." In *Latin Christianity: Its Founder, Tertullian*, translated by Peter Holmes, edited by Alexander Roberts and James Donaldson, 243-65, vol. 3 of *The Ante-Nicene Fathers*. Grand Rapids, MI: Eerdmans, 1951.

Thiébaux, Marcelle, ed. *The Writings of Medieval Women: An Anthology*. London: Routledge, 1994.

Thijesen, J. M. M. "What Really Happened on 7 March 1277? Bishop Tempier's Condemnation and Its Institutional Context." In *Texts and Contexts in Ancient and Medieval Science*, edited by Edith Sylla and Michael McVaugh, 84-114. Leiden: Brill, 1997.

Thompson, Craig R. Introduction to *Ten Colloquies* by Desiderius Erasmus, vii–xxx. Indianapolis: Bobbs-Merrill, 1957.

———. *Universities in Tudor England*. Washington, DC: Folger Shakespeare Library, 1959.

Thompson, Livingstone. *Modern Science*. Bern, Switzerland: Peter Lang, 2009.

Thompson, R. M. *A Descriptive Catalogue of the Medieval Manuscripts of Merton College*. Cambridge, UK: D. S. Brewer, 2009.

Thomson, S. Harrison. "Grosseteste's Topical Concordance of the Bible and the Fathers." *Speculum* 9, no. 2 (1934): 139-144.

Thornton, Dora. *The Scholar in His Study: Ownership and Experience in Renaissance Italy*. New Haven, CT: Yale University Press, 1997.

Tierney, Brian. "Public Expediency and Natural Law: A Fourteenth-Century Discussion on the Origins of Government and Property." In *Authority and Power*, edited by Brian Tierney and Peter Lineham. Cambridge: Cambridge University Press, 1980.

Tolan, John Victor. *Petrus Alfonsi and His Medieval Readers*. Gainesville: University of Florida Press, 1993.

Torchia, Joseph. *Restless Mind: Curiositas and the Scope of Inquiry in St. Augustine's Psychology*. Marquette, WI: Marquette University Press, 2013.

Tosi, Arturo. "The Accademia della Crusca in Italy: Past and Present." *Language Policy* 10, no. 4 (2011): 289-303.

Tracy, James D. *Erasmus of the Low Countries*. Berkeley: University of California Press, 1997.

Translation of the First Charter, Granted to the President, Council and Fellows of the Royal Society of London by King Charles the Second, A.D. 1662. Royal Society, London, online.

Trevor-Roper, Hugh. *Archbishop Laud, 1573-1645*. 3rd ed. London: Macmillan, 1988.

Triggs, Chris. "Academic Freedom, Copyright and the Academic Exception." *Workplace: A Journal for Academic Labor* 13 (2005): 60-79.

Tuchman, Gaye. *Wannabe U: Inside the Corporate University*. Chicago: University of Chicago Press, 2009.

Tuck, Richard. *Natural Rights Theories: Their Origin and Development*. Cambridge: Cambridge University Press, 1979.

Tully, James H. "Aboriginal Property and Western Theory: Recovering a Middle Ground." *Social Philosophy and Policy* 11, no. 2 (1994): 153-80.

———. *An Approach to Political Philosophy: Locke in Contexts*. Cambridge: Cambridge University Press, 1993.

———. "Conclusion: Consent, Hegemony, Dissent in Treaty Negotiations." In *Consent among Peoples*, edited by J. Webber and C. MacLeod. Vancouver: University of British Columbia Press, 2010.

———. *A Discourse on Property: John Locke and His Adversaries*. Cambridge: Cambridge University Press, 1980.

———. "Property, Self-Government and Consent." *Canadian Journal of Political Science* 28, no. 1 (1995): 105-32.

———. *Public Philosophy in a New Key*. 2 vols. Cambridge: Cambridge University Press, 2008.

Turner, James. *Philology: The Forgotten Origins of the Modern Humanities*. Princeton, NJ: Princeton University Press, 2014.

Twigg, John. *The University of Cambridge and the English Revolution, 1625-1688*. Cambridge, UK: Boydell and Brewer, 1990.

Ullman, Walter. *Law and Politics in the Middle Ages: An Introduction to the Sources of Medieval Political Ideas*. Ithaca, NY: Cornell University Press, 1973.

United Nations Educational, Social, and Cultural Organization (UNESCO). "Open Access Policy concerning UNESCO Publications." Paris, July 31, 2013, online.

"University Statutes (1634-6), Title 18, Section 5." Translated by Simon Neal and Andrew Hegarty. In *Beginnings to 1780*, vol. 1 of *The History of Oxford University Press*, edited by Ian Gadd, 659-60. Oxford: Oxford University Press, 2013.

Vacandard, Elphège. "Arnold of Brescia." In *Catholic Encyclopedia*. Vol. 1. New York: Robert Appleton, 1907. Online.

Vaisey, David. "Thomas Hyde and Manuscript Collecting at the Bodleian." In *The Foundations of Scholarship: Libraries and Collecting, 1650-1750; Papers Presented at a Clark Library Seminar, 9 March 1985*, edited by David Vaisey and David McKitterick, 3-27. Los Angeles: William Andrews Clark Memorial Library, University of California, Los Angeles, 1992.

Vanderputten, Steven. *Reform, Conflict and the Shaping of Corporate Identities: Collected Studies on Benedictine Monasticism, 1050-1150*. Berlin: Lit Verlag, 2013.

Van Engen, John. "The 'Crisis of Cenobitism' Reconsidered." *Speculum* 61 (1986): 269-304.

Veit, Raphaela. "Greek Roots, Arab Authoring, Latin Overlay." In *Vehicles of Transmission, Translation, and Transformation in Medieval Textual Culture*, edited by Robert Wisnovsky, Faith Wallis, Jamie C. Fumo, and Carlos Fraenkel, 353-69. Turnhout, Belgium: Brepols, 2011.

Verger, Jacques. *Men of Learning in Europe at the End of the Middle Ages*. Translated by Lisa Neal and Steven Randall. Notre Dame, IN: University of Notre Dame Press, 2000.

Vernon, R., Gerald McDonnell, and A. Schmidt. "The Geophysical Evaluation of an Iron-Working Complex: Rievaulx and Environs, North Yorkshire." *Archaeological Prospection* 5, no. 4 (1999): 181-201.

Vessey, Mark. "Erasmus' Jerome: The Publishing of a Christian Author." *Erasmus of Rotterdam Society Yearbook* 14 (1994): 62-99.

———. Introduction to *Augustine and the Disciplines: From "Classiacum" to "Confessions,"* edited by Karla Pollmann and Mark Vessey, 1-21. Oxford: Oxford University Press.

———. "Jerome's Origen: The Making of a Christian Literary Persona." *Studia Patristica* 28 (1993): 135-45.

Waddell, Helen. *The Wandering Scholars of the Middle Ages.* 6th ed. London: Constable, 1932.

Waldron, Jeremy. "Enough and as Good Left for Others." *Philosophical Quarterly* 29, no. 117 (1979): 319-28.

———. *God, Locke, and Equality: Christian Foundations of John Locke's Political Thought.* Cambridge: Cambridge University Press, 2002.

———. "John Locke: Social Contract versus Political Anthropology." *Review of Politics* 51, no. 1 (1989): 3-28.

———. *The Right to Private Property.* Oxford: Oxford University Press, 1988.

Wallis, John. "A Copy of the Account, which Dr. Wallis Gave to Dr. Bernard, one of the Delegates for Printing, Jan 23 1691." In *Philosophical Experiments and Observations of the Late Eminent Dr. Robert Hooke,* 217-25. London: W. and J. Innys, 1726.

Walzer, Richard, "Early Islamic Philosophy." In *The Cambridge History of Later Greek and Early Mediaeval Philosophy,* edited by A. H. Armstrong, 641-69. Cambridge: Cambridge University Press, 1970.

———. "The Rise of Islamic Philosophy." *Oriens* 3, ng. 1 (1950): 1-19.

Ward, J. C. "Fashions in Monastic Endowment: The Foundations of the Clare Family, 1066-1314." *Journal of Ecclesiastical History* 32, no. 4 (1981): 427-51.

Ware, Mark, and Michael Mabe. *The STM Report: An Overview of Scientific and Scholarly Journals Publishing.* 4th ed. London: International Association of Scientific, Technical and Medical Publishers, 2015, online.

Watts, Edwards. "Justinian, Malalas, and the End of Athenian Philosophical Teaching in A.D. 529." *Journal of Roman Studies* 94 (2004): 168-82.

Webber, Teresa. "Monastic and Cathedral Book Collections." In *The Cambridge History of Libraries in Britain and Ireland,* vol. 1, *To 1640,* edited by Elisabeth Leedham-Green and Teresa Webber. Cambridge: Cambridge University Press, 2006.

Weber, Max. *Economy and Society: An Outline of Interpretative Sociology.* 2 vols. Edited by Guenther Roth and Claus Wittich. Berkeley: University of California Press, 1978.

———. *The Protestant Ethic and the Rise of Capitalism.* Translated by Talcott Parsons. New York: HarperCollins Academic, 1991.

Webster, Charles. *The Great Instauration: Science, Medicine and Reform 1626-1660.* London: Duckworth, 1975.

Weil, Rachel. "Sometimes a Scepter Is Only a Scepter: Pornography and Politics in Restoration England." In *The Invention of Pornography: Obscenity and Origins of Modernity, 1500-1800,* edited by Lynn Hunt, 125-53. New York: Zone, 1996.

Wells, Joseph. *Wadham College.* London: Routledge/Thoemmes, 1898.

Wemple, Susan Fonay. *Women in Frankish Society: Marriage and the Cloister, 500-900.* Philadelphia: University of Pennsylvania Press, 1985.

West, Andrew Fleming. *Alcuin and the Rise of the Christian Schools.* London: Heinemann, 1899.

Westfall, Richard S. *Never at Rest: A Biography of Isaac Newton.* Cambridge: Cambridge University Press, 1983.

Wilder, Craig Steven. *Ebony and Ivy: Race, Slavery, and the Troubled History of America's Universities*. New York: Bloomsbury, 2014.

Wilkins, John, and Seth Ward. *Vindiciae academiarum Containing, Some Briefe Animadversions upon Mr Websters Book, Stiled, "The Examination of Academies."* Oxford: Leonard Lichfield, 1654.

Wilkinson, Louise J. *"The Rules of Robert Grosseteste* Reconsidered: The Lady as Estate and Household Manager in Thirteenth-Century England." In *The Medieval Household in Christian Europe, 800–c. 1550*, edited by Cordelia Beattie, Anna Maslakovic, and Sarah Rees Jones, 293–307. Turnhout, Belgium: Brepols, 2003.

Williams, Megan Hale. *The Monk and the Book: Jerome and the Making of Christian Scholarship*. Chicago: Chicago University Press, 2006.

Williamson, George. "The Restoration Revolt against Enthusiasm." *Studies in Philology* 30, no. 4 (1933).

Willinsky, John. *The Access Principle: The Case for Open Access to Research and Scholarship*. Cambridge, MA: MIT Press, 2006.

———. *Empire of Words: The Reign of the OED*. Princeton, NJ: Princeton University Press, 1994.

———. *Learning to Divide the World: Education at Empire's End*. Minneapolis: University of Minneapolis Press, 1998.

———. *The New Literacy: Redefining Reading and Writing in the Schools*. New York: Routledge, 1990.

———. "The Publisher's Pushback against NIH's Public Access Policy and Scholarly Publishing Sustainability." *PLOS Biology* 7, no. 1 (2009): e30.

———. "To Publish and Publish and Publish." *Language Arts* 62, no. 6 (1985): 619–23.

———. *The Well-Tempered Tongue: The Politics of Standard English in the High School*. New York: Teachers College Press, 1988.

Wilshire, Leland E. "The Condemnations of 1277 and the Intellectual Climate of the Medieval University." In the *Intellectual Climate of the Early University: Essays in Honor of Otto Gründler*, edited by Nancy van Deusen, 151–93. Kalamazoo, MI: Medieval Institute Publications, 1977.

———. "Were the Oxford Condemnations of 1277 Directed against Aquinas?" *New Scholasticism* 48, no. 1 (1974): 125–32.

Winstanley, Gerrard. *A Letter to the Lord Fairfax and His Council Of War . . . That the Common People Ought to Dig, Plow, Plant, and Dwell upon the Commons, without . . . Paying Rent to Any*. London: Giles Calvert, 1649.

Wippel, John F. "The Parisian Condemnations of 1270 and 1277." In *A Companion to Philosophy in the Middle Ages*, edited by Jorge J. E. Garcia and Timothy N. Noone, 65–73. Oxford: Blackwell, 2002.

Withier, George. *The Schollers Purgatory*. London: G. Wood, 1624.

Witt, Ronald G. *The Two Latin Cultures and the Foundation of Renaissance Humanism in Medieval Italy*. Cambridge: Cambridge University Press, 2012.

Wood, Anthony. *The History and Antiquities of the University of Oxford*, vol. 2. Translated by John Gutch. Oxford: Oxford University Press, 1746.

———. *Life and Times of Anthony Wood: Antiquary of Oxford, 1663–1695, Described by Himself*, vol. 3, *1682–1695*. Oxford: Oxford University Press, 1894.

Wood, Ellen Meiksins. "Radicalism, Capitalism and Historical Contexts: Not Only a Reply to Richard Ashcraft on John Locke." *History of Political Thought* 15, no. 3 (1994): 323–72.

Wood, Ian N. "The Gifts of Wearmouth and Jarrow." In *The Languages of Gift in the Early Middle Ages*, edited by Wendy Davies and Paul Fouracre, 89–115. Cambridge: Cambridge University Press, 2010.

Wood, Rega. "The Influence of Arabic Aristotelianism on Scholastic Natural Philosophy: Projectile Motion, the Place of the Universe, and Elemental Composition." In *The Cambridge History of Medieval Philosophy*, edited by Robert Pasnau, 247–26. Cambridge: Cambridge University Press, 2009.

Woodhouse, J. R., "Borghini and the Foundations of the Accademia della Crusca." In *Italian Academies of the Sixteenth Century*, edited by David Chambers and F. Quiviger, 165-73. London: Warburg Institute, 1995.

Woolf, Virginia. *A Room of One's Own and Three Guineas*. London: Hogarth, 1948.

Woolhouse, Roger S. *Locke: A Biography*. Cambridge: Cambridge University Press, 2007.

Wootton, David. *Modern Political Thought: Readings from Machiavelli to Nietzsche*. Cambridge, MA: Hackett, 2008.

"The World's 60 Largest Book Publishers, 2012." *Publisher's Weekly*, July 19, 2013.

Wright, Louis B. "Some Early 'Friends' of Libraries." *Huntington Library Quarterly* 2, no. 3 (1939): 355-69.

Xalabarder, Raquel. *Study on Copyright Limitations and Exceptions for Educational Activities in North America, Europe, Caucasus, Central Asia and Israel*. Geneva: World Intellectual Property Organization, 2009.

Yates, Frances A. "The Italian Academies." In *Renaissance and Reform: The Italian Contribution; Collected Essays*, 6-29. London: Routledge, 1983.

Yocum, Demetrio S. *Petrarch's Humanist Writing and Carthusian Monasticism: The Secret Language of the Self*. Turnhout, Belgium: Brepols, 2013.

Yolton, Jean S. *John Locke: A Descriptive Bibliography*. Bristol, UK: Thoemmes, 1998.

Zimmermann, F. W. "Al-Kindī." In *Religion, Learning and Science in the 'Abbasid Period*, edited by M. J. L. Young, J. D. Latham , R. B. Serjeant, 364-69. Cambridge: Cambridge University Press, 2014.

Index

Plato: Academy of, 79–80; patronage and, 79
Platonic Academy of Florence, 212
Pliny the Elder, 5, 57–58
Porete, Marguerite, 112
Press Act of 1662, 300. *See also* Licensing of
the Press Act of 1662
presses. *See* printing
press regulation, during English Civil War and
Commonwealth, 300
The Principia (Newton), 231–32
printing: Locke's reflections on regulation of,
303–7; role of, in spread of humanism, 212–
13; spread of learning and, 290
properties of learning, 314–18
property: Locke's communal principle of, 281–
82; Locke's ideas about, 279–81; Locke's
increase of common stock principle of,
288–89; Locke's labor principle of, 284–
86; Locke's natural limit of, 286–87;
Locke's self-possession principle of, 282–
84, 283n28; Locke's seven principles of,
281–91; Locke's social contract principle of,
287–88; Locke's spoilage proviso of, 287;
right of responsible use and, 291–95; rights
of, First Nations people in Canada and, 295.
See also intellectual property
Proslogion (Anselm of Canterbury), 90–92
public access. *See* open access
publishing, scholarly: financing, 321; open access of, 3; radical changes in, 4; understanding principles and patterns of, 11–12

Radegund of Poitiers, Saint, 44–46, 48, 283
reading: glosses and, 67–71; *Rule of Benedict*
and, 38–41
*The Reasonableness of Christianity as Delivered
in Scriptures* (Locke), 306
Recchi, Nardo Antonio, 222
responsible use, right of, and property, 291–95
Robert of Courçon (cardinal), 169–70
Royal Society of London, 223–39; autonomy
of, 226–27; charter of, 225–26; clubbishness
of, 239; credibility of, 228; meetings of, 227–
28; motto of, 228; open access and, 236–37;
openness of, 229; *Philosophical Transactions*,
233–35; printing program of, 229–32
Rule for Virgins (Caesarius), 45
Rule of Benedict (Saint Benedict), 22, 36–42,
37n64, 48, 66, 94, 164, 282, 315; Anselm of
Canterbury and, 90; authorship of, 41; Bede

and, 54; Cistercians and, 94–95; communal
property and, 41, 315; possessions and, 41;
reading and, 38–40; structure of, 38; ways
monastics resolved paradox of, 111

scholarly publishing, 255–67; financing, 321;
open access of, 3; radical changes in, 4;
understanding principles and patterns of,
11–12
scholars, wandering (*vagantes*), 118, 150
scholasticism: Anselm of Canterbury as
founder of, 90, 94; Petrarch and, 184
schools, 101–2, 156; almonry, 67n86, 67n87;
cathedral, 97; charitable, 67; elementary,
Dominicans and Franciscans founding of,
167–68; palace, during Carolingian Renaissance, 64
Schreck, Johann, 222
scientific academies, 216–23. *See also* Royal
Society of London
scientific inquiry, Venerable Bede and, 57–59
Sci-Hub (website), 1–2
script, development of, 61
scriptoria, 61, 63, 81
self-possession principle, of property, 282–84
Sens, Council of. *See* Council of Sens
Shaftesbury, 1st Earl of (Anthony Ashley Cooper),
273, 275–76, 277, 300
Sheldon, Gilbert 261
Siger of Brabant, 173
Smith, Adam, 284n32
social contract principle, of property, 287–88
sources, authenticity of, Saint Jerome and,
28–29
spiritualism, Bernard of Clairvaux and, 94–95
spoilage proviso, of property, 287
sponsorship property, of learning, 316
Sprat, Thomas, 227–29
Stationers' Company of London, 251; book
piracy and, 307–10; Locke and, 302–3;
Oxford University Press and, 260–71;
piracy of books and, 307–10; University of
Cambridge and, 254–55
Statute of Anne (1710), 7–8, 269, 295, 310–16,
319; learning and, 314
Strauss, Leo, 292, 292n47
studium generale, 153–54, 157n14; in Bologna,
156–57
subscriptions: for learned books, 214; scholarly journals and, 3–4

sufficiency proviso, of property, 286–87
Swartz, Aaron, 11–12
Sweynheim, Konrad, 209–11
Swift, Jonathan, 216
Sylvester II (pope), 117–18

Tempier, Etienne, 176
Tertullian, Qintus, 25
texts, learned, properties of working with, 7
Theodosius, Macrobius Ambrosius, 49
Theodulf of Orléans, 61, 64–65
Thomas, Thomas, 255–56
Thomas Aquinas, Saint, 136, 165–66, 173–76,
282; Aristotle and, 173–74; communal property and, 175; intellectual responsibility and,
175; open approach to teaching of, 175–76;
theology of property and authorship of, 175
Toledo, Spain, as center of Arabic translation
to Latin, 141–42
tourism, medieval manuscript, 118
translation movements, 118–20. See also Islamic
learning; Latin Translation Movement
transubstantiation, doctrine of, 81, 81n31
Trinity College, Cambridge, England, 245
Tully, James, responsible use of Locke's work
and, 291–95
Two Treatises of Government (Locke), 16, 132,
273–74, 277, 279n18; historical influence
of, 291–95; ideas about property in, 279–
81; publication of, 274–75. See also Locke,
John

universities, medieval: dominance of Aristotle
and, 157–58; founding of, by royal decrees,
157; influx of Islamic learning through
translation movement and, 154–55; international, 5n11; mystery of origins of, 153–
54; organization of, 153; women excluded
from, 101–2
universities, modern: campus capitalism and,
13; innovation and, 13–14; loss of distinction of, from commercial sectors, 14
University of Bologna, 156–57; bookmaking
regulations of, 179
University of Cambridge, 159; establishment
of press by, 254; first printer of, 255–56;
granting of printing privileges to, 253–54
University of Oxford: appointment of William
Laud as chancellor of, 257–61; Bodley's
building of library of, 247–53; earliest

accounts of, 158–59; founding of press at,
256–57; gifts and endowments to, 163;
Great Charter of, 260; Grosseteste and,
160–65; state of libraries of, during time
of Edward VI, 245–47; welfare system of,
162–63. See also Christ Church, college of;
Oxford University Press
University of Paris, 110, 169–79; access and
use rights issues and, 169–70; attainment
of academic freedom, 177–78; autonomy
struggles of, 171; book trade and, 178–79,
178n107; Dominicans and, 166; early ten-
sions at, 169; establishing academic freedom at, 171–72; Great Dispersion of, 171;
housing issues, 170–71; scribal culture of,
178; teaching of Aristotle at, 172; Tempier's
condemnation against, 176–77; Thomas
Aquinas and, 173–76
Urban II (pope), 148
use property, of learning, 316
Utopia (More), 197

vagantes (wandering scholars), 118, 150
Valla, Lorenzo, 197, 197n77
Venetian glassmakers, intellectual protection
and, 180
Vivarium, library of, 43–44
Vocabolario della lingua italiana (dictionary),
214–16

Wallis, John, 224, 237, 265
wandering scholars (vagantes), 118, 150
Ward, Seth, 224, 237
wealth, problem of excess, 83–85
Weber, Max, 21–22, 33
Wilkins, John, 223–24, 237
William III (king of England), 277
Williamson, Joseph, 262
Willis, Thomas, 224
Wolsey, Cardinal Thomas, 242
women: as benefactors to monasteries, 77;
contributions of, to monasticism, 101–2;
exclusion of, from cathedral schools and
medieval universities, 101–2, 111–12; Northern European semimonastic communities
(béguinages) of, 112; restraint of, within
monasteries, and Charlemagne, 64
Wren, Sir Christopher, 224, 261

Yates, Thomas, 262, 264–65